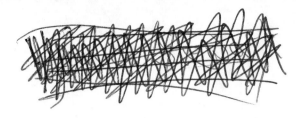

W9-BBY-908

Scott Mitchell
James Atkinson

SAMS
Teach Yourself

Active Server™
Pages 3.0

in 21 Days

SAMS

A Division of Macmillan USA
201 West 103rd St., Indianapolis, Indiana, 46290 USA

Sams Teach Yourself Active Server Pages 3.0 in 21 Days

Copyright ©2000 by Sams Publishing

International Standard Book Number: 0-672-31863-6

Library of Congress Catalog Card Number: 99-067299

Printed in the United States of America

First Printing: January, 2000

02   01   00   4

Trademarks

All terms mentioned in this book that are known to be trademarks or service marks have been appropriately capitalized. Sams Publishing cannot attest to the accuracy of this information. Use of a term in this book should not be regarded as affecting the validity of any trademark or service mark.

Active Server Pages is a trademark of Microsoft Corporation

Warning and Disclaimer

Every effort has been made to make this book as complete and as accurate as possible, but no warranty or fitness is implied. The information provided is on an "as is" basis. The authors and the publisher shall have neither liability nor responsibility to any person or entity with respect to any loss or damages arising from the information contained in this book or programs accompanying it.

PUBLISHER
Bradley Jones

ACQUISITIONS EDITOR
Chris Webb

DEVELOPMENT EDITOR
Kevin Howard

MANAGING EDITOR
Lisa Wilson

PROJECT EDITOR
Paul Schneider

COPY EDITOR
Geneil Breeze

INDEXER
Rebecca Salerno

PROOFREADER
Jill Mazurczyk

TECHNICAL EDITORS
Steve Banick
Jill Bobbin

TEAM COORDINATOR
Meggo Barthlow

SOFTWARE SPECIALIST
Todd Pfeffer

INTERIOR DESIGNER
Gary Adair

COVER DESIGNER
Aren Howell

COPYWRITER
Eric Borgert

EDITORIAL ASSISTANT
Angela Boley

PRODUCTION
Dan Harris
Liz Johnston

Contents at a Glance

Appendixes

Table of Contents

About the Authors

JAMES ATKINSON is one of the founders and head developers of 4GuysFromRolla.com, a leading Active Server Pages informational site, and has several years of experience in Internet development. In addition to his accomplishments as a programmer, he is recognized for his skills in mathematics and journalism. James holds a Bachelor's degrees in Applied Mathematics and Computer Science from the University of Missouri-Rolla.

SCOTT MITCHELL is a programmer, consultant, writer, and speaker for a plethora of interesting computing topics. Scott is known best for his work on the award-winning Web site, 4GuysFromRolla.com, which provides thorough tutorials and reference material for learning and perfecting Active Server Pages skills. Scott, who has been programming since age 10, is passionate about all computer-related topics, although his main interests focus on distributed applications. Scott, a former Microsoft employee, has recently started his own consulting company.

Dedication

To my family, whose unconditional love and support have given me the strength, determination, and fortitude to accomplish any goal. ——*Scott Mitchell*

To my father, Gene, my mother, Sue, and my sister, Catherine, for their love and support, and to the best teacher ever, Stanley Miller, for encouraging and challenging me. ——*James Atkinson*

Acknowledgments

None of this would have been possible without Scott Pope's assistance in introducing me to Active Server Pages. His encouragement assisted both James and me in writing this book. I'd also like to thank my truest and closest friends for their constant support and good will.

What acknowledgement would be complete without mentioning Todd Callister (or Transmitted, as his close friends like to refer to him)? He deserves the utmost recognition for reason upon reason and unquestionably deserves an entire book written about him and his witty sense of humor. A greater friend does not exist.

Finally, I'd like to acknowledge all those people in the ASP community and at various places of employment who have helped me along the way: Charles Carroll, Bill Wilkinson, Bill Graziano, Sean Baird, David Besch, and Henry Crevensten. These people have taught me so much, from Active Server Pages and database programming to running a successful Web site and business. Thank you! —Scott Mitchell

I thank Chris Webb, Kevin Howard, and the rest of the Sams group for being patient with a couple of college kids.

I could not have done any of this without my friends, especially the other three founders of 4GuysFromRolla.com: co-author Scott Mitchell, Justin Miller, and Scott Pope. Thanks guys, for all your friendship and support.

Most of all, I thank the loyal visitors who have made 4GuysFromRolla.com number one! —James Atkinson

Tell Us What You Think!

As the reader of this book, *you* are our most important critic and commentator. We value your opinion and want to know what we're doing right, what we could do better, what areas you'd like to see us publish in, and any other words of wisdom you're willing to pass our way.

As a Publisher for Sams, I welcome your comments. You can fax, email, or write me directly to let me know what you did or didn't like about this book—as well as what we can do to make our books stronger.

Please note that I cannot help you with technical problems related to the topic of this book, and that due to the high volume of mail I receive, I might not be able to reply to every message.

When you write, please be sure to include this book's title and author as well as your name and phone or fax number. I will carefully review your comments and share them with the author and editors who worked on the book.

Fax:	317-581-4770
Email:	adv_prog@mcp.com
Mail:	Bradley Jones, Publisher
	Sams Publishing
	201 West 103rd Street
	Indianapolis, IN 46290 USA

Introduction

Over the next 21 days, you will learn how to create dynamic Web pages using Microsoft's Active Server Pages. With the Internet becoming a central part of both business and pleasure, there is high demand today for developers who can create data-driven Web sites. The following 21 days' lessons will teach you everything you need to know to create your own interactive Web sites utilizing Active Server Pages technology.

Active Server Pages allows for powerful Web site creation by combining programmatic code with standard HTML. If you've never written a program before, you will successfully learn how to program using VBScript, the most commonly used Active Server Pages programming language.

Each of the 21 days is presented in a tutorial style that focuses on both theory and application. When a new topic is presented, the theory and background behind the topic are discussed first. Then real-world examples, accompanied by code, are examined. Commonly asked questions about the day's topics are addressed. At the end of each day's lesson, questions and exercises are presented to allow you to test your mastery of the topic before moving on.

The first seven lessons—Week 1—introduce you to Active Server Pages and VBScript, as well as important programming concepts. Week 2 looks at creating Web pages whose output is based on user input. Week 3 looks at databases and how your pages can use them to store and retrieve information. At the end of each week, you'll find a Bonus Project in the Week-in-Review section, which ties together the material learned throughout the week into a complete, real-world application.

As with most computer topics, much more information about ASP is available than you *need* to know in most real-world situations. The 21 days' tutorials strive to present as complete a picture as possible while focusing on the aspects of Active Server Pages used most in the real world. Such topics will be covered in detail, with numerous code examples. The exercises at the end of each hour-long day provide a chance for you to get your feet wet with the topics covered in the day's lesson. We think you'll find a nice balance between theory and application, with added focus on the topics and problems that most Active Server Pages developers face.

With the explosive growth of the Internet in our everyday lives, being able to create dynamic, user-responsive Web sites is one of the most in-demand technical skills. Not only is the dynamic Web site design market a hot one, but it is also a fun and interesting one! This book will serve as your guide to this exciting field, teaching you the ins and outs of Active Server Pages programming and data-driven Web site design.

To help make it easier, we have placed our source code and examples on the publisher's web site located at http://www.mcp.com/info. Just enter this book's ISBN number from the back cover into the form presented and you will be taken to the download area.

If you're ready and excited to learn Active Server Pages, this book is for you! Whether you are a hobbyist or a professional, *Sams Teach Yourself Active Server Pages 3.0 in 21 Days* will provide the background needed to program just about any Active Server Pages application.

WEEK 1

At a Glance

This week you will learn how to create dynamic Web pages using Active Server Pages. We will begin with a discussion of what Active Server Pages are and how you can use them to enhance your Internet or intranet Web site. We'll then delve into the VBScript programming language, the most commonly used language for Active Server Pages. You'll be amazed at how quickly you will be creating your own ASP pages!

Where You're Going

This week begins with an introduction to Active Server Pages, commonly abbreviated as ASP. To run ASP pages, you need to have a Web server installed on your computer that supports Active Server Pages. Microsoft provides two free Web servers—one intended for Windows NT and Windows 2000, and the other intended for Windows 95 and Windows 98. We'll look into installing the appropriate Web server on your computer so that you can run ASP pages.

ASP pages are scripts, or short snippets of code interpreted by the Web server to perform a particular task. Many scripting programming languages can be used on your ASP pages, such as VBScript and JScript. Throughout the book, we will use VBScript for our example scripts. If you've ever programmed in Visual Basic, you'll find the VBScript syntax nearly identical to the syntax used in Visual Basic. For those who are new to VBScript, don't worry! Throughout this week we will step through all the important aspects of VBScript.

When creating ASP pages, you are, essentially, writing small programs. You can think of each ASP page as its own, discrete program. Because you will be writing your own programs, we will be discussing programming logic throughout this week.

1

2

3

4

5

6

7

One of the nicest things about Active Server Pages, and the main reason why they are so commonly used in industry, is that ASP pages are *easy* to create. As we'll show on Day 1, "Getting Started with Active Server Pages," you can write an ASP script with as little as one line of code! ASP's greatest asset is that powerful and useful Web pages can be created easily!

If you've had programming experience in the past, you'll find Active Server Pages easy to learn. If you're new to programming, you'll come to appreciate the ease with which ASP pages can be created and executed. Regardless of your experience, you'll find ASP programming fun and be amazed at what you can accomplish with ASP.

WEEK 1

DAY 1

Getting Started with Active Server Pages

Active Server Pages are Microsoft's solution to creating dynamic Web pages. With the explosion of the Internet and the World Wide Web into our everyday lives, Web site creation is quickly becoming one of the fastest growing sectors.

In the early days of the World Wide Web, Web site design consisted primarily of creating fancy graphics and nice-looking, easy-to-read Web pages. As today's Web sites have become user interactive, the steps in Web site design have changed. Although creating a pleasant-looking Web site is still important, the primary focus has shifted from graphical design to programmatic design. For example, imagine that you wanted to create a Web site from which you could sell widgets. The programmatic design, creating the Web pages that will collect and store user billing information, for example, is more pressing than deciding what background color to use.

Enter Active Server Pages. If you need to build a dynamic Web site—one that can interact with users—Active Server Pages are an easy-to-use solution. Today, you take your first step into the world of Active Server Pages!

Today, you will learn the following:

- What Active Server Pages (ASP) are
- When Active Server Pages need to be used in place of static HTML files
- How ASP differs from client-side scripting
- What software is required to serve ASP pages from a computer
- How to install Microsoft's Internet Information Server and Microsoft's Personal Web Server
- How to run ASP pages on a non-Microsoft Web server
- How to create ASP pages
- How to view the output of an ASP page

What Are Active Server Pages?

Over the past couple of years, we have seen some major changes concerning the Internet. Initially, the Internet served as a medium for members of government and education institutions to communicate. With the advent of the World Wide Web, the Internet became a multimedia, user-friendly environment. Originally, the Internet served as a place for enthusiasts to create personal home pages, but as more people began going "online," the Internet transformed into an informational resource for the common man. When the number of people online reached a critical mass, companies that sold products and services began to spring up. These companies had no physical presence, only a virtual one. For example, you can buy a book from Amazon.com's Internet site, but you won't be able to find an Amazon.com bookstore in your neighborhood.

As the Internet has matured into a viable marketplace, Web site design has changed in step. In the early days of the World Wide Web, HTML was used to create static Web pages. Today, though, static Web pages are quickly becoming obsolete. Imagine if Amazon.com was composed of nothing but static Web pages—you couldn't search its inventory; you couldn't place an order online; you couldn't read other users' comments. It is a safe bet that Amazon.com wouldn't sell many books if it didn't use dynamic Web pages.

You can create dynamic Web pages in many ways. Microsoft's solution to building dynamic Web pages is through the use of Active Server Pages, commonly abbreviated ASP.

 Note   Many large Web sites use Active Server Pages to serve dynamic Web content. For example, Buy.com, HotBot.com, and Dell.com use Active Server Pages to build their interactive, dynamic Web sites.

Active Server Pages contain two parts: programmatic code and embedded HTML. The programmatic code can be written in a number of *scripting languages*.

NEW TERM A *scripting language* is a particular syntax used to execute commands on a computer.

A program composed of commands from a particular scripting language is referred to as a *script*.

Some popular Web-related scripting languages include VBScript and JavaScript. When creating an ASP page, you can use one of four programming languages:

- VBScript—Similar to Visual Basic's syntax, the most commonly used scripting language for Active Server Pages
- JScript—Similar to JavaScript
- PerlScript—Similar to Perl
- Python—A powerful scripting language commonly used for Web development

Most ASP pages are created using VBScript. VBScript has the most English-like syntax of the four scripting languages and is similar to Visual Basic's syntax, which many Web developers have experience with.

Note Throughout this book, we will present examples using VBScript.

Recall that an ASP page can contain embedded HTML. This allows for existing static Web pages to be easily converted into dynamic ASP pages. Finally, an ASP page must contain an .ASP extension.

Understanding the Client-Server Model

Have you ever wondered what, exactly, happens when you type a URL into your browser's Address window? The Internet operates on a *client-server model*.

NEW TERM In a *client-server model*, two computers work together to perform a task. A client computer requests some needed information from a server computer. The server returns this information, and the client acts on it.

Many everyday activities mimic the client-server model. For example, a map at a large mall performs the role of the server, whereas those strolling through the mall are the clients. If one of these clients wants to know how to reach Sears, he would consult this map, requesting a particular piece of information—namely, "How do I get to Sears from here?" After the client (the mall shopper) has received the information from the server (the map), he leaves, headed in the correct direction. The client-server model typically has many more clients than servers. For example, many mall shoppers are requesting information from just a few maps spread throughout the mall.

The Internet runs on a client-server model as well. With the Internet, the server is a particular *Web server*.

Note

> A *Web server* is a computer that contains all the Web pages for a particular Web site and has special software installed to send these Web pages to Web browsers that request them.

The client, on the Internet, is a Web browser. When you visit a static Web page through a Web browser, the following steps occur:

1. The client (the Web browser) locates the Web server specified by the first part of the URL (www.Something.com).

2. The client then requests the static Web page specified by the second part of the URL (/index.htm).

3. The Web server sends the contents of that particular file to the client in HTML format.

4. The client receives the HTML sent by the server and renders it for you, the user.

Figure 1.1 illustrates this transaction.

FIGURE 1.1

The Internet is based on a client-server model.

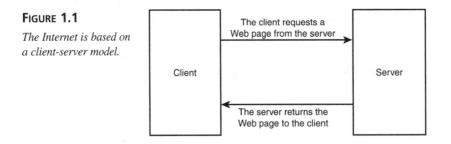

In this transaction, the Web server acts passively, like the mall map in the previous example. The Web server sits around idly, waiting for a client to request a static Web page. After such a page is requested, the Web server sends that page to the client and then returns to idly wait for the next request. With this series of steps, only static Web pages can be sent to the client. To allow for dynamic Web pages, the Web server must play a more active role.

As mentioned earlier today, ASP pages contain a combination of HTML and program-matic code. This code, which can be written in many different languages, allows ASP pages to be dynamic; however, the Web server has to process this programmatic code *before* sending the HTML to the client. When a Web browser requests an ASP page, the following steps occur:

1. The client (the Web browser) locates the Web server specified by the first part of the URL (www.Something.com).

2. The client then requests the ASP page specified by the second part of the URL (/default.asp).

3. The Web server reads the ASP file and *processes* the code.

4. After the ASP page has been completely *processed* by the Web server, the output is sent in HTML format to the client.

5. The client receives the HTML sent by the server and renders it for you, the user.

The client cannot tell the difference between an ASP page and a static Web page because, in both cases, it receives just HTML. When the Web server *processes* an ASP page, all the programmatic code is interpreted on the server—none of it is sent to the client. Figure 1.2 graphically represents this transaction.

FIGURE 1.2

The Web server plays a more active role when an ASP page is requested by the client.

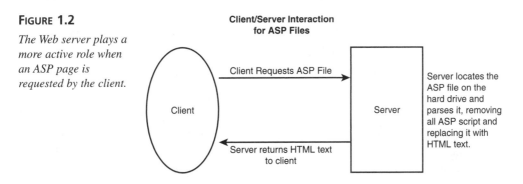

Client/Server Interaction for ASP Files

We've just looked at the two ways a Web server responds to a client's request. If the request is for a static HTML page, the server simply sends back the contents of the Web page. If, however, the request is for an ASP page, the Web server first processes the ASP page and then sends the resulting HTML output to the client. How, though, does the Web server determine whether the client is requesting a static HTML page or an ASP page? The Web server determines this by the extension of the Web page being requested. This is why when you create an ASP page you must give it an .ASP extension. This way, the Web server knows to process the programmatic code *before* sending the output to the client.

Let's briefly look at an example ASP page. Listing 1.1 contains code that displays the current date and time. To execute the code in Listing 1.1, you first need to install a Web server on your computer. We will discuss how to do this later today in "Running ASP Pages." For now, just examine the code in Listing 1.1 to get a feeling for what an ASP page looks like.

LISTING 1.1 An ASP Page Displaying the Current Date and Time

```
1:  <%@ Language=VBSCRIPT %>
2:  <HTML>
3:  <BODY>
4:    The current time is
5:    <% Response.Write Time() %>
6:  </BODY>
7:  </HTML>
```

ANALYSIS Note that the ASP code is surrounded by a <% and %>. When an ASP page is requested from a Web server, the Web server fully processes all the code between <% and %> before sending the output to the client. The code in Listing 1.1 probably looks a lot like a regular HTML file. This embedded HTML (lines 2, 3, 6, and 7) makes it easy to create ASP pages from existing HTML documents. In fact, the only ASP code is on lines 1 and 5. Line 1 informs the Web server what scripting language this particular ASP page is using. Recall that an ASP page can use one of four scripting languages. As mentioned earlier, all the examples in this book will be coded in VBScript. To specify the scripting language for an ASP page, you use the @LANGUAGE directive (line 1). If you wanted to use JScript instead of VBScript in this example, you could change line 1 to the following:

```
<%@ LANGUAGE=JScript %>
```

The second line of ASP code (line 5) displays the current date and time. The Time() function is a VBScript function that we will discuss in more detail on Day 5, "Using VBScript's Built-in Functions." The Response.Write outputs the results of the Time() function to the client. This Response object and the Response.Write method are discussed in more detail on Day 7, "Using the Response Object."

If you have a Microsoft Web server already running on your computer, you can test the code in Listing 1.1. Create a file named CurrentTime.asp and place it in your Web site's root directory. Next, load your favorite browser and visit the ASP page you just created. The URL you want to type in is

```
http://machineName/CurrentTime.asp
```

where *machineName* is the name of your computer.

> **Tip**
>
> The following URL will also work:
>
> http://localhost/CurrentTime.asp

Figure 1.3 displays the output of Listing 1.1 when viewed through a browser.

FIGURE 1.3

The current date and time is displayed.

Remember that the browser just receives HTML text from the Web server—it does not receive any of the ASP code that was between the <% and %> delimiters. You can see exactly what the browser received from the client by viewing the HTML source code the browser received. To see this in Internet Explorer, select View, Source from the menu. This opens up Notepad and shows you the source code received. Listing 1.2 shows the source code received by the browser when visiting CurrentTime.asp.

LISTING 1.2   The Browser Receives Only HTML

```
1:  <HTML>
2:  <BODY>
3:    The current time is
4:    3:26:57 PM
5:  </BODY>
6:  </HTML>
```

ANALYSIS Listing 1.2 contains the HTML source code received by the browser. Note that the ASP code in Listing 1.1 is not apparent in Listing 1.2. In fact, when line 5 in Listing 1.1 was processed, the output was 3:26:57 PM. This is what was sent to the client. All the code in Listing 1.1 that is surrounded by the delimiters <% and %> was processed. Some of the processing of ASP code results in an HTML output, such as the Time function returning the current time, 3:26:57 PM, specifically. It is important to understand that the browser received nothing but HTML. This topic is discussed in further detail later today in "Creating Your First ASP Page."

How ASP Differs from Client-Side Scripting Technologies

When using ASP, it is vitally important to understand that ASP code exists on the server only. ASP code, which is code surrounded by the <% and %> delimiters, is processed completely on the server. The client cannot access this ASP code.

If you've created Web pages before, you might be familiar with *client-side scripting*.

NEW TERM *Client-side scripting* is programmatic code in an HTML file that runs on the browser.

Client-side scripting code is simply HTML code and is denoted by the <SCRIPT> HTML tag. Client-side scripting is commonly written using the JavaScript programming language due to the fact that Netscape Navigator only supports the JavaScript scripting language for client-side scripting. Listing 1.3 contains a static HTML page that contains client-side scripting code.

LISTING 1.3 The Browser Receives Only HTML

```
1:  <HTML>
2:  <HEAD>
3:    <SCRIPT LANGUAGE="JavaScript">
4:    <!--
5:      alert("Hello world!");
6:    // -->
7:    </SCRIPT>
8:  </HEAD>
9:  <BODY>
10:   Welcome to my web page!
11: </BODY>
12: </HTML>
```

ANALYSIS The code in Listing 1.3 includes raw HTML (lines 1 through 3, and lines 7 through 12) and client-side JavaScript code (lines 4 through 6). Listing 1.3 is nothing more than a static HTML file. If the contents of Listing 1.3 were entered into a Web page named ClientSideScripting.htm, the entire contents would be sent to the browser when the client requested the Web page. The browser, when rendering the HTML, would display a message box when the `alert` method was reached (line 5). Figure 1.4 shows the output of Listing 1.3 when viewed through a browser.

FIGURE 1.4

Use client-side scripting to display message boxes on the client's computer.

You can have client-side scripting code in an ASP page because client-side scripting is HTML code, as far as the Web server is concerned. When developing ASP pages, though, it is important to remember that client-side scripting and ASP code are two different things and cannot interact with one another. ASP scripts are *server-side scripts*.

NEW TERM *Server-side scripts* are scripts that execute on the Web server. These scripts are processed and their output is sent to the client.

Table 1.1 outlines the differences between client-side scripting and server-side ASP scripting.

TABLE 1.1 Differences Between Client-Side Scripting and Server-Side ASP Code

Method	Differences
Client-side scripting	A client-side script is not processed at all by the Web server, only by the client. It is the client's responsibility to execute any and all client-side scripts.
Server-side scripting	Server-side scripts are processed completely on the Web server. The client does not receive any code from server-side scripts; rather, the client receives just the output of the server-side scripts. Client-side scripts and server-side scripts cannot interact with one another because the client-side scripts are executed on the client, after the server-side scripts have finished processing completely.

It is important to understand that client-side scripts and server-side scripts are two completely separate entities. For a detailed discussion on the differences between client-side scripting and server-side scripting, check out the following article on 4GuysFromRolla.com: "ASP Basics: What's Happening Back There?" (`http://www.4guysfromrolla.com/webtech/082399-1.shtml`).

Caution
A common pitfall beginning ASP developers make is to assume that their client-side scripts can interact with their server-side ASP code. Understanding the differences between the client and the server is important.

Running ASP Pages

To execute ASP pages on your computer, you need to be running a Web server. Free products are available from Microsoft that allow you to run a Web server on both Windows 95 and 98, as well as on Windows NT and Windows 2000.

If you do not have a Web server installed that can handle ASP pages, when you request an ASP page through a browser, you receive a dialog asking you whether you want to save the ASP file to disk. For example, create a file with an .ASP extension and copy into it the contents of Listing 1.1. Next, open this file in your browser of choice. You see a dialog asking you whether you want to Save the file to disk (see Figure 1.5).

Recall that a Web server capable of handling ASP pages *processes* the requested ASP page *before* it is sent to the client. During this processing, two things occur:

1. The programmatic code in the ASP page is interpreted by the Web server.
2. The Web server informs the browser that it is sending HTML information, at which point the Web server sends the output of the ASP page. The browser, receiving this raw HTML, renders it for the user.

If you do not have a Web server installed, though, and try to view an ASP page through your browser, the second step is not accomplished. That is, the browser isn't informed that the ASP page contains HTML code. The browser doesn't know what to do with an .ASP file and tries to see whether any other programs know what to do with the .ASP file extension. If a program is installed on your computer that has associated the .ASP file extension with itself, this program is launched. For example, both Visual InterDev and Microsoft FrontPage associate the .ASP extension. If you have one of these programs installed on your computer and attempt to view an ASP page through your browser before you have installed a Web server, Visual InterDev or FrontPage is launched automatically. If, however, there are no programs installed on your computer that associate the .ASP file extension, then you are prompted with the dialog in Figure 1.5.

> **Tip**
>
> After you install a Web server, you will be able to view ASP pages through your browser.

1

Setting Up Personal Web Server

When creating a professional Web site, it is important that the Web site run on a computer that has Windows NT Server or Windows 2000 installed. However, not many people run Windows NT Server or Windows 2000 on their personal computers. For this reason, Microsoft created a stripped-down version of its professional Web server. This stripped-down version is called Personal Web Server (PWS) and is intended to run on Microsoft Windows 95 or 98, or Microsoft Windows NT Workstation.

Personal Web Server can be downloaded for free from Microsoft's Web site at http://www.microsoft.com/msdownload/ntoptionpack/askwiz.asp. (Beware, this is around a 35 MB download!) Many Microsoft products also ship with Personal Web Server—for example, FrontPage 98 and 2000 and Visual Studio, Microsoft's collection of programming tools and languages.

After you have a copy of the PWS, run the Setup program. After a few informational screens, you are prompted with your first choice—what type of installation to perform. Figure 1.6 shows the option you are presented with. You can customize what components and documentation to install by selecting the Custom option. The default options will suit you well, though, so we recommend just selecting the Typical installation.

FIGURE 1.6

Choose what type of installation to perform.

After you select the Typical or Minimum installation, a dialog prompts you to enter the directory to select as your default Web publishing home directory (see Figure 1.7). If you chose to perform the Custom install, you see this screen after you select which components to install.

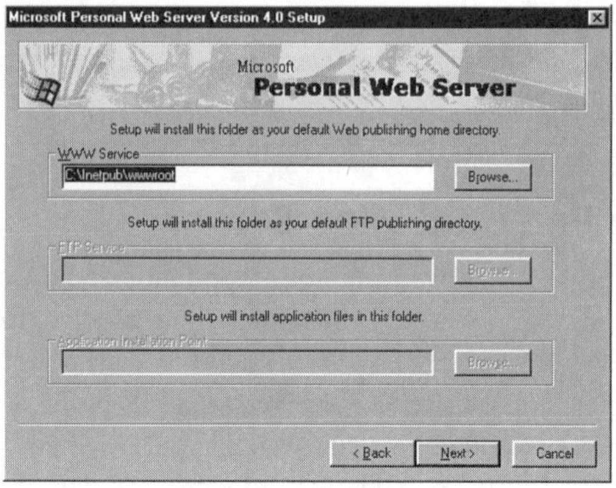

FIGURE 1.7

Enter the directory where you plan on placing your Web site's files.

A Web page is requested from a Web server with a URL, like the following:

`http://www.InventoryResellers/Inventory/ShowInventory.asp`

The first part of the URL, `www.InventoryResellers.com`, is the domain name. This name identifies what Web server this Web site exists on. The remainder of the URL determines what directory and file the user is requesting. In the example, the user is requesting a file named `ShowInventory.asp` from the `/Inventory` directory. `/Inventory/ShowInventory.asp` is referred to as the *virtual address*.

New Term   A *virtual address* is the directory and filename requested through the URL.

The Web server needs to map the virtual address to a *physical address*.

New Term   A *physical address* is a fully qualified path for a specific file.

In the dialog in Figure 1.7, you need to specify the *root physical address*.

New Term   The *root physical address* determines the starting physical address directory.

For example, if you set the *root physical address* to `C:\InetPub\wwwroot` (as shown in Figure 1.7), the following virtual addresses

```
http://yourServer/default.asp
http://yourServer/datetime/CurrentTime.asp
http://yourServer/Inventory/Books/New/index.asp
```

would translate to the following physical addresses

```
C:\InetPub\wwwroot\default.asp
C:\InetPub\wwwroot\datetime\CurrentTime.asp
C:\InetPub\wwwroot\Inventory\Books\index.asp
```

> **Tip**
>
> You can enter any directory name into the dialog shown in Figure 1.7. However, it is a convention to use InetPub\wwwroot as your Web's root physical address.

After you select your Web's root physical address, the Setup program starts installing the needed files to your computer. When the installation is complete, you will need to reboot your computer.

After rebooting, you'll notice a new icon in your System Tray. Double-clicking this icon brings up the Personal Web Manager dialog, which contains five panes, each pane presenting different information and serving a different purpose. The default pane is the Main pane, shown in Figure 1.8.

FIGURE 1.8

The Main pane allows you to stop and start the Web server and shows Web server statistics.

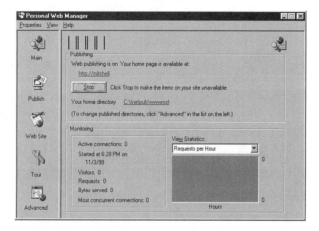

You can stop the Web server by clicking the Stop button. If you try to request a page when the Web server is stopped, you receive an error that the browser could not establish a connection to the Web server. Figure 1.9 displays the error message you see if you try to request a page from your Web server through Internet Explorer 5.0 when the Web server is stopped.

FIGURE 1.9

You cannot view Web pages from a stopped Web server.

The Main pane also contains statistical information about the Web site's activity. You can view stats on the Requests per Hour, Requests per Day, Visitors per Hour, or Visitors per Day.

Another useful pane in the Personal Web Manager dialog is the Advanced pane, which
can be seen in Figure 1.10. This pane contains the Web site's directory structure and
three Web site properties that you can alter. You can edit the permissions for a particular
directory by clicking the directory name and then clicking Edit Properties.

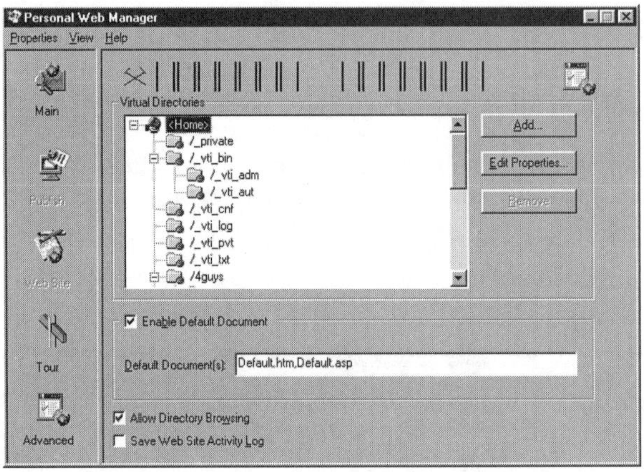

FIGURE 1.10

*To edit the Web site's
properties, visit the
Advanced pane.*

You can alter three Web site-wide properties in the Advanced pane. The first, Enable
Default Document, determines whether to load a default document if the user does not
request a specific file in the URL. For example, if you have the Default Document(s) set
to `Default.htm,Default.asp` (which is the default), if the user visits a URL such as

```
http://yourServer/
```

the Web server checks to see whether a document named `Default.htm` exists in your root
physical directory. If it does, it is displayed; if it does not, the Web server checks to see
whether a document named `Default.asp` exists. If it does not, a 404 Error is returned to
the browser, indicating that the requested file was not found. If you have Enable Default
Document unselected, the Web server does not check for `Default.htm` or `Default.asp`
when a user does not explicitly specify a filename in the URL. Rather, a 404 Error is
immediately returned. In the Default Document(s) text box, you can choose the filenames
the Web server should look for when the user does not specify the filename.

The next option in the Advanced pane is Allow Directory Browsing. If this is selected and
the user requests a URL that does not contain a filename—and a `Default.htm` or
`Default.asp` (or whatever Default Document(s) you specified) does not exist—then the
contents of that directory are listed in the Web browser. This option is off by default
because more often than not Webmasters do not want to let their users browse their directories. However, if you are going to be the only one accessing your Web site, directory
browsing can be a helpful feature. Figure 1.11 shows the contents of my root directory
when directory browsing is enabled.

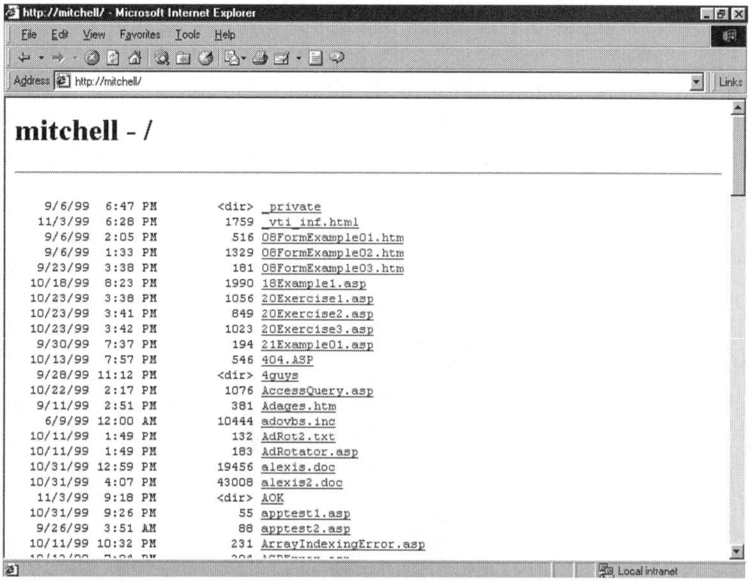

FIGURE 1.11

The contents of your directories will be listed if you have Allow Directory Browsing enabled.

The last option in the Advanced pane is Save Web Site Activity Log. If this option is checked, daily Web site logs are saved. These logs indicate who has connected to your computer, when, and what files they requested. These logs are saved in the Log File\W3SPC1 directory of your Windows System directory.

Setting Up Internet Information Server

Internet Information Server (IIS) is Microsoft's professional Web server. The latest version of IIS is 5.0, which ships with Windows 2000. ASP 3.0 ships with IIS 5.0 and is installed automatically when IIS 5.0 is installed.

If you are running Windows NT Server, you need to use IIS 4.0. IIS 4.0 can be found on the Windows NT Option Pack 4.0, which can be downloaded for free from Microsoft's Web site at http://www.microsoft.com/msdownload/ntoptionpack/askwiz.asp.

> **Caution**
>
> IIS 4.0 does not support ASP 3.0. If you are running Windows NT Server, you will have to run IIS 4.0. If you install IIS 4.0, ASP 2.0 will be installed automatically. The installation of IIS 4.0 is nearly identical to the installation of IIS 5.0. Both provide an easy to follow wizard to help you along the installation process.

IIS 5.0 is shipped with Windows 2000, although it is not installed by default when Windows 2000 is installed. To install IIS 5.0, choose Start, Programs, Administrative Tools, Configure Your Server. A dialog box appears that has several configuration options in the left pane. Choose the bottommost option from the left pane, labeled Advanced. On clicking the Advanced button, four new options appear: Cluster Service, Message Queuing, Support Tools, and Optional Components. Click the Optional Component option. In the right-hand pane, a description of the Option Components option appears, as well as a hyperlink labeled Start. Figure 1.12 shows what the Configure Your Server dialog should look like.

FIGURE 1.12

IIS is considered an Optional Component in Windows 2000.

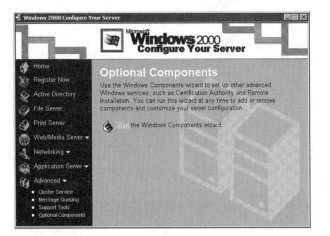

Go ahead and click the Start hyperlink—this launches the Windows Components Wizard. The Windows 2000 Components Wizard displays the Windows 2000 optional components; through this wizard, you can install and uninstall optional components. Scroll down until you see the Internet Information Services (IIS) option. Figure 1.13 shows what you should see.

FIGURE 1.13

You can install or uninstall IIS and its related components through the Windows 2000 Components Wizard.

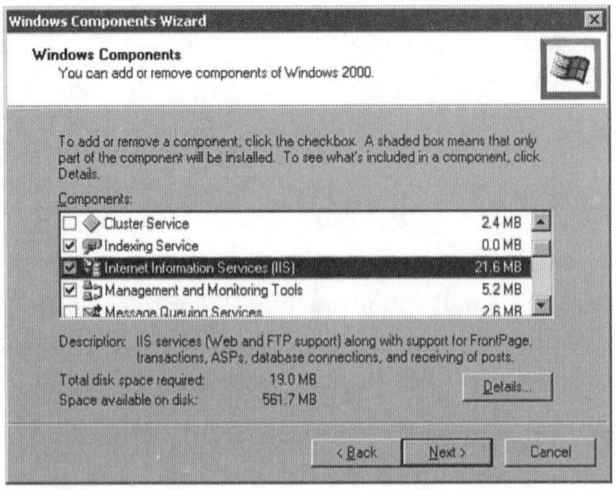

The Internet Information Services (IIS) component contains a number of subcomponents other than the World Wide Web server, such as an FTP Server and SMTP service. To decide what IIS components to install, click the Internet Information Services (IIS) component in the Windows 2000 Components Wizard and then click the Details button. You see a list of components that can be installed with IIS. The options that you should make sure are selected are Common Files, Documentation, Internet Information Services Snap-In, and World Wide Web Server. If you plan on using Visual InterDev or Microsoft FrontPage to edit your Web site, be sure to also install the FrontPage 2000 Server Extensions. Of course, it doesn't hurt to install other IIS subcomponents. Figure 1.14 shows the Internet Information Services (IIS) subcomponents.

FIGURE 1.14

When installing IIS, you need to decide what subcomponents to install.

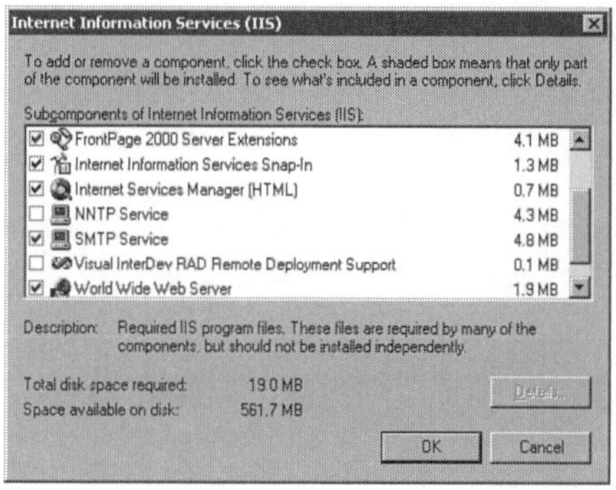

After you have selected all the IIS subcomponents you want to install, click OK, which takes you back to the Windows 2000 Components Wizard. To start installing IIS 5.0, click the Next button. When the installation is complete, you can access the *Internet Services Manager.*

NEW TERM   The *Internet Services Manager* allows you to configure IIS's properties and settings.

To launch the Internet Services Manager, choose Start, Programs, Administrative Tools, Internet Services Manager. The Internet Services Manager allows you to configure your Web site, FTP server, and SMTP service. Figure 11.15 shows the Internet Services Manager.

The Internet Services Manager displays the directory structure for your Web site. You can view and edit your Web site's properties by right-clicking the Web site name (Default Web Site) and clicking Properties. This opens a Web Site Properties dialog, shown in Figure 1.16, which contains many tabs, each with a number of options.

Figure 1.15

To edit your Web site's properties, visit the Internet Services Manager.

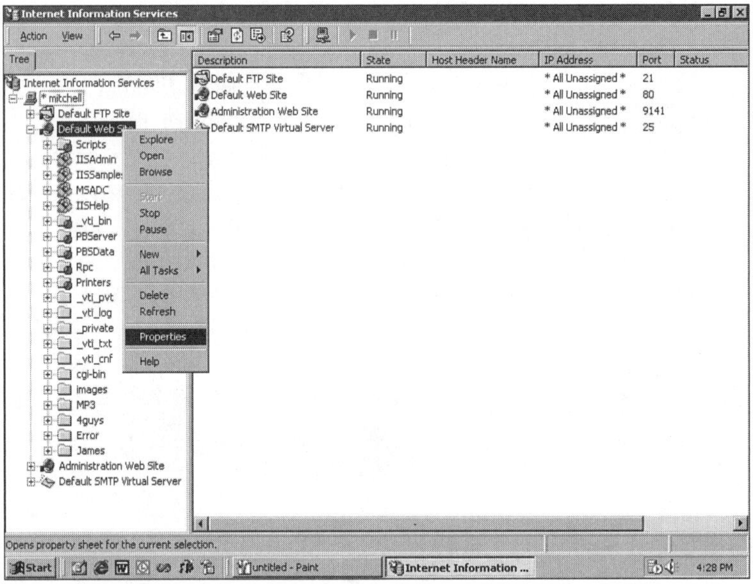

Figure 1.16

The Web Site Properties dialog lists all the editable properties for your Web site.

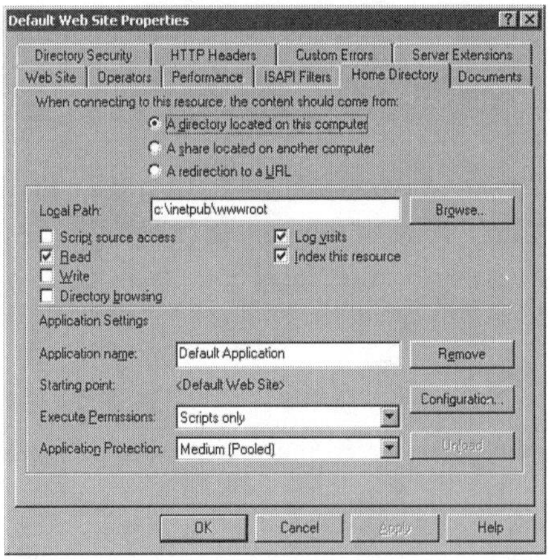

This dialog, as you'll note, contains 10 tabs full of options. Throughout the course of this book, we will discuss many of these tabs and their options, but for now, we are only going to focus on a select few options in the Home Directory tab (refer to Figure 1.16).

Note the Local Path option. The directory entered here is the root physical directory and defaults to \InetPub\wwwroot on the drive that Windows 2000 is installed on. You can alter this value if you choose, but, as discussed earlier today in "Setting Up Personal Web Server," the standard convention is to leave the root physical directory as \InetPub\wwwroot.

1

Below the Local Path option is a series of check boxes. Two of these check boxes are similar to the options in the Personal Web Server Properties dialog: Directory Browsing and Log Visits. Both of these options are identical to the options through Personal Web Server. By selecting Directory Browsing, you allow the contents of a directory to be displayed if a visitor enters the URL of a directory that does not contain any files that match the Default Document(s). Selecting the Log Visits option enables Web site activity logging. More information can be obtained on both of these topics by clicking the Help button at the bottom of the Web Site Properties dialog.

Note   The Custom Errors tab in the Web Site Properties dialog is discussed on Day 14, "Debugging Your ASP Scripts and Handling Errors."

Now that you've installed IIS, you can visit your Web site. As with PWS, you can access your computer's Web site by typing

```
http://localhost
http://yourServer
```

into your favorite browser.

Using ASP Without IIS or PWS

Because Microsoft's Web servers only run on the various Microsoft Windows products, you may think that if you want to use ASP pages, you *must* use IIS or PWS as your Web server. This is not the case, however, thanks to a couple of companies that have created software to allow ASP pages to run on various Web servers and platforms.

One of these products is Halcyon Software's Instant ASP, often abbreviated as iASP. Another such product, created by Chili!Soft, is Chili!ASP. These products can run on many non-IIS Web servers, such as the following:

- Apache
- Sun Web Server
- Java Web Server
- Netscape Enterprise Server

These products can also run on a number of platforms, including

- Linux
- Sun Solaris
- Apple Mac OS
- IBM/AIX

To learn more about iASP, check out Halcyon Software's Web site, `http://www.halcyonsoft.com`. To learn more about Chili!ASP, visit Chili!Soft's home page at `http://www.chilisoft.com`.

Creating ASP Pages

ASP pages, like regular HTML Web pages, are simply text files on the Web server. To create an ASP page, all you really need, after you've installed the Web server, is a text editor, such as Notepad.

> **Note**
>
> Notepad is commonly used for creating and editing ASP pages, although it lacks the functionality of editors designed specifically for ASP development.

Let's create our first ASP page using Notepad. Start by opening up Notepad (choose Start, Programs, Accessories, Notepad). Create an ASP page that displays the square roots of the numbers between 1 and 10. Don't worry if you do not understand the VBScript syntax used—we will discuss the VBScript language throughout the remainder of this week. Listing 1.4 contains the code that you should type into Notepad.

LISTING 1.4 VBScript Code that Displays the Square Roots of the Numbers Between 1 and 10

```
1:  <%@ Language=VBScript %>
2:  <% Option Explicit %>
3:
4:  <HTML>
5:  <BODY>
6:    <B>Square Roots</B><BR>
7:  <%
8:    Dim iLoop
9:    For iLoop = 1 to 10
10:     Response.Write iLoop & ": " & Sqr(iLoop) & "<BR>"
11:   Next
12: %>
13:
14: </BODY>
15: </HTML>
```

ANALYSIS The code in Listing 1.4 displays the square roots of the numbers between 1 and 10, inclusive. Line 1 starts the ASP code with the @LANGUAGE directive, which was discussed in the section "Understanding the Client-Server Model." Line 2 uses the

Option Explicit statement—this requires that all variables used in the ASP page be explicitly defined. If you are unfamiliar with variables with respect to programming, don't worry! Day 3, "Working with Variables," is dedicated to this topic.

Lines 4 through 6 contain the embedded HTML code. Then line 7 begins another ASP block, performing a For loop from 1 to 10. For loops are discussed on Day 4, "Understanding VBScript Control Structures." Line 10 displays both the current looping iteration and its square root. The Sqr function, which generates the square root of a number, is discussed on Day 5. Finally, lines 14 and 15 end the ASP page coding with more embedded HTML.

Now that you've typed this code into Notepad, you need to save it as an ASP page. If you wanted to let your users access this page via the following URL

http://yourServer/SquareRoot.asp

you would need to save the file as SquareRoot.asp and place it in your root physical directory. Recall that the root physical directory is specified by the Web Site's Properties dialog and defaults to C:\InetPub\wwwroot. So, save the Notepad document in C:\InetPub\wwwroot (or whatever your root physical directory is) and name it SquareRoot.asp. Now, open up your browser of choice and enter the following into the Address window:

http://yourServer/SquareRoot.asp

replacing yourServer with your computer's machine name. Your browser should then display SquareRoot.asp, whose output is shown in Figure 1.17.

FIGURE 1.17

The square roots of the first 10 natural numbers are displayed.

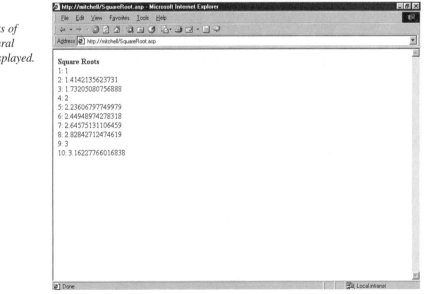

Remember from the previous discussion in "Understanding the Client-Server Model" that the browser, which serves as the client, only receives the finalized HTML from the Web server. If you view the HTML source in your browser after visiting `SquareRoot.asp`, you will see only HTML—none of the server-side VBScript that generated the 10 square roots.

Creating ASP pages using Notepad has advantages and disadvantages. First, its advantages:

- Speed—Notepad is a small, efficient text editor. In the next two sections, we will look at how to create ASP pages with more advanced development tools. Although these tools have their own advantages, they require more disk space and memory and run slower than Notepad.
- Easy to use—Because Notepad doesn't offer many options (after all, its sole purpose is to serve as a text editor), you won't find yourself reading help files.

When compared to the advanced development tools of today, though, Notepad can seem lacking. Notepad's disadvantages are usually based on its lack of options and include the following:

- No Web site maintenance—With Visual InterDev or Microsoft FrontPage, you can manage your entire Web site. With Notepad, you can only edit or create one file at a time.
- No color-coded syntax—When using FrontPage and InterDev, two popular web development editors from Microsoft, different pieces of your code turn different colors. This makes it easier to check for syntax errors in both HTML tags and VBScript code.
- No drag-and-drop Web page creation tools—Both InterDev and FrontPage allow you to create the HTML aspects of a Web page by simply dragging and dropping certain objects and elements onto a Web page. With Notepad, you need to have a good understanding of the HTML tags you plan on using.

What editor to use to create and manage your ASP pages depends on your preferences. If you prefer a robust editor, chances are you'll find Visual InterDev or Microsoft FrontPage to your liking. However, if you'd rather have a bare bones editor, Notepad is the way to go. The next two sections look at using Visual InterDev and Microsoft FrontPage to create and edit ASP pages.

Using Visual InterDev

Microsoft's Visual InterDev serves as a unified development editor for the Visual Studio suite. InterDev is most commonly used, though, to manage Web sites. To manage a Web site with Visual InterDev, the Web site must have FrontPage Server Extensions installed. Recall from "Setting Up Internet Information Server," that FrontPage 2000 Extensions were one of the optional subcomponents that could be installed with IIS 5.0. With Personal Web Server, FrontPage server extensions are installed by default. With PWS, you can check to make sure that FrontPage extensions are installed by running the FrontPage Server Administrator (choose Start, Programs, Microsoft Personal Webserver, FrontPage Server Administrator).

To manage a Web site using Visual InterDev, you need to create a new Web project. To do this, launch Visual InterDev. You initially see a New Project dialog (see Figure 1.18). Enter the name of the new Web project into the Name text box and click Open.

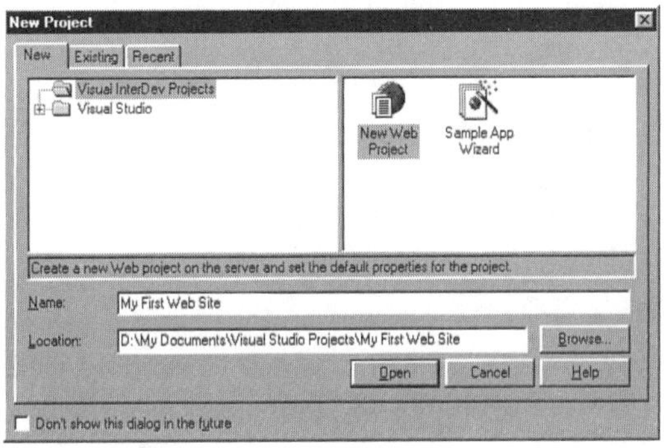

FIGURE 1.18

Create a new Web project through the New Project dialog.

After you create your new Web project, InterDev steps you through a wizard. In the first step, you need to specify the Web server to connect to. If you plan on managing the Web server on your computer, enter localhost as the server name. If you are managing an external Web site, enter the domain name of the Web site, www.domainname.com. Because you are going to be working on your local Web, just enter localhost for now and then click Next. Figure 1.19 shows the first step of the wizard.

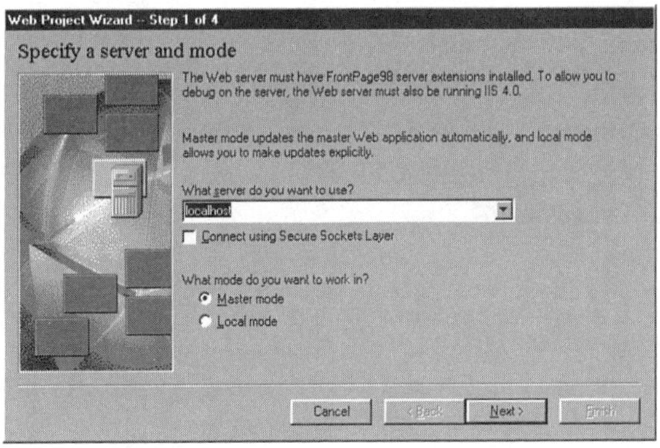

FIGURE 1.19

Enter the name of the Web site you want to manage through InterDev.

The next step of the wizard asks whether you want to Create a New Web Application or Connect to an Existing Web Application. Choose to Connect to an Existing Web Application, specifically the <Root Web> and click Next. At this point, you might be asked to select what Themes you want to apply to your Web site. Chose None, and proceed until you reach the final stage and click Finish.

The files in your Web directory are shown in a tree control in the right-hand pane in Visual InterDev. You can double-click one of these files to edit it. To create a new ASP page, right-click the server name, click Add, and then Active Server Page.

Visual InterDev is a rich editing environment, one that allows you to easily develop ASP pages. Visual InterDev also adds a database application interface, which can be helpful when you start creating ASP pages that interact with databases (as we'll discuss during Week 3). A thorough discussion of Visual InterDev is beyond the scope of this book. To learn more about Visual InterDev, check out the official InterDev Web site at http://msdn.microsoft.com/vinterdev/ and *Sams Teach Yourself Visual InterDev 6 in 24 Hours*.

Using FrontPage

In the early days of the World Wide Web, no graphical tools were available to create Web pages. Developers had to use simple text editors, such as Notepad, to create HTML pages. As the popularity of the Web grew, several HTML editors came out. One of these editors was Microsoft's FrontPage, a tool used by many Web developers to quickly build professional-looking Web pages. FrontPage focuses on creating HTML elements by allowing the user to simply type in the contents of the Web page and drag and drop in images and links to other Web pages. FrontPage removes the need to know HTML tags by heart.

Although FrontPage may be useful for building HTML Web pages, it has shortcomings when using it to design ASP pages. You cannot simply drag and drop code, and because ASP pages contain scripting code, you cannot create the code for ASP pages as easily as you can create the HTML for a Web page.

Despite this limitation, FrontPage is still often used to create Web pages. Developers use FrontPage's GUI system to create the HTML for a Web page and then view the HTML source of the page created with FrontPage to add in the ASP code. Figure 1.20 shows FrontPage in use.

FrontPage, like InterDev, contains many intricacies and nuances. To learn more about FrontPage, visit http://www.microsoft.com/frontpage/ online, or pick up a copy of *Sams Teach Yourself Microsoft FrontPage 2000 in 21 Days*.

FIGURE **1.20**

FrontPage excels at HTML Web page design.

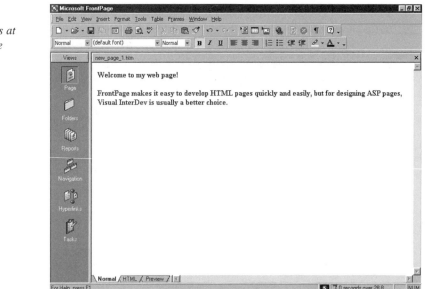

Creating Your First ASP Pages

To create ASP pages, you need access to a computer with a Web server that supports Active Server Pages technology. In "Running ASP Pages," we showed how to set up and install two free Microsoft Web servers: Personal Web Server and Internet Information Server. At this point, you should either have an ASP-enabled Web server installed on your computer, or have access to a computer that has such a Web server already installed.

After you have a Web server installed, you can create ASP pages in your Web site's root physical directory, or in subdirectories of the root physical directory, and view the result of these ASP pages through a standard Web browser. Because ASP pages are processed completely on the server-side and only return HTML to the client, any Web browser can be used to view ASP pages. There are no restrictions on the client-side.

You now have the elements necessary to create and visit ASP pages. Over the next four days, you will learn the ins and outs of the VBScript scripting language, the most commonly used scripting language for ASP pages. Although at this point you may not be familiar with VBScript, let's look at an example ASP page. This will help you become familiar with the notation and VBScript syntax. Furthermore, it will show you some neat things you can do with Active Server Pages.

Imagine that, depending on the time of the day, you want a Web page to display a different message. For example, if the time is 11:00 AM, you want to display Good Morning!, whereas if the time is 5:00 PM, you want to display Good Evening!

Using static HTML pages, you would have to edit the HTML page twice a day—once before noon and once after, altering the Web page and changing its message. With ASP pages, however, you can use programmatic code to determine the current time and display a custom message based on the time. Listing 1.5 contains the code for an ASP page that displays a custom message based on the current time.

LISTING 1.5   Displaying a Different Message Depending on the Time of Day

```
 1:  <%@ Language=VBScript %>
 2:  <% Option Explicit %>
 3:
 4:  <HTML>
 5:  <BODY>
 6:    The current time is <%=Time()%>
 7:    <P>
 8:  <%
 9:    If DatePart("h",Time()) >= 12 then
10:       'Is is after noon
11:       Response.Write "Good Evening!"
12:    Else
13:       'Is is before noon
14:       Response.Write "Good Morning!"
15:    End If
16: %>
17:
18: </BODY>
19: </HTML>
```

ANALYSIS To view the output of Listing 1.5, create an ASP page named `TimeBasedMessage.asp` and save this file in your Web's root physical directory. Enter the code in Listing 1.5, save the file, and then view it through your browser of choice using the following URL:

`http://localhost/TimeBasedMessage.asp`

Let's look over the code in Listing 1.5. Line 1 begins with the @LANGUAGE directive, which informs the Web server what scripting language the current ASP page is using and will be discussed in more depth tomorrow, Day 2, "Dissecting Your First ASP Script." Always include this directive in the first line of your ASP pages. Line 2, Option Explicit, is another line of code that should *always* be used in *every* ASP page you create. When Option Explicit is used, all variables must be explicitly declared. We'll discuss Option Explicit in greater detail on Day 3.

Line 6 displays the current system time using the Time() function. This function is discussed on Day 5. The notation for displaying the results of the function, <%=...%> will be discussed tomorrow. For the time being, realize that <%=...%> shares the same functionality as Response.Write, which outputs information to the client.

Lines 8 through 16 are an ASP code block, denoted by the <% and %> delimiters. An If statement is used on line 9 to determine whether the current time is after or at noon or before noon. We will discuss If statements and other control statements in Day 4. The DatePart, which is used here to get just the hour portion of the current time, is discussed on Day 5.

Figure 1.21 shows the output of Listing 1.5 when viewed through a browser.

FIGURE 1.21

A custom message is displayed depending on the current system time.

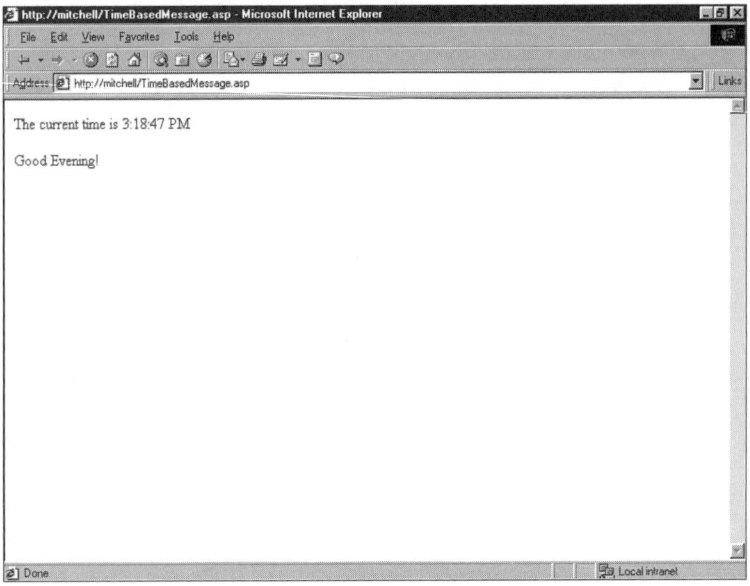

Congratulations on creating a fully functional ASP page! The rest of this week will explore the VBScript language. Because the advantage of using ASP pages is the capability to execute programmatic code, having a solid understanding of the VBScript language is vital.

Summary

You have taken you first step toward becoming an Active Server Pages developer. Today, we looked at the client-server model and how it relates to the Internet, and, more specifically, to ASP pages. When a static HTML page is requested from a Web server, the page is just sent, as is, to the client (refer to Figure 1.1). When an ASP page is requested, though, the Web server processes the programmatic code, translating it to raw HTML. When this processing of the programmatic code is complete, the HTML generated is sent to the client (refer to Figure 1.2). Because an ASP page returns HTML, the Web browser does not notice any difference between the results of an ASP page or a static HTML page.

To process ASP pages on your computer, you need to install an ASP-enabled Web server. Microsoft makes two Web servers that are ASP-enabled: Personal Web Server (PWS), which is intended for Microsoft Windows 95 and 98, and Windows NT Workstation; and Internet Information Server (IIS), which is intended for Windows 2000 or Windows NT Server 4.0. IIS is currently at version 5.0, which ships with Windows 2000. IIS 5.0 comes with ASP 3.0, whereas earlier versions, as well as Personal Web Server, can run only ASP 2.0. These Microsoft Web servers are free and can be downloaded from Microsoft's Web site.

If you don't run Microsoft Windows, or don't want to use one of Microsoft's Web servers, you can use a third-party component to execute ASP pages on a non-Microsoft Web server. Halcyon Software's iASP and Chili!Soft's Chili!ASP allow for Active Server Pages to be run on non-Microsoft Web servers and on non-Microsoft platforms. To find out more about these products, be sure to visit these vendors' Web sites.

To create an ASP page, all you really need is a text editor, such as Notepad. More professional tools are available, though, such as Microsoft's Visual InterDev or FrontPage. Because ASP pages are simply text files that exist in the root physical directory or one of the root physical directory's subdirectories, any editor will do. To view an ASP page, launch your browser of choice and visit the appropriate URL.

We concluded today's lesson by looking at an example ASP page that displayed a message depending on the current system time (refer to Listing 1.5). This example script leads nicely into tomorrow's lesson, where we'll examine the essential elements of an ASP page.

Q&A

Q Is there anyway to view the output of an ASP page without having a Web server installed?

A No. You can view the contents of an ASP page by using Notepad or any other text editor, but you cannot *execute* an ASP page and view its HTML results without having an ASP-enabled Web server installed. Of course, if the ASP page does not exist on your machine but rather on a Web server somewhere else, you can view the output of that ASP page using a standard Web browser.

Q How does ASP 3.0 differ from ASP 2.0?

A ASP 3.0, which is only available through IIS 5.0, contains some new features from ASP 2.0 and increased performance in certain areas. Some of the new functionality in ASP 3.0 is discussed on Day 13, "Reading and Writing Files on the Web Server," and Day 14, "Debugging Your ASP Scripts and Handling Errors." Throughout the book, if we discuss a feature new to ASP 3.0, we'll be sure to mention it!

Q How do I put my ASP pages on the Internet? I have installed a Web server on my computer, but only I can access these ASP pages.

A To place your ASP-enabled Web site on the Internet, you will need to work with a Web hosting company. These companies have direct connections to the Internet and can help you get your Web site on the Internet for a small monthly fee. By working with these companies, you can have your own domain name and Internet site. To find a recommended list of Web site hosts that support ASP, be sure to check out `http://www.4GuysFromRolla.com/webtech/hosts.shtml`.

Workshop

The Workshop provides quiz questions to help you solidify your understanding of the material covered and exercises to provide you with experience in using what you've learned. Try to understand the quiz and exercise answers before continuing to tomorrow's lesson. Quiz answers are provided in Appendix A, and exercise answers can be found at `http://www.mcp.com/info`.

Quiz

1. True or False: The Internet is based on the client-server model.
2. How does a Web server handle ASP page requests differently than static HTML page requests?
3. What Microsoft Web server is needed to run ASP pages on Windows 95, Windows 98, or Windows NT Workstation?
4. What version of Internet Information Server do you need to be running to use ASP 3.0?
5. True or False: ASP pages can only be run on Microsoft Web servers.
6. What is the default root physical directory when installing both Personal Web Server and Internet Information Server?
7. If you created an ASP file in `C:\InetPub\wwwroot\scripts\hello.asp`, where `C:\InetPub\wwwroot` was your Web's root physical directory, what URL could you use to access `hello.asp` from your machine?
8. True or False: Notepad can be used to create and edit ASP pages?

Exercise

1. Today, we looked at how to create and execute ASP pages. For this exercise, create an ASP page named `HelloWorld.asp`, which contains the following code:

```
1:  <%@ Language = VBSCRIPT %>
2:  <% Option Explicit %>
3:  <%
4:      Response.Write "Hello, world!"
5:  %>
```

What will the output be? Save this file to your root physical directory and visit it through a browser. What URL will you use to visit this ASP page?

DAY 2

Dissecting Your First ASP Script

Yesterday, you typed in your very first ASP script. Today, we will break that script down and look at what each of its components does. By the end of the day, you should have a solid grasp on the overall structure of an ASP page, so you will be prepared for the programming topics of the next few days. Today, you will learn the following:

- How to write pages with ASP code in them
- How to send output from the ASP to the HTML
- What the languages of ASP are
- How to comment your code
- How ASP generates the page seen by the user

Today, you will also see several previews of things to come. If you are not already an experienced programmer, this will include many new concepts that are only touched on briefly. Do not worry. They will be explained in greater detail on Day 3, "Working with Variables," and Day 4, "Understanding VBScript Control Structures."

Understanding ASP Scripts

Yesterday, you glanced at several ASP scripts. Today, we will examine them in greater depth, to understand their structure. To begin, the last example from Day 1 is listed again in Listing 2.1. This is an ASP page that prints out "Good Evening!" if the current time is past noon, and "Good Morning!" otherwise.

LISTING 2.1   Your First ASP Script

```
1.  <%@ Language=VBScript %>
2.  <% Option Explicit %>
3.
4.  <HTML>
5.    <BODY>
6.      The current time is <%=Time()%>
7.      <P>
8.  <%
9.      If DatePart("h",Time()) >= 12 then
10.        'Is is after noon
11.        Response.Write "Good Evening!"
12.      Else
13.        'Is is before noon
14.        Response.Write "Good Morning!"
15.      End If
16. %>
17.
18.    </BODY>
19. </HTML>
```

We will examine several parts of this in detail.

ANALYSIS   The first things we will look at are the <% and %> tags. You should be familiar with HTML tags. For example, you know that text in between <B> and </B> will appear in bold. Well, these tags are similar. The text that appears in between <% and %> is designated as ASP code. This is what the server processes before it sends the page to the Web browser. For example, on lines 8 and 16 you see the opening and closing tags. That means that the stuff on lines 9 through 15 is ASP code.

Try taking lines 8 and 16 out and view this page through your Web browser. You will see something like Figure 2.1. What has happened?

Without the tags <% and %>, your server does not know to treat the text from lines 9 through 15 as ASP code. Instead, it thinks that it is simple text, like in any HTML page. Forgetting one or both tags is a common cause of error among beginning ASP programmers. Fortunately, it is easily corrected.

FIGURE 2.1

Viewing Listing 2.1 without the <%...%> tags.

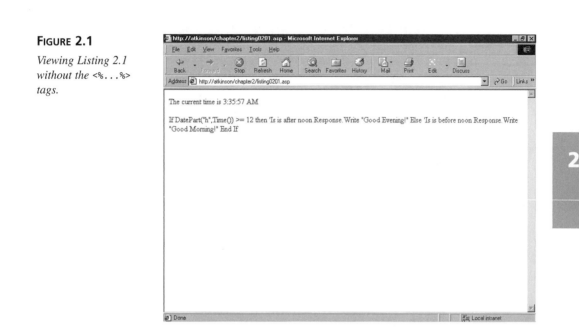

2

 Note

The <%...%> tags are not the only way to mark ASP code. You may be familiar with the HTML <SCRIPT>...</SCRIPT> tags. They can be used, too, as we will see in the section "Writing ASP Code Without Using <%...%>."

You are certainly not limited to only one pair of ASP tags on a page. Listing 2.2 is equivalent to Listing 2.1.

Caution

Although Listing 2.2 works just like Listing 2.1, it is confusing and more prone to typos. See the analysis of Listing 2.2 for more details.

LISTING 2.2 Equivalent to Listing 2.1

```
1.  <%@ Language=VBScript %>
2.  <% Option Explicit %>
3.
4.   <HTML>
5.     <BODY>
6.     The current time is <%=Time()%>
7.     <P>
8.  <%
9.     If DatePart("h",Time()) >= 12 then
10. %>
```

continues

LISTING 2.2   continued

```
11.   <%
12.        'Is is after noon
13.   %>
14.   <%
15.        Response.Write "Good Evening!"
16.   %>
17.   <%
18.     Else
19.   %>
20.   <%
21.        'Is is before noon
22.   %>
23.   <%
24.        Response.Write "Good Morning!"
25.   %>
26.   <%
27.     End If
28.   %>
29.
30.     </BODY>
31.   </HTML>
```

ANALYSIS   Here we have used a pair of tags for each line of ASP code. There is an opening tag on line 8, then a single line of code, then a closing tag, followed by another opening tag, and so forth. This is inefficient and difficult to read. In HTML, it would be like making an entire sentence boldface by making each word boldface individually. Otherwise, though, it is perfectly legal and does exactly the same thing as Listing 2.1.

There is something you need to be careful about. Although it is okay to have HTML tags within HTML tags, it is not okay to have ASP tags within ASP tags. The following will generate an error:

```
<%
<%
   Response.Write "Good Morning!"
%>
%>
```

You can put ASP code within HTML tags, as long as you use <%...%>. Try the example shown in Listing 2.3.

LISTING 2.3   ASP Code Inside HTML Tags

```
1.   <%@ Language=VBScript %>
2.   <% Option Explicit %>
3.   <HTML>
4.     <BODY>
```

```
5.      <B>
6.      <%
7.          Response.Write "Hello"
8.      %>
9.      </B>
10.     <%
11.         Response.Write " World"
12.     %>
13.   </BODY>
14. </HTML>
```

Save this file as `listing0203.asp`. Be sure to put it in the folder you configured PWS for.

ANALYSIS Line 8 opens an ordinary HTML boldface tag. Then, line 6 begins a block of ASP code. Line 7 writes a word out, line 8 closes the ASP block, and line 9 closes the boldface tag. Lines 10 through 12 create another block of ASP code that prints out the rest of the message.

Figure 2.2 shows how this page looks in your Web browser. Notice that the HTML bold tags affect the ASP code on line 7, but not the ASP code on line 11.

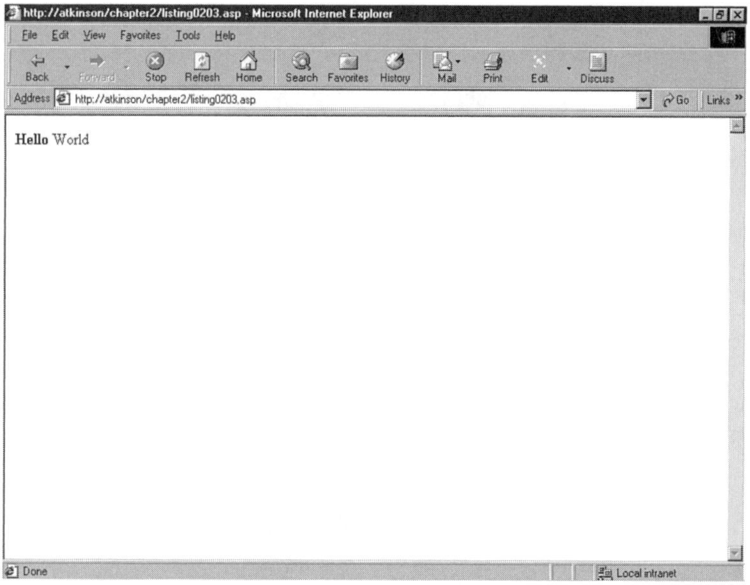

FIGURE 2.2

Viewing Listing 2.3.

There is nothing special about putting the ASP tags on a separate line from the actual ASP code. All four of the following are equivalent:

1.

```
<%
```

```
        Response.Write "Hello"
    %>
```

2.

```
    <%  Response.Write "Hello" %>
```

3.

```
    <%  Response.Write "Hello"
    %>
```

4.

```
        <%

        Response.Write "Hello"
    %>
```

We will generally write ASP statements like number 1 for readability. All four are perfectly legal, though, and exactly the same as far as the server is concerned.

What Does `Response.Write` Do?

This subject will be covered in greater detail on Day 7, "Using the `Response` Object." For now, you only need to know that `Response.Write` is used to go from ASP on the server to the HTML seen in the user's Web browser.

For example, consider the following code:

```
<B>
<%
   Response.Write "Hello"
%>
</B>
```

The text "Hello" is sent to the output stream. The result sent to the user is <B>Hello</B>, so in the Web browser, the user will see the word "Hello" printed in boldface.

If the text written by `Response.Write` contains HTML tags, they will be interpreted as such by the user's Web browser. So the following will also cause "Hello" to be displayed in boldface in the user's browser:

```
<%
   Response.Write "<B>Hello</B>"
%>
```

Be careful that you do not forget one or both of the quotation marks.

Listing 2.4 gives a slightly longer, though still fairly simple, ASP script. This page, when viewed through the Web browser, will produce the output shown in Figure 2.3.

LISTING 2.4 A Longer Example of `Response.Write`

```
1.   <%@ Language=VBScript %>
2.   <% Option Explicit %>
3.   <HTML>
4.     <BODY>
5.       I can count to five!
6.     <%
7.           Response.Write "<BR>1"
8.           Response.Write "<BR>2"
9.           Response.Write "<BR>3"
10.          Response.Write "<BR>4"
11.          Response.Write "<BR>5"
12.    %>
13.    </BODY>
14.   </HTML>
```

ANALYSIS Line 1 will be explained later today, in the section "What's with the <%@ LAN-GUAGE=VBSCRIPT%>?". Line 2 will be explained on Day 3. For now, just remember that two lines should be at the top of every ASP page you write.

Lines 3 and 4 should be familiar to you. Their matching closing tags are on lines 13 and 14. Line 5 is a simple message, written the way you would normally write it.

Line 6 opens a block of ASP code. Now, on lines 7 through 11, you can see five lines of `Response.Write`, back to back.

Line 12 closes the block of ASP code. This is important. Without line 12, lines 13 and 14 would be interpreted as ASP code.

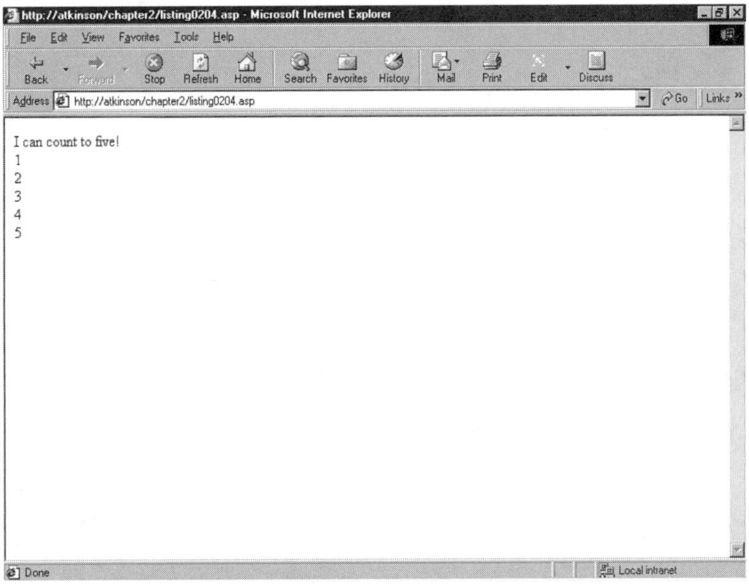

FIGURE 2.3

Output of Listing 2.4.

At this point, this may all seem a little pointless. After all, you have not done much with ASP that could not be done easier without ASP. You might say to yourself that you could write a plain HTML page that does the same thing as Listing 2.4 in a lot fewer characters. You would be correct. What if you wanted to print the numbers 1 to 100, instead? Listing 2.5 will do that.

LISTING 2.5   A Preview of Things to Come

```
1.    <%@ Language=VBScript %>
2.    <% Option Explicit %>
3.    <HTML>
4.      <BODY>
5.        I can count to one hundred!
6.      <%
7.          Dim iCount
8.          For iCount = 1 to 100
9.             Response.Write "<BR>"
10.            Response.Write iCount
11.          Next
12.      %>
13.      </BODY>
14.    </HTML>
```

Okay, so this is still kind of a silly example. Nevertheless, it should help to illustrate how ASP expands the capabilities of your pages.

ANALYSIS   Line 7, by the way, declares a variable for use in your script. Variables are discussed further on Day 3. Lines 8 and 11 are an example of a control structure called a loop. Control structures are discussed further on Day 4.

The <%= Shortcut

You can use a shortcut in place of Response.Write. The following two are equivalent:

```
<%= expression %>
```

and

```
<%
   Response.Write expression
%>
```

You can see an example of the shortcut being used on line 6 of Listing 2.1.

```
The current time is <%=Time()%>
```

The preceding line is really no different than this:

```
The current time is
<%
```

```
    Response.Write Time()
%>
```

Notice that the shortcut only works outside an ASP block. For example, each of the following will result in an error:

```
<%
    Response.Write "The current time is"
    <%=Time() %>
%>
```

and

```
<%
    Response.Write "The current time is"
    =Time()
%>
```

So, you have three different ways of sending data to the HTML. The first is to simply not put it inside an ASP block in the first place. The second is to use Response.Write, and the third is to use the shortcut. Listing 2.6 uses all three methods.

LISTING 2.6 Three Different Ways of Writing Text

```
1.  <%@ Language=VBScript %>
2.  <% Option Explicit %>
3.  <HTML>
4.    <BODY>
5.      First
6.      <%
7.          Response.Write "Second"
8.      %>
9.      <%= "Third" %>
10.   </BODY>
11. </HTML>
```

ANALYSIS Line 5 prints "First" using normal text outside of ASP tags. Line 7 uses Response.Write inside of the ASP tags. Line 9 uses the shortcut. For now, do not worry about using the shortcut. On Day 7, you will learn more about when you should use each method.

What's with the `<%@ LANGUAGE=VBSCRIPT%>`?

At the very top of your first script, you will see a line that reads `<%@ LANGUAGE=VBSCRIPT%>`. This line sets the language that ASP will use.

Yes, you may not have realized it, but ASP is not a language. It is a server technology. The language we have been using to program is actually VBScript. VBScript is not the only language you can use with ASP, though. JavaScript, for example, can be used, as shown in Listing 2.7.

LISTING 2.7 ASP Using JavaScript

```
1.   <%@ Language=JavaScript %>
2.   <HTML>
3.     <BODY>
4.   <%
5.       d = new Date();
6.       if (d.getHours() > 12)
7.           Response.Write("Good Evening");
8.       else
9.           Response.Write("Good Morning");
10.  %>
11.    </BODY>
12.  </HTML>
```

This prints out "Good Evening" if it is past noon, and "Good Morning" otherwise, just as Listing 2.1 does. This is still ASP, just with a different language.

ANALYSIS Line 1 sets the language as JavaScript. The code on lines 5 through 9 is then interpreted as JavaScript. It is difficult to tell the differences between JavaScript and VBScript from this one small example.

JavaScript is not used much for server-side scripting. VBScript is generally considered easier to learn. So, we will not be using JavaScript for server-side scripting in this book. If you really want to learn JavaScript, refer to a book such as *Sams Teach Yourself JavaScript 1.3 in 24 Hours*. It is not too different from the C, C++, and Java programming languages; so if you have experience with them, it should be easy to pick up.

Note

JavaScript is the preferred language for client-side scripting. This is mainly because when you are doing client-side scripting, you have to be concerned about browser compatibility. Only Microsoft Internet Explorer supports VBScript, whereas both major browsers support JavaScript. When doing server-side scripting, however, it does not matter whether the Web browser supports the language. The Web browser will never even see server-side scripting code. For more information, see the discussion of server-side processing later today in the section "What Your ASP Script Returned to the Browser."

VBScript's primary advantage is being easy to learn. VBScript is based on the popular Visual Basic. If you have used Visual Basic, the transition will be even easier.

VBScript is also the default language for ASP. This means that if you are planning to use VBScript, the `<%@ LANGUAGE=...%>` line is not really necessary. If you leave it out, the server will assume that you mean to use VBScript. Still, it is a good idea to go ahead and include that line anyway. It makes your code a little easier for others to figure out.

VBScript and JavaScript are not the only two languages you can use with ASP, by the way. PerlScript, Python, and Jscript (Microsoft's version of JavaScript) can be used, too. Even if you already know one of these languages, it is worth learning VBScript because it is so commonly used.

Writing ASP Code Without Using <%...%>

As mentioned n the section "What's with the <%@ LANGUAGE=VBSCRIPT%>?" there is a way to write ASP code without using <%...%>. We will not use it in this book, but it is worth taking a quick look at, since you might encounter it sometime.

You may recall from yesterday that we discussed the differences between client-side scripting and server-side scripting. Client-side scripting is run on the user's computer, after the page has been downloaded. If you have ever looked at client-side scripting, you probably recognize the HTML <SCRIPT> and </SCRIPT> tags. They are used to insert client-side scripting code into an HTML page.

For example, you might see something like this:

```
<SCRIPT LANGUAGE=JAVASCRIPT>
   d = new Date();
   if (d.getHours() > 12)
      document.write("Good Evening");
   else
      document.write("Good Morning");
</SCRIPT>
```

This does pretty much the same thing as Listing 2.1, only on the client-side, with JavaScript. document.write is used in place of Response.Write because this is being run on the client side. Do not worry about understanding this. It is just provided as an example of client-side scripting.

The same tag can be used to insert server-side scripting code, too. All it needs is an extra directive to specify that the server should execute it:

```
<SCRIPT LANGUAGE=JAVASCRIPT RUNAT=SERVER>
   d = new Date();
   if (d.getHours() > 12)
      response.write("Good Evening");
   else
      response.write("Good Morning");
</SCRIPT>
```

Now this will be run as server-side JavaScript. You can use VBScript this way, too:

```
<SCRIPT LANGUAGE=VBSCRIPT RUNAT=SERVER>
   If DatePart("h",Time()) >= 12 then
      Response.Write "Good Evening!"
   Else
```

2

```
        Response.Write "Good Morning!"
      End If
</SCRIPT>
```

As mentioned earlier, we will not use this method in this book. Why? Well, for one thing, the other way is simpler (fewer characters to type) and used more. Finally, there is an extra complication if you use <SCRIPT> for your server-side scripting: order of execution.

The output of Listing 2.8 can be seen in Figure 2.4, and the output of Listing 2.9 can be seen in Figure 2.5. Compare the two listings and their output.

LISTING 2.8 Using <SCRIPT> for Server-Side Scripting

```
1.  <HTML>
2.    <BODY>
3.      <SCRIPT LANGUAGE=VBSCRIPT RUNAT=SERVER>
4.          Response.Write("First")
5.      </SCRIPT>
6.      Second
7.    </BODY>
8.  </HTML>
```

FIGURE 2.4

Looking at the order of execution of <SCRIPT>.

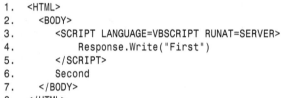

LISTING 2.9   Using <%...%> for Server-Side Scripting

```
1.   <HTML>
2.     <BODY>
3.       <%
4.            Response.Write("First")
5.       %>
6.       Second
7.     </BODY>
8.   </HTML>
```

FIGURE 2.5

Looking at the order of execution with
<%...%>.

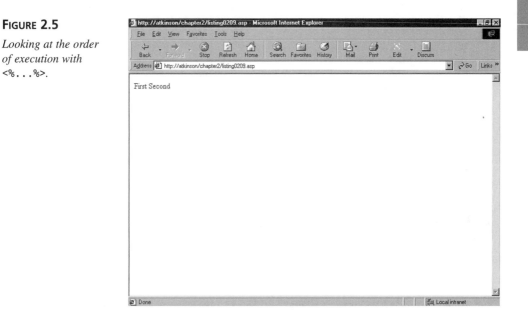

Notice how in the version that uses <SCRIPT>, the word "First" comes after "Second" (refer to Figure 2.4)? This is because <SCRIPT> is always executed last. This makes things counterintuitive.

You can even mix <SCRIPT> and <%...%> in the same page. Listing 2.10 demonstrates the different kinds of scripting all in one page.

LISTING 2.10   All the Different Kinds of Scripting

```
1.   <%@ Language=VBScript %>
2.   <% Option Explicit %>
3.   <HTML>
4.     <BODY>
5.       I am HTML<P>
```

continues

LISTING 2.10   continued

```
6.
7.      <%
8.        Response.Write "I am server-side VBScript using <% <P>"
9.      %>
10.
11.   <SCRIPT LANGUAGE=JAVASCRIPT>
12.     document.write("I am client-side JavaScript<P>");
13.   </SCRIPT>
14.
15.   <SCRIPT LANGUAGE=VBSCRIPT>
16.     document.write("I am client-side VBScript<P>")
17.   </SCRIPT>
18.
19.   <SCRIPT LANGUAGE=JAVASCRIPT RUNAT=SERVER>
20.     response.write("I am server-side JavaScript using the SCRIPT tag<P>");
21.   </SCRIPT>
22.
23.   <SCRIPT LANGUAGE=VBSCRIPT RUNAT=SERVER>
24.     response.write("I am server-side VBScript using the SCRIPT tag<P>")
25.   </SCRIPT>
26.
27.     </BODY>
28.   </HTML>
```

ANALYSIS   Line 5 writes the message "I am HTML" using, of course, plain HTML.

Lines 7 and 9 declare an ASP block using the <% and %>. Line 8 uses Response.Write to write a similar message from within the ASP.

Lines 11 through 13 use client-side JavaScript. Lines 15 through 17 use client-side VBScript. This is only supported in Internet Explorer.

Lines 19 through 21 are server-side JavaScript code, using the <SCRIPT> tag. Notice the RUNAT=SERVER being used to specify this. Lines 23 through 25 are server-side VBScript code, again using the <SCRIPT> tag.

As you can imagine, sorting out when everything is executed is difficult. This is why we will avoid using <SCRIPT> for server-side scripting altogether. You can see the results of this script in Figure 2.6. Are they what you would have expected?

Comments

You may be familiar with the notion of comments from your work with HTML. If you are not, comments are lines inserted into code for the benefit of the programmer and anyone trying to understand the code. Comments do not affect the actual execution of the script.

FIGURE 2.6

Looking at the
</SCRIPT> HTML
order of execution from
Listing 2.10.

2

Look back to Listing 2.1. Lines 10 and 13 are comments. You can remove them without changing anything as far as the system is concerned. Either way, the end-user will see exactly the same thing.

In VBScript, comments are indicated using the single quote ('). Any line that begins with a single quote is a comment line.

Many programmers get lazy and do not use comments in their code. This is a bad practice. It makes things a little more difficult for themselves and a lot more difficult for anyone who might need to read and change the code later. Different people think differently and write code differently. Commenting allows you to put into English the logic that you are using.

Commenting is not terribly important in the simple scripts we will be looking at over the next few days. When you get to more complex projects, though, it is essential. If anyone else will ever need to read your code, you must comment it and give him some guidelines about what does what.

By the way, the single quote only works inside ASP code (inside the <%...%>). To comment in HTML, you should use <!-- and -->. For example

```
<%
    'this is a VBScript comment
%>
<!-- this is an HTML comment -->
```

In Jscript, comments are indicated using two forward-slashes (//) like this:

```
<%
    // This is a Jscript comment.
%>
```

The first step is knowing how to comment. The second is knowing when. Anytime you have code where the logic is a bit tricky, you should put a comment to explain it. You should also comment blocks of related code, such as loops, subroutines, and functions. If some of these terms make no sense to you now, they will after Day 4.

> **Note**
>
> Bear in mind when you're commenting that ASP comments are not even sent to the client. HTML comments are sent, but not displayed by their browser. The client can still see HTML comments by using the View, Source command. This might be a factor in how you comment if you have information you specifically want the user to be able to access or not be able to access.

Line Continuation Character

Sometimes, you may encounter a single statement you want to execute that is really long. In fact, it may be so long that trying to put it all on one line is awkward. Take, for example, the following line:

```
Response.Write "Supercalifragilisticexpialadocious"
```

You might decide that it would be better to use two lines for this expression. Try viewing Listing 2.11 in your Web browser.

LISTING 2.11   Breaking Up a Statement into Two Lines

```
1.   <%@ Language=VBScript %>
2.   <% Option Explicit %>
3.   <HTML>
4.     <BODY>
5.       <%
6.         Response.Write
7.             "Supercalifragilisticexpialadocious"
8.       %>
9.     </BODY>
10.  </HTML>
```

You get an error message because VBScript uses line breaks to figure out where a statement ends. Because of this, lines 6 and 7 are treated as separate commands. This is not what you want, as shown in Figure 2.7.

FIGURE 2.7

Viewing the error generated by Listing 2.11.

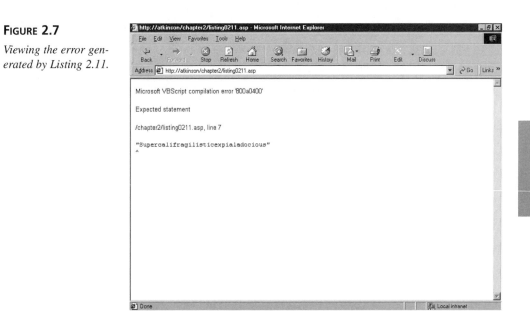

That is why we use the line continuation character. The line continuation character for VBScript is the underscore (_). Putting it on the end of a line says "continued on the next line." Try adding an underscore on the end of line 6 (see Listing 2.12).

LISTING 2.12 Breaking Up a Statement into Two Lines the Right Way

```
1.  <%@ Language=VBScript %>
2.  <% Option Explicit %>
3.  <HTML>
4.    <BODY>
5.      <%
6.        Response.Write _
7.          "Supercalifragilisticexpialadocious"
8.      %>
9.    </BODY>
10. </HTML>
```

Now you get the results you intended (see Figure 2.8).

In fact, you could use several line continuation characters on several lines, as shown in Listing 2.13. It is pointless, but it is legal.

FIGURE 2.8

Viewing Listing 2.12.

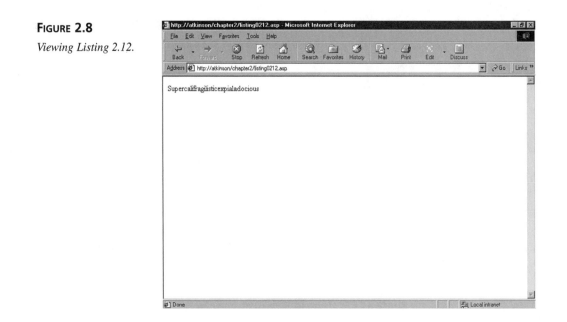

LISTING 2.13 Using the Line Continuation Character Some More

```
1.  <%@ Language=VBScript %>
2.  <% Option Explicit %>
3.  <HTML>
4.    <BODY>
5.      <%
6.          Response.Write _
7.                  _
8.                  _
9.                  _
10.                 _
11.         "Supercalifragilisticexpialadocious"
12.     %>
13.   </BODY>
14. </HTML>
```

What happens if you try putting the line continuation character in the middle of an output, as in Listing 2.14? You will get an error.

LISTING 2.14 Breaking Up a Statement in the Middle of a Text String

```
1.  <%@ Language=VBScript %>
2.  <% Option Explicit %>
3.  <HTML>
4.    <BODY>
5.      <%
```

```
6.        Response.Write "Supercal _
7.     ifragilisticexpialadocious"
8.       %>
9.     </BODY>
10. </HTML>
```

This does not work because the underscore is inside the double quotes. This means that the system will think you want to print the underscore. It will not interpret it as "continued on next line."

Things to Come

There are still several things in Listing 2.1 that we have not discussed yet today.

The significance of line 2 will be covered on Day 3.

How the script makes the decision to display "Good Morning" or "Good Evening" is covered on Day 4's discussion of control structures.

Time and DatePart (see lines 6 and 9) are two of the functions discussed on Day 5, "Using VBScript's Built-in Functions."

What Your ASP Script Returned to the Browser

Questions commonly asked by beginning ASP programmers might be "How can I use ASP to make this image change when the mouse moves over it?" or "How can I use ASP to keep people from entering bad data in this form?" The answer to both questions is you can't. This does not mean, of course, that these tasks cannot be accomplished. They can, but ASP is not the answer.

These beginning programmers are trying to use server-side scripting to solve client-side problems. When the page is sent to the user, ASP's work is finished. It generates an HTML document and sends it on, and it is finished until the user requests the next document. If you are looking for something to happen after the page is downloaded, you are looking for client-side solutions. Client-side JavaScript is probably what you need.

It is an easy mistake to make. When you look at an ASP page you are working on, you see the HTML and the ASP at once. The idea that they are executed at different times is difficult to grasp.

Figure 2.9 shows the source code the Web browser gets when it loads the page in Listing 2.1.

You can see that the Web browser has no idea that the page it received is anything special. It looks like plain, static HTML to the browser. This does not mean that ASP is not powerful. It really is quite powerful. It's just that when the ASP is finished, it needs to be able to express itself in terms of normal HTML.

FIGURE **2.9**

Viewing the source
code received by the
browser for Listing 2.1.

Think about Listing 2.1 again. It displays the current time at the top when you view it. It figures out what the current time is, converts it to text, and inserts it into the HTML. This is still a dynamic Web site. A person who visits the site at 1 p.m. sees a different page than the one who visits at 5 p.m., even if you have not made any changes to the actual ASP file.

The ASP Process

You may still be a little unclear on how server-side scripting works, so let's take a look at what happens when you view an ASP page in your browser (see Figure 2.10).

FIGURE **2.10**

A look at what
happens when you
view an ASP page.

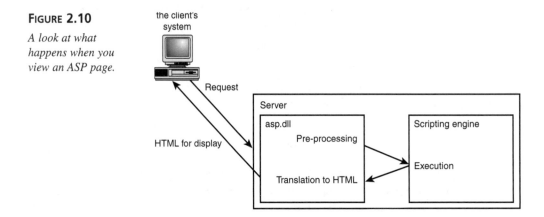

Figure 2.10 provides a picture of the process ASP goes through to send a page to the user. There are five stages that we will concern ourselves with at this point:

1. Request—The Web browser contacts the server and tells it what page it wants to see.
2. Preprocessing—The `asp.dll` file does some initial processing on the requested script. At the moment, you do not need to worry about what this processing is.
3. Execution—The scripting engine executes the instructions in the script.
4. Translation—ASP translates the results of the execution into HTML.
5. Display—The HTML is sent back to the Web browser, which processes the tags and displays the page.

Try to bear this process in mind as you go through this book. Remember that the ASP process ends when the page is sent back to the user. Everything you want it to do must be done by then.

Summary

Today, we looked some more at what ASP is and what an ASP script looks like.

ASP is a server-side technology, which means that it should be finished by the time the page is downloaded. It does all its work and then generates an ordinary HTML page that is sent to the browser.

ASP code is separated from normal ASP code by one of two sets of tags. The first, simplest, and most commonly used are the `<%...%>` tags. The other option is to use `<SCRIPT>` and `</SCRIPT>`, which are more commonly used for client-side scripting. By specifying `RUNAT=SERVER`, though, they can be used for server-side scripting, too. There is, however, the complication that code inside `<SCRIPT>` and `</SCRIPT>` is executed last.

`Response.Write` is used to send output from an ASP block to the HTML. So, if you had this

```
<B>
<% Response.Write "Hello" %>
</B>
```

the user's Web browser would received this:

```
<B>Hello</B>
```

There is a shortcut alternative to `Response.Write`. The following are equivalent:

```
<% Response.Write "Hello" %>
```

and

```
<%= "Hello" %>
```

Several programming languages can be used with ASP. VBScript, which is based on Microsoft's Visual Basic, is by far the favorite. It is easy to learn and has many nice features. JavaScript and PerlScript are two of the others that can be used but are far less popular. JavaScript does remain the language of choice for client-side scripting, though.

The language to be used is specified by putting the directive

```
<%@ Language=name_of_the_language %>
```

at the top of the page. VBScript is the default language for ASP, so it is not truly necessary to include this line if you are using VBScript. It is, however, recommended, for clarity.

Comment lines are lines of text that are solely for the benefit of the programmers working on the page. They do not affect script execution. They can be used to provide a helpful explanation of what a particular line or block of code does. In VBScript, comment lines start with a single quote ('). In HTML, comments are put between <!-- and --> .

When a statement is so long that you want to break it up, you can use the line continuation character to tell the system that the statement is "continued on the next line." For VBScript, the line continuation character is the underscore (_).

Q&A

Q Can server-side scripting and client-side scripting coexist?

A Sure. You can certainly use both in the same page. There are many circumstances in which you will want to. You just have to remember that they can coexist, but they cannot really cooperate. They cannot share data or communicate back and forth.

Q So what can server-side scripting do that client-side scripting can't?

A At this point it may look like ASP is pretty limiting. Nothing could be farther from the truth. The power of ASP comes in when you use it to access data on the server. By the time you finish this book, you will be able to use ASP to read and write to files and databases. With this, your pages can save and recall information, adding a whole new dimension to them.

Workshop

The Workshop provides quiz questions to help you solidify your understanding of the material covered and exercises to provide you with experience in using what you've learned. Try to understand the quiz and exercise answers before continuing to tomorrow's lesson. Quiz answers are provided in Appendix A, and exercise answers can be found at http://www.mcp.com/info.

Quiz

1. What is wrong with this code:

```
<% Response.Write "Hello, World"
   %>
%>
```

2. What kind of scripting is the `<SCRIPT>` tag used for?

3. How are comments written in VBScript?

4. What does the underscore character mean?

5. What does `Response.Write` do?

6. What is the shortcut alternative to `Response.Write`?

7. Is it possible to write a page that displays the current time using ASP?

8. Is it possible to write a ticking clock using ASP?

Exercises

1. Consider the following ASP Script:

```
1.   <%@ Language=VBScript %>
2.   <% Option Explicit %>
3.   <HTML>
4.     <BODY>
5.     Today is:
6.       <!--
7.            print the current date
8.       -->
9.       <%= Date() %>,
10.      a
11.      <%
12.          Dim arrDOW
13.          arrDOW = Array("Sunday", "Monday", "Tuesday", "Wednesday", _
14.                  "Thursday", "Friday", "Saturday")
15.          Response.Write arrDOW(DatePart("w", Date()) - 1)
16.          Response.Write " and the current time is "
17.          'print the time
18.          Response.Write Time()
19.      %>
20.    </BODY>
21.  </HTML>
```

What language is this written in?

2. Find an example of a VBScript comment.

3. Find an example of an HTML comment.

4. What lines, besides the first two, contain ASP code?

5. Find all the uses of `Response.Write` in this script.

6. Find all the uses of the shortcut alternative to `Response.Write` in this script.

7. Convert the shortcut into a `Response.Write`.

DAY **3**

Working with Variables

Now that you know what ASP is and what an ASP page looks like, it is time to get into some programming topics. Today, you will learn about variables and operators. These are fundamental to moving and manipulating data in ASP and VBScript. Without these, your pages would have no way of remembering the information they are told and would be unable to perform basic computations using that information. Today, you will learn the following:

- What a variable is
- What the different types of variables are
- Good programming techniques with variables
- What operators are found in VBScript and how to use them
- What operator precedence is and how it affects programmers

What Is a Variable?

If you have never programmed before, you may wonder what the term *variable* means. A variable is a small section of a computer's memory that you give a name to. Think of a variable as a box into which you can put numbers, letters, dates, and more. This information can now be carried around and manipulated by referring to the name you gave it. For example, as illustrated in Figure 3.1, you might put the number 3 into a variable. Then you might add 1 to it. Or you could decide that you do not want that number after all, and so you replace it with 5. All these things, and more, are possible with variables.

FIGURE 3.1

A variable may be thought of as a box that data is put into.

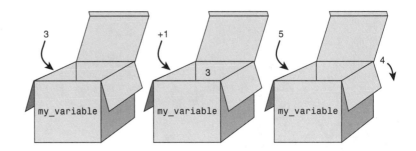

Data Types

There are many different types of data that you might want to be able to store into a variable: numbers, words, dates, and many more. In this section, you will look at a few of the most important data types that can be stored in variables and discuss the way in which VBScript does this.

Integer

An *integer* is a whole number—that is, a number with no fractional portion. For example, 1, 3, 9, and -4 are all integers, but 1.2, 0.9, and -5.5 are not.

Two other data types are related to the integer: byte and long. A long can store a larger range of numbers than an integer. A byte stores fewer. You do not have to worry too much about which range your numeric values fall into. VBScript handles the issue for you.

Floating-point Numbers

Floating-point numbers may have a decimal. 1.5, -3.4, 4.1, and even 5.0 are all floating-point numbers. It is important to note, however, that although integers are stored exactly, that is not necessarily true of floating-point numbers. Floating-point numbers are often rounded or truncated to fit into the space allotted for them.

Single and Double data types are associated with floating-point numbers. The difference between the two has to do with the precision used to store the number. Doubles require twice as much memory as singles, but can obviously hold a much greater range of numbers and to greater precision than can singles. Again, in VBScript, you do not have to worry about the distinction too much.

By the way, in working with floating-point numbers, you may sometimes see them in scientific notation. If you are not familiar with scientific notation or have forgotten it, the E in the numbers means "10 to the power of." So, for example, 3E5 is 300,000.

String

A string can hold any sequence of letters, numbers, and symbols. Strings are distinguished from code, variable names, and numbers by putting them between double quotation marks. `"My name is Fred."`, `"20mph"`, and `"14"` are all possible strings. Even the empty string `""` can be treated like a string in most cases.

You have already encountered strings in the first two days. When we would use a statement like `Response.Write "Hello"`, the `"Hello"` is a string value. It is not stored in a variable, but it is the same kind of data. String values will be used often in sending output like this. They are also used when we start reading in data from the user, in Days 8 and later.

Do	Don't
DO remember when using digits in strings that there is a difference between a string of digits and a number. The string "14" is handled differently than the integer value 14.	**DON'T** confuse a string variable's name with the value it contains. A string variable called `black` might contain a value of `"white"`.

Date

A nice feature of VBScript that is missing in other programming languages is its date handling. Although it is possible to represent the date using strings and/or integers, this variable type simplifies things. A date variable can hold either a date or a time, and VBScript's various date functions and operators make the formatting and printing of date-related information easy. They will be discussed thoroughly on Day 5, "Using VBScript's Built-in Functions."

Boolean

A Boolean variable may hold a value of either `True` or `False`. Boolean variables are generally used when a decision needs to be made. The value of the variable can determine which of two actions should be taken. This is done with control structure, which will be discussed on Day 4, "Understanding VBScript Control Structures."

Currency

A single precision number would work fine for storing monetary values, but VBScript provides a special data type for money that works with several special VBScript functions and displays nicer. In Day 5 we will discuss the FormatCurrency function, which allows you to customize how currency values are displayed.

Object

This refers to special objects. It is used a lot in performing database operations and will be covered in Week 3.

What Are Variant Variables?

In most programming languages, a distinction must be made between variables of different types. A variable used to contain a string cannot later be used to contain an integer. This is not true in VBScript. VBScript uses *variant variables*, which are variables that may contain values of any type.

What Does It Mean to Declare a Variable?

Many programming languages require that, before you use a variable, you tell the system what type of data you intend to put into the variable and what you want it to be called. For example, in the C++ programming language, you might say

```
int my_variable;
my_variable = 2;
```

NEW TERM   The first line tells the system that you want to use a variable that you will call my_variable, and that you want to be able to put integer data into it. This is an example of an *explicit declaration*. You explicitly tell the system what variable you want to create. The second line begins to use that variable by putting the value 2 into it.

If you are familiar with C or C++, this should look familiar to you. If you are not, you need not be concerned with it. VBScript makes things a little easier. In VBScript, it is not necessary to specify integer, real, char, or whatever when you create a variable. In VBScript, all variables are declared using the keyword dim. This is because VBScript uses the aforementioned variant variables. Therefore, the VBScript equivalent of the preceding statements would be as follows:

```
dim my_variable
my_variable = 2
```

Here the first line declares my_variable without specifying that my_variable will represent an integer.

NEW TERM Further, it is not even necessary to include the first line at all. In VBScript, it would be acceptable to simply use the second line with no prior mention of my_variable whatsoever. This is called an *implicit declaration*. That is, the system figures out on its own that you want to create a variable named my_variable.

Why Use Explicit Declarations in VBScript?

Now that you can see that explicit declarations are not necessary in VBScript, you may well be wondering why anyone would want them. Try putting Listing 3.1 into your editor of choice. Name the file Typo1.asp.

LISTING 3.1 Mistyping a Variable Without Using Option Explicit

```
 1: <%@ Language=VBScript %>
 2: <% myfirstvariable = 2 %>
 3: <HTML>
 4:   <BODY>
 5:     The variable named "myfirstvariable" has a value of
 6: <%
 7:       Response.Write(myfirtvariable)
 8: %>
 9:   </BODY>
10: </HTML>
```

Notice that in line 7, the variable name has been misspelled. This is deliberate. Now try viewing this page. You get no error message, but the result is not what the programmer had intended. In this simple example, you could probably find the problem with no great difficulty. Imagine, though, a longer page with 200 lines. Finding the typo might be a bit more of a challenge!

That is why the following line is often included in active server pages, especially ones of any great length:

```
<% Option Explicit %>
```

Adding this immediately following the <%@ Language=...%> line will cause VBScript to require explicit declarations of all variables. So let's try adding this line into the previous example. Name the new file Typo2.asp. It should now look like Listing 3.2.

LISTING 3.2 Declaring Variables with Option Explicit

```
<%@ Language=VBScript %>
<% Option Explicit %>
<% myfirstvariable = 2 %>
<HTML>
```

continues

LISTING 3.2 continued

```
<BODY>
  The variable named "myfirstvariable" has a value of
<%
  Response.Write(myfirtvariable)
%>
</BODY>
</HTML>
```

You get an error message when you try to view this in your Web browser. It says something like, "Variable is undefined: 'myfirstvariable'." Do you know what is causing this error?

It's the work of that Option Explicit. You did not declare the variable "myfirstvariable" explicitly. So, let's do that, and call this Typo3.asp. This version can be found in Listing 3.3.

LISTING 3.3 Finding the Typo with Option Explicit

```
<%@ Language=VBScript %>
<% Option Explicit %>
<% Dim myfirstvariable
   myfirstvariable = 2
%>
<HTML>
<BODY>
   The variable named "myfirstvariable" has a value of
 <%
   Response.Write(myfirtvariable)
 %>
</BODY>
</HTML>
```

So that is fixed now. Try viewing it again. You will still get an error message. Now it says "Variable is undefined: 'myfirtvariable'." This makes fixing the problem easy because you know you didn't mean to have any variables named 'myfirtvariable'. Also notice that below that it tells you what file the error is in and what line number it is on. You can see the full error message in Figure 3.2. This is much better than when you had a page with incorrect results, but no error message.

Now all you have to do is go down to line 10 and fix your typo!

FIGURE 3.2

Because we used
`Option Explicit,` *we*
see our error.

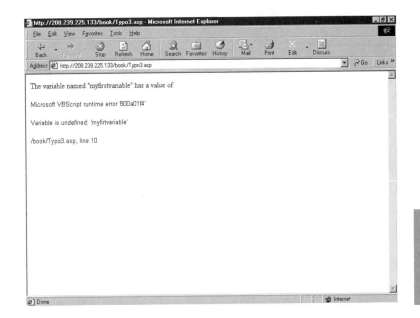

How Do You Name a Variable?

The rules you should follow in deciding what to name your variables can be divided into two groups. The first group of rules helps you avoid error messages. The second group of rules helps make you a better programmer and makes your code easier to read and fix.

Syntax Requirements on Variables

These are rules that you must follow, or the system will not be able to run your code.

- Do not use spaces, periods, or dashes. Using any of these anywhere in a variable name will cause an error. Instead, if you want to spread things out, try using the underscore (_). For example, `my_first_variable` would be an acceptable variable name, whereas `my first variable` would not.

- Variable names must begin with a letter. Underscores and numbers are fine in your variable names, as long as they are not the first character. Variable names must begin with a letter. For example, `variable_number_2` works, but "2nd_variable" does not.

- Variable names should be no longer than 255 characters.

- Do not use reserved words (keywords). Reserved words are words that have special meaning in the language. For example, `Dim` is a reserved word. If you use InterDev, reserved words appear in blue. You may use such words as part of a variable name, but not as the whole name. For example, `my_dim` is okay for a variable name, but `dim` is not. If you follow the style guidelines described in the next section, you should have no trouble with this rule.

- Do not reuse variable names. You can reuse variables. Just be aware that you cannot have the same name refer to two different variables.

Caution

> Unlike C/C++, VBScript, which is used with ASP, is not case sensitive. This means that the way you capitalize variable names, function calls, or key-words does not matter. If you have a variable named `myvar`, you can refer to the same variable as `MyVar`, `MYVAR`, and so on.

Style Guidelines on Variable Names

Certain conventions are generally followed by programmers. These conventions are not outright required by the system, but they make it easier for you to program and make it easier for others to read your code. Ultimately, it is up to you whether you follow them. Over time, you will probably develop your own modified version of these guidelines as you figure out what works best for you. For the remainder of this book, we will follow these guidelines.

- Include variable type in name. As mentioned earlier, VBScript uses the variant variable, so there is no built-in requirement that you use a particular variable for only one data type. It is, however, a good convention to follow. It makes your code easier for others to read, but what's more, it makes things easier for you as you write it. The convention in this book is to use the prefixes on variables shown in Table 3.1. For example, a date variable that was going to hold your birthday would probably be called `dtBirthday`.

- Use descriptive names. Many programmers try to save a little typing by using one-letter variable names. Those programmers spend any time they saved when typing now debugging their code! Imagine reading through 100 lines of code and coming across a line like `x = 5`. What does this mean? What is x? If a variable is a `String` that will hold a user's name, give it a name like `strUserName`. If it is a `Single` to hold someone's salary, call it `sngSalary`.

- Declare all variables at the top. If, even after using good names, you have trouble remembering what you called a particular variable, it is nice to know exactly where to look to find it. Some languages actually require this.

TABLE 3.1 Suggested Type Prefixes for Variable Names

Variable Type	Prefix
Integer	i
Single	sng
Double	dbl

Variable Type	Prefix
String	str
Date	dt
Boolean	bol
Currency	cur
Object	obj

Do	Don't
DO choose your variable names bearing in mind that you need to be able to look back at your code and understand it!	**DON'T** use one variable for several different purposes. It makes code confusing when you change the meaning of things as you go along!

3

Constants

A constant is a little like a variable in that you give it a name and store data in it. Unlike variables, however, constants are assigned a value when they are declared, and that value cannot be changed. VBScript has several constants built into it. A few of these are listed in Table 3.2. For example, the constant vbInteger is declared to be equivalent to the number 2. In your code, you could either refer to the number directly or using the constant name. Typing the number directly may involve fewer keystrokes, but using the constant name makes your code a little easier to read. It also helps save you from having to memorize many numbers. You will see more about this particular set of constants later.

You may also find it useful at times to declare your own constants for use on your pages. For example, if you were creating a page to sell merchandise, you might find you need to use the sales tax rate several times within the page. If you did not make a constant for the tax rate, you would need to refer to a strange decimal number like 0.0625 a lot. Plus, if the tax rate ever changed, you would have to update several lines of code. Put a simple declaration like this at the top of your page, though, and you can refer to TAXRATE throughout the rest of the page and make updates easily:

```
Const TAXRATE = 0.0625
```

It is suggested that you use all capital letters to refer to constants to help distinguish them from your variables.

Arrays

There is another major data type that we have not yet discussed. A *variable array* is a sequence of variables, with the same name, but distinguished by an *index*.

If we return to the comparison we made earlier between a variable and a box, a variable array may be seen as a row of boxes. This is shown in Figure 3.3.

Arrays will often be used to group data of the same type. For example, you might have an array of strings containing the email addresses of your users. When used in conjunction with the loop structures discussed in Day 4, arrays can simplify working with multiple data values.

FIGURE 3.3

A variable array may be thought of as row of boxes that data is put into.

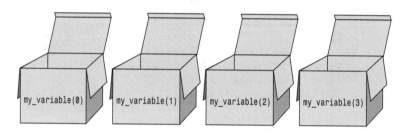

Try creating and using a variable array called `arrDays`. First, declare the variable array, like this:

```
Dim arrDays(6)
```

 The (6) in parentheses indicates the array's *upper bound*. The upper bound is the largest index that will identify a valid location in the array.

 The array's *lower bound* is (0). That is, zero is the smallest index that identifies a valid location in the array. Zero is the lower bound of any array.

So what are your variables? In this case, you have seven: `arrDays(0)`, `arrDays(1)`, `arrDays(2)`, `arrDays(3)`, `arrDays(4)`, `arrDays(5)`, and `arrDays(6)`. The numbers in parentheses are the variables' indexes, and they run from zero to six. Now type in Listing 3.4 and call your file ArrayReference.asp.

LISTING 3.4   Demonstrating Ways of Referencing Array Elements

```
1:    <%@ Language=VBScript %>
2:    <% Option Explicit
3:        Dim arrDays(6), iIndex
4:    %>
5:    <HTML>
6:        <BODY>
7:    <%
8:            iIndex = 3
9:            arrDays(0) = "Sunday"

10:            arrDays(1) = "Monday"
11:            arrDays(2) = "Tuesday"
```

```
12:           arrDays(3) = "Wednesday"
13:           arrDays(4) = "Thursday"
14:           arrDays(5) = "Friday"
15:           arrDays(6) = "Saturday"
16:           Response.Write("iIndex has a value of ")
17:           Response.Write(iIndex)
18:    %>
19:       <BR>
20:       arrDays(1) has a value of
21:    <%
22:           Response.Write(arrDays(1))
23:    %>
24:        <BR>
25:       arrDays(iIndex) has a value of
26:    <%
27:           Response.Write(arrDays(iIndex))
28:    %>
29:        <BR>
30:       arrDays(2+3) has a value of
31:    <%
32:           Response.Write(arrDays(2+3))
33:    %>
34:        <BR>
35:       arrDays(iIndex+1) has a value of
36:    <%
37:           Response.Write(arrDays(iIndex+1))
38:    %>
39:        </BODY>
40:    </HTML>
```

Listing 3.4 shows a few of the ways specific array elements can be accessed. Line 22 shows a direct reference to element number 1. Line 27 shows referencing an element using a variable. Lines 32 and 37 show referencing elements with expressions. Anything that has a value of an integer within the correct range will work. Figure 3.4 shows the results of this code.

> **Caution**
>
> When using variables to index arrays, make sure that the variables fall within the correct range.

Much more can be done with arrays, as you'll see over the next couple of weeks. One more thing worth mentioning, however, is the Array function, which is used to quickly assign values to each element in an array. For example, in Listing 3.4, lines 9 through 15 could be replaced with the following single line:

```
ArrDays = Array("Sunday", "Monday", "Tuesday", "Wednesday", "Thursday",
"Friday", "Saturday")
```

FIGURE 3.4

Array elements may be referenced with any numerical expression.

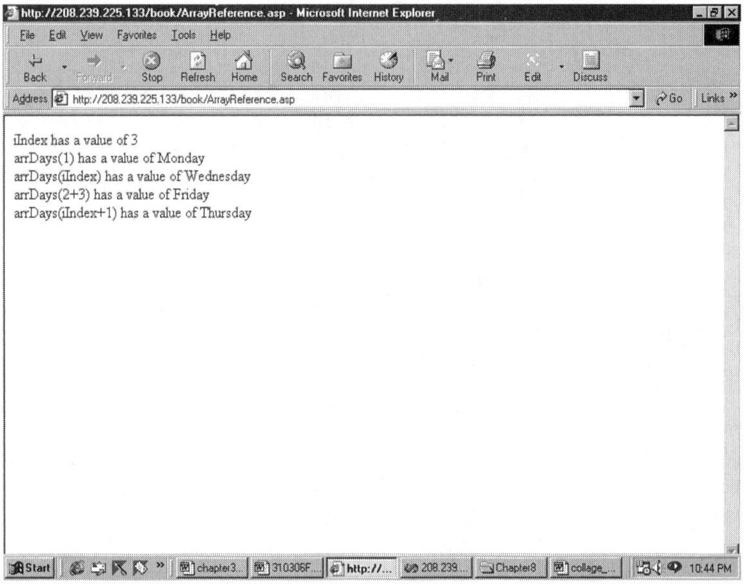

```
http://208.239.225.133/book/ArrayReference.asp - Microsoft Internet Explorer
File  Edit  View  Favorites  Tools  Help

Back   Forward   Stop   Refresh   Home   Search  Favorites  History   Mail   Print   Edit   Discuss
Address  http://208.239.225.133/book/ArrayReference.asp                              Go   Links

iIndex has a value of 3
arrDays(1) has a value of Monday
arrDays(iIndex) has a value of Wednesday
arrDays(2+3) has a value of Friday
arrDays(iIndex+1) has a value of Thursday
```

> **Note**
>
> Array was not included in VBScript 1.0. Make sure that you are using 2.0 or later if you want to use this function. Otherwise, you must assign values to array elements one at a time.

How Do You Determine Your Variable's Type?

Two functions are useful in determining the data type being stored in a variable. The first is VarType, which is used like this:

```
VarType(variable_name)
```

VarType returns an integer code that corresponds to the data type as shown in Table 3.2.

TABLE 3.2   VarType Codes for Data Types

Value	Constant	Data Type
0	vbEmpty	Empty (This is the type for a variable that has not been used yet. In other words, Empty is the default data type.)
1	vbNull	Null (No valid data)
2	vbInteger	Integer
3	vbLong	Long
4	vbSingle	Single
5	vbDouble	Double

Value	Constant	Data Type
6	vbCurrency	Currency
7	vbDate	Date
8	vbString	String
9	vbObject	Object
10	vbError	Error
11	vbBoolean	Boolean
12	vbVariant	Variant (used with vbArray)
13	vbDataObject	Data Access Object
14	vbDecimal	Decimal
17	vbByte	Byte
8192	vbArray	Array (VBScript uses 8192 as a base for arrays and adds the code for the data type to indicate an array. 8204 indicates a variant array, the only real kind of array in VBScript.)

3

The other, and perhaps nicer, function to do this is TypeName. TypeName returns a string with the name of the data type rather than a code. It is used the same way as VarType. The return values for TypeName, and their meanings, are listed in Table 3.3.

TABLE 3.3 TypeName Codes for Data Types

Return Value	Data Type
Empty	Empty (uninitialized)
Null	Null (no valid data)
Integer	Integer
Byte	Byte
Long	Long
Single	Single
Double	Double
Currency	Currency
Date	Date
String	String
Error	Error
Boolean	Boolean
object type	Returns the type of object, if it is recognized.

continues

TABLE 3.3 continued

Return Value	Data Type
Unknown	Unknown object type
Object	Generic Object
Nothing	Object variable that points to nothing

A variable that has not been given a value yet is of type `Empty`.

The `Null` type is used in conjunction with databases, when dealing with sets of data that are empty. Databases are covered more in Days 15 through 21.

The last four data types relate to objects, which are discussed in Day 6.

Try typing Listing 3.5 into your editor, naming the file FindType.asp.

LISTING 3.5   Exploring `VarType` and `TypeName`

```
 1: <%@ Language=VBScript %>
 2: <% Option Explicit
 3:     Dim strName, iAge
 4: %>
 5: <HTML>
 6:     <BODY>
 7: <%
 8:         Response.Write("Before assigning a value, strName is of type ")
 9:         Response.Write(TypeName(strName))
10:         Response.Write(", which is type number ")
11:         Response.Write(VarType(strName))
12: %>
13:         <BR>
14: <%
15:         strName = "James"
16:         iAge = 21
17:         Response.Write("Now strName is of type ")
18:         Response.Write(TypeName(strName))
19:         Response.Write(", which is type number ")
20:         Response.Write(VarType(strName))
21: %>
22:         <BR>
23: <%
24:         Response.Write("Now iAge is of type ")
25:         Response.Write(TypeName(iAge))
26:         Response.Write(", which is type number ")
27:         Response.Write(VarType(iAge))
28: %>
29:     </BODY>
30: </HTML>
```

ANALYSIS Line 8 uses `Response.Write` to print a message. `Response.Write` was discussed in Day 2. Line 9 writes the results of calling `TypeName` with `strName`. Since `strName` has not yet been given a value, `TypeName` should return `"Empty"`. Line 10 writes another message, and line 11 writes the results of `VarType`.

Lines 15 and 16 assign values to the variables `strName` and `iAge`. The assignment operator is discussed a little later. Now when line 18 calls `TypeName(strName)`, the result should no longer be `"Empty"`. Instead, since line 15 gives `strName` a string value, this should print `"String"`. Then, when line 20 calls `VarType`, the result should be the number 8, which corresponds to the string data type.

Lines 24 through 27 perform similar operations with iAge. Since line 16 gives `iAge` a value equal to the integer 21, `TypeName(iAge)` should give a value of `"Integer"` and `VarType(iAge)` should return 2.

If you are looking for one data type in particular, you might prefer to use one of a series of VBScript functions designed for this purpose. `IsNumeric`, for example, returns a Boolean value of `True` if the variable given to it has numeric data, and `False` otherwise. Other functions along this line are `IsArray`, `IsDate`, `IsEmpty`, `IsNull`, and `IsObject`. So, for example, let's assume that you have a variable `sngSalary` appropriately declared and give it a value as follows:

```
sngSalary = "100000.00"
```

Then calling `IsDate(sngSalary)` will return a value of `False`, but `IsNumeric(sngSalary)` will return a value of `True`.

VBScript Operators

Operators allow us to work with data, combining, changing, or replacing it. There are five major classes of operators we will deal with. The first is assignment, which you have already seen a little of.

Assignment Operator

So far today we have discussed variables and mentioned that data may be stored in them without explaining how to do so. The most common way to accomplish this is through the *assignment operator*. The assignment operator, in VBScript, is the equals sign (=). The assignment operator takes whatever is on the right-hand side of it and stores it in the variable on the left-hand side of it.

For example, consider the following code:

```
<% Dim iVar
   iVar = 3
   iVar = 5
%>
```

3

If you have not done any programming before, you may be wondering how iVar could equal 3 and 5 at the same time. It does not. You must be careful not to confuse the assignment operator with mathematical equality. The third statement does not say iVar equals 5. Rather, it says 5 is stored in iVar. For a little review, we shall step through this code line-by-line.

The first line is the variable declaration, as discussed previously. At this point, a value of Empty is stored in iVar.

The next line assigns a value of 3 to iVar. So in the box labeled iVar, there is now a 3.

Finally, a value of 5 is assigned to iVar. The 3 that was in there before is gone now. Be careful with this when you are programming. Do not overwrite variables with new values until you are sure that you are finished with the previous value.

If it is absolutely necessary to overwrite a value you plan to use later, you might create a second variable to hold onto it:

```
<% Dim iVar, iOldVar
   iVar = 3
   iOldVar = iVar
   iVar = 5
%>
```

Here, the first line declares two variables now: iVar and iOldVar. Both begin with an empty value.

The next line assigns a value of 3 into iVar. At this point, iOldVar still has an empty value.

The third line might be a bit confusing if you are new to programming. Assignment may be done not just with explicit values such as 3 or 5 on the right, but also with variables. Following this statement, both iOldVar and iVar will have values of 3 stored in them.

Finally, iVar is assigned a value of 5. This does not affect iOldVar. Line 3 copied what was in iVar into iOldVar, but it did not establish any kind of permanent connection between iVar and iOldVar. This way, iVar can be used with its new value, but if you still need to use the old value of iVar, it is available.

Now look at one last version of this code before going on to a new topic:

```
<% Dim iVar
   iVar = 3
   5 = iVar
%>
```

Do you think this code will work? Reread the first paragraph on the assignment operator if you are not sure.

The answer is No. This code is not valid. The first two lines are carried out as expected, but the third is meaningless. The assignment operator copies what is on the right into the variable on the left. In this case, the number 5—not a variable—is on the left. 5 cannot be the name of a variable since all variable names must begin with letters (see the section "Syntax Requirements on Variables" earlier in today's lesson).

I have been using integers in these examples, but I needn't have. The assignment operator works with singles, doubles, strings, Booleans, and so on, just as well.

```
strName = "John Smith"
bol_The_Assignment_Operator_Is_Powerful = True
dtJills_Birthday = #03/06/1946#
```

Note Surrounding the date with #s keeps it from being evaluated as three divided by six divided by 1946.

3

You might have noticed that Listing 3.5 used the assignment operator. Listing 3.6 is a modified version of that code to show off the assignment operator a bit more. The file is called `AssignmentDemo.asp`.

LISTING 3.6 Demonstration of the Assignment Operator

```
 1: <%@ Language=VBScript %>
 2: <% Option Explicit
 3:    Dim strName, iAge
 4: %>
 5: <HTML>
 6:    <BODY>
 7: <%
 8:        Response.Write("Before assigning a value, strName has value ")
 9:        Response.Write(strName)
10: %>
11:        <BR>
12: <%
13:        strName = "James"
14:        iAge = 21
15:        Response.Write("Now strName has value ")
16:        Response.Write(strName)
17: %>
18:        <BR>
19: <%
20:        Response.Write("Now iAge has value ")
21:        Response.Write(iAge)
22: %>
23:    </BODY>
24: </HTML>
```

Line 3 declares the two variables we will use: `strName` and `iAge`.

Lines 8 and 9 write a message that demonstrates the value that `strName` has before we use the assignment operator to set it.

Lines 13 and 14 set the values of the two variables. Lines 15 and 16 show the new value given to `strName`. Looking at the output, you can now verify that the assignment was successful. Lines 20 and 21 similarly display the new value given to `iAge`.

Mathematical Operators

Now that you can put values into variables, it is time to start using those values. We begin with the operations VBScript can perform that are classified as mathematical operators. They include addition, subtraction, negation, multiplication, division, and exponentiation, all of which you have probably seen before, as well as integer division, modulus, and string concatenation, which may be new.

Addition

Addition takes the form *argument + argument* where each argument may be a number, a numerical variable, or another numerical expression:

```
<% Dim iSum
   iSum = 3 + 5
%>
```

This is one of the simplest cases, where both arguments are numbers. When the code is run, the variable `iSum` ends with a value of 8.

The next example demonstrates how a variable may be used as an argument:

```
<% Dim sngSum, sngLeft
   sngLeft = 3.2
   sngSum = sngLeft + 1.1
%>
```

In this case the result, as you may have guessed, is 4.3. The value in `sngLeft` is added to 1.1 and stored into `sngSum`. `sngLeft` is unaffected by the addition.

Let's take a look at another tricky example.

```
<% Dim iCount
  iCount = 2
  iCount = iCount + 1
%>
```

This case may seem strange to you at first. How can `iCount` be equal to `iCount` plus 1? First, remember that the equals sign refers to the assignment operator. Let's step through this line-by-line. The first line, as you have seen before, is the declaration. The variable iCount is created, with an empty value. The second line assigns a value of 2 to iCount. In the third line, the 2 is retrieved from iCount. Then 1 is added to that value, giving 3. 3 is then sent to the assignment operator, which stores it in iCount. So, at the end of this code, iCount holds a value of 3. The 2 formerly in iCount has been overwritten.

Notice that the 1 is added to iCount before the assignment is carried out. Everything on the right side of an assignment operator is executed before the assignment. Table 3.4 lists the order in which operations are carried out.

TABLE 3.4   Operator Precedence

Precedence	Operators
Highest (done first)	Anything in parentheses
	Exponentiation (^)
	Negation (-)
	Multiplication, Division (*, /)
	Integer Division (\)
	Modulus (Mod)
	Addition, Subtraction (+, -)
	String Concatenation (&)
	Equality (=)
	Inequality (<>)
	Less than (<)
	Greater than (>)
	Less than or equal to (<=)
	Greater than or equal to (>=)
	Not
	And
	Or
	Xor
	Eqv
Lowest (done last)	Imp

Subtraction

Now that you know how to add, you may well wonder how to subtract. Subtraction works much like addition, taking the form *argument - argument*. Any combinations you might have used with addition will again work for subtraction. One difference, however, is that with subtraction the order of arguments is important. For example, 3 - 5 is certainly much different from 5 - 3. In the following code, can you tell what value iCount will have after the code is finished?

```
<% Dim iCount
   iCount = 3
   iCount = iCount + 1
   iCount = iCount - 2
%>
```

The answer you should come up with is 2. iCount begins as 3, adding 1 makes it 4, and subtracting 2 makes it 2.

Multiplication

Multiplication should be easy for you. The symbol for multiplication is the asterisk (*). Multiplication follows the same form as the other operations we have covered so far. Multiplication does introduce a new complication, though.

NEW TERM Think about the expression 3 * 5 + 2. What should this expression evaluate to? If you perform the addition first, the result is 21. If you perform the multiplication first, the result is 17. Which is correct? You should remember from math class that multiplication is performed before addition, making the correct answer 17. VBScript knows this, too. This understanding that multiplication comes before addition is an example of *precedence*. Precedence is a set of rules for the order in which operations should be performed. Multiplication is said to have higher precedence than addition. Table 3.4 offers a complete listing of operator precedence in VBScript.

If you wanted to evaluate the addition first, there is a way. Perhaps you remember from math class that whatever is in parentheses is carried out first. VBScript works the same way. Putting parentheses into the previous expression gives you 3 * (5 + 2), which evaluates to 21. Parentheses can be used with any operation to force it to be evaluated in a certain order.

> **Tip**
>
> You can use the parentheses even when not absolutely necessary to make the meaning of an expression clearer. Parentheses can also be used when you cannot remember the operator precedence.

Division

VBScript has two different kinds of division. The first is the kind you are probably most familiar with. Standard division is represented with the slash (/). It takes two numerical values and returns their floating-point quotient. For example, 5 / 2 returns 2.5, and 4 / 5 returns 0.8.

Some divisions will result in decimals that do not terminate. In these cases, the best approximation the system can store is used. For example, in the case of 1 / 3, the computer cannot store an infinitely repeating decimal like 0.33333…. Also, be careful to avoid division by zero. Dividing by zero, or a number so close to zero that the computer thinks it is zero, results in an error.

Integer Division

Chances are, before you knew what decimals were, you learned division like this:

5 divided by 3 is 1 with a remainder of 2.

Together, the integer division and modulus operators allow you to do this kind of division in VBScript. The integer division operator, represented with the backslash (\), returns the quotient. So, for example

5 \ 3 returns 1

4 \ 2 returns 2

0 \ 8 returns 0

1 \ 2 returns 0

Unlike most other programming languages, integer division is even defined when the terms are floating-point numbers. When a term in an integer division operator is a floating-point number, it is rounded to the nearest integer and then integer division is applied. For example

4 \ 2.2 returns 2

8.3 \ 2.6 returns 2

Modulus

Going along with integer division is the modulus operator. Whereas integer division returns the quotient when the two numbers are divided, modulus returns instead the remainder. For example

5 Mod 3 returns 2

4 Mod 2 returns 0

0 Mod 8 returns 8

1 Mod 2 returns 1

4 Mod 2.2 returns 0

8.3 Mod 2.6 returns 2

The usefulness of these last two operators may not be apparent right now, but, in truth, they are very powerful.

Notice that the Mod operator repeats.

0 Mod 3 returns 0

1 Mod 3 returns 1

2 Mod 3 returns 2

3 Mod 3 returns 0

4 Mod 3 returns 1

5 Mod 3 returns 2

and so forth. This can make the Mod operator useful when you need something to behave in a cyclical manner. Mod can also help you check whether one number divides evenly into another. If a Mod b returns 0, b divides evenly into a.

Exponentiation

In VBScript, the exponentiation operator is represented by the carat symbol (^). If you do not recall much about exponentiation, a^b = a*a*a... *a (b times). For example

$3^3 = 3*3*3 = 27$

$5^2 = 5*5 = 25$

$6^3 = 6*6*6 = 216$

Also, note that exponentiation is executed from left to right. This means that if you have an expression such as 2^3^2, the 2^3 is carried out first and then raised to the second power.

$2^3{}^2 = 8^2 = 64$

Negation

Negation is the operation that converts a positive number to a negative number and vice versa. It is equivalent to multiplying by -1. Negation is denoted using the same symbol, the dash (-), as subtraction.

NEW TERM   The difference between negation and subtraction is that subtraction—like addition, multiplication, and the other operations discussed so far—is a *binary operation*. A binary operation is one that takes two arguments.

NEW TERM   Negation, on the other hand, is a *unary operation*. It takes only one argument. So the dash means subtraction when it is between two numerical values and negation when it is just in front of one.

Listing 3.7 puts together a few of the arithmetic operations covered so far. Take a good look at it and make sure that you can follow what is happening.

LISTING 3.7   Putting the Arithmetic Operators Together

```
 1: <%@ Language=VBScript %>
 2: <% Option Explicit
 3:    Dim iTerm1, iTerm2, sngArithmetic, sngGeometric
 4: %>
 5: <HTML>
 6:    <BODY>
 7: <%
 8:       iTerm1 = 5
 9:       iTerm2 = 16
10:       Response.Write("We are computing the averages of ")
11:       Response.Write(iTerm1)
12:       Response.Write(" and ")
13:       Response.Write(iTerm2)
14: %>
15:       <BR>
16: <%
17:       sngArithmetic = iTerm1 + iTerm2
18:       sngArithmetic = sngArithmetic / 2
19:       sngGeometric = (iTerm1 * iTerm2)^0.5
20:       Response.Write("Their arithmetic mean is ")
21:       Response.Write(sngArithmetic)
22:       Response.Write(" and their geometric mean is ")
23:       Response.Write(sngGeometric)
24: %>
25:    </BODY>
26: </HTML>
```

Line 3 declares the variables this script will use. Line 8 initializes one of the variables with the number 5. Line 9 initializes the other with 16. Lines 10 through 13 print a message that tells the user what numbers are being used for the calculations.

Lines 17 and 18 proceed to calculate the arithmetic mean of the two numbers. The arithmetic mean is simply the standard average you learned in school. Line 17 takes the two numbers, adds them together, and stores the result in sngArithmetic. Then line 18 divides sngArithmetic by 2 and stores the result in sngArithmetic. Notice that the slash is used, indicating that we are performing floating-point division rather than integer division. sngArithmetic now holds the average of the two numbers.

Line 19 computes the geometric mean. If you have not seen the geometric mean of two numbers before, it is simply the square root of their products. To calculate it, we first multiply the two numbers. Then, the result is raised to the power 0.5. Raising a number to the power 0.5 is the same as finding its square root. Notice the parentheses that are used on line 19. They are necessary. Without them, the exponentiation would be performed first, and then the multiplication. Refer back to Table 3.4 for more about operator precedence.

Lines 20 through 23 print out some closing messages. The values of sngArithmetic and sngGeometric are displayed.

You can see the output of this listing in Figure 3.5.

FIGURE 3.5

Operators may be put together to form more complex expressions.

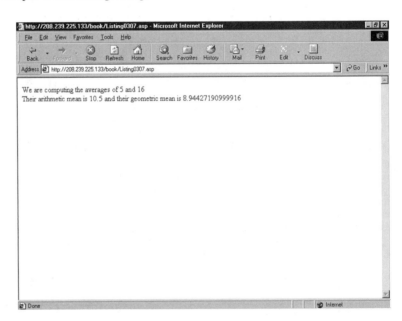

Concatenation

The arithmetic operations we have discussed have been operations on numbers. Concatenation, though, is an operation between two strings. The two strings are joined together, becoming one string. Concatenation may be represented by either the plus sign (+) or the ampersand (&), but the ampersand is preferred to avoid confusion with addition. Look at a few examples:

```
"Hello" & "World" becomes "HelloWorld"

"Hello " & "World" becomes "Hello World"

"My name is " & "John Smith" becomes "My name is John Smith"
```

Like the numerical operations, concatenation may be used several times in one statement, as in the following:

```
"Welcome," & " John Smith, " & "to the wonderful world of strings"
```

becomes

```
"Welcome, John Smith, to the wonderful world of strings"
```

Listing 3.8 demonstrates how string concatenation can make life a little easier. Instead of constantly using Response.Write as was done in Listing 3.7, you can collect data, put it together with the concatenation operator, and write it out together.

LISTING 3.8   Simplifying Things with String Concatenation

```
 1: <%@ Language=VBScript %>
 2: <% Option Explicit
 3:     Dim iTerm1, iTerm2, sngArithmetic, sngGeometric, strOut
 4: %>
 5: <HTML>
 6:   <BODY>
 7: <%
 8:      iTerm1 = 5
 9:      iTerm2 = 16
10:      strOut = "We are computing the averages of " & iTerm1 & _
11:           " and " & iTerm2 & "<BR>"
12:      Response.Write(strOut)
13:      sngArithmetic = iTerm1 + iTerm2
14:      sngArithmetic = sngArithmetic / 2
15:      sngGeometric = (iTerm1 * iTerm2)^0.5
16:      strOut = "Their arithmetic mean is " & sngArithmetic & _
17:           " and their geometric mean is " & sngGeometric
18:      Response.Write(strOut)
19: %>
20:   </BODY>
21: </HTML>
```

This listing does the same thing as Listing 3.7. The only difference is that we were able to cut down on calls to Response.Write by using the string concatenation operator.

Lines 10 and 11 take all the output that was displayed on lines 10 through 13 of Listing 3.7, and concatenate them together. Then, line 12 needs only one Response.Write to send the entire message to the output at once.

Lines 13 through 15 perform the same computations as before. Now, lines 16 and 17 concatenate the output strings. Once again, strOut is used to hold the result. Then, line 18 simply needs to write strOut to output.

Comparison Operators

The comparison operators make comparisons between two arguments and evaluate to either True or False. The VBScript comparison operators are equality (=), inequality (<>), less than (<), greater than (>), less than or equal to (<=), and greater than or equal to (>=). You probably worked with all these in math class, but in case you are a bit unsure about them, Table 3.5 provides a little review.

TABLE 3.5 Comparison Operators

Operator	True When...	False When...
A = B	A and B are the same	A and B are different
A > B	A larger than B	A same as or smaller than B
A < B	A smaller than B	A same as or bigger than B
A >= B	A bigger than or same as B	B bigger than A
A <= B	A smaller than or same as B	A bigger than B
A <> B	A and B different	A and B the same

A few examples

3 > 4	False
5 > 4	True
4 >= 3	True
4 >= 4	True
3 < 3	False
2 <> 9	True

Comparison operators can also be used to compare strings. In this case, it compares them alphabetically. The string that comes first alphabetically is treated like it is less than the one that comes later. It treats uppercase letters like they come before lowercase letters. So "Alligator" comes before "aardvark," which comes before "alligator." This means that "Alligator" < "aardvark" would return true, and "alligator" < "aardvark" would return false.

Logical Operators

The last set of operators allows you to join together and manipulate Boolean expressions such as those in the "Comparison Operators" section. They are And, Or, Not, the exclusive or (XOR), equivalence (EQV), and implication (IMP).

If you have had some logic courses, you should find using these operators comes naturally. All these, except NOT, take two Boolean values and return a Boolean value. AND returns true when both of its arguments are true. Table 3.6 describes when each logical operator evaluates to True and to False.

TABLE 3.6 Logical Operators

Operator	True When...	False When...
A AND B	A and B both true	Either A or B is false
A OR B	One of A or B is true	Both A and B are false
NOT A	A is false	A is true
A XOR B	A or B true, but not both	Both true or both false
A EQV B	Both false or both true	One is false; other is true
A IMP B	A is false or B is true	A is true and B is false

Logical operators are usually put together with comparison operators in the same line.

A few examples

(3 < 4) AND (4 < 5)	evaluates to True
(4 <> 4) OR (6 < 7)	evaluates to True
(4 < 2) AND bolExpr	evaluates to False

Notice in that last case, we do not know based on the information shown what the value of bolExpr is. However, because it is an AND statement and we know the first part is false, the whole statement is false regardless.

Summary

Today you learned how VBScript stores data with variables and how to manipulate the data stored. Variables give a section of memory a name and may be used to store integers, floating-point numbers, strings, dates, Boolean values, and more. Good variable names should have no characters besides letters, numbers, and the underscore. They should be descriptive and indicate the data type they will store. Using Option Explicit requires that all variables be declared, which makes fixing errors easier.

Arrays are a special kind of variable that can store several pieces of data. They are referenced using the index number of that particular piece.

Constants are used for data that will be repeated and that do not change within the page.

Variables are given values using the assignment operator.

Arithmetic operators return numerical data. They include addition, subtraction, multiplication, division, negation, integer division, modulus, and exponentiation. All but negation are binary operations, which means that they require two numbers to be carried out.

String concatenation is a bit like an arithmetic operator for strings. It takes two strings and joins them.

Comparison operators are all binary. They take two arguments, which may be strings, numerical, dates, and more, and compare them. They return a Boolean value; that is, they return either true or false.

Logical operators are also binary, except for NOT. They take Boolean arguments and return Boolean values.

Arithmetic, string concatenation, comparison, and logical operators can all be joined together in long sequences. Parentheses and operator precedence help sort out the meaning of these long expressions.

Q&A

Q Why would an array be more useful than a bunch of separate variables?

A An array is more useful when the data is related (such as an array of customer names). As discussed, individual elements can be accessed with a variable (as in arrDays(iIndex)). Combined with the control structures covered in tomorrow's lesson, this allows you to perform actions on all the data in the array with only a few lines of code, even if it is an array of hundreds!

Q I am performing a comparison on what should be two identical floating-point values, but I am not getting the right answer. What is going on?

A The problem could be a matter of precision. Computers can only hold so many decimal places. Numbers, though, can have any number of decimal places. So, sometimes when you perform arithmetic with floating-point values, a few little digits get rounded, and you get an answer that is just a teeny-tiny bit away from what you should get. This can cause problems when you make comparisons, or when you divide by something really close to zero. Memory is getting cheaper, and this is less of a problem than it used to be, but it can still pop up once in a while.

Workshop

The Workshop provides quiz questions to help you solidify your understanding of the material covered and exercises to provide you with experience in using what you've learned. Try to understand the quiz and exercise answers before continuing to tomorrow's lesson. Quiz answers are provided in Appendix A, and exercise answers can be found at http://www.mcp.com/info.

Quiz

1. What effect does putting `<% Option Explicit %>` at the top of your page have?
2. What does 5 `Mod` 2 evaluate to? 7 `Mod` 9?
3. What does 3 * 5 + 2 ^ 2 - 6 evaluate to, according to the correct rules of precedence?
4. How would you parenthesize 3 * 5 + 2 ^ 2 - 6 to make its meaning clearer?
5. What does ("Banana" < "banana") AND (4 < 4) evaluate to?
6. What does ("Banana" < "banana") OR (4 < 4) evaluate to?
7. What data type do the comparison and logical operators evaluate to?
8. What is 5 / 2? 5 \ 2?

Exercises

1. Write a VBScript statement using either `VarType` or `TypeName` that is equivalent to the `IsDate` function.
2. Write a statement that calculates the length of the hypotenuse of a right triangle. Assume the lengths of the other two sides are stored in `sngSide1` and `sngSide2`. If you have forgotten, the square of the hypotenuse equals the sum of the squares of the other two sides.
3. Write the explicit declaration for variables that will store a user's name, age, email address, and birth date. Choose good names according to the guidelines discussed today.

3

Understanding VBScript Control Structures

It would be pretty silly to use ASP for pages that would always look the same. The power of ASP comes in building dynamic Web sites. In order to be dynamic, a page needs to be able to make decisions and do different things under different circumstances. This is where control structures come in. If you have programming experience, you should find VBScript's control structures familiar. If not, that is okay. We will introduce you to the logic of control structures and the reasons for using them. Today, you will learn the following:

- What control structures are and why we use them
- What conditional logic is
- What looping logic is
- What branching logic is
- How to use the control structures of VBScript

What Is a Control Structure?

A *control structure* is a programming structure that allows your program to make decisions based on the information it is given.

In the first two days, most of the scripts you saw were completely linear. The system would carry out the instructions from the top to the bottom.

Now you can control the flow of the program, which gives your pages greater flexibility.

A program that always follows the same sequence of steps would not be very useful. When you use your word processor, you expect different things to happen based on what buttons you press, which options you have turned on, and so forth. Control structures give programs that kind of flexibility, and you need them for your pages.

Types of Controls

There are three major types of control structures that programmers use. They allow control over if, when, and how many times certain instructions are executed. Mastering the use of these control structures is critical to becoming skilled as a programmer. Fortunately, the logic behind them is very natural.

Conditional Logic

Conditional logic allows you to specify a sequence of events to happen if certain circumstances are met. For example, in a word processor, if you click on File and then New, you are probably presented with several options as to what you want to create. Depending on which one of those you select, you are presented with a different interface, different options, and so on. This is because your word processor is employing conditional logic.

Suppose that you work in a factory. Your boss might say to you, "If the widget is defective, throw it to the side. Otherwise, put it in the box." There is no way to rephrase this instruction without requiring a decision in the middle. This is an example of how conditional logic increases the power of our language.

This capability is important in programming Web pages, too. If someone types in a password to log in, you need to check whether his or her password matches the one on file. If it does, you display one page; otherwise, you give him or her an error.

Looping Logic

Looping logic allows you to write code that will be executed multiple times. If you wanted your code to execute twice, you might just type it twice. What if you wanted it to be carried out a hundred times? Worse, what if you did not know how many times it would need to be carried out? How would you like a word processor that would only spell check the first ten words? You expect it to be flexible enough to keep spell checking until it is done.

To continue the factory analogy: your boss might give instructions, such as, "Put widget into the box until it is full," or "Stamp each widget with the model number." It would be difficult to put these kinds of instructions in plain, linear terms without knowing exactly how many widgets there are. Both of these instructions use looping logic.

You need this kind of flexibility in your pages, too. If you were writing a page for an online store, you would want it to add up all the user's purchases. A script that stopped at five items and required at least five items would be useless.

Branching Logic

Branching logic is closely related to the other two kinds of control structures. It involves leaving the normal flow of the program to execute a new sequence of steps.

In the factory, your boss might announce: "Everyone, stop what you are doing for the moment to work on a special project."

You have already used branching logic in a few of the examples from previous days. Functions, such as `TypeVar` and `IsNumeric`, are one kind of branching logic.

Control Structure Examples

NEW TERM Control structures do not, by themselves, cause visible changes in data or output. Instead, they determine what actions are taken in what order. The statements that do the actual work are called *action statements*.

Consider again the factory worker instruction, "If the widget is defective, throw it to the side. Otherwise, put it in the box." In this instruction, "throw it to the side" and "put it in the box" are action statements. The rest is the control structure, guiding what should happen when.

Conditional Logic Controls

Conditional logic tests a condition or a series of conditions and, based on the result, chooses what code should be executed.

If...Then Statements

The `If...Then` statement is one of the most commonly used control structures. It takes the form

```
If condition Then
    code block
End If
```

`condition` is a Boolean expression like we covered yesterday. When `condition` evaluates to `True`, the action statements are carried out, and then whatever comes after `End If` is carried out. If `condition` evaluates to `False`, the action statements are skipped and only what comes after `End If` is carried out.

So when would you use this structure? Well, say that you are working on a page with a user registration form where users can indicate whether they want to receive email updates about your product. You probably have a check box for this purpose, and your code would probably look something like this:

```
if bolBox_is_checked Then
    'Put the code to add the user to the mailing list here.
End if
    'Continue with the rest of the registration.
```

NEW TERM This is just pseudo-code. Do not type this into your editor. *Pseudo-code* looks like code but does not have all the details. This is just for illustration purposes. By the time you finish this book, though, you will know all you need to fill in the blanks!

So let's get to a full example. The following code segment computes the absolute value of a number. The absolute value is the positive part of the number. We need to check whether the number is negative, and if so, take the negation of it. Otherwise, leave it alone.

```
If sngNumber < 0 Then
    sngNumber = -sngNumber
End if
```

In a simple case like this where there is only one line of code to be executed, the code may be put on the same line as the `If`, and the `End If` may be omitted.

```
If sngNumber < 0 Then sngNumber = -sngNumber
```

Now look at a little longer example. Say that you want code to turn a numerical grade into letter grade, like in school. So if iGrade is greater than or equal to 90, it is an "A." If it is between 80 and 90, a "B," and so forth. Your code might look like Listing 4.1.

LISTING 4.1   First Version of the Grade Finding Code

```
 1: <%@Language = VBScript %>
 2: <% Option Explicit %>
 3: <HTML><BODY>
 4: <%
 5:    Dim iGrade, strLetterGrade
 6:    iGrade = 85
 7:    If iGrade >= 90 Then
 8:       strLetterGrade = "A"
 9:    End If
10:    If (iGrade >= 80) AND (iGrade < 90) Then
11:       strLetterGrade = "B"
12:    End If
13:    If (iGrade >= 70) AND (iGrade < 80) Then
14:       strLetterGrade = "C"
15:    End If
16:    If (iGrade >= 60) AND (iGrade < 70) Then
17:       strLetterGrade = "D"
18:    End If
19:    If (iGrade < 60) Then
20:       strLetterGrade = "F"
21:    End If
22:    Response.Write("The numerical grade is " & iGrade)
23:    Response.Write(" and the letter grade is " & strLetterGrade)
24: %>
25: </BODY></HTML>
```

Line 5 declares the variables we will use in this script. iGrade will be used to hold the numerical grade. strLetterGrade will be used to hold the letter grade, once our script figures it out.

Line 6 sets the value of iGrade. In a real-world example, the value would be read in from the user, or a database, or something. Since we have not yet covered these topics, we shall simply code the value in, as on line 6.

Lines 7 through 9 say that if iGrade is greater than or equal to 90, the letter grade is an "A." If iGrade is not greater than or equal to 90, the code on line 8 is not executed.

Lines 10 through 12 say that if iGrade is greater than or equal to 80, and less than 90, the letter grade is a "B." Again, if the condition specified on line 10 is not true, line 11 is not executed.

Lines 13 through 15 say that if iGrade is greater than or equal to 70, and less than 80, the letter grade is a "C." Lines 16 through 18 then say that if iGrade is less than 70, but greater than or equal to 60, the letter grade is a "D."

Lines 19 through 21 finish the decision-making process by checking if iGrade is less than 60. If so, the letter grade is an "F."

Lines 22 and 23 display an appropriate message, including the numerical grade in iGrade, and the letter grade in strLetterGrade.

Let's step through what happens in the particular case where iGrade is 85.

First, iGrade is compared to 90. It is not greater than or equal to 90, so the code on line 8 is not executed. Instead, the system moves on to line 10. iGrade is indeed greater than or equal to 80, so the second part of the condition is looked at. iGrade is less than 90, so the entire condition is true. This means that the code inside is executed. strLetterGrade is set to "B".

Now we move on to the next statement. iGrade is compared to 70. It is greater than or equal to 70, so it is compared with 80. iGrade is not less than 80, so the condition fails and the code on line 14 does not execute. The system skips to line 16. iGrade is greater than or equal to 60, but not less than 70, so the condition fails. The system moves on to line 19. iGrade is not less than 60, so the condition fails.

Look carefully at this and make sure that you understand each step. Try changing iGrade's value.

> **Note**
>
> Notice that I indent the code inside the If statement a little. This is for readability and will be used throughout this book. It is a good thing for you to do in your code. The spacing makes clearer what code is affected by what control structure and makes it easier for you to keep your logic straight.

You may notice that the script seems to be doing a lot of unnecessary work. Once it figures out that the letter grade should be a "B", there is no reason to keep checking. If...Then...Else expands the If...Then structure to avoid this unnecessary work.

If...Then...Else Statements

Sometimes it is useful to have a segment of code that executes only if the condition fails. You can add an else statement to the if...then structure:

```
If condition Then
    code block 1
Else
```

```
    code block 2
End If
```

Now if `condition` evaluates to `True`, `code block 1` is executed. If it evaluates to `False`, `code block 2` is executed.

For example, you might write a statement like this:

```
If (sngValue > 5)
    Response.Write("Big")
Else
    Response.Write("Small")
```

NEW TERM Note that either code block may contain `if...then` statements within it. These are called *nested If statements* and might look like this:

```
If condition1 Then
    code block 1
    If condition2 Then
        code block 2
    Else
        code block 3
    End if
Else
    code block 4
End if
```

Looking at this, can you tell which code blocks are executed under what circumstances? `code block 1` is executed if `condition1` is `True`, regardless of `condition2`. `code block 2` is executed if `condition1` and `condition2` are `True`. `code block 3` is executed if `condition1` is `True` and `condition2` is `False`. `code block 4` is executed if `condition1` is `False` regardless of `condition2`.

Listing 4.2 modifies the letter grade code using nested `If` statements. This time, the declarations, initializations, and some other parts have been left out. By now, you should know how to put these in yourself. Call the file GradeFind2.asp.

LISTING 4.2 Second Version of Grade Finding Code Uses Nested If Statements

```
1: If iGrade >= 90 Then
2:      strLetterGrade = "A"
3: Else
4:     If iGrade >= 80 Then
5:          strLetterGrade = "B"
6:     Else
7:         If iGrade >= 70 Then
8:             strLetterGrade = "C"
9:         Else
```

continues

LISTING 4.2   continued

```
10:             If iGrade >= 60 Then
11:                 strLetterGrade = "D"
12:             Else
13:                 strLetterGrade = "F"
14:             End if
15:         End If
16:     End If
17: End If
```

Line 1 checks if iGrade is greater than or equal to 90. If so, line 2 is executed and strLetterGrade is set to "A". Then, the system skips to whatever comes after line 17, if anything. Only if the condition is false is line 4 executed.

Line 4 checks whether iGrade is greater than or equal to 80. If so, it knows the grade must be a "B." If iGrade were greater than or equal to 90, this code would not be executed in the first place. So, if line 4 is being executed, it knows that iGrade is less than 90. Only when iGrade is not greater than or equal to 80 will the code between lines 6 and 16 have a chance to execute.

Line 7 checks whether iGrade is greater than or equal to 70. Again, iGrade must have been less than 80 for this part of the script to execute. If iGrade is greater than or equal to 70, the letter grade is set as "C," and the system skips over lines 10 through 14. If not, it goes to line 10.

Line 10 checks whether iGrade is greater than or equal to 60. If so, the letter grade is a "D." If not, the letter grade must be less than 60, which is an "F."

Notice how once the letter grade is found, the rest of the code can be skipped. For example, if the grade is found to be a "B," lines 7 to 15 are skipped since they are inside the Else part of the structure.

Sometimes nested If statements can be simplified using the logical operators discussed in Day 3, "Working with Variables." Be careful, though, because using the wrong logical operator, or the wrong order, can cause a different meaning than you intended. Review the descriptions from yesterday and think about what you want to do.

For example, consider the following:

```
If Not (day_of_week = "Saturday") Then
   If Not (day_of_week = "Sunday") Then
      Response.Write "Today is a weekday."
   End If
End If
```

This code checks a variable called day_of_week. If it is not equal to "Saturday," it checks if it is equal to "Sunday." If not, today must be a weekday, and a message saying so is displayed. This can be reduced one If...Then statement like this:

```
If Not (day_of_week = "Saturday") And Not (day_of_week = "Sunday") Then
     Response.Write "Today is a weekday."
End If
```

This says that if day_of_week is not "Saturday" and it is not "Sunday", then print the message about the weekday. Notice that we used And to put the conditions together. Using Or in place of And does not work.

```
If Not (day_of_week = "Saturday") Or Not (day_of_week = "Sunday") Then
     Response.Write "Today is a weekday."
End If
```

Using Or like this will not work. Suppose day_of_week was "Saturday". Then, Not (day_of_week = "Sunday") evaluates to True, causing the entire condition to be True.

ElseIf Statement

The ElseIf statement simplifies one common type of nested If structure. An If statement that looks like this:

```
If condition1 Then
    code block 1
Else
    If condition2 Then
        code block 2 ...
```

can be changed to this:

```
If condition1 Then
    code block 1
ElseIf condition2 Then
        code block 2 ...
```

The ElseIf functions as a combined If and Else. Bear in mind two things when you are using ElseIf.

- ElseIf may not appear after an Else. You can use repeated ElseIf statements, followed by an Else if you want, but no ElseIf statements may follow an Else.
- ElseIf does not require an End If of its own, but the original If still does.

Listing 4.3 further updates the grade-finding script by using the ElseIf statement to simplify the nesting.

LISTING 4.3   Third Version of Grade Finding Code Uses ElseIf

```
1: <%@Language = VBScript %>
2: <% Option Explicit %>
3:  <HTML>
4:    <BODY>
5:  <%
6:  Dim iGrade, strLetterGrade
7:  iGrade = 85
8:  If iGrade >= 90 Then
9:      strLetterGrade = "A"
10: ElseIf (iGrade >= 80) Then
11:         strLetterGrade = "B"
12:     ElseIf (iGrade >= 70) Then
13:             strLetterGrade = "C"
14:         ElseIf (iGrade >= 60) Then
15:                 strLetterGrade = "D"
16:             Else
17:                 strLetterGrade = "F"
18: End If
19: Response.Write("The numerical grade is " & iGrade)
20: Response.Write(" and the letter grade is " & strLetterGrade)
21: %>
22:    </BODY>
23:  </HTML>
```

This does pretty much the same thing as Listing 4.2. The only difference is that we were able to clean things up a little by combining Else statements and If statements, and getting rid of some of the End If statements. You can see the output of this script in Figure 4.1.

Select Case Statements

Even with the addition of the ElseIf, it can still be unwieldy to use nested If statements if you are going more than two or three levels deep. You have probably used a keystroke-driven program before, where choosing "A" would cause one thing to happen, "B" something else, and so on. Programs like that might have 10, 20, or more possible choices. Would you want to write If statements 20 levels deep to figure out what to do next?

This is why the Select Case statement is available. Select Case allows you to specify a sequence of code blocks, one of which will be carried out depending on the value of a numerical or string expression. The syntax looks like this:

```
Select Case expression
Case value1
    Code for when expression equals value1
Case value2
    Code for when expression equals value2
...
Case valueN
    Code for when expression equals valuen
End Select
```

FIGURE 4.1

Using ElseIf *to simplify nested* Ifs.

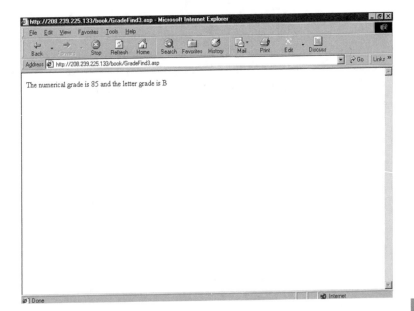

The numerical grade is 85 and the letter grade is B

4

Suppose that you have two numbers and, depending on what command is in a string, you want to add, multiply, subtract, or divide them. Using Select Case, it would look like this:

```
1:    <%
2:    Dim strOperation, sngValue1, sngValue2
3:    sngValue1 = 5
4:    sngValue2 = 2.3
5:    strOperation = "Multiply"
6:    Select Case strOperation
7:    Case "Add"
8:       Response.write (sngValue1 + sngValue2)
9:    Case "Subtract"
10:      Response.write (sngValue1 - sngValue2)
11:   Case "Multiply"
12:      Response.write (sngValue1 * sngValue2)
13:   Case "Divide"
14:      Response.write (sngValue1 / sngValue2)
15:   End Select
16:   %>
```

Can you see why this would be preferable over using many nested If statements in this kind of circumstance? Line 6 starts the Select Case statement. It specifies that the value we are going to be looking at is the value of strOperation, set on line 5. When the code is run, strOperation is checked against the values specified on lines 7, 9, 11, and 13. Line 11 matches, so the instructions beneath it are carried out.

Try changing the value of strOperation to "Add" and then to "ADD". You do not get the same result with "ADD" because "ADD" is not specified as a case to check for. What if you wanted all capital letters to be a valid way to specify an operation? You could add four new cases to the code, but VBScript provides a better way. VBScript allows you to use a comma (,) to specify a sequence of values to check.

```
1:     <%
2:     Dim strOperation, sngValue1, sngValue2
3:     sngValue1 = 5
4:     sngValue2 = 2.3
5:     strOperation = "Multiply"
6:     Select Case strOperation
7:     Case "Add", "ADD"
8:        Response.write (sngValue1 + sngValue2)
9:     Case "Subtract", "SUBTRACT"
10:        Response.write (sngValue1 - sngValue2)
11:     Case "Multiply", "MULTIPLY"
12:        Response.write (sngValue1 * sngValue2)
13:     Case "Divide", "DIVIDE"
14:        Response.write (sngValue1 / sngValue2)
15:     End Select
16:     %>
```

This version allows you to use "Add" or "ADD" (though not "add") to refer to addition. With either one, the Case statement on line 7 will find a match, and line 8 will be executed.

Now try changing strOperation to something not listed as a choice. What is printed out?

Nothing is printed out because you have not specified any actions for when strOperation does not match any of the choices. Because you cannot anticipate everything that a user might type in, it is useful to have a default case to catch typos and the like. Using Case Else does this. Case Else works, as you might expect, much like the Else statements in the previous sections did. If no match can be made among any choice listed, the code specified under Case Else is executed:

```
1:     <%
2:     Dim strOperation, sngValue1, sngValue2
3:     sngValue1 = 5
4:     sngValue2 = 2.3
5:     strOperation = "Multiply"
6:     Select Case strOperation
7:     Case "Add", "ADD"
8:        Response.write (sngValue1 + sngValue2)
9:     Case "Subtract", "SUBTRACT"
10:        Response.write (sngValue1 - sngValue2)
11:     Case "Multiply", "MULTIPLY"
```

```
12:        Response.write (sngValue1 * sngValue2)
13:    Case "Divide", "DIVIDE"
14:        Response.write (sngValue1 / sngValue2)
15:    Case Else
16:        Response.write("Invalid operation")
17:    End Select
18:    %>
```

This is almost the same as what we had before. Line 15 adds the `Case Else`. If no match is found between `strOperation` and any of the `Case` statements on lines 7, 9, 11, and 13, line 16 will be executed. Line 16 displays a message letting the user know of their error.

Now the code covers the choices we want and displays an error if another choice is used.

Do	Don't
DO use `Select Case` when you have a sequence of values to check for one variable. **DO** use the `Case Else` statement often to catch mistakes.	**DON'T** use a lot of nested `If` statements. It becomes difficult to sort out very quickly.

4

You can also use what you have just learned to adapt the grade finding program to use `Select Case` instead of `If` (see Listing 4.4).

LISTING 4.4 Fourth Version of Grade Finding Code Uses `Select Case`

```
Select Case iGrade
Case 90, 91, 92, 93, 94, 95, 96, 97, 98, 99, 100
    strLetterGrade = "A"
Case 80, 81, 82, 83, 84, 85, 86, 87, 88, 89
    strLetterGrade = "B"
Case 70, 71, 72, 73, 74, 75, 76, 77, 78, 79
    strLetterGrade = "C"
Case 60, 61, 62, 63, 64, 65, 66, 67, 68, 69
    strLetterGrade = "D"
Case Else
    strLetterGrade = "F"
End Select
```

This looks kind of ugly, and it is not really an improvement over Listing 4.3. Still, it does work, as long as grades cannot exceed 100.

This is one drawback to the Select Case. There must be only a finite number of choic-
es. Trying to specify an action for any number greater than 100 cannot be done. Also,
Case statements are only really useful where the number of choices is not too big.
Managing a large list of choices, such as in Listing 4.4, becomes difficult and tedious.
Trying to specify code to be executed for all values greater than 5, for example, cannot
reasonably be done.

Note

> If you have used Visual Basic case statements before, you should be aware
> that the is and to keywords cannot be used in VBScript. This means that
> statements such as Case is <3 or Case 5 to 10 are illegal.

Also, be sure that only one of your options can ever be true at once. Putting 3, 4, 5 as
one option and 5, 6, 7 as another will result in only the first being carried out when the
value is 5.

Looping Logic Controls

Looping logic executes a block of code repeatedly until certain conditions are met, or
while certain conditions are true.

Do...Loop Statements

The Do...Loop takes one of two forms. The first, Do While...Loop executes a block of code
while certain conditions are true. The second, Do Until...Loop, executes a block of code
until a certain condition is met.

Do While...Loop Statements

The Do While...Loop takes the following form:

```
Do While condition
    Code block
Loop
```

The code block is executed as long as condition is True. If condition is False the
first time the Do statement is encountered, the loop does not execute at all.

The following example counts from 1 to 10 using the Do While...Loop:

```
iCount = 1
Do While iCount <= 10
    Response.Write(iCount)
    iCount = iCount + 1
Loop
```

The first line sets iCount to 1. Then the system executes the Do While line. While checks to make sure that the condition is True. Because 1 is certainly less than or equal to 10, the condition is True, and the code inside the loop is executed. Next, "1" is printed to the screen, and iCount takes a value of 2. The Loop statement sends the system back to the Do While line. iCount is still less than or equal to 10, so the code inside the loop is carried out again. A "2" is printed, and iCount becomes 3.

This continues with iCount taking values of 3, 4, 5, 6, 7, 8, 9, and 10. With iCount holding the value of 10, the condition is still met, and so the code inside the loop is executed again. A "10" is printed to the screen, and iCount becomes 11. When iCount is 11, the loop condition fails, and the loop stops running. The next code to be executed is whatever comes after Loop.

In the output from this code, you can see that we put all the numbers on the same line, so that they run together. If this is not what you want, you can insert a <BR> in the loop. Listing 4.5 shows the full version of this code, with the <BR>.

LISTING 4.5   Simple Counting Script with Do While

```
<%@Language = VBScript %>
<% Option Explicit %>
<HTML>
    <BODY>
<%
    Dim iCount
    iCount = 1
    Do While iCount <= 10
       Response.Write(iCount)
%>
<BR>
<%
       iCount = iCount + 1
    Loop
%>
    </BODY>
</HTML>
```

After you type this in, view it in a Web browser. Each number is on a separate line now. If you view the code, you notice that the <BR> is listed 10 times in the code, although it is only typed once in the ASP code. HTML tags that fall within ASP control structures are affected by the control structure, too.

This loop structure can also take another form:

```
Do
Code block
Loop While condition
```

The only difference between this form and the other one is that in this case, the code inside the loop will always execute at least once. The *condition* is not tested until after the *code block*. So, even if the *condition* is False from the start, the code inside the block will execute once.

Compare the following two segments of code and the output they produce:

```
iCount = 11
Do While iCount <= 10
   Response.Write(iCount)
   iCount = iCount + 1
Loop

iCount = 11
Do
   Response.Write(iCount)
   iCount = iCount + 1
Loop While iCount <= 10
```

In the first code segment, no output will be generated. This is because iCount already has a value greater than 10 when it reaches the Do While statement.

In the second code segment, the value of iCount is not checked until the body of the loop has already executed once. This means that 11 will be printed to the screen and iCount will be incremented to 12. Then, when the condition is checked, it will fail since iCount is greater than 10. Thus, although the body of the loop has executed once, it will not execute a second time.

Do Until...Loop Statements

Do Until...Loop statements are much like Do While...Loop statements. The only difference with Do Until...Loop is that the loop executes until the *condition* becomes True, not False. Anything that one of the Do...Loops can do, the other can do also. The only difference is whether the *condition* is written positively or negatively.

The following counting to 10 script demonstrates using the Until instead of the While:

```
<%
   Dim iCount
   iCount = 1
   Do Until iCount > 10
      Response.Write(iCount)
%>
<BR>
<%
      iCount = iCount + 1
   Loop
%>
```

Listing 4.6 shows code to factor out all the 2s from a number using a Do Until…Loop.

LISTING 4.6   Factoring Out 2s Using Do Until…Loop

```
<%@Language = VBScript %>
<% Option Explicit %>
<HTML><BODY>
<%
    Dim iNumber
    iNumber = 72
    Do Until ((iNumber Mod 2) = 1)
        iNumber = iNumber \ 2
%>
<BR>
<%
    Loop
    Response.Write(iNumber)
%>
</BODY></HTML>
As with While, Until may also be put at the bottom, with the same result:
Do
Code block
Loop Until condition
```

Again, the *condition* will not be checked until after the *code block* has executed once.

Most of the time, you will write loops that are exited only when the loop condition fails. Occasionally, however, it may be necessary to exit a Do…Loop abruptly. If so, you would use the Exit Do statement. Often, the Exit Do is used along with an If…Then to exit immediately if an unexpected situation occurs. Exit Do works for all forms of the Do…Loop.

While…Wend **Statements**

While…Wend statements are the same as the Do While…Loop. The syntax is included because it is more familiar to some programmers. The While statement replaces the words Do While, and Wend replaces the Loop statement. Otherwise, While…Wend works exactly the same as a Do While…Loop:

```
1:  <%
2:      Dim iCount
3:      iCount = 1
4:      While iCount <= 10
5:          Response.Write(iCount)
6:  %>
7:  <BR>
8:  <%
```

4

```
9:          iCount = iCount + 1
10:    Wend
11: %>
```

If you replaced While on line 4 with Do While, and Wend on line 10 with Loop, the result would work exactly the same.

For...Next Statements

The For...Next loop is used when the number of times the code should execute is known before the loop begins. It executes a code block a specified number of times, while incrementing a counter. It takes the following form:

```
For counter_variable = start_value to stop_value Step step_value
    code block
Next
```

The counter_variable is a numeric variable that keeps track of which time through the loop you are on. start_value is the first value that counter_variable takes. The first time through the loop, counter_variable has a value of start_value. The next time through, it takes a value of start_value + step_value. Assuming that step_value is positive, the loop keeps executing until counter_variable is greater than stop_value. Each time through, counter_variable is increased by step_value.

You can do the simple counting program with the For...Next loop:

```
For iCount = 1 to 10 step 1
    Response.Write(iCount)
Loop
```

Notice that for this kind of simple loop, the For...Next is much better than the Do While...Loop. The For...Next handles the counter initialization and increments it for you.

Try changing the step_value to 2. Then you will get only the odd numbers between 1 and 10. Notice that although iCount never equals 10, the loop stops correctly.

> **Note**
>
> step_value may be negative. In this case, each time through step_value is still added to counter_variable. But when step_value is negative, the loop stops executing when counter_variable is less than stop_value.

If start_value is greater than stop_value and step_value is positive, the code block will not execute at all. Likewise, if stop_value is greater than start_value and step_value is negative, the code block will not execute.

Specifying a step_value is optional. If the keyword Step and the step_value are omitted, a step_value of 1 is assumed. You can see this in the following example.

This code segment adds the integers from 1 to 10 and puts the sum into iSum:

```
iSum = 0
For iCounter = 1 to 10
    iSum = iSum + iCounter
Next
```

The following code segment computes the factorial of a non-negative integer. If you are not familiar with factorials, the factorial of x is x * (x–1) * (x–2) * ... * 2 * 1. The factorial of 0 is defined to be 1. In this particular case, we will be computing the factorial of 6.

```
iNumber = 6
iFactorial = 1
For iCounter = 1 to iNumber
    iFactorial = iFactorial * iCounter
Next
```

This time we are using a variable as our *stop_value*. This is fine, as long as it is defined before we begin the loop. If iNumber is 0, the loop will not execute at all, and 1 is the value in iFactorial, as it should be.

If it is necessary to exit a For...Next or For Each...Next loop abruptly, Exit For may be used.

For Each...Next Statements

The For Each...Next construct is used to iterate through each element in a group. Suppose that you had an array of usernames and you wanted to print each name to the screen. One way would be to use the For...Next and a counter.

```
For iCounter = 0 to arraySize
    Response.Write(arrUserNames(iCounter))
Next
```

The For Each...Next offers an alternative:

```
For Each strName in arrUserNames
    Response.Write(strName)
Next
```

For simple things like this, it does not make much difference which approach you use. When you get to objects collections, you will find For Each...Next very useful.

Infinite Loops

If there is nothing in your code block that will eventually cause *condition* to be False, the code will execute indefinitely. This is called an *infinite loop* and will make visitors to your page very unhappy.

One way to get an infinite loop is to change the wrong values. For example:

```
Do While iCount > 0
  Response.Write(iFactor * iCount)
  iFactor = iFactor - 1
Loop
```

Nothing in the code block here will ever cause iCount to change. If it is greater than 0 when the loop starts, it will always be, and the loop will not stop.

It is not always obvious that your code will result in an infinite loop. You may get loops that are infinite only in certain circumstances.

```
Do While iCount <> 0
  Response.Write(3 * iCount)
  iCount = iCount - 1
Loop
```

This loop will be infinite when iCount is negative or not an integer. The rest of the time it will run normally. When you test a loop like this, you might come to the conclusion that it works. But, if you do not put in measures to prevent negative or non-integer values from reaching the loop, it can cause serious problems.

Do	Don't
DO use For…Next whenever it can be applied. **DO** remember to check your loops carefully. What will they do if they receive bad data?	**DON'T** modify the value of your counter inside the body of your For…Next loop. It makes code hard to follow and can have unpredictable results.

Nesting Loops

Just like conditional controls, loops may be nested within loops. Listing 4.7 shows a script that prints out a multiplication table for 1 through 10. Save this file as TimesTable.asp. When you view it, you may notice it is a little messy. You could use HTML tables to straighten it out if you want. For the purposes of demonstrating nested loops, it is not necessary.

Listing 4.7 Multiplication Table with Nested Loops

```
1: <%@Language = VBScript %>
2: <% Option Explicit %>
3: <HTML>
4:    <BODY>
5:    <%
```

```
 6:        Dim iTerm1, iTerm2
 7:        For iTerm1 = 1 to 10
 8:           For iTerm2 = 1 to 10
 9:              Response.Write (iTerm1 * iTerm2)
10:              Response.Write (" ")
11:           Next
12:    %>
13:    <BR>
14:    <%
15:        Next
16:    %>
17:    </BODY>
18: </HTML>
```

Printing the multiplication table requires two loops. One loop moves across, and the other, down.

Line 6 declares the variables we will use. Since we will need two loops, we need two loop counters: iTerm1 and iTerm2.

Line 7 begins the first, or outer loop. iTerm1 will go from 1 to 10. Line 8 begins a second, inner loop inside of the first loop. iTerm2 will go from 1 to 10. Lines 9 and 10 print out the product of iTerm1 and iTerm2, with a space for readability.

The Next keyword on line 11 will end the inner loop. The outer loop contains the <BR> on line 13 and ends on line 15.

Notice that the inner loop executes ten times for each iteration of the outer loop. This means that the code inside the inner loop really executes 100 times. iTerm1 takes on a value of 1. iTerm2 will go from 1 to 10 while iTerm1 is still 1. Then, iTerm1 becomes 2, and iTerm2 goes from 1 to 10 again.

The output of this script is shown in Figure 4.2. Look at it and make sure you understand why lines 9 and 10 are executed 100 times.

If you use the Exit For or Exit Do within nested loops, it will only quit the loop immediately containing it. It will not quit all the loops.

Branching Logic Controls

There are two kinds of branching logic controls: subroutines and functions. Subroutines perform actions. Functions compute values. You have already seen some of the built-in functions VBScript has.

Branching logic is often used for code that is repeated throughout a script or may need to be changed often. Putting it into a function or subroutine can improve readability, shorten the length of your code, and make it easier to maintain and improve.

FIGURE 4.2

Using nested loops.

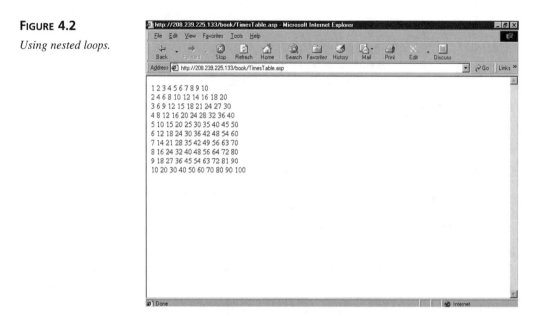

Both kinds can get complex as you use more object-oriented techniques. You will learn more about those on Day 6, "Working with Objects."

Using Subroutines

Subroutines (also called *procedures*) perform actions. The simplest kind is written like this:

```
Sub name
    code block
End Sub
```

Create a subroutine that prints a heading for you:

```
Sub subHeading
    Response.Write("<P align=right>")
    Response.Write("Your name<BR>")
    Response.Write("Your site name<HR>")
End Sub
```

Now, if somewhere in your page you want your heading to be printed, you would type this line:

```
SubHeading
```

NEW TERM   *Calling* a subroutine tells the system to execute the subroutine, and then return to normal script execution.

subHeading is now a replacement for the code that prints out the header. So you could write a page like Listing 4.8. Save it as PrintHeader1.asp.

LISTING 4.8 Simple Subroutine Example

```
 1: <%@Language = VBScript %>
 2: <% Option Explicit %>
 3: <HTML>
 4:    <BODY>
 5: <%
 6:    Sub subHeading
 7:        Response.Write("<P align=right>")
 8:        Response.Write("Your name<BR>")
 9:        Response.Write("Your site name<HR>")
10:    End Sub
11:    subHeading
12:    subHeading
13:    subHeading
14: %>
15:    </BODY>
16: </HTML>
```

Lines 6 through 10 define the subroutine subHeading. It will print an HTML paragraph tag, your name, your site's name, and an HTML <HR> tag. Line 11 calls subHeading, as do lines 12 and 13. So subHeading is called three times, which will print the heading on the screen three times.

View this in your browser. You can see that your heading was printed three times. That is because you call subHeading three times. Nothing is printed when you create your subroutine, only later when you call it.

Obviously, this is a trivial example. Nevertheless, you may already be able to see some advantages of using subroutines. You had less to type than if you had typed your heading three times. And if you change the name of your site, you only need to change one line rather than three.

It is inefficient to call subHeading three times like that. If you want something to appear multiple times, you already know a better way, right? A loop. In this case, you would use a For…Next loop because you want it to print a fixed number of times. Now you have a decision to make. Do you want the loop to go inside the subroutine or around the subroutine call? That is, you could change your subroutine to look like this:

```
Sub subHeading
   For iCounter = …
      Response.Write(…
```

```
     ...
   Next
End Sub
```

Or you could change the way you call it:

```
For iCounter = ...
   subHeading
Next
```

When faced with a decision like this, you have to figure out how you will want to use your subroutine in the future. If you will want it to print multiple times every time you use your subroutine, it makes sense to go ahead and put your loop inside the subroutine. Let's assume that this is what you want. Listing 4.9 does this.

Listing 4.9   Simple Subroutine Example with Loop

```
 1: <%@Language = VBScript %>
 2: <% Option Explicit %>
 3: <HTML>
 4:    <BODY>
 5: <%
 6:    Dim iCounter
 7:    Sub subHeading
 8:       For iCounter = 1 to 3
 9:          Response.Write("<P align=right>")
10:          Response.Write("Your name<BR>")
11:          Response.Write("Your site name<HR>")
12:       Next
13:    End Sub
14:    subHeading
15: %>
16:    </BODY>
17: </HTML>
```

With the For...Next loop on line 8, the subroutine subHeading will print the header information three times. Now subHeading need only be called once, as on line 14, in order to print the heading information three times.

This makes things easy. Whenever you want your heading to print three times in your page, just call subHeading. Now I want to complicate things a bit more with a question. What if sometimes you want it to print three times, and other times you want it to print a different number of times—maybe once, twice, five times, or zero times? This subroutine would not let you.

Think about what you have learned today about the loop structures. With the For…Next loop, you can specify variable start and stop values. So create a variable to represent the stop value. Listing 4.10 adds such a variable called iNumTimes. Whatever number is in iNumTimes when subHeading is called, that is how many times the loop will execute.

LISTING 4.10 Simple Subroutine Example with Variable Stop Value in Loop

```
 1: <%@Language = VBScript %>
 2: <% Option Explicit %>
 3: <HTML>
 4:   <BODY>
 5: <%
 6:    Dim iNumTimes, iCounter
 7:    Sub subHeading
 8:      For iCounter = 1 to iNumTimes
 9:        Response.Write("<P align=right>")
10:        Response.Write("Your name<BR>")
11:        Response.Write("Your site name<HR>")
12:      Next
13:    End Sub
14:    iNumTimes = 3
15:    subHeading
16:    Response.Write("Now two times")
17:    INumTimes = 2
18:    subHeading
19: %>
20:   </BODY>
21: </HTML>
```

ANALYSIS Lines 7 through 13 create the subroutine. Notice on line 8 that the upper bound of the loop is given by the variable iNumTimes. iNumTimes is set to 3 on line 14, and then subHeading is called. Because iNumTimes is 3, the loop will execute three times and the header information will be printed three times. Line 17 sets iNumTimes to 2 and calls subHeading again. The header information will be printed two more times.

Listing 4.10 will work. You can see its results in Figure 4.3. Now you can specify how many times the heading should print with iNumTimes. Unfortunately, you are not finished yet. What we have just done is very bad programming style. Subroutines should be kept separate from the main part of the script. subHeading shares two variables with the main part.

Suppose you started using iNumTimes for something else after line 18. Then, forgetting, you called subHeading expecting it to print the heading twice. You might not get the results you expect.

The next section, "Argument Passing", will help us to solve this problem.

4

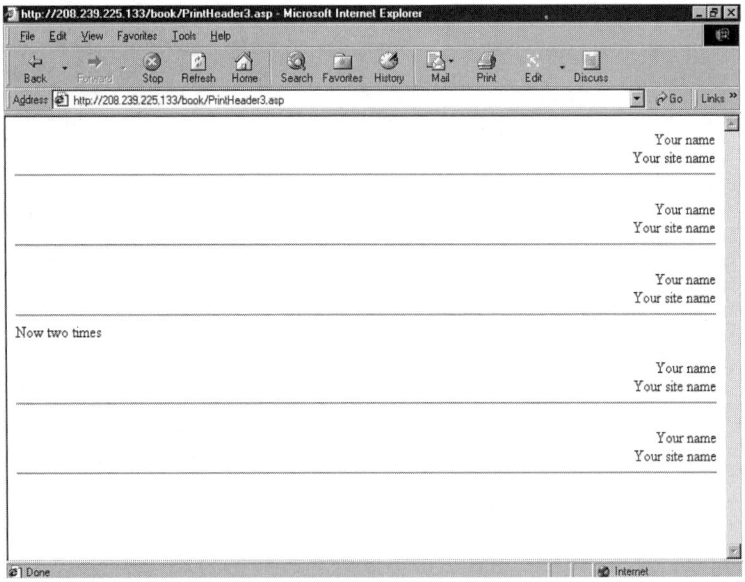

Figure 4.3

*Simple subroutine
works, but uses bad
programming style.*

Argument Passing

An *argument* is a way of sending data and variables to a subroutine or a function without
violating separateness. Values for the arguments are specified when the subroutine (or
function) is called. The subroutine (or function) can then access and manipulate the data
through specially defined variables.

Subroutines and functions should be as separate from the rest of your scripts as possible.
The subroutine in Listing 4.10 uses two variables that are declared in the main program!
You can fix one of them easily. Move the declaration of iCounter inside the subroutine.
Now try adding a Response.Write(iCounter) to the main part of your script as in
Listing 4.11.

LISTING 4.11 Simple Subroutine with Declaration Inside It

```
1: <%@Language = VBScript %>
2: <% Option Explicit %>
3: <HTML>
4:   <BODY>
5: <%
6:     Dim iNumTimes
7:     Sub subHeading
8:         Dim iCounter
9:         For iCounter = 1 to iNumTimes
```

```
10:            Response.Write("<P align=right>")
11:            Response.Write("Your name<BR>")
12:            Response.Write("Your site name<HR>")
13:        Next
14:    End Sub
15:    iNumTimes = 4
16:    subHeading
17:    Response.Write(iCounter)
18: %>
19:    </BODY>
20: </HTML>
```

This is a lot like Listing 4.10. The declaration for the iCounter variable is on line 8 now, inside the function. Lines 15 and 16 call subHeading, using iNumTimes to set the number of times the loop executes. Line 17 then tries to print out the value of iCounter. What happens when you view this page in your browser?

You get an error message because the variable iCounter has no meaning outside the subroutine. So, when line 17 tries to access it, it causes an error. iCounter's *scope* is limited to the subroutine.

New Term Variables declared in the main part of your script are *global*. They can be accessed by any subroutine or function in the page.

New Term iCounter, however, was declared inside a subroutine and is *local* to that subroutine. Nothing outside subHeading can access it. However, if subHeading had subroutines inside it, those subroutines could access iCounter.

This is probably all very confusing right now. That's okay. For the time being, just remember that you declared iCounter inside a subroutine and you can only use it inside that subroutine.

Now this is good. You got rid of one of the variables that was connecting the subroutine to the main program. The other one is a bit trickier. You need to set the value of iNumTimes outside the subroutine. If you declare it inside the subroutine, you cannot access it outside subHeading.

This is why subroutines can take arguments. Using argument passing, write the subHeading subroutine as in Listing 4.12.

LISTING 4.12 Simple Subroutine with Argument Passing

```
1:    <%@Language = VBScript %>
2:    <% Option Explicit %>
3:    <HTML>
```

continues

Listing 4.12 continued

```
4:        <BODY>
5:    <%
6:        Dim iNumTimes
7:        Sub subHeading (iNumTimes)
8:            Dim iCounter
9:            For iCounter = 1 to iNumTimes
10:               Response.Write("<P align=right>")
11:               Response.Write("Your name<BR>")
12:               Response.Write("Your site name<HR>")
13:           Next
14:       End Sub
15:       iNumTimes = 4
16:       subHeading iNumTimes
17:       Response.Write("iNumTimes is " & iNumTimes)
18:   %>
19:       </BODY>
20:   </HTML>
```

On line 7, you see how the first line of a subroutine with arguments looks. The argument name is in parentheses following the name of the subroutine. If you had more than one argument, they would be written as a list with commas between them. Listing 4.15 shows such a subroutine.

On line 16, you see how the subroutine is called with arguments. The name of the subroutine is followed by the variable or value being passed. If there was more than one argument, they would be written, again, as a comma-delimited list.

NEW TERM   Now the iNumTimes in the main part of the script is different from the iNumTimes in the subroutine. When line 16 calls subHeading, the value stored in the variable iNumTimes is copied into an argument called iNumTimes. This is called *passing by value*. If you change the value of the iNumTimes that is inside the subroutine, it will not affect the value of the iNumTimes outside the subroutine. This is to prevent subroutines and functions from messing up data they should not be messing up.

In fact, try adding

```
iNumTimes = iNumTimes + 1
```

between lines 13 and 14 and viewing the page again. You will see no effect. Try moving the line you just added to between lines 8 and 9 in Listing 4.12. Now you will see an extra heading because you have changed the value of the iNumTimes inside the subroutine. It does not affect things outside the subroutine, but it does inside. The number printed at the bottom still is 4, not 5.

In fact, because there is no longer any connection between the two iNumTimes, the fact that they have the same name is now unimportant. So change iNumTimes in your main script to iNumHeadings and take out the line you added a minute ago. Listing 4.13 reflects these changes.

LISTING 4.13 Simple Subroutine with Argument Passing

```
 1:   <%@Language = VBScript %>
 2:   <% Option Explicit %>
 3:   <HTML>
 4:     <BODY>
 5:   <%
 6:      Dim iNumHeadings
 7:      Sub subHeading (iNumTimes)
 8:         Dim iCounter
 9:         For iCounter = 1 to iNumTimes
10:            Response.Write("<P align=right>")
11:            Response.Write("Your name<BR>")
12:            Response.Write("Your site name<HR>")
13:         Next
14:      End Sub
15:      iNumHeadings = 4
16:      subHeading iNumHeadings
17:      Response.Write("iNumHeadings is " & iNumHeadings)
18:   %>
19:     </BODY>
20:   </HTML>
```

It still works just like Listing 4.12. You can even go further. It is not necessary to use a variable when you call a subroutine. Take a look at Listing 4.14.

LISTING 4.14 Simple Subroutine with Argument Passing

```
 1:   <%@Language = VBScript %>
 2:   <% Option Explicit %>
 3:   <HTML>
 4:     <BODY>
 5:   <%
 6:      Sub subHeading (iNumTimes)
 7:         Dim iCounter
 8:         For iCounter = 1 to iNumTimes
 9:            Response.Write("<P align=right>")
10:            Response.Write("Your name<BR>")
11:            Response.Write("Your site name<HR>")
12:         Next
13:      End Sub
14:      subHeading 4
15:   %>
16:     </BODY>
17:   </HTML>
```

4

You can even call your subroutine with a number, or with anything that evaluates to a number. Now you have a truly versatile version of this subroutine. As long as you have subHeading created like it is in lines 6 through 13, you can call anywhere on the page with a numerical variable, a number, or a numerical expression.

This is one of the toughest concepts you will encounter this week. You should read over what we have done so far a second time.

Now we will look at another subroutine. This one prints out the elements of an array from iStartVal to iStopVal:

```
1:      Sub subPrintArray(arrToPrint, iStartValue, iStopValue)
2:          Dim iCounter
3:          For iCounter = iStartValue to iStopValue
4:              Response.Write(arrToPrint(iCounter))
5:              Response.Write("<BR>")
6:          Next
7:      End Sub
```

ANALYSIS Line 1 creates a subroutine called subPrintArray that takes three arguments. The first one is called arrToPrint, the second iStartValue, and the third is iStopValue. Line 2 declares a variable called iCounter. iCounter is local to subPrintArray. The main script cannot access iCounter. Line 3 begins a For…Next loop. iCounter begins at iStartValue and increases until it passes iStopValue. No step value is specified, so iCounter will increase one at a time. Line 4 prints to the screen the value of arrToPrint in location number iCounter. Line 5 adds a line break between array elements. Line 6 ends the For…Next statement. Line 7 ends the subroutine.

Listing 4.15 puts this subroutine into a full ASP page.

LISTING 4.15   Another Simple Subroutine with Argument Passing

```
1:      <%@Language = VBScript %>
2:      <% Option Explicit %>
3:      <HTML>
4:        <BODY>
5:      <%
6:      Dim arrPrimeNos, arrNames
7:      Sub subPrintArray(arrToPrint, iStartValue, iStopValue)
8:          Dim iCounter
9:          For iCounter = iStartValue to iStopValue
10:             Response.Write(arrToPrint(iCounter))
11:             Response.Write("<BR>")
12:         Next
13:       End Sub
14:     arrPrimeNos = Array(2, 3, 5, 7, 11, 13, 17, 19)
15:     arrNames = Array("John", "Mary", "Frank", "Scott")
```

```
16:    subPrintArray arrNames, 2, 3
17:    subPrintArray arrPrimeNos, 0, 4
18:    subPrintArray arrNames, 1, 3
19:  %>
20:    </BODY>
21:    </HTML>
```

ANALYSIS Lines 1 through 6 should be familiar to you by now. Lines 7 through 13 are discussed above, when we created the subPrintArray function. Line 14 uses the Array function mentioned yesterday to initialize the array arrPrimeNos. It now contains the first eight prime numbers. Line 15 uses the Array function to initialize the array arrNames. It now contains four names. Line 16 makes a call to the subroutine subPrintArray, passing arrNames, the number 2, and the number 3. This causes the number 2 and 3 elements of arrNames to be printed to the screen. Line 17 makes a call to subPrintArray, passing arrPrimeNos, 0, and 4. This causes elements number 0 through 4 of arrPrimeNos to be printed. Line 18 makes a call to subPrintArray, passing arrNames, 1, and 3. This causes elements number 1 through 3 of arrNames to be printed.

Figure 4.4 shows the output of the page we have just created. Look at it and verify that the subPrintArray subroutine does what we intended.

4

FIGURE 4.4

The results of the subroutine to print part of an array.

There are other ways to call subroutines, but they do not add any power or ease to the language. They are discussed in Appendix B, "VBScript Reference."

Do	Don't
DO apply the same good variable naming techniques to the names of your arguments.	**DON'T** use global variables in your subroutines and functions.

Using Functions

Functions compute values. You may wonder at first how this is different from what subroutines do. Subroutines do not evaluate to anything. The only way you would ever call a subroutine is on a line by itself. Functions, on the other hand, return values. This means that a function call can be put into an expression, have things added to it, and so on.

Creating a function is much like creating a subroutine. Replace Sub with Function and End Sub with End Function. More importantly, you must include a line that tells what value the function should return. The line should look like this:

```
Function_name = some_value
```

Now try creating a function. We will reuse some code written earlier to compute an absolute value in the section on If…Then:

```
If sngNumber < 0 Then
   sngNumber = -sngNumber
End if
```

Turn this into a function:

```
Function sngAbsoluteValue(sngNumber)
   If sngNumber < 0 Then
      sngNumber = -sngNumber
   End if
   sngAbsoluteValue = sngNumber
End Function
```

Functions use passing by value, just like subroutines, so the line

```
sngNumber = -sngNumber
```

does not change anything in the script that calls this.

Speaking of which, you may be wondering how to call a function. The syntax of the function call is

```
Functionname (argumentlist)
```

If it has no arguments, it may be called with either empty parentheses or no parentheses at all.

So in the case of the absolute value function, it would look like sngAbsoluteValue(-5) or sngAbsoluteValue(*variable_name*). However, it would not make sense to put a function call on a line by itself. Function calls return values. You should put that value someplace. You might assign it to variable, write it to the screen, or even use it in the call of another function. For example,

```
sngMyNumber = sngAbsoluteValue(sngMyNumber)
```

replaces sngMyNumber with its absolute value.

> **Note**
>
> If you really need to call a function and want to discard the value it returns, you can use the Call statement, like this:
>
> ```
> Call function_name(arguments)
> ```
>
> Generally, however, if you are writing a function, but are not going to use the value the function returns, you should use a subroutine instead. That is what subroutines are for, after all, and it will make your code cleaner.

We also wrote code to compute the factorial of a number in the section on For...Next:

```
iFactorial = 1
For iCounter = 1 to iNumber
   iFactorial = iFactorial * iCounter
Next
```

So the function would look like this:

```
Function iFactorial (iNumber)
   Dim iCounter
   iFactorial = 1
   For iCounter = 1 to iNumber
      iFactorial = iFactorial * iCounter
   Next
End Function
```

Just as with subroutines, you want to keep the function as separate from the main script as possible. You use an argument for iNumber and declare iCounter inside the function to accomplish this. However, it is not good programming style to use iFactorial so much within the function. It would be better to create a temporary variable and copy the value over at the end.

```
Function iFactorial (iNumber)
   Dim iCounter, iTemp
   iTemp = 1
   For iCounter = 1 to iNumber
      iTemp = iTemp * iCounter
```

```
    Next
    iFactorial = iTemp
End Function
```

You may have noticed that, for the code in this book, we have adopted the convention of giving subroutine names a prefix of "sub" and giving function names the same prefix as the data type they return. Many people use no prefix at all on subroutines and functions. The choice is up to you on the code you write.

If you ever need to quit a function or subroutine abruptly, use Exit Function or Exit Subroutine, respectively.

Summary

With so many new structures you have learned today, you may feel overwhelmed. That is nothing to feel bad about. This is a difficult day. You may often find yourself having difficulty deciding which control structure to use. Here is a quick guide.

Do you need some code to only execute under certain circumstances? If so, you probably need some sort of conditional structure. If your circumstances are a yes/no kind of thing, you want an If…Then or If…Then…Else. If it is more multiple-choice, you probably should go with a Select Case.

Do you need some code to execute more than once at a time? If so, you probably need some sort of looping structure. If you know how often it needs to be executed, or have that number stored in a variable prior to the loop, use a For…Next. Otherwise, you need a Do…Loop of some sort.

Do you have code that you reuse often in different places? If so, you probably should use a branching structure. Do you want calculations to be performed? If so, a function is probably the way to go. Subroutines are generally good for things like printing output.

Use arguments and local variables to keep subroutines and functions distanced from the main script. Using passing of arguments by value also serves this purpose by preventing rogue procedures from changing the data.

Q&A

Q How do I pass arguments to a procedure by reference?

A Passing by reference means passing so that the procedure can change the values in the calling program. VBScript does not directly support this. One way to get around that is to pass arguments inside an array.

Q Why would I want to use an Exit statement to terminate a control structure abruptly?

A The most common reason is if bad data gets into the loop somehow. It might be the wrong kind of data, it might be data outside the correct range, or something like that. Whatever the problem, it is better for you to check for it and use an Exit statement than for your script to fail and give visitors to your site a cryptic error message!

Workshop

The Workshop provides quiz questions to help you solidify your understanding of the material covered and exercises to provide you with experience in using what you've learned. Try to understand the quiz and exercise answers before continuing to tomorrow's lesson. Quiz answers are provided in Appendix A, and exercise answers can be found at `http://www.mcp.com/info`.

Quiz

1. Under what circumstance is it better to use a For…Next than a Do While…Loop?

2. What is wrong with this code?
```
If (sngArea > 5)
    Response.Write("Big")
Else
    Response.Write("Small")
End if
```

3. What does it mean for a variable to be global?

Exercises

1. Write a function called iSumSeries that computes the sum of the integers from iStart to iStop.

2. Write a function that computes the greatest common divisor of two integers.

DAY 5

Using VBScript's Built-in Functions

After yesterday's difficult lesson, you get to take things a little easier today. Today's discussion involves using some of the functions that are built-in to VBScript. These functions do not add the same kind of power as the topics of the past two days, but they make life a little easier for us. Today, you will learn the following:

- What a typecasting is
- What functions are available for formatting
- What built-in math functions VBScript has
- How VBScript helps manipulate dates
- How to use VBScript's powerful string functions

Typecasting Variables

There are many reasons that you might want to be able to change between data types. Often, when data entered through an HTML form is sent to an ASP page, it does not arrive in the desired format. Or, maybe there will be times that you have data you want to treat like a string part of the time and like a number part of the time. Typecasting is the way it is all done.

What Is Typecasting and Why Should I Typecast?

Typecasting converts between data subtypes. For example, typecasting could turn the string value "455" into an integer value, 455. It could also be used to go the other direction, from an integer to a string. Or, it could turn the string "12/3/97" into a date value.

Why typecast? You may remember from Day 3, "Working with Variables," that some operators do different things for different data types. For example, if you have two strings, "+" joins them together. If you have two numbers, though, "+" adds them. This is all well and good, but what if you had two strings of digits, like "236" and "355" and you wanted to add them like numbers? Applying addition directly gives "236" + "355" is "236355". In a situation like this, you need typecasting.

How to Typecast Your Variables

VBScript has a long list of typecasting functions.

Cint(*expression*) casts *expression* to an integer. If *expression* is a floating-point value or a currency value, it is rounded. If it is a string that looks like a number, it is turned into that number and then rounded if necessary. If it is a string that contains letters, an error results. If it is a Boolean value of True, it becomes -1. False becomes 0. It also must be within the range that an integer can store.

Caution

> If the expression to be cast is outside the range that an integer can represent, an error is generated. For example, Cint("300000000") will produce an error because 300000000 is too big.

Examples:

- Cint("33") returns 33.
- Cint(44.6) returns 45.
- Cint(True) returns -1.

Clng(*expression*) casts *expression* to a long.

Examples:

- `Clng("435896640")` returns 435896640.

`Cbyte(expression)` casts *expression* to a byte value provided that the *expression* falls between 0 and 255. The *expression* should be numeric or something that can be cast to a number.

Examples:

- `...Cdbl(expression)` casts *expression* to a double. *expression* should be numeric or something that can be cast to a number.

Examples:

- `Cdbl("4.55")` returns 4.55.
- `Cdbl("0.000000556")` returns 0.000000556.

`Csng(expression)` casts *expression* to a single. It works like `Cdbl()`, but must fall within the range represented by a single.

Examples:

- `Csng("0.000000556")` returns 5.56E-07.

`Cbool(expression)` casts *expression* to a Boolean value. If expression is zero, the result is False. Otherwise, the result is True. *expression* should be numeric or something that can be cast to a number.

Examples:

- `Cbool(5)` returns True.
- `Cbool("3.25")` returns True.
- `Cbool("A")` generates an error.
- `Cbool(0.1)` returns True.

`Ccur(expression)` casts *expression* to a currency value. *expression* should be numeric or something that can be cast to a number.

Examples:

- `Ccur(4)` returns 4.
- `Ccur("9.12355")` returns 9.1236.
- `Ccur(-2)` returns -2.

`Cdate(expression)` casts *expression* to a date value. *expression* should be numeric or something that can be cast to a number, or a string of a commonly used date format. `DateValue(expression)` or `TimeValue(expression)` can also be used for this.

5

Examples:

- Cdate(4) returns 1/3/1900.
- Cdate("4.445") returns 1/3/1900 10:40:48 AM.
- Cdate("4-5-98") returns 4/5/98.
- Cdate("April-5-98") returns 4/5/98.
- DateValue("4-5-98") returns 4/5/98.
- DateValue("April 5, 1998") returns 4/5/98.
- TimeValue("2:23 PM") returns 2:23:00 PM.

> **Caution**   The format that dates are displayed in depends on your system settings. The examples here assume the American format (mm/dd/yy).

Cstr(*expression*) casts *expression* to a string. *expression* can be any kind of data.

Examples:

- Cstr(4.5) returns "4.5".

Formatting Functions

Four functions help to format data to be displayed the way you want it. All of them return a string.

FormatDateTime is used to format date/time data. It has one required argument, the expression to be formatted, and one optional argument that allows you to specify a format. Five different constants stand for possible formats. Unfortunately, they vary from system to system, so you will have to check yours to see what they look like.

- vbGeneralDate—Displays date, if present, as short date. Displays time, if present, as long time. Value is 0. This is the default setting if no format is specified.
- vbLongDate—Displays date using long date format, as specified in system settings. Value is 1.
- vbShortDate—Displays date using short date format, as specified in system settings. Value is 2.
- vbLongTime—Displays time using long time format, as specified in system settings. Value is 3.
- vbShortTime—Displays time using short time format, as specified in system settings. Value is 4.

So if you wanted to print the current date to the screen in short date format, you would write

```
Response.Write FormatDateTime(Date, vbShortDate)
```

or

```
Response.Write FormatDateTime(Date, 2)
```

`FormatCurrency` is used to format monetary values. It can have up to five arguments. The first is the currency value to be formatted.

The second argument is the number of digits after the decimal place that should be shown. Or, you may use -1 to indicate that the system's default should be used.

NEW TERM   The third, fourth, and fifth arguments are *Tristate* options, which means that they have three possible values. If the value is -2, it means use the system default. Notice that this is different than with the number of digits, where -1 specifies system default. With Tristate options, -1 means to turn on the option. 0 means the to turn off the option.

For example, `FormatCurrency` (amount, -1, -2, -2, -2) specifies to use system default for the number of digits and all three Tristate options, while `FormatCurrency` (amount, -1, -1, -1, -1) specifies to use the system default for the number of digits, but explicitly turns on all three of the Tristate options.

The third argument to `FormatCurrency` specifies whether to include leading zeroes on values less than one. For example, show 0.25 or .25?

The fourth argument to `FormatCurrency` specifies whether to enclose negative values in parentheses. For example, ($4) or -$4?

The fifth argument to `FormatCurrency` specifies whether to use the delimiter specified in the computer's settings to group digits. In the U.S., the delimiter is the comma. For example, 4,000 or 4000?

A few examples follow:

`FormatCurrency`(*amount*, -1, -2, -2, -2) specifies to use all the system defaults. It would be equivalent to say `FormatCurrency`(*amount*).

`FormatCurrency`(*amount*, 2, -1, 0, -1) specifies two decimal places, shows the leading zeroes, uses a negative sign rather than parentheses on negative values, and uses the delimiter.

5

Caution	Many of the functions discussed today have several optional arguments. Most of the time, if you want to use one of the later optional arguments, you must do one of two things.

One way is to include all the optional arguments that precede it. For example, if you want to specify no delimiter, and use system defaults for the other options, you could do this:

`FormatCurrency(amount, -1, -2, -2, 0)`

The other way is to put spaces where the other optional arguments would go. To specify no delimiter and use all the other defaults, you could do this:

`FormatCurrency(amount, , , , 0)`

You must leave the commas in. `FormatCurrency(amount, 0)` would be interpreted as setting zero digits after the decimal place.

You can also mix specifying values and using spaces.

`FormatCurrency(amount, 4, ,-2, -1).`

This says 4 decimal places should be shown, leading zeros would be system default, use of parentheses is also left to system default, and the delimiter would be used.

In fact, it is not a bad idea to go ahead and specify all the arguments. It helps you learn what options these functions have.

FormatNumber is used to format numerical values. It is almost exactly like FormatCurrency. The only difference is that FormatNumber does not display a dollar sign. The options all work exactly the same.

FormatPercent works like the previous two. The options are the same, but it turns the value it is given into a percentage. `FormatPercent(0.45, 1, -1, 0, 0)` returns `45.0%`.

Math Functions

You may recognize many of VBScript's built-in mathematical functions. Most are simple to use. Table 5.1 provides a quick reference to the ones that are available. You probably will not need most of these very often, so you do not need to memorize these. You can refer back to this as a reference when you do.

TABLE 5.1   Built-in Math Functions

Function	Meaning
Abs(number)	Absolute value
Atn(number)	Arctangent
Cos(number)	Cosine

Function	Meaning
Exp(*number*)	e ^ *number*
Fix(*number*)	Integer portion
Hex(*number*)	Base 10 to hexadecimal
Int(*number*)	Integer portion
Log(*number*)	Natural logarithm
Oct(*number*)	Base 10 to octal
Rnd	Random number
Round(*number*)	Round to integer
Round(*number*, *dec*)	Round to *dec* decimals
Sgn(*number*)	Sign
Sin(*number*)	Sine
Sqr(*number*) (*number* > 0)	Square root
Tan(*number*)	Tangent

Many of these will probably look familiar to you from your math classes, but in case you have forgotten, here's a little explanation of what they all mean.

Abs(*number*) returns the absolute value of the number, which is the positive part. If *number* is greater than or equal to zero, *number* is returned. If *number* is less than zero, the negation of *number* is returned.

Exp(*number*) raises e (approximately 2.71828) to the power *number*. So Exp(2) returns e^2, which is approximately 7.38905

Note

> You may have noticed that both Fix(*number*) and Int(*number*) mean integer portion. The difference between Fix(*number*) and Int(*number*) comes in their handling of negative values. Both return the integer portion of *number*, but with negative values; Int returns the first integer less than or equal to *number*, whereas Fix returns the first integer greater than or equal to *number*.

So Fix(-4.5) returns -4, and Int(-4.5) returns -5.

Hex(*number*) and Oct(*number*) return strings consisting of the *number* converted to hexadecimal and octal bases, respectively.

So Hex(435) returns "1B3", and Oct(435) returns "663".

Log(*number*) returns the base e (approx. 2.71828) logarithm of *number*. If you want a logarithm of a different base, use this formula, where B is the new base:

```
LogB(number) = Log(number)/Log(B)
```

Rnd returns a random number less than one and greater than or equal to zero. Rnd should be used following the statement Randomize.

By itself, Randomize uses the system timer to initialize the random number generator. Randomize *number* uses *number* to initialize the random number generator. Usually, it does not matter which way you want to use randomize.

If you want to use random numbers in a page, put a Randomize statement at the top of the page, and call Rnd whenever you need a random number.

```
Randomize
...
sngMyVariable = Rnd
```

This stores a random number into sngMyVariable.

Strictly speaking, the numbers generated by Randomize and Rnd are not random. Computers cannot pick random numbers. However, these numbers should be random enough for your purposes.

If you want a random number between ranges other than zero and one, use an expression like this:

```
(upperbound - lowerbound) * Rnd + lowerbound
```

This will return a random number greater than or equal to lowerbound and less than upperbound. If you want an integer, use the same expression inside of a Cint().

 Note

> Rnd can take an argument.
>
> Rnd *number*
>
> *number* affects the way the random number is generated. If number is less than zero, the same number is generated every time, using *number* as the seed. If *number* equals zero, the most recently generated number is returned. If *number* is greater than zero, the result is the same as leaving *number* out.

Round(*number*) rounds *number* to the nearest integer. Round(*number*, *dec*) rounds to *dec* decimal places.

Round(4.556) returns 5, whereas Round(4.556, 2) returns 4.56.

The trigonometric functions Sin, Cos, and Tan all take the number to be in radians. Atn returns a number in radians. If you have forgotten, multiply by 180/pi to go from radians to degrees, and by pi/180 to go from degrees to radians. Also, because among the inverse trig functions, only arctangent is defined, you may need to use the following equations:

```
arcsin(x) = arctan(x/sqrt(1 - x^2))
```

```
arccos(x) = arctan(sqrt(1 - x^2)/x)
```

Here is the code for the arcsin function:

```
Function Arcsin(sngNumber)
If abs(sngNumber) > 1 Then
   'use some special value to indicate an error has occurred
   ' -2 is used here
   Arcsin = -2
Else
   Arcsin = Atn(sngNumber / Sqr(1 - sngNumber ^ 2))
End If
End Function
```

If you are not familiar with trigonometry, do not worry too much about these functions. They are not needed often in ASP.

Sgn(*number*) returns 1 if *number* is greater than zero, 0 if *number* equals zero, and -1 if *number* is less than zero.

Date Functions

As mentioned on Day 3, VBScript offers a wide variety of built-in functions to make working with dates easier.

Working with Date Values

The first set of date functions we will examine allow you to find and manipulate dates and times.

Note

You may recall that you refer to a particular date by putting it inside two pound signs (#). However, when working with these functions, you may omit the year and let the system assume the current year. If you want to do this, put the date in double quotes instead. For example, #9/18/99# is used to explicitly refer to November 18, 1999. If you instead wanted to refer to November 18 of the current year, whatever that might be, you would write "9/18". This is sometimes handy in writing code to prevent it from needing to be changed every year.

5

`Date` returns the current date. It can then be stored into a date/time variable, written to the screen, and so on.

Examples:

```
dtToday = Date
```

```
Response.Write("Today is " & Date)
```

`Time` returns the current time. It can then be stored into a date/time variable, written to the screen, and so on.

Examples:

```
dtCurrentTime = Time
```

```
Response.Write("Current time is " & Time)
```

`Now` returns the current date and time.

Examples:

```
dtRightNow = Now
```

`DateAdd(`*interval*`, `*number*`, `*date*`)` is used to add to the date specified by *date*. *interval* is a string that represents whether you want to add days, months, years, and so on. Table 5.2 lists the possibilities and the code used. *number* indicates the number of *interval*s you want to add; that is, the number of days, months, years, and so on, that you want to add.

Note   The `DateAdd` function takes into account worries such as "Is tomorrow the start of a new month?" and "Is it a leap year?"

Examples (assuming date in mm/dd/yy format):

- `DateAdd("m", 1, #12/7/90#)` would return 1/7/91.
- `DateAdd("d", 1, Date)` would return tomorrow's date.
- `DateAdd("yyyy", 5, #2/7/88#)` would return 2/7/93.
- `DateAdd` will not return an invalid date.
- `DateAdd("m", 1, #8/31/99#)` will return 9/30/99, not 9/31/99.

TABLE 5.2 Interval Values for `DateAdd`

Value	Meaning
`"yyyy"`	Year
`"q"`	Quarter
`"m"`	Month
`"y"`	Day of year (same as Day)
`"d"`	Day
`"w"`	Weekday (same as Day)
`"ww"`	Week of year (Week)
`"h"`	Hour
`"n"`	Minute
`"s"`	Second

`DateDiff` is used to find the time between two dates. It takes this form:

`DateDiff(interval, date1, date2, first_dow, first_woy)`

interval is one of the values from Table 5.3. `DateDiff` returns the number of *interval*s between *date1* and *date2*. If *date2* comes after *date1*, the return value is positive. If *date2* precedes *date1*, it is negative.

first_dow is an optional argument that allows you to specify what day of the week to consider the first day of the week. The values used to indicate what to consider the first day of the week are listed in Table 5.5.

first_woy is another optional argument. It allows you to specify what week to consider the first week of the year. Table 5.6 lists the values you can choose.

Examples:

- `DateDiff("m", #12/3/89#, #11/8/90#)` returns 11.
- `DateDiff("d", #1/2/93#, #1/8/93#)` returns 6. Notice that `DateDiff` counts the second date but not the first one.
- `DateDiff("w", date1, date2)` takes the day of the week that *date1* falls on and counts how many of that day are between *date1* and *date2*, counting *date2* but not *date1*.
- `DateDiff("ww", date1, date2)` returns the number of calendar weeks between *date1* and *date2*. By default, this means counting the number of Sundays between the two dates, counting *date2* if it is a Sunday, but not *date1* no matter what it is.
- `DateDiff("ww", date1, date2, 4)` counts the number of Wednesdays between the two dates, counting *date2* if it is a Wednesday, but never *date1*.

TABLE 5.3   Interval Values for `DateDiff`

Value	Meaning
"yyyy"	Year
"q"	Quarter
"m"	Month
"y"	Day of year (same as Day)
"d"	Day
"w"	Weekday
"ww"	Week of year(Week)
"h"	Hour
"n"	Minute
"s"	Second

You know to specify a date using pound signs, but what if you want to create a date value using a month stored in one variable and a day stored in another? You cannot say `#iMonthVar/iDayVar/99#` or anything like that. Instead, you need a function for this. `DateSerial` takes a year, month, and day and puts them together into a date value. The year, month, and day may be in variables, specified directly, or expressions.

`dtImportantDate = DateSerial(67, 5, iDayVar)` creates a date value of May iDayVarth, 1967, and stores it into `dtImportantDate`.

Note that values need not fall within the standard ranges for days or months. `DateSerial(99, 5, 1 - 3)` returns 4/28/99. In other words, it returns a value of three days before May 1, 1999. As you can see, `DateSerial` offers a lot of flexibility in creating date values.

`TimeSerial` is similar to `DateSerial` but is called with a desired hour, minute, and second.

`dtImportantTime = TimeSerial(3, 0 - 5, 0 - 20)` creates a value of 20 seconds before 5 minutes before 3:00 in the morning. In other words, 2:54:40 A.M.

`Timer` returns the number of seconds elapsed since midnight. It can be useful in determining the amount of time it takes a section of your code to execute.

```
iStartTime = Timer
   code to time
iEndTime = Timer
iSecondsElapsed = iEndTime - iStartTime
```

Breaking Down Date Values

Often when programming, you may find it useful for your code to know the current month, but not need the rest of the date information.

`DatePart` allows you to retrieve only a specific part of a date/time value. You can use it to retrieve the current year, quarter, month, day of the year (from 1 to 365), day of the month, day of the week, week of the year (from 1 to 52), hour (from 0 to 23), minute, or second. It has two required arguments and two optional ones. The required arguments are a string code for what you want to retrieve and the date value to retrieve it from. The codes for the first argument are listed in Table 5.4.

The optional arguments accepted by DatePart are codes to indicate the first day of the week and the first week of the year. They work the same as the optional arguments to `DateDiff`.

TABLE 5.4 Interval Values for `DatePart`

Value	Meaning
`"yyyy"`	Year
`"q"`	Quarter
`"m"`	Month
`"y"`	Day of year
`"d"`	Day
`"w"`	Weekday
`"ww"`	Week of year
`"h"`	Hour
`"n"`	Minute
`"s"`	Second

Examples:

- `DatePart("m", #9/17/67#)` returns 9 since September is the ninth month.
- `DatePart("y", #9/11/96#)` returns 255 since September 11 is the 255th day of the year.
- DatePart also allows you to specify what to consider the first day of the week to be. This is useful with the interval codes `"w"` and `"ww"`. For example,
    - `DatePart("w", #9/18/99#, 3)` means consider Tuesday as the first day of the week. 9/18/99 is a Saturday, so this returns 5.

- `DatePart("w", #9/18/99#, 6)` returns 2. The 6 indicates that Friday should be considered the first day of the week. Saturday, then is the second.
- `DatePart("ww", #9/18/99#, 2, 1)` means consider Monday the first day of the week and the week of January 1 to be the first week of the year.

TABLE 5.5   Day of the Week Constants

Value	Name	Meaning
0	vbUseSystem	National Language Support API Setting
1	vbSunday	Sunday (default)
2	vbMonday	Monday
3	vbTuesday	Tuesday
4	vbWednesday	Wednesday
5	vbThursday	Thursday
6	vbFriday	Friday
7	vbSaturday	Saturday

TABLE 5.6   First Week of the Year Constants

Value	Name	Meaning
0	vbUseSystem	National Language Support API Setting
1	vbFirstJan1	Week of January 1
2	vbFirstFourDays	First week with four days of new year
3	vbFirstFullWeek	First full week

There is also a series of functions that serve basically the same purpose as the `DatePart` function.

`Year(date)` returns the year portion from *date* (a number).

`Month(date)` returns the month portion from *date* (a number).

`MonthName(monthNumber, abbrev)` returns a string with the name of the month. *monthNumber* is an integer from 1 to 12. *abbrev* is an optional argument that indicates whether to return the whole month or just an abbreviation. The default is `False`, which means that the full name is returned.

`MonthName(11)` returns `"November"`.

`MonthName(11, False)` returns `"November"`.

`MonthName(11, True)` returns `"Nov"`.

Day(*date*) returns the day portion from *date* (a number).

Weekday(*date*) returns the day of the week of *date* (a number, see Table 5.5).

Hour(*time*) returns the hour portion from *time*.

Minute(*time*) returns the minute portion from *time*.

Second(*time*) returns the second portion from *time*.

The following example uses a few of the date functions we have discussed:

```
 1: <%
 2:     Dim iCounter, dtWeekBegan, dtIterate, arrWeekDays
 3:     arrWeekDays = Array("", "Sunday", "Monday", "Tuesday", _
 4:     "Wednesday", "Thursday", "Friday", "Saturday")
 5:     dtWeekBegan = DateAdd("d", 1 - Weekday(Date), Date)
 6:     For iCounter = 0 to 6
 7:         dtIterate = DateAdd("d", iCounter, dtWeekBegan)
 8:         Response.Write(arrWeekDays(Weekday(dtIterate)) & ", ")
 9:         Response.Write(dtIterate & "<BR>")
10:     Next
11: %>
```

ANALYSIS   This prints out the days and date of the current week, starting at Sunday. Notice line 3 makes use of the Array function mentioned in Day 3 to quickly set the value of the array arrWeekDays. Line 5 uses DateAdd to calculate the date that the current week began on. The expression 1 - Weekday(Date) calculates how many days ago Sunday was as a negative number, which is then added to the current date. It then steps through the days using a For...Next loop. Each time through the loop, the current value of the loop counter is added to the date the week began (line 7). The day of the week is retrieved from that date as a number, as in line 8, and the array arrWeekDays is used to convert from the day number returned by Weekday to a string of the day's name.

5

String Functions

Perhaps VBScript's greatest advantage over other programming languages is its library of powerful, yet easy-to-use string manipulating functions. They allow you to retrieve and change part or all of a string or a series of strings. Many programmers find string manipulation to be one of the most annoying and tiresome aspects of programming, but VBScript makes things much easier.

UCase(*string*) returns *string* with all its lowercase letters converted to uppercase letters. For example, UCase("John Smith") returns "JOHN SMITH".

Similarly, LCase(*string*) returns *string* with all its uppercase letters converted to lowercase letters. Neither of these functions affects the numbers or special characters that may appear in the string.

LTrim(*string*) removes all the spaces from the left side of *string*. For example, LTrim(" Hello, John ") would return "Hello, John ".

Similar to LTrim is the function RTrim(*string*), which removes all the spaces from the right side of *string*. RTrim(" Hello, John ") returns " Hello, John".

Trim(*string*) removes spaces from both the left and the right sides.

You may remember this example from the discussion of the Select Case statement yesterday:

```
<%
Select Case strOperation
Case "Add"
    Response.write (sngValue1 + sngValue2)
Case "Subtract"
    Response.write (sngValue1 - sngValue2)
Case "Multiply"
    Response.write (sngValue1 * sngValue2)
Case "Divide"
    Response.write (sngValue1 / sngValue2)
End Select
%>
```

We mentioned the limitations of this also on yesterday. If the user entered "multiply" or "MULTIPLY" or "Multiply ", the code would fail. Using the string functions we have discussed, you can improve this. Listing 5.1 makes this improvement.

LISTING 5.1   Removing Case-Sensitivity with UCase

```
 1:    <%
 2:        Dim sngValue1, sngValue2, strOperation
 3:        sngValue1 = 44.3
 4:        sngValue2 = 4
 5:        strOperation = "MulTipLY"
 6:    Select Case UCase(Trim(strOperation))
 7:    Case "ADD"
 8:        Response.write (sngValue1 + sngValue2)
 9:    Case "SUBTRACT"
10:        Response.write (sngValue1 - sngValue2)
11:    Case "MULTIPLY"
12:        Response.write (sngValue1 * sngValue2)
13:    Case "DIVIDE"
14:        Response.write (sngValue1 / sngValue2)
15:    End Select
16:    %>
```

ANALYSIS   One line 6, Trim and Ucase are used on the string containing the operation. The UCase function removes the case-sensitivity of our code. No matter how the user enters the command, it will be converted to all capital letters. Trim removes any stray spaces that may come before or after the command. Now when the Select Case makes its comparisons on lines 7, 9, 11, and 13, it will be using a string that is in all uppercase with no extra spaces on the sides. In this case, `"MulTipLY"` is converted to `"MULTIPLY"` before any comparisons are made. Therefore, it will match `"MULTIPLY"` on line 11, and the two numbers will be multiplied.

`Space(number)` returns a string consisting of *number* spaces. So, `Space(4)` would return `" "`. This is sometimes useful in formatting. `"John Smith" & Space(25) & "555-4343"` would put 25 spaces between the name and the phone number. Of course, HTML does not display spaces, so this can only be used in special circumstances. It could be used in writing to a text file, to space things out. Writing to files on the server is discussed more in Day 13. You could also use this function for output that will go between <PRE> and </PRE> tags, since spaces are displayed there.

`String(number, character)` returns a string consisting of *character* repeated *number* times. `String(3, "$")` would return `"$$$"`. `String(number, " ")` would have the same result as `Space(number)`.

`Len(string)` returns the number of characters in *string*. `Len("Sue Jones")` is 9.

Len can also be used to determine the number of bytes required by a variable:

```
iVariable = 99
Response.Write(Len(iVariable))
```

This will print out the number 2.

If you want to find the number of bytes required to store a string, you can use `LenB(string)`.

`StrReverse(string)` returns *string* with the characters in reverse order. So, `StrReverse("Active Server Pages")` would return `"segaP revreS evitcA"`.

`StrComp(string1, string2, comparetype)` is used to perform string comparisons. If *comparetype* is zero or omitted, the two strings are compared the same way they were with < on Day 3. That is, uppercase letters come before lowercase letters. This is a binary comparison. If *comparetype* is one, the two strings are compared as if upper- and lowercase letters are the same. This is a textual comparison. `StrComp` returns -1 if *string1* is less than *string2*, 0 if they are the same, and 1 if *string1* is greater than *string2*. So `StrComp("John", "JOHN")` will return 1. `StrComp("John", "JOHN", 0)` will also return 1. `StrComp("John", "JOHN", 1)` will return 0, indicating that they are the same, textually.

Note

The `ComparisonType` values can also be referred to using built-in VBScript constants `vbBinaryCompare` (0) and `vbTextCompare` (1).

`Right(`*`string, number`*`)` returns the *number* rightmost characters of *string*. So `Right("soda pop", 3)` would return `"pop"`. `Right("John Doe", 6)` would return `"hn Doe"`.

`RightB(`*`string, number`*`)` works like `Right`, but *number* is taken to be a number of bytes rather than characters.

`Left(`*`string, number`*`)`, as you may guess, returns the *number* leftmost characters of *string*. `Left("soda pop", 4)` would return `"soda"`.

`LeftB(`*`string, number`*`)` works like `Left`, but *number* is taken to be a number of bytes rather than characters.

`Mid(`*`string, start, length`*`)` returns *length* characters from *string*, starting at position *start*.

`Mid("Happy New Year", 7, 3)` returns `"New"`.

`Mid("Wizard of Oz", 8, 9)` returns `"of Oz"`. When the length is greater than the number of characters left in the string, the rest of the string is returned. Also, if the length is not specified, the rest of the string starting at the specified starting position is returned.

`Mid("Wizard of Oz", 8)` returns `"of Oz"`.

`MidB(`*`string, start, length`*`)` works like `Mid`, but *start* and *length* are both taken to be byte numbers rather than character numbers. `MidB("Happy New Year", 13, 6)` returns `"New"`.

`InStr(`*`start, string1, string2, comparetype`*`)` is used to check if and where *string2* occurs within *string1*. *start* is an optional argument that specifies where in *string1* to start looking for *string2*. *comparetype* is an optional argument that specifies which type of comparison to perform. If *comparetype* is 0, a binary comparison is performed, and uppercase letters are distinct from lowercase letters. If *comparetype* is 1, a textual comparison is performed, and uppercase and lowercase letters are the same. If *comparetype* is specified, *start* must also be specified.

`InStr` returns zero if *string1* is empty (`""`), if *string2* is not found in *string1*, or if *start* is greater than the length of *string1*. It returns Null if either string is Null. It returns *start* if *string2* is empty. If *string2* is successfully found in *string1*, it returns the starting position where it is first found.

Some examples:

- `InStr("Teach Yourself ASP", "self")` returns 11 because the "s" of `"self"` is the eleventh character of `"Teach Yourself ASP"`.
- `InStr("Teach Yourself ASP", "yourself")` returns 0 because `"yourself"` with a lower case "y" is not found in the string.

- InStr(1, "Teach Yourself ASP", "yourself", 0) specifies to start looking at position 1, but is still looking for "yourself" with a lower case "y" and cannot find it. So, it returns 0.

- InStr(1, "Teach Yourself ASP", "yourself", 1) has no more case-sensitivity because of the one in the *comparetype* position. Therefore, it matches "yourself" to "Yourself". "Yourself" begins at character 7, and so it returns 7.

- InStr(8, "Teach Yourself ASP", "yourself", 1) returns 0. It is not case-sensitive in this case, but it starts looking at position 8. This means it is really searching through the string "ourself ASP" and therefore does not find "yourself".

- InStr(8, "Teach Yourself ASP", "", 1) returns 8. It starts looking at position 8 for an empty string. When InStr is told to look for an empty string, it returns the first position it checks.

- InStr(1, "", "yourself", 1) returns 0 because it cannot find "yourself" in an empty string.

InStrB works like InStr except that the start position and return value are byte positions, not character positions.

Similar to InStr is InStrRev. InStrRev starts looking for a match at the right side of the string rather than the left side. It also takes its arguments in a different order: InStrRev(*string1*, *string2*, *start*, *comparetype*). *start* is by default -1, which means to start at the end of the string.

InStrRev("Teach Yourself ASP", "yourself", -1, 1) returns 7. It starts from the last character since -1 is used as the start value. It works from the end to the beginning, but still numbers the character positions from left to right. Therefore, "yourself" is still found at position 7.

InStrRev("Teach Yourself ASP", "yourself", 16, 1) returns 7. It starts from the sixteenth position (in this case, the "A" in "ASP") and works forward. Again, "yourself" is found in position 7.

Listing 5.2 puts a few of the string functions we have learned together, to create two new functions.

LISTING 5.2   RemoveAll.asp: Function to Remove the Occurrences of a Sub-string from a String

```
1: <%@ Language=VBScript %>
2: <% Option Explicit %>
3: <HTML>
4:    <BODY>
5: <%
```

continues

LISTING 5.2 continued

```
 6:    Dim strMain
 7:    'this function removes the first occurrence of strRemove
 8:    'from strExpression
 9:    Function RemoveOnce(strExpression, strRemove)
10:      Dim iStartPos, iStopPos, strLeft, strRight
11:      Dim iLeftLen, iRightLen
12:      'find the starting position of strRemove
13:      iStartPos = InStr(1, strExpression, strRemove, 1)
14:      'find the ending position of strRemove
15:      iStopPos = iStartPos + Len(strRemove) - 1
16:      'find the length of the portion of strExpression
17:      'to the left of the occurrence of strRemove
18:      iLeftLen = iStartPos - 1
19:      'find the length of the portion of strExpression
20:      'to the right of the occurrence of strRemove
21:      iRightLen = Len(strExpression) - iStopPos
22:      strLeft = Left(strExpression, iLeftLen)
23:      strRight = Right(strExpression, iRightLen)
24:      'join the left part and the right part together
25:      RemoveOnce = strLeft & strRight
26:    End Function
27:    Function RemoveAll(strExpression, strRemove)
28:      Dim strExpressionCopy
29:      StrExpressionCopy = strExpression
30:      'while there are still instances of strRemove in
31:      'strExpressionCopy, remove them.
32:      Do While InStr(1, strExpressionCopy, strRemove, 1) <> 0
33:        strExpressionCopy = RemoveOnce(strExpressionCopy, strRemove)
34:      Loop
35:      RemoveAll = strExpressionCopy
36:    End Function
37:    strMain = "To be, or not to be. That is the question."
38:    Response.Write(strMain)
39:    Response.Write("<BR>")
40:    Response.Write(RemoveAll(strMain, "to"))
41: %>
42:    </BODY>
43: </HTML>
```

ANALYSIS Lines 9 through 26 of Listing 5.2 use Len, Left, Right, and InStr to create a function that removes the first occurrence of strRemove in strExpression. It does this basically by finding the part of strRemove to the left of strExpression and the part to the right, breaking them off and putting them together without the middle part.

First it determines the starting position of the first occurrence of the sub-string. This is done on line 13 using InStr. It then calculates the ending position of that occurrence on line 15. Then, it calculates the length of the part to the left of the sub-string (line 18) and retrieves that part using the function Left (line 22). It also calculates the length of the part to the right of the sub-string (line 21) and retrieves that part using Right (line 23).

Line 25 concatenates the two parts together and assigns the resulting string to RemoveOnce. This causes RemoveOnce to return that string.

Lines 27 to 36 of Listing 5.2 also create a function to remove every occurrence of a sub-string from a larger string. It makes use of the previous function by applying RemoveOnce repeatedly until the sub-string can no longer be found.

On line 29, strExpression is copied into strExpressionCopy, just to make sure nothing is changed. While an occurrence of strRemove is still in strExpressionCopy, the InStr statement on line 32 will return the starting position, not zero. On line 33, RemoveOnce is applied to strExpressionCopy, which then replaces the previous version of strExpressionCopy. This repeats until InStr can no longer find strRemove in strExpressionCopy.

Lines 37 through 40 demonstrate the RemoveAll function by removing every occurrence of "to" from "To be, or not to be. That is the question."

Now all you need to do to use this is insert this into your page and then call RemoveAll(*strExpression, strToRemove*).

Try applying this function to remove every occurrence of "cowboy" from "cowcowboyboy". It will first remove "cowboy" from the middle, leaving the string as "cowboy". Then this occurrence of "cowboy" is removed. This function could be modified to not remove occurrences that result from the removal of previous occurrences. This is left as an exercise to the interested reader.

strExpression is copied into strExpressionCopy just to make sure that nothing is changed. If an occurrence of strRemove is still in strExpressionCopy, InStr will return the starting position, not zero. strExpressionCopy is then replaced with the version of strExpressionCopy with an occurrence taken out. This repeats until InStr can no longer find strRemove in strExpressionCopy.

Now all you need to do to use the RemoveAll function is copy the two function definitions into your page and then call RemoveAll(*strExpression, strToRemove*). Figure 5.1 demonstrates the use of this function to remove all occurrences of "to" from "To be, or not to be, that is the question".

Replace(*string, find, replace, start, count, comparetype*) is used to replace occurrences of *find* with *replace* in *string*. You have probably used find and replace in your word processor and other editors before; this is just a programming version.

FIGURE 5.1

The two functions remove all occurrences of one string in another.

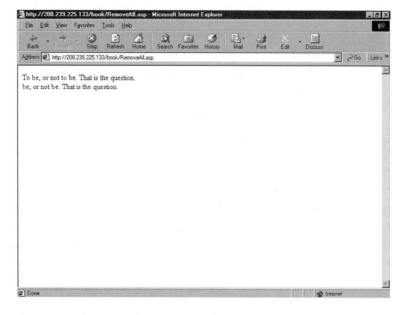

Caution

start, *count*, and *comparetype* are optional, but if you want to use one, you must use the ones that come before it, or leave the commas in place.

start indicates where the resulting string will start and where to start searching for *find*. It defaults to 1.

```
Replace("Johnny rode a bike to school", "bike", "bus", 1)
```

This statement returns "Johnny rode a bus to school", as you might expect.

```
Replace("Johnny rode a bike to school", "bike", "bus", 8)
```

This, on the other hand returns "rode a bus to school". *count* indicates how many times to perform the replacement. By default, *count* is -1, which means to replace every occurrence. *comparetype* is the same as in InStr. If it is zero, lowercase and uppercase letters are treated as being different. If it is one, they are treated as being the same. The default value is zero. Filter(*arrStrings*, *SearchFor*, *include*, *comparetype*) searches an array of strings, *arrStrings*, and returns a subset of the array. *include* is a Boolean value. If *include* is True, Filter searches through all the strings in *arrStrings* and returns an array containing the strings that contain *SearchFor*. If *include* is False, Filter returns an array of the strings that do not contain *SearchFor*. *include* is optional and defaults to True. *comparetype* works the same as in the other string functions we have discussed.

```
arrStrings = Array("July", "August", "September", "October")
arrStrings = Filter(arrStrings, "ber", True, 0)
```

This code searches through arrStrings looking for strings with "ber" in them. It then replaces arrStrings with this new, smaller array of strings. Following the execution of these statements, arrStrings will be an array of two elements. arrStrings(0) contains "September", and arrStrings(1) contains "October".

Split(expression, delimiter, count, comparetype) takes a string and splits it up into an array of strings. This can be a powerful function. If you have a string "Monday Tuesday Wednesday" that you want to break up into three strings "Monday", "Tuesday", and "Wednesday", you would use Split. expression is the string to be split up. delimiter indicates what is used to separate the sub-strings in expression. This is optional; by default the delimiter is the space. count is used to specify a maximum number of sub-strings to be created. The default for count is -1, which means no limit. comparetype is useful when the delimiter you have chosen is a letter. For example:

Split("MondayVTuesdayVWednesdayVThursday", "v", -1, 0) returns an array of one element, "MondayVTuesdayVWednesdayVThursday"

Split("MondayVTuesdayVWednesdayVThursday", "v", -1, 1) returns the array of four elements, "Monday", "Tuesday", "Wednesday", and "Thursday".

Listing 5.3 uses Split to take a sentence and print each word of it on a separate line.

LISTING 5.3 Using Split

```
 1: <%@ Language=VBScript %>
 2: <% Option Explicit %>
 3: <HTML>
 4:   <BODY>
 5: <%
 6:   Dim strSentence, arrWords, strOneWord
 7:   strSentence = "The quick brown fox jumped over the lazy dog."
 8:   'in case there are any spaces on the sides, trim
 9:   strSentence = Trim(strSentence)
10:   'do the split
11:   arrWords = Split(strSentence, " ", -1, 1)
12:   For Each strOneWord in arrWords
13:       Response.Write(strOneWord)
14:       Response.Write("<BR>")
15:   Next
16: %>
17:   </BODY>
18: </HTML>
```

5

ANALYSIS   Take a look at Listing 5.3. Line 6 declares the variables that we will use. strSentence will hold the string that will be split up using Split. arrWords will be the array that will contain the pieces after strSentence has been split. strOneWord will be used to iterate through arrWords.

Line 7 assigns the sentence "The quick brown fox jumped over the lazy dog" to strSentence. Line 9 trims any extra spaces off the ends of strSentence. There are none in this case, but if we did not know that, this might be important. Since we will be using spaces to separate words, extra spaces on the end would be interpreted as separating words of length zero.

Line 11 actually uses the Split function. The string to be split is strSentence and the delimiter is the space. The value for count in this case is -1, so Split will separate the string everywhere it finds a space. The comparetype is set to one, although in this case it does not really matter. A space is a space, regardless of case sensitivity.

Line 12 iterates through each element of the array arrWords. strOneWord is used as our loop variable in this case. On line 13, strOneWord is written to the screen. Then, line 14 adds a <BR> to force the words to be on separate lines. Line 15 ends the loop.

Figure 5.2 shows the output of Listing 5.3. You can see that each word in the sentence is now on a separate line.

FIGURE 5.2

Split can make parsing strings a little easier.

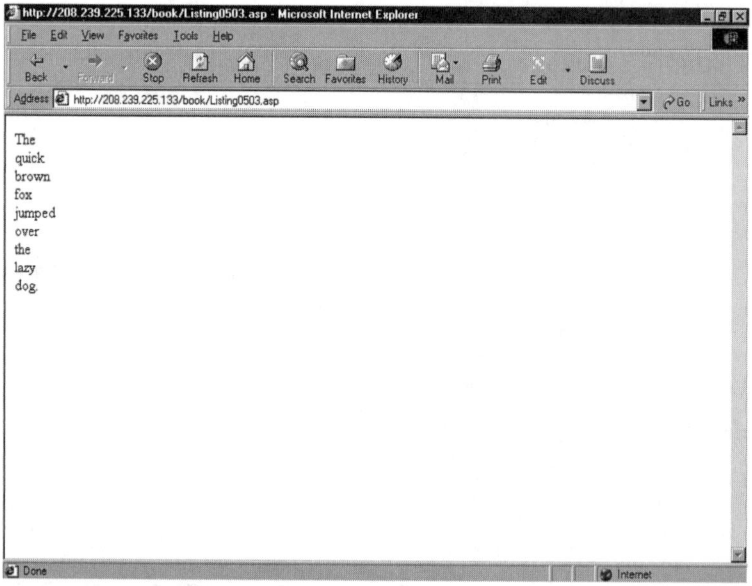

delimiter need not be only one character. If your string were "Monday, Tuesday, Wednesday, Thursday", you would use a delimiter of ", ". If *delimiter* is zero length

(""), an array of one element consisting of the whole string is returned. If *expression* is zero length, Split returns an array of no elements.

Join(*stringarray*, *delimiter*) does just the opposite of Split. It takes an array of strings and joins them into one string, using *delimiter* to separate them. *delimiter* is optional; the space is again the default.

```
arrDays = Array("Monday", "Tuesday", "Wednesday")
strDays = Join(arrDays, ";")
Response.Write(strDays)
```

This code will print to the screen "Monday;Tuesday;Wednesday".

Other Functions

When you use functions such as Split and Filter, you often end up with arrays of unknown size. There are two ways to iterate through such arrays. One is to use the For Each...Next statement. The other is to use the For...Next loop in conjunction with two functions: LBound and UBound. LBound(*array*) returns the smallest valid index for *array*. This will normally be zero. UBound(*array*) returns the largest valid index for *array*. This is the index of the last element in the array.

So for an array, arrWhatever, you can access the first and last elements like this: arrWhatever(LBound(arrWhatever)) and arrWhatever(UBound(arrWhatever)). If you wanted to iterate through an array of unknown size, you could do something like this:

```
For iIndex = LBound(MyArray) to UBound(MyArray)
   code to work with MyArray(iIndex)
Next
```

All the characters on the keyboard, plus many other, special characters, have an ANSI character code. It is basically an integer that represents that particular character. If you ever want to know the character code for a particular character, use the Asc function. Asc(*string*) returns the code for the first character of *string*. For example, Asc("Apple") returns 65, and Asc("A") also returns 65. Asc("a"), however, is 97. To go the other way, from code to character, use the Chr function. Chr(*integer*) returns a string consisting of the character that matches *integer*. For example, Chr(65) returns "A".

Here is an example of a use of these functions. This piece of code prints the letters from "A" to "Z" on separate lines.

```
<%
   Dim iCounter
   For iCounter = Asc("A") to Asc("Z")
      Response.Write(Chr(iCounter) & "<BR>")
   Next
%>
```

5

These functions are more important in languages that do not have such good string functions as VBScript. They can still come in handy in VBScript when you get into some more complex string parsing. Also, there are some characters that do not match keys on the keyboard. With the Chr function, you can still access and print these characters. For example, Chr(169) will return a string containing the copyright character. Chr(153) returns the little TM.

We have covered a lot of functions in this Day. Here is a rundown of the most important.

- Cint(*expression*) casts expression to an integer.
- Cstr(*expression*) casts expression to a string.
- Date returns the current date. Time returns the current time.
- DateAdd(*interval, number, date*) adds *number intervals* to *date*. interval is a code from Table 5.2 that represents days, weeks, months, years, and more.
- DateSerial(*year, month, day*) creates flexible date values.
- DatePart(*code, date*) retrieves part of the date information from *date*.
- UCase(*string*) returns *string*, with all the lower case letters converted to upper case letters.
- LCase(*string*) returns *string* converted to lower case letters.
- Left(*string, number*), Right(*string, number*) and Mid(*string, start, length*) are used to retrieve part of a string.
- InStr(*start, string1, string2, comparetype*) is used to check if and where *string2* occurs within *string1*, starting from the end of *string1*.
- InStrRev(*string1, string2, start, comparetype*) is similar, but starts from the end of *string1*.
- Replace(*string, find, replace, start, count, comparetype*) is used to replace occurrences of *find* with *replace* in *string*.
- Filter(*arrStrings, SearchFor, include, comparetype*) searches an array of strings, *arrStrings*, and returns a subset of the array.
- Split(*expression, delimiter, count, comparetype*) takes a string and splits it up into an array of strings.
- Join(*stringarray, delimiter*) does just the opposite of Split. It takes an array of strings and joins them into one string, using *delimiter* to separate them.
- LBound(*array*) returns the smallest valid index for *array*. UBound(*array*) returns the largest valid index for *array*.

Now take a look at a lengthier piece of code that will tie a few concepts from this day together. Say that you want to be able to evaluate a string expression such as "3 times 5" into a numerical answer. Begin by breaking up the string, using Split. Assuming that the expression is in a string variable called strCompute, the Split statement should look like this:

```
arrExpression = Split(strCompute, " ", -1, 1)
```

It really does not matter about the type of comparison you use because you are using space as the delimiter. Following this statement, if strCompute was a valid expression, arrExpression(0) has the first number we will use, in string form. arrExpression(1) should have the first word of the command: either "plus", "times", "minus", or "divided". Now the Select Case statement should look a bit like the earlier example. This time, you want to use arrExpression(1) as the variable that determines the action you take:

```
 1: <%
 2:    Select Case UCase(Trim(arrExpression(1)))
 3:    Case "PLUS"
 4:        dblValue1 = Cdbl(arrExpression(0))
 5:        dblValue2 = Cdbl(arrExpression(2))
 6:        Response.Write (dblValue1 + dblValue2)
 7:    Case "MINUS"
 8:        dblValue1 = Cdbl(arrExpression(0))
 9:        dblValue2 = Cdbl(arrExpression(2))
10:        Response.Write (dblValue1 - dblValue2)
11:    Case "TIMES"
12:        dblValue1 = Cdbl(arrExpression(0))
13:        dblValue2 = Cdbl(arrExpression(2))
14:        Response.Write (dblValue1 * dblValue2)
15:    Case "DIVIDED"
16:        dblValue1 = Cdbl(arrExpression(0))
17:        dblValue2 = Cdbl(arrExpression(3))
18:        Response.Write (dblValue1 / dblValue2)
19:    End Select
20: %>
```

ANALYSIS This code will determine which operation to perform. Line 2 trims the extra spaces off arrExpression(1), and then converts it to upper case. This keeps little things like different capitalization or extra leading spaces from preventing a match. Line 3 compares this result to "PLUS". If it is a match, we get one value from arrExpression(0) and the other from arrExpression(2), convert both to type double using Cdbl, and store them into two variables (lines 4 and 5). Finally, we write their sum to the screen.

Line 7 compares the string to "MINUS". If there is a match, we do essentially the same thing as in the "PLUS" case. The only difference is that we write their difference to the screen instead of the sum (line 10). Line 11 compares the string to "TIMES". If there is a match, we do the same thing again, but write out the product (line 14).

5

Line 15 compares the string to "DIVIDED". Notice that we do things a little differently
in the case of division. For division, the command the user will use is `"divided by"`. But
the two words will be separated by `Split`. This is not a serious complication. Simply
take `arrExpression(3)` to be the second number, rather than `arrExpression(2)`.
`arrExpression(2)`, in this case, will contain the string "by". Notice that this code does
not actually check to make sure that the "by" part is typed correctly. We can fix this,
though, and do so in Listing 5.4. One other thing we want is to be able to give the user
an error message if they type a bad command. Listing 5.4 implements this, too.

LISTING 5.4   EvalExpr.asp: Putting Some Functions Together

```
 1: <%@ Language=VBScript %>
 2: <% Option Explicit %>
 3: <HTML>
 4:    <BODY>
 5: <%
 6:    Dim strCompute, arrExpression
 7:    Dim dblValue1, dblValue2
 8:    strCompute = "44.67 times 4"
 9:    'in case there are any spaces on the sides, trim
10:    strCompute = Trim(strCompute)
11:    'do the split
12:    arrExpression = Split(strCompute, " ", -1, 1)
13:    Response.Write(UCase(strCompute) & " = ")
14:    'determine the operation
15:    Select Case UCase(arrExpression(1))
16:    Case "PLUS"
17:       dblValue1 = Cdbl(arrExpression(0))
18:       dblValue2 = Cdbl(arrExpression(2))
19:       Response.Write (dblValue1 + dblValue2)
20:    Case "MINUS"
21:       dblValue1 = Cdbl(arrExpression(0))
22:       dblValue2 = Cdbl(arrExpression(2))
23:       Response.Write (dblValue1 - dblValue2)
24:    Case "TIMES"
25:       dblValue1 = Cdbl(arrExpression(0))
26:       dblValue2 = Cdbl(arrExpression(2))
27:       Response.Write (dblValue1 * dblValue2)
28:    Case "DIVIDED"
29:       If UCase(arrExpression(2)) = "BY" Then
30:        '"divided by" is a two word command
31:          dblValue1 = Cdbl(arrExpression(0))
32:          dblValue2 = Cdbl(arrExpression(3))
33:          Response.Write (dblValue1 / dblValue2)
34:       Else
35:          Response.Write("invalid operator")
```

```
36:          End if
37:      Case ELSE
38:          Response.Write("invalid operator")
39:      End Select
40: %>
41:      </BODY>
42: </HTML>
```

ANALYSIS Look at listing 5.4. Lines 6 and 7 declare the variables we will use. strCompute will hold the string with the expression to calculate. arrExpression is the array that will hold the words after they have been separated using Split. dblValue1 will hold the first value we compute with and dblValue2 will hold the second value we compute with.

Line 8 assigns the string "44.67 times 4" to strCompute. In a more real-world sort of situation, this would probably come as input from the user. We have not covered receiving input yet, though. That will be discussed in Day 8. For now, we simply code in the string ourselves. Line 10 trims the string of any extra spaces on the ends.

Line 12 performs the split. The space is used as a delimiter, with no limit on the number of times to split. The comparison type does not matter, but has been set to case insensitive. The results of the split are stored in arrExpression.

Line 13 writes out strCompute, just so that we can see the string we entered. Line 15 begins the select, which works pretty much the same as in the code we looked at earlier. One difference worth noting is on line 29. The If…Then…Else statement will check to make sure the word "DIVIDED" is followed by "BY". If so, the computation is performed as before. If not, an error is printed. Lines 37 and 38 add the Case ELSE. If no match is found among the other choices, these lines will print out an error message.

Even with the error checking you do, many things could cause your code to fail. Too many spaces in some places, for example, could cause problems. This code also does not check for invalid numbers. Still, it is a start. Another way it might be improved would be to create separate functions to handle PLUS, MINUS, TIMES, and DIVIDED BY. This would make the code in the Select Case a little easier to read.

Figure 5.3 shows the output of Listing 5.4. As you can see, the script is no longer case sensitive. Even though the word "times" is in lower case on line 8, it is converted to all uppercase so that our comparison will work.

FIGURE 5.3

Using the string functions can improve the flexibility of your code.

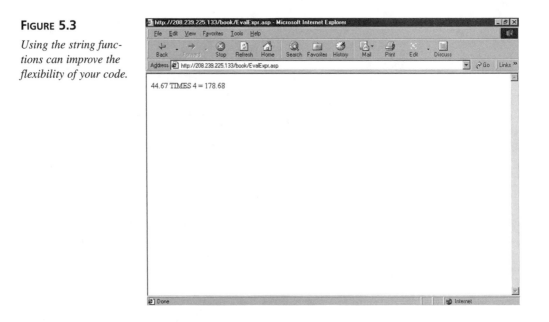

Summary

This day covered a lot of VBScript functions. VBScript has a very rich library of functions for dealing with dates and strings. The sheer number of them may seem overwhelming at first. It is more important at this point that you be aware of the capabilities of VBScript than to memorize all the syntaxes. You can always bookmark this day to come back to it as a reference.

VBScript has a set of functions to typecast data. Typecasting converts one data type to another. You can do this with functions like Cint, Cstr, Cdbl, and others.

There are also a lot of functions to handle formatting. FormatDateTime, FormatCurrency, FormatNumber, and FormatPercent all give us greater control over how dates and numeric values are displayed.

VBScript provides some basic mathematical functions. They include the exponential function, Exp, trigonometric functions Sin, Cos, Tan, and Rnd and Randomize to generate random numbers.

One of the best features of VBScript is its date functions. Trying to code your own date functions that are smart enough to take into account all the exceptions and complications that can arise would be maddening.

Date returns the current date, Time the current time and Now returns both together. DatePart(*part,date*) is used to retrieve part of date.

DateAdd(*interval, number, date*) adds *number intervals* to *date*. If *number* is negative, the result is an earlier date/time. DateAdd makes things easier by taking care of things like leap years for us. It is one of the most useful date functions VBScript provides.

DateDiff(*interval, date1, date2*) is used to compute the amount of time elapsed between *date1* and *date2*. Specifically, it returns the number of *interval*s between the two dates.

VBScript also has a remarkable set of string manipulation functions. UCase and LCase are used to convert a string to all upper- or all lowercase letters respectively.

Left(*string, n*) and Right(*string, n*) are used to retrieve the leftmost and rightmost *n* characters of *string* while Mid(*string, start, length*)returns a chunk from the middle.

InStr(*start, string1, string2, comparetype*) searches for *string2* in *string1* and returns the position where it is found. Replace(*string, find, replace, start, count, comparetype*) searches and replaces occurrences of *find* with *replace* in *string*.

Another useful string function, Split, is used to break a string up into an array of strings. Join does just the opposite, taking an array of strings and joining them into one string.

Two other useful functions are LBound and UBound. They are used to determine the bounds of an array. LBound returns the smallest valid index value, while UBound returns the largest.

All of these functions add a lot to our capabilities in programming with VBScript. If you are new to programming, you may not realize it, but these solve some of the biggest headaches programmers encounter. String and date manipulation in particular can be a real nightmare in other languages. Master the functions in this Day, though, and you have nothing to fear.

5

Q&A

Q Why are Split and Join useful?

A There will be times when data can be more easily passed or stored in string form rather than an array. In those cases, Split and Join are used to convert between the two. You will see this more on Day 9, "Collecting the Form Information."

Q Why do dates range from the years 100 to 9999?

A Well, you can specify years from 0 to 9999. It's just that the system will assume you mean 1985 when you type 85, and so on.

Workshop

The Workshop provides quiz questions to help you solidify your understanding of the material covered and exercises to provide you with experience in using what you've learned. Try to understand the quiz and exercise answers before continuing to tomorrow's lesson. Quiz answers are provided in Appendix A, and exercise answers can be found at `http://www.mcp.com/info`.

Quiz

1. What function would you use to find out how many weeks there were between September 19, 1999, and April 15, 2000?

2. What function would you use if you had an array of names and you wanted to find all the Johnsons?

3. What function would you use if you wanted to change every mention of Frank Johnson to Frank Smith in a particular string?

4. What function would you use to find out what day of the week your birthday will fall on in the year 2020?

5. What are the differences between `InStr` and `InStrRev`?

6. What function would you use to perform comparisons between two strings without distinguishing between upper- and lowercase letters?

7. Describe what the `Split` function does.

8. What is the term for converting one data type to another?

Exercises

1. Given a person's birth date, write the code to determine his or her current age.

2. Code a function to determine the base-10 logarithm of a number.

3. Write the code to turn a comma-delimited string of names into a semicolon-delimited string.

4. Given an array of names, write the code to determine whether the name Bill Miller is in the array, without using a loop or `Filter`.

DAY **6**

Working with Objects

A popular buzzword in programming is "object-oriented programming." Today, you will get a high-level overview of objects, including what they are and how they can help you in your ASP programming. Today, you will learn the following:

- What objects are
- Components of objects
- Actions that can be performed on objects
- Available ASP built-in objects
- What a collection is

What Are Objects?

Think about your car. You know that when you want to start your car, you put the key into the ignition and turn it. You probably have not thought too much about everything that happens when you turn that key. You do, however, know the result you expect. Your car executes a sequence of steps to get ready for your next instruction.

Imagine if you had to specify each step yourself. It would be difficult to keep it straight. You might occasionally forget a step and cause serious damage. Further, if you ever wanted to drive a different car, you would have to learn a whole new set of instructions.

It is much easier to simply remember to put the key in the ignition and turn it. This is an instruction you can remember, and you can apply to any car.

This is the object-oriented way of thinking about your car. You think about a couple of general things: the things that describe your car and the things you can tell it to do. An object is a reusable piece of software that contains related data and functions that represent some real-life thing.

Why would objects be useful in the pages you write? Objects help increase the level of abstraction in our pages. Say that you want to display a randomly chosen banner. You could read in the list of banners to choose from, run the random number generator, and write the code for the <IMG SRC=...> tag. You could do all these things every time you wanted to display a banner. But wouldn't it be easier to write all that into an object that represents a random banner? From then on, you would only need to write something like RandomBanner.Display to display a banner. Then, if you wanted to change or add to your banner displaying system, you would only need to change one piece of code instead of many.

And wouldn't it be even better to find out that someone else had already written an object that would do it all for you?

Using functions helps to improve the simplicity and readability of your code, and objects takes that to the next level. Pages can then be built from objects rather than low-level statements.

The Building Blocks of Objects

Like your car, programming objects are composed of the things that describe them and the things that can be done with them. The things that describe the object are called properties. The things you can do with an object are called methods.

Properties

Properties describe an object. If you were treating your car like an object, some of the properties might be

- Color
- Manufacturer
- Model
- What year it was made

These are things about your car that tend not to change. This is not all you need to completely describe your car, though. Probably even more important is describing the things that change often:

- Is it stopped or moving?
- How fast is it moving?
- Is it in forward or reverse?
- Are the headlights on?

All this information and more is needed to fully describe your car. Examining your car at particular moment in time, we might be able to describe it like this:

- Manufacturer: Ford
- Model: Explorer
- Year: 1995
- Color: Silver
- Speed: 55 mph
- Headlights: On

FIGURE 6.1

An object consists of properties and methods.

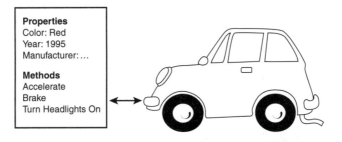

If you had an object to represent a random banner, you might have properties to represent things such as the URL a user is taken to when that banner is displayed, which would change for different banners. You might also have properties to represent the height and width of the image, which would probably be the same for all your banners.

In programming, properties work pretty much the same as variables. You access properties of an object in the following way:

```
ObjectVariableName.Property
```

So if you had an object variable called objLesson, with a property called Name, you would set a value for the property Name like this:

```
<% objLesson.Name = "Joe" %>
```

And you would write the value of Name like this:

```
<% Response.Write(objLesson.Name) %>
```

Some properties are hidden. Just like you do not know all of Ford's trade secrets for making your car, you will not know everything that goes into building most of the objects you will use. Some properties may be hidden from you, just as parts inside your car are hidden from you. That does not matter, though. As long as you follow the documentation, you do not need to see everything.

Methods

Methods are the things you can do with an object. A few of your car's methods might be:

- Accelerate
- Brake
- Change gears
- Turn on headlights
- Check speed

You may notice that the method "Change gears" is, by itself, pretty meaningless. Change to which gear? That method requires more information. It receives that information based on how you move the shift stick. Accelerate needs more information and gets it based on how you press the pedal.

Methods associated with programming objects may also need information. They receive it in much the same way as the functions and subroutines we have discussed during the last two days did. Functions and subroutines receive arguments. So, too, do methods. Methods, like functions, may have zero, one, or more arguments.

Methods often affect the values of properties. For example, when you use "accelerate," the value of the property "speed" should change.

Methods are also often used to retrieve the values of properties. You might want to know what your current speed is. To find out, you would look at the speedometer. "Displaying the speed on the speedometer" is another example of a method. Unlike "accelerate," it does not change the speed. It merely tells you what the speed is.

Figure 6.2 shows what some of the methods of a car would be. You can see that some methods, such as "Accelerate" change properties of the car. Other methods, such as "check speed" give you information about the properties of the car.

FIGURE 6.2

Methods are often used to set and retrieve property values.

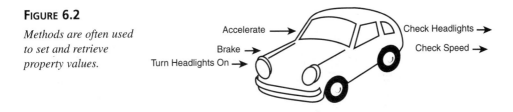

Accelerate →

Brake →

Turn Headlights On →

Check Headlights →

Check Speed →

Methods can also tell you the value of properties. They do this by returning values, the same way functions return values.

Methods are accessed like this:

```
ObjectVariableName.Method
```

Most methods behave just like the functions and subroutines discussed in the last two days. If you had a method called `Go` in `objLesson` and it returned a value, you could store the value in a variable like this:

```
MyVariable = objLesson.Go
```

or write it to the browser like this:

```
Response.Write(objLesson.Go)
```

If another method called `Compute` took a numerical argument, you would write the result to the screen like this:

```
Response.Write(objLesson.Compute(4.5))
```

or

```
Response.Write(objLesson.Compute(sngMyNumber))
```

So again, there is not much difference between an object's method and a function.

Like properties, methods may be hidden.

Instances of Objects

One important thing to understand is the difference between an *instance* of an object and the object itself. In the car analogy, the object is "car." Your specific car would be one instance of "car." Your neighbor's car would be another instance of "car." The properties of "car" would be manufacturer, model, year, and so on. All instances of "car" have some value for each of these things, but they may be different values. Your car is a Ford, and your neighbor's is a Chevrolet. Both have the property "Manufacturer," but they each have different values for that property. Figure 6.3 illustrates how two separate instances can have different values for the properties.

6

FIGURE 6.3

Two instances of the same object have the same properties but different values.

Properties	**Methods**		**Properties**	**Methods**
Color: Blue	Accelerate		Color: Red	Accelerate
Year: 1990	Brake		Year: 1995	Brake
Doors: 4	Turn headlights on		Doors: 2	Turn headlights on

Built-in ASP Objects

You may not realize it, but you have already been using an ASP object. During the last few days, you have been using `Response.Write` without really knowing what it is. `Response` is one of the six objects built-in to ASP.

Response Object

`Response` is used to send output. The `Write` method sends output to the user's Web browser. `Response` can also control how and when data is sent and write cookies to store information. The `Response` object is discussed more thoroughly tomorrow, Day 7, "Using the `Response` Object," and cookies are discussed more on Day 10, "Working with the `Request` Object."

Request Object

`Request` is used to retrieve data from the client. When the client's Web browser makes a request for a particular page, it sends some information along to the server. That data is packaged together in the `Request` object. Some of it may be useful to the requested page; some of it may not be. `Request` allows the page to retrieve what it needs—cookie information, information from a form, query string data, and more.

NEW TERM *Query string* data is the extra stuff sometimes attached at the end of a URL. It might look like `"?firstname=John&lastname=Smith"`. You have probably seen query string data before, but may not know much about it.

Application Object

`Application` is used to share information among several clients visiting the same group of pages. In ASP, the term *application* refers to all the .asp pages in a directory and its subdirectories. Only one instance of the `Application` object is created per application.

It is shared among all the clients accessing that application. The `Application` object is discussed more on Day 11, "Maintaining Persistent Information on the Web."

Session Object

A session, on the other hand, refers to a single client accessing an application. Therefore, a new instance of the `Session` object is created for each session. `Session` is important to carrying information as a client travels between pages because `Session` variables persist for the entire session. One page can store data into a `Session` variable, and that data can be accessed from other pages in the session. Day 11 covers the `Session` object in greater detail.

Server Object

The `Server` object provides a few basic properties and methods. Probably the most important of these is the `CreateObject` method. `CreateObject` is used to create an instance of a server component. Components are packages of related objects that you can use in your pages. They make common ASP tasks easier, and add a great deal of power to your pages. `CreateObject` is used in conjunction with the `Set` statement like this:

```
<% Set objInstance = Server.CreateObject("Class.Component") %>
```

You will see `CreateObject` more throughout this book.

The property `ScriptTimeout` can be used to specify the length of time the script may be allowed to execute before an error occurs.

```
<% Server.ScriptTimeout = 90 %>
```

This specifies that if the script is still executing after 90 seconds, it should give up and produce an error message.

`HTMLEncode` and `URLEncode` are two methods that apply encoding to a string. `HTMLEncode` goes through the string and replaces the character "<" with "<" and ">" with ">". This causes the Web browser to display the text literally rather than interpret it as HTML tags. For example, `<%=Server.HTMLEncode("<P align=right>")%>` returns the string `"&lt;P align=right&gt;"`, which the Web browser displays as `<P align=right>` rather than applying the tag. This is useful if you need to display HTML source code on your page.

`URLEncode` applies URL encoding. Often, you may want to pass data to another page as part of the URL. This is done through the query string. Certain characters, such as the ampersand (&) have special meanings to the query string and can cause problems if you try to use them in your data. URLEncode can help encode that data so it can be safely passed as part of the query string. The query string is discussed more in chapter 8.

The `MapPath` method converts a virtual path into a physical path. So, if your script is in C:\mypage\www\, `Server.MapPath("scripts/test.asp")` would return

6

C:\mypage\www\scripts\test.asp. Various objects, such as the `FileSystemObject`, may require physical paths rather than virtual paths. `MapPath` will be used for this purpose in Day 13.

`ObjectContext` **Object**

The `ObjectContext` object is used to link ASP and the Microsoft Transaction Server. MTS is used to make web sites more scalable and improve the performance of other components. This is an advanced tool that will not be used in this book.

`ASPError` **Object**

The `ASPError` object is new to ASP. It allows you to obtain information about script errors in your pages. It will not be covered further in this book. If you want more information about it, you should look at the MSDN web page (`http://www.msdn.microsoft.com`).

Collections

Sometimes, values need to be grouped together. For example, a query string may contain any number of names and values. In these cases, a *collection* is used to store the data. A collection is a set of name/value pairs. The query string `"?firstname=John&lastname=Smith"` contains two name/value pairs. The first pair has the name `"firstname"` and the value `"John"`. The second has the name `"lastname"` and the value `"Smith"`. When this data is stored in the `Request` object, it is stored in `QueryString`, which is a collection.

Suppose that you have an object instance named `Texas` that contains a collection `namedCities`. Further suppose that one of the pairs in `namedCities` has the name `"Capital"`. The value that corresponds to `"Capital"` could be found using the `Item` method, like this:

```
Texas.Cities.Item("Capital")
```

This retrieves the value that corresponds to the name `"Capital"`. To print out each name/value pair in Cities, you would use the `For Each...Next` statement as follows:

```
For Each varItem in Texas.Cities
    Response.Write(varItem & " = " & Texas.Cities.Item(varItem) & "<BR>")
Next
```

`Item` is the default method for collections, so `Texas.Cities("Capital")` is equivalent to `Texas.Cities.Item("Capital")`.

You can also access a value in a collection using an index number. Index numbers in collections work about like index numbers for arrays. For example, `Texas.Cities(2)` would refer to one element of the collection, and `Texas.Cities(3)` would be another. However, this is usually not useful because a pair's index number might change.

For example, `Texas.Cities("LargestCity")` might have index number 5 at one point and index number 4 later. So, depending on where it is in your code, `Texas.Cities(5)` might or might not be the same as `Texas.Cities("LargestCity")`.

Be careful about using the index number. However, if all you need to do is iterate through the pairs, the index number works fine:

```
For iCount = 1 to 5
    Response.Write(iCount & "th value = ")
    Response.Write(Texas.Cities(iCount) & "<BR>")
Next
```

You may recall that array index numbers start at zero. For collections, index numbers start at one. This code will work if there are five pairs in `Cities`. If you do not know how many pairs there are, use the `Count` property.

```
For iCount = 1 to Bob.Frank.Count
    Response.Write(iCount & "th value = ")
    Response.Write(Bob.Frank(iCount) & "<BR>")
Next
```

The `Request` object and the `QueryString` collection are discussed more on Day 9, "Collecting the Form Information," and Day 10, "Working with the `Request` Object," but let's look at a quick example in Listing 6.1.

LISTING 6.1   Using Collections

```
 1:    <%@ Language=VBScript %>
 2:    <% Option Explicit %>
 3:    <HTML>
 4:        <BODY>
 5:    <%
 6:        Dim varItem
 7:        For Each varItem in Request.QueryString
 8:            Response.Write(varItem & " = ")
 9:            Response.Write(Request.QueryString(varItem) & "<BR>")
10:        Next
11:    %>
12:        </BODY>

13:    </HTML>
```

6

This listing uses `For Each` (line 7) to iterate through all the name/value pairs in the `QueryString` collection. For each one, the name (line 8) and the value (line 9) is printed. Try viewing this script in your browser, passing in some values on the QueryString. For example, you might call it like this:

```
listing0601.asp?firstname=Jim&lastname=Smith&age=23&day=Tuesday
```

This passes in four name/value pairs. `firstname` has value `"Jim"`, `lastname` has value `"Smith"`, age has value `"23"`, and day has value `"Tuesday"`. Figure 6.4 shows the results of passing these into listing 6.1.

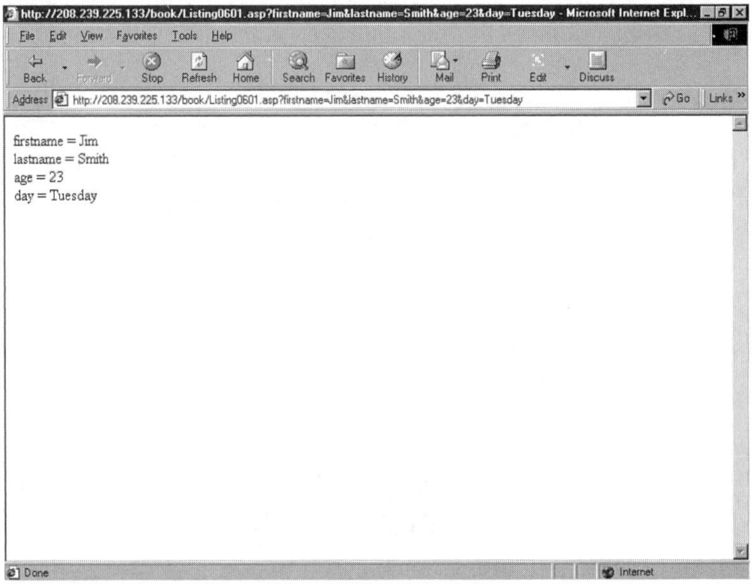

FIGURE **6.4**

Looping through a collection (QueryString).

Working with Objects

For most of today, we have been dealing in theory. Now, we will write some code to demonstrate how objects are used.

The most powerful objects you will use generally are either the built-in ASP objects or separate ASP components. Many books have been written on ASP components. It is a complicated subject and is beyond the scope of this book. However, it is possible to create simple objects within your VBScript code. We will do this using the VBScript `Class` statement. Listing 6.2 shows a simple class.

LISTING 6.2   Simple Object with No Methods

```
<%
Class Car
    public Color
    public CurrentSpeed
    public HeadlightsOn
End Class
%>
```

Listing 6.2 creates an object called `Car`, which contains three properties and no methods. Its three properties are `Color`, `CurrentSpeed`, and `HeadlightsOn`. The keyword `public` specifies that all three of them can be accessed from outside the class.

NEW TERM Notice that we have not yet created any instances of `Car`. Creating an instance of an object is called *instantiation*.

In ASP, creating an instance of an object is a two-step process. First, declare a variable normally, using `Dim`. Normal variable naming requirements apply, and it's a good idea to begin the name with `obj` to indicate what it is. Second, use the `Set` statement to make your variable an instance of the appropriate object.

```
Set variablename = objectexpression
```

objectexpression is either the name of an object, another instance of the same object type, or the keyword `New` followed by a class name. Because we are using a class name, we will use the last form. So, if you want to create an instance of `Car` called `objMyCar`, you would do this:

```
Dim objMyCar
Set objMyCar = New Car
```

This creates a single instance of `Car`. You could now set the `Color` property of `objMyCar` like this:

```
objMyCar.Color = "Blue"
```

It would not, however, make any sense to write a statement like

```
Car.Color = "Blue"
```

The class `Car` defines what cars will look like and what guidelines they follow. It does not actually create any cars.

If you wanted a second instance of `Car` called `objJoesCar`, and set its color as `"Black"`, you would do it like this:

```
Dim objJoesCar
Set objJoesCar = New Car
objJoesCar.Color = "Black"
```

`objMyCar` would still have a value of `"Blue"`. Changing the value of a property of one instance of `Car` does not affect the value of that property in any other instance of `Car`. The fact that Joe's car is black does not change the color of your car.

Let's expand `Car` a bit. So far, to change the value of a property, we have been doing it directly, as in

```
objMyCar.Color = "Silver"
```

6

However, this is not always the best way to change the value of a property. Often, objects have properties that should not be changed, should only be changed in special circumstances, or require some other kind of special attention. Rather than leaving it to the user to understand those special circumstances, properties can be changed through methods included in the object. We can add such methods to `Car`, as shown in Listing 6.3.

LISTING 6.3   Simple Object with Methods

```
<%
Class Car
    public Model
    public CurrentSpeed
    public HeadlightsOn
    public Sub Accelerate(PercentAccel)
            CurrentSpeed = CurrentSpeed * (1 + PercentAccel * 0.01)
        End Sub
End Class
%>
```

This adds a method called `Accelerate` that increases `CurrentSpeed` by the percentage specified by `PercentAccel`. Now there are two ways to change the current speed. The first is the direct approach:

```
objMyCar.CurrentSpeed = 26
```

The second way uses the new method:

```
objMyCar.Accelerate(50)
```

One nice feature of VBScript's `Class` statements is the capability to hide properties altogether. Special subroutines can be used to take their place. This allows the programmer to work with the properties the same way he or she is used to, but keeps the inner workings of the object secret and protected.

Listing 6.4 contains a more complex VBScript class. It contains hidden properties and some of those special subroutines. The result is an object with a lot of power. Yet, you can use it without knowing how it works. The idea is to protect you from having to worry about a lot of details. Do not worry too much about what the code in this listing means yet. Just type it in, or copy it from the web site. Either way, save the file as `CarDefinition.asp`. Then type in Listing 6.5 and call it `UsingCar.asp`.

LISTING 6.4   Car Object's Definition

```
1:    <%
2:        Class Car
3:            private internal_color
```

```
4:          private internal_speed
5:          private internal_headlights
6:          private Sub Class_Initialize()
7:                  internal_speed = 0
8:                  internal_color = "WHITE"
9:                  internal_headlights = FALSE
10:             End Sub
11:     public Property Get CurrentSpeed
12:             CurrentSpeed = internal_speed
13:             End Property
14:     public Property Let CurrentSpeed(ByVal iSpeedIn)
15:             internal_speed = iSpeedIn
16:             End Property
17:     public Property Get Color
18:             Color = internal_color
19:             End Property
20:     public Property Let Color(ByVal strColorIn)
21:             internal_color = Ucase(strColorIn)
22:             End Property
23:     public Sub TurnHeadlightsOn
24:             internal_headlights = True
25:             End Sub
26:     public Sub TurnHeadlightsOff
27:             internal_headlights = False
28:             End Sub
29:     public Function CheckHeadlights
30:             if internal_headlights then
31:                 CheckHeadlights = "ON"
32:             else
33:                 CheckHeadlights = "OFF"
34:             end if
35:             End Function
36:     public Sub Accelerate(PercentAccel)
37:             Dim sngMultiplier
38:             sngMultiplier = (1 + PercentAccel * 0.01)
39:             internal_speed = internal_speed * sngMultiplier
40:             End Sub
41:  End Class
42: %>
```

6

Listing 6.4 defines the car object. As mentioned before, you do not need to worry too much about how this listing works, but here is a quick look at it. Basically, the Class statement on line 2 tells VBScript what we are defining. Lines 3 through 5 define three properties. The private keyword is used with each, so they are only accessible within the object. If you want to modify them, you have to go through special methods.

Lines 6 through 10 define a method. It is also private. When you create a new instance of the car object, this method will run. It initializes the values of the three private properties. This will be discussed more in the section "Events".

Lines 11 through 13 and 14 through 16 define two related methods. These two methods, together, allow us to pretend we have a property called CurrentSpeed. Lines 11 through 13 set how we can read the value of CurrentSpeed using the Property Get statement. Lines 14 through 16 set how we can assign the value of the property. With these two methods together, we can treat CurrentSpeed as if it were a normal property of the object. Lines 17 through 22 define a similar "property" called Color. You can use Property Get and Property Let to control how values are given to your data. If you only want to allow certain values, you can control this. Line 21 converts the user's data into upper case before saving it, for example.

Lines 23 through 25 and 26 through 28 create two more traditional methods, for turning the headlights on or off. Lines 29 through 35 create a method that checks the headlights and returns "ON" or "OFF".

Lines 36 through 40 create one more method, which increases the speed by a specified percentage.

This is probably all a bit confusing for you. That is okay; writing objects and components is a pretty advanced topic. For now, what you should know is that we have a Car object. For all our purposes, it has two properties, CurrentSpeed and Color. It has two methods for controlling the headlights, TurnHeadlightsOn and TurnHeadlightsOff, and one for finding out the current status of the headlights, called CheckHeadlights. Finally, there is an Accelerate method.

If you want to find out more about VBScript's class statement, you can read about it on the Web:

```
http://www.4guysfromrolla.com/webtech/092399-1.shtml
```

LISTING 6.5   More Complex Object with Methods

```
1:    <%@ Language=VBScript %>
2:    <% Option Explicit %>
3:    <HTML>
4:        <BODY>
5:    <!--#include file="CarDefinition.asp"-->
6:    <%
7:        Dim objMyCar
8:        Set objMyCar = New Car
9:        Response.Write("The car is " & objMyCar.Color)
10:       Response.Write("<BR>")
11:       Response.Write("The headlights are ")
12:       Response.Write(objMyCar.CheckHeadlights)
13:       Response.Write("<BR>")
14:       objMyCar.CurrentSpeed = 44
15:       Response.Write("My car is currently travelling at ")
16:       Response.Write(objMyCar.CurrentSpeed & ".")
17:       Response.Write("<BR>")
```

```
18:        objMyCar.Accelerate(25)
19:        Response.Write("My car is currently travelling at ")
20:        Response.Write(objMyCar.CurrentSpeed & ".")
21:        Response.Write("<BR>")
22:        objMyCar.TurnHeadlightsOn
23:        Response.Write("The headlights are ")
24:        Response.Write(objMyCar.CheckHeadlights)
25:        objMyCar.Color = "blue"
26:        Response.Write("<BR>")
27:        Response.Write("The car is " & objMyCar.Color)
28:        Set objMyCar = Nothing
29:    %>
30:        </BODY>
31:    </HTML>
```

ANALYSIS Line 5 of Listing 6.5 is a server-side include. Server-side includes will be discussed more in Day 13. For now, all you need to know is that the server will insert `CarDefinition.asp` into `UsingCar.asp`. This breaks up our script to keep it from getting too long and difficult to follow.

Rather than worrying about how `CarDefinition.asp` works at the moment, let's look at what it can do. You still declare an instance of car like before, as you can see in lines 7 and 8 of Listing 6.5.

Now if you want to set `CurrentSpeed`, you may do so directly, as before. This is done in line 14. You can also affect the current speed using `Accelerate`, as in line 18. You write the current speed to the screen the same way, too, as in lines 16 and 20.

If you want to turn on the headlights, use `objMyCar.TurnHeadlightsOn`, as in line 22. To turn them off, use `objMyCar.TurnHeadlightsOff`. To find out whether they are on or off, use `objMyCar.CheckHeadlights`, as in lines 12 and 24.

Line 25 shows how to set the color property of the car. Finding out what color the car is works like you would expect, too, as in line 27.

Notice, though, that no matter how you typed `"blue"`, it is stored all in capital letters. Normally, if you typed something like

```
variablename = "blue"
```

you would expect it to be stored exactly as you typed it. That is not the case here because `objMyCar.Color` is not really a variable. The data is being stored in a property that is hidden from you. `Color` acts as sort of an interface between you and the data hidden in this object. For some reason, when this object was written, it was decided not to allow lowercase letters in that particular value. Why? It does not matter. Whatever the reason, the writer chose not to make you remember this rule. Instead, he built barriers into the object. This is not to restrict your freedom. It is to help you, so that you do not have to know anything about the interior working of this object.

6

In fact, when you set CurrentSpeed, the same thing happened. It appeared that CurrentSpeed was a simple property of Car, as in the earlier versions. In truth, though, CurrentSpeed is now another interface between you and the hidden data. Does CurrentSpeed do anything special to protect the data? In this case, no, but it does not matter. Again, the important thing is to know how to use the object, not what is going on "behind the scenes" of the object.

Figure 6.5 shows the results of viewing Listing 6.5. Compare the output with the code to make sure you understand how to set and change properties, and call methods.

FIGURE 6.5

Using the Car object.

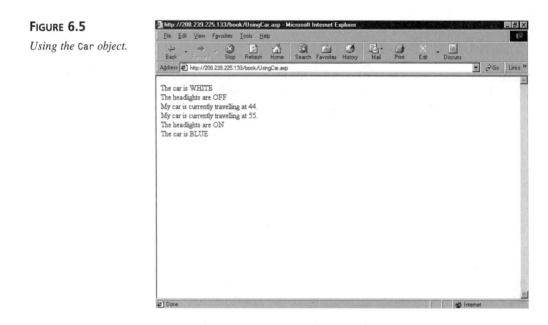

In this version of Car, we have three hidden properties: internal_color, internal_speed, and internal_headlights. They are hidden because the keyword private is used instead of public. Try changing line 14 of Listing 6.5 to

```
objMyCar.internal_speed = 44
```

This gives you an error message. Because of the keyword private, you cannot modify internal_speed directly. In fact, you cannot retrieve internal_speed directly either. Try changing line 16 to

```
Response.Write(objMyCar.internal_speed & ".")
```

The only way to access the properties of Car is to go through the methods Accelerate, TurnHeadlightsOn, TurnHeadlightsOff, and CheckHeadlights, or the special subroutines CurrentSpeed and Color. The special subroutines are created using Property Let and Property Get.

In line 23 of Listing 6.5, Set is used again. This time, it frees up the memory used by the objMyCar instance of Car. Following line 28, objMyCar is back to being an empty variable. Doing this frees up memory the system may need. A general guideline to follow is, "instantiate late, free early." You should wait as late in your code as possible before you use the first Set statement to create an instance. You should also free the memory as soon as possible. As soon as you know you are finished using an object, Set it to Nothing.

Although memory is getting cheaper, a Web server may deal with thousands of visitors. It does not hurt to minimize memory use in your pages!

Events

A third part of the object is the capability of the object to alert you that something has happened. If you have a fairly new car, it may beep at you to bring your attention to a problem: if your door is not closed, if your seat belt is not buckled, and so on. Some programming objects do something similar.

Now if your car wants to warn you about something, it could just light up a warning on your dashboard. Then it is up to the driver to check the dashboard and notice the problem. This is fine, if it is not something too urgent. If it is urgent, though, it is important to get the driver's attention immediately. This is why the car beeps. This is also why we need *events*. Events are what objects use to let the user know that something important just happened. Some possible events your car might generate include "Driver not buckled in", or "Engine overheating". If you have a car alarm, "Person touching car" might be another.

NEW TERM Unlike methods and properties, events are different from anything we have discussed before. When an event is generated, special code called an *event handler* can be executed. For example, with the event "Engine Overheating" your car would automatically start taking actions to try to cool it down.

Generating events of your own is difficult and will not be discussed in this book. Writing event handlers to deal with existing events is not too difficult, though. Two commonly handled events are Initialize and Terminate. Initialize is the event generated when an instance of the object is created. Terminate is the event generated when an instance of the object is destroyed (set to Nothing).

If you will recall Listing 6.4, lines 6 through 10 created a private method called Class_Initialize. This name designates the method as an event handler for the Initialize event. When an instance of Car is created, Class_Initialize is called.

Figure 6.6 adds events to complete our picture of what an object is.

6

Figure 6.6

Events send out alerts that something important has happened.

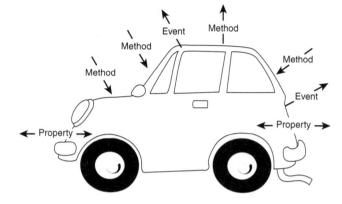

For example, lines 6 through 10 in Listing 6.4 create an event handler for the Initialize event of the Car object. It sets the car's color to white, the speed to 0, and the headlights to off before you do anything with it. These become the default values for the properties of Car.

Summary

In today's lesson we discussed objects, which consist of properties, methods, and events. A property is a value that describes the object. A method is something you can do with the object. An event is something the object generates to alert your program to take special action.

Properties are accessed like this:

```
ObjectInstanceName.PropertyName
```

Methods are accessed like this:

```
ObjectInstanceName.MethodName
```

Or, if they have arguments, like this:

```
ObjectInstanceName.MethodName(argument list)
```

Often, an object will have methods and properties that are hidden and cannot be directly accessed. This is nothing to be concerned about. You probably won't even know they are there. Just make sure that you know how to use the object in question.

It is important to remember the difference between an object and an instance of an object. If Car is an object, your car in particular is an instance of Car.

ASP has seven built-in objects, five of which we will cover in this book.

- `Response` is used to send data as output.

- `Request` is used to access data sent by the client.

- `Application` is used to share data among several clients accessing the same group of pages.

- `Session` is used to carry data along as the client moves from page to page.

- `Server` provides some basic utilities including `CreateObject`, which is used to create instances of server components.

A collection is a set of name/value pairs. A particular value may be accessed like this:

```
ObjectName.CollectionName(Name)
```

Or all the pairs may be stepped through using `For Each...Next`.

Q&A

Q Why is object-oriented programming so popular?

A Object-oriented programming results in modular code. You may notice as you get a bit more experience with ASP that many of your pages are similar. This is because they perform related tasks. Using OOP, you can save yourself a lot of repeated code.

Q What does it mean when I see something like `Request("name")` without any property or method name?

A Some objects can have default properties. These properties can be accessed without using their names, just the object name. In the case of Request, it will start searching through its collections, looking for the matching variable. It goes in this order: `QueryString`, `Form`, `Cookies`, `ClientCertificate`, `ServerVariables`.

Workshop

The Workshop provides quiz questions to help you solidify your understanding of the material covered and exercises to provide you with experience in using what you've learned. Try to understand the quiz and exercise answers before continuing to tomorrow's lesson. Quiz answers are provided in Appendix A, and exercise answers can be found at `http://www.mcp.com/info`.

6

Quiz

1. What is a collection?
2. What three things make up an object?
3. What does `Set objectVariable = Nothing` do?
4. What built-in object would you use to read a client's cookies?
5. What built-in object is used to share data among clients?
6. What method of `Server` converts virtual paths to physical paths?

Exercises

1. Suppose that you want an object to represent a desk lamp. What properties and methods would you need? Assume that the lamp has three settings: off, dim, and full power. Do not worry about coding the object, just design it.

2. Suppose that you want an object to represent a microwave. What properties, methods, and events would you need? It can have variable power and time settings and should beep when the food is done. Do not worry about coding the object, just design it.

DAY 7

Using the Response Object

One of the built-in ASP objects discussed on Day 6, "Working with Objects," was the Response object. You have seen the Response object before. You have been using its Write method since the first day of this book. Now we will discuss the other methods and properties that can make the Response object invaluable to your pages. Today, you will learn the following:

- What the Response object is
- How the Response object can write HTML to the Web browser
- How the Response object can send visitors to another page
- How the Response object can control the buffering of your pages
- How the Response object can control the caching of your pages

What Is the Response Object?

The Response object is one of the six built-in ASP objects. Response is used to send output to the client. This output might be text displayed in a browser window, cookie data (see Day 10, Working with the Request Object"), or it might have to do with how your pages are sent to the client and stored.

Dissecting the Response Object

`Response` allows you to send information to the browser and control how information is sent to the browser. It has several methods and properties. This section covers about half of them. The others are more advanced and much less commonly used.

Sending HTML to the Browser

The most common use of the `Response` object is to send data to the client's Web browser to be displayed as part of a Web page. It does this in two different ways. The first is to use the `Write` method, as we have throughout most of this book. The other is to use the shortcut `<%=…%>`.

Response.Write

We have been using `Response.Write` since the first day of this book. Without it, ASP would be pretty useless. You should be familiar with using `Response.Write` by now. Although so far we have always used parentheses with `Response.Write`, they are actually optional: `Response.Write(expression)` is the same as `Response.Write expression`.

One important issue in using `Response.Write` is that the string being written cannot contain "%>". If you need to write a string that contains "%>", use "%\>". Since we use %> to indicate the end of a block of ASP code, putting it in your strings will confuse the system.

`Response.Write("<HR WIDTH=50%>")` will result in an error because the server will interpret the "%>" as the closer to a block of ASP code.

`Response.Write("<HR WIDTH=50%\>")` will write `"<HR WIDTH=50%>"` to the HTTP.

Because the double quote (") is used to indicate the beginning and end of a string, writing strings that contain double quotes can cause problems. There are several ways around this, though. One way is to use the single quote in your string, if possible.

For example, in HTML, `<IMG SRC="banner.gif">` is equivalent to `<IMG SRC='banner.gif'>`.

So, instead of using

`Response.Write("<IMG SRC="banner.gif">")`

which will cause problems, you could use

`Response.Write("<IMG SRC='banner.gif'>")`

Sometimes, though, you need to use double quotes. In this case, putting two double quotes together will have the effect of including a double quote within your string. For example, if you write

```
Response.Write("<IMG SRC=""banner.gif"">")
```

the browser will receive <IMG SRC="banner.gif">.

As mentioned on Day 6, Server.HTMLEncode can be used to send text encoded so that the browser will not interpret it as HTML. For example,

```
Response.Write(Server.HTMLEncode("<P align=right>"))
```

will cause <P align=right> to be printed to the screen without being interpreted as HTML.

Listing 7.1 demonstrates the different ways of sending text containing quotation marks. It also demonstrates the use of Server.HTMLEncode to send text so that the browser does not interpret it.

LISTING 7.1 Special Characters with Response.Write

```
1:  <%@ Language=VBScript %>
2:  <% Option Explicit %>
3:  <HTML>
4:   <BODY>
5:   <A HREF="index.html">click here</a>
6:   <BR>
7:  <%
8:    Response.Write("<A HREF=""index.html"">click here</a>")
9:    Response.Write("<BR>")
10:   Response.Write("<A HREF='index.html'>click here</a>")
11:   Response.Write("<BR>")
12:   Response.Write(Server.HTMLEncode("<BR>"))
13: %>
14:  </BODY>
15: </HTML>
```

In Listing 7.1, line 5 writes an HTML link statement normally. Line 8 writes that link statement using Response.Write and double double quotes. Line 10 writes basically the same statement yet again, using single quotes rather than double. Finally, line 12 demonstrates Server.HTMLEncode.

Figure 7.1 shows Listing 7.1 as it appears in the browser window. Notice the <BR> that is displayed, rather than interpreted as HTML. Figure 7.2 shows Listing 7.1 as it appears when you click on "View Source". You can see how the three links look to the browser. You can also see how the HTML encoded "<BR>" arrives at the browser.

7

FIGURE 7.1

*Viewing the output of
Listing 7.1 in a
browser window.*

FIGURE 7.2

*Viewing the source code
received by the browser
from Listing 7.1.*

Using <%=

As you have >seen elsewhere in this book, a shortcut can be used in place of
Response.Write.

<%=*expression* %> is equivalent to <% Response.Write(*expression*) %>.

So the question is, when should you use which method? Note that the shortcut can only be used to send a single expression.

First, consider a script that looks like this:

```
1:   <%@ Language=VBScript %>
2:   <% Option Explicit %>
3:   <HTML>
4:    <BODY>
5:    <%
6:      Dim iCounter
7:      For iCounter = 0 to 6
8:          Response.Write(DateAdd("d", iCounter, Date))
9:          Response.Write("<BR>")
10:     Next
11:   %>
12:    </BODY>
13: </HTML>
```

Given a long block of ASP code, it makes sense to go ahead and use `Response.Write`, as is done here on lines 8 and 9.

Here is the same >script with <%= used instead of `Response.Write`.

```
1:   <%@ Language=VBScript %>
2:   <% Option Explicit %>
3:   <HTML>
4:    <BODY>
5:    <%
6:      Dim iCounter
7:      For iCounter = 0 to 6
8:    %>
9:    <%=DateAdd("d", iCounter, Date) %>
10:    <BR>
11:    <% Next %>
12:    </BODY>
13: </HTML>
```

To use the shortcut in the middle of a long block of ASP code would require that you first add a closing %> (line 8), and then reopen with a <%=; close again with a %> (line 9) and finally reopen with a <% (line 11). That is a lot of opening and closing of ASP code sections. This hurts the readability of your code, and worse, may hurt performance, too. So, it makes more sense to go ahead with the `Response.Write`.

Sometimes, though, your scripts may look more like this:

```
1:   <%@ Language=VBScript %>
2:    <HTML>
3:     <BODY>
4:       Hello. My name is Joe. This is my page.
5:       <P>
```

7

```
6:      Today is <%=Date %>
7:    </BODY>
8: </HTML>
```

If you had a long block of HTML where you needed a single line of output from the ASP, it would probably be better to use the shortcut. The shortcut is used in the preceding code example, on line 6, and it looks readable.

Here is what it would look like to use Response.Write in this case:

```
1: <%@ Language=VBScript %>
2:    <HTML>
3:     <BODY>
4:        Hello. My name is Joe. This is my page.
5:        <P>
6:        Today is
7:      <%
8:          Response.Write(Date)
9:      %>
10:    </BODY>
11: </HTML>
```

Response.Write is used on line 8. It is a little less readable and several more keystrokes than the shortcut.

Buffering ASP Pages

In addition to sending output to the client, Response can control how and when output is sent to the client. Output can be sent two different ways: buffered or unbuffered. Unbuffered output is sent immediately. Buffered output is not sent until the script is finished, or until a special command is given to send it. For example, let's say that you have a script with one Response.Write at the top and another one later. Without buffering, the first one is sent to the client immediately before the later Response.Write is executed. With buffering, though, all the output is collected in a buffer on the server and sent at once.

Response.Buffer

In IIS version 5.0, buffering is turned on by default. In the previous versions, buffering was turned off by default. In either case, you can specify whether you want buffering using the Response property Buffer. Response.Buffer = True turns on buffering, Response.Buffer = False turns it off. You must be careful, though. If you want to set buffering, you must do it before you send any output. Put it up at the top, immediately after the Option Explicit.

Buffering may seem unimportant. In most of your pages, the buffering setting will not matter. In some circumstances it is helpful to be able to specify it, though. If you have a page that will take a long time to finish processing, you might want to turn off buffering so that users can start reading part of your output while the rest is processing. Alternatively, you might not want your users to see anything until the whole thing is done. You might even want to let them see a part of the output and wait until the page is done before sending the rest.

Listing 7.2 shows you the buffer at work. It shows how output can be generated at two different times, yet arrive at the client together.

LISTING 7.2   Using the Buffer

```
1.  <%@ Language=VBScript %>
2.  <% Option Explicit %>
3.  <% Response.Buffer = True %>
4.  <HTML>
5.    <BODY>
6.  <%
7.      Dim lngCounter, lngTimeWaster
8.      Response.Write("It is now: " & Now)
9.      Response.Write("<BR>")
10.     For lngCounter = 1 to 5000000
11.         lngTimeWaster = lngTimeWaster + 1
12.     Next
13.     Response.Write("It is now: " & Now)
14. %>
15.   </BODY>
16. </HTML>
```

ANALYSIS   Listing 7.2 demonstrates a little more how the buffer works. On line 8, the current time is written to the buffer. Lines 10-12 are a For…Next loop whose only purpose is to eat up some time. Then, the new current time is written to the buffer on line 13. The script ends after line 16, and the output is sent to the client. View the output of this in your Web browser. It should take some time to load. Look at the two times. They should be different. Even though both are sent to the client at the same time, they are evaluated and written to the buffer at different times. If the two times are the same, try changing the 5000000 to something larger.

Figure 7.3 shows the output of Listing 7.2. Though both lines of output arrive at the browser at the same time, they clearly were generated at very different times.

Also try removing line 3. Can you see the difference in how it loads into your browser?

Response.Clear

Suppose that you have buffering turned on. As your script is executing, output is being sent to the buffer. Calling Response.Clear causes that buffer to be wiped out. Why would this be desirable? Maybe you have a page that you do not want to be viewed

under a special set of circumstances. If the page will not know that those circumstances have been met until late in the script, `Response.Clear` might be the best way to go.

FIGURE 7.3

The output of Listing 7.2.

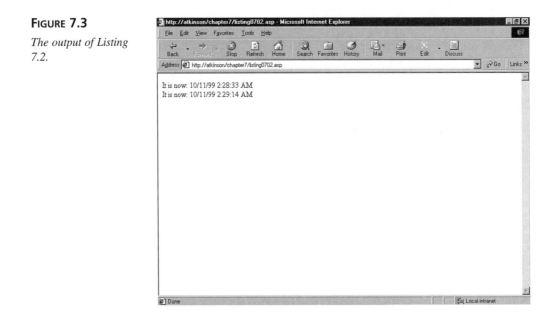

Listing 7.3 demonstrates the use of `Response.Buffer` and `Response.Clear`.

LISTING 7.3   `Response.Buffer` and `Response.Clear`

```
1.  <%@ Language=VBScript %>
2.  <% Option Explicit %>
3.  <% Response.Buffer = True %>
4.  <HTML>
5.    <BODY>
6.  <%
7.      Response.Write("Before Response.Clear")
8.      Response.Clear
9.      Response.Write("After Response.Clear")
10. %>
11.   </BODY>
12. </HTML>
```

ANALYSIS   Line 3 turns on buffering. Depending on what version of IIS you are using, as well as your system settings, this may be your default. Nevertheless, on pages where buffering matters, it is good to go ahead and specify it, just in case your system settings change. Lines 4 and 5 write a couple of standard HTML tags to the buffer. Line 7 writes a line of output to the buffer. This output is not delivered to the client yet, though.

It merely resides in the system buffer for the moment. Line 8 clears out the buffer. That line of output that was sitting there is destroyed. The two tags written to the buffer earlier are lost, too. Line 9 writes a new line of output to the buffer. The script finishes with line 12, and the output in the buffer is sent. This includes the text written on line 9, plus the tags on lines 11 and 12.

Take a look at Figure 7.4. This is the source code as the browser receives it. You can see from this that neither the tags on lines 4 and 5 nor the output of line 7 of Listing 7.3 ever make it to the browser.

FIGURE 7.4

Viewing the source code received by the browser from Listing 7.3.

Response.Flush

Like Response.Clear, Response.Flush flushes all the data from the system buffer. However, Response.Flush first sends it to the client. This is useful when you want to send a chunk of the output on to the client. Like Response.Clear, Response.Flush produces an error message when buffering is turned off.

Listing 7.4 writes three messages to the output buffer, and uses Flush and Clear to determine which are sent.

7

LISTING 7.4 Adding Response.Flush

```
1:  <%@ Language=VBScript %>
2:  <% Option Explicit %>
```

continues

LISTING 7.4   continued

```
3:  <% Response.Buffer = True %>
4:  <HTML>
5:    <BODY>
6:  <%
7:      Response.Write("Before Clear and Flush<BR>")
8:      Response.Flush
9:      Response.Write("After Flush, before Clear<BR>")
10:     Response.Clear
11:     Response.Write("After Clear and Flush<BR>")
12: %>
13:   </BODY>
14: </HTML>
```

ANALYSIS   Notice that line 3 is still there to specify that buffering be turned on. Lines 4 and 5 write a couple of standard HTML tags to the buffer. Line 7 writes a line of output to the buffer. Line 8 flushes, sending that output to the client and clearing the buffer. Line 9 writes a new line of output to the buffer. Line 10 clears the buffer, destroying one line of output. It does not, however, affect the line that was already sent. Line 12 writes another line to the buffer. The script finishes with line 14, and the remaining output in the buffer is sent to the client.

Remember Listing 7.2? It took it awhile to load. When users encounter a page like that, they tend to get impatient. They may think something has gone wrong. They might abort execution or leave the site. To prevent this on pages that you know will take awhile to execute, you can use Flush to go ahead and send the first part of the output. This gives the user something to look at and keeps them from giving up on the rest of the page. Listing 7.5 adds Response.Flush to Listing 7.2.

LISTING 7.5   Using Response.Flush on Pages That Will Take a While to Finish Executing

```
1:  <%@ Language=VBScript %>
2:  <% Option Explicit %>
3:  <% Response.Buffer = True %>
4:  <HTML>
5:    <BODY>
6:  <%
7:      Dim lngCounter, lngTimeWaster
8:      Response.Write("It is now: " & Now)
9:      Response.Write("<BR>")
10:     Response.Flush
11:     For lngCounter = 1 to 5000000
12:         lngTimeWaster = lngTimeWaster + 1
13:     Next
14:     Response.Write("It is now: " & Now)
15: %>
16:   </BODY>
17: </HTML>
```

ANALYSIS Now the first part of the output will go ahead and be sent while the loop is executing. The user will see the output from lines 8 and 9, and will be more likely to wait for the loop to stop executing.

Response.End

Response.End ends execution of the script. If buffering is turned on and there is any buffered data, it is sent. Any statements after the Response.End are not carried out. This is a more abrupt end than simply allowing the script to end on its own, and so should be avoided if possible. It can be useful, though, when problems (such as bad data) are detected to prevent them from making things worse.

Listing 7.6 demonstrates the use of Response.End to halt execution of a script early. Because of the Response.End, some of the code in this listing will never be executed.

LISTING 7.6 Using Response.End

```
1.  <%@ Language=VBScript %>
2.  <% Option Explicit %>
3.  <% Response.Buffer = True %>
4.  <HTML>
5.    <BODY>
6.  <%
7.      Response.Write("Before End and Flush<BR>")
8.      Response.Flush
9.      Response.Write("After Flush, before End<BR>")
10.     Response.End
11.     Response.Write("After End")
12. %>
13.   </BODY>
14. </HTML>
```

ANALYSIS In Listing 7.6, the Response.Flush on line 8 will cause the tags on lines 4 and 5, and the output on line 7 to be sent to the browser. Then, the output on line 9 is sent to the buffer. The Response.End on line 10 will send the buffer data and end execution of the script. This means that output of line 11 and the HTML tags on lines 13 and 14 will never even be sent to the buffer. This is bad form, of course, since the HTML received by the browser has opening <HTML> and <BODY> tags but no corresponding closing tags. Most browsers can handle it, though. Look at the output in Figure 7.5 and verify this. You can see that the "After End" line from Listing 7.6 does not print.

7

FIGURE 7.5

Viewing the output of Listing 7.6.

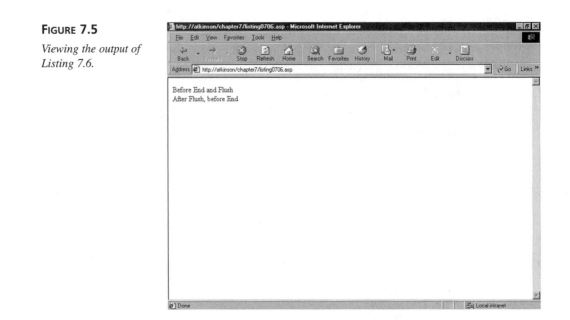

If you want to end execution of the script and not send the contents of the buffer, simply call a `Response.Clear` before the `Response.End`.

Let's get to an example that is a bit more "real world." Listing 7.7 shows how you might use buffering on a Web page to keep unregistered users from accessing it.

LISTING 7.7   Using `Response.End` for a "Members Only" Page

```
1:  <%@ Language=VBScript %>
2:  <% Option Explicit %>
3:  <% Response.Buffer = True %>
4:  <HTML>
5:    <BODY>
6:       Welcome to the Members' page!
7:  <%
8:     Dim bolPasswordMatch, strRealPasswd, strEnteredPasswd
9:     strRealPasswd = "bill"
10:    strEnteredPasswd = "bill"
11:    bolPasswordMatch = (strEnteredPasswd = strRealPasswd)
12:    if Not bolPasswordMatch then
13:       Response.Clear
14:       Response.Write "Invalid password."
15:       Response.Write "You must be a registered user."
16:       Response.End
17:    end if
18: %>
19:       <P>More members-only content
20:    </BODY>
21: </HTML>
```

ANALYSIS   Listing 7.7 takes a password entered by the user and compares it to a password that is coded into the page. If the two passwords match, the user is valid and is allowed to see the page. If they do not match, several things happen. First, the buffer is cleared to prevent the user from seeing the welcome message (line 13). Then an error is written to the buffer (lines 14 and 15). Then, to prevent the unregistered user from seeing the rest of the page (such as line 19), Response.End is used (line 16). The Response.End will terminate execution of the script before it gets to any of the members-only content.

Figure 7.6 shows the output of Listing 7.7 when the passwords match. Try changing the value of strEnteredPasswd (line 9) so that you can see what happens when the passwords do not match.

FIGURE 7.6

Viewing the output of Listing 7.7.

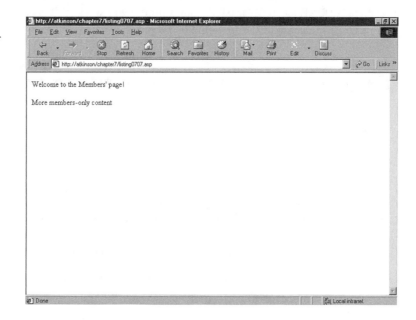

Of course, in a real version of this, the password would be entered into a form. Forms and reading from them are covered on Day 8, "Communicating with the User," and Day 9, "Collecting the Form Information."

Sending the User to Another Page

You have HTML probably encountered Web pages that were on the screen for just a few seconds and then suddenly took you to another page. This can be done in many ways. One way uses the META tag:

```
<META HTTP-EQUIV=REFRESH CONTENT="2;URL=http://www.macmillan.com">
```

This causes the browser to be sent to www.macmillan.com after 2 seconds.

7

This can also be done with client-side scripting like JavaScript, using the window object like this:

```
<script language="JavaScript">
<!--
      window.location='anotherpage.html';
// -->
</script>
```

The `Response` object offers yet another way.

Response.Redirect

`Response.Redirect URL` takes the user to the page `URL`. If it is within the same site, a relative URL (such as "products/index.html") will work. If it is a separate site, the full address including `http://` should be provided.

> **Note**   `Response.Redirect = URL` is equivalent to `Response.Redirect URL`.

Every time a client makes a request for a particular ASP page, an object context is created. An object context holds things such as the `Session` and `Request` objects and some server variables (the `Request` object is discussed on Day 10, "Working with the `Request` Object," and the `Session` object is discussed on Day 11, "Maintaining Persistent Information on the Web"). `Response.Redirect` works by telling the client to make a request for a new page. The client does so, and a new object context is created for the new page. It only works if nothing has been sent to the client yet. This means that you should either put the `Response.Redirect` before any output is sent or use buffering.

The error message you will get if you do not follow this rule looks like this:

```
Response object error 'ASP 0156 : 80004005'
Header Error
/common/test.asp, line 6
The HTTP headers are already written to the client browser.
Any HTTP header modifications must be made before writing
page content.
```

You also get this same error message for putting your `Response.Buffer` after output has already been written.

Listings 7.8 and 7.9 implement the password checking system from Listing 7.7 a little differently. Now instead of one file containing both versions of the page, it is broken up into two pages. Listing 7.8 checks the passwords and displays the error message if they do not match. If the passwords do match, the user is taken to Listing 7.9, which has the member's content.

LISTING 7.8   Using `Response.Redirect` (verify.asp)

```
 1: <%@ Language=VBScript %>
 2: <% Option Explicit %>
 3: <% Response.Buffer = True %>
 4: <HTML>
 5:   <BODY>
 6: <%
 7:     Dim bolPasswordMatch, strRealPasswd, strEnteredPasswd
 8:     strRealPasswd = "bill"
 9:     strEnteredPasswd = "bill"
10:     bolPasswordMatch = (strEnteredPasswd = strRealPasswd)
11:     if bolPasswordMatch then
12:        Response.Redirect "members.html"
13:     else
14:        Response.Write "Invalid password."
15:     end if
16: %>
17:   </BODY>
18: </HTML>
```

LISTING 7.9   Using `Response.Redirect` (members.html)

```
 1: <HTML>
 2:   <BODY>
 3:      Welcome to the member's page!
 4:   </BODY>
 5: </HTML>
```

Type in Listing 7.8 and save the file as verify.asp. Type in Listing 7.9 and save it as members.html.

Listing 7.8 is a page to compare the password a user typed in with the real password. Then, based on that comparison, the user is either sent to the page members.html or given an error message. Line 3 of Listing 7.8 turns on buffering. Lines 8 and 9 set the value of the two password strings. In a real page, one password would come from the form the user typed it into, and the other would probably come from a database. Databases and forms are discussed later (on Days 8-10 and 15-21), but this will suffice for demonstrational purposes. Line 10 sets a Boolean variable so that it equals True if the two passwords are equal and False otherwise. If that value is True, a Response.Redirect takes the user to the next page. Remember, you cannot do a Response.Redirect if you have already written to the page. Because you are using buffering, though, and have not yet performed a Response.Flush, no output has been sent to the client yet. If the value of bolPasswordMatch is False, an error message reading "Invalid Password" is displayed (lines 13-14). Then the script ends, and the contents of the buffer are sent to the client. Try changing the value of strEnteredPasswd (line 9) so that you can see what happens in both cases.

7

Listings 7.10 and 7.11 create a random link page, using `Response.Redirect` and the `Rnd` function. Users go to the page in Listing 7.11. When they click on the link, they will be taken to one of seven sites.

LISTING **7.10**   Using `Response.Redirect` to Create a Random Link Page

```
1:  <%@ Language=VBScript %>
2:  <% Option Explicit %>
3:  <%
4:     Response.Buffer = True
5:     Randomize
6:     Dim arrSites(6), iSites
7:     arrSites(0) = "http://www.4guysfromrolla.com"
8:     arrSites(1) = "http://www.cnn.com"
9:     arrSites(2) = "http://www.yahoo.com"
10:    arrSites(3) = "http://www.microsoft.com"
11:    arrSites(4) = "http://www.macmillan.com"
12:    arrSites(5) = "http://www.go.com"
13:    arrSites(6) = "http://www.netscape.com"
14:    iSites = Cint(6*Rnd)
15:    Response.Redirect arrSites(iSites)
16: %>
```

LISTING **7.11**   Using `Response.Redirect` to Create a Random Link Page

```
1:  <HTML>
2:    <BODY>
3:      Click <a href="randomlink.asp">here</a> to be taken
4:      to a random page
5:    </BODY>
6:  </HTML>
```

ANALYSIS   Be sure to save Listing 7.10 as randomlink.asp. Lines 7 through 13 of Listing 7.10 initialize an array with some URLs. Line 14 uses the `Rnd` function to choose a random number. We want the random number to range from 0 to 6, rather than 0 to 1, so it is multiplied by 6. Then, to be sure we have an integer, we use `Cint`. Now `iSites` is a randomly chosen integer between 0 and 6, so line 15 does a `Response.Redirect` on the `iSites` element of `arrSites`.

Notice that in this case line 4 is optional. Nowhere in `randomlink.asp` is anything written to output (except the `Response.Redirect`). Buffering does not hurt, but it is not necessary in this case.

Cookies

Have you ever returned to a Web page you had visited earlier to find that it remembered you? Cookies are small files that Web sites you visit can save on your computer. Cookies tell that Web site things such as who you are and what you did when you visited the page before. `Response` includes a collection called `Cookies` that can be used to write cookies. Reading and writing cookies is discussed more on Day 10.

Caching Your ASP Pages

You have probably noticed that when you visit a Web page, leave it for just a moment, and return, your browser does not have to re-download the page. This is because it has cached that page. Cache is special space on your computer where your Web browser stores pages that it has been to recently for quick access. HTML pages and graphics can be stored in the cache. `Response` has two properties that can be used to determine how long an ASP page may be cached.

The Caching Dilemma

Cache speeds up Web surfing, but it causes some problems, too. If a client is loading a page from cache rather than the server, there is a possibility that the version on the server has changed, and the client is missing the update.

Active Server Pages are dynamic. Often, the contents of an ASP page as viewed by the client changes even if the actual ASP code is the same. Some ASP code is time-dependent. The time it is executed affects its content. Other code is dependent on previous events. Visiting page A after page B causes it to look different than if you just visited page A.

In situations like this, caching can cause all sorts of problems. It may not seem important, whether a user is seeing the page from now or the page from 5 minutes ago. Sometimes it is not important; often, it is.

Imagine a Web site with a virtual shopping cart. You view the cart's contents at one point and then go shopping some more. You add a few more items to the cart and then view the contents again. Imagine the confusion of not seeing the items you just added. What happened? The "view contents" page was cached.

When do you need to turn off caching? For the pages you have done so far, it was not important to turn off caching. In the days to come, you will basically have to ask yourself "Does it matter if the user is seeing a current-to-the-second copy of this page?" If you are not sure that the answer is "No," then go ahead and turn off caching.

How do you turn off caching? In the next two sections, we will cover a couple of ways to do it using `Response`. These techniques are certainly useful and worthwhile to learn. Unfortunately, they do not solve the problem completely. Neither Netscape nor Internet

7

Explorer can be 100% counted on to handle caching the way you expect or intend. Many expert developers go to great, seemingly extreme lengths to combat the problem.

Response.Expires

Expires is a property of Response used to specify how long from now a page should be kept in cache.

Response.Expires = *Number* tells the browser that the cached version of the page should expire after *Number* minutes.

Response.Expires = 5 tells the browser that the cached version of the page should expire in 5 minutes.

Response.Expires = 1440 tells the browser that the cached version should expire in a day.

What if you want it to expire immediately?

Response.Expires = -1500 tells the browser that the page should not be cached. Why not use Response.Expires = 0? That might work, but it might not. The server computes the time that it should expire and sends it to the client. If the client's computer were 3 minutes behind the server, it would think it should cache the page for 3 minutes. -1500 minutes ago is the same as 25 hours ago and should be plenty to make sure that the page is not cached. You should also be careful about using really precise positive values, too. Setting Response.Expires = 1 might cause the page to be cached for 0 minutes, or up to 4 minutes or so.

Let's take a look at caching in action. Type in Listing 7.12.

LISTING 7.12   Using Response.Expires

```
1.  <%@ Language=VBScript %>
2.  <% Option Explicit %>
3.  <% Response.Expires = 3 %>
4.  <HTML>
5.    <BODY>
6.      The time is currently <%= Now %>
7.    </BODY>
8.  </HTML>
```

Listing 7.12 uses Response.Expires on line 3. It is a good idea to put it at the top, just so that people will know where to find it. The only thing this page does is to write out the time it is executed on line 6.

Save Listing 7.12 as listing0712.asp and try viewing it in your web browser. Write down the time it says to the second. Now leave the page and go to a favorite Web page of yours. Click a couple of links. Now go back to listing0712.asp. A few seconds have passed, but the page should still read the exact same time it did before. Now go surf around for about 3 minutes. Go back to listing0712.asp again. Now has it changed? It should. You set the cached version to expire after 3 minutes. Three minutes have passed, and so now when you view the page, it is retrieving a new, up-to-date copy.

Response.ExpiresAbsolute

`Response.ExpiresAbsolute = Date Time` tells the browser that the cached version of the page should expire on the date *Date* at the time *Time*. If *Date* is omitted, the current date is assumed. If *Time* is omitted, the cached page expires at midnight.

`<% Response.ExpiresAbsolute = #June 2, 2001 18:16:00# %>` specifies that the cached page should expire at 6:16 pm on June 2, 2001.

`<% Response.ExpiresAbsolute = #March 5, 2000# %>` specifies that the cached page should expire at midnight, March 5, 2000.

`<% Response.ExpiresAbsolute = #11:05:20# %>` specifies that the cached page should expire on the current day at 20 seconds past 11:05 am.

`Response.ExpiresAbsolute` can also be used to force immediate expiration.

`<% Response.ExpiresAbsolute = DateAdd("d", -1, Now) %>` sets the expiration date at one day ago. This can also be done with the expression `<% Response.ExpiresAbsolute = Now() - 1 %>`.

Summary

Today we discussed the most important properties and methods of the `Response` object. The most important use of `Response` is sending information to the client. This is done with the `Write` method or the `<%=…%>` shortcut.

`Response` can also control when information is sent to the client. `Response.Buffer` is a property that determines whether output is collected in a buffer or sent directly to the client. If it is collected in a buffer, it is sent to the client after the script has ended. It can also be sent before the script ends with `Response.Flush`. `Response.Flush` empties the buffer and sends the data to the client. `Response.Clear`, on the other hand, empties the buffer, destroying the data. `Response.End` flushes the buffer and then ends execution of the script regardless of what follows it.

`Response` can send the client to a different page using the `Redirect` method. `Redirect` can send the client either to a different page within the same site or to an entirely separate site. It only works, though, if no data has been sent to the client yet. For this reason, `Redirect` is often used in conjunction with `Response.Buffer`.

7

`Response` can be used to write cookies. Cookies are little files residing on the client's computer that tell the page a little about the client. This is discussed more on Day 10.

`Response` can also set how long an ASP page should be cached on the client's system. Caching refers to saving pages on the client's machine for quick retrieval. If pages are cached for too long, the client may not be seeing updates made to your site. Some ASP pages should not be cached at all because they depend too heavily on data that changes. No caching at all slows down Web browsing and places more demand on your server.

`Response.Expires` is used to specify how many minutes from now the cached version of the page should expire. If you do not want the page to be cached at all, you should specify a negative value such as -1500. `Response.ExpiresAbsolute` is used to specify a date and time the cached version of the page should expire.

Q&A

Q Is there a better way than `Response.Redirect` to take a user to a new page?

A Yes! `Server.Transfer` and `Server.Execute`, both discussed on Day 13, "Reading and Writing Files on the Web Server," offer a new way that will, for most purposes, work better than `Response.Redirect`. As mentioned today, `Response.Redirect` requires sending an instruction to the client and receiving a request from the client, as well as the creation of a new object context. These two methods, however, do not require that extra communication and allow sharing of object contexts between the two pages.

Q Is there any other way to force immediate expiration of the cached version of a page?

A Certainly. There are many different ways. Phil Paxton's suggestion for a "cache-buster," is to use a randomly generated URL. Adding a `"?NoCache=Rnd"`, where `Rnd` is a randomly generated number to the end (see Day 6 and Day 9 for more about the query string), causes the browsers to think it is a different page every time.

Workshop

The Workshop provides quiz questions to help you solidify your understanding of the material covered and exercises to provide you with experience in using what you've learned. Try to understand the quiz and exercise answers before continuing to tomorrow's lesson. Quiz answers are provided in Appendix A, and exercise answers can be found at `http://www.mcp.com/info`.

Quiz

1. If you have a long block of HTML code and you need to retrieve a single ASP value, which should you use: `Response.Write` or `<%=…?`

2. What is the difference between `Response.Flush` and `Response.Clear`?

3. What is the difference between `Response.Expires` and `Response.ExpiresAbsolutely`?

4. Why should a negative value for `Response.Expires` be used to force the page to expire immediately?

5. True or False: Using `Response.Flush` without buffering turned on will produce an error.

6. True or False: Using `Response.End` without buffering turned on will produce an error.

7. True or False: Using `Response.Clear` without buffering turned on will produce an error.

Exercises

1. Write a `Response.Write` statement to send `<A HREF="aboutme.html">` to the browser.

2. Write the code that sends the user to another page if it is an odd-numbered day and prints a message if it is an even-numbered day.

3. Write a statement using `Response.ExpiresAbsolute` that is equivalent to the following:

```
Response.Expires = 5
```

4. Write the code to have the cached version of the current page expire the first of the next month.

7

WEEK 1

In Review

In the Week at a Glance, we wagered that you would find Active Server Pages programming fun and would be amazed at what you can do with an ASP page. We hope we won that wager! You've come a long way since Day 1, when you learned the basics of ASP programming. You're now able to write your own useful ASP pages and are on your way to becoming an advanced ASP developer!

Bonus Project 1

Creating a Calendar

At the end of each week, you'll find a Bonus Project that applies the lessons learned throughout the given week. Each Bonus Project contains a complete, working application, and each successive Bonus Project builds on the previous Bonus Project. It is highly recommended that you take the time to try these Bonus Projects out on your computer. Learning a programming language is like learning a foreign language—practice makes perfect! To truly master the VBScript scripting language and Active Server Pages programming, you must roll up your sleeves and get your hands dirty.

This first Bonus Project demonstrates how to use ASP pages to dynamically tailor the contents of a Web page. Specifically, the current month and year's calendar will be generated.

The Bonus Project programs are intended to tie together the lessons learned in the preceding week. Today's Bonus Project program uses variables (Day 3), arrays (Day 3), control structures (Day 4), VBScript's built-in functions (Day 5), and user-defined functions (Day 4). Don't feel restricted to entering in

1

2

3

4

5

6

7

the presented code verbatim. Experiment with the Bonus Projects! Try entering different things to see what results those changes make. As you become more familiar with VBScript and ASP in the future, feel free to come back to this Bonus Project and add new functionality.

Building the Calendar

This Bonus Project displays a calendar for the current month and year. We've often found that it helps to have a solid understanding of what you want to accomplish before you begin writing code.

> **Tip**
>
> Building a solid understanding of a project's requirements is often referred to as software design. Day 21, "Practicing Intelligent Application Design," discusses the importance of and the steps involved in software design.

So, what exactly do you want this calendar to look like? It would be nice to create a calendar that looks as much like an actual calendar as possible. Figure BP1.1 shows what you want your calendar to look like.

FIGURE BP1.1

Your "Web" calendar should look like a normal, "paper" calendar.

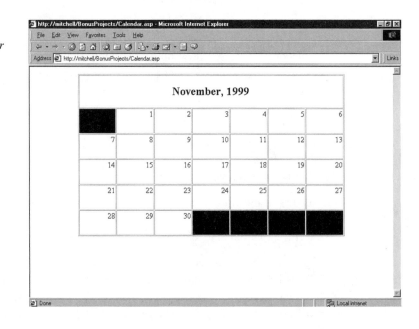

Now that you know where you are going, you need to determine how to get there! In your ASP page, what will you need to code to produce the output shown in Figure BP1.1?

1. Determine the current month and year

2. Determine the name of the current month

3. Determine the weekday of the first day of the current month

4. Determine the total number of days in the current month

5. Determine how many rows you will need in your calendar to display all the days in the month

6. Create a two-dimensional grid using the HTML TABLE tag, displaying the appropriate day number in the corresponding TABLE cell

7. Black out those TABLE cells that do not contain a date

To display your calendar, use one ASP page, Calendar.asp. Throughout this Bonus Project we are going to look at snippets within Calendar.asp and will tie all these code snippets together near the end of this Bonus Project. Each snippet of code we'll examine accomplishes one of the preceding steps.

Begin by determining the current month and year. To accomplish this, you can use the Date() function, which was discussed on Day 5, "Using VBScript's Built-in Functions." The Date() function returns the Web server's current system date. Assign the value of the Date() function to a variable, dbCurrentDate. Listing BP1.1 contains this code.

LISTING BP1.1 Using the Date() Function to Obtain the Current Date

```
1: 'We need to obtain the current date.
2: 'To do this, we will store the result of the
3: 'Date() function into a variable named dbCurrentDate
4:  Dim dbCurrentDate
5:  dbCurrentDate = Date()
```

ANALYSIS Listing BP1.1 creates a variable named dbCurrentDate (line 4) and assigns it the value of the Date() function (line 5). You will use the dbCurrentDate variable many times in the rest of Calendar.asp.

dbCurrentDate contains the current system date. As Figure BP1.1 shows, you want to display the current name and year at the top of the calendar. Usually, when you want to display a date variable, you use the FormatDateTime function, which was discussed on Day 5. However, there is no FormatDateTime format that displays just the month's name and the year. To display just the month name and year, you need to write your own function that receives, as input, the ordinal value of a month and outputs the name of the

month. For example, if you pass your function the value 8, it should return the string
August. Listing BP1.2 contains this function, GetMonthName.

LISTING BP1.2   Using a Custom Function to Obtain the Name of the Current Month

```
 1:     'We will want to be able to determine the month name
 2:     'for a given month.  So, let's create a function that
 3:     'takes the numeric value of a month and displays the name of
 4:     'the month (i.e., GetMonthName(8) would output August)
 5:     Function GetMonthName(iMonth)
 6:       Select Case iMonth
 7:         Case 1:
 8:           GetMonthName = "January"
 9:         Case 2:
10:           GetMonthName = "February"
11:         Case 3:
12:           GetMonthName = "March"
13:         Case 4:
14:           GetMonthName = "April"
15:         Case 5:
16:           GetMonthName = "May"
17:         Case 6:
18:           GetMonthName = "June"
19:         Case 7:
20:           GetMonthName = "July"
21:         Case 8:
22:           GetMonthName = "August"
23:         Case 9:
24:           GetMonthName = "September"
25:         Case 10:
26:           GetMonthName = "October"
27:         Case 11:
28:           GetMonthName = "November"
29:         Case 12:
30:           GetMonthName = "December"
31:         Case Else:
32:           GetMonthName = "**INVALID MONTH**"
33:       End Select
34:     End Function
```

ANALYSIS   GetMonthName, the function shown in Listing BP1.2, expects one parameter,
iMonth, which represents the ordinal value of the current month. Starting at line 6,
a Select Case is used to map the ordinal month value to the correct month name. Recall
that we discussed the Select Case control structure on Day 4, "Understanding VBScript
Control Structures." Line 31 contains a Case Else just in case iMonth is not between 1
and 12. In this case, GetMonthName returns **INVALID MONTH** (line 32).

Now that you have a function that can return the name of a given month, you can display the month name of a Date variable using the Month function. The Month function, which was discussed on Day 5, returns the month value of a Date variable. For example, you can obtain the current month by using the Month function to obtain the month of the Date() function:

```
Response.Write "The current month is " & Month(Date())
```

Unfortunately, the Month function returns an ordinal value, so the preceding line of code might output The current month is 2. To display the name of the current month, you could use the GetMonthName function:

```
Response.Write "The current month is " & GetMonthName(Month(Date()))
```

The output of the preceding line of code would contain the name of the current month. For example, the code might output The current month is February.

At this point, you have a variable, dbCurrentDate, that contains the current system date. Also, you have a function, GetMonthName, that you can use to display the name of the current month. Now you need to decide how you are going to build up the calendar, making sure that each day of the month corresponds to the correct day of the week on the calendar. To accomplish this, you have to determine what day of the week the first day of the current month occurs on and how many days there are in the current month.

It is helpful to think of a calendar as a two-dimensional matrix that contains 7 columns and up to 6 rows. Therefore, a calendar can contain up to 42 unique "cells" (7 * 6 = 42). Using this information, you can represent a calendar with an array of 42 elements. The first element in the array represents the first cell, or the first Sunday, on the calendar, the second element in the array represents the first Monday on the calendar, and so on. Figure BP1.2 contains a graphical representation of this array.

If you place the days of the month in the correct positions in this array, you can later loop through this array, outputting the correct format of the calendar. For example, if the first day of the current month happens on a Tuesday, the third element of the array would be assigned a value of 1 because the first Tuesday of the calendar corresponds to the first day of the month. Then, the fourth element of the array would be assigned the value 2, and so on. This would continue as many times as there are days in the current month.

To populate this array, you need to know only two pieces of information:

- The weekday on which the first day of the current month occurs
- How many days are in the current month

FIGURE BP1.2

*An array can be used
to represent a calendar.*

Array Representation of a Calendar

First Sunday	First Monday	First Tuesday	First Thursday	• • •	First Saturday	Second Sunday	Second Monday	• • •
1	2	3	4		7	8	9	

Each element in the array corresponds to a particular day of the week on the calendar. The 1st element corresponds to the first Sunday, and each 7th element in the array after the 1st element (i.e., the 8th, the 15th...) is a consecutive Sunday.

Since there can be at most 6 weeks in a calendar, this array should contain 42 elements.

After you have this information, you can populate this array by using the following loop:

```
For iLoop = 1 to DaysInMonth
    aCalendarArray(iLoop + iFirstWeekday - 1) = iLoop
Next
```

iFirstWeekday is a numeric value, corresponding to a day of the week, where Sunday is represented by 1, Monday by 2, and so on.

Listing BP1.3 contains the complete code needed to execute this loop.

LISTING BP1.3   Populating an Array that Corresponds to the Calendar

```
1:     'We will create an array that will store the 42 possible
2:     'days of the month.
3:     Dim aCalendarDays(42)
4:
5:     'Into aCalendarDays, we will place the days of the current
6:     'month.  We will use the DatePart function to determine
7:     'when the first day of the month is
8:     Dim iFirstWeekday
9:     iFirstWeekday = DatePart("w",DateSerial(Year(dbCurrentDate), _
10:                             Month(dbCurrentDate), 1))
11:
12:    'Now, we want to loop from 1 to the number of days in the
13:    'current month, populating the array aCalendarDays
14:    Dim iDaysInMonth
15:    iDaysInMonth = DatePart("d",DateSerial(Year(dbCurrentDate), _
16:                             Month(dbCurrentDate)+1, 1-1))
17:    Dim iLoop
18:    For iLoop = 1 to iDaysInMonth
19:       aCalendarDays(iLoop + iFirstWeekday - 1) = iLoop
20:    Next
```

ANALYSIS   Listing BP1.3 contains the code that will populate the array that corresponds to the calendar. Before you can populate this array, you must first create it. Because a calendar can only have 42 cells at most, line 3 creates this array, aCalendarDays, with 42 elements. Next, you need to determine what weekday the first day of the month occurs on. You can use the DatePart function, which was discussed on Day 5, to determine what weekday a given date occurred on. Because you don't want to determine the weekday of the current day, you *do not* want to do the following:

```
iFirstWeekday = DatePart("w", dbCurrentDate)
```

That will obtain the weekday of the current date. Rather, you are interested in the weekday that the *first* date of the month occurred on. You can use DateSerial (also discussed on Day 5) to construct a new date object, one that corresponds to the first of the month (line 9 and 10). After line 9 executes, iFirstWeekday will contain the ordinal value of the weekday that the first day of the current month and year occurred on.

Next, line 15 determines the total number of days in the current month. You do this by using the DatePart function to obtain the day that the last day of the current month occurs on. To obtain the last day of the current month, you do a little trick with DateSerial, informing it to return the date that is equal to the year of the current year, the month *after* the current month, and one day *before* the first of that month. This will generate the day before the first day of the next month—the last day of the current month. After you have obtained these two values, you are ready for the loop, which starts on line 18. This loop populates the aCalendarDays array.

> **Tip**
> One of the most powerful features of VBScript's date functions is the capability for DateSerial to generate dates by using simple arithmetic. For an article on the advantages of using arithmetic to enhance DateSerial, visit http://www.4guysfromrolla.com/webtech/110398-1.shtml.

Now that you have the array, you need to display the array as an HTML TABLE. To do so, though, you first need to determine how many rows you need for your table. Recall that you will need six at most, but you may need just four or five. To determine how many rows you need, apply the following formula:

```
iRows = 6 - INT((42 - (iFirstWeekday + iDaysInMonth)) / 7)
```

Recall from Day 5 that the INT function truncates a number. The preceding formula calculates the number of days between the end of the array (42) and the last element in the array that was explicitly assigned a value. It then takes this number, divides it by 7, and truncates the value to find out how many weeks it represents. This is then subtracted from 6, which is the most rows that will be used.

After you know how many rows you need, you can create two For loops. The first For loop will iterate through the number of needed rows, whereas the second For loop will iterate through the number of needed columns (7). Inside these loops will be the HTML code to properly display the TABLE. Listing BP1.4 contains the code to loop through the array aCalendarDays and display the calendar.

LISTING BP1.4   Looping Through the Array aCalendarDays to Display the Calendar

```
1:    'Now that we have our populated array, we need to display the
2:    'array in calendar form.  We will create a table of 7 columns,
3:    'one for each day of the week.  The number of rows we will use
4:    'will be 6, the total number of possible rows, minus 42 (the upper
5:    'bound of the aCalendarDays array) minus the last array position
6:    'used (iFirstWeekday + iDaysInMonth) divided by seven, the number of
7:    'days in the week!  Simple, eh!!  :)
8:    Dim iColumns, iRows
9:    iColumns = 7
10:   iRows = 6 - Int((42 - (iFirstWeekDay + iDaysInMonth)) / 7)
11:
12:   'Now, create the table
13: %>
14:
15:   <TABLE ALIGN=CENTER BORDER=1 CELLSPACING=1 WIDTH=75% HEIGHT=75%>
16:     <TH COLSPAN=7>
17:       <FONT SIZE=+2>
18: <%
19:   'Display the month and year
20:   Response.Write GetMonthName(Month(dbCurrentDate))
21:   Response.Write ", " & Year(dbCurrentDate)
22: %>
23:       </FONT>
24:     </TH>
25: <%
26:   'Now, loop through 1 through iRows, then 1 through iColumns
27:   Dim iRowsLoop, iColumnsLoop
28:   For iRowsLoop = 1 to iRows
29:     'Create a new row
30:     Response.Write "<TR>"
31:     For iColumnsLoop = 1 to iColumns
32:       'Create a new column
33:       'If there is a day there, display it, else black out the cell
34:       If aCalendarDays((iRowsLoop-1)*7 + iColumnsLoop) > 0 then
35:         'Display the date
36:         Response.Write "<TD VALIGN=TOP ALIGN=RIGHT WIDTH=""14%"">"
37:         Response.Write aCalendarDays((iRowsLoop-1)*7 + iColumnsLoop)
38:         Response.Write "</TD>"
39:       Else
40:         'Black out the cell
41:         Response.Write "<TD BGCOLOR=BLACK> </TD>"
42:       End If
43:     Next
```

```
44:
45:    'Close the row
46:       Response.Write "</TR>"
47:    Next
48: %>
49:
50:    </TABLE>
```

ANALYSIS Listing BP1.4 loops through the array aCalendarDays, creating the HTML TABLE needed to display the calendar. To create the TABLE, you must know how many rows you need. To calculate this, you apply the formula discussed earlier in this Bonus Project. In Listing BP1.4, the formula is applied on line 10, and the value is assigned to the variable iRows.

Next, starting at line 15, you drop out of your ASP code block and use embedded HTML to create a TABLE. Lines 18 through 22 return to an ASP code block and output the name of the current month and the current year. Note that line 20 uses the custom function, GetMonthName, discussed in Listing BP1.2.

To display the columns and rows within the table, you need to use two For loops. The first loop, which begins on line 28, iterates from 1 to iRows, the number of rows needed by the calendar to display the current month. The second loop is nested inside the first and loops from 1 to the number of columns that you need, which is 7 (line 31). Each time you loop through a row, you output a <TR> tag (line 30), which represents a new row in the TABLE. After the inner, column loop has completed, the row loop outputs a closing row tag, </TR> (line 46).

You need to determine whether the aCalendarDays array has a value for the specific column and row in the TABLE you're currently at. You can map the current column and row in the TABLE to a specific value in the array by using the following equation:

```
aCalendarDays((iRowsLoop-1)*7 + iColumnsLoop)
```

Study this formula briefly and confirm that it will generate the correct array value for a specific column and row in the calendar.

To determine whether the array contains a value at the current row and column in the calendar, test to see whether the value of the array element corresponding to the calendar's row and column is greater than zero (line 34). If it is, you need to output the day value stored in the array (line 37); otherwise, you want to create the TABLE cell so that it contains all black (line 41). Finally, line 50 displays the closing TABLE tag, </TABLE>.

The Complete Code

You have looked at the code for `Calendar.asp` broken up into many pieces. Looking at certain sections at a time makes it easier to understand how these sections work together. Now that you've looked at the code in pieces, though, it's time to look at the code as a whole. Listing BP1.5 contains the complete code for `Calendar.asp`.

LISTING BP1.5   The Complete Code for `Calendar.asp`

```
 1: <%@ Language = VBSCRIPT %>
 2: <% Option Explicit %>
 3:
 4: <HTML>
 5: <BODY>
 6:
 7: <%
 8:    '************************************************
 9:    'Display a calendar based upon the current date
10:    '************************************************
11:
12:    'To accomplish this, we need to perform a number of tasks.
13:    'First, we will want to be able to determine the month name
14:    'for a given month.  So, let's create a function that
15:    'takes the numeric value of a month and displays the name of
16:    'the month (i.e., GetMonthName(8) would output August)
17:    Function GetMonthName(iMonth)
18:      Select Case iMonth
19:        Case 1:
20:          GetMonthName = "January"
21:        Case 2:
22:          GetMonthName = "February"
23:        Case 3:
24:          GetMonthName = "March"
25:        Case 4:
26:          GetMonthName = "April"
27:        Case 5:
28:          GetMonthName = "May"
29:        Case 6:
30:          GetMonthName = "June"
31:        Case 7:
32:          GetMonthName = "July"
33:        Case 8:
34:          GetMonthName = "August"
35:        Case 9:
36:          GetMonthName = "September"
37:        Case 10:
38:          GetMonthName = "October"
39:        Case 11:
40:          GetMonthName = "November"
```

```
41:        Case 12:
42:           GetMonthName = "December"
43:        Case Else:
44:           GetMonthName = "**INVALID MONTH**"
45:     End Select
46:  End Function
47:
48:  'Next, we need to obtain the current
49:  'date.  To do this, we will store the result of the
50:  'Date() function into a variable named dbCurrentDate
51:  Dim dbCurrentDate
52:  dbCurrentDate = Date()
53:
54:  'Now, we need to display a calendar.  At most, a calendar
55:  'can have six weeks.  Since a week contains seven days,
56:  'we will show, at most, 42 calendar cells.  We will use
57:  'a TABLE to generate this calendar
58:
59:  'We will create an array that will store the 42 possible
60:  'days of the month.
61:  Dim aCalendarDays(42)
62:
63:  'Into aCalendarDays, we will place the days of the current
64:  'month.  We will use the DatePart function to determine
65:  'when the first day of the month is
66:  Dim iFirstWeekday
67:  iFirstWeekday = DatePart("w",DateSerial(Year(dbCurrentDate), _
68:                           Month(dbCurrentDate), 1))
69:
70:  'Now, we want to loop from 1 to the number of days in the
71:  'current month, populating the array aCalendarDays
72:  Dim iDaysInMonth
73:  iDaysInMonth = DatePart("d",DateSerial(Year(dbCurrentDate), _
74:                          Month(dbCurrentDate)+1, 1-1))
75:  Dim iLoop
76:  For iLoop = 1 to iDaysInMonth
77:     aCalendarDays(iLoop + iFirstWeekday - 1) = iLoop
78:  Next
79:
80:  'Now that we have our populated array, we need to display the
81:  'array in calendar form.  We will create a table of 7 columns,
82:  'one for each day of the week.  The number of rows we will use
83:  'will be 6, the total number of possible rows, minus 42 (the upper
84:  'bound of the aCalendarDays array) minus the last array position
85:  'used (iFirstWeekday + iDaysInMonth) divided by seven, the number of
86:  'days in the week!  Simple, eh!!  :)
87:  Dim iColumns, iRows
88:  iColumns = 7
89:  iRows = 6 - Int((42 - (iFirstWeekDay + iDaysInMonth)) / 7)
90:
```

continues

LISTING BP1.5   continued

```
91:    'Now, create the table
92:  %>
93:
94:    <TABLE ALIGN=CENTER BORDER=1 CELLSPACING=1 WIDTH=75% HEIGHT=75%>
95:      <TH COLSPAN=7>
96:        <FONT SIZE=+2>
97:  <%
98:    'Display the month and year
99:    Response.Write GetMonthName(Month(dbCurrentDate))
100:   Response.Write ", " & Year(dbCurrentDate)
101: %>
102:        </FONT>
103:      </TH>
104: <%
105:   'Now, loop through 1 through iRows, then 1 through iColumns
106:   Dim iRowsLoop, iColumnsLoop
107:   For iRowsLoop = 1 to iRows
108:     'Create a new row
109:     Response.Write "<TR>"
110:     For iColumnsLoop = 1 to iColumns
111:       'Create a new column
112:       'If there is a day there, display it, else black out the cell
113:       If aCalendarDays((iRowsLoop-1)*7 + iColumnsLoop) > 0 then
114:         'Display the date
115:         Response.Write "<TD VALIGN=TOP ALIGN=RIGHT WIDTH=""14%"">"
116:         Response.Write aCalendarDays((iRowsLoop-1)*7 + iColumnsLoop)
117:         Response.Write "</TD>"
118:       Else
119:         'Black out the cell
120:         Response.Write "<TD BGCOLOR=BLACK> </TD>"
121:       End If
122:     Next
123:
124:     'Close the row
125:     Response.Write "</TR>"
126:   Next
127: %>
128:
129: </TABLE>
130: </BODY>
131: </HTML>
```

ANALYSIS   Note that the code in Listing BP1.5 is made up of the snippets of code listed in Listing BP1.1 through Listing BP1.4. Some trivial code has also been added, such as lines 1 through 6 and lines 130 and 131. There you have it—Calendar.asp! Figures BP1.3 and BP1.4 show Calendar.asp in action.

FIGURE BP1.3

A calendar for August, 1978.

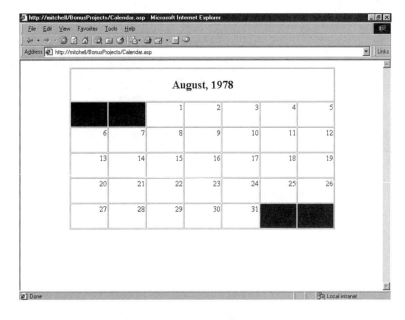

FIGURE BP1.4

A calendar for January, 2000.

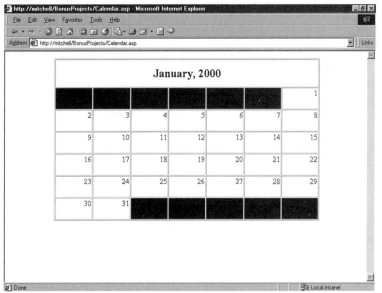

To display a calendar for a month that is not the current month, we altered line 52 in Listing BP1.5, so that dbCurrentDate was explicitly set to the preferred date. For example, to generate the output shown in Figure BP1.3, we altered line 52, setting it equal to:

```
DbCurrentDate = "8/1/1978"
```

In the second Bonus Project, we will look at how to let the user select what month and year she is interested in viewing a calendar for.

You have completed your first Bonus Project—congratulations! Hopefully, this Bonus Project has served as an opportunity to hone your VBScript coding skills. Future Bonus Projects will build on the calendar application created today. As you learn more VBScript and ASP in the coming days, you are encouraged to come back to this Bonus Project and work on extending the calendar application.

WEEK 2

8

9

10

11

12

13

14

At a Glance

Congratulations on completing your first week of Active Server Pages programming! Hopefully, you have had a lot of fun writing your own dynamic Web pages. Using Active Server Pages really simplifies the process of creating dynamic Web pages—in the past, complicated CGI scripts were required. With so much media attention being focused on the importance of the Internet, it is exciting to be able to write Web pages that dynamically interact with the visitor. In this coming week, you'll look at some ways to extend the power of your ASP scripts.

Where You're Going

This week's lessons concentrate on improving the usability of our ASP pages. In Day 8, "Communicating with the User," we'll discuss how to create text boxes, list boxes, check boxes, and radio buttons on a Web page. In Day 9, "Collecting the Form Information," we'll examine how we can use ASP pages to collect and process the information the user entered into these text boxes, list boxes, check boxes, and radio buttons. Being able to receive inputs from your visitors and make decisions based these inputs will greatly increase the usefulness of your ASP pages.

We will also look at some standard components you can use with your Active Server Pages. The components, written by Microsoft, allow for you to easily add new functionality to your existing ASP pages. The nice thing about these components is that they already have been written for you! One such component, which we'll discuss in Day 12, "Working with Common ASP Components," is the Ad Rotator component. Using this component, we'll add randomly rotating advertising banners on our ASP pages!

The ASP pages we looked at throughout the first week did not interact with other files on the Web server. This week we'll examine how to read and write files to and from our Web server. Being able to access the Web server's file system is useful since we can use files on the Web server for a number of purposes. These uses are discussed in detail in Day 13, "Reading and Writing Files on the Web Server."

This week concludes with a discussion on debugging. No one writes perfect code, and it is important to be able to test your code and find errors. Also, we'll look at how to use the ASPError object, a build-in ASP object, to gracefully handle errors when they do occur. Debugging existing errors and gracefully handling run-time errors are two of the most important aspects of any type of programming, be it ASP programming, Visual Basic programming, or C++ programming.

DAY **8**

Communicating with the User

So far you have seen how to use ASP to send information to the browser, but you have yet to learn how to obtain information from the user. Today's lesson demonstrates how to collect information from your users. Plenty of real-world situations require user feedback. How useful would a search engine be if you couldn't enter keywords? How practical would an online store be if users could not enter their billing and shipping information?

The four general methods of acquiring information from a user are through the use of a text box, a list box, a check box, or a radio button. In today's lesson, you will examine these ways of collecting information from the user in detail. You will also look at sending the information to an ASP page for processing.

Today, you will learn the following:

- How to collect information from your users
- How to use the <FORM> tag
- How to use the <INPUT> tag

- How to send a user's information to an ASP page for processing
- How to use text boxes to gather information
- How to use list boxes to gather information
- How to use check boxes to gather information
- How to use radio buttons to gather information

Receiving Information from the User

Last week we created ASP pages that would accomplish various tasks based on static data. For example, in Week 1's Week in Review, we created a calendar program to display the current month with information about events that will occur during the month. Although the idea is pretty cool, it's also impractical the way it is currently written. What if a user wants to view events that will occur two months into the future? Or perhaps a user wants to see all the events that occurred last month. Without having any way to receive input from the user, you cannot accommodate requests on a user-by-user basis. Every user is stuck seeing the same thing. There is no customization! To put these types of issues in a practical, albeit simple, context, consider the following real-world scenario.

Imagine that you were put in charge of creating a Web site for Company XYZ, a creator of widgets. What would you want on the Web site? Here are some possible features:

- You would want to let the users search for information on a particular widget.
- If a user was interested in receiving the company's widget catalog, you would need to collect the user's name and mailing address.
- You might want to allow customers to purchase widgets online. In this scenario, you would need to collect the customer's order information, as well as her billing and shipping information.

All these situations require input from the user. However, being able to collect information is not useful unless you have a way of *processing* the information as well. You can accomplish both of these tasks by using a *form*.

What Are Forms?

Recall from Day 1, "Getting Started with Active Server Pages," that the Internet is based upon the client-server model. When you visit a Web page, your browser, the client, makes a request to the Web server, asking for a particular Web page. The Web server responds by sending the requested document to the client. When requesting an ASP page, the web server first processes the ASP code *before* sending the resulting web page back to the client. What, though, if we want our ASP page to make decisions based upon a user's input? To accomplish this, we need to use forms.

8

A *form* has two duties: to collect information from the user and to send that information to a separate Web page for processing. Through the use of a form, an ASP page can acquire the user's input, and make programmatic decisions based on that input.

While surfing the Net, chances are you've used an assortment of forms designed for a variety of purposes. For example, whenever you submit personal information to a Web site, you are using a form. Whenever you type the keywords into your favorite search engine, you are using a form. Forms are the heart and soul of the World Wide Web.

Forms provide one mechanism to pass information from one Web page to another. As we'll discuss in Day 11, "Maintaining Persistent Information on the Web," the Internet is inherently stateless, and continuing information from one Web page to the next is not a trivial task. Forms provide one mechanism of passing information from one Web page to another. Forms also allow for the user to enter detailed information using a variety of input controls, such as text boxes, list boxes, check boxes, and radio buttons. We'll discuss these input controls, or *form fields* as they're called, in "Using Form Fields."

Creating Forms

Creating a form is straightforward and simple. It requires as little as two lines of HTML, as shown in Listing 8.1.

LISTING 8.1 A Form is Created Using the <FORM> Tag

```
1:  <FORM METHOD=POST ACTION="somePage.asp">
2:  </FORM>
```

ANALYSIS Listing 8.1 uses the HTML tag <FORM> to create a simple form. The <FORM> tag has two properties: METHOD and ACTION.

- METHOD—The METHOD tag can be set to either GET or POST. We will discuss the METHOD property in more detail in "The Difference Between GET and POST."

- ACTION—The ACTION tag specifies what page will be called when the form is submitted. Usually, this is an ASP page that will process the information entered by the user.

A form is *submitted* when the user confirms that he is finished entering the information, usually by clicking a button. If there is just one input field in the form, such as a text box, the user can simply press Enter to submit the form.

Using Form Fields

The form in Listing 8.1 serves no function. It has no text boxes for users to enter information into. It has no list boxes, radio buttons, or check boxes either. On a Web site, this form would be useless; however, it does demonstrate how a <FORM> tag is used. To be useful, a form must contain one or more *form fields*: objects inside a form that are used to collect information from the user.

Each text box, list box, check box, or radio button in a form is a form field. You need a way to create form fields within your form.

To create text boxes, check boxes, and radio buttons, use the <INPUT> tag. The <INPUT> tag has a number of properties, but we will only concentrate on the following three:

- NAME—The NAME tag uniquely identifies each element in the form. You will use the NAME tag in tomorrow's lesson when you use ASP to process the user's input.

- TYPE—The TYPE tag determines what type of form field is displayed. To display a text box, set TYPE equal to TEXT. To create a check box, assign TYPE equal to CHECKBOX.

- VALUE—The VALUE tag determines the default value for the form field. This property is important when processing the information submitted by list boxes, check boxes, and radio buttons.

To create list boxes, use the <SELECT> tag in conjunction with the <OPTION> tag. Each option in the list box needs an <OPTION> tag. The <SELECT> tag is only used once, encompassing many <OPTION> tags. Let's say that you want a list box that lists the months of the year. You would need 12 <OPTION> tags enclosed by a <SELECT> tag, like so:

```
<SELECT NAME=Month>
    <OPTION VALUE="January">January
    <OPTION VALUE="February">February
    <OPTION VALUE="March">March
    ...
    <OPTION VALUE="November">November
    <OPTION VALUE="December">December
</SELECT>
```

The VALUE property in the <OPTION> tags serves as a unique identifier for each separate option in the list box. We will discuss list boxes in "List Boxes."

Putting it All Together

Now that you know how to create forms and form fields, let's create a form that asks for the user's name, age, and sex. This form would need a number of form fields. First, we would need a text box for the user's name. We could also use a text box for the user's age; however, if we were only interested in what age group our user fit in, we could use a list box. Finally, to obtain the user's sex, we will use two radio buttons, one labeled Male and the other labeled Female. Listing 8.2 contains the HTML code that will generate these form fields.

LISTING 8.2   A Form to Collect Generic User Information

```
 1:   <FORM METHOD=POST ACTION="somePage.asp">
 2:      What is your name?
 3:      <INPUT TYPE=TEXT NAME=Name>
 4:      <P>
 5:
 6:      How old are you?
 7:      <SELECT NAME=Age>
 8:        <OPTION VALUE="Under 21">Under 21
 9:        <OPTION VALUE="21 - 50">21 - 50
10:        <OPTION VALUE="Over 50">Over 50
11:      </SELECT>
12:      <P>
13:
14:      Sex:<BR>
15:      <INPUT TYPE=RADIO NAME=Sex VALUE=Male>
16:      Male
17:      <BR>
18:      <INPUT TYPE=RADIO NAME=Sex VALUE=Female>
19:      Female
20:      <BR>
21:
22:      <INPUT TYPE=SUBMIT VALUE="Send us your Information!">
23:  </FORM>
```

ANALYSIS   The code in Listing 8.2 creates a form that contains a number of form fields. These form fields are used to collect information from the user. Each form field is created using either the <INPUT> tag, for text boxes, check boxes, and radio buttons, or the <SELECT> and <OPTION> tags, for list boxes.

For example, our users will be presented with a text box to enter their names into. This text box was created using the <INPUT> tag (line 3) with its TYPE property set to TEXT. The list box that contains the various age ranges is created on line 7 with the <SELECT> tag. Each option for the list box is created using the <OPTION> tag (lines 8, 9, and 10).

Finally, the two radio buttons are created on lines 15 and 18. These are both created using the <INPUT> tag with the TYPE property set to RADIO.

Line 22 in Listing 8.2 also demonstrates the use of a valid submit button. All forms you create should contain a submit button. A *submit button*, when clicked, submits the form. To create a submit button, you use the <INPUT> tag with TYPE set equal to the keyword SUBMIT. The VALUE tag determines the submit button's label. If you do not include a VALUE for your submit button, the browser will decide what to label the submit button. (Internet Explorer 5.0, for example, will label the submit button as Submit Query.)

Note

Under close inspection, you'll notice that the properties in the INPUT and FORM tags are all capitalized. For your reference, HTML is *not* case sensitive. In other words, the following two lines are functionally identical:

<InPUt Type=Text NamE=naME>

and

<INPUT TYPE=TEXT NAME=Name>

As a coding convention, it is recommended that you fully capitalize your tags and their properties. Following this convention will make your code easier to read, and will clearly differentiate between the HTML tags and regular text within your Web page. In all the examples throughout this book, you'll note such capitalization of the HTML tags.

The form created by the code in Listing 8.2 can be seen in Figure 8.1. Take a few moments to look over the HTML in Listing 8.2 and compare it with the output in Figure 8.1.

Designing Forms

When creating forms, keep a couple of things in mind. First, make sure that the form has a submit button. In the preceding section, we discussed how to create a submit button by using the <INPUT> tag. It is imperative that every form have a submit button.

Second, it is important that the form be easy for the user to complete. You have four form fields at your disposal: the text box, list box, check box, and radio button. Make sure that the type of form field you use best fits the information needing to be collected. For example, if you are going to ask for a user's mailing address, it makes more sense to have a list box that contains the 50 states than to have the user type in the name of his or her state of residency. This topic is discussed in "Using the Different Form Fields."

FIGURE 8.1

This form uses a text box, a list box, and two radio buttons.

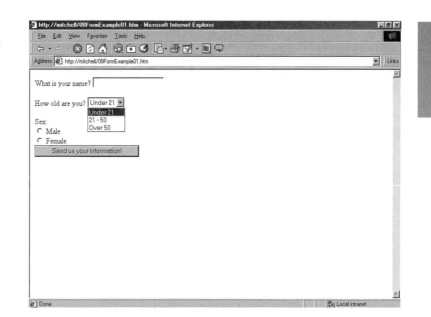

In "Receiving Information from the User," we mentioned Company XYZ, a hypothetical company that created widgets, and pretended that you were put in charge of developing its Web site. One requested feature was to have a form where a user could enter his mailing address and receive a widget catalog through the mail. Let's look at how you could create such a form.

The first thing to do is ask, "What information do I need from the user?" In this case, the information you need is the user's name, street address, city, state, and zip code. Let's say, though, that you also wanted to obtain some background information on the user as well, such as how often he purchases widgets. Finally, Company XYZ has requested that you ask their users whether they want to subscribe to the Company XYZ online newsletter.

Based on these requirements, you need the following form fields:

- Text boxes would work well for entering the first and last names of the customer, as well as for the street address and zip code.

- A list box should be employed so that the users can select their states, instead of typing state names or postal abbreviations. A large list box, containing 50 states, may seem unwieldy, but resist the temptation to use a text box. When using a text box, you are allowing users to enter *anything*, where a list box requires them to choose one of the viable options. If you permitted your users to type in the names of their states, you could receive several different values for one particular state. For example, users who live in Missouri might enter values like: Missouri, MO, Misoury, or Misery. Using a list box eliminates the potential for data entry errors by the user. We will discuss what form fields are best suited for what purposes in "Using the Different Form Fields."

- Radio buttons would work well for the background information on the user's widget buying habits.

- A simple check box would suffice for the online newsletter subscription.

After you decide what form fields you'll need, it's then just a matter of writing the HTML. Listing 8.3 presents the HTML code for the Company XYZ form.

LISTING 8.3   The Widget Catalog Request Form

```
 1:  <FONT FACE=Arial SIZE=3>
 2:  <B>Please enter the following information to receive
 3:  your free Widget catalog by mail</B>
 4:  </FONT><HR>
 5:
 6:  <FORM METHOD=POST ACTION="catalog.asp">
 7:     First Name: <INPUT TYPE=TEXT NAME=FirstName>
 8:     <BR>
 9:    Last Name: <INPUT TYPE=TEXT NAME=LastName>
10:     <BR>
11:     Street Address: <INPUT TYPE=TEXT NAME=StreetAddress>
12:     <BR>
13:     City: <INPUT TYPE=TEXT NAME=City SIZE=10>,
14:     State:
15:     <SELECT NAME=State>
16:        ...
17:        <OPTION VALUE="IL">Illinois
18:        <OPTION VALUE="IN">Indiana
19:        <OPTION VALUE="IA">Iowa
20:        <OPTION VALUE="KS">Kansas
21:        ...
22:     </SELECT>
23:
24:     Zip: <INPUT TYPE=TEXT NAME=Zip SIZE=6>
25:     <BR>
26:
27:     <INPUT TYPE=CHECKBOX NAME=Newsletter VALUE=Yes>
28:     Please sign me up to receive your on-line newsletter!
29:     <BR>
30:
31:     How often do you buy Widgets?<BR>
32:     <INPUT TYPE=RADIO NAME=PurchaseRate VALUE=Low>
33:     Once a year<BR>
```

```
34:     <INPUT TYPE=RADIO NAME=PurchaseRate VALUE=Fair>
35:     Once a month<BR>
36:     <INPUT TYPE=RADIO NAME=PurchaseRate VALUE=High>
37:     Several times a month<BR>
38:
39:     <INPUT TYPE=SUBMIT VALUE="Submit Information!">
40: </FORM>
```

ANALYSIS Listing 8.3 creates a form to gather a user's mailing information so that he can be sent a free catalog. Whenever creating a form, start by deciding what information is required from the user and then create the form fields necessary to obtain this information. To obtain a mailing address, we need the user to enter his first and last name, his street address, his city, state, and zip code. All of these, with exception of the state, are accomplished using text boxes. We also want to query the user on his widget buying habits. This is accomplished using three radio buttons.

In Listing 8.3, the form is created using the <FORM> tag on line 6. Over the next several lines, the text boxes for the user's first and last name and street address are created (lines 7, 9, and 13, respectively).

On line 15, the list box containing the 50 states is created. For brevity, only four of the 50 states are shown in Listing 8.3 (lines 17 through 20). An <OPTION> tag is used for each state.

On line 24, the text box for the zip code is created. This text box's SIZE property is set to 6, which causes the text box to be only six characters long. Note that this does not place any restriction on the number of characters the user can enter into this text box—rather, it simply displays the text box as only 6 characters wide.

Lastly, three radio buttons are created, asking the user when he last purchased a widget. These radio buttons (lines 32, 34, and 36) allow the user to select at least one of the three options.

Tip

Because forms are HTML code, many HTML editors, such as FrontPage, make it quick and easy to design forms. For larger forms, much time can be saved by the use of such an editor.

Figure 8.2 shows how the form in Listing 8.3 appears in a browser. Again, look over Listing 8.3 and compare the HTML tags with the final output. You'll have a better understanding of how to use form fields if you take the time to examine the HTML tags and their corresponding output.

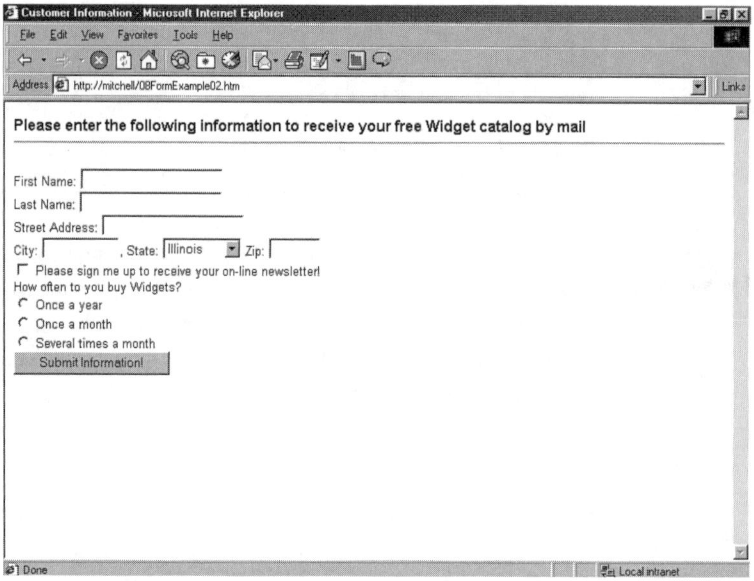

FIGURE 8.2

This form collects the information needed for sending a widget catalog.

Congratulations, you have just designed and created a useful, complex form that uses each of the four types of form fields. In "Using the Different Form Fields" we'll discuss each type of form field in detail.

Submitting Forms

Using a standard Web browser, a user can surf to a Web page with a form on it and enter information. When the user does this, the information he is typing in has not yet been sent to the Web server. This information is not available for the Web server to process until the user submits the form by clicking the form's submit button.

It would be nice to be able to send this information to an ASP page, which could then determine what the user entered into the form and act on that information. The <FORM> tag offers two properties that allow you to send form information to an ASP page for processing: the ACTION property and the METHOD property.

Using the ACTION Property

The ACTION property of a form can be set to any valid URL. When a user submits the form, the URL specified in the ACTION property is called, and the values in the form fields are passed. In Listing 8.3, the form's ACTION property is set to catalog.asp. When the user clicks the submit button, the form field values are sent to catalog.asp as the user's browser is redirected to catalog.asp.

8

> **Note**
>
> The ACTION property does not have to be set to an ASP page. The ACTION property can be set to any Web page name on your Web server (such as a CGI script) or to a script on another server altogether, or it could be left out completely. Note that if you do not specify the ACTION property in a form, when a user submits the form, the current page is reloaded.
>
> In the examples in this book, we will *always* specify the ACTION property in our forms. Also, because this book deals with ASP, the ACTION property will always be set to an ASP page.

The second property of the <FORM> tag is called METHOD and can be set to either GET or POST. The METHOD determines how the form field values are passed to the ASP page specified in the form's ACTION property.

The Difference Between GET and POST

There are, not surprisingly, two ways through which information can be passed from a form to an ASP page. The first method uses the querystring and is the method used when a form's METHOD property is set to GET. The other method, POST, hides the user's information by not using the querystring.

NEW TERM   The *querystring* is additional information sent to a Web page appended to the end of the URL.

The querystring is made up of name/value pairs, in the following form:

```
VariableName=ValueOfVariable
```

For example, if a URL were to appear as

```
http://www.yourserver.com/someFile.asp?name=Scott
```

the querystring would be

```
?name=scott
```

Note that the start of the querystring is denoted by a question mark (?).

The querystring can contain multiple name/value pairs. When more than one name/value pairs is in the querystring, each name/value pair is separated by an ampersand (&). For example, if both the name and age were stored in the querystring, the querystring might look like this:

```
?name=scott&age=21
```

Remember that the querystring is always appended to the URL, so in your browser's address pane, the full URL of the page would appear as follows:

```
http://www.yourserver.com/someFile.asp?name=Scott&age=21
```

> **Caution**
>
> If you have a vast number of form fields in your form, it quickly becomes apparent that the querystring will become very long! Strive to keep the length of the total URL fewer than 255 characters. This 255 character limitation was a shortcoming of older browsers. Today's web browsers do not have this limitation; however, you have no guarantee that all of your Web site's visitors will be using up to date browsers, and therefore you should strive to keep the length of the total URL fewer than 255 characters. That means if you are going to have a vast number of form fields, it might be wise to set the form's METHOD to POST. We'll discuss how POST differs from GET shortly.

In Listing 8.4, you'll find a simple form that has its METHOD property set to GET. This form doesn't really do anything complex; it simply demonstrates how form values can be passed through the querystring.

LISTING 8.4   Creating a Form Where METHOD=GET

```
1:  <FORM METHOD=GET ACTION="GetMethodExample.asp">
2:    Name: <INPUT TYPE=TEXT NAME=Name>
3:    <BR>
4:    Age: <INPUT TYPE=TEXT NAME=Age>
5:    <BR>
6:    <INPUT TYPE=SUBMIT>
7:  </FORM>
```

ANALYSIS   For this example, the ASP file GetMethodExample.asp does nothing useful; it simply prints a message about the querystring. The complete code for GetMethodExample.asp is shown in Listing 8.5. Note the Address bar in Figure 8.3, which shows how the querystring is appended to the URL and contains two name/value pairs:

```
?Name=Scott&Age=21
```

FIGURE 8.3

The form field values are stored as name/value pairs in the querystring.

In Listing 8.4, we examined how to create a form using the GET method. When this form is submitted, the ASP page specified by the form's ACTION property is called, and values the user entered are passed to this page. How they are passed depends upon the form's METHOD property. In Listing 8.4, in line 1, the form's METHOD is set to GET. When the form is submitted, the user's inputs are passed through the querystring to GetMethodExample.asp, and the output is shown in Figure 8.3.

Let's take a moment to examine the code for GetMethodExample.asp. Note that it outputs the contents of the querystring. Listing 8.5 shows the code for GetMethodExample.asp:

LISTING 8.5 Outputting the Contents of the querystring

```
1:  Note the A<U>d</U>dress bar above.
2:  <P>
3:  The querystring is set to:<BR>
4:  <%=Request.Querystring%>
```

ANALYSIS Listing 8.5, the code for `GetMethodExample.asp`, is fairly straightforward. The only non-HTML code used is on line 4, where the contents of the `Request.QueryString` collection are outputted. The `Request.QueryString` is discussed in detail in tomorrow's lesson, "Collecting the Form Information." As you'll learn tomorrow, the `Request.QueryString` collection contains the information passed in the querystring.

There are three ways to pass information to an ASP page through the querystring. You've already seen the first way, which is to set a form's `METHOD` property as `GET`. Another way is to use the `HREF` tag, which creates a link in your Web page. If you wanted to allow a user to click a link that would take him directly to `someFile.asp`, passing in a querystring of

```
?Name=Scott&Age=21
```

you would simply need to create an `HREF` tag:

```
<A HREF="someFile.asp?Name=Scott&Age=21">Click Me!</A>
```

This method proves useful when you want to provide a quick link that passes some pre-determined information to a Web page. Rather than creating a bulky form, using a hyperlink provides a quicker way to submit a default response. We will examine using this method to quickly pass information from one Web page to another in Day 9, "Collecting the Form Information."

The third and final way to pass information to an ASP page through the querystring is to simply type in the full URL with the querystring into your browser. For example, you could enter

```
http://www.yourserver.com/someFile.asp?Name=Scott&Age=21
```

into your browser's Address bar, which would be equivalent to using either of the other two methods.

Caution

Although passing form information through the querystring might seem harmless, imagine if you have a form where you want the user to enter his password or some other type of sensitive information. When the information is passed through the querystring, this sensitive information appears on the screen. Furthermore, the browser might save the full URL in the Histories folder, which could be a security threat if multiple individuals used the computer.

If you are going to ask for private information, it is best *not* to set `METHOD` to `GET`. When the `METHOD` property is set to `POST`, the information being passed is hidden, and, therefore, setting `METHOD=POST` is preferred when collecting sensitive information from your users.

8

One disadvantage with using GET is that the form field values are exposed through the Address bar. Also, some older clients do not support URLs longer than 255 characters, which means that you should always make sure that the Web page's URL plus the querystring is less than 255 characters. You can hide these variables being passed and get rid of the 255 character limitation by simply setting the METHOD property to POST instead of GET.

When using POST, the data is still passed in name/value pairs to the ASP page specified by the form's ACTION property. Instead of being appended to the URL, however, the name/value pairs are hidden from the Address bar. Therefore, if you plan to ask your users to enter private information, it is best to use POST.

When using a form whose METHOD is set to POST, the form field values are sent through the HTTP headers. These headers are bits of information that the web browser sends to the web server when requesting a Web page. HTTP headers and their uses are discussed in detail in Day 10, "Working with the Request Object."

Reading Form Values from an ASP Page

Now that you know how to send form field values to an ASP page, you may find yourself wondering how to read these form field values in your ASP pages. Day 9 is dedicated to this discussion, but I think it only fair that I give you a sneak peek today!

You read form field values by using the Request object. The Request object contains two *collections* used to read form data:

- QueryString collection—The QueryString collection is used to access the name/value pairs passed through the querystring.

- Form collection—The Form collection is used to access the name/value pairs passed by a form that has its METHOD property set to POST.

A *collection* is a set of name/value pairs, similar to a two-column matrix. Suppose that you wanted to list the months of the year and how many days were in each month. Table 8.1 shows such a two-column matrix. In a collection, you refer to each row by the left column of the matrix, which gives you the value, or the right column of the matrix. For example, say that you named your collection DaysInMonths. If you requested the value of

DaysInMonth("August")

you would get the value 31.

TABLE 8.1 DaysInMonths Collection Illustrated as a Matrix

Name	Value
…	…
June	30
July	31
August	31
September	30
…	…

We will discuss collections in more detail during Day 9. For now, just remember that a collection is a set of name/value pairs. To refer to a particular value, you need to know its name and refer to it as:

```
NameOfCollection(Name)
```

Because you want to read the values from a form in an ASP page, you will need two Web pages: one page that contains the HTML code for the form and another page, an ASP page, that processes the information entered into the form.

Let's start by creating the page that will have the form on it. For this example, we'll create a form that asks for the user's name and date of birth. We will name this page BirthdateForm.htm. Create this HTML page and enter the code in Listing 8.6. You can see the output of BirthdateForm.htm in Figure 8.4.

LISTING 8.6 The HTML Code for BirthdateForm.htm

```
 1: <HTML>
 2: <BODY>
 3:     <B>Please enter your name and birthdate:</B><BR>
 4:
 5:     <FORM METHOD=POST ACTION="YourAge.asp">
 6:         Your name: <INPUT TYPE=TEXT NAME=Name>
 7:         <BR>
 8:
 9:         Your Birthdate (in MM/DD/YY format):<BR>
10:         <INPUT TYPE=TEXT NAME=Birthdate>
11:
12:         <P>
13:         <INPUT TYPE=SUBMIT VALUE="Send!">
14:     </FORM>
15: </BODY>
16: </HTML>
```

ANALYSIS The form created in Listing 8.6 is fairly straightforward. The form consists of two form fields: a text box for the user to enter his name (line 6) and a text box for the user to enter his date of birth (line 10). In line 5, we set the form's ACTION property to YourAge.asp. This is the ASP page that will be called when the user submits the form.

You need to create YourAge.asp in the same directory as BirthdateForm.htm. The code for YourAge.asp can be found in Listing 8.7. Although some of the ASP code present in YourAge.asp might be new, we will cover it in detail during Day 9. The output for YourAge.asp can be seen in Figure 8.5.

Note When you need to collect information from a user, you generally need two separate pages: a page with the HTML code for the form, and an ASP page that will process the form. The page that displays the form can be either an HTML page or an ASP page. However, the page that processes the form cannot be an HTML page and will always be an ASP page in our examples.

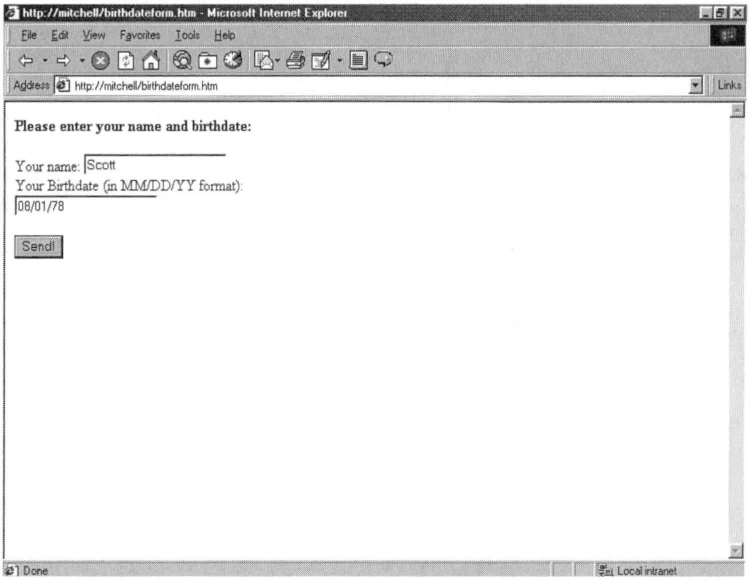

FIGURE 8.4

BirthdateForm.htm, *when viewed through a browser.*

It is important to understand how the form's ACTION property works. If you specify a simple filename, such as ACTION="someFile.asp", it is important that someFile.asp exists in the same directory as the page that displays the form. In our example with

BirthdateForm.htm, we set the form's ACTION property as ACTION="YourAge.asp" (line 5). This requires that both YourAge.asp and BirthdateFile.htm exist in the same directory. If YourAge.asp does not exist in the same directory as BirthdateForm.htm, when the user submits the form she will receive a 404 Error. A 404 Error occurs when the browser asks the Web server for a Web page that does not exist. Although YourAge.asp may exist, if it does not exist in the same directory as BirthdateForm.htm, a 404 Error will occur.

With a slight modification of the form's ACTION property, you can have these two files exist in different directories, or even on different Web servers. This topic will be discussed in "Revisiting the ACTION property."

LISTING 8.7   The Code for YourAge.asp

```
 1:  <%@ Language=VBScript %>
 2:  <% Option Explicit %>
 3:  <%
 4:      'Read in the form field variables
 5:      Dim strName, dtBirthDate
 6:      strName = Request.Form("Name")
 7:      dtBirthDate = Request.Form("Birthdate")
 8:
 9:      Dim iDaysOld
10:      iDaysOld = DateDiff("d", dtBirthDate, Date)
11: %>
12: <HTML>
13: <BODY>
14:
15:     Hello <%=strName%>!
16:     You were born on <%=dtBirthDate%>.
17:     <BR>
18:     That makes you <%=iDaysOld%> days old.
19: </BODY>
20: </HTML>
```

ANALYSIS   Although the code in Listing 8.7 uses the Request object (lines 6 and 7), which we have not formerly discussed, you should be familiar with the rest of the ASP code. We've used the shorthand notation for Response.Write (<%= ... %>) before (lines 15, 16, and 18), and on Day 5, "Using VBScript's Built-in Functions," we discussed how to use DateDiff (line 10), one of the many powerful date functions available with VBScript. YourAge.asp simply reads in the name and birth date that the user entered into the form in BirthdateForm.htm (lines 6 and 7). It then takes this information and uses DateDiff to calculate the number of days that have passed since the user's date of birth (line 10). Finally, YourAge.asp prints out a welcome message with the user's name and birth date, and then displays the number of days since the user's date of birth (lines 15 through 18).

FIGURE 8.5

YourAge.asp *after the form in* BirthdateForm.htm *is submitted.*

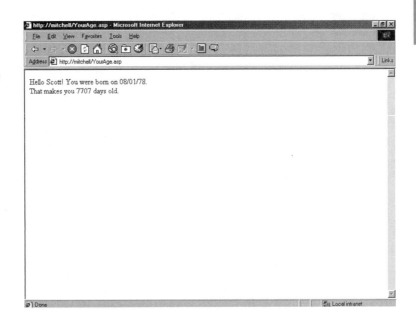

Caution

Imagine, for a moment, that in BirthdateForm.htm the user entered her date of birth as "Yellow school bus." Obviously "Yellow school bus" is not a valid birth date, so how can you ensure that YourAge.asp will be sent valid data from BirthdateForm.htm?

One method is to use *client-side form validation*. We will discuss this in further detail in "Client-Side Form Validation."

In "What Are Forms?", I mentioned that collecting user input is a two-step process. The first step is to create a Web page that contains the HTML code needed to properly display a form for users to enter their information into. We refer to this Web page as the *form creation web page*. The second step is to create an ASP page that will use the Request object to read the form field values entered by the user and decide what to do with this information. This script is referred to as the *form processing script*. In Listing 8.6, BirthdateForm.htm was the form creation web page, and, in Listing 8.7, YourAge.asp was the form processing script.

NEW TERM   A *form creation Web page* is the HTML or ASP page created to display the form. In today's lesson, we've shown several examples of form creation Web pages: Listing 8.2, Listing 8.3, Listing 8.4, and Listing 8.6.

NEW TERM   A *form processing script* is the ASP page created to collect the values a user enters into the form fields. This ASP page is also responsible for processing the information in the form fields. We've shown one form processing script in today's lesson, `YourAge.asp`. The code for this form processing script can be found in Listing 8.7.

> **Note**
>
> We've defined a form processing script as the ASP page that collects and processes the information entered into the form fields. This processing may be performing a simple task, such as displaying the form field values. In `YourAge.asp`, the processing was fairly simple: We calculated the number of days that had elapsed between the user's birth date and the current date; we then displayed this information.
>
> In later lessons we will begin to do more complex processing, such as searching a database based on the form field values.

Although `YourAge.asp` might not perform a terribly useful task, it does demonstrate the capability to collect and process input from the user. We hope you find this exciting because, in our opinion, it really is an amazing feat! From your personal computer, you can enter values into an ASP script that is being executed on a Web server that could be located on another continent. We can remember trying out form-based ASP scripts several years ago for the first time. Creating an ASP script that could gather input was exciting because it was then that we realized just how powerful ASP is!

Before you continue with the remainder of today's lesson, let's take a moment to pause and reflect over what you've learned so far today. At this point, you know what forms are and how they can be used to gather information from the user. You learned how to use the ACTION and METHOD properties of forms. Finally, you looked at an example of reading form field values from an ASP page.

Using Advanced Form Techniques

Now that we've covered some of the basics of forms, it's time to discuss some of the more advanced form techniques. We've focused most of our attention so far on the various types of form fields, and less attention on the actual <FORM> tag. The <FORM> tag is used to encapsulate the form fields. Each form field is responsible for gathering a discrete chunk of information from the user, while the form is responsible for gathering this information and sending it to an ASP page for processing.

8

To accomplish this feat, the <FORM> tag has two properties: METHOD and ACTION. The METHOD property determines *how* the information is passed to the form processing script. Recall that the METHOD property can be set to either GET or POST. The ACTION property determines to what form processing script to send the users' information.

The form field information is not sent to the form processing script until the form is submitted. A form is submitted when the submit button is clicked by the user. In "Creating Forms," we covered the basics of forms, and discussed how to create simple forms. In "Revisiting the ACTION Property" and "Client-Side Form Validation," the next two sections, we will be discussing the ACTION property in more detail, as well as other advanced form techniques.

Revisiting the ACTION Property

Up until this point we've specified the ACTION property as a simple filename, such as YourAge.asp or GetMethodExample.asp. Although there is nothing wrong with this, it restricts you to placing your form creation Web pages and form processing scripts in the same directory. What do you do, though, if you want to have your form creation Web page and form processing scripts in different directories? What if you want your form processing script on another Web server altogether? The ACTION property can be used to allow for either of these two scenarios.

Assume that you have a directory called scripts, which you create in the root directory. In the scripts directory, you place all your form processing scripts.

Note

> Recall from Day 1, "Getting Started with Active Server Pages," that the *root directory* is the base directory for your Web site. For example, if you access a Web page like this:
>
> http://www.yourserver.com/someFile.asp
>
> then someFile.asp is in the root directory. If you have to access someFile.asp like so:
>
> http://www.yourserver.com/someDirectory/someFile.asp
>
> then someFile.asp is in the directory someDirectory.

Now, let's say that you plan on creating FormCreationWebPage.asp and FormProcessingScript.asp to handle form creation and form processing, respectively. If you place FormProcessingScript.asp in the scripts directory, then in the form in FormCreationWebPage.asp, you would need to set the ACTION property as follows:

ACTION="/scripts/FormProcessingScript.asp"

Note the leading forward slash (`/`), then the directory name (`scripts`), and finally the form processing script filename (`FormProcessingScript.asp`). This is the syntax used to specify the directory and filename of the form processing script.

Not only can you have form processing scripts in different directories on your Web site, you can have the form processing script on a completely different Web server. Imagine that you wanted to create an eCommerce site where users could purchase goods online. What type of forms would you need there?

NEW TERM An *eCommerce* site is a Web site that sells products online. There are several popular eCommerce sites on the Internet. Amazon.com, which is the most talked about eCommerce site in the media these days, is a good example.

For starters, you would need to create a form where users could enter their credit card information for billing purposes. You would need to verify that the credit card information entered is valid and carry through the billing transaction, debiting the customer and crediting you, the seller. To do so, you would need to send the credit information to a company that specializes in processing and validating credit card transactions. This company would have its own form processing script that would expect, perhaps, a credit card number, a credit card type, and an expiration date.

In creating this form on your site, you would want to set the `ACTION` property to the full URL of the form processing script. For this example, let's assume that the credit card processing company's Web site is `http://www.CreditProcessors.com` and that the actual form processing script is in the `cgi-bin` directory and named `ProcessCard.asp`. To send this page the form field values when the user submits the form, all you need to do is set the form's `ACTION` property as follows:

```
ACTION="http://www.CreditProcessors.com/cgi-bin/ProcessCard.asp
```

In fact, you can use this technique to refer to form processing scripts on your own Web server.

```
ACTION="http://www.yourserver.com/scripts/FormProcessingScript.asp
```

By being able to specify a complete URL as the `ACTION` property for a form, you can send your form field data to any ASP script on any Web server. In the discussed example of the credit card transaction and processing company, you are beginning to reap the benefits of distributed computing. Three separate computers are involved with this transaction:

- The user's computer, with which he uses a browser to visit and fill in a form.
- The Web server, which sends the browser the HTML to display the form. This web server is the eCommerce site which actually sells the goods to the web visitor, displaying the available products and their prices.

8

- The credit card transaction company's Web server, which collects the user's and the company's information and debits and credits their accounts respectively.

Pretty amazing!

Client-Side Form Validation

In "Reading Form Values from an ASP Page," you saw an example of creating an HTML page to display a form to collect the user's name and birth date. This HTML page was named BirthdateForm.htm and is presented in Listing 8.6. We also created an ASP page that read the form field values, calculated the number of days between the user's date of birth and the current date, and displayed this calculation, as well as the user's name and birth date. This ASP page, named YourAge.asp, is available for review in Listing 8.6.

Suppose that in the Birth date form field, the user entered an ill-formatted date. For the moment, let's assume that the user entered Thirty years ago as the value for the Birth date field. What would happen? What should happen?

The form would submit normally and would pass the "Thirty years ago" as the value of the Birth date field. The ASP page would read in the form field value with no problem but would generate an error on line 10 of Listing 8.6 when trying to use the DateDiff function. The DateDiff function, which we discussed on Day 5, expects properly formatted dates as its parameters and generates an error if improperly formatted dates are used.

Now that we know what *will* happen, what *should* happen instead? It would be nice to be able to determine whether any form field values were improperly formatted *before* the form was submitted. If any form field values were incorrectly formatted, you would want to alert the user and not allow the user to submit the form until the form field values were properly formatted.

Checking the user's form fields for validity *before* the form is submitted is known as *client-side form validation*: the process of using a client-side scripting language, such as JavaScript, to validate form fields.

Client-side form validation can be bewildering for those who do not have a solid programming background. Client-side form validation scripting requires the use of a client-side scripting language. The only client-side scripting language supported by both Internet Explorer and Netscape Navigator is JavaScript, which is similar in syntax to the C programming language.

We will not discuss client-side form validation in detail. Many great books are dedicated to this topic, such as *Sams Teach Yourself JavaScript 1.3 in 24 Hours*. Form validation can also occur on the web server. This type of form validation is referred to as *server-side form validation* and, like client-side form validation, it serves as a means to ensuring proper form field entries. *Server-side form validation* checks the formatting of the form fields *after* the form is submitted. With server-side form validation, it is the form processing script's responsibility to guarantee that the form fields have the proper formatting.

> **Tip**
>
> Many HTML editors, such as FrontPage, can be used to automatically enter client-side form validation scripts into your HTML code.

Using the Different Form Fields

The examples in today's lesson have used all four types of form fields. Although we used the various types of form fields, we skimmed over the details of each form field type. This section covers the more intricate details of each type of form field.

> **Caution**
>
> Whenever you want to place a form field within your Web page, make sure that you place it *after* a <FORM> tag and *before* that <FORM> tag's associated closing tag (</FORM>). Netscape Navigator will not display form fields that are not encapsulated by <FORM> ... </FORM>.

There are times when a list box makes more sense than a text box, or when it's easier to use a series of radio buttons as opposed to a series of check boxes. Table 8.2 lists each form field type and discusses what circumstances each form field type is best suited for.

TABLE 8.2 Choosing the Best Form Field Type

Form Field Type	When to Use
Text box	When you need to allow the user to enter a string of characters or a number, the text box is the best option. If, however, the input is restricted, such as in the case with a user choosing his state of residency, it may be wiser to use a list box or a series of radio buttons.
List box	If you want to restrict the user to selecting an item among a set of acceptable answers, a list box is usually the best choice, especially when the set of acceptable answers is large.
Check box	Anytime you have multiple, related, Yes/No options that can be mixed and matched in any number of ways, you will want to use a series of check boxes. Also, anytime you have a simple Yes/No type question, such as, "Do you want to receive updates on our products via email?", a check box will do nicely.
Radio button	Whenever you have a set of options that are mutually exclusive—that is, only none or one of the options out of the set of options can be selected, radio buttons are the way to go. Radio buttons can also be used in place of list boxes when the number of unique options is not too great.

8

Text Boxes

Text boxes can be created using the INPUT tag. Text boxes are not the only form field type that is created via the INPUT tag: check boxes and radio buttons are created similarly. To specify that you want to create a text box and not a check box or radio button, you must set the INPUT's TYPE property to TEXT. Other important properties are the NAME, SIZE, and VALUE properties. The NAME property, common among all form field types, uniquely identifies the form field.

The form processing script also uses the value of the NAME property. Recall that the form processing script interprets the form field values as a set of name/value pairs. That is, to retrieve the information the user entered into a specific form field, the form processing script must know the form field's name. This name is specified by the NAME property in the INPUT tag in the form creation Web page.

This probably sounds a little confusing. Perhaps an example will clear things up. For this example, we will create a new ASP page that will contain a form. We'll name this ASP page SimpleForm.asp, and set the form's ACTION property to collectInfo.asp. The code for SimpleForm.asp is shown in Listing 8.8. Figure 8.6 displays SimpleForm.asp when viewed through a browser. Note that in Figure 8.6 the user has entered two values into the text boxes.

LISTING 8.8 SimpleForm.asp Creates a Form with Two Form Fields

```
1:  <%@ Language=VBScript %>
2:  <% Option Explicit %>
3:
4:  <HTML>
5:  <BODY>
6:     <FORM METHOD=POST ACTION="collectInfo.asp">
7:        TextBox1:
8:        <INPUT TYPE=TEXT NAME=TextBox1>
9:        <BR>
10:       TextBox2:
11:       <INPUT TYPE=TEXT NAME=TextBox2>
12:       <P>
13:       <INPUT TYPE=SUBMIT>
14:    </FORM>
15: </BODY>
16: </HTML>
```

ANALYSIS Listing 8.8 demonstrates how to create form fields within a form. We start by creating a form using the <FORM> tag (line 6). Whenever you use the <FORM> tag, you should have a closing form tag as well (line 14). The closing form tag, </FORM>, identifies the end of a form. All of your form fields should be placed between the <FORM>and </FORM> tags.

In Listing 8.8 we create two text boxes on lines 8 and 11. Text boxes are created using the <INPUT> tag with its TYPE property set to TEXT. The NAME property is responsible for uniquely identifying each text box. Finally, we add a submit button to our form (line 13). The form created in Listing 8.8 contains two text boxes and a submit button; Figure 8.6 displays the output of Listing 8.8 when viewed through a browser.

When this form is submitted, the user will be redirected to the ASP page

FIGURE 8.6

SimpleForm.asp *when viewed through a browser. The user has entered two values for the text boxes.*

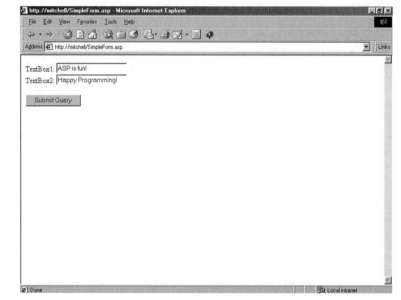

collectInfo.asp. collectInfo.asp can easily read the form variables by using the Request object. If we wanted to store the user's two text box entries into two separate variables, we could do so with some simple code. The code for collectInfo.asp, shown in Listing 8.9, demonstrates how to use the name of the form field to obtain the form field's value.

LISTING 8.9   Store the Values of the Form Fields into Two Variables

```
1:  <%@ Language=VBScript %>
2:  <% Option Explicit %>
3:  <%
4:      'Create two variables to hold the values from
5:      'TextBox1 and TextBox2
6:      Dim strTextBox1, strTextBox2
7:
```

```
 8:     'Read in the form field values using the Request object
 9:     strTextBox1 = Request.Form("TextBox1")
10:     strTextBox2 = Request.Form("TextBox2")
11:     'Output the values of strTextBox1 and strTextBox2
12:     Response.Write "TextBox1 = " & strTextBox1
13:     Response.Write "<BR>TextBox2 = " & strTextBox2
14: %>
```

ANALYSIS The values of strTextBox1 and strTextBox2 in collectInfo.asp depend on what the user entered into the text boxes in SimpleForm.asp. These two variables are declared on line 6, and are assigned the values passed in through the Request.Form collection on lines 9 and 10. In Figure 8.6, the user entered the value ASP is fun! into the first text box (whose NAME property is set to TextBox1), and Happy Programming! into the second (whose NAME property is set to TextBox2). What are the values of the variables in collectInfo.asp? In this example, strTextBox1 would be equal to Happy Programming, and strTextBox2 would be equal to Happy Programming!, exactly the values entered into the form fields.

Besides the NAME and TYPE properties, there are a couple of other interesting text box properties. The first is the VALUE property, which allows you to set the default response in the text box. For example, if you have a text box where you want the user to type in the country she lives in, you might decide to have the text box show United States by default. To do so, all you need to do is create the text box and set the VALUE property correctly:

```
<INPUT TYPE=TEXT NAME=Country VALUE="United States">
```

Another neat property is the SIZE property, which determines how many characters long the text box is. If you create a text box for a user to enter his email address, that text box might need to be 20 characters long. If you want the user to enter a shorter string, perhaps an area code, a text box of length 3 would suffice. If you want to create a small text box to inquire for the user's area code, you might do so with the following code:

```
<INPUT TYPE=TEXT NAME=AreaCode SIZE=3>
```

Note The SIZE property does not force the user's input to be less than a certain length. The SIZE property only determines how many characters wide the text box will be.

In Listing 8.10, you'll find the code for an HTML page that creates a form and displays three text boxes. One text box has its VALUE property set. The other two text boxes have differing SIZE property values. Figure 8.7 illustrates how the browser renders the user of the VALUE and SIZE properties.

LISTING 8.10 Working with the VALUE and SIZE Properties

```
 1:   <HTML>
 2:   <BODY>
 3:     <FORM METHOD=GET ACTION="/scripts/someFile.asp">
 4:       This INPUT box has its VALUE property set to "United States":
 5:       <BR>
 6:       <INPUT TYPE=TEXT NAME=Country VALUE="United States">
 7:       <P>
 8:       This INPUT box has its SIZE property set to 3:<BR>
 9:       <INPUT TYPE=TEXT NAME=AreaCode SIZE=3>
10:       <P>
11:       This INPUT box has its SIZE property set to 25
12:       and its VALUE property set to "Hi, mom!"<BR>
13:       <INPUT TYPE=TEXT NAME=Hi VALUE="Hi, mom!" SIZE=25>
14:     </FORM>
15:   </BODY>
16:   </HTML>
```

ANALYSIS In Listing 8.10 we create three text boxes. Recall that text boxes are created using the <INPUT>tag. In line 6 we create our first text box, setting the VALUE property to United States. The VALUE property, when used with text boxes, indicates the entry a text box will contain by default. When a user visits this page, the first text box will already contain the words United States. The text box created on line 13 also makes use of the VALUE property.

The text boxes created on lines 9 and 13 demonstrate the use of the SIZE property. The SIZE property determines how many characters wide the text box will be. If you expect that your users will only enter a few characters into a given text box, it is a good idea to use the SIZE property to make the text box smaller. When a user sees a small text box, they instantly realize that the text box is to only contain a few characters. On line 9 we query the visitor for their age. Since it is ludicrous to expect this to be more than three characters long, we create the text box with SIZE=3.

Note | The order with which you place properties in a form field is unimportant. For example, these two lines are functionally identical:
`<INPUT NAME=City SIZE=20 VALUE="Chicago" TYPE=TEXT>`
and
`<INPUT VALUE="Boston" TYPE=TEXT SIZE=20 NAME=City>`

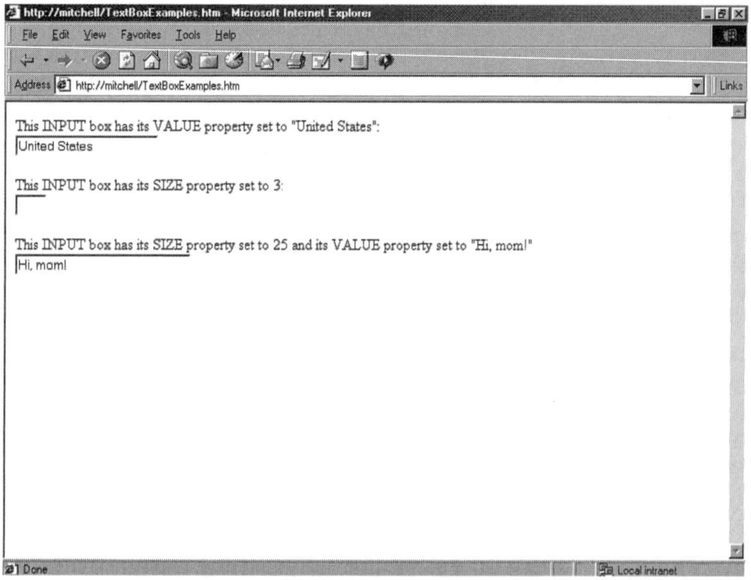

FIGURE 8.7

*Note the text boxes'
differing sizes and
default values.*

List Boxes

There are times when a text box just won't cut it. Perhaps you want to restrict the user to a specific set of choices. For example, if you want users to specify their states of residency, you don't want to use a text box because someone might misspell a state's name or enter 41 as his state of residency. When you need the user to choose a response to a particular set of valid options, it is best to use a list box.

Of all the form field types, the list box is the oddball, being the only one that isn't created via the `<INPUT>` tag. Rather, the list box uses two tags, the `<SELECT>` and the `<OPTION>` tags. The `<SELECT>` tag indicates that a list box will be created, whereas each `<OPTION>` tag represents a unique choice for the list box.

The `<SELECT>` tag has two properties that we will discuss: the NAME property and the SIZE property. The NAME property serves the same purpose as with the text box form field type—it uniquely identifies the particular list box. The SIZE property determines how many list box options are shown at one time. The default value for the SIZE property is 1, which means that a list box, by default, will show only one option at a time. Figure 8.8 displays a list box with the default SIZE property and a list box with a SIZE property of 5.

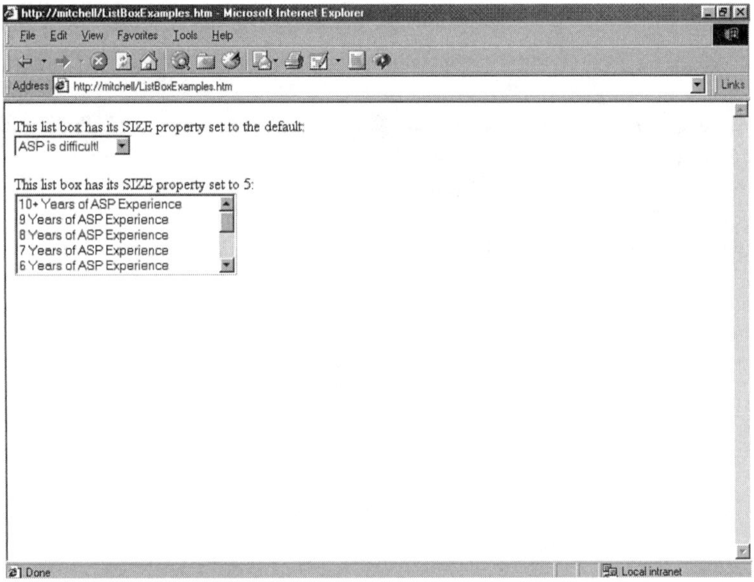

FIGURE **8.8**

Two list boxes with different SIZE *values.*

The <OPTION> tag has two important properties. The first is the VALUE property, which uniquely identifies each separate list box option. When the user selects a list box option and submits the form, the form processing script is passed the string in the VALUE property of the selected list box item. The VALUE property does not determine what is displayed in the list box. Rather, the text that appears *after* the <OPTION> tag is displayed in the list box. Examine the code in Listing 8.11. This is the code that, when viewed through a browser, appears in Figure 8.8.

LISTING 8.11 Understanding the <OPTION> Tag

```
1:  <HTML>
2:  <BODY>
3:    <FORM METHOD=GET ACTION="/scripts/someFile.asp">
4:       This list box has its SIZE property set to the default:
5:       <BR>
6:       <SELECT NAME=ASPopinion>
7:          <OPTION VALUE="5">I like ASP a lot!
8:          <OPTION VALUE="4">ASP sure is neat.
```

```
9:            <OPTION VALUE="3">It's Interesting.
10:           <OPTION VALUE="2">ASP is difficult!
11:           <OPTION VALUE="1">Ah!
12:        </SELECT>
13:        <P>
14:        This list box has its SIZE property set to 5:
15:        <BR>
16:        <SELECT NAME=Experience SIZE=5>
17:           <OPTION VALUE="10">10+ Years of ASP Experience
18:           <OPTION VALUE="9">9 Years of ASP Experience
19:           <OPTION VALUE="8">8 Years of ASP Experience
20:           <OPTION VALUE="7">7 Years of ASP Experience
21:           <OPTION VALUE="6">6 Years of ASP Experience
22:           <OPTION VALUE="5">5 Years of ASP Experience
23:           <OPTION VALUE="4">4 Years of ASP Experience
24:           <OPTION VALUE="3">3 Years of ASP Experience
25:           <OPTION VALUE="2">2 Years of ASP Experience
26:           <OPTION VALUE="1">1 Year of ASP Experience
27:           <OPTION VALUE="0">Less than a year of ASP Experience
28:        </SELECT>
29:     </FORM>
30: </BODY>
31: </HTML>
```

ANALYSIS   If you compare the code in Listing 8.11 to the output shown in Figure 8.8, you'll notice that the text after the <OPTION> tag is displayed in the list box. Look at line 7 in Listing 8.11 and the first list box in Figure 8.8. Notice how the text in the list box reads: I like ASP a lot! This is, not coincidentally, the text that follows after the <OPTION> tag.

The text that is displayed and the text that is sent to the form processing script when the form is submitted can be two completely different values. The form processing script is sent the value in the <OPTION> tag's VALUE property, not what is displayed as the list box's text in the browser. To help you understand this concept, let's look at an example. The following code creates a simple list box that contains two options, Yes and No. The <OPTION> tags that define these two options each have a unique VALUE.

```
<FORM METHOD=POST ACTION="/scripts/processListBox.asp">
    <SELECT NAME=YesOrNo SIZE=1>
        <OPTION VALUE="YesChoice">Yes
        <OPTION VALUE="NoChoice">No
    </SELECT>
    <P>
    <INPUT TYPE=SUBMIT VALUE="Voice your Opinion!">
</FORM>
```

The form processing script, `/scripts/processListBox.asp`, could determine what list box option was selected with `Request.Form("YesOrNo")`. YesOrNo is the value of the `<SELECT>` tag's NAME property and is what the form processing script would use to refer to the list box. The value of `Request.Form("YesOrNo")` would depend on what list box option the user chooses. If the user chooses Yes, `Request.Form("YesOrNo")` would be equal to YesChoice. If, on the other hand, the user chooses the option labeled No, `Request.Form("YesOrNo")` would be equal to NoChoice.

> **Note**
>
> When you want to read the value of a list box in the form processing script, you need to refer to it by the NAME property in the `<SELECT>` tag. The value of the list box is equivalent to the VALUE property of the selected list box option. We will discuss retrieving the list box values in form processing scripts in much more detail during Day 9.

One other interesting property for `<OPTION>` tags deserves mentioning. Notice that in a list box, the option selected by default is the first `<OPTION>` tag. You can change that by using the SELECTED property of the `<OPTION>` tag. Just place the word SELECTED within the `<OPTION>` tag that you want to have selected by default. If you created a list box like the following:

```
<FORM>
    <SELECT NAME=DefaultTest>
        <OPTION VALUE="1">1GuyFromRolla
        <OPTION VALUE="2">2GuysFromRolla
        <OPTION VALUE="3">3GuysFromRolla
        <OPTION VALUE="4" SELECTED>4GuysFromRolla
    </SELECT>
</FORM>
```

the preceding code, if viewed through a browser, would have the last list box option selected by default.

Check Boxes

Suppose that you were asked to create a way for a large eCommerce Web site to ascertain the interests of its visitors. You might want to know what product lines customers are interested in. Rather than asking the user to type into a text box what product lines they are interested in, it would make more sense to use a series of check boxes to limit the choices to those that make sense for your business. Further, check boxes are useful if there is a group of related Yes/No type questions that are not mutually exclusive. That is, there are a number of Yes/No type questions, and the user should be able to answer each question in the affirmative or negative.

8

For the user interests example, you might ask the users to choose what product lines they are interested in. You then might list several product lines such as Home Electronics, Major Appliances, and Stereos. It would be nice to have a series of check boxes next to each product line name, so that the user could check the product lines that interest them. In this example, we'd have three check boxes, one for each of three product lines.

Check boxes are created with the <INPUT> tag. For a check box, you need to set the TYPE property to TYPE=CHECKBOX. The NAME property is slightly different for a check box. Rather than having a unique NAME for each check box, you can group check boxes by giving them all the same NAME. In the product line example, you would want to give all three check boxes the same NAME. The VALUE property needs to be unique among check boxes that have the same NAME. The VALUE property is what the form processing script will receive when referring to the check box group. This topic will be covered in more detail on Day 9.

Let's write some HTML to create a form to query users about their interests in the three product lines. The code will create three check boxes. When creating a check box, the <INPUT> tag only creates the check box. You need to use HTML to label the check box. Listing 8.12, when viewed through a browser, can be seen in Figure 8.9.

LISTING 8.12   Users Can Select Their Interests Via a Series of Checkboxes.

```
 1:  <HTML>
 2:  <BODY>
 3:      <FORM METHOD=POST ACTION="/scripts/someFile.asp">
 4:          What Product Lines are you Interested in?<BR>
 5:          <INPUT TYPE=CHECKBOX NAME=ProductLine VALUE=HomeElectronics>
 6:          Home Electronics
 7:          <BR>
 8:          <INPUT TYPE=CHECKBOX NAME=ProductLine VALUE=MajorAppliances>
 9:          Major Appliances
10:          <BR>
11:          <INPUT TYPE=CHECKBOX NAME=ProductLine VALUE=Stereos>
12:          Stereos
13:          <P>
14:          <INPUT TYPE=SUBMIT>
15:      </FORM>
16:  </BODY>
17:  </HTML>
```

ANALYSIS Listing 8.12 creates three checkboxes. Recall that checkboxes are created using the <INPUT> tag with the TYPE property set to CHECKBOX. In lines 5, 8, and 11 we create our three related checkboxes, each with the same NAME.

Each checkbox in the group of related checkboxes will be uniquely identified in the form processing script via the INPUT tag's VALUE property.

The INPUT tag simply creates a checkbox; we have to supply our own label for the checkbox. A checkbox's label is denoted by the text that follows the INPUT tag used to create the checkbox. In Listing 8.12, the three checkbox labels are Home Electronics, Major Appliances, and Stereos. Line 5 creates our first checkbox, which, on line 6, is labeled Home Electronics. Note how the other two labels follow each of their respective checkboxes.

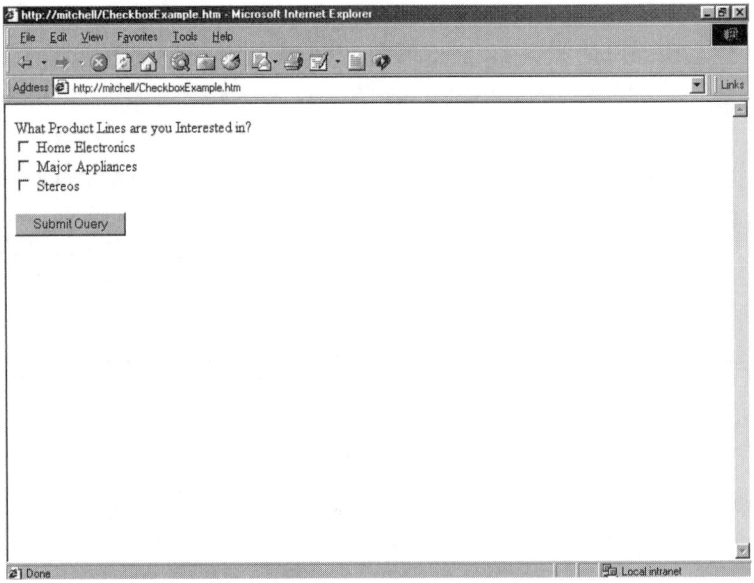

FIGURE 8.9

Three related check boxes.

Tip

Related check boxes should all have their NAME property set to the same value. Their VALUE properties should differ, though. The NAME is what uniquely identifies each check box grouping, and the VALUE is what uniquely identifies each check box within a group of check boxes.

Notice that the check boxes are unchecked by default. There may be times, though, that you would like to have a checkbox checked by default. For example, if the majority of users, in your opinion, will check the checkbox, why not have it checked by default? Another reason to check a checkbox by default is to persuade your users to select that particular option. For example, when you enter contact information at many Web sites, there is often a checkbox labeled, "Receive email information about our products?"

Since the Web site wants to encourage you to receive its product information, this is often checked by default.

If you want to have a check box initially checked when the user loads the HTML page, insert the keyword CHECKED into the <INPUT> tag. The following line would create a check box that is checked by default:

```
<INPUT TYPE=CHECKBOX NAME=ProductLine VALUE=Stereos CHECKED>
```

Radio Buttons

Radio buttons and check boxes are a lot alike. Both radio buttons and check boxes are used to group options that users can choose from. Looking back at the last example, we created a form that listed three product lines and asked users to select which ones they were interested in. Because we wanted to let the users select one, two, or three product lines that they were interested in, we used check boxes to facilitate our information gathering. However, what if we wanted to let the user select only one product line? Perhaps we want to ask users what is their most favorite product line. Check boxes wouldn't work in this situation, but radio buttons would.

Check boxes allow users to select none, one, or many of the available options among a group of related options. Radio buttons, on the other hand, only allow none or one of the options to be selected from a group of options. Let's examine how you can use radio buttons to query users for their favorite product line. The code in Listing 8.13 creates a form with three radio buttons, and the output can be seen in Figure 8.10.

LISTING 8.13   Radio Buttons Allow the User to Select One Option, at Most

```
 1:  <HTML>
 2:  <BODY>
 3:      <FORM METHOD=POST ACTION="/scripts/someFile.asp">
 4:          What Product Lines are you most interested in?<BR>
 5:          <INPUT TYPE=RADIO NAME=ProductLine VALUE=HomeElectronics>
 6:          Home Electronics
 7:          <BR>
 8:          <INPUT TYPE=RADIO NAME=ProductLine VALUE=MajorAppliances>
 9:          Major Appliances
10:          <BR>
11:          <INPUT TYPE=RADIO NAME=ProductLine VALUE=Stereos>
12:          Stereos
13:          <P>
14:          <INPUT TYPE=SUBMIT>
15:      </FORM>
16:  </BODY>
17:  </HTML>
```

ANALYSIS The three radio buttons in Listing 8.13 are related radio buttons; that is, they each share the same NAME (ProductLine). Each radio button is created with an `<INPUT>` tag with its TYPE set to RADIO. Lines 5, 8, and 11 contain the three INPUT tags responsible for creating our three radio buttons.

The text that follows the radio button will be the radio button's label. Our first radio button's label is Home Electronics, and is created in line 6. Major Appliances and Stereos are the other two labels, shown on lines 9 and 12 respectively.

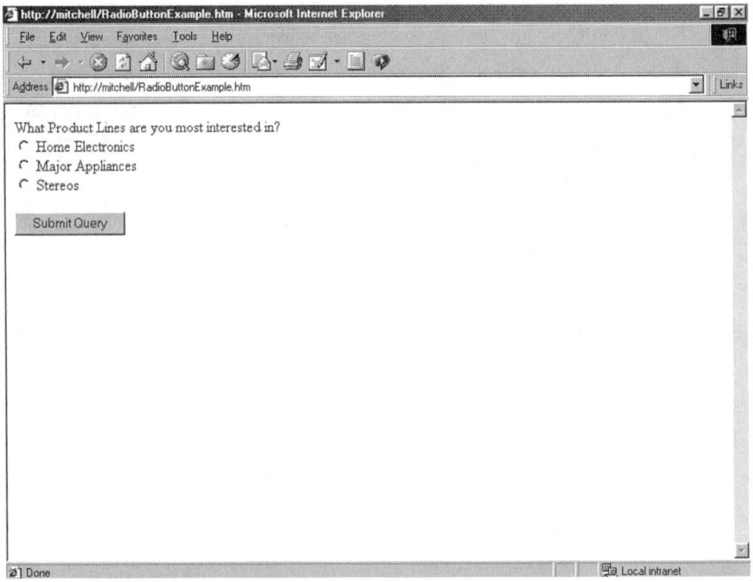

FIGURE 8.10

Radio buttons force the user to choose zero or one of the three options.

Note the syntax of the `<INPUT>` tag when creating a radio button. It looks a lot like the syntax when we created a check box. The only change is the value of the TYPE property from TYPE=CHECKBOX to TYPE=RADIO. Again, with radio buttons, as with check boxes, related radio buttons have their NAME properties equal but different values for their VALUE properties.

You can also use the CHECKED keyword to have a radio button selected by default. Again, its syntax is identical to the syntax for having a check box selected by default. The following line would create a radio button that is checked by default:

```
<INPUT TYPE=RADIO NAME=ProductLine VALUE=Stereos CHECKED>
```

> **Caution**
>
> Because radio buttons only allow one option to be selected among a group of options, you cannot have multiple radio buttons with the CHECKED keyword. If you do, though, don't worry, you won't cause an error. When there are multiple related radio buttons with the CHECK keyword, the *last* radio button will be the one that is selected by default.

We mentioned earlier in this section that radio buttons ensure that the user selects none or one of the related options. However, if you use the CHECKED keyword to have a radio button selected by default, you restrict the user to having to choose an option. Without a radio button selected by default, the user can simply not choose a radio button option. If, however, one of the radio buttons is selected by default, there is no way the user can unselect that option! So, if you use radio buttons for options that must have a response, such as gender, then it is wise to have one of the radio buttons selected by default. That way, the user cannot submit the form without having selected one of the radio button options.

Choosing your Checkboxes and Radio Buttons

Checkboxes and radio buttons are used as a means to select one or many options from a set of related options. It is important, then, that you carefully choose how to label each option, so that each option, in the set of related options, is unique. When using checkboxes and radio buttons, you want to present your user with a series of unique options.

For example, imagine that you wanted to ask the user what parts of the United States they've visited. You could create a series of checkboxes from which the user could select what places he or she has visited. If you made a series of checkboxes titled:

- The South
- The East Coast
- The West
- The Midwest
- The Southeast

what would the users who had visited both the South and the East coast check? Would they check just the Southeast checkbox? Would they check the East Coast and South checkboxes? Or would they check all three? This is why it is important when creating both checkboxes and radio buttons to choose options that are distinct from one another.

Summary

Today's lesson explained how to collect information from your users using forms. Just about every site on the Internet these days allows users to submit information. The information gathered from the user might be as simple as a query for a search engine, or as complex as an order form for an eCommerce site.

We also discussed a number of useful HTML tags in depth and examined how to use <FORM>, <INPUT>, and <SELECT> tags to create forms. A form, when submitted, sends the values entered into its form fields to a form processing script, which can be an ASP page. This form processing script reads the form field values entered by the user and makes decisions based on these values.

Today's lesson also detailed the four types of form fields: text boxes, list boxes, check boxes, and radio buttons. Although each form field type is fairly similar, there are some minor differences in creating and correctly using each of them. Each form field type is also best suited for a specific role. Text boxes are useful when the user needs to enter a string or number. List boxes are needed when there is a certain set of information the user must select from. Check boxes and radio buttons are a must when there is a related group of options you want to have your users select from.

Tomorrow's lesson, Day 9, explores how you can read and process the values of a form using an ASP page as the form processing script.

Q&A

Q When do I need to use a form?

A Anytime you need information from your users, you need to use a form. With some tasks, it is obvious that you would need to use a form. If you wanted to have a form where a user could enter feedback and have it emailed to the Web site administrator, you would definitely need to use a form. There are some less obvious cases, though. In many Internet sites, you'll see a list box that has the various "sections" of the site listed. If you select a section, you are instantly redirected to the corresponding Web page. This uses a form. The rule of thumb is that anytime you need to place a form field, be it a text box, list box, check box, or radio button, you need to use a form.

Q Should I use METHOD=GET or METHOD=POST in my forms?

A That depends on what type of information you plan on collecting from your user. If you plan on having many form fields in your form, it is best to go with METHOD=POST. Setting the METHOD property equal to GET uses the querystring to transfer the form field values. Always strive to keep your querystring and URL less than 255 characters. For this reason, it is often best to use METHOD=POST when you have many form fields.

Also, if you plan on asking your user to enter sensitive data into a form, such as billing information or a password, it is best to use METHOD=POST because, when using METHOD=GET, the form field values are shown in the Address bar.

Personally, I just about always set the METHOD property to POST. There are very few occasions when you *need* to have the form's METHOD property set to GET. We recommend that you, too, follow suit and create your forms with METHOD=POST as the default.

Q Do different browsers display forms differently?

A Because forms are strictly HTML code, it is the browser's responsibility to render a form. Unfortunately, there are slight differences between all browsers in the appearance of the form fields. However, the functionality of the form fields is constant across browsers. One caveat, though: Netscape Navigator requires that *all* form fields be encompassed by <FORM> ... </FORM> tags. That means, if you create an HTML page that contains the following code:

```
<HTML>
<BODY>
  <INPUT TYPE=TEXT NAME=TextBox>
</BODY>
</HTML>
```

Netscape Navigator *won't* display the text box. You would need to change the code so that the <INPUT> tag was encased by a pair of starting and closing <FORM> tags. For the text box to display in Netscape Navigator, you would need to change the code so that it appeared like this:

```
<HTML>
<BODY>
  <FORM>
      <INPUT TYPE=TEXT NAME=TextBox>
  </FORM>
</BODY>
</HTML>
```

Internet Explorer, however, isn't so picky; either code snippet will display a text box in Internet Explorer.

Workshop

The Workshop provides quiz questions to help you solidify your understanding of the material covered and exercises to provide you with experience in using what you've learned. Try to understand the quiz and exercise answers before continuing to tomorrow's lesson. Quiz answers are provided in Appendix A, and exercise answers can be found at `http://www.mcp.com/info`.

Quiz

1. What are the two properties for the `<FORM>` tag?

2. What are the roles of the form creation Web page and the form processing script?

3. How can you create a text box that is 50 characters wide?

4. Can you have the form processing script exist in a different directory than the form creation Web page?

5. What property of the `<INPUT>` and `<SELECT>` tag uniquely identifies each form field, or each group of related form fields?

6. How does a program determine which item the user has selected?

7. How do you create a submit button in a form?

8. How do you create a check box that is checked by default?

9. What property of the `<OPTION>` tag is used to uniquely identify what list box option was selected by the user?

10. How do you create a text box that has a value entered by default?

Exercises

1. Create an HTML page that displays a form to collect users' programming experience. It should ask users to enter their names and select which programming languages they are familiar with. The list of programming languages they can choose from should include: VisualBasic, C, HTML, and Fortran. Feel free to add other programming languages to the list. Users should also be asked to enter how many years of experience they have with computer programming. Take the time to think through the form layout and what form fields will be needed.

2. Write the HTML code needed to produce a form that looks like the form in Figure 8.11.

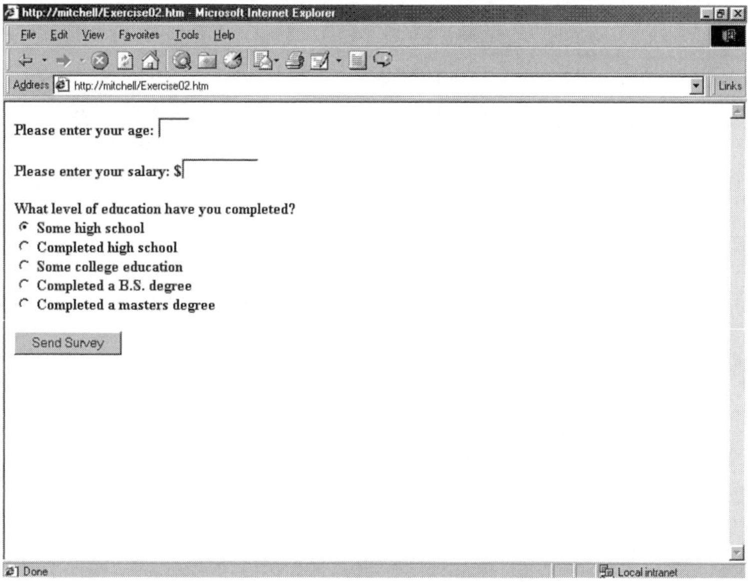

FIGURE 8.11
What HTML code would generate this form?

WEEK 2

DAY 9

Collecting the Form Information

Yesterday's lesson, Day 8, "Communicating with the User," discussed how to collect information by using forms and form fields. You looked at how to use text boxes, list boxes, check boxes, and radio buttons to gather information from users. Whereas yesterday's lesson focused on creating forms for information entry, today's lesson will focus on how to read and process that information.

We will introduce the `Request` object in today's lesson. The `Request` object is a built-in ASP object that is used to read form values in a form processing script. After you obtain the form field values, you can use that input to guide the execution of your form processing script.

Today's lesson is important. Being able to collect and process information from users is one thing that makes ASP so useful. Until yesterday's lesson, the user has not been able to direct the outcome or output of an ASP page. Now, with the use of forms and the `Request` object, the user's input will affect the execution of an ASP script.

Today, you will learn the following:

- How to use the `Request` object to read form field values
- The difference between the `Request.QueryString` and the `Request.Form` collections
- How text box values can be accessed in the form processing script
- How list box values can be accessed in the form processing script
- How check box values can be accessed in the form processing script
- How radio button values can be accessed in the form processing script
- How to pass information through the querystring to simulate form data

Retrieving the Results of a Form

Yesterday, you learned how to create forms. These forms gave users the capability to submit input. Recall that two steps are involved when working with forms. The first is to create the form creation Web page, which is the HTML or ASP page that contains the HTML code to display the form. Yesterday's lesson was dedicated to this topic. The second step is to create the form processing script. This is an ASP page that is specified in the form's `ACTION` property.

The form processing script has two main responsibilities:

- Read in the form field values.
- Process this information.

The first responsibility, reading in the form field values, is done using the `Request` object. Before we discuss in detail the process of reading the form field values, let's quickly review the two ways form field values can be passed to the form processing script.

Recall that the form's `METHOD` property determines the way that the form field values are sent to the form processing script. If the `METHOD` property is set to `GET`, the form field values are passed through the querystring. The querystring is a string appended to the end of the URL. For example, if your browser loads up the following URL:

```
http://www.yourserver.com/someFile.asp?Gender=Male&Age=34
```

the querystring is everything to the right of, and including, the question mark (?). Remember that form information is passed as a series of name/value pairs. You can think of it as a variable/value pairing. The names of the two variables passed in the preceding querystring are `Gender` and `Age`. The values of these variables are `Male` and `34`, respectively.

Note

The formatting of the querystring is important. A properly formatted querystring consists of a question mark followed by a list of name/value pairs. Each name/value pair needs to be in the form `VariableName=Value`. Between each name/value pair, there needs to be an ampersand (&). There can be no spaces in the querystring.

9

Caution

If the querystring is improperly formatted, there is no guarantee that the form processing script will read the form field values correctly. This is yet another reason why using `METHOD=POST` is preferred over `METHOD=GET`.

The `METHOD` property does not have to be set to `GET`, though; it can also be set to `POST`. When the `METHOD` property is set to `POST`, the form field values are not passed through the querystring; they are passed in the HTTP headers. (Don't worry about the specifics of how form field values are passed when you set the `METHOD` property to `POST`. Just know that they are "hidden" from view and do not have the same length and formatting restrictions as passing form field values through the querystring.)

Knowing how the information is passed into the form processing script is important. You will write different code if the form has its `METHOD` property set to `GET` than if the `METHOD` property is set to `POST`.

Using the Request Object

To read the values of a form field, you need to use the `Request` object. The `Request` object has four collections in total, but today's lesson only concentrates on two of those four. Table 9.1 summarizes the two collections we will use today.

TABLE 9.1 Useful `Request` Object Collections

Form Collection	When to Use
QueryString	When the form field values are being passed through the querystring, use this collection. So if you create a form with `METHOD=GET`, this is the `Request` collection you'll want to use.
Form	When the form is created with its `METHOD` property set to `POST`, use this `Request` collection.

To use these collections, you use the following syntax:

```
Request.QueryString(variableName)
Request.Form(variableName)
```

The *variableName* is always the NAME property from the form field that you are interested in. For example, let's say that you created a text box in your form creation Web page with its NAME property set to Age. If, in your form processing script, you wanted to save the value of the text box into a variable named iAge, you could do so with the code in Listing 9.1 (assuming that the form's METHOD property was set to GET).

LISTING 9.1   Reading a Text Box Form Field Value Using the Request Object

```
 1: <%@ Language=VBScript %>
 2: <% Option Explicit %>
 3: <%
 4:     'Create a variable named iAge and store
 5:     'into it the form field "Age"
 6:     Dim iAge
 7:     iAge = Request.QueryString("Age")
 8:
 9:     Response.Write "iAge = " & iAge
10: %>
```

ANALYSIS   To read a variable, you just need to use the correct Request collection and specify the NAME of the form field. This is demonstrated on line 7 in Listing 9.1.

Caution

What happens if the form field values are being passed through the querystring and you use the Request.Form collection? What if the form was created with METHOD=POST and you use the Request.QueryString collection?

Using the incorrect collection returns a zero length string. In the preceding example code, if the form was submitted with METHOD=POST, iAge would be equal to an empty string after line 7 in Listing 9.1 was executed.

If you haven't guessed, such a mistake is difficult to debug! For this reason, be careful to use the correct collection when reading form field values.

Remember that the form field values are passed to the form processing script via a string of name/value pairs. Each name and value is separated by an equals sign (=), and each name/value pair is separated from one another with an ampersand (&). For example, the string might look like this:

```
Age=21&Gender=Male
```

You can access each one of these variables separately by using the Request.QueryString or Request.Form collections. What collection you would use depends on the form's METHOD property. It is possible, though, to read the entire string in one shot. To do so, simply specify the collection name. The following code would assign the name/value string passed through the querystring to the variable strFormFieldValues:

```
1:  <%
2:      Dim strFormFieldValues
3:      strFormFieldValues = Request.QueryString
4:  %>
```

If the form field values were sent via the POST METHOD, you would want to modify line 3
to read

```
strFormFieldValues = Request.Form
```

9

Note

> There are only a few scenarios where it's helpful to read the entire
> name/value pairs string. Usually it makes more sense to read one name/value
> pair at a time using the Request.Form(variableName) and
> Request.QueryString(variableName) notation.

One nice thing about collections is that you can easily step through all the items using a
For Each...Next control structure. This control structure was discussed on Day 4,
"Understanding VBScript Control Structures," and is used often with collections. Let's
create two ASP pages, ExampleForm.asp and ListFormValues.asp, which will be a
form creation Web page and a form processing script, respectively. Listing 9.2 shows the
code for ExampleForm.asp, whereas Listing 9.3 shows the code for
ListForumValues.asp.

LISTING 9.2   ExampleForm.asp, Which Creates a Simple Form

```
1:  <HTML>
2:  <BODY>
3:    <FORM METHOD=GET ACTION="ListFormValues.asp">
4:      TextBox1:<BR>
5:      <INPUT TYPE=TEXT NAME=TextBox1>
6:      <P>
7:      TextBox2:<BR>
8:      <INPUT TYPE=TEXT NAME=TextBox2>
9:      <P>
10:      TextBox3:<BR>
11:      <INPUT TYPE=TEXT NAME=TextBox3>
12:      <P>
13:      <INPUT TYPE=SUBMIT VALUE="Submit Form">
14:    </FORM>
15: </BODY>
16: </HTML>
```

ANALYSIS   ExampleForm.asp in Listing 9.2 is fairly straightforward. It simply creates
three text boxes named TextBox1, TextBox2, and TextBox3 (lines 5, 8, and
11, respectively). The form's ACTION property is set to the form processing script,

ListFormValues.asp, in Listing 9.3. When you run this script, go ahead and enter text into each of the text boxes before submitting the form. Note the results of the form processing script.

LISTING 9.3   `ListFormValues.asp` Displays All the Form Field Values

```
 1:  <%@ Language=VBScript %>
 2:  <% Option Explicit %>
 3:  <%
 4:     Dim strName
 5:
 6:     'List the form values in the Request.QueryString collection
 7:     For Each strName in Request.QueryString
 8:        Response.Write strName & " - " & Request.QueryString(strName)
 9:        Response.Write "<BR>"
10:     Next
11: %>
```

ANALYSIS   Pause for a moment and examine Listing 9.3. What are we doing here? First, note that we use the `Request.QueryString` collection. This is because the form in `ExampleForm.asp` was created with `METHOD=GET`. Next, look at the `For Each...Next` loop. This construct loops through the `Request.QueryString` collection one name at a time. Recall that collections are nothing more than a set of name/value pairs. So, if you can obtain the name, you can find the value by querying the collection. That's exactly what we're doing in line 8.

Because `ExampleForm.asp` (see Listing 9.2) contains three form fields, the `For Each... next` loop will execute exactly three times. Table 9.2 demonstrates the states of the variables throughout the three cycles of the loop.

TABLE 9.2   A Step-by-Step Dissection of the `For Each...Next` Loop in Listing 9.3

Loop	Variable	Value
1	strName	TextBox1
	Request.QueryString(strName)	Value of the text box with its NAME property set to TextBox1
2	strName	TextBox2
	Request.QueryString(strName)	Value of the text box with its NAME property set to TextBox2
3	strName	TextBox3
	Request.QueryString(strName)	Value of the text box with its NAME property set to TextBox3

Note that over the course of three iterations, strName is set to each name in the Request.QueryString's name/value pairs. Figure 9.1 demonstrates the output of Listing 9.3. Note that the values in the text boxes in ExampleForm.asp were entered as Active, Server, and Pages. You can ascertain this from inspection of the querystring in Figure 9.1.

FIGURE 9.1

List the values passed in by the form.

Now that you've seen how to use the Request.QueryString and Request.Form collections, we'll let you in on a little secret that will make life much easier. Rather than worrying about which of the two collections to use, use the following syntax:

```
Request("variableName")
```

When you do not specify the collection, the Request object is smart enough to check both collections for you. So, if you create a form with the METHOD property set to either GET or POST and the form contains a text box with its NAME property set to Age, this code will correctly read the value of the form field:

```
<%@ Language=VBScript %>
<% Option Explicit %>
<%
    'Create a variable named iAge and store
    'into it the form field "Age"
    Dim iAge
    iAge = Request("Age")
%>
```

> **Note**
>
> When a collection type is not specified, the `Request` object searches the querystring first. If the variable name isn't found there, the HTTP headers, which contain the form field values when the form uses METHOD=POST, is searched. If the variable name is not found in either place, an empty string is returned.

> **Tip**
>
> Do not explicitly specify the collection name when using the `Request` object to read a form field value. Simply using `Request(variableName)` will find the correct form field value.

Now that we've touched on the basics of the `Request` object, let's examine how you would use the `Request` object to read values from each of the four form field types.

Retrieving Text Box Values

Recall that you create a text box with the `<INPUT>` tag. There are a number of properties you can set to alter the appearance of the text box in the form, but after the form is submitted and the data sent to the form processing script, all you care about is the `NAME` property. The value of the `NAME` property is what you use to reference the value of a particular text box.

Let's say that in the form creation web page, you create a text box with the following code:

```
<INPUT TYPE=TEXT NAME=PhoneNumber">
```

In the form processing script, you would obtain the value of this text box with the following ASP code:

```
<%
   Dim strPhoneNumber
   strPhoneNumber = Request("PhoneNumber")
%>
```

Let's look at an example form processing script that reads in a number of text box values. The first step is to create the form creation Web page. Name this Web page `Adages.htm` and have it display a form that asks for the user's name and three adages. Listing 9.4 shows the code for `Adages.htm`, and Figure 9.2 shows the form with values entered into all the text boxes.

LISTING 9.4 `Adages.htm`, Which Creates Four Text Boxes

```
1:  <HTML>
2:  <BODY>
3:    <FORM METHOD=POST ACTION="ListAdages.asp">
4:      Name: <INPUT TYPE=TEXT NAME=Name>
```

```
 5:      <BR>
 6:
 7:      Please enter three adages:<BR>
 8:      <INPUT TYPE=TEXT NAME=Adage1 SIZE=50><BR>
 9:      <INPUT TYPE=TEXT NAME=Adage2 SIZE=50><BR>
10:      <INPUT TYPE=TEXT NAME=Adage3 SIZE=50><BR>
11:
12:      <P>
13:      <INPUT TYPE=SUBMIT VALUE="Share your Adages">
14:   </FORM>
15: </BODY>
16: </HTML>
```

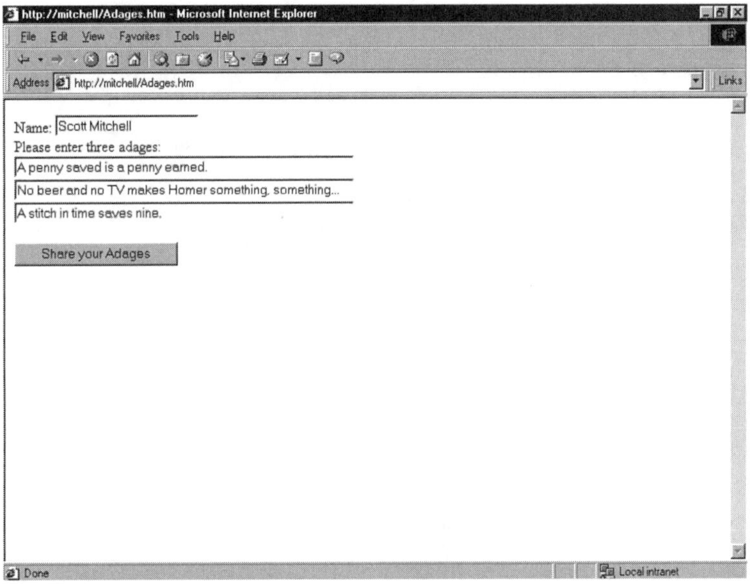

9

FIGURE 9.2

A form with four text boxes.

ANALYSIS Take a few moments to look over Listing 9.4. The form's METHOD property is set to POST (line 3). This means that the form field values will be hidden from the user. If we had used METHOD=GET, the form field values would have been passed through the querystring. In this situation, it was wise to use METHOD=POST because the user might enter some lengthy proverbs! Recall that you should strive to keep the querystring length less than 255 characters. If you are going to be asking for information that could be lengthy, it is best to set the form's METHOD property to POST. Also, using METHOD=POST keeps the users' input out of the querystring. If requesting sensitive information from your users, be sure to set the Form's METHOD property to POST.

The form in Listing 9.4 also creates several text boxes. The first text box prompts the user for her name (line 4), while the next three prompts the user for her three favorite

adages (lines 8 through 10). Finally, on line 13, a submit button is created titled Share
your Adages.

Now let's create the form processing script, ListAdages.asp. This ASP page will read in
the form field values and then print out the user's name and a list of his favorite adages.

It simplifies things if, in your form processing scripts, the first thing you do is read in all
your form field values. After you have completed this step, you can decide what exactly
you want to do with this information. Listing 9.5 shows the code for ListAdages.asp.

LISTING 9.5   ListAdages.asp Uses the Request Object to List the Form Field Values

```
 1: <%@ Language=VBScript %>
 2: <% Option Explicit %>
 3: <%
 4:      'Declare our form field value variables
 5:      Dim strName
 6:      Dim strAdage1, strAdage2, strAdage3
 7:
 8:      'Now, use the Request object to read the
 9:      'form field values into our variables
10:      strName = Request("Name")
11:      strAdage1 = Request("Adage1")
12:      strAdage2 = Request("Adage2")
13:      strAdage3 = Request("Adage3")
14: %>
15: <HTML>
16: <BODY>
17:      Hello <%=strName%>!
18:      <P>Your three favorite adages are:<BR>
19:      <LI><%=strAdage1%>
20:      <LI><%=strAdage2%>
21:      <LI><%=strAdage3%>
22: </BODY>
23: </HTML>
```

ANALYSIS   Note lines 4 through 13. All form processing scripts should start similarly. First,
declare your variables that will hold the form field values. Next, read the form
field values into the variables, using the Request object. By following these starting steps
for every form processing script, you will find your code easier to read and understand,
which leads to less buggy code.

You don't *have* to read your form field values into variables to use them. For example,
line 19 in Listing 9.5 sends the contents of strAdage1 to the browser. StrAdage1 is a
variable that was declared on line 6 and assigned to Request("Adage1") in line 11.

An alternative to declaring form field value variables is to just use the Request object wherever you'd normally use a form field value variable. For example, in line 19, you could have written <%=Request("Adage1")%> and achieved the same output.

However, it is recommended that you always declare and use form field variables in your form processing scripts. This will lead to easier-to-read code.

The output of ListAdages.asp is straightforward. Line 17 outputs the value that the user entered as his name, whereas lines 19 through 21 display the three adages entered by the user. When submitted with the form data shown in Figure 9.2, the output of ListAdages.asp can be seen in Figure 9.3.

FIGURE 9.3

ListAdages.asp *displays the four text box values from* Adages.htm.

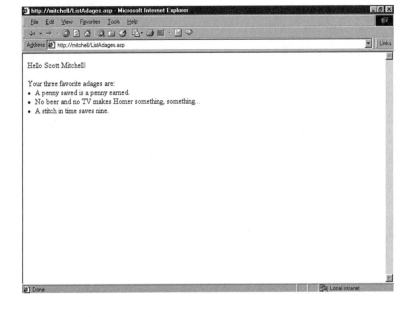

Retrieving List Box Values

Now that you've seen how to read text box values, let's examine how you read list box values. Recall that a list box is created with two HTML tags: <SELECT> and <OPTION>. For each list box, there is one opening and closing <SELECT> tag pair (<SELECT> ... </SELECT>). Inside the opening and closing <SELECT> tag pair, there are several <OPTION> tags. For each selectable choice in the list box, there needs to be an <OPTION> tag.

For example, if you wanted to create a list box that contained the seven days of the week, you would need seven <OPTION> tags. These tags would need to be in between a pair of opening and closing <SELECT> tags. Here is the HTML that would create such a list box:

```
1:  <SELECT NAME=DaysOfTheWeek>
2:    <OPTION VALUE="0">Sunday
3:    <OPTION VALUE="1">Monday
4:    <OPTION VALUE="2">Tuesday
5:    <OPTION VALUE="3">Wednesday
6:    <OPTION VALUE="4">Thursday
7:    <OPTION VALUE="5">Friday
8:    <OPTION VALUE="6">Saturday
9:  </SELECT>
```

The NAME property of the <SELECT> tag uniquely identifies the list box. The VALUE property of the <OPTION> tags uniquely identifies each list box choice. To obtain the list box selection the user made, the form processing script uses the Request object in the following manner:

```
Request(nameOfListBox)
```

The value returned from the preceding snippet of code is the contents of the VALUE property of the <OPTION> tag that was selected. Imagine that a user was shown the days of the week list box and chose Tuesday, and that the following code was placed in the form processing script:

```
Dim iDayOfWeek
iDayOfWeek = Request("DaysOfTheWeek")
```

iDayOfWeek would equal 2. This is because the user selected the Tuesday option, which has its VALUE property set to 2.

> **Note**
>
> The VALUE property of the <OPTION> tag can be set to any string. Usually the VALUE property is set to a number or a short string without any spaces, but this is not required.

On Day 7, "Using the Response Object," we discussed the Response object and how you could use the Redirect method to transfer users from one Web page to another. Using Response.Redirect in conjunction with list boxes, you can create a small form that lists the subsections of your sites. Users can then navigate through the site by selecting the subsection in the list box!

The first step is to create a form that contains the navigation list box. Suppose that you run a news media site, similar to CNN.com or ABCNEWS.com. On the site, you have various types of news, such as US News, World Affairs, Sports, Business, Technology, and others. Listing 9.6 shows the code that creates the list box.

LISTING 9.6   Navigation List Box Is Created Using This HTML Code

```
 1:  <FORM METHOD=POST ACTION="/scripts/Redirect.asp">
 2:      <SELECT NAME=SubsectionURL>
 3:          <OPTION VALUE="/USNews/default.asp">US News
 4:          <OPTION VALUE="/WorldAffairs/default.asp">World Affairs
 5:          <OPTION VALUE="/Business/default.asp">Business
 6:          <OPTION VALUE="/Sports/default.asp">Sports
 7:          <OPTION VALUE="/Technology/default.asp">Technology
 8:      </SELECT>
 9:      <INPUT TYPE=SUBMIT VALUE="Go!">
10:  </FORM>
```

ANALYSIS   The code in Listing 9.6 can be inserted into any HTML or ASP page that you want to show the subsection navigation list box. Right now, you need to cut and paste the preceding code snippet, but on Day 13, "Reading and Writing Files on the Web Server," you will examine an easier alternative. Note that the form's ACTION property is set to an ASP page in the /scripts directory. It is important in this case because if you specified the ACTION tag as simply ACTION="Redirect.asp", you would need to have Redirect.asp in every single directory that contained an HTML or ASP page that used the preceding form. By specifying the ACTION property as ACTION="/scripts/Redirect.asp", you only need one copy of Redirect.asp.

Figure 9.4 shows the code from Listing 9.6 when viewed through a browser. Because the navigation list box would be inserted into a Web page that already has existing content, Figure 9.5 shows a content-rich Web page with the navigation list box in the upper right-hand corner.

Tip   To embed the navigation list box into an HTML page, simply insert the code from Listing 9.6.

To quickly review, the code in Listing 9.6 displays a list box that contains the subsections of your Web site. The user can select an option and click the button labeled Go! to be immediately taken to the chosen subsection. Redirect.asp, the form processing script, needs to read in the selected <OPTION> tag's VALUE parameter and redirect the user to the specified URL by using Response.Redirect.

The code for Redirect.asp can be found in Listing 9.7. Redirect.asp only needs to do two things: read in the form field value for the navigation list box and redirect the user to the URL of the selected subsection. Because you set the <OPTION> tag VALUE properties to the URLs of the various subsections, you can simply redirect the user to the value of

Request("SubsectionURL"). That's exactly what Redirect.asp does, except rather than use Request("SubsectionURL") directly, it reads the value of Request("SubsectionURL") into a variable named strRedirectURL.

FIGURE 9.4

The navigation list box.

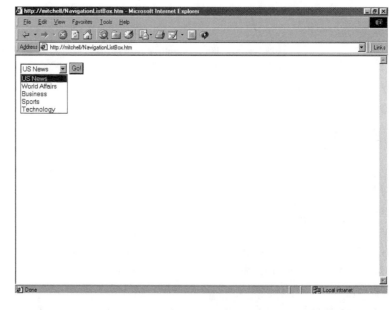

FIGURE 9.5

The navigation list box when embedded in a content-rich HTML page.

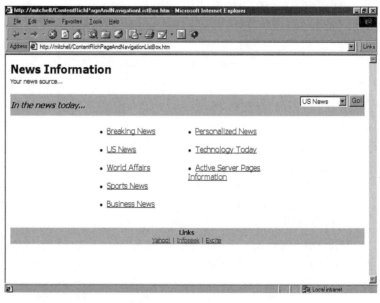

LISTING 9.7   Navigation List Box Is Created Using This HTML Code

```
1:  <%@ Language=VBScript %>
2:  <% Option Explicit %>
3:  <%
4:      'Read in the list box option value
5:      Dim strRedirectURL
6:      strRedirectURL = Request("SubsectionURL")
7:
8:      'Since the value of the list box's OPTION tags
9:      'are URLs, we can simply use Response.Redirect
10:     'to send the user to the URL specified by the
11:     'form field value
12:     Response.Redirect strRedirectURL
13: %>
```

ANALYSIS   Listing 9.7 redirects the user to the Web page they selected in the list box created in Listing 9.6. The URL of the Web page that the user needs to be redirected to is passed in through a form field named SubsectionURL. This form field value is stored into a variable named strRedirectURL (line 6). The Response.Redirect method is then used (line 12) to automatically send the user to the appropriate Web page. We discussed the Response.Redirect method in Day 7, "Using the Response Object."

Note   Response.Redirect automatically sends the user to the URL specified. The Response object was discussed in detail on Day 7.

Retrieving Check Box Values

Recall from yesterday that check boxes are used to group related choices. For example, say that you wanted to ask users what languages they speak. You could list several commonly spoken languages with a check box next to each one. A user could then check all the languages that she speaks.

Check boxes are created using the <INPUT> tag with its TYPE property set to CHECKBOX. Because check boxes are used to group related options, all related check boxes should have identical values for their NAME properties. Related check boxes are uniquely identified from one another by their VALUE properties. When creating related check boxes, be sure to give them all the same NAME but different VALUEs.

Reading check box values in a form processing script is slightly more complicated than reading text box or list box values. Because multiple check boxes can have the same NAME property, you don't receive one single value when you use the following:

Request(*checkboxName*)

When you request a group of related check boxes, you receive a comma-delimited list of the VALUEs of the selected check boxes.

NEW TERM A *comma-delimited* list is a series of items, each item being separated by a comma. If there is only one item, there is no comma present. Some examples of comma-delimited lists include: 2, 4, 8, 19; 34; and Bob, Frank, Sue.

Imagine that you have three check boxes created with the following code:

```
<INPUT TYPE=CHECKBOX NAME=RelatedGroup VALUE=Checkbox1>
Checkbox 1
<BR>
<INPUT TYPE=CHECKBOX NAME=RelatedGroup VALUE=Checkbox2>
Checkbox 2
<BR>
<INPUT TYPE=CHECKBOX NAME=RelatedGroup VALUE=Checkbox3>
Checkbox 3
<BR>
```

If, in the form processing script, you had the following code:

```
<%@ Language=VBScript %>
<% Option Explicit %>
<%
    Dim strRelatedGroupCheckBoxes
    strRelatedGroupCheckBoxes = Request("RelatedGroup")
%>
```

the value of strRelatedGroupCheckBoxes would depend on which check boxes were checked. Imagine that the check boxes with the VALUE properties set to Checkbox1 and Checkbox3 were checked. In this scenario, strRelatedGroupCheckBoxes would be equal to Checkbox1, Checkbox3. If just Checkbox2 were checked, strRelatedGroupCheckBoxes would be equal to Checkbox2. If no check boxes were checked, strRelatedGroupCheckBoxes would be an empty string.

Note Request(checkboxName) returns a comma-delimited list of all the check boxes that have been checked and that have their NAME property equal to checkboxName.

You might be wondering how you can use these comma-delimited lists. Say, for instance, that you wanted to determine whether the user checked a particular check box, or you wanted to display a listing of all the check boxes checked. To accommodate these needs, you can create an array to hold all the selected check boxes. You then use the split function to load the selected check boxes into the array. Examine Listing 9.8 to see how you can accomplish this.

LISTING 9.8 To Determine the Selected Check Boxes, Use an Array and the split Function

```
1:  <%@ Language=VBScript %>
2:  <% Option Explicit %>
3:  <%
4:      Dim strCheckBoxString
5:      strCheckBoxString = Request("Languages")
6:
7:      Dim aCheckBoxArray
8:      aCheckBoxArray = split(strCheckBoxString, ",")
9:  %>
```

ANALYSIS The code in Listing 9.8 is responsible for splitting the comma-delimited list of selected check boxes into an array. Line 5 reads the comma-delimited list of selected check boxes into the variable strCheckBoxString. Line 7 declares aCheckBoxArray as a variant, which later is assigned to the array returned by the split function in line 8.

Recall that split takes a delimited list and parses the list into an array. Line 8, in Listing 9.8, uses the split function as follows:

```
aCheckBoxArray = split(strCheckBoxString, ",")
```

strCheckBoxString is the delimited list, and because it is a comma-delimited list, the second parameter of the split function is a comma. split creates an array and iterates through strCheckBoxString, adding an element to the array for each item in the comma-delimited list. Finally, aCheckBoxArray is set to the array generated by split.

The number of elements in the aCheckBoxArray depends on how many items were in the comma-delimited list strCheckBoxString. If no checkboxes were checked, then strCheckBoxString would be an empty string, containing no items. In this case, the split function would return an array with zero elements; therefore, aCheckBoxArray would have zero elements. If just one check box had been checked, strCheckBoxString would contain the single VALUE property of the checked check box, and the aCheckBoxArray would have just one element. If two or more check boxes were checked, strCheckBoxString would contain a comma-delimited list of all the selected check boxes. In this case, aCheckBoxArray would have as many elements as there were selected check boxes.

Now that you have an array of the checked check boxes, what can you do with it? Well, you'll surely want to be able to iterate through the array. By stepping through the array, you can do things like display the contents of the array or determine whether a particular value is in the array. Let's look at a code snippet that demonstrates how to iterate through the aCheckBoxArray array.

```
1:   'Create a looping variable and step through the array
2:   Dim iLoop
3:   For iLoop = LBound(aCheckBoxArray) to UBound(aCheckBoxArray)
4:      Response.Write aCheckBoxArray(iLoop) & "<BR>"
5:   Next
```

The preceding code steps through aCheckBoxArray one element at a time and prints out the contents of the array. If you want to determine whether a particular check box was checked, you can use similar logic. Say that you presented users with a series of check boxes that were labeled with various country names, and you asked them to check which nations they've visited. Assume that the VALUE property for each check box was the country's name. If you wanted to determine whether the user has visited France, you could use the following code:

```
1:    'What are we looking for?
2:    Dim strFindCheckbox
3:    strFindCheckbox = "France"
4:
5:    Dim iLoop
6:    For iLoop = LBound(aCheckBoxArray) to UBound(aCheckBoxArray)
7:       If strFindCheckbox = aCheckBoxArray(iLoop) then
8:           'The checkbox has been checked.
9:           'Perform whatever processing is needed.
10:      End If
11:  Next
```

If you are a little confused at this point, don't worry. We've just discussed a complex topic. This is the part of forms that most people have some trouble understanding at first. To help clear things up a bit, we are going to look at an example of using a group of related check boxes next. After that, we'll examine an alternative approach to using check boxes that many people have an easier time understanding.

At the beginning of "Retrieving Check Box Values," we talked about using a group of related check boxes to ask users what languages they spoke. Let's implement this example.

The first thing you need to do is create a form creation Web page. Call this Web page Languages.asp. Languages.asp should simply list some popularly spoken languages, presenting a check box next to each language name. The code for Languages.asp can be seen in Listing 9.9. Figure 9.6 shows Languages.asp when viewed through a browser.

LISTING 9.9   Languages.asp Creates a Form That Asks Users What Languages They Speak

```
1:   <HTML>
2:   <BODY>
3:      <FORM METHOD=GET ACTION="ListLanguages.asp">
4:         <B>Please check all of the languages that you speak.</B>
5:         <BR>
```

```
6:          <INPUT TYPE=CHECKBOX NAME=Languages VALUE=English>
7:          English<BR>
8:
9:          <INPUT TYPE=CHECKBOX NAME=Languages VALUE=French>
10:         French<BR>
11:
12:         <INPUT TYPE=CHECKBOX NAME=Languages VALUE=Spanish>
13:         Spanish<BR>
14:
15:         <INPUT TYPE=CHECKBOX NAME=Languages VALUE=German>
16:         German<BR>
17:
18:         <INPUT TYPE=CHECKBOX NAME=Languages VALUE=Italian>
19:         Italian<BR>
20:
21:         <P>
22:         <INPUT TYPE=SUBMIT>
23:      </FORM>
24: </BODY>
25: </HTML>
```

9

FIGURE 9.6

*What languages do
you speak?*

ANALYSIS Examine the code in Listing 9.9. You'll notice that we're using a form with
METHOD=GET. This is so that you can see how the querystring appears when
using a series of check boxes with the same NAME. Each check box has the same NAME
but different VALUE.

For each language that the user speaks, you want to display "Hello, World!" in the selected language. If a user selected English and French as the two languages he speaks, you would want to output the following:

```
Hello, World!
Bonjour, Monde!
```

In `ListLanguages.asp`, the form processing script, you would need to do the following things: Read in the comma-delimited check box string; parse the string into an array; loop through the array; if a particular language was spoken, you would want to output "Hello, World!" in that particular language. This may sound complicated, but if you work on it one step at a time, it becomes much simpler. Let's start with the first step, reading in the comma-delimited check box string:

```
1:  <%@ Language=VBScript %>
2:  <% Option Explicit %>
3:  <%
4:      Dim strLanguagesSpoken
5:      strLanguagesSpoken = Request("Languages")
```

The preceding code snippet is easy to dissect. Line 4 creates a variable named `strLanguagesSpoken` to hold the comma-delimited check box string, and line 5 assigns the check box string to the variable. The second step is to parse the check box string into an array. Use the `split` function just like you did in Listing 9.8:

```
6:      Dim aLanguagesSpoken
7:      aLanguagesSpoken = split(strLanguagesSpoken, ",")
```

Here you create an array named `aLanguagesSpoken` and assign it to the array returned by `split(strLanguagesSpoken, ",")`. At this point, you have an array of all the selected check box VALUEs. Now all you need to do is loop through the array and display "Hello, World!" in the correct language!

```
8:      Dim iLoop
9:      For iLoop = LBound(aLanguagesSpoken) to UBound(aLanguagesSpoken)
10:         Select Case Trim(aLanguagesSpoken(iLoop))
11:             Case "English":
12:                 Response.Write "Hello, World!<BR>"
13:             Case "French":
14:                 Response.Write "Bonjour, Monde!<BR>"
15:             Case "Spanish":
16:                 Response.Write "Halo, Mundo!<BR>"
17:             Case "German":
18:                 Response.Write "Hallo, Welt!<BR>"
19:             Case "Italian":
20:                 Response.Write "Ciao, Mondo!<BR>"
```

```
21:      End Select
22:    Next
23: %>
```

This last section of code is a bit more complex. A For ... Next loop starts on line 9 to loop through the array of selected check boxes. We then use a Select Case to determine the VALUE of the currently selected check box. If the selected check box you're currently working on had its VALUE equal to English, "Hello, World!" is printed. If the selected check box had its VALUE equal to French, Bonjour, Monde! would be displayed. Note that each of the Case statements corresponds to one of the VALUE properties in Listing 9.9.

Now that you've examined ListLanguages.asp in piecemeal, it's time to display the entire, unbroken code. Take the time to look over the code in whole. The more ASP code you work with and read, the more ASP will become like a second language. The complete code for ListLanguages.asp can be found in Listing 9.10. Figure 9.7 depicts some example output for ListLanguages.asp.

LISTING 9.10 ListLanguages.asp Demonstrates How to Iterate Through an Array of Selected Check Boxes

```
 1: <%@ Language=VBScript %>
 2: <% Option Explicit %>
 3: <%
 4:     Dim strLanguagesSpoken
 5:     strLanguagesSpoken = Request("Languages")
 6:
 7:     Dim aLanguagesSpoken
 8:     aLanguagesSpoken = split(strLanguagesSpoken, ",")
 9:
10:     Dim iLoop
11:     For iLoop = LBound(aLanguagesSpoken) to UBound(aLanguagesSpoken)
12:       Select Case Trim(aLanguagesSpoken(iLoop))
13:         Case "English":
14:           Response.Write "Hello, World!<BR>"
15:         Case "French":
16:           Response.Write "Bonjour, Monde!<BR>"
17:         Case "Spanish":
18:           Response.Write "Halo, Mundo!<BR>"
19:         Case "German":
20:           Response.Write "Hallo, Welt!<BR>"
21:         Case "Italian":
22:           Response.Write "Ciao, Mondo!<BR>"
23:       End Select
24:    Next
25: %>
```

> **Caution**
>
> Unfortunately, comma-delimited lists put spaces after each comma. In the preceding example, `strLanguagesSpoken` might equal `English, French, German`. Note the spaces after the commas. When `split` breaks up this comma-delimited list into an array, it doesn't get rid of those spaces, so all the elements in the array *except* for the first one, have a leading space! This is why, in line 12, we use the `Trim` statement. Recall from Day 5, "Using VBScript's Built-in Functions," that the `Trim` statement removes leading and trailing spaces from a string.

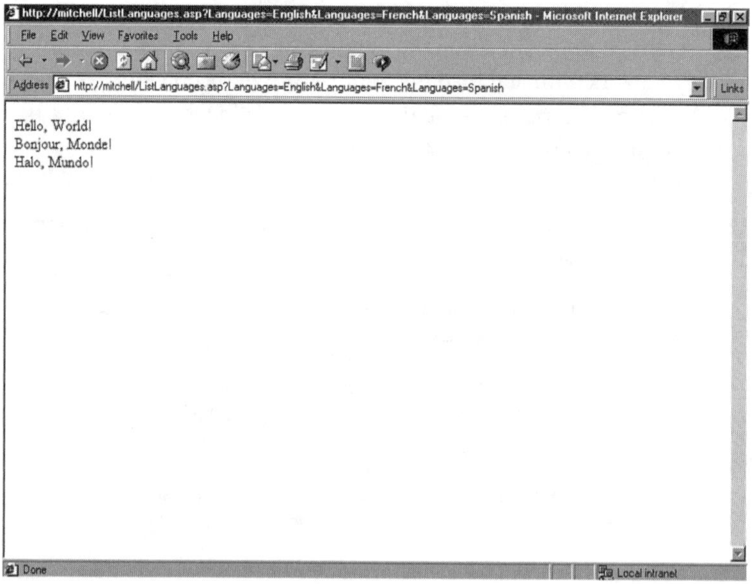

FIGURE 9.7

Output is based on the check box selections.

Note the querystring in Figure 9.7. Whereas the `Request` object returns a comma-delimited list when you have multiple related check boxes selected, the querystring passes multiple name/value pairs. The querystring, in this example, reads:

```
?Languages=English&Languages=French&Languages=Spanish
```

There is an alternative way to using check boxes. Until now, we've used check boxes to group related items. We constructed related check boxes by setting the NAME property to a common value. For a moment, imagine that a group of related items contained only one item. Because you would only want one check box, that sole check box would have a unique NAME property from all other form fields. How would you create such a check box in the form creation Web page? How would you determine whether the check box had been checked in the form processing script?

You would create the checkbox with an <INPUT> tag, like we've been doing. This check box, though, would have a unique value for its NAME property. Let's say that you wanted to create a check box that would ask users whether they like Active Server Pages. The following code creates a single check box:

```
<INPUT TYPE=CHECKBOX NAME=LikeASP VALUE="Yes">Do you like ASP?
```

To determine whether the check box was checked, in the form processing script you would want to use the following code:

```
1:  <%
2:      Dim strLikeASP
3:      strLikeASP = Request("LikeASP")
4:
5:      If strLikeASP = "Yes" then
6:          'The user likes ASP!
7:          Response.Write "I like ASP too!"
8:      Else
9:          'The user does not like ASP...
10:         Response.Write "That's too bad, ASP is fun!"
11:     End If
12: %>
```

Notice that we didn't use the split function or create any arrays. When there is only one check box, Request(*checkboxName*) can only be one of two things: Either an empty string, which means that the user did not check the check box; or a string containing the VALUE of the check box, which indicates that the user did check the check box.

Because you only have one check box to check for, you simply store Request(*checkboxName*) into strLikeASP. Line 5 has an If statement to determine whether the check box was checked. Remember, if the check box was checked, strLikeASP will equal the VALUE property specified in the <INPUT> tag. If, however, the check box was not checked, strLikeASP will be an empty string.

Note

> If you have multiple check boxes with identical NAME properties, or if you have just one check box, Request(checkboxName) returns the same thing: a comma-delimited list of the VALUE properties of the checked check boxes. Of course, in the case where there is one check box with a unique NAME, Request(checkboxName) will have, at most, one item in its comma-delimited list.

Now that you know how to create and process a check box with a unique NAME, what's to stop you from using several more on a page? You can even use a series of check boxes, each with unique NAMEs, rather than giving a series of related check boxes all the same

NAME. Let's reexamine the earlier example, where you asked the users to select which languages they speak.

Listing 9.9 shows the code that displayed the form using related check boxes. Each check box had its NAME property set to Languages but was assigned a unique VALUE. Listing 9.11 displays the same form as Listing 9.9, but instead uses a series of independent check boxes. Each of these check boxes has a unique NAME property.

LISTING 9.11   Here We Use a Series of Check Boxes with Unique NAMEs

```
 1:  <HTML>
 2:  <BODY>
 3:     <FORM METHOD=GET ACTION="ListLanguages2.asp">
 4:        <B>Please check all of the languages that you speak.</B>
 5:        <BR>
 6:        <INPUT TYPE=CHECKBOX NAME=English VALUE=Yes>
 7:        English<BR>
 8:
 9:        <INPUT TYPE=CHECKBOX NAME=French VALUE=Yes>
10:        French<BR>
11:
12:        <INPUT TYPE=CHECKBOX NAME=Spanish VALUE=Yes>
13:        Spanish<BR>
14:
15:        <INPUT TYPE=CHECKBOX NAME=German VALUE=Yes>
16:        German<BR>
17:
18:        <INPUT TYPE=CHECKBOX NAME=Italian VALUE=Yes>
19:        Italian<BR>
20:
21:        <P>
22:        <INPUT TYPE=SUBMIT>
23:     </FORM>
24:  </BODY>
25:  </HTML>
```

ANALYSIS   The code in Listing 9.11 differs from Listing 9.9 only in the NAME and VALUE properties for each of the check boxes. This change in Listing 9.11 does not affect the display of the form through a browser. To see how Listing 9.11 appears when viewed through a browser, refer to Figure 9.6.

The form processing script needs to be modified as well. Rather than creating an array using split, as in Listing 9.10, you will now read in one check box form field value at a time using Request(checkboxName). Rather than using a For ... Next loop to step through the check boxes, as in Listing 9.10, you will now have an If statement for each check box to determine whether that particular check box was checked. The revised code for the form processing script can be seen in Listing 9.12.

LISTING 9.12   Here We Determine Which Check Boxes Were Checked

```
 1:  <%@ Language=VBScript %>
 2:  <% Option Explicit %>
 3:  <%
 4:      'Create a variable for each checkbox
 5:      Dim strEnglish, strFrench, strSpanish
 6:      Dim strGerman, strItalian
 7:
 8:      'Read in the checkbox values
 9:      strEnglish = Request("English")
10:      strFrench = Request("French")
11:      strSpanish = Request("Spanish")
12:      strGerman = Request("German")
13:      strItalian = Request("Italian")
14:
15:      'Now determine which checkboxes were checked
16:      'We will use five If statements to do this.
17:      If strEnglish = "Yes" then
18:          Response.Write "Hello, World!<BR>"
19:      End If
20:
21:      If strFrench = "Yes" then
22:          Response.Write "Bonjour, Monde!<BR>"
23:      End If
24:
25:      If strSpanish = "Yes" then
26:          Response.Write "Halo, Mundo!<BR>"
27:      End If
28:
29:      If strGerman = "Yes" then
30:          Response.Write "Hallo, Welt!<BR>"
31:      End If
32:
33:      If strItalian = "Yes" then
34:          Response.Write "Ciao, Mondo!<BR>"
35:      End If
36: %>
```

ANALYSIS Let's quickly examine Listing 9.12. The first thing it does is create five variables to hold the values of the five check box VALUEs. Lines 9 through 13 use the Request object to read the form field values into the respective variables. Finally, an If statement is applied to determine whether a check box has been checked. If the check box was checked, the respective variable will be equal to the VALUE property, which was set to Yes for all the check boxes.

The output for Listing 9.12 is identical to that of Listing 9.10. The only difference worth noting is the querystring. In Figure 9.7, the querystring is as follows:

```
?Languages=English&Languages=French&Languages=Spanish
```

For each check box checked, there is a name/value pair with its name as Languages. This was because each check box had a similar NAME value, namely Languages. In Figure 9.8, the output of Listing 9.12, the querystring is slightly different:

?English=Yes&French=Yes&Spanish=Yes

Once again, only the check boxes that were checked show up in the querystring. However, because each check box has a unique name, each name in the querystring (English, French, and Spanish) is unique as well.

FIGURE 9.8

Note the name/value pairs in the querystring.

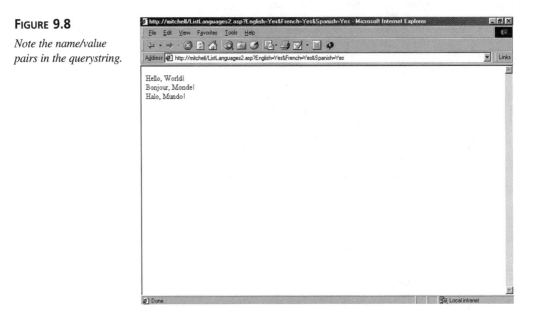

Note

When a check box is checked, its VALUE property is passed to the form processing script. You do not have to explicitly specify the VALUE property for check boxes, though. If you create a check box without the VALUE property, like so:

```
<INPUT TYPE=CHEFCKBOX NAME=MyCheckbox>
```

the VALUE is implicitly set to on. If you had not explicitly set the VALUE property in any of the check boxes in Listing 9.11, you would have to modify Listing 9.12's conditional statements. For example, line 17 in Listing 9.12 would change to the following:

```
If strEnglish = "on" then
```

This is because the VALUE for the check box English would have been implicitly set as on.

You've seen two approaches for determining whether a check box has been checked. With the first approach, we created the related check boxes by using the same NAME but unique VALUEs. We determined which of the related check boxes had been checked by first creating an array using split and then iterating through that array. With the second approach, we gave each check box a unique NAME. To determine which check boxes were checked, we first read in each check box VALUE into a separate variable and then performed an If statement to see whether the variable was an empty string.

9

Note

Note how the two methods to using check boxes differ. One method creates related check boxes with identical NAMEs and unique VALUEs; the other method creates check boxes with unique NAMEs and identical VALUEs.

These two methods differ in the logic they employ to determine what check boxes were checked. In the first method, where we have identical NAMEs and unique VALUEs, we are obtaining a list of check boxes that have been checked. In the second method, where we have unique NAMEs and identical VALUEs, we are examining each check box one at a time, asking whether it has been checked.

You may be wondering what approach is best. Is it better to give related check boxes the same NAME or different NAMEs? Is it wiser to use an array to iterate through the list of checked check boxes, or does it make more sense to use an If statement for each check box to determine whether it's checked?

The choice is up to you. Many people find that using unique NAMEs for each check box is much easier because they don't have to bother with creating and iterating through arrays. Personally, we prefer the former method, but the decision is up to you. There are some rare times when using check boxes with identical NAMEs can lead to more elegant form processing scripts, but these situations are beyond the scope of this book.

Retrieving Radio Button Values

Yesterday's lesson concluded with a discussion of the fourth and final form field type, the radio button. Radio buttons are used when you want to present users with a group of options, from which they can only pick none or one. For example, if you were building an eCommerce site and needed a form for shoppers to enter their billing information, you might use a radio button to ask what type of credit card the shopper wants to use. You would list the credit cards that were acceptable forms of payment, with a radio button next to each one.

Radio buttons are created using the <INPUT> tag with its TYPE property set to RADIO. Related radio buttons are used similarly to related check boxes. It is important that related radio buttons have the same NAME and different VALUEs.

Related radio buttons are a set of radio buttons from which only one radio button can be selected. If you accepted four types of credit cards, you would need four related radio buttons.

> **Tip**
>
> Of all the radio buttons on a Web page that have the same NAME, the user can only choose one. This is why it is important to give related radio buttons the same NAME.

When the form processing script uses Request(*radioButtonName*), it returns the VALUE of the selected radio button option. If no option was selected, Request(*radioButtonName*) returns an empty string.

Radio buttons are good form field types for online questionnaires and surveys. The first step is to create the form creation Web page, which we'll name Questionnaire.asp. The questionnaire will mimic those "career interests" questionnaires we've all seen. This example questionnaire will have four questions with five answers each, ranging from Strongly Disagree to Strongly Agree. The form processing script will collect this information and determine whether the questionnaire-taker would enjoy a career in computer science. Listing 9.13 shows the code for Questionnaire.asp, and Figure 9.9 shows Questionnaire.asp when viewed through a browser.

LISTING 9.13   An Example of Using Radio Buttons

```
1:  <%@ Language=VBScript %>
2:  <HTML>
3:  <BODY>
4:    <FORM METHOD=POST ACTION="QuestionnaireResults.asp">
5:      <B>Please take the time to fill out this questionnaire.</B>
6:      <BR>This will help determine if you would enjoy a
7:      profession as a computer scientist!
8:      <P>
9:
10:     1. I like to work on problems<BR>
11:     <INPUT TYPE=RADIO NAME=Question1 VALUE=4>
12:     Strongly Agree<BR>
13:     <INPUT TYPE=RADIO NAME=Question1 VALUE=3>
14:     Agree<BR>
15:     <INPUT TYPE=RADIO NAME=Question1 VALUE=2 CHECKED>
16:     No Opinion<BR>
17:     <INPUT TYPE=RADIO NAME=Question1 VALUE=1>
18:     Disagree<BR>
```

```
19:     <INPUT TYPE=RADIO NAME=Question1 VALUE=0>
20:     Strongly Disagree<BR>
21:     <P>
22:
23:     2. I find mathematics interesting<BR>
24:     <INPUT TYPE=RADIO NAME=Question2 VALUE=4>
25:     Strongly Agree<BR>
26:     <INPUT TYPE=RADIO NAME=Question2 VALUE=3>
27:     Agree<BR>
28:     <INPUT TYPE=RADIO NAME=Question2 VALUE=2 CHECKED>
29:     No Opinion<BR>
30:     <INPUT TYPE=RADIO NAME=Question2 VALUE=1>
31:     Disagree<BR>
32:     <INPUT TYPE=RADIO NAME=Question2 VALUE=0>
33:     Strongly Disagree<BR>
34:     <P>
35:
36:     3. I enjoy fixing and tinkering with gadgets<BR>
37:     <INPUT TYPE=RADIO NAME=Question3 VALUE=4>
38:     Strongly Agree<BR>
39:     <INPUT TYPE=RADIO NAME=Question3 VALUE=3>
40:     Agree<BR>
41:     <INPUT TYPE=RADIO NAME=Question3 VALUE=2 CHECKED>
42:     No Opinion<BR>
43:     <INPUT TYPE=RADIO NAME=Question3 VALUE=1>
44:     Disagree<BR>
45:     <INPUT TYPE=RADIO NAME=Question3 VALUE=0>
46:     Strongly Disagree<BR>
47:     <P>
48:
49:     4. Being social isn't important to me<BR>
50:     <INPUT TYPE=RADIO NAME=Question4 VALUE=4>
51:     Strongly Agree<BR>
52:     <INPUT TYPE=RADIO NAME=Question4 VALUE=3>
53:     Agree<BR>
54:     <INPUT TYPE=RADIO NAME=Question4 VALUE=2 CHECKED>
55:     No Opinion<BR>
56:     <INPUT TYPE=RADIO NAME=Question4 VALUE=1>
57:     Disagree<BR>
58:     <INPUT TYPE=RADIO NAME=Question4 VALUE=0>
59:     Strongly Disagree<BR>
60:     <P>
61:
62:     <INPUT TYPE=SUBMIT VALUE="Completed Questionnaire">
63:   </FORM>
64: </BODY>
65: </HTML>
```

9

FIGURE 9.9

Is computer science for you?

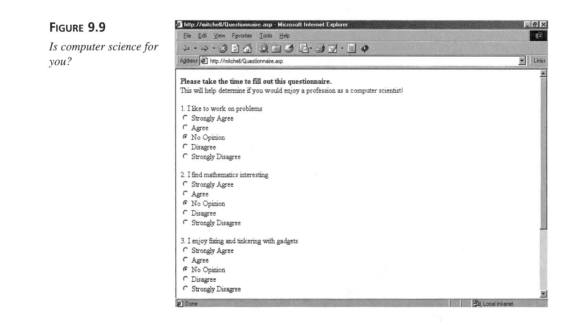

ANALYSIS Listing 9.13 has four related radio button groups, one for each question. Note that each related radio button group has its own common NAME among the individual radio buttons. Also note that in each related radio button group, each individual radio button has a unique VALUE. Because you want to make sure that the person taking the questionnaire answers every question, the CHECKED keyword has No Opinion selected by default. The CHECKED keyword was discussed yesterday.

It's now time to write the form processing script, QuestionnaireResults.asp. In QuestionnaireResults.asp, you want to first read in the answers selected for the four questions. Next, you need to apply some formula to determine whether the person taking the questionnaire would enjoy a career in the computer science field. Note that we set the VALUE for each radio button option to be a number, 0 through 4. If the person taking the questionnaire averages a 3 or higher per question, we'll recommend that they enter the computer science field.

Listing 9.14 contains the code for QuestionnaireResults.asp.

LISTING 9.14 Determine whether the Questionnaire-Taker Should Be a Computer Scientist

```
1:  <%@ Language=VBScript %>
2:  <% Option Explicit %>
3:  <%
4:      'Declare the variables that will hold the
5:      'values for the chosen radio buttons
6:      Dim iQuestion1, iQuestion2
```

```
 7:     Dim iQuestion3, iQuestion4
 8:
 9:     'Read in the selected radio buttons
10:     iQuestion1 = Request("Question1")
11:     iQuestion2 = Request("Question2")
12:     iQuestion3 = Request("Question3")
13:     iQuestion4 = Request("Question4")
14:
15:     'Sum up the Question scores
16:     Dim iSum
17:     iSum = iQuestion1 + iQuestion2 + iQuestion3 + iQuestion4
18:
19:     'Average the questions
20:     Dim iAverage
21:     iAverage = iSum / 4
22:
23:     'If iAverage is greater than or equal to 3, then we
24:     'need to recommend the computer science field!
25:     If iAverage >= 3 then
26:         Response.Write "Computer Science is for you!"
27:     Else
28:         Response.Write "Computer Science is not for everyone..."
29:     End If
30: %>
```

9

ANALYSIS Lines 10 through 13 read in the chosen responses for the four questions. Recall that Request(*radioButtonName*) returns the radio button that the user selected. Line 17 sums up the four questions, and line 21 divides the sum by 4 to obtain the average question value. Finally, line 25 uses an If statement to determine whether the average is greater than or equal to 3.

Today, you've examined reading all four form field types in the form processing scripts. Now that you've looked at each form field type individually, let's focus on an example that combines all four. In this example, you create a system that predicts the user's life expectancy based on a series of questions.

The first step is to create the form creation Web page, LifeExpectancy.asp. This page creates a form in which you ask the user a number of questions concerning age, gender, vitamin usage, and general disposition. These values are read into CalculateLifeExpectancy.asp, the form processing script, which determines the life expectancy of the user. The form processing script displays the life expectancy along with how many estimated seconds the person has left to live.

Listing 9.15 shows the code for LifeExpectancy.asp. Figure 9.10 displays the life expectancy calculation form with some values entered into the form fields.

LISTING 9.15   Calculating One's Life Expectancy Has Never Been So Easy!

```
 1:  <HTML>
 2:  <BODY>
 3:    <FORM METHOD=POST ACTION="CalculateLifeExpectancy.asp">
 4:      <B>Enter the below information to calculate your
 5:      estimated life expectancy!</B><HR>
 6:
 7:      How old are you? <INPUT TYPE=TEXT NAME=Age SIZE=3><BR>
 8:      What is your gender?<BR>
 9:      <INPUT TYPE=RADIO NAME=Gender VALUE=Male CHECKED>
10:      Male<BR>
11:      <INPUT TYPE=RADIO NAME=Gender VALUE=Female>Female
12:      <P>
13:      What vitamins do you take regularly?<BR>
14:      <INPUT TYPE=CHECKBOX NAME=E>Vitamin E<BR>
15:      <INPUT TYPE=CHECKBOX NAME=A>Vitamin A<BR>
16:      <INPUT TYPE=CHECKBOX NAME=B12>Vitamin B12<BR>
17:      <INPUT TYPE=CHECKBOX NAME=C>Vitamin C<BR>
18:      <INPUT TYPE=CHECKBOX NAME=ASP>Vitamin ASP<BR>
19:      <P>
20:      What is your general disposition?<BR>
21:      <SELECT NAME=Attitude>
22:        <OPTION VALUE=Poor>Pessimistic
23:        <OPTION VALUE=Average>Realistic
24:        <OPTION VALUE=High>Optimistic
25:      </SELECT>
26:      <P>
27:      <INPUT TYPE=SUBMIT VALUE="Calculate Life Expectancy">
28:    </FORM>
29:  </BODY>
30:  </HTML>
```

ANALYSIS Note that Listing 9.15 uses each form field type. The form processing script, `CalculateLifeExpectancy.asp`, reads in these values and uses the input to calculate the user's life expectancy. The algorithm used to calculate life expectancy can be seen in Listing 9.16 on lines 17 through 61 and is explained fairly thoroughly with comments. Of course this algorithm is not scientific, so please don't worry if you try out this example and it calculates a short life expectancy for you!

FIGURE 9.10

How long do you have to live?

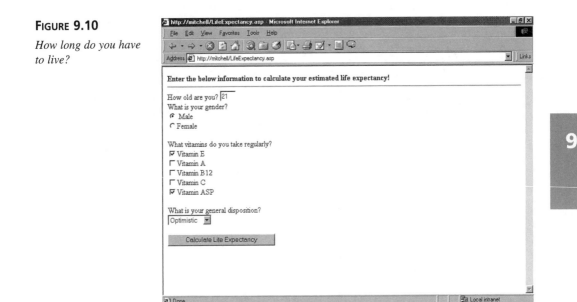

LISTING 9.16   CalculateLifeExpectancy.asp Determines One's Life Expectancy

```
1:  <%@ Language=VBScript %>
2:  <% Option Explicit %>
3:  <%
4:      'Read in the form field values
5:      Dim iAge, strGender, strE, strA
6:      Dim strB12, strC, strASP, strAttitude
7:
8:      iAge = Request("Age")
9:      strGender = Request("Gender")
10:     strE = Request("E")
11:     strA = Request("A")
12:     strB12 = Request("B12")
13:     strC = Request("C")
14:     strASP = Request("ASP")
15:     strAttitude = Request("Attitude")
16:
17:     'We will calculate the user's life expectancy by
18:     'calculating the number of estimated days they have
19:     'left to live.  We assume the average man has
20:     '26,300 days of life, while the average woman has
21:     '28,500 days of life.
22:     const iDaysMale = 26300
23:     const iDaysFemale = 28500
24:
25:     'First, find out how many days the person has currently
```

continues

LISTING 9.16   continued

```
26:    'been alive.  (The users age times 365, since 365 days/year)
27:    Dim iDaysAlive
28:    iDaysAlive = iAge * 365
29:
30:    'Now, find out how many days they have left to live by
31:    'subtracting the expected total days of life by the days
32:    'of life lived thus far (based upon gender)
33:    Dim iDaysToLive
34:
35:    If strGender = "Male" then
36:        iDaysToLive = iDaysMale - iDaysAlive
37:    Else
38:        'The user is a woman
39:        iDaysToLive = iDaysFemale - iDaysAlive
40:    End If
41:
42:    'Now, add to their expected days to live based on what vitamins
43:    'they take regularly.  Add 30 days to life expectancy for each
44:    'vitamin taken regularly
45:    If strE = "on" then iDaysToLive = iDaysToLive + 30
46:    If strA = "on" then iDaysToLive = iDaysToLive + 30
47:    If strB12 = "on" then iDaysToLive = iDaysToLive + 30
48:    If strC = "on" then iDaysToLive = iDaysToLive + 30
49:    If strASP = "on" then iDaysToLive = iDaysToLive + 30
50:
51:    'Now, if their attitude is pessimistic, subtract 365 days from
52:    'their life expectancy.  If it is optimistic, add 365 days.  If
53:    'it is average, do nothing
54:    Select Case strAttitude
55:      Case "Pessimistic":
56:        iDaysToLive = iDaysToLive - 365
57:      Case "Optimistic":
58:        iDaysToLive = iDaysToLive + 365
59:      Case "Average":
60:        'Do nothing
61:    End Select
62:
63:    'We now know how many days we expect the person left to live.
64:    'If this is less than 0, they are lucky!
65:    If iDaysToLive < 0 then
66:      Response.Write "You are lucky to be alive!<BR>"
67:      Response.Write "You are " & Abs(iDaysToLive) & _
68:          " days past your life expectancy!"
69:    Else
```

```
70:     'Display how many days they have left to live
71:     Response.Write "You should live for another " & _
72:        FormatNumber(iDaysToLive,0) & " days.<BR>"
73:
74:     'Display how many seconds they have left to live
75:     '(There are 86,400 seconds in a day
76:     Response.Write "You have " & FormatNumber(iDaysToLive * 86400,0) & _
77:        " seconds left to live.  Make the most of it!"
78:   End If
79: %>
```

9

ANALYSIS Take a few moments to examine the code in Listing 9.16. Note how the first step for all form processing scripts is the same: Read in the form field values. In Listing 9.16 we read in each of the form field values from lines 8 through 15.

The next step is to process the information. In `CalculateLifeExpectancy.asp`, you use the form field values to determine the estimated number of days left to live. To accomplish this, you begin by declaring how many days the average male and female live (lines 22 and 23). Next, you calculate the total number of days the person has lived by multiplying their age by 365, the number of days in a year (line 28). Next, we calculate the total number of days left to live by subtracting the number of days the user has been alive from the number of days the user is expected to live (lines 35 through 40).

We then determine what vitamins the user is taking by determining if the various form field check boxes have been selected. If a check box was checked, the corresponding form field value should equal on. In lines 45 through 49 we add an expected 30 days of life for each vitamin regularly taken by the user. Finally, we take into effect the user's outlook on life. If they are pessimistic, we decrease their life expectancy (line 56), and, if they're optimistic, we increase their life expectancy (line 58).

Once we have calculated the precise number of days the user has left to live, we display a custom message based upon how many days they are expected to live. If the user has lived longer than expected, the code from line 66 through 68 is executed and the user is shown how many days past their life expectancy they've lived. Otherwise, the code from line 70 through line 77 is executed. The user is told how many more days and seconds they are expected to live (lines 71 and 76, respectively).

Figure 9.11 displays the results of the form processing script with the form field values shown in Figure 9.10.

FIGURE 9.11

*The number of days
and seconds left to live.*

Using the Querystring to Send Information

Today's lesson has focused on how to process information in a form processing script. You've examined each of the four form field types and have viewed examples on how to use them. Each example, though, has used a form to send the information to the form processing script. However, you aren't restricted to using forms to send information from one ASP page to another.

An alternative method is to pass information straight through the querystring. Recall that when you use a form with the METHOD property set to GET, the form field values are passed through the querystring in name/value pairs, with each pair separated by an ampersand (&). So, if you wanted to pass information to a form processing script *without* using a form, you could use the querystring to trick the form processing script into thinking it was receiving form field values from a form.

There are many situations when being able to pass information through the querystring is helpful. During Week 3, you'll start to use the querystring to send information to an ASP page quite often! For now, though, a common use for the querystring would be to save your user's time.

Imagine that you needed to know what country your users lived in. You would want to provide a list box with a list of all the nations of the world, from which the user could select her country of residence. The drawback to this approach would be that your users would have to spend time picking through the list of countries to find her own.

What if the majority of visitors to your site resided in the United States? Could you provide a mechanism so that US citizens wouldn't have to take the time to find their country among the list? If you placed a hyperlink above the list box that read, I live in the United States, the majority of your visitors would only have to click a simple link as opposed to finding United States in the list of nations. Listing 9.17 shows an example of using the querystring to expedite the data entry process.

LISTING 9.17   An Example of Passing Information Through the Querystring

```
1:  <%@ Language=VBScript %>
2:  <HTML>
3:  <BODY>
4:    <FORM METHOD=POST ACTION="CountryProcessor.asp">
5:      <B>What country do you live in?</B><BR>
6:      <A HREF="CountryProcessor.asp?Country=UnitedStates">
7:       I live in the United States
8:      </A>
9:      <P>
10:     <SELECT NAME=Country>
11:       <OPTION VALUE="Angola">Angola
12:       <OPTION VALUE="Australia">Australia
13:       <OPTION VALUE="Austria">Austria
14:       ...
15:     </SELECT>
16:     <P>
17:     <INPUT TYPE=SUBMIT>
18:    </FORM>
19: </BODY>
20: </HTML>
```

ANALYSIS   Note the hyperlink created on line 6. When clicked, it loads the form processing script (CountryProcessor.asp), passing in one name/value pair, Country=UnitedStates. Note that the name part of the name/value pair, Country, is the same as the list box's NAME property. Also, if United States were also listed in the list box, you'd expect the VALUE property of the <OPTION> tag to be equal to UnitedStates, the value part of the name/value pair.

Note   When you pass information through the querystring as a supplement to using a form, you are tricking the form processing script into thinking it is receiving information via a form. For this reason, it is vital that the name/value pairs you pass through the querystring match up to the NAME and VALUE properties of your form fields.

Passing information through the querystring is discussed in further detail in Day 10, "Working with the `Request` Object."

Summary

Today's lesson explained how to process the information collected through the use of forms. Collecting information is wasted effort if there is no way to process that information. With the use of an ASP form processing script, though, form field values can be read, and programmatic decisions can be made based on these values.

Today, we discussed the specifics of reading the value of each form field type. Although the general methodology is similar among all four form field types, there are nuances that required examination. You learned how to read the values of text boxes and list boxes. You studied the two approaches you can take to determine what check boxes the user checked. You also looked at how to determine what radio button the user selected out of a group of related radio buttons.

Today's lesson concluded with a discussion on how to send information via the querystring as a complement to using a form. The `Request` object searches the querystring for name/value pairs in a specified format. You can take advantage of this fact and pass information from one ASP page to another using a properly formatted querystring. In later lessons, you will do this frequently!

Tomorrow's lesson explores the `Request` object in greater detail. The `Request` object, aside from reading form field values, also can read cookies and HTTP headers.

Q&A

Q Is there ever a time when I would want to use `Request.QueryString(variableName)` or `Request.Form(variableName)` instead of just `Request(variableName)`?

A If you are reading a single form field value, `Request(variableName)` will do the trick 99% of the time. If you want to use a `For Each...Next` loop to iterate through all the form fields, however, you do need to use the correct collection. The following code causes an error:

```
<%
  Dim strName
  For Each strName in Request
    ...
  Next
%>
```

Rarely will Request(*variableName*) not read a form field value as expected. Simply using Request searches both the QueryString and Form collections. The only time that Request(*variableName*) won't work is when you have two bits of information with the same NAME in *both* the querystring (where the Request.QueryString collection searches) and the HTTP headers (where the Request.Form collection searches).

This can only happen in one scenario. First, create a form. Set the form's METHOD property to POST. Next, create a form field and set its NAME property to some value. Let's choose SomeValue for this example. Now, set the form's ACTION property to

URLOfFormProcessingScript.asp?SomeValue=Something

The problem here is that the NAME SomeValue is being used in both the querystring and through the form that's using METHOD=POST. To read the value from the form, you would need to use Request.Form("SomeValue"), and to read the value from the querystring, you could use either Request("SomeValue") or Request.QueryString("SomeValue").

Q What happens if multiple text boxes or list boxes have non-unique NAME properties?

A When a form is submitted, every single form field is passed to the form processing script in name/value pairs. Even if the form contains several form fields with the same name, each form field receives its own name/value pair. Imagine a form that has three text boxes, each with the NAME TextBox. When the form is submitted, the form processing script will be sent:

TextBox=*Value1*&TextBox=*Value2*&TextBox=*Value3*

where *Value1* is the value of the first text box, *Value2* the value of the second text box, and so on. Note how each name of the name/value pairs is TextBox. This is because each text box in the form was given the same NAME property.

When the Request object is asked to retrieve the value for TextBox, it observes that TextBox is the name of three name/value pairs. Noting this, the Request object returns one string: a comma-delimited list of the three TextBox values. You can iterate through this comma-delimited list by using the split function as shown earlier in today's lesson.

Q When is the best time to use the querystring to pass information from one ASP page to another?

A It is essential to understand that passing information through the querystring cannot be used as a replacement for forms. If you need to collect information from your users, you need to use a form. You can use hyperlinks with information-loaded querystrings to supplement forms. If a form has a common response, a quick hyperlink preloaded with the common response(s) can serve to complement a form.

Passing information through the querystring will be used extensively to help maintain state from one ASP page to another. That topic, however, is for Day 11, "Maintaining Persistent Information on the Web."

Workshop

The Workshop provides quiz questions to help you solidify your understanding of the material covered and exercises to provide you with experience in using what you've learned. Try to understand the quiz and exercise answers before continuing to tomorrow's lesson. Quiz answers are provided in Appendix A, and exercise answers can be found at `http://www.mcp.com/info`.

Quiz

1. What is the difference between the `Request.QueryString` collection and the `Request.Form` collection?

2. How can you read the entire querystring into a single variable?

3. The querystring is made up of name/value pairs. What character separates one name/value pair from another in the querystring?

4. If you created a form with a text box whose `NAME` property was set to `TextBox`, how would you read the contents of the text box into a variable named `strTextBox`?

5. Why do you need to use the `split` function when you create multiple form fields with the identical `NAME` properties?

6. What are related radio buttons?

7. How do you create a group of related radio buttons?

8. What is the syntax needed to loop through all the form field values from a form that had its `METHOD` property set to `POST`?

9. If you fail to explicitly specify the `VALUE` property in a check box, what is it implicitly set to?

10. If you had the following code:
    ```
    What is your gender?<BR>
    <INPUT TYPE=RADIO NAME=Gender VALUE=Male>Male<BR>
    <INPUT TYPE=RADIO NAME=Gender VALUE=Female>Female
    ```

    could the form send the following querystring to the form processing script?

    ```
    Gender=Male&Gender=Female
    ```

Exercises

1. Create a calculator-type form. It should contain three list boxes. The first and third
   list boxes should list the numbers 0 through 9. The middle list box should list the
   following mathematical operators: +, -, *, and /. The user should be able to select
   the two numbers and the operation, submit the form, and be shown the answer.

2. Given the following form, create a form processing script to display all the form
   field values in a nice-looking report.

```
<FORM METHOD=POST ACTION="Report.asp">
  Please enter you customer information:<BR>
  First Name: <INPUT TYPE=TEXT NAME=FirstName><BR>
  Last Name: <INPUT TYPE=TEXT NAME=LastName><BR>
  Phone Number: <INPUT TYPE=TEXT NAME=PhoneNumber><BR>
  <INPUT TYPE=CHECKBOX NAME=Newsletter CHECKED>
  Receive our free newsletter<BR>
  When is the best time to contact you?<BR>
  <INPUT TYPE=RADIO NAME=Contact VALUE=Day CHECKED>Day<BR>
  <INPUT TYPE=RADIO NAME=Contact VALUE=Night>Night<BR>
  <INPUT TYPE=RADIO NAME=Contact VALUE=Never>Never
  <P>
  <INPUT TYPE=SUBMIT>
</FORM>
```

9

DAY **10**

Working with the Request Object

In yesterday's lesson, Day 9, "Collecting the Form Information," you examined how the Request object could be used to read form field values in a form processing script. Specifically, we discussed the Request object's Querystring and Form collections. The Request object, though, can do more than just read form field values. Today's lesson focuses on two different collections of the Request object: the ServerVariables collection and the Cookies collection.

Each time you visit a Web page, your browser sends a good deal of information to the Web server. This information can be accessed by the ServerVariables collection. Also, the Web server has many environment variables that you can access with the ServerVariables collection. We will discuss what information, exactly, is exchanged between the browser and the Web server, and how you can obtain this information. We'll also define what Web server environment variables are and how you can use them in your ASP pages.

The other Request collection we'll examine in today's lesson is the Cookies collection. Through the use of cookies, your Web pages can store small bits of information on the client's computer. These bits of information can be used to identify a return visitor, or to customize the content of your Web pages for each unique visitor.

The `Request` object is useful for reading form field values. However, the `Request` object is not limited to form processing. Today's lesson explores the other functionality inherent in the `Request` object.

Today, you will learn the following:

- What information a browser sends to a Web server
- What HTTP headers are
- How to use the `ServerVariables` collection
- How to determine what browsers are being used to visit your site
- What cookies are
- How to read cookies using the `Request` object
- How to write cookies using the `Response` object

Accessing the HTTP Headers

On Day 1, "Getting Started with Active Server Pages," we discussed the client-server model. The client, in this case a Web browser, communicates with the server, requesting a Web page. The server processes that request and responds by sending the Web page contents to the browser for rendering. Figure 10.1 demonstrates the client-server model graphically.

FIGURE 10.1

The Internet is based on the client-server model.

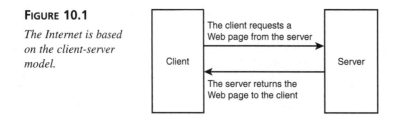

When the client requests a Web page from the server, it not only sends the URL of the Web page requested but also some additional information. This extra information consists of useful facts about the client. For example, this added information can include what browser is being used, what operating system the client is running, and what URL the user just came from. Each piece of additional information is referred to as a *request header*.

NEW TERM A *request header* is a single line of text that your browser sends to the Web server when requesting to view any Web page. A browser can send no headers, or several headers. Mainstream browsers all send a set of common headers.

> **Note**
>
> Headers sent to the Web server from the client (the browser) are called request headers because they're sent when the client requests a particular Web page.

NEW TERM When the server sends back the requested Web page to the client, it also sends a set of headers, known as *response headers*. Response headers are additional bits of information about the Web page being sent to the client. Both the request headers and the response headers are referred to, more generally, as *HTTP headers*.

NEW TERM An *HTTP header* is a single piece of information, sent either from the client to the server, when requesting a page, or from the server to the client, when responding to a page request.

10

> **Note**
>
> HTTP headers do not appear in the Web page that you view on your browser. With Internet Explorer, you can view the response headers that the Web server sends to your browser by loading a Web page and choosing File, Properties from the menu. Figure 10.2 shows the response headers sent by http://www.go.com/ (Protocol, Type, Connection, and so on).
>
> You can read the request headers that the browser sends to the Web server by using the Request object. We'll cover this topic later in "Reading the HTTP Headers with Request.ServerVariables."

FIGURE 10.2

Response headers can be viewed through your browser.

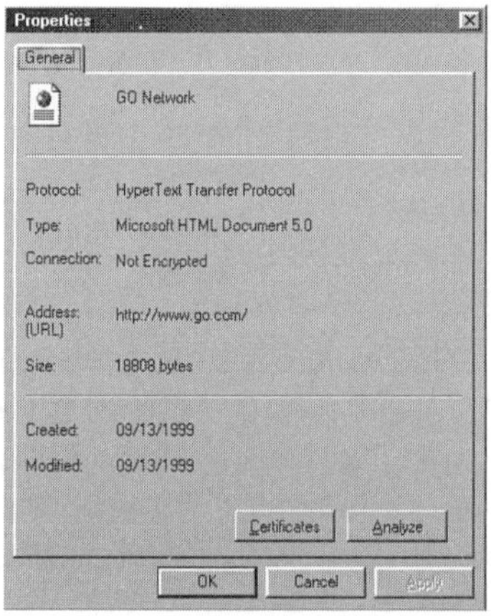

Useful HTTP Headers

Because today's lesson concentrates on the Request object, we will focus on the request headers. Rarely do you need to send a custom response header. However, if you do need to send such a header, you can do so using the AddHeader method of the Response object. The syntax for the AddHeader method is as follows:

```
Response.AddHeader HeaderName, HeaderValue
```

What headers does the browser send to the Web server? Technically, the browser *could* send any header it chose to. Thankfully, there is a standard set of headers that the vast majority of browsers send to the Web server. Of these headers, one of the most useful ones is the User-Agent header.

The User-Agent header contains information about the browser being used and the client's operating system. This information can be used by an ASP page to customize the content based on what browser the visitor is using. For example, Netscape Navigator and Internet Explorer differ in the way they handle *style sheets*. If you wanted to use style sheets on your Web site, you could use ASP to first determine what browser was requesting the ASP page and then tailor the style sheet definitions to correspond with the particular browser.

NEW TERM   *Style sheets* are HTML tags that help determine how Web pages are displayed in the browser. Style sheets were first implemented in Internet Explorer and Netscape Navigator 4. Style sheets are an advanced HTML subject, however, and will not be discussed further in this book.

Another useful header is the Referer header. If the user has reached a Web page via a hyperlink on another Web page, the Referer header will contain the URL of the Web page that had the hyperlink. This header can be useful for reporting purposes because you can track how your visitors are finding your site. Also, if you want to create a Web page that users can only access through a link on your site, you can check the Referer property to make sure that the visitor did not reach the page from an outside Web site.

Table 10.1 contains a listing of all standard HTTP headers that can be read by the Request.ServerVariables.

TABLE 10.1   Standard HTTP Headers

HTTP Header Name	Description
HTTP_ACCEPT	A list of the MIME types the client will accept.
HTTP_ACCEPT_LANGUAGE	What type of languages the browser expects. These are human languages, such as en-us, to represent, English, United States.
HTTP_CONNECTION	The type of connection established between the client and the Web server.

HTTP Header Name	Description
HTTP_HOST	The hostname of the client computer.
HTTP_USER_AGENT	The browser type and version, and operating system information of the client.
HTTP_REFERER	The full URL of the Web page containing the hyperlink used to reach the currently executing ASP page.
HTTP_COOKIE	The cookies sent from the browser.

Reading the HTTP Headers with `Request.ServerVariables`

Using ASP, you can read the headers that the browser sends to the Web server using the `Request` object. Specifically, you use the `ServerVariables` collection of the `Request` object. Recall that collections are used to store name/value pairs, and to obtain the value you need to know the name. To display all the HTTP headers, you can simply issue the following statement:

```
<%= Request.ServerVariables("ALL_RAW")%>
```

This displays the *exact* list of headers sent by the browser to the Web server. To display a formatted list of headers, use the following command:

```
<%= Request.ServerVariables("ALL_HTTP")%>
```

To display a specific HTTP header, use the following form:

```
<%= Request.ServerVariables("HTTP_HeaderName")%>
```

Note that you must prefix the name of the header with `HTTP_`. Also, if the header name contains any dashes (-), you can replace the dash with an underscore (_). If you wanted to display the `User-Agent` header, you could do so with either one of the following two lines of code:

```
1: <%= Request.ServerVariables("HTTP_USER-AGENT")%>
2: <%= Request.ServerVariables("HTTP_USER_AGENT")%>
```

Line 1 requests the HTTP header using the literal name of the `User-Agent` header. Line 2, however, replaces the dash in the header name with an underscore. Either approach generates the same value.

Let's create an ASP page named `HTTPHeaders.asp` that simply displays all the HTTP headers, both in the raw and formatted versions. Listing 10.1 shows the code for `HTTPHeaders.asp`. Figure 10.3 depicts the output of `HTTPHeaders.asp` when viewed through a browser.

10

LISTING 10.1 Request.ServerVariables Can Be Used to Display the HTTP Headers

```
 1: <%@ Language=VBScript %>
 2: <% Option Explicit %>
 3: <HTML>
 4: <BODY>
 5:   These are the unformatted HTTP headers.  These are the <i>exact</i>
 6:   headers that the web server was sent by the browser when this page
 7:   was requested!<BR>
 8:   <PRE>
 9: <%=Request.ServerVariables("ALL_RAW")%>
10:   </PRE>
11:
12:   <P>
13:   These are the formatted HTTP headers.  Note that all headers are
14:   capitalized and begin with the <CODE>HTTP_</CODE> prefix.<BR>
15:   <PRE>
16: <%=Request.ServerVariables("ALL_HTTP")%>
17:   </PRE>
18: </BODY>
19: </HTML>
```

ANALYSIS Listing 10.1 displays the ALL_RAW and ALL_HTTP HTTP headers. To read the HTTP headers, the Request.ServerVariables collection is used. On line 9, we output the contents of the ALL_RAW HTTP header, which contains the *exact* headers sent by the Web browser. On line 16, the contents of the ALL_HTTP HTTP header are displayed. This HTTP header contains a formatted version of the ALL_RAW HTTP header. The output of Listing 10.1, when viewed through a browser, is shown in Figure 10.3.

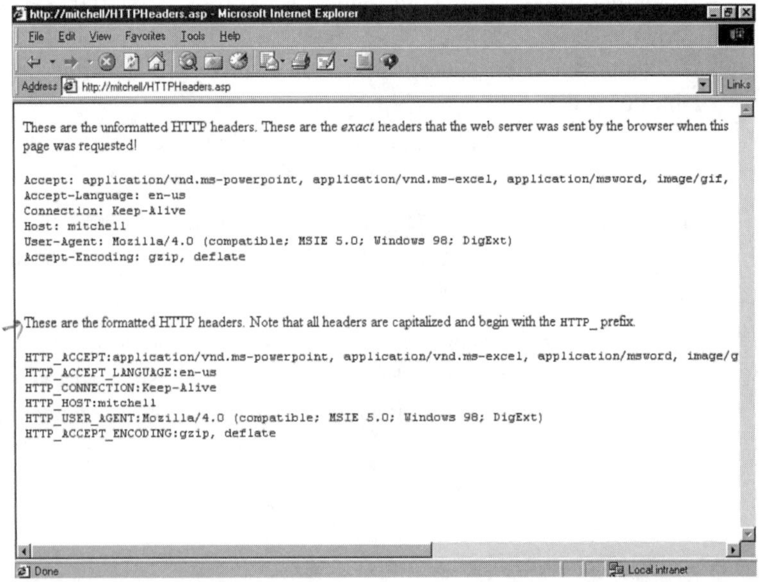

FIGURE 10.3

ASP can read the request headers sent to the Web server.

Note how `Request.ServerVariables("ALL_HTTP")` formats the list of HTTP headers. All header names are capitalized and prefixed by `HTTP_`. Also, all dashes in the header names are replaced with underscores, and the space between the colon at the value of the header is removed. `Request.ServerVariables("ALL_RAW")` performs no formatting to the request headers.

Examine the headers and values present in Figure 10.3. The only header listed in Figure 10.3 that we'll be concentrating on is the `User-Agent` header. From this header, you (and the Web server) can tell that we're using Microsoft Internet Explorer 5.0 (`MSIE 5.0`) and Windows 98. In Listing 10.2, we create a script that reads the `User-Agent` header to determine what browser is being used by the current Web visitor.

You may notice that the `Referer` header is missing. This is because the `Referer` header is only present if the page was reached through a hyperlink on a different Web page. When creating the screen shot, we typed in the URL of the Web page into the browser's Address bar. Figure 10.4 shows that we reached `HTTPHeaders.asp` via a link in `Referer.asp`, which was created with the following code:

```
<A HREF="HTTPHeaders.asp">Click to view HTTPHeader.asp</A>
```

10

FIGURE 10.4

Note the `Referer` *header that was not present in Figure 10.3.*

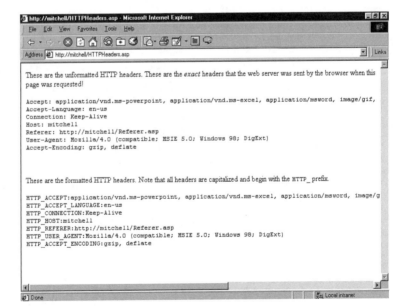

One useful purpose of the `User-Agent` header is that it can be used to determine the visitor's browser type and version, as well as the visitor's operating system. Because Netscape Navigator and Internet Explorer display Web pages differently and because each different browser supports different, unique technologies, there are times when you need to tailor the output of your ASP pages for your visitors based on the type of browser being used.

The User-Agent header differs among the browsers, which makes it a bit tricky to determine what type and version of browser your visitor is using. Fortunately, there is a helpful ASP component that comes standard with ASP. This component, called the Browser Capabilities Component, will be used to determine the visitor's browser specifications on Day 12, "Working with Common ASP Components." For today, however, we will use the User-Agent header.

The User-Agent header follows this standard:

- Both Internet Explorer and Netscape Navigator begin their User-Agent headers with the word Mozilla.

- Netscape Navigator follows the word Mozilla with a forward slash and then the version number. For example, Netscape Navigator Version 4.61 would start off its User-Agent header with Mozilla/4.61.

- Internet Explorer has a set of parameters in a string following Mozilla. This string starts with a parenthesis, and a semicolon delimits each parameter. The second parameter is the characters MSIE followed by the version number.

- Netscape Navigator's User-Agent header also contains a parameterized string surrounded by parentheses. In this string, the operating system is the first parameter.

- Internet Explorer sends the operating system as the third parameter of the parameterized string.

Here are a couple of example User-Agent headers. Line 1 is a User-Agent header from a client running Windows 98 and using Internet Explorer 4.01. Line 2 contains the User-Agent header of a client running Windows NT 5.0 and using Internet Explorer 5.01. Finally, line 3 contains the User-Agent header of a client running Netscape Navigator 4.5 for Windows NT:

```
1: Mozilla/4.0 (compatible; MSIE 4.01; Windows 98)
2: Mozilla/4.0 (compatible; MSIE 5.01; Windows NT 5.0)
3: Mozilla/4.5   (WinNT; I)
```

The code in Listing 10.2 uses an assortment of string manipulation functions, along with split, to determine what type of browser the current visitor is using.

LISTING 10.2   The User-Agent Header Identifies the Visitor's Browser Type and Version

```
1:  <%@ Language=VBScript %>
2:  <% Option Explicit %>
3:  <%
4:      'Read in the User-Agent header
```

```
 5:      Dim strUserAgent
 6:      strUserAgent = Request.ServerVariables("HTTP_USER_AGENT")
 7:
 8:      'If the first seven characters are "Mozilla" then the
 9:      'browser is either Internet Explorer or Netscape Navigator
10:
11:      'If the first seven characters are NOT "Mozilla", then
12:      'we are dealing with some unknown browser type
13:
14:      Dim bolOther, bolIE, bolNN, strVersion, strOS
15:      bolOther = True
16:
17:      If Left(strUserAgent, 7) = "Mozilla" then
18:         'Internet Explorer or Netscape Navigator is being used
19:         bolOther = False
20:      End If
21:
22:      Dim aParenthesisTerms, strParenString
23:
24:      If bolOther = False then
25:         'If the characters "MSIE" are in the User-Agent header,
26:         'then we are dealing with IE
27:         If InStr(1, strUserAgent, "MSIE") > 1 then
28:            bolIE = True
29:            bolNN = False
30:            'The user agent string contains a string surrounded
31:            'by parenthesis.  For IE, the second and third items
32:            'in the parenthesis are the MSIE VersionNumber and OS.
33:
34:            'So, use split to create an array of the terms
35:            strParenString = Mid(strUserAgent, InStr(1,strUserAgent,"(") + 1,
_
36:                               Len(strUserAgent))
37:
38:            aParenthesisTerms = split(strParenString, ";")
39:
40:            strVersion = Right(aParenthesisTerms(1), _
41:                               Len(aParenthesisTerms(1)) - 5)
42:            strOS = aParenthesisTerms(2)
43:            If Right(strOS,1) = ")" then
44:               strOS = Left(strOS, Len(strOS) - 1)
45:            End If
46:         Else
47:            'The user is visiting with Netscape
48:            bolNN = True
49:            bolIE = False
50:            'The OS is represented by the first term in the
51:            'parenthesis, while the version is after
52:            '"Mozilla/" and before the left bracket
53:
54:            'So, use split to create an array of the terms
```

continues

Listing 10.2 continued

```
55:            strParenString = Mid(strUserAgent, InStr(1,strUserAgent,"(") + 1, _
56:                            Len(strUserAgent))
57:
58:            aParenthesisTerms = split(strParenString, ";")
59:
60:            If InStr(1,strUserAgent,"[") > 1 then
61:                strVersion = Mid(strUserAgent, 9, _
62:                            InStr(1,strUserAgent,"[") - 9)
63:            Else
64:                strVersion = Mid(strUserAgent, 9, _
65:                            InStr(1,strUserAgent,"(") - 9)
66:            End If
67:
68:            strOS = aParenthesisTerms(0)
69:            If Right(strOS,1) = ")" then
70:                strOS = Left(strOS, Len(strOS) - 1)
71:            End If
72:
73:        End If
74:    End If
75: %>
76:
77: <HTML>
78: <BODY>
79:   <B>Your undecoded <CODE>User-Agent</CODE> string:</B><BR>
80:   <%=strUserAgent%>
81:   <P>
82:
83: <%
84:   If bolIE then Response.Write "You are using Internet Explorer."
85:   If bolNN then Response.Write "You are using Netscape Navigator."
86:
87:   If bolOther then
88:     Response.Write "You are using a non-standard browser."
89:   Else
90:     Response.Write "<BR>Your browser's version is " & strVersion
91:     Response.Write "<BR>OS: " & strOS
92:   End If
93: %>
94: </BODY>
95: </HTML>
```

Analysis Let's take some time to examine the code in Listing 10.2. The script starts out with reading the User-Agent header in line 6. Line 17 checks to see whether the client is visiting the site with either Netscape Navigator or Internet Explorer. If the visitor is using Netscape Navigator or Internet Explorer, the If statement is entered at line 24. From there, if MSIE is found within the User-Agent header, then the If statement is entered at line 27, or else the client is using Netscape Navigator, and the Else statement at line 46 starts processing. We use some of the string functions discussed on Day 5, "Using VBScript's Built-in Functions," to parse out the version and operating system information. Finally, lines 79 through 93 display the browser type and version, as well as the operating system information to the visitor. Figure 10.5 shows the output of Listing 10.2 on my personal computer, which uses Internet Explorer 5.0 and is running Windows 98.

FIGURE 10.5

The User-Agent *header dissected.*

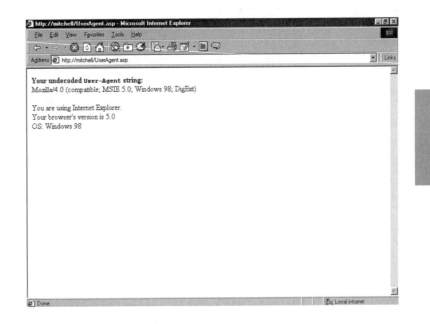

Accessing the Environment Variables

The HTTP headers are useful for obtaining information about the current visitor but tell you nothing about the Web server or the ASP page that is being requested by the client. Imagine that you wanted to determine the full URL of the requested ASP page. You couldn't use the HTTP headers to access this server information because the HTTP headers only communicate information about the client. To obtain such information, you have to use the Web server's *environment variables*.

NEW TERM *Environment variables* are bits of information that the Web server makes available to any program that requests them. Environment variables contain information such as the name of the Web server, the URL of the currently processing ASP page, or the name of the Web server software being used.

Caution

> When you request a single environment variable or HTTP header from the `Request.ServerVariables` collection, *all* the environment variables and HTTP headers are loaded into the collection. Loading all the environment variables and HTTP headers can cause a performance decrease on your Web site.
>
> Because this performance hit is not too great, do not stop using the `Request.ServerVariables` collection altogether. Simply take care to use the collection only when necessary.

Useful Environment Variables

There are many useful environment variables. Anytime you need to gather information about the Web server or an executing ASP script, chances are you can use one of the environment variables.

Throughout today's lesson and the rest of the book, you will use a number of environment variables. You'll find that many built-in ASP objects mirror certain facets of the `Request.ServerVariables` collection. For example, the full querystring, which, as discussed on Day 9, can be displayed by issuing the following command:

```
<%= Request.QueryString%>
```

can also be displayed using the `QUERY_STRING` environment variable. `<%= Request.ServerVariables("QUERY_STRING")%>` will also display the full querystring.

Just about every commonly referenced environment variable can be referenced using one of ASP's intrinsic objects. The environment variables that can only be accessed using the `Request.ServerVariables` collection include miscellaneous information about the Web server, such as the HTTP protocol being used, the Web server's IP address, and the HTTP port number.

Table 10.2 lists some frequently used environment variables.

TABLE 10.2 Commonly Used Environment Variables

Environment Variable	Description
URL	The URL of the ASP page from after `http://www.yourWebServer.com/` up to the querystring
PATH_INFO	The same as the URL environment variable
PATH_TRANSLATED	The full, physical path of the currently executing ASP page
APPL_PHYSICAL_PATH	The physical address of the Web's root directory
QUERY_STRING	The querystring (equivalent to `Request.QueryString`)
SERVER_NAME	The Web server's computer name
SERVER_SOFTWARE	The name of the Web server software; for example, `Microsoft-IIS/5.0`

Reading the Environment Variables Using `Request.ServerVariables`

The environment variables are accessed much like the HTTP headers. The `Request.ServerVariables` collection is used in the following format:

`Request.ServerVariables(environmentVariableName)`

Because `Request.ServerVariables` is a collection, you can display the contents using a `For Each...Next` loop. Because the `ServerVariables` collection contains both environment variables and HTTP headers, both will be displayed when listing the contents of the collection. Listing 10.3, `ListAllServerVariables.asp`, contains ASP code that lists all the items in the `Request.ServerVariables` collection.

LISTING 10.3   The `Request.ServerVariables` Contains all the HTTP Headers and Environment Variables

```
 1:  <%@ Language=VBScript %>
 2:  <% Option Explicit %>
 3:  <%
 4:      'Use a For Each ... Next loop to iterate through
 5:      'the Request.ServerVariables collection
 6:      Dim strName
 7:      For Each strName in Request.ServerVariables
 8:        Response.Write strName & ": " & _
 9:              Request.ServerVariables(strName) & "<BR>"
10:      Next
11: %>
```

ANALYSIS   The code in Listing 10.3 lists all of the environment variables and HTTP headers in the `ServerVariables` collection. Since the HTTP headers and environment variables are stored in a collection, we can list the entire contents of this collection using a `For Each...Next` loop, which we do from lines 7 through 10 in Listing 10.3. Each HTTP header or environment variable name (stored in `strName`) is output, along with the corresponding value, on lines 8 and 9. Figure 10.6 displays the listing of the environment variables and HTTP headers.

Many environment variables do not contain a value. For example, the environment variables prefixed with `CERT` all contain empty strings as their values. This is because these variables are used only when the client and server use *certificates*.

NEW TERM   When a browser and Web server communicate over a secure channel, *certificates* are used to ensure the identity of the client to the server. Certificates are only used when a Secure Socket Layer (SSL) is used on the Web server. This topic is beyond the focus of this book and will not be covered in detail.

10

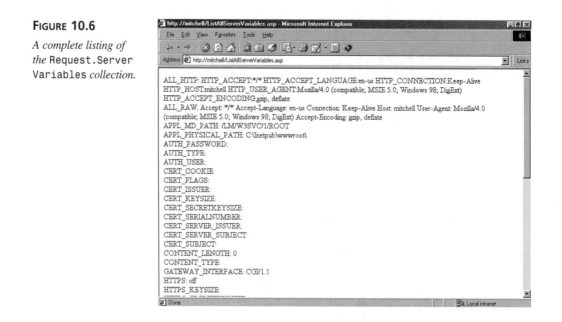

FIGURE 10.6

A complete listing of the Request.Server Variables *collection.*

You cannot expect all environment variables to have values at all times, just like you cannot assume that all HTTP headers will have values at all times. When a Web server is not using SSL, the certificate environment variables are empty strings, much like the Referer HTTP header contains an empty string when the page is not visited via a hyperlink.

Note

Many environment variables are empty strings the majority of the time. There are also some that are never empty strings, such as URL, PATH_INFO, and PATH_TRANSLATED.

If you wanted to display the URL of the currently running ASP page, you would use the URL environment variable. For example, create an ASP page in the directory /scripts named MyASPPage.asp. In MyASPPage.asp, insert the following code:

```
You are visiting
<%=Request.ServerVariables("URL")%>
```

The output of the ASP page would be:

```
You are visiting /scripts/MyASPPage.asp
```

Note that the URL environment variable does not show the http://*webserverName*, simply the full virtual path and filename. Another environment variable, SERVER_NAME, contains the actual hostname of the Web server. You can use the SERVER_NAME environment variable in conjunction with the URL environment variable to retrieve the *full* URL of the ASP page. Listing 10.4 shows an amended MyASPPage.asp that displays the full URL.

LISTING 10.4   Environment Variables Can Determine the URL of an ASP Page

```
 1:  <%@ Language=VBScript %>
 2:  <% Option Explicit %>
 3:  <%
 4:      'Use the URL and SERVER_NAME environment variables
 5:      'to determine the full URL of this ASP page
 6:      Dim strFullURL, strServerName, strDirectoryFileName
 7:      strServerName = Request.ServerVariables("SERVER_NAME")
 8:      strDirectoryFileName = Request.ServerVariables("URL")
 9:
10:      strFullURL = "http://" & strServerName & strDirectoryFileName
11:      Response.Write "You are visiting " & strFullURL
12:  %>
```

ANALYSIS   When viewed through a browser on my computer, the code in Listing 10.4 generates the following output:

```
You are visiting http://mitchell/scripts/MyASPPage.asp
```

On Day 1, we discussed how a Web address maps to a physical address. For example, when the browser requests an HTML or ASP page from my Web server, the Web address might be http://mitchell/SomeDirectory/someASPPage.asp. Of course, someASPPage.asp exists somewhere on my Web server's hard drive. This location on my hard drive is known as the file's physical path.

On Day 13, "Reading and Writing Files on the Web Server," you will use an ASP component that can read and write files on the server. For this component to work properly, the physical address of the file must be known. So, how can you determine the physical address of an ASP page? One method is to use the environment variable PATH_TRANS-LATED. This returns the physical path and filename of the currently executing ASP page. For example, if you created an ASP page named FileName.asp in the /scripts directory and typed in the following code:

```
<% Response.Write Request.ServerVariables("PATH_TRANSLATED") %>
```

the output of FileName.asp, when viewed through a browser, would be:

```
C:\Inetpub\wwwroot\scripts\FileName.asp
```

assuming that you set up your Web site to map the root Web address to C:\Inetpub\wwwroot. While obtaining the full path and filename of the current ASP page, sometimes you need to have *just* the physical address of the root Web address.

10

This value is stored in an environment variable named APPL_PHYSICAL_PATH. Because the APPL_PHYSICAL_PATH environment variable only returns the Web site's root physical address, in a given Web site, the value of APPL_PHYSICAL_PATH won't change from one ASP page to another. If you create an ASP page named RootPhysicalPath.asp in your /scripts directory and type in the following code:

```
<%= Request.ServerVariables("APPL_PHYSICAL_PATH")%>
```

the output would be C:\Inetpub\wwwroot\. If you copied the preceding code into a differently named ASP page in a different directory, you would still receive C:\Inetpub\wwwroot as your output. Because the APPL_PHYSICAL_PATH environment variable returns just the Web's root physical path, the filename and location of the ASP page does not affect the value of the environment variable.

> **Note**
>
> The difference between PATH_TRANSLATED and APPL_PHYSICAL_PATH is that PATH_TRANSLATED obtains the physical path of the executing ASP page. APPL_PHYSICAL_PATH retrieves *just* the root Web's physical address.

In summary, the Request.ServerVariables collection serves two purposes: to read the HTTP headers sent from the browser to the Web server and to read the Web server's environment variables. HTTP headers give you insight into what browser and operating system your users have installed, whereas the environment variables provide information on the Web server. Now that you've examined the ServerVariables collection, the remainder of today's lesson will focus on the Cookies collections.

Using Cookies

As discussed on Day 1, the design of the Internet is based on a client-server model. If a client wants to view a particular HTML or ASP page, the browser and the Web server need to conduct a short discussion with one another. First, a request for a Web page is sent to the Web server; assuming that the page is found, the Web server returns the requested page. After this point, the conversation between the client and server is over.

It is important to understand that this conversation between browser and Web server is an impersonal one. The Web server does not keep tabs on what clients it has spoken with recently, or what requests were made. For this reason, Web sites are often referred to as *stateless*.

NEW TERM An application is said to have *state* if it persists information for each user. In a Web site, this is not the case. For example, if you fill out a form on a Web page and then revisit the form at some later time, the form fields will not contain the values you entered earlier. Rather, the form fields will be blank. Because Web sites lack state, they are said to be *stateless*.

Web sites do not have to be stateless, though. The `Session` object, a built-in ASP object, is designed to persist user information while the user is visiting the Web site. Although the `Session` object is easy to use, it has a couple drawbacks.

First, information stored in the `Session` object is stored in the Web server's memory for the duration of each user's visit. If you have hundreds or thousands of concurrent users visiting your Web site, using the `Session` object can cause a performance hit on your server. Second, the `Session` only maintains state while the user is visiting the site. If you want to maintain state over the course of days, weeks, or years, the `Session` object will not suffice. Despite the `Session` object's drawbacks, it is an easy mechanism to use to maintain state for short periods of time. The `Session` object will be thoroughly discussed tomorrow, Day 11, "Maintaining Persistent Information on the Web."

To persist user information over a lengthy duration, use *cookies*.

10

What Are Cookies?

Cookies are small bits of information, such as strings and numeric values, stored on the client's computer for a specified amount of time. When cookies are created on the client's computer, the developer needs to specify when they expire. After a cookie expires, it will automatically remove itself from the client's computer.

When cookies first appeared in Netscape Navigator 2.0 several years ago, many people viewed cookies as a security threat. Because cookies can save information on your computer, people feared that cookies would remove the enjoyed anonymity of the Internet. This attitude is not widely held today, although, personally, I think there will always be a small set of Web users who will never accept cookies.

Today, the vast majority of Web sites use cookies, saving all sorts of information to prevent the user from having to reenter that information. For example, if you have an account on a Web site such as MyYahoo!, a cookie with your username is saved on your computer so that you don't have to enter your username and password every time you visit the site.

> **Caution**
>
> All browsers provide users with an option to not accept cookies on their computers. All modern browsers accept cookies by default; however, there is no guarantee that all your users will accept cookies.

When one Web site writes a cookie to a client's computer, only that Web site can later read the cookie's value. It is the browser's responsibility to keep track of which Web site created what cookie, and only allow cookies to be read by the proper Web sites.

Cookies can be stored in one of two ways on the client's computer. Let's say that you wanted to store three values on your visitors' computers: the last time they visited your site, their names, and their browser information (via the `User-Agent` HTTP header). One way that these morsels of information could be stored on the client's computer would be to use three separate cookies. You could have cookies named `LastVisit`, `Name`, and `UserAgentString`. The other approach involves *keys*.

NEW TERM Each cookie can optionally have a set of *keys*. Each key can be used to save a tidbit of information. Each cookie can have anywhere from zero to many keys, just like a collection can have zero to many elements. Using keys allows you to create more logically structured cookies. For example, if you wanted to use cookies to save a user's information, it would make more sense logically to create a single cookie named `UserInfomation` with a key for each piece of information you want to save, as opposed to creating unique cookies for each piece of information.

How to Read Cookies Using the `Request` Object

Cookies are stored and read using the HTTP headers. Each time the browser requests a Web page, it sends the cookies that the current Web site created. You can use the `Cookie` HTTP header to read the cookies. For example, if you create an ASP page on your Web server that contains the following code:

```
<%= Request.ServerVariables("COOKIE")%>
```

you will see a listing of all the current cookies on the client's computer that were created by scripts on your Web site. This list is made up of name/value pairs, with each name and value separated by an equals sign (=), and each name/value pair separated from one another by a semicolon. Thankfully, you don't have to parse the cookie values out of this environment variable—the `Request` object already does this for you!

The `Request` object contains yet another collection, the `Cookies` collection. This collection is used to read the values of cookies, and, because it is a collection, the syntax to read a cookie is as follows:

```
Request.Cookies(cookieName)[(keyName)]
```

Each cookie can have zero to many keys. To determine whether a cookie has keys, use the `HasKeys` method of the `Cookies` collection. For example, suppose that there was a cookie on the client's computer named `UserInformation` that was created on your Web site, and you ran the following code:

```
1:  <%
2:    If Request.Cookies("UserInformation").HasKeys then
3:      Response.Write "UserInformation has keys!"
4:    Else
```

```
5:      Response.Write "UserInformation does not have any keys..."
6:   End If
7: %>
```

On line 2, you access the cookie using `Request.Cookies("UserInformation")` because you are checking the cookie named `UserInformation`. You then use the `HasKeys` property to determine whether the `UserInformation` cookie has any keys. If the `UserInformation` cookie does not exist at all on the client's computer, `HasKeys` will always return `False`.

If a cookie does have keys, you can access the key by first specifying the cookie and then adding (*keyName*). Earlier we discussed using keys to save user information, such as the user's last visit to the site, name, and browser information. If you had a cookie named `UserInformation` that had three keys, `LastVisit`, `Name`, and `UserAgentString`, the following code would display the values of the three keys:

```
1: <%
2:    Response.Write "Last Visit to the site: " & _
3:              Request.Cookies("UserInformation")("LastVisit")
4:    Response.Write "<BR>Your name: " & _
5:              Request.Cookies("UserInformation")("Name")
6:    Response.Write "<BR>User-Agent Information: " & _
7:              Request.Cookies("UserInformation")("UserAgentString")
8: %>
```

Note the syntax for reading key values in lines 3, 5, and 7. You simply specify the cookie name using `Request.Cookies(cookieName)` and then append (*keyName*) to read the key.

Tip

Always strive to use keys. Rather than creating a cookie for each and every bit of information you want to store on your visitors' computers, group the related values into keys and create just one or two actual cookies.

Because `Request.Cookies` is a collection, you can iterate through the entire collection of cookies one item at a time. Listing 10.5 displays the code that will iterate through all the cookies that you've created.

LISTING 10.5   A Listing of Cookies

```
1: <%@ Language=VBScript %>
2: <% Option Explicit %>
3: <%
4:   Dim strCookieName, strKeyName
5:   For Each strCookieName in Request.Cookies
6:     'If the current cookie has keys, we need to iterate
```

continues

Listing 10.5 continued

```
 7:      'through the keys, using a For Each ... Next
 8:      If Request.Cookies(strCookieName).HasKeys then
 9:        For Each strKeyName in Request.Cookies(strCookieName)
10:          Response.Write strCookieName & "(" & _
11:                  strKeyName & ") = " & _
12:                  Request.Cookies(strCookieName)(strKeyName)
13:          Response.Write "<BR>"
14:        Next
15:      Else
16:        'We don't have any keys for this cookie, so just
17:        'display the value of the cookie
18:        Response.Write strCookieName & " = " & _
19:                  Request.Cookies(strCookieName)
20:      End If
21:
22:      Response.Write "<BR>"
23:    Next
24: %>
```

ANALYSIS Line 8 uses the HasKeys property to determine whether the current cookie has any keys. If it does, the code iterates through the keys collection using a For Each ... Next loop, just as with any other collection. If the cookie *does not* have any keys, that is, if HasKeys equals False, then line 17 simply prints out the name and value of the cookie.

Of course, Listing 10.5 won't display anything if you have not created any cookies on the client's computer. Listing 10.6, which is in the following section, "How to Write Cookies Using the Response Object," of today's lesson, contains ASP code that will create the UserInformation cookie we've been discussing. Listing 10.6 creates the UserInformation cookie with its three keys.

How to Write Cookies Using the Response Object

Now that you know how to read cookies from the client's computer, it's about time that you learn how to write them. Earlier today, we discussed response headers—the HTTP headers that the Web server sends to the browser before it sends the actual Web page requested by the client. Cookies are written to the client's computer through the use of the response headers. Therefore, it's not surprising to find that cookies are written to the browser using the Response object.

The Response object, like the Request object, has a Cookies collection. The following code writes a cookie to the client's computer:

```
Response.Cookies("MyFirstCookie") = "Hello, World!"
```

Cookies can contain any simple data type. This includes all data types except for arrays and objects. Cookies can store strings, numbers, dates, currencies, and Boolean values.

You can also use the Response.Cookies collection to create cookies with keys. The following code creates three keys in the cookie MyFirstCookieWithKeys:

```
Response.Cookies("MyFirstCookieWithKeys")("Key1") = 6.5
Response.Cookies("MyFirstCookieWithKeys")("Key2") = "4GuysFromRolla"
Response.Cookies("MyFirstCookieWithKeys")("Key3") = True
```

If you create a cookie and set it to some value and then create keys for that cookie, the cookie's initial value will be erased. A cookie cannot contain both a value and keys. Keys in cookies take precedence over cookie values.

10

Listing 10.5 contains ASP code that displays all the cookies created on a client's computer. Figure 10.7 displays Listing 10.5's output *after* the code in Listing 10.6 has been run. Listing 10.6 creates the cookie UserInformation, a cookie to keep track of a visitor's name, User-Agent header, and last time he visited the site. These three values are each a key in the UserInformation cookie.

LISTING 10.6   Create the UserInformation Cookie and Keys

```
1:  <%@ Language=VBScript %>
2:  <% Option Explicit %>
3:  <%
4:      'Create the UserInformation cookie and
5:      'associated keys
6:
7:      Response.Cookies("UserInformation")("LastVisit") = Now
8:      Response.Cookies("UserInformation")("Name") = "Scott"
9:      Response.Cookies("UserInformation")("UserAgentString") = _
10:             Request.ServerVariables("HTTP_USER_AGENT")
11:
12:     Response.Redirect "ListAllCookies.asp"
13: %>
```

ANALYSIS Listing 10.6 creates a cookie named UserInformation that contains three keys: LastVisit, Name, and UserAgentString. These three keys are set on lines 7 through 10, using the Response.Cookies collection. Next, the user is redirected to ListAllCookies.asp (line 12), the code shown in Listing 10.5 that lists all of the cookies in the Request.Cookies collection. When visiting CreateCookies.asp, the code shown in Listing 10.6, a cookie is created with three keys; the user is then sent to `ListAllCookies.asp`. The output of `ListAllCookies.asp`, when reached through a redirection from `CreateCookies.asp`, is shown in Figure 10.7.

```
http://mitchell/ListAllCookies.asp - Microsoft Internet Explorer
File  Edit  View  Favorites  Tools  Help
Address  http://mitchell/ListAllCookies.asp                        Links

UserInformation(LASTVISIT) = 9/19/99 8:01:58 PM
UserInformation(NAME) = Scott
UserInformation(USERAGENTSTRING) = Mozilla/4.0 (compatible; MSIE 5.0; Windows 98; DigExt)

Done                                              Local intranet
```

> **Note**
>
> The Cookies collections for both the Request and Response objects look strikingly alike. They both have similar syntax. The major difference is that Response.Cookies *writes* cookies to the client's computer, whereas Request.Cookies *reads* cookies from the client's computer.

In "What Are Cookies?" we talked about cookies expiring after a determined amount of time. When a cookie expires, it deletes itself from the client's computer. When creating cookies, you can specify when the cookie should expire using the Expires property. If you do not specify this value, the cookie is set to expire when the user closes his or her browser. That means that the cookie created in Listing 10.6 will delete itself from the user's computer once the user shuts down his or her browser.

If all you want to do is maintain state for the duration of the user's visit to your site, using cookies with the default Expires property is ideal. However, cookies are often used to persist state over days, weeks, or years. To accommodate for this lengthy a period, the Expires property must be set explicitly.

The Expires property expects to receive a specific date when to expire. For example, the following code will set our UserInformation cookie to expire on August 1, 2000:

```
Response.Cookies("UserInformation").Expires = #August 1, 2000#
```

In VBScript, you can specify a literal date by surrounding it with pound signs (#). There are also many other ways that you could specify the expiration date. The following list illustrates other methods of setting the Expires property to a fixed date.

- #January 27, 2001#
- "1/27/2001"
- CDate("1/27/2001")
- DateSerial(2001, 1, 27)

All the methods listed are valid ways to set the Expires property. However, what if you want the cookie to expire a fixed number of days or weeks from the current date? To do this, use the Date function, which was first discussed on Day 5. The Date function allows you to add a number to it to increment or decrement the date value returned. For example, if you wanted to obtain a date five days in the future, Date + 5 would do the trick. Date - 5 would return a date five days in the past.

This syntax is helpful when setting the Expires property of the Cookies collection. Rarely do you want cookies to expire on a specific date. Far more often you want your cookies to expire a certain number of days, weeks, or months in the future. Let's say that you wanted to set the cookie MyCookie to expire in a week from the current date:

```
Response.Cookies("MyCookie").Expires = Date + 7
```

Note

> If the Expires property is set to a date prior to the current date, the cookie will expire when the user closes her browser.

Keep in mind that cookies can only be read by a specified Web site. There is a Domain property that you can set using the Response.Cookies collection. This property, which is equal to your Web site's domain name by default, allows you to enter a different domain name.

The Path property also determines how cookies can be read. This property can be set to allow cookies to only be read by ASP pages in certain directories. By default, this property is set to your Web site's root directory, which allows cookies created by an ASP page existing in any directory to be read by an ASP page existing in any directory.

Caution

It is strongly suggested that you do not change or alter the `Domain` or `Path` properties. If you leave both properties as the defaults, you will have no trouble reading the cookies you've created on your Web site. If you set your `Domain` or `Path` incorrectly, you may not be able to successfully read the cookies you write on your clients' computers.

Yet another property is the `Secure` property. This write-only, Boolean property determines whether a cookie will be sent through a nonsecure protocol. If this property is set to `True`, the cookie will only be sent when accessing a page using the HTTPS protocol. If this property is set to `False`, its default value, then the cookie will be transmitted over both HTTP and HTTPS.

Now that we've examined the various properties associated with the `Response.Cookies` collection, let's look at an example of cookies in use. Imagine that you were asked to create the search interface for a Web site. Such an interface would require a form that contained a text box, where the users could enter search terms. Figure 10.8 shows a suitable interface for searching a Web site.

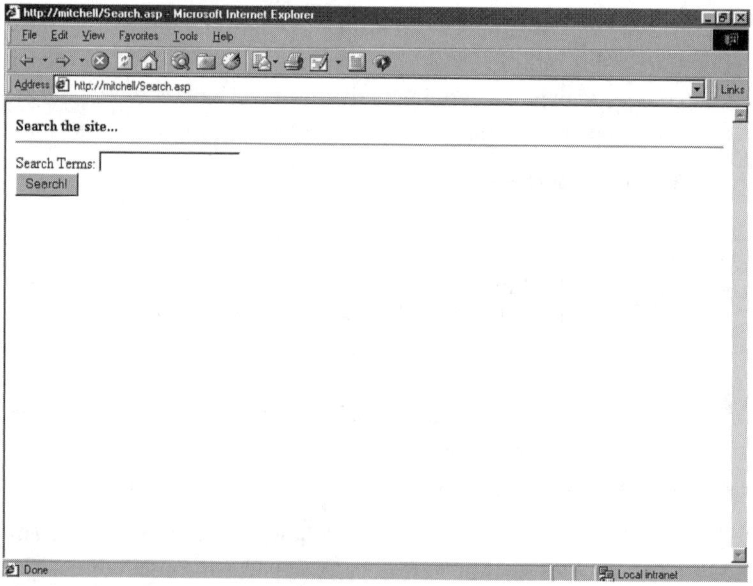

FIGURE **10.8**

A simple "Search the Site" interface.

A neat addition to this search interface would be the capability to have the user's previous search appear, by default, in the Search Terms text box. Another neat feature would be to list the last date the user searched the site. Both these features can be easily implemented with the use of a cookie. Create one cookie, `LastSearch`, and give it two keys, `Terms` and

Date. These two keys will store the user's previous search terms and the date the search was last used. Listing 10.7 displays the code used to generate the search interface.

LISTING 10.7 Using Cookies to Enhance the Search Interface

```
 1: <%@ Language=VBScript %>
 2: <% Option Explicit %>
 3: <%
 4:     'Read the cookie value that stores the previous
 5:     'search terms and last date searched.
 6:
 7:     Dim strSearchTerms, dateSearchDate
 8:     strSearchTerms = Request.Cookies("LastSearch")("Terms")
 9:     dateSearchDate = Request.Cookies("LastSearch")("Date")
10: %>
11:
12: <HTML>
13: <BODY>
14:   <FORM METHOD=POST ACTION="RunSearch.asp">
15:       <B>Search the site...</B>
16: <%
17:     If IsDate(dateSearchDate) then
18:         Response.Write " (Site last searched on " & _
19:                 dateSearchDate & ")"
20:     End If
21: %>
22:       <HR>
23:       Search Terms:
24:       <INPUT TYPE=TEXT NAME=Terms VALUE="<%=strSearchTerms%>">
25:       <BR>
26:       <INPUT TYPE=SUBMIT VALUE="Search!">
27:   </FORM>
28: </BODY>
29: </HTML>
```

ANALYSIS Let's take a moment to dissect Listing 10.7. First, lines 8 and 9 read in the values of the cookie's keys. Remember, if the cookie does not exist on the client's computer, then these two keys will contain empty strings. Line 14 creates a form with its METHOD property set to POST and its ACTION property set to RunSearch.asp.

Lines 16 through 21 display the date the user last searched the site. Line 17 uses the IsDate function to determine whether dateSearchDate is a valid date variable. If dateSearchDate is a valid date, meaning that the LastSearch cookie exists, then a short message is shown so that the user can see when he last searched the site.

Line 24 creates the search text box. Note that the VALUE property is set to strSearchTerms, which contains the user's last search terms. Recall from Day 8, "Communicating with the User," that the VALUE property of text boxes determines what is

10

inserted into the text box by default. If the cookie does not exist on the client's computer, strSearchTerms will be equal to an empty string. In this case, an empty string will be the text box's default value, which is what it should be in this instance because the user's last search terms are unknown.

After the search form is submitted, RunSearch.asp is called. In RunSearch.asp, the first thing you need to do is write the search terms and current date to the LastSearch cookie. Listing 10.8 contains the code in RunSearch.asp that is responsible for writing the cookie to the client's computer.

LISTING 10.8   Using Cookies to Enhance the Search Interface

```
 1:  <%@ Language=VBScript %>
 2:  <% Option Explicit %>
 3:  <%
 4:      'Read in the search terms from the form
 5:      Dim strTerms
 6:      strTerms = Request("Terms")
 7:
 8:      'Now, write the cookie LastSearch
 9:      Response.Cookies("LastSearch")("Terms") = strTerms
10:      Response.Cookies("LastSearch")("Date") = Date
11:      Response.Cookies("LastSearch").Expires = Date + 365
12:
13:      'Execute search...
14:      ...
15:
16:  %>
17:
18:  <HTML>
19:  <BODY>
20:
21:  <B>The cookies are set.</B>
22:
23:  To try another search, <A HREF="search.asp">click here</A>.
24:
25:  </BODY>
26:  </HTML>
```

Listing 10.8 begins by reading the value of the Terms form field. After you have the search terms, you write the cookie LastSearch to the client's computer. Lines 9 and 10 create the two keys, Terms and Date. Set the Terms key equal to the search terms the user entered and the Date key to the current date. Finally, set the Expires property so that the cookie will expire one year from the current date.

Through the use of cookies, you have created a mechanism to store the user's search terms and date searched. Cookies can be used for simple customization on a user-by-user basis. Because the previous search terms are saved on the client's computer, each visitor to your Web site would feel as though the search interface was personally customized for him. Figure 10.9 shows the search interface some time after the user has performed a search. The user's own last search terms have been entered by default into the search terms text box, and the date the user last searched the site is shown as well.

FIGURE **10.9**

It remembers your previous search terms!

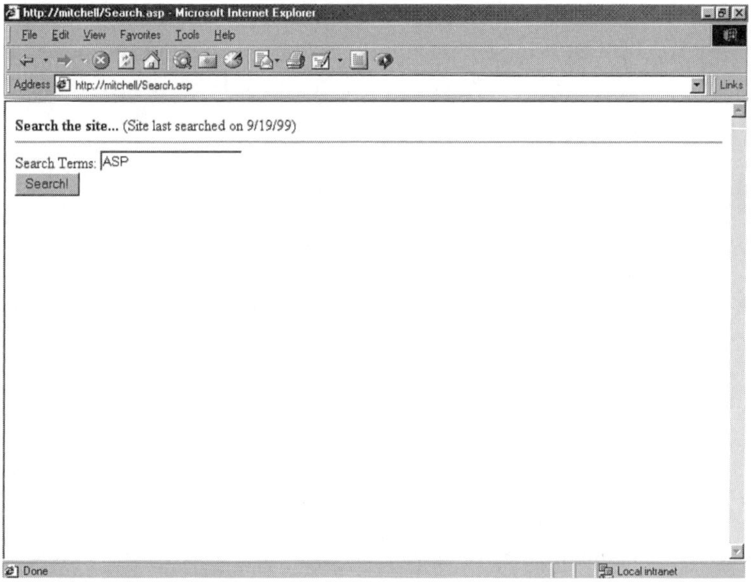

Advantages and Disadvantages of Using Cookies

Maintaining state over the Web is tricky business. Because a Web server may receive requests from hundreds, if not thousands, of clients, it is implausible to expect the server to maintain state for all the clients for any significant length of time. It therefore makes sense to persist long-term information on the client's computer. This is accomplished through the use of cookies.

Cookies are great to use when small amounts of data need to be preserved over time. Cookies allow simple data types to be saved on the client's computer for days, months, or even years. Tomorrow, Day 11, we will examine methods of persisting state by saving user information on the Web server. When user information is stored on the Web server, the Web site's performance will decrease as the number of concurrent users increases. Cookies provide a mechanism for saving simple user information *without* causing a performance hit on the Web server.

To summarize, cookies contain the following advantages:

- Since cookies persist on the client's computer, space does not need to be allocated on the web server to store user-specific information.
- Cookies can save small amounts of information for very long periods of time — weeks, months, or even years!
- Cookies can be used to customize a user's visit to your web site. For a good article on allowing a user to fully customize your site, be sure to read Christopher Miller's great article, "Creating a Customized Home Page." (`http://www.4guysfrom-rolla.com/webtech/051599-1.shtml`)

Cookies have disadvantages as well. There is no guarantee that your cookies will be successfully written to a client's computer because any user can set up his browser to refuse cookies. Also, cookies can only be used to save simple data types, such as strings, dates, and numbers. If you need to save an array or an object for each user, you cannot use cookies; rather, you will have to use one of the techniques that we're going to discuss tomorrow. When using cookies, beware of the following disadvantages:

- Users can choose not to accept cookies on their Web browsers.
- Cookies are unable to save large objects, arrays, or other complex data types. Cookies can *only* save string, date, or numeric data types.

Don't think that cookies are useless because of their limitations. Although cookies are not a cure-all, they do have their time and place. If you need to maintain state for a significant length of time and can do so by saving only simple data types, then cookies are absolutely the best approach. Learning how to read and write cookies is a topic that many books quickly glaze over. However, it is important that you have a solid understanding of how and when to use cookies. Such an understanding will make you a better ASP developer.

Summary

Today we examined two useful `Request` object collections—the `ServerVariables` and `Cookies` collections. We started by examining the `ServerVariables` collection, which is used to read both the HTTP headers and the server's environment variables. We concluded with a thorough discussion of using cookies.

HTTP headers are pieces of information the browser and Web server send to one another. Request headers are headers that the browser sends to the Web server and include such headers as `Referer` and `User-Agent`. Response headers are information that the Web server sends to the browser. Together, the response and request headers are referred to as the HTTP headers. HTTP headers are read using the `ServerVariables` collection. To read an HTTP header, the header name must be prefixed with `HTTP_`. For example, to read the `Referer` HTTP header, use the following syntax:

```
Request.ServerVariables("HTTP_REFERER")
```

Environment variables contain information about the Web server, such as the URL of the currently executing ASP script, the Web server's IP address, and other miscellaneous information. The `ServerVariables` can access an environment variable with the following syntax:

```
Request.ServerVariables(environmentVariableName)
```

Cookies, which we examined in the latter half of today's lesson, can be used to maintain state for lengthy periods of time. Cookies are stored on the client's computer for a specified amount of time and can only be read by the Web site that created them. Cookies are read using the `Request.Cookies` collection and written using the `Response.Cookies` collection. When using cookies, it is important to remember that cookies can only be used to store simple data types and that some users may elect not to accept cookies.

Tomorrow's lesson is a more in-depth look at how to maintain state on the Web. We will explore two more ASP objects: the `Application` object and the `Session` object. These objects can be used to help persist information.

10

Q&A

Q Why do the querystring and cookie strings exist in the `ServerVariables` collection *and* the `Request` object?

A The cookie string exists in the `ServerVariables` collection because the browser sends the cookies associated with a particular Web site each time a page is requested. This cookie information is sent in the form of a delimited name/value pair string and is sent through the request headers. Because it is sent through the headers, the `ServerVariables` collection has access to it. The querystring is stored in the `ServerVariables` collection because when a URL request is made, the Web server takes the querystring from the URL and saves it in an environment variable.

The querystring and cookie information are also available through the `Request` object's `querystring` and `Cookies` collection, respectively. This is done to provide an easy way to access the querystring and the cookies. It is much easier, as a developer, to work with a collection as opposed to working with a delimited string. The `Request` object makes our lives easier by parsing the querystring and cookie strings into two easy-to-use collections. Always use `Request.QueryString` and `Request.Cookies` as opposed to `Request.ServerVariables("QUERY_STRING")` and `Request.ServerVariables("HTTP_COOKIE")`.

Q **Is there a way to determine whether a user has his browser set up to not accept cookies?**

A Unfortunately, there is not a property associated with the `Cookies` collection that reveals whether the user will accept cookies. You can, however, determine whether a user accepts cookies by writing a cookie on one page and then trying to read it on another. If your cookie exists on the second page, then the user can accept cookies. Here is some example code. To determine whether the user will accept cookies, first, the user must be sent to `AcceptCookies.asp`:

```
<% 'FILE: AcceptCookies.asp
   'Write a cookie
   Response.Cookies("TEST") = "testing"
   'Redirect the user to DetermineCookieAcceptance.asp
   Response.Redirect "DetermineCookieAcceptance.asp"
%>
```

`AcceptCookies.asp` writes a cookie and then immediately sends the user to `DetermineCookieAcceptance.asp`. In `DetermineCookieAcceptance.asp`, we will determine whether the cookie `TEST` is an empty string. If it is, then the cookie was not successfully written because the user does not accept cookies.

```
<% 'FILE: DetermineCookieAcceptance.asp
   'Read in the cookie.  If it is not an empty string,
   'the user accepts cookies
   If Len(Response.Cookies("TEST")) = 0 then
      'The user has his browser set to not accept cookies
      Response.Write "You do not accept cookies!"
   Else
      'Ah, good; the user accepts cookies!!
      Response.Write "You accept cookies."
   End If
%>
```

Unfortunately, a more elegant approach is not available.

Q **How many cookies should I save on the client's computer?**

A Because the browser sends all the cookies you've created each time it requests a page on your Web site, it makes sense to keep the total number of cookies per user at a reasonably low number. Cookies should only be used to store small, simple information that needs to persist for days, months, or years. If you have information that only needs to be persisted for a few minutes or for the user's duration on your Web site, there are alternative approaches that are easier to work with. These alternatives are discussed in detail tomorrow.

If you have a large amount of data that needs to be stored for each user, perhaps a database is the best option. Databases allow massive amounts of information to be logically stored on the Web server. Week 3 is dedicated solely to the discussion of databases.

Knowing *when* to use cookies is as important as knowing *how*. If you need to store small quantities of simple data types that need to persist for days, months, or years, cookies are definitely the way to go. If you need to store large amounts of information, information for short periods of time, or complex types of information, such as arrays and objects, then cookies are not the solution.

Q   What types of information are cookies used to store most often?

A   Many sites use cookies to present a visitor with a custom look and feel. At many news Web sites, you can select what types of news stories interest you. This information is usually saved via a cookie on your computer. Then, when you return to the site, your cookie is read, and only the news items you are interested in are listed. Cookies are well designed to allow for this type of simple customization.

Workshop

The Workshop provides quiz questions to help you solidify your understanding of the material covered and exercises to provide you with experience in using what you've learned. Try to understand the quiz and exercise answers before continuing to tomorrow's lesson. Quiz answers are provided in Appendix A, and exercise answers can be found at `http://www.mcp.com/info`.

Quiz

1. What is the name of the response header that sends detailed information about the browser and operating system being used by the client?

2. What HTTP header can you check to determine whether your visitor reached your page through a hyperlink on a different Web page?

3. What environment variable returns the physical address of your Web's root directory?

4. When using the `ServerVariables` collection to obtain an HTTP header, what five characters must prefix the name of the HTTP header?

5. What does the `URL` environment variable contain?

6. What kinds of data types can a cookie not store?

7. When writing a cookie to a client's computer, what properties can you set?

8. If a cookie is created with its `Expires` property set to some date in the past, when will the cookie expire?

9. What happens to a cookie when it expires?

10. What functionality does the `HasKeys` property serve?

Exercises

1. Create two ASP pages: ValidLink.asp and InvalidLink.asp. Next, create a third ASP page, VisitMe.asp. In both ValidLink.asp and InvalidLink.asp, simply create a hyperlink that, when clicked, takes the user to VisitMe.asp. In VisitMe.asp, determine what page the user came from. If the user came via InvalidLink.asp, display a message telling him that he can only reach VisitMe.asp through ValidLink.asp. If the user came from ValidLink.asp, display a welcome message and the visitor's User-Agent string.

   If you have an ASP page that you only want visitors to reach when coming through another page, this technique works well.

2. Create an ASP page named DeleteAllCookies.asp. Write code that will delete all the cookies your Web site has created on the client's computer. (Hint: Remember that cookies are deleted when they expire!)

DAY 11

Maintaining Persistent Information on the Web

Yesterday, Day 10, "Working with the Request Object," we discussed how the Request and Response objects could be used to read and write cookies on clients' computers. Cookies, which can save small bits of simple information on the user's computer, can be used to maintain state over long periods of time. Although cookies offer an easy way to persist information over time, they do have limitations.

To combat these shortcomings, ASP provides two built-in objects: the Session object and the Application object. The Session object is designed to maintain state for each visitor to your Web site for the duration of his or her visit. The Application object provides a mechanism to persist non-user-specific information for great lengths of time. By using these two objects, you can maintain state across your Web site.

The Session and Application objects are easier to use than cookies. Because both the Session and Application objects can save arrays and objects, something cookies *can't* do, many developers prefer to use these two objects in place of using cookies. There is one caveat, though: Because the Session and Application objects save their information in the Web server's memory, these two objects, if overused, can lead to major performance degradation on the Web server. Advantages and disadvantages of using the `Session` and `Application` objects are discussed later today in the sections "The `Session` Object" and "The `Application` Object," respectively.

Today, you will learn the following:

- Different methods of maintaining state on the Internet
- What the `Session` object is
- Advantages and disadvantages of the `Session` object
- What the `Application` object is
- Advantages and disadvantages of the `Application` object
- How to initialize the `Session` and `Application` objects
- What `Global.asa` is, and what purpose it serves

It's a Fact: The Web Is Stateless

Have you ever wondered what, exactly, happens when you type in a URL into your browser's Address bar? After yesterday, you probably have a better understanding of the detailed conversation that goes on between the client and the Web server. Recall from Day 1, "Getting Started with Active Server Pages," that the Internet is based on a client-server model, where your Web browser is the client, and the Web server is the server. Figure 11.1 provides a graphical representation of the client-server model.

FIGURE 11.1

The Internet is based on the client-server model.

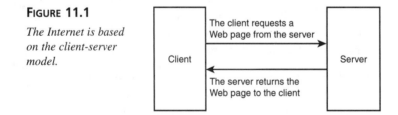

In the client-server model, the client opens up a channel of communication with the server and requests a resource. The server receives the request, locates the resource being requested, and sends it to the client, closing the channel of communication. This is an impersonal transaction between the client and server. The server does not keep open its channel of communication with the client. The server is not concerned with who it has talked to recently, what it has sent recently, or what it thinks a particular client will request next. The server does one job, and it does it well: wait for a request from the client and then process that request.

Due to this impersonal communication between a Web browser and a Web server, user information is not persisted from one request to another. Imagine that you wanted to create a form that would query the user for his or her name. After the user entered his or her name, it would be nice to display a personal greeting on each Web page on your Web site. To display a personalized welcome message, you would need some way of remembering each user's name. Saving such information is referred to as maintaining state, or persisting state.

Ways to Maintain State

Because the client-server model does not make maintaining state inherently easy, you must examine some advanced techniques to maintain state. No doubt you'll find that some of the methods that can be used to persist state seem rather obtuse.

Later today, in the section "Passing Information Through the Querystring," we'll look at how to maintain state by sending state information through the querystring. Using this approach can lead to a syntactical headache, and you may find yourself wondering why maintaining state through the querystring appears to be so confusing. Keep in mind that the client-server model does not lend itself to state persistence; therefore, some methods of maintaining state can be unwieldy.

Thankfully, ASP provides some built-in objects and collections to help maintain state. The `Cookies` collection, which was discussed yesterday, can be used to maintain simple state information over lengthy periods of time. The `Session` and `Application` objects, discussed later today in the sections "The `Session` Object" and "The `Application` Object," can also be used to maintain state. By using Active Server Pages, state maintenance is easier to understand.

You are going to examine other, non-ASP specific approaches as well, though. Each method of maintaining state has its time and place. Being knowledgeable on each of these methods enables you to make the best decision regarding how to implement state persistence.

Passing Information Through the Querystring

When you only need to maintain state for the duration of a user's visit to your site, you have a couple of options. If you only need to save simple data types, a series of cookies will suffice. If more complex data types need to be used, you can store this information through the `Session` object. (The `Session` object uses cookies to uniquely identify each visitor to your site. We discuss the inner workings of the `Session` object later today in "The `Session` Object.") The drawback to both these methods is that if the user has cookies disabled, your Web site will appear to be stateless.

Although the vast majority of Web surfers today have cookies enabled, if it is essential that your site maintain state for *all* your visitors, cookies and session variables just won't do. If this is ever the case, and all you need to persist is simple data types, you can store your state information in the querystring.

Recall from Day 9, "Collecting the Form Information," that the Request object can process information from the querystring if it is formatted in name/value pairs, with each name and value separated by an equals sign (=), and each name/value pair separated from one another by an ampersand (&). For example, a querystring that contained my name and age might look like:

?Name=Scott&Age=21

Imagine that when users first come to your Web site, you ask them to enter their name. You would need to create a form that contained a text box where users could enter their names, and the form also would need a submit button. Listing 11.1 shows the HTML needed to create such a form.

LISTING 11.1   What Is Your Name?

```
1:  <FORM METHOD=GET ACTION="Welcome.asp">
2:    What is your name?<BR>
3:    <INPUT TYPE=TEXT NAME=Name>
4:    <P>
5:    <INPUT TYPE=SUBMIT VALUE="Login">
6:  </FORM>
```

ANALYSIS   Line 1 in Listing 11.1 creates the form with the METHOD property set to GET. This sends the results of the form through the querystring. The code in Listing 11.1 also creates a text box for the users to enter their names (line 3) and a submit button (line 5). Figure 11.2 shows the code for Listing 11.1 when viewed through a browser. I have taken the liberty to enter my name in the text box.

When the form created in Listing 11.1 is submitted, Welcome.asp, the form processing script, is called. Welcome.asp is passed the name of the user through the querystring. The information you want to persist is the user's name, which is in the querystring. It's obvious that Welcome.asp can ascertain the user's name (via Request.QueryString("Name")), but how can you ensure that other Web pages on your site will have access to this information?

The secret is to make sure that each and every ASP page contains the same querystring that Welcome.asp contains. If you can ensure uniformity of the querystring across your Web site, then each ASP page that needed to obtain the user's name could do so by using Request.QueryString("Name"). The question now is how can each Web page on your site have the same querystring as Welcome.asp.

Day 9 discussed how you could pass information through the querystring using hyperlinks. A hyperlink is created with the following syntax:

<A HREF="URL">The title of the link</A>

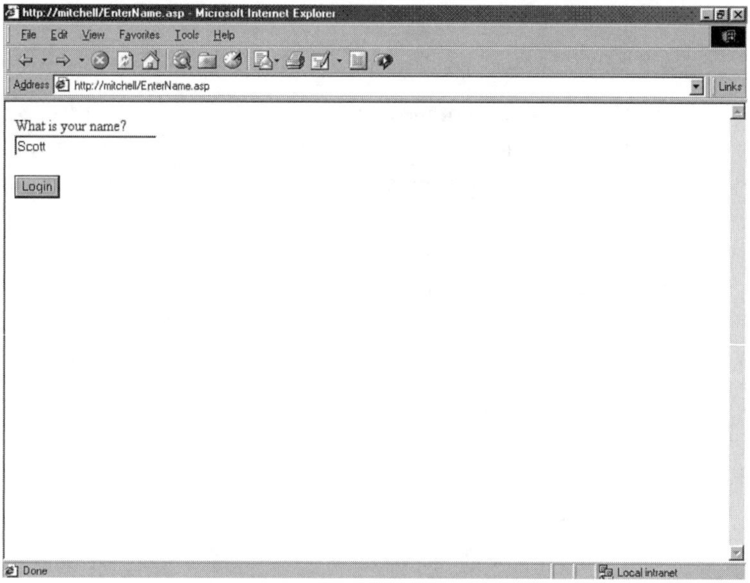

FIGURE 11.2

The Web site will now persist the users' names.

To pass the querystring to the URL, you need to append a question mark (?) followed by the querystring. The following code would create a hyperlink titled `Click Me` that would pass to `ClickMe.asp` the querystring `Name=Scott`:

```
<A HREF="ClickMe.asp?Name=Scott">Click Me</A>
```

Creating hyperlinks with a static querystring, however, will not suffice. You need the hyperlink URL's querystring to be equal to the current querystring in `Welcome.asp`. This way, you will maintain state for each user. Recall from Day 9 that for an ASP page, the entire, current querystring can be read using `Request.QueryString`. You can create all your hyperlinks so that they pass the current querystring by using the following syntax:

```
<A HREF="somePage.asp?<%=Request.QueryString%>">Click Me</A>
```

The preceding syntax will create a hyperlink that, when clicked, will pass the ASP page `somePage.asp` the current querystring. Recall that when an ASP page is requested from a Web server, *all* the ASP code is processed on the server—the client is sent pure HTML. The client does not receive

```
<A HREF="somePage.asp?<%=Request.QueryString%>">Click Me</A>
```

Rather, the value of `Request.QueryString` is inserted after `somePage.asp?`. For example, say that `Welcome.asp`'s querystring is `Name=James`. If you create a hyperlink in `Welcome.asp` using the following syntax:

```
<A HREF="somePage.asp?<%=Request.QueryString%>">Click Me</A>
```

the Web browser, when visiting `Welcome.asp`, would receive the HTML as follows:

```
<A HREF="somePage.asp?Name=James">Click Me</A>
```

Now that you have sent the querystring `Welcome.asp` you received to `somePage.asp`, `somePage.asp` can access the user's name with `Request.QueryString("Name")`. Listing 11.1 created a form where the user could enter her name. This form, when submitted, sent the user's name to `Welcome.asp` through the querystring. All the hyperlinks in `Welcome.asp` need to pass the current querystring to their respective URLs. The code for `Welcome.asp` can be seen in Listing 11.2.

LISTING 11.2   Inserting the Current Querystring into all the Hyperlinks

```
1:  <%@ Language=VBScript %>
2:  <% Option Explicit %>
3:  <%
4:       'Read the Name
5:       Dim strName
6:       strName = Request.QueryString("Name")
7:  %>
8:  <HTML>
9:  <BODY>
10:   Hello <%=strName%>!
11:   <P>
12:   What interests you?<BR>
13:   <LI><A HREF="sports.asp?<%=Request.QueryString%>">Sports</A><BR>
14:   <LI><A HREF="politics.asp?<%=Request.QueryString%>">Politics</A><BR>
15:   <LI><A HREF="fashion.asp?<%=Request.QueryString%>">Fashion</A><BR>
16:   <LI><A HREF="events.asp?<%=Request.QueryString%>">Current Events</A><BR>
17:  </BODY>
18:  </HTML>
```

ANALYSIS   `Welcome.asp` starts by reading in the user's name (line 6). When using the querystring to maintain state, all the ASP pages on your Web site should start out by reading the persistent information; in this case, the user's name. Line 10 displays a personalized greeting, and lines 13 through 16 create a series of hyperlinks. Notice that each hyperlink passes its URL the current querystring using `Request.QueryString`. Figure 11.3 shows `Welcome.asp` when viewed through a browser.

You might be wondering what the HTML the browser received from `Welcome.asp` looked like. Listing 11.3 reveals the exact HTML received by the browser when `Welcome.asp` was sent `Name=Scott` in the querystring.

FIGURE **11.3**

A custom message is shown.

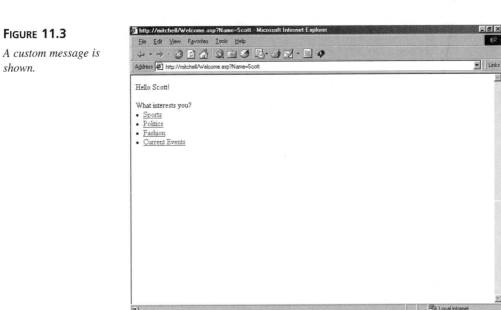

LISTING **11.3**   The HTML Received by the Browser When Visiting `Welcome.asp`

```
 1:  <HTML>
 2:  <BODY>
 3:    Hello Scott!
 4:    <P>
 5:    What interests you?<BR>
 6:    <LI><A HREF="sports.asp?Name=Scott">Sports</A><BR>
 7:    <LI><A HREF="politics.asp?Name=Scott">Politics</A><BR>
 8:    <LI><A HREF="fashion.asp?Name=Scott">Fashion</A><BR>
 9:    <LI><A HREF="events.asp?Name=Scott">Current Events</A><BR>
10:  </BODY>
11:  </HTML>
```

ANALYSIS   Notice in lines 6 through 9 that the querystring, `Name=Scott`, was appended to the URL in the hyperlink. This ensures that when any of these hyperlinks are clicked, it will be sent the current URL. This ensures that the user's name will persist on the next ASP page on your site that the user reaches via a hyperlink.

Note

To have the user's name be maintained throughout your Web pages, every page must be passed the user's name through the querystring. To ensure that every page is passed the user's name through the querystring, *every* hyperlink on *every* ASP page must have `?<%=Request.QueryString%>` appended to it! This may seem like a burden and a headache—it is.

The querystring solution for maintaining state is not without pitfalls. Imagine that a user entered her information and surfed through a couple of pages on your site by clicking the hyperlinks—so far, so good. Now, imagine that the user wants to visit a specific URL on your site, so she types it in the Address bar. The user will reach that URL without having passed the persistent information. At this point, state has been lost. The querystring method also is a development headache. If you forget to append the querystring to a hyperlink's URL, when that hyperlink is clicked, state will be lost because the querystring won't contain the maintained information. Also, the querystring method cannot persist objects because it would be impossible to express an object via the querystring. Finally, keep in mind that the querystring method can only persist data while the user is on your Web site. The second the user leaves your site, state is lost.

The querystring approach, despite its disadvantages, will always work with any browser, whether or not the user has disabled cookies. Also, the querystring approach is free of the performance concerns that plague you when dealing with the `Session` object, which is discussed in length later today in "The `Session` Object." If, for the duration of a user's visit, you must have information persisted, regardless of whether the user has cookies enabled, the querystring approach is the way to go.

Using Cookies

Yesterday's lesson discussed how cookies could be used to maintain simple state information over long periods of times. Cookies are small text files written to the client's computer. As you learned yesterday, cookies can be written to the client's computer using the `Response.Cookies` collection and can be read using the `Request.Cookies` collection.

Cookies can persist on the client's computer for a variable amount of time. When writing a cookie to the client's computer, you can set when the cookie expires. This can be in a day, a week, or even a year. Cookies allow a user's state to be maintained beyond the current visit. The section "Passing Information Through the Querystring" earlier today looked at persisting a user's name throughout all the ASP pages on your Web site. Let's examine how you can use cookies to maintain this information.

Listing 11.1 created a simple form in which the user was prompted to enter his or her name. This form, when submitted, passed the user's name through the querystring to `Welcome.asp`, the form processing script. Because you are going to use cookies to maintain state in this example, you don't need to worry about having all the hyperlinks in `Welcome.asp` passing along the querystring information. All you need to do in `Welcome.asp` is write the name of the user to a cookie. Listing 11.4 shows `Welcome.asp`, modified to use cookies to maintain the user's name.

LISTING 11.4   Using Cookies to Maintain State

```
 1: <%@ Language=VBScript %>
 2: <% Option Explicit %>
 3: <%
 4:      'Read in the Name from the form
 5:      Dim strName
 6:      strName = Request("Name")
 7:
 8:      'Write the user's name to a cookie
 9:      Response.Cookies("UserName") = strName
10:
11:      'Set the cookie to expire in a week
12:    Response.Cookies("UserName").Expires = Date() + 7
13: %>
14:
15: <HTML>
16: <BODY>
17:   Hello <%=strName%>!
18:   <P>
19:   What interests you?<BR>
20:   <LI><A HREF="sports.asp">Sports</A><BR>
21:   <LI><A HREF="politics.asp">Politics</A><BR>
22:   <LI><A HREF="fashion.asp">Fashion</A><BR>
23:   <LI><A HREF="events.asp">Current Events</A><BR>10: </BODY>
24: </HTML>
```

ANALYSIS   To maintain state using cookies, you only need to write the cookie to the client's computer once: when the user enters the information that you want to persist. After the user enters his or her name into the form created by Listing 11.1, Welcome.asp, shown in Listing 11.4, is called. Line 6 starts off by reading the user's name into the variable strName. Line 9 then creates a cookie named UserName and writes to it the user's name. Line 12 sets the cookie to expire in seven days. Assuming that the user accepts cookies, the user's name will be persisted for a week.

Line 17 simply print outs the personalized welcome message. Lines 20 through 23 create a series of hyperlinks. Notice that with the cookie method you don't need to bother with appending the current querystring to the hyperlinks. The output of Listing 11.4, when viewed through a browser, is no different than that of Listing 11.2. The output can be seen in Figure 11.3.

You can read the user's name from any other ASP page on your site by using the Request.Cookies collection to access the UserName cookie. On each page that you wanted to display your personalized greeting, you could simply add the following ASP code:

```
<%
  Dim strName
  strName = Request.Cookies("UserName")
  Response.Write "Hello " & strName & "!"
%>
```

11

> **Caution**
>
> Recall from Day 10, that some people set their browsers to not accept cookies. If such a person were to visit your site, his name would not be persisted. The only way to persist information for these types of users is to use the querystring method discussed in the earlier section "Passing Information Through the Querystring."

Using the Session Object

Active Server Pages comes with a built-in object to help developers maintain state on a user-by-user basis. This object is called the Session object and can be accessed through any ASP page on your Web site. The Session object can store any kind of data type, from numbers and strings to arrays and objects!

The Session is used to maintain state *only* for the duration of a user's visit to your Web site. When each new user comes to your site, memory on the Web server is allocated to store the Session object for that user. This memory is released if the user does not visit your Web site for a certain length of time. This time period is 10 minutes, by default but can be set to a shorter or lengthier period. We will discuss the finer details of the Session object in "The Session Object."

Each variable stored in the Session object is referred to as a *session variable*. You can create session variables with the following syntax:

```
Session(sessionVariableName) = value
```

where sessionVariableName is a string. The following lines of code create a number of session variables:

```
1:  Session("Today") = Date()
2:  Session("WelcomeMessage") = "Hello, world!"
3:  Session("Age") = 21
```

ANALYSIS Line 1 creates a session variable named Today, which stores the current date. Line 2 creates a session variable named WelcomeMessage, which contains a string. Finally, line 3 stores a numeric value in the session variable named Age.

Each time you create a new variable in the Session object, that bit of memory for each unique user increases, and the new variable is stored in that memory space. These variables are persisted for each user as long as the user keeps making page requests of the Web site. Therefore, the session variables can be used to maintain state.

In both the sections "Passing Information through the Querystring" and "Using Cookies," you saw an example where the user would enter his or name. The name would then be shown in a personalized greeting on each Web page. You already know how to accomplish this with cookies and the querystring method—let's examine how you would use the Session object.

You only need to slightly modify the code in Listing 11.4 to use the Session object to maintain state. Listing 11.5 contains the new code for Welcome.asp.

LISTING 11.5   Using the Session Object to Maintain State

```
1: <%@ Language=VBScript %>
2: <% Option Explicit %>
3: <%
4:     'Read in the Name from the form
5:     Dim strName
6:     strName = Request("Name")
7:
8:     'Write the user's name to a session variable
9:     Session("UserName") = strName
10: %>
11:
12: <HTML>
13: <BODY>
14:   Hello <%=strName%>!
15:   <P>
16:   What interests you?<BR>
17:   <LI><A HREF="sports.asp">Sports</A><BR>
18:   <LI><A HREF="politics.asp">Politics</A><BR>
19:   <LI><A HREF="fashion.asp">Fashion</A><BR>
20:   <LI><A HREF="events.asp">Current Events</A><BR>
21: </BODY>
22: </HTML>
```

ANALYSIS   To maintain state using the Session object, you need to create a session variable for each bit of information that needs to be persisted. Because you only need to save the user's name, you can use just one session variable. Listing 11.5 starts off by reading in the name the user entered in the previous form (line 6). Next, on line 9, a single session variable, named UserName, is created. This session variable is then assigned the value of strName.

Lines 12 through 21 have not changed from Listing 11.4. Line 14 simply prints out a personalized welcome message, whereas lines 17 through 20 create a series of hyperlinks. Notice that when using session variables, you don't need to bother with appending the current querystring to the hyperlinks. Again, the output of Listing 11.5, when viewed through a browser, is no different from that of Listing 11.2 or Listing 11.4. The output can be seen in Figure 11.3.

To obtain the user's name in any other ASP page on your Web site, all you have to do is read the value of your session variable. Session variables are read using the following syntax:

```
SomeVariable = Session(sessionVariableName)
```

You can display your personalized greeting on any ASP page with the following code:

```
<%
  Dim strName
  strName = Session("UserName")
  Response.Write "Hello " & strName & "!"
%>
```

The `Session` object uniquely identifies visitors via cookies. This means that session variables will **not** persist across ASP pages if the user has cookies disabled. Once again, the only sure-fire way to guarantee that state will be maintained for *all* your visitors is to use the querystring method. However, because the vast majority of users accept cookies, most Active Server Pages developers feel comfortable using cookies or the `Session` object to maintain state. A more detailed discussion is dedicated to this matter later today in the section "The `Session` Object."

Using the `Application` Object

The `Application` object is another intrinsic ASP object to help maintain state. You may wonder how the `Application` and `Session` objects differ, if they both are designed to maintain state on your Web site. Whereas the `Session` object is designed to maintain state on a user-by-user basis, the `Application` object is designed to maintain state globally, across the entire Web site. The `Application` object, like the `Session` object, can store an assortment of variables of any type. Each variable stored in the `Application` is referred to as an *application variable*.

Application variables are sometimes referred to as global variables because any user can access any application variable from any ASP page. It is important to keep in mind that there is only one instance of the `Application` object for your Web site. Every single user to your Web site has access to the exact same set of application variables.

Imagine that two users visit your site and that there exists an application variable named `DefaultMessage`, which contains the string `Welcome to my Web site!`. Imagine that the first user visits an ASP page that changes the application variable `DefaultMessage` to `Hello, there!`. After this change has been made, the second user visits another ASP page that displays the application variable `DefaultMessage`. The second user will see `Hello, there!` through his browser. Because there is only one instance of the `Application` object and because any user on any ASP page can alter application variables, when the first user changes the value of an application variable, the results are immediately noticed by the second user.

You may be wondering how the `Application` object can be used to maintain state. Because the `Application` object is global among all users, you should not try to use application variables to maintain state on a user-by-user basis. However, if you have some global piece of information that you want to save for the entire Web site, application variables are often the way to go, especially if the information changes often.

We will discuss when and how to use application variables in greater detail later today in the section "The `Application` Object."

Do	Don't
	DON'T store user-specific information in the `Application` object. If you need to store information specific to each user, use the `Session` object instead.

Choosing the Approach that Works for You

So far we've examined the four methods of maintaining state. The first three approaches examined—using the querystring, using cookies, and using session variables—can be used to maintain state on a user-by-user basis. The final method discussed—using the `Application` object—can be used to maintain Web site-wide state.

Now that you've studied the four methods of persisting state, which method should you choose? Because each approach has strong points and weak points, the method to use depends largely on the situation. Table 11.1 presents all four methods of maintaining state and lists under what conditions to use what method.

TABLE 11.1 Approaches to Maintaining State

Methods	When to Use
Querystring method	When using the querystring method to persist state, make sure that each hyperlink passes on the current querystring to the next ASP page. This leads to a maintenance headache. The nice thing about the querystring method, though, is that it doesn't require the user to have cookies enabled. If you need to persist simple data types for only the duration of the user's visit to the site and it is imperative that even users who have cookies disabled have their state maintained, then the querystring method is the way to go.
Cookies	If you need to maintain state for periods longer than the duration of the user's visit, then cookies are your only option. Cookies can only save simple data types (strings, numbers, dates) and can be rejected by the client's computer. Cookies, though, require no overhead on the Web server because they are stored on the client's machine. If performance is a big concern, or if you need to persist information for days, weeks, or months, then cookies are the best choice!

continues

TABLE 11.1 continued

Methods	When to Use
Session variables	If you only need to maintain state for the duration of your users' visits, using session variables may be the way to go. The Session object, unlike cookies, can store any variable type. However, the Session object resides on the Web server. If you receive many concurrent users or place large objects in the Session object, your Web server's performance will degrade. Session variables are the best choice when you need to maintain state only for the user's visit to your site.
Application variables	Application variables can be used to maintain information that is global to the entire Web site. The Application object should not be used to maintain state on a user-by-user basis. Application variables are a wise choice when you have some piece of information that changes often and that is global to the entire Web site. For example, if you ran a Web site that had a message board where users could post their questions, you might want to display on all your Web pages the time and date the last post was made. This information should be stored in an application variable because it changes often and is global to the Web site.

Now that we've examined four ways to maintain state, we are going to delve into the Session and Application objects. Both of these built-in objects are useful but often misused. Because the Session and Application objects reside on the Web server, misusing these two objects can lead to a performance hit. The next two sections, "The Session Object" and "The Application Object," discuss not only how to use these objects but also how *not* to use these objects.

The Session Object

The Session object is an intrinsic ASP object designed to maintain state on a user-by-user basis. Each user is assigned his own Session object. Because each user has his own Session object, each user's unique data can be saved. Figure 11.4 graphically shows that each user is assigned his own Session.

It is helpful to think of the Session object as a warehouse. When each new user arrives at the site, she receives her own warehouse. Throughout the site, any ASP page can deposit or retrieve information into a user's warehouse. Such a collection of user-specific information can prove useful.

For example, many of today's eCommerce sites have a shopping cart system, where, as you browse through the site, if you see an item you want to purchase, you can simply click it to add it to your shopping cart. When you are ready to "check out," you visit a page that summarizes your purchases, presents a total charge, and asks for your billing and shipping information. The shopping cart is your personal warehouse, holding the information on your specific items.

FIGURE 11.4

An instance of the
Session object exists
for each client.

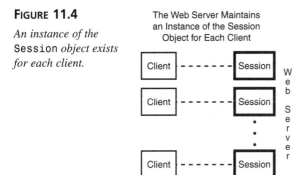

When a visitor reaches your site, his "personal warehouse" is, technically, a new instance of the Session object. This object is created specifically for this particular user, serving as a vault of user-specific information. A user's Session object instance is often referred to simply as the user's *Session*.

Because each user is assigned his own Session, each instance needs to be uniquely identifiable. A numeric ID, referred to as the SessionID, is used to identify that a particular Session belongs to a particular user. To list the SessionID for a user's Session, you can use the following syntax:

```
Session.SessionID
```

The SessionID is a numeric value, uniquely identifying each Session from other another. The following line of code would display, to each visitor, his or her unique SessionID:

```
<% Response.Write "Your SessionID is " & Session.SessionID %>
```

Figure 11.5 shows the output of the preceding line of code.

The SessionID is guaranteed to be unique for each separate session as long as the Web server is running. However, if the Web server is restarted, new SessionIDs might be duplicates of older SessionIDs. For this reason, it is unwise to use the SessionID as a unique identifier in a database. Week 3 will discuss databases in detail.

11

The SessionID *is a numeric value uniquely identifying each* Session *object.*

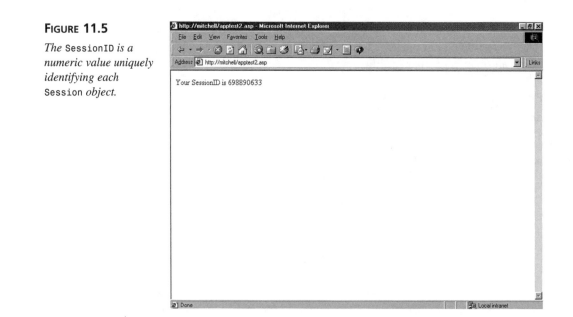

The SessionID is stored in two locations: the Web server and the client. Each Session that is managed by the Web server contains its own SessionID. This SessionID is also stored on the client's computer, in the form of a cookie. Because the SessionID is saved on both the client and the Web server, the Web server can establish what Sessions belong to what clients.

Imagine that you have an ASP page that contains the following simple line of code:

```
<% Response.Write "Your name is " & Session("Name") %>
```

The preceding line would display Your name is, followed by the value in the session variable Name. What, exactly, happens when a user visits this page? Because each visitor can have a different value for the session variable Name, how is the correct value selected? Recall from yesterday's lesson that each time a Web page is requested from the Web server, a number of HTTP headers are sent. One of the HTTP headers is the Cookie header, which contains all the cookies on the client's computer that were created by the Web site. If session variables are being used on your Web site, one of these cookies contains the SessionID associated with a particular Session on the Web server. This cookie is matched up with the correct Session, and the Name variable is displayed.

Using cookies to associate a particular client with a particular Session has its drawbacks. What happens if the user has set up his browser to not accept cookies? If this is the case, this user cannot have his own "personal warehouse," and state will not be persisted for this user. Although the majority of Web surfers today have cookies enabled, there is no guarantee that *all* your visitors accept cookies. There is, however, a way to use session variables with users who do not accept cookies. This workaround is discussed later today in the section "Session Variables Without Cookies."

Because each user's Session is created and stored in the Web server's memory, it is important to have this memory freed up when the visitor is no longer at your site. Due to the client-server model, you cannot determine when someone leaves your site. However, you can keep track of the last time a specific user accessed your site. If a specific user has not accessed your site for a particular amount of time, her Session is freed from the Web server's memory. The amount of time that passes before a user's Session is freed is referred to as the *session timeout*.

> **Note**
>
> IIS 5.0 is scheduled to have the default session timeout to 10 minutes. However, with Windows 2000 Release Candidate 2, the default session timeout is still at 20 minutes. With IIS 4.0, the default session timeout is, and has always been, 20 minutes.

You can set the session timeout by using the Timeout property of the Session object. You can assign the Timeout property a numeric value, representing the number of minutes before a user's Session times out and destroys itself. For example, if you want to set the session timeout to 5 minutes, use the following line of code:

```
'The Session object is set to timeout in five minutes!
Session.Timeout = 5
```

If you want to destroy the user's Session explicitly, before the session timeout occurs, use the Abandon method. Some personalized sites have a LogOut button available that, when clicked, removes any saved information, such as cookies and session variables. The LogOut button, when clicked, should display a LogOut message and call the Session object's Abandon method. Listing 11.6 shows the code for LogOut.asp, which simply displays a short message informing the user that she has been logged out and destroys the user's Session through a call to Session.Abandon.

LISTING 11.6   Using Session.Abandon to Destroy the User's Session Object

```
1:  <%@ Language=VBScript %>
2:  <% Option Explicit %>
3:  <%
4:      'Destroy the user's session
5:      Session.Abandon
6:  %>
7:
```

continues

LISTING **11.6** continued

```
 8:  <HTML>
 9:  <BODY>
10:   You have been logged out.  Your Session variables have
11:   been destroyed!
12:  </BODY>
13:  </HTML>
```

ANALYSIS Because each user has her own instance of a Session object, the memory requirements on your Web server increase as the number of concurrent users on your Web site increases. Therefore, it helps to free the memory associated with a user's Session as soon as possible. Listing 11.6 demonstrates how to remove a user's Session object by using the Abandon method of the Session object (line 5).

When each new user visits your site, he is given a "personal warehouse," into which your ASP pages can store and retrieve user-specific information. The Session object acts as the warehouse itself. Each warehouse contains its own unique, numeric ID, called the SessionID. After a warehouse has not been accessed for a set length of time, the warehouse is demolished, freeing up real estate for another warehouse. This length of time is the session timeout and can be accessed via the Timeout property of the Session object. Finally, use the Abandon method if you need to explicitly destroy a Session prematurely.

Now that you've examined the role of the Session object, it's time to discuss how to write and read the variables stored inside the Session object. These session variables are responsible for saving the user's information, thereby maintaining state across the Web application. The next section, "Using Session Variables," discusses the intricacies of session variables.

Using Session Variables

As discussed in the previous section, an instance of the Session object serves as a warehouse for a specific user's information. What use is a warehouse, though, if you put nothing inside it? If you have a user-specific piece of information that you need to persist, you need to save this information to a variable and put that variable into the user's Session. Such variables are referred to as session variables.

To write a value to a session variable, use the following syntax:

```
Session(sessionVariableName) = Value
```

This, essentially, stores a variable into a user's personal warehouse. A session variable can be read by using:

```
Value = Session(sessionVariableName)
```

Imagine that you were creating a site, and at the top of each Web page you wanted to put a quote of the day. It would be nice to present the user with an option to hide the quote. Listing 11.7 shows the source code for an ASP page that shows both the quote of the day and an option to hide the quote.

LISTING 11.7   Hiding the Quote of the Day

```
1:  <%@ Language=VBScript %>
2:  <% Option Explicit %>
3:  <%
4:      'Do we want to show the quote of the day?
5:      If Session("ShowQuote") = False then
6:          'The user doesn't want to see the quote
7:          'Show them an option to see the quote again
8:  %>
9:          <A HREF="/scripts/ShowQuote.asp">Show Quote of the Day</A>
10: <%
11:     Else
12:         'The user wants to see the quote, so show it!
13: %>
14:         A stitch in time saves nine.<BR>
15:         <A HREF="/scripts/HideQuote.asp">Hide Quote</A>
16: <%
17:     End If
18: %>
19:
20:   <P><HR><P>
21:   <I>Blah blah blah blah...</I>
```

ANALYSIS   The code in Listing 11.7 first determines whether the user is interested in seeing the quote of the day. In line 5, an If statement determines whether the session variable ShowQuote is False. If ShowQuote is False, you don't want to show the quote of the day. Line 9 provides a hyperlink that, when clicked, allows users to see the quotes of the day. If, on the other hand, ShowQuote is not False, the code after the Else on line 11 is executed. Line 14 displays a famous quote from Ben Franklin, and line 15 provides a link that, when clicked, turns off the quote of the day. Figure 11.6 shows the output of Listing 11.7 when a user visits the site for the first time.

In Figure 11.6, the quote of the day isn't shown on the user's first visit. This is because the session variable ShowQuote has not yet been created in the user's Session. Because ShowQuote doesn't yet exist, when you ask for ShowQuote in line 5 of Listing 11.7, you are returned an empty string, which evaluates to False. There's nothing wrong with this unless you want to have the quote of the day shown by default. Later today, in the section, "Initializing Application and Session Variables," we will discuss how to have session variables created automatically upon a new user's visit.

11

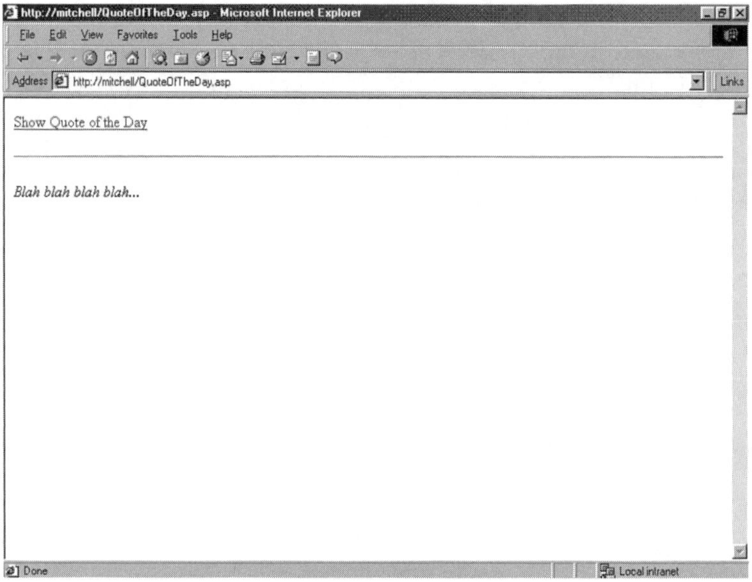

FIGURE 11.6

Initially, the user won't see the quote of the day.

Note Figure 11.6 and line 9 in Listing 11.7. If the ShowQuote session variable is False, you need to provide the user with a link to start showing the quotes of the day again. This link, if clicked, will take the user to ShowQuote.asp. This ASP page needs to "turn on" the quote of the day. This is done by setting the ShowQuote session variable to True. After ShowQuote has been set to True, ShowQuote.asp needs to redirect the user back to the page he came from. Listing 11.8 presents the code for ShowQuote.asp.

LISTING 11.8 ShowQuote.asp "Turning On" the Quote of the Day

```
1:  <%@ Language=VBScript %>
2:  <% Option Explicit %>
3:  <%
4:      'Set ShowQuote to True
5:      Session("ShowQuote") = True
6:
7:      'Send the user back to the page from which they came
8:      Response.Redirect Request.ServerVariables("HTTP_REFERER")
9:  %>
```

ANALYSIS ShowQuote.asp needs to do two things: set the ShowQuote session variable to True, thereby turning on the quote of the day; and redirect the user back to the page from which he came. The first task is accomplished on line 5. The second task is completed on line 8, using the Redirect method of the Response object. The user is sent to the URL specified by the Referer HTTP header, which is the URL of the page he came from. The Request.ServerVariables collection and the HTTP headers were discussed on Day 10.

By clicking the Show Quote of the Day hyperlink in Figure 11.6 (created on line 9 in Listing 11.7), ShowQuote.asp was loaded. ShowQuote.asp then set the ShowQuote session variable to True and sent the user back to the Web page he came from. When the user arrives back at the page he started on, the quote is now showing. Figure 11.7 shows the results of the code in Listing 11.7 *after* the user clicks the Show Quote of the Day hyperlink. Figure 11.8 presents a diagram of the steps taken to show and hide the quote of the day.

FIGURE 11.7

The quote of the day is now showing.

```
http://mitchell/QuoteOfTheDay.asp - Microsoft Internet Explorer
File   Edit   View   Favorites   Tools   Help
Address  http://mitchell/QuoteOfTheDay.asp                          Links

A stitch in time saves nine.
Hide Quote


Blah blah blah blah...




                                                        Local intranet
```

11

FIGURE 11.8

The steps involved in showing/hiding the quote of the day.

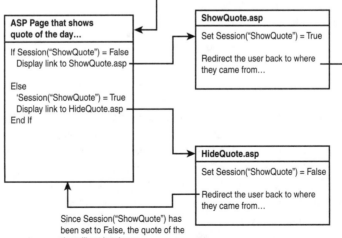

ASP Page that shows quote of the day...

If Session("ShowQuote") = False
   Display link to ShowQuote.asp

Else
   'Session("ShowQuote") = True
   Display link to HideQuote.asp
End If

ShowQuote.asp

Set Session("ShowQuote") = True

Redirect the user back to where they came from...

HideQuote.asp

Set Session("ShowQuote") = False

Redirect the user back to where they came from...

Since Session("ShowQuote") has been set to False, the quote of the day will not be shown...

When the quote of the day is shown, not only do you need to display the quote of the day, you also need to provide the user with an option to turn off the quote of the day. Line 15 in Listing 11.7 creates a link to HideQuote.asp, which needs to do nearly the exact same thing as ShowQuote.asp. HideQuote.asp should set the ShowQuote session variable to False and then redirect the user back to the page he came from. The code for HideQuote.asp can be found in Listing 11.8. After turning off the quote of the day, the output is the same as when you initially visited. You no longer see a quote but instead see the Show Quote of the Day hyperlink. This output was shown previously in Figure 11.6.

The Session object can be used to store *any* type of variable. With cookies, you are restricted to only saving simple data types on the client's computer. The Session object, however, can be used to store arrays. To show this, create an ASP page named CreateSessionArray.asp and enter the code shown in Listing 11.9.

LISTING 11.9   Using the Session Object to Store Arrays

```
 1:  <%@ Language=VBScript %>
 2:  <% Option Explicit %>
 3:  <%
 4:      'Create an array
 5:      Dim aSentence(4)
 6:      aSentence(0) = "I "
 7:      aSentence(1) = "like "
 8:      aSentence(2) = "Active "
 9:      aSentence(3) = "Server "
10:      aSentence(4) = "Pages!"
11:
12:      Dim iLoop
13:      For iLoop = LBound(aSentence) to UBound(aSentence)
14:          Response.Write aSentence(iLoop)
15:      Next
16:
17:      'Store the array in the Session object
18:      Session("Sentence") = aSentence
19: %>
```

ANALYSIS   Listing 11.9 starts out by creating an array, aSentence (line 5). This array contains five elements, 0 through 4. Lines 6 through 10 set the values of each of these five array elements. Next, the contents of the array are printed out. Line 13 uses the LBound and UBound functions to iterate through the array aSentence one element at a time. Recall from Day 5, "Using VBScript's Built-in Functions," that the LBound function returns the starting index of an array, while UBound returns the ending index, or upper bound, of an array. UBound and LBound can be used in conjunction with a For loop to iterate through an array. Refer to Appendix B for a more thorough description of LBound and UBound.

Next, line 14 prints out the current element on each iteration of the loop. Finally, line 18 creates a session variable named Sentence and sets it equal to the array aSentence. Note how simple it is to set a session variable equal to an array. The output of Listing 11.9 is I like Active Server Pages!

Now that you have your array in a session variable, you can access the contents of that array on another ASP page. Listing 11.10 shows the code for PrintSessionArray.asp, which, as the name suggests, prints out the contents of the Sentence session variable array.

LISTING 11.10   Displaying the Contents of the Session Variable Array

```
 1:  <%@ Language=VBScript %>
 2:  <% Option Explicit %>
 3:  <%
 4:    Dim iLoop
 5:
 6:    'First, make sure that the Session variable
 7:    'Sentence is a valid array
 8:    If IsArray(Session("Sentence")) then
 9:      'Print out each element in the array
10:      For iLoop = LBound(Session("Sentence")) to UBound(Session("Sentence"))
11:        Response.Write Session("Sentence")(iLoop)
12:      Next
13:    Else
14:      'If Session("Sentence") is not a valid array,
15:      'display an error message
16:      Response.Write "No sentence to process!"
17:    End If
18: %>
```

ANALYSIS   The code in Listing 11.10 displays the contents of the Sentence session variable array, if it exists. Before attempting to read from Session("Sentence"), line 8 checks to make sure that Sentence is a valid array by using the IsArray function. If the user had not visited CreateSessionArray.asp prior to visiting PrintSessionArray.asp, the session variable Sentence would not have existed and would have returned an empty string. Passing LBound an empty string, as opposed to an array, would have generated an error. Therefore, it is essential that you first check to make sure that Sentence is a valid array.

If Sentence is an array, line 10 loops through each element of the array, displaying the contents of each element (line 11), similar to lines 13 through 15 in Listing 11.9. The syntax for referring to a specific element in a session variable array may seem a bit confusing (line 11). With an array, you refer to a specific variable with ArrayName(index). When you store an array in the Session object, the ArrayName is Session(sessionVariableName). Therefore, to read an element from a session variable array, the syntax is Session(sessionVariableName)(index).

11

If you were to leave out the If statement starting on line 8, an error would occur when you asked to compute LBound(Session("Sentence")). The error message displayed would read:

```
Microsoft VBScript runtime error '800a000d'

Type mismatch: 'LBound'

/PrintSessionArray.asp, line 9
```

Because the If statement is on line 8, if the Sentence session variable array hasn't been created, IsArray(Session("Sentence")) will return False, and the code following the Else statement on line 13 will execute. Line 16 simply displays an error message, indicating to the user that there was no sentence to display. This type of error message is preferred to the VBScript runtime error message shown previously.

The Session object can also contain session variable objects, although it is vital that, as a developer, you use prudence when placing objects into the Session object. Because each user has his own Session, if your Web site has many concurrent users, Session scoped objects can quickly eat the Web server's memory. Objects should only be placed in the Session on small Internet or intranet sites, where the number of concurrent users is guaranteed to be low. The ramifications of using session variable objects are discussed in detail later today in the section "Pitfalls of Session Variables."

Recall from Day 6, "Working with Objects," that to create and store a new instance of an object into a variable, the Set keyword must be used. When storing an object in the Session, the Set keyword is also used, as in the following example:

```
Set Session(sessionVariableName) = ObjectInstance
```

The following lines of code show how to set a session variable to an instance of an object:

```
1: Set Session("MyDict") = Server.CreateObject("Scripting.Dictionary")
2: Set Session("Connection") = Server.CreateObject("ADODB.Connection")
3: Set Session("CustomObject") = Server.CreateObject("My.Object")
```

ANALYSIS Line 1 creates a session variable named MyDict that is an instance of the Scripting.Dictionary object. Line 2 creates an instance of the ADODB.Connection object, storing it in the session variable Connection. Similarly, line 3 creates an instance of an object named My.Object and assigns it to the session variable CustomObject. Although these three examples create instances of objects as session variables, it is not wise to place such objects in the Session, due to performance and memory concerns. This topic is addressed later today in the section "Pitfalls of Session Variables."

The Session object provides two collections containing the session variables.

- Contents contains the non-object session variables.
- StaticObjects contains session variable objects.

The code in Listing 11.11 displays all the non-object session variables in a user's Session.

LISTING 11.11 The `Contents` Collection Contains All Non-Object Session Variables

```
1:  <%@ Language=VBScript %>
2:  <% Option Explicit %>
3:  <%
4:     'How many session variables are there?
5:     Response.Write "There are " & Session.Contents.Count & _
6:              " Session variables<P>"
7:
8:     Dim strName, iLoop
9:     'Use a For Each ... Next to loop through the entire collection
10:    For Each strName in Session.Contents
11:      'Is this session variable an array?
12:      If IsArray(Session(strName)) then
13:        'If it is an array, loop through each element one at a time
14:        For iLoop = LBound(Session(strName)) to UBound(Session(strName))
15:          Response.Write strName & "(" & iLoop & ") - " & _
16:                Session(strName)(iLoop) & "<BR>"
17:        Next
18:      Else
19:        'We aren't dealing with an array, so just display the variable
20:        Response.Write strName & " - " & Session.Contents(strName) & "<BR>"
21:      End If
22:    Next
23: %>
```

ANALYSIS Listing 11.11 displays all the user's session variables and values. Line 5 uses the `Count` property of the `Contents` collection to display the number of session variables. Line 10 starts the `For Each...Next` loop through the `Contents` collection. Because the `Contents` collection contains all non-object session variables, it also contains session variable arrays. For this reason, before you display a session variable, you need to first determine whether it is an array. Line 12 accomplishes this, using the `IsArray` function. This is identical to the syntax used on line 8 in Listing 11.10 to determine whether a session variable is an array.

If the session variable is an array, lines 14 through 17 are executed. Line 14 is a `For` loop, which iterates through each element in the session variable array. The contents of each session variable array element are displayed (line 16). If, however, the session variable is *not* an array, the `Else` block starting on line 18 is executed. The session variable's name and value are then displayed (line 20). Figure 11.9 shows an example of the output of Listing 11.11.

11

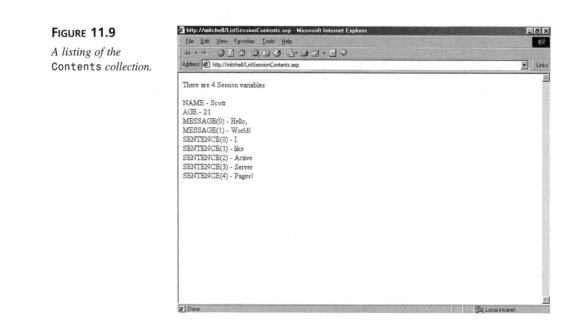

Before running this page, I created another session variable array, Message. As you can see, there are four session variables, two of which are arrays, and two of which are not. These session variables, except for Message, were all created with earlier examples in today's lesson. Specifically, Name was created in Listing 11.5, Age in an example in the section "Using the Session Object," and Sentence in Listing 11.9.

The other session variable collection, StaticObjects, cannot be used to list session variable objects created in an ASP page. Objects created in this manner are referred to as *dynamic objects* because they are created on-the-fly, only when a user visits an ASP page that contains code similar to the following:

```
Set Session(sessionVariableName) = ObjectInstance
```

Rather, the StaticObjects collection, as its name implies, can only be used to iterate through static objects in the Session object. Static objects are objects that are created for each user when she first visits the site. We will discuss how to create such objects later in today's lesson, in the section "Initializing Application and Session Variables." The syntax for iterating through the StaticObjects collection is straightforward. You can access each static object in a user's Session by issuing a For Each...Next construct. The following example lists all the session variable names that are holding a static object instance:

```
Dim strName
For Each strName in Session.StaticObjects
    Response.Write strName & "<BR>"
Next
```

Using these two collections, Contents and StaticObjects, you can loop through the session variables stored in a user's Session (except for session variable objects created on an ASP page). When using the Session object to maintain state on your Web site, it helps to think of the Session object itself as a warehouse and session variables as the goods inside the warehouse. Because each user has her own Session, each user can have unique session variables values. This allows for user-specific state to be maintained across a Web site.

Pitfalls of Session Variables

When using session variables in your Web application, try to avoid a few common pitfalls:

- Pitfall 1—Placing objects in a user's Session
- Pitfall 2—Setting the Timeout property to a non-optimal value
- Pitfall 3—Creating unnecessary session variables

Because each user is assigned her own instance of the Session object, the more concurrent users visiting your site, the more Session instances are needed. If you start placing large objects into each user's Session, each Session object will grow, requiring more of the Web server's memory. As more and larger Session objects are instantiated, the slower your Web server will become. For this reason, it is wise to keep objects out of the Session.

Sometimes an object needs to be used on nearly every ASP page. Some developers place large objects into the user's Session, reasoning that creating the object once will lead to a performance boost over creating the object every time a page is loaded. Don't fall into this trap! Microsoft recommends that you wait to create objects as late as possible and destroy them as soon as possible. This technique leads to the best performance. Again, resist the urge to place objects in your users' Sessions.

Another common pitfall that developers experience when using the Session object is setting the Timeout property to an optimal value. Recall that after a particular user has not accessed your Web site for a specific duration, the user's Session will be freed from memory. This length of time before the Session terminates itself is referred to as the session timeout and can be set using the Session object's Timeout property. Do not set this value too high. Imagine, for a moment, that you set the Session's Timeout property to 120 minutes. When a new visitor comes, a Session is created for that user. If the user browses your site for a while and then leaves, the memory resources allocated for that user will remain present for another 2 hours.

Imagine that, on average, every half-hour, 100 users come to your site as 100 users leave. The net effect is an average of 100 users on your site at any given time. You would expect to have decent performance, but a poorly set Timeout would thrash your Web server's memory. When the first 100 users come, 100 Sessions are created. When they leave half an hour later and a new 100 users come, another 100 Sessions are created. However, the

11

first 100 Sessions aren't freed from the Web server's memory and won't be for another 2 hours. Your Web server will soon have 500 Session object instances in memory, even though there are only 100 concurrent users on your site. Table 11.2 displays the growth of user Sessions on a Web site with its session timeout set to 120 minutes.

TABLE 11.2 A High Timeout Property Wastes Memory

Time	Concurrent Users	Total Sessions	Explanation
0:00	100	100	At time 0, 100 new users come to your site. Hence, 100 Sessions are created.
0:30	100	200	Your 100 initial visitors have left (although their Sessions won't be removed until the start of time 2:30. 100 new visitors have come to the site, adding another 100 Sessions.
1:00	100	300	Another 100 new visitors come, adding a new 100 Sessions. 200 Sessions exist from the first two groups of 100 visitors.
1:30	100	400	Another 100 new visitors replaced the 100 from the half-hour period before.
2:00	100	500	Yet another 100 visitors arrived. You now have *500 Sessions* for only 100 concurrent users! What a waste of memory!
2:30	100	500	A new 100 users come, but the first 100 visitors from time 0 have their 100 Sessions removed. As long as you keep receiving 100 new users every half hour, you will remain at 500 total Sessions.
3:00	100	500	...

Be careful not to set your Timeout property too low, either. Imagine that you decided to set the session timeout to 1 minute. Although this will surely keep the Web server's performance up to par, your visitors will find your site annoying to use because, if they don't visit a page within 1 minute, their Session will have expired. When the Session is lost, state is lost because the Session is used to maintain state.

If you were creating an eCommerce site that used session variables to maintain the state of a shopping cart, setting the Timeout property to 1 minute would surely aggravate your users. If a user placed a few items in his cart and then, perhaps, sent an email or performed some other activity that kept him from browsing your Web site for longer than 1 minute, when the user went back to continue shopping, his cart would be empty.

For these reasons, choosing an appropriate session timeout value is important. IIS 5.0 should set the default session timeout to 10 minutes, which is a good value for most Web applications. (Note that the beta version of IIS 5.0 shipped with Windows 2000 Release Candidate 2 has the session timeout set to 20 minutes.) If, however, you know that your users will spend long periods of time viewing your Web pages, it would make more sense to up the session timeout. If you expected several hundred concurrent users, it might be beneficial to lower your session timeout from 10 minutes. The best way to determine what timeout value works best for your particular Web site is to simply try various timeout values during high loads and note the performance of your Web server.

The Session is easy to use. It's simple to use session variables anytime you need to maintain state. They are easy to program and work across all ASP pages. This leads us to the third pitfall—creating unneeded session variables. It is easy to become a bit overzealous when using session variables. If you are using session variables to store information that is not user specific, use the Application object instead. For example, many Web sites have a standard navigation footer at the bottom of all of their Web pages. This *navigation footer* displays a list of links to the site's various sections. When you use the Session object to store non-user-specific values, you are wasting your Web server's resources. Why should each user have the text navigation footer stored in his Session, when every user sees the same footer?

11

> **Note**
>
> If you want to have a navigation footer on your Web site, or any other kind of static information that needs to appear on all your ASP pages, optimal performance can be achieved through the use of *include files*. We will discuss how to include files on Day 13, "Reading and Writing Files on the Web Server."

Before deciding to use the Session object, carefully consider a few issues. Do you *need* to maintain state via the Session object? Could cookies be used instead? Because the Session object carries with it potentially grave performance consequences, it is important to ask yourself the following questions before deciding to use the Session object:

- How many concurrent users do I expect on my Web site at any given time?
- How many session variables do I plan on using?
- Can I maintain state using an alternative approach?

If you expect many concurrent users, you should *not* use any session variables. The number of concurrent users that your Web site can handle before showing signs of performance degradation depends on the hardware you use to run your Web site. When I develop ASP applications, if the number of concurrent users is expected to be more than 50, I try my best to refrain from using session variables.

Session Variables Without Cookies

Because each user has his own `Session`, the Web server needs some way to tie a particular user to a particular `Session` object instance. This is done through a unique
`SessionID`, which links together the `Session` and the user. The `SessionID` is found both
on the particular `Session` object instance, and on the client's computer, in the form of a
cookie. When the user requests an ASP page that uses session variables, the user's session cookie can be read and matched up to an existing `Session` in memory.

What happens, though, if the user has configured her browser not to accept cookies?
Because the Web server cannot associate the user with a particular `Session`, all session
variables accessed by this user will return empty strings. You will not be able to maintain
state for this user, or any other user who does not accept cookies.

To remedy this problem, Microsoft has created an *ISAPI filter* that will *simulate* cookies
for users who have configured their browsers not to accept cookies.

NEW TERM   An *ISAPI filter* is a small, low-level program that enhances a Web server by pro-
            viding additional functionality. *ISAPI* is an acronym for Internet Server
Application Programming Interface.

This ISAPI filter, named *Cookie Munger*, can be downloaded for free from Microsoft's
Web site (http://www.microsoft.com). By using this ISAPI filter on your Web server,
those who do not accept cookies can still utilize session variables.

When a user who accepts cookies visits your site, Cookie Munger does nothing.
However, when a user who does not accept cookies visits your site, the following transactions occur:

1. When a page is requested, Cookie Munger generates a `SessionID` for that particular client.

2. The ASP page takes that `SessionID` and can map it to a particular `Session` object
   instance.

3. When an ASP page is sent to a client that does not accept cookies, Cookie Munger
   parses the HTML for hyperlinks. At the end of the hyperlink URL, Cookie Munger
   adds the synthesized `SessionID` for the client.

4. When a client requests a URL that has the `SessionID` appended to the end, Cookie
   Munger removes the appended `SessionID`, calls the ASP page requested, and
   passes the `SessionID` to the ASP page.

Through these four steps, Cookie Munger allows state to be maintained via session variables for those who do not accept cookies.

If Cookie Munger can be used to allow all visitors to use session variables, you may be wondering why it isn't installed with IIS by default. Because Cookie Munger has to process every ASP page being requested and process every outgoing ASP response, this can place a tremendous burden on your Web server, especially for high volume sites. Cookie Munger should only be used for low volume sites where it is necessary for all users to be able to store and retrieve session variables. For more information on Cookie Munger, visit Microsoft's Web site.

The Application Object

ASP, along with the Session object, provides another intrinsic object to aid in state maintenance. The Application object can be used to persist information for the entire Web site. You can also think of the Application as a warehouse, except that with the Application there is only one warehouse, regardless of the number of users. Each user, when requesting or storing information in the Application warehouse, is working with the same warehouse. Figure 11.10 shows how a single Application object instance is used by all the Web site's users.

FIGURE 11.10

Only one instance of the Application *object exists.*

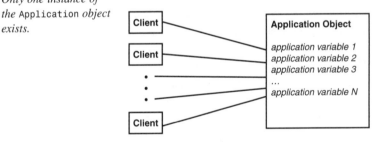

Each Client Accesses the Same Application Object
Since There Is Only One Application Object per Web Application

The Application object, like the Session object, can be populated with bits of information, referred to as *application variables*. Application variables are assigned and read just like session variables. In the following code, line 1 shows how to assign a value to an application variable, whereas line 2 demonstrates how to read the contents of an application variable:

```
1:  Application(applicationVariableName) = Value
2:  Variable = Application(applicationVariableName)
```

Because only one instance of the Application object exists for the entire Web site, it should only be used to store information that is specific to the entire Web site. The Application object, like the Session object, exists in the Web server's memory. Because there is only one instance of the Application object, you can be more liberal with the types of objects you place inside the `Application` object. However, some common mistakes are still made concerning the usage of the `Application` object. This topic is addressed in detail later today in the section "Pitfalls of Application Variables."

Using Application Variables

For an `Application` warehouse to serve any functional purpose, you need to be able to insert and retrieve information from it. These bits of information—referred to as application variables— can be of any data type and are read and retrieved in a fashion similar to session variables. The following two lines of code demonstrate how application variables can be retrieved:

```
1:  dtSomeDate = Application("LastMessageDate")
2:  strEmail = Application("WebmasterEmailAddress")
```

Line 1 reads the `LastMessageDate` application variable into `dtSomeDate`. Earlier today, in the section "Using the `Application` Object," we discussed a scenario concerning a message forum Web site. It might be neat to track the last date and time of a post and display that tidbit of information on the Web site. This example is an excellent choice for using application variables, and line 1 shows how you could read the `LastMessageDate` application variable. Line 2 reads the contents of the `WebmasterEmailAddress` application variable, storing it in the variable `strEmail`.

Because only one `Application` object is shared among all users, you must take care when updating application variable values. Because many people can visit your site simultaneously, when you update an application variable, you must ensure that only one user can update it at a time. The `Application` object provides a method named `Lock`, which should be called before updating any application variables. When this method is called, no other users can update any application variables until the `UnLock` method is called, or the page that issued the `Lock` command finishes processing. So, if you wanted to set the `LastMessageDate` to the current date and time, you could use the following code:

```
1:  Application.Lock
2:  Application("LastMessageDate") = Now()
3:  Application.UnLock
```

Line 1 locks the `Application` object, so that no other users can update application variables while the current user updates `LastMessageDate`. Next, `LastMessageDate` is set to the Web server's current date and time (line 2), and finally, in line 3, the `Application` object is unlocked. Anytime you alter the value of an application variable, make sure to surround the statement with `Application.Lock` and `Application.UnLock`.

Application variables can store any type of variable. The syntax for storing arrays and objects is identical to the syntax for storing such variables with the `Session` object. Remember, when storing objects in the `Application` object, you must use the `Set` keyword to obtain an instance of the object:

```
Set Application(applicationVariableName) = ObjectInstance
```

The `Application` object also contains two collections that reveal the application variables. These collections, `Contents` and `StaticObjects`, are used much like the `Session` object's `Contents` and `StaticObjects` collections. The code in Listing 11.12 uses the `Application` object's `Contents` collection to list all the application variables.

LISTING 11.12 The `Contents` Collection Contains All Non-Object Application Variables

```
 1:  <%@ Language=VBScript %>
 2:  <% Option Explicit %>
 3:  <%
 4:    'How many session variables are there?
 5:    Response.Write "There are " & Application.Contents.Count & _
 6:              " Application variables<P>"
 7:    Dim strName, iLoop
 8:    'Use a For Each ... Next to loop through the entire collection
 9:    For Each strName in Application.Contents
10:      'Is this session variable an array?
11:      If IsArray(Application(strName)) then
12:        'If it is an array, loop through each element one at a time
13:        For iLoop = LBound(Application(strName)) to _
14:                                    UBound(Application (strName))
15:          Response.Write strName & "(" & iLoop & ") - " & _
16:              Application(strName)(iLoop) & "<BR>"
17:        Next
18:      Else
19:        'We aren't dealing with an array, so just display the variable
20:        Response.Write strName & " - " & _
21:                    Application.Contents(strName) & "<BR>"
22:      End If
23:    Next
24:  %>
```

ANALYSIS Listing 11.12 displays all the user's application variables and values. Take a moment to compare Listing 11.12 to Listing 11.11. Note that the *only* change made was replacing every instance of `Session` with `Application`. The `Session` and `Application` objects are similar in both purpose and syntax. The major difference between the two objects is that the `Session` object stores unique information about each user, whereas the `Application` object stores information general to all users.

Due to the similarities between Listing 11.11 and Listing 11.12, only a brief analysis of the code in Listing 11.12 is given here. For a more detailed explanation, see the analysis following Listing 11.11. Listing 11.12, starts off by displaying the total number of application variables (line 5). Line 9 starts a `For Each...Next` loop through the

`Contents` collection. Because the `Contents` collection can contain arrays, before you display an application variable, you need to first determine whether it is an array. Line 11 accomplishes this, using the `IsArray` function.

If the application variable is an array, lines 13 through 17 are executed. Line 13, a `For` loop, iterates through each element in the application variable array, displaying the contents of each element (line 15). If, however, the application variable is *not* an array, the `Else` block starting on line 18 is executed. The application variable's name and value are displayed on line 20.

Pitfalls of Application Variables

Because only one instance of the `Application` object exists for the entire Web application, application variables can be used more liberally than session variables. However, the `Application` object does take up memory on the Web server, so only items that *need* to be stored in application scope should be entered into the `Application` object. Two common pitfalls should be avoided when working with application variables:

- Pitfall 1—Do not put objects into the `Application` object unless vitally needed.
- Pitfall 2—Only create application variables that are necessary. Why create unneeded application variables when they'll only waste your Web server's memory?

A common pitfall among developers is wanting to place objects in the `Application`. One object that is particularly alluring to put into the `Application` is the `ADO Connection` object, which is used to connect to a database. We'll discuss this object in detail during Week 3. It may seem like a good idea to create a single database connection object and have all users communicate to a database through that object. However, as with most other objects, it is always best to wait to create the object until you need it. In fact, the `ADO Connection` object will degrade your server's performance if put into the `Application` object.

Like the `Session` object, the `Application` object is easy to use, and the temptation to create a plethora of application variables is high indeed. Many developers use the `Application` object to store many Web site-wide constants—for example, a navigational footer common to all Web pages, or perhaps the Webmaster's email address. Although it's better to place these items in the `Application` object than in the `Session` object, they belong best in a static text file on the Web server. This text file can then be *included* into any ASP page that needs to display the navigation footer or the Webmaster's email address. We will discuss how to include files on Day 13.

Sometimes, however, the use of application variables is preferred to include files. If the data you need to store changes often, such as the last post to a message board, then the information should be stored in the `Application` object. Include files should only be used if the data is static and not susceptible to frequent change.

Although you can afford to be less prudent when creating application variables than you can be when creating session variables, you should still strive to use the minimum needed amount of such variables. Because the Application object persists in the Web server's memory, the fewer the application variables stored within it, the less drain on the Web server's performance. Therefore, the Application should remain free of objects and contain only needed application variables.

Initializing Application and Session Variables

Recall that the Session and Application objects serve as warehouses for session and application variables, respectively. When the user first visits the site, a new Session warehouse is created. What is inside this warehouse by default? Initially, the warehouse is empty. Attempting to retrieve a nonexistent session variable from the users Session returns an empty string.

However, the Session and Application objects both have an event you can use to initialize the contents of your users Session and your Web site's Application. This event is called the OnStart event, and it occurs at different times for the Session and Application objects. The Session's OnStart event occurs whenever a new user comes to the site. This is when a new Session object instance is created for this particular user. In the OnStart event, you can create the session variables you plan to use and initialize them to certain values. The Application's OnStart event fires when the first Session object is instantiated—that is, when the first Session's OnStart event fires.

To create and initialize session and application variables, you need to write event handlers for the OnStart events. Listing 11.13 displays the OnStart event handler for both the Session and Application objects.

LISTING 11.13 Initializing Application and Session Variables in the OnStart Events

```
1:    Sub Application_OnStart()
2:        Application("LastPost") = ""
3:    End Sub
4:
5:    Sub Session_OnStart()
6:        Session("LogonTime") = Now()
7:        Session("Name") = ""
8:
9:        Dim aPi(2)
10:       aPi(0) = 3
11:       aPi(1) = 1
12:       aPi(2) = 4
13:       Session("Pi") = aPi
14:   End Sub
```

11

ANALYSIS Listing 11.13 displays the OnStart event handlers for the Session and Application objects. The Application object's OnStart event handler begins on line 1. A single application variable, LastPost, is initialized to a blank string (line 2). The Session object's OnStart event handler begins on line 5. Line 6 creates a session variable named LogonTime that is initialized to the Web server's current date and time. Next, a session variable, Name, is created and initialized to an empty string (line 7). Line 9 creates aPi, an array, and lines 10 through 13, set the three elements of aPi. Line 13 creates the final session variable, setting it equal to aPi.

Note the syntax for creating an event handler (lines 1 and 5). First, a subroutine is created and named with the object's name, followed by an underscore, and then followed by the event name. Because the OnStart event passes in no parameters, no arguments are in the event handler definition.

Whenever these events fire, the functions in Listing 11.13 are executed. The OnStart event for the Session object occurs whenever a new visitor (one that does not already have a Session instance) arrives at the site. If your Web site experiences a lot of traffic, this event can fire hundreds, or even thousands of times an hour. The Application's OnStart event, however, fires only once, right before the first Session is created. If you restart your Web server, though, the next visit after restarting causes the Application object's OnStart event to fire.

Creating a Global.asa File

We've looked at the code to handle the OnStart event of the Session and Application objects, but we've not discussed *where* we should place the code shown in Listing 11.13. To handle Session and Application events, a special file needs to be created. This file must be named, precisely, Global.asa and needs to be placed in the root directory of your Web site. When a new user comes to your site and Global.asa exists, the correct event handler in Global.asa is executed.

What should Global.asa look like? Listing 11.13 showed the syntax for the OnStart event handler, but Global.asa also needs a couple extra lines to run properly. Listing 11.14 shows a complete Global.asa, incorporating the event handlers shown in Listing 11.13.

LISTING 11.14 A Complete Global.asa

```
1: <SCRIPT LANGUAGE=VBScript RUNAT=Server>
2:     Sub Application_OnStart()
3:         Application("LastPost") = ""
4:     End Sub
5:
6:     Sub Session_OnStart()
```

```
7:        Session("LogonTime") = Now()
8:        Session("Name") = ""
9:
10:       Dim aPi(2)
11:       aPi(0) = 3
12:       aPi(1) = 1
13:       aPi(2) = 4
14:       Session("Pi") = aPi
15:   End Sub
16: </SCRIPT>
```

ANALYSIS   Listing 11.14 shows a complete Global.asa file. For this to take effect, it needs to be placed in the Web's root directory. Note that lines 2 through 15 are identical to lines 1 through 14 in Listing 11.13. The only difference between the two listings is that Listing 11.14 contains the <SCRIPT> tag (lines 1 and 16). The <SCRIPT> tag on line 1 contains two properties, LANGUAGE and RUNAT. LANGUAGE determines what language the <SCRIPT> block will be written in. RUNAT determines whether the <SCRIPT> block will be run on the Web server, or passed to the client. We discussed the <SCRIPT> block notation for writing ASP on Day 2, "Dissecting Your First ASP Script." Line 16 contains the close of the <SCRIPT> tag, specifying that the <SCRIPT> block has ended.

11

Note   Global.asa should only contain initialization of session and application variables. In fact, all the session and application variables that you use on your Web site should be created and initialized in Global.asa.

Both the Session and Application objects support another event, the OnEnd event. For the Session object, this event is fired when a user's Session times out, or when the Session.Abandon is called. The Application object's OnEnd event is fired when the Web server is being shut down. You can perform any cleanup maintenance in these two event handlers. For example, if you created any session variables in the OnStart event handler, you should explicitly delete those objects in the OnEnd event handler.

In the Session object's OnEnd event handler, the only built-in objects available are the Session, Application, and Server objects. In the Application object's OnEnd, only the Application and Server objects are available for use. This is understandable because the Application's OnEnd event handler isn't fired until the last Session is destroyed. Listing 11.15 shows a complete Global.asa, one that contains an OnStart and OnEnd event handler for both the Session and Application object.

LISTING 11.15 Global.asa Containing the OnEnd Event

```
 1: <SCRIPT LANGUAGE=VBScript RUNAT=Server>
 2:    Sub Application_OnStart()
 3:      'Create an object in the Application scope
 4:      Set Application("MyDict") = _
 5:                    Server.CreateObject("Scripting.Dictionary")
 6:      End Sub
 7:
 8:    Sub Application_OnEnd()
 9:      'Explicitly free the Application Variable object
10:      Set Application("MyDict") = Nothing
11:    End Sub
12:
13:
14:    Sub Session_OnStart()
15:      'Create an object in the session scope.  This is
16:      'not wise, but we are doing it to illustrate how
17:      'the OnEnd event should be used
18:      Set Session("MyObject") = Server.CreateObject("My.Obj")
19:    End Sub
20:
21:    Sub Session_OnEnd()
22:      'Explicitly free the session variable object
23:      Set Session("MyObject") = Nothing
24:    End Sub
25: </SCRIPT>
```

ANALYSIS Listing 11.15 enhances the Global.asa file by adding the OnEnd event handlers for the Session and Application objects. Listing 11.15 begins with the OnStart event handler for the Application object (line 2). In this event handler, an application variable named MyDict is created that holds an instance of the Dictionary object (line 4). On line 8, the OnEnd event for the Application object is placed. Note how the subroutine's definition is similar to that of the OnStart event handler. The only difference is that in place of OnStart, OnEnd is used instead. Line 10 explicitly frees the MyDict application variable by setting it equal to Nothing.

The Session object's OnStart event handler is coded on line 14. When a new Session is created, a session variable named MyObject is created and set equal to an instance of the My.Obj object (line 18). Placing an object in the Session, of course, could lead to performance degradation on high volume Web sites. On line 21, the OnEnd event handler for the Session object starts. Finally, on line 23, the session variable MyObject is explicitly destroyed by setting it equal to Nothing.

Note that the OnEnd event handlers are only being used to explicitly free objects. Rarely do you place anything else in the OnEnd event handlers. Because the Session object's OnEnd event handler occurs a while after the user has left your site (depending on the

Session.Timeout property), you cannot display a message to them, or redirect them to another page. The OnEnd event handlers should do nothing more than simply clean up the objects created by the OnStart event handlers.

Do	Don't
DO use Global.asa to create and initialize all your session and application variables with the OnStart event handlers. Also, Global.asa should contain the OnEnd event handlers to explicitly free any session or application variable objects.	DON'T use Global.asa to try to redirect users to other pages or to display or retrieve information.

Summary

Today we examined a number of approaches to maintaining state. We looked at how to use the querystring to pass state information around from one page to another via hyperlinks. We also looked at using cookies to persist state. The bulk of the day, though, concentrated on using the Session and Application objects.

The Session object is a built-in ASP object designed to persist user-specific information. New visitors are granted their own Sessions, which serve as warehouses for session variables. These session variables are bits of personalized information, different for each user. Because a Session object instance exists for each user, it is important to use session variables sparingly. The more session variables used, the more memory consumed by each Session object instance. If your site has many concurrent users, such memory consumption may affect the Web server's performance.

The Application object is another intrinsic ASP object. The purpose of the Application object, however, is to maintain Web site-specific information. Only one instance of the Application object exists for the entire Web application. Each client accesses this one instance when retrieving or setting Application information. Because multiple users can modify application variables at the same time, it is important to Lock the Application object before modifying any application variables. After you have made your updates to the application variables, be sure to UnLock the Application object.

Finally, we discussed how to initialize your application and session variables using the OnStart event handler of the Application and Session objects. The Session and Application objects have one other event as well, the OnEnd event, which should be used to explicitly free any session or application level objects. The event handlers for both the `Application` and `Session` objects need to be placed in a file in the Web's root directory named `Global.asa`. Placing these event handlers here ensures that they will be executed when the `OnStart` and `OnEnd` events fire.

Tomorrow we will examine some standard ASP components. These components, written by Microsoft, provide some powerful functionality and can help make your Web site easier to manage and update. We will also talk briefly about the built-in `Server` object and how it is used to instantiate objects.

Q&A

Q Do I need to have a `Global.asa` even if I don't need event handlers for `OnStart` and `OnEnd`?

A If you plan on using session or application variables at all on your site, you should have a `Global.asa`. The `OnStart` event for the `Application` and `Session` objects should be used to initialize your session and application variables. If, for some reason, you want to use session or application variables on your site but do not want to initialize them in the `OnStart` event handler, you should still create a *blank Global.asa* file. A blank `Global.asa` file contains the four event handlers but places no code inside these event handlers. Here is an example of a blank `Global.asa` file:

```
<SCRIPT LANGUAGE=vbscript RUNAT=SERVER>
Sub Application_OnStart()
End Sub

Sub Application_OnEnd()
End Sub


Sub Session_OnStart()
End Sub

Sub Session_OnEnd()
End Sub
</SCRIPT>
```

If you plan on using session or application variables on your Web site, always have a `Global.asa` file in your Web's root directory. If you don't want to write any event handlers for the `Application` or `Session` objects' `OnStart` or `OnEnd` events, simply use a blank `Global.asa`.

Q When initializing application variables in the `OnStart` event of the `Application` object, do I need to first `Lock` and then `UnLock` the `Application` object?

A Whenever you alter the contents of an application variable in an ASP page, it is important to use the Lock and UnLock methods of the Application object. However, Locking and UnLocking in the Application object's OnStart event is not necessary. Why is it important to Lock and UnLock on ASP pages but not in the Application's OnStart event?

With ASP pages, because every user accesses the same instance of the Application object, when one user changes an application variable's value, the change affects all other users. Because multiple users may be trying to update the same application variable simultaneously, to prevent the application variable data from being corrupted, it is important to Lock the Application object before altering a variable. When finished, UnLock the Application object. This will allow the next user to alter an application variable.

The Application object's OnStart event, however, only fires once, when the first instance of the Session object is created. Because this only happens once, when the first user is visiting since the Web server was last restarted, there are no concurrency issues. Therefore, using the Lock and UnLock methods in the OnStart event of the Application object is unneeded.

Q **What method of state maintenance is best?**

A This depends on a number of factors. Because performance is important on a Web server, you want to make sure that you choose a state maintenance method that will not greatly impair the performance of your Web site. The use of session variables can lead to serious performance degradation if they are not properly used. First and foremost, it is vitally important *not* to place objects into the Session. Second, be sure not to create unneeded session variables. Finally, make sure that you have set a reasonable value for the Timeout property.

If you want to maintain state for a period longer than the user's visit to your site, you will need to use cookies. Some Web surfers, unfortunately, will have their browsers set up not to receive cookies. However, these people are in the minority. If you need to ensure that every user can have state maintained, whether or not they accept cookies, you will need to use the querystring method discussed in the section "Passing Information Through the Querystring," or you will have to use Cookie Munger to simulate cookie usage.

11

Workshop

The Workshop provides quiz questions to help you solidify your understanding of the material covered and exercises to provide you with experience in using what you've learned. Try to understand the quiz and exercise answers before continuing to tomorrow's lesson. Quiz answers are provided in Appendix A, and exercise answers can be found at http://www.mcp.com/info.

Quiz

1. Will the querystring method of maintaining state work if the user has configured her browser not to accept cookies?

2. If you need to maintain user-specific state for weeks at a time, should you use the querystring method, the cookies method, or the Session object?

3. What does the Timeout property of the Session object do?

4. True or False: Objects should be put into the user's Session.

5. Why is it important to Lock and UnLock the Application object before altering the values of application variables?

6. In what file should you place the code for the OnStart and OnEnd events of the Application and Session objects?

7. What is Cookie Munger used for?

8. What collection, present in both the Session and Application objects, contains all the non-object variables?

9. What property of the Session object uniquely identifies each Session instance?

10. When does the Application object's OnEnd event fire?

Exercises

1. Start by creating a blank Global.asa file. Next, add code to the Session object's OnStart event handler that will create a session variable named LogOnTime. LogOnTime should be initialized to the Web server's current date and time. On an ASP page, have a message print out, You arrived at this site at, and then have it display the LogOnTime session variable.

2. Write a program that will use session variables to determine whether a user has cookies enabled. Remember that for a user's session variables to be saved, he must have cookies enabled. (Hint: Because a user needs to accept cookies to have his session variables persisted, if you write a session variable on one ASP page, transfer to another ASP page, and that session variable does not exist, what does that tell you about the user's cookie acceptance?)

DAY **12**

Working with Common ASP Components

As you develop ASP pages, some of the code you will need is already written and packaged into a component. All you need to do is use it. This chapter will teach you how to do that by looking at three of the most common components that Microsoft provides for developers. Today, you will learn the following:

- How components make things easier for you
- How to create and delete instances of components
- How to use the Ad Rotator component
- How to use the Content Linker component
- How to use the Browser Capabilities component

Using Components

Using code that has already been written is essential. If everybody had to build everything from scratch, computing would not have gotten too far. Fortunately, there are many ways to reuse code. Copy and paste might work for small things, but it's too unwieldy for larger pieces of code. This is why components are used. Components package the things you need together, keeping them separate, yet accessible.

Components can be a tremendous help, but only if you know how to use them. Some details will differ from component to component. You need to read the documentation carefully for any component you plan to use. Just about any ASP problem you can think of has a component solution, so it is well worth learning to use them.

Components Make Life Easy

There are some things that Web programmers need to do constantly. When a task becomes common like this, someone will write a component to handle it. Some components are available on the Web for free, and some are for sale. Still others are included by Microsoft with IIS. Rather than reinventing the wheel all the time, learn to use these components. The components covered in this chapter make it easy to display a randomly chosen advertising graphic, add hassle-free navigational controls, and tailor your site to the user's browser.

Using a Component in ASP

You need to know two things before you begin using components: how to create instances of them and what to do when you are finished with them. These topics were covered as they pertain to objects in general on Day 6, "Working with Objects."

Instantiating Components

You instantiate these built-in components using `Set` and the `CreateObject` method of the `Server` object. Just as before, the first step is to declare the variable that will hold the instance of the component. You usually begin the variable name with "obj," just so that you can remember what it is. Instantiating a component looks like this:

```
Dim objWhatever
Set objWhatever = Server.CreateObject("classname.componentname")
```

For the components discussed in this chapter, `classname` is `"MSWC"`. MSWC is the package these components are in.

Generally, the variable should be declared at the beginning, but the object should be instantiated no sooner than it has to be.

For most components, you will not need more than one instance of it per page.

Freeing the Memory Associated with Components

When you create an instance of a component, ASP sets aside some memory especially for it. It is important that you explicitly free this memory when you are finished with that component. Although ASP *should* handle this for you, it is not terribly wise to rely on it.

If ASP fails, you can face all kinds of problems. Web servers tend to stay on 24 hours per day for long periods of time. If memory is getting used and not freed on your pages, a small problem has plenty of time to grow into a big one.

Explicitly free the memory associated with obj*Whatever* like this:

```
Set objWhatever = Nothing
```

Many sites have crashed simply because someone forgot this important step.

Developing with Microsoft's ASP Components

Three components are probably already installed on your system. Microsoft includes the Ad Rotator, Content Linker, and Browser Capabilities components with Personal Web Server and IIS. These three are pretty easy to use and can be very handy.

Ad Rotator

Ads are everywhere on the Web. For better or for worse, the 440 by 60 banner ad has become as instantly recognizable a part of the Web as the "www.com." Microsoft makes it easy to add a random changing banner to your site with the Ad Rotator component.

Using the Ad Rotator

You need three components to use the Ad Rotator. The first is a file that tells the Ad Rotator what images to use, what to link them to, and so on. This file is called the rotator schedule file. The second part is an ASP page that handles redirecting the user to the appropriate URL. The third part is the actual page that will display the ads.

The first thing to do is create a rotator schedule file. This is done like this:

```
 1: REDIRECT URL
 2: WIDTH pixel_width
 3: HEIGHT pixel_height
 4: BORDER border_thickness
 5: *
 6: FirstImageURL
 7: HomepageURL
 8: AltText
 9: Weight
10: SecondImageURL
11: HomepageURL
12: AltText
13: Weight
14: …
```

ANALYSIS The first four lines affect every banner.

12

URL (line 1) is the URL of an ASP page or a .dll of yours that will handle redirecting the user to the correct page. This option allows you to control what happens when a user clicks the banner. You can force the new page to open in a separate window. You will probably want to record for your statistics that someone has clicked that banner. This can be either a full URL or a relative one. Specifying a URL is optional. Simply omit the line if you want the current page to handle redirection.

pixel_width (line 2) specifies the width of the banners in pixels. This line is also optional. The default is 440.

pixel_height (line 3) specifies the height of the banners in pixels. This line is also optional. The default is 60.

border_thickness (line 4) specifies the thickness, in pixels, of the border that is drawn around the image. This line is optional. The default value is 1.

The asterisk on line 5 is important. It indicates where the first section of the file ends and the second section begins. It must be on a line by itself. The second section consists of four lines per ad.

FirstImageURL (line 6) is a URL that specifies where to find the graphic to display for this ad. It may be either a relative URL or a full one.

HomepageURL (line 7) is the URL that the user should be taken to when he clicks the link. This URL is then passed on to the redirect URL. If there is no page they should be taken to, a hyphen (-) should be used.

AltText (line 8) is the text that should be displayed when the user has graphics turned off. It is also displayed before the image has loaded and when the user moves his/her mouse over the image.

Weight (line 9) is a number between 0 and 10,000 that indicates how the ad should be weighted. If all the ads in the list have the same *Weight*, they will all be equally likely to appear. If there were three ads, one of weight 10 and two of weight 20, the one of weight 10 would appear 20% of the time, and the other would each appear 40% of the time. The fraction of the time an ad will appear is computed by dividing its weight by the sum of all the weights in the file. If the sum of all the *Weight*s in the file is more than 10,000, an error will occur.

Many sites that sell advertising have a standard weight that most ads are given. Then they allow advertisers to pay extra to have their ad appear twice as often as normal. In this case, that ad would be given a weight equal to twice the normal weight. You might also allow an advertiser to buy one block and use four different ads. In this case, each ad would be given a weight of one-fourth the normal weight.

You can specify any number of banners to be displayed. Simply repeat the pattern. Each banner needs four lines of information.

So let's create a rotator schedule file that has four ads. Save Listing 12.1 as `AdList.txt`.

LISTING 12.1   Creating a Rotator Schedule File

```
 1:    REDIRECT AdRedirect.asp
 2:    WIDTH 440
 3:    HEIGHT 60
 4:    BORDER 1
 5:    *
 6:    banners/advertise.gif
 7:    AdvertiseHere.asp
 8:    Advertise with this site
 9:    15
10:    banners/companyX.gif
11:    -
12:    Sponsored by CompanyX
13:    20
14:    banners/companyY.gif
15:    http://www.CompanyY.com
16:    Shop at Company Y
17:    20
18:    banners/companyZ.gif
19:    http://www.CompanyZ.com
20:    Win cash at Company Z!
21:    20
```

ANALYSIS   The first line is the redirect page, which will be created in a moment. The next three specify image width, height, and border thickness. The example uses the default values, so it is not necessary to include these lines, but it does not hurt anything to go ahead and include them. Line 5 is the separator again.

Line 6 specifies the URL to the graphic. For this example, you are assuming that the banners are in a subdirectory of the current one, called banners. This first ad, as you can probably tell, is an ad encouraging businesses to advertise on the site. The remaining three are for companies X, Y, and Z. Their ads are weighted a bit more heavily than the first one. Notice that Company X does not have a Web page.

Now create a redirect page. It will be called like this:

`AdRedirect.asp?URL=HomepageURL&image=imageURL`

So the simplest redirect page looks like this:

`<% Response.Redirect(Request.QueryString("url")) %>`

12

This will do for now, so go ahead and save this in a file called AdRedirect.asp.

Now all you have left to do is write the pages that are going to include the ads. This is done using the GetAdvertisement method. GetAdvertisement randomly chooses one of the ads in the list file and generates the HTML code to display it, with the appropriate link. If the Company Z ad were chosen, the code would look like this:

```
<A HREF="AdRedirect.asp?url=
http://www.CompanyZ.com&image=banners/companyZ.gif" >
<IMG SRC="banners/companyZ.gif"
ALT="Half-price sale at Company Z!" WIDTH=440
HEIGHT=60 BORDER=1></A>
```

If the ad chosen has no Web page, the image is displayed without a link but with a border.

Listing 12.2 is an example page that uses the Ad Rotator and the AdList.txt you already made to display a banner at the top and bottom.

LISTING 12.2   A Page that Displays Ads

```
 1:  <%@ Language=VBScript %>
 2:  <% Option Explicit %>

 3:  <%
 4:      Dim objAd
 5:      Set objAd = Server.CreateObject("MSWC.AdRotator")
 6:  %>

 7:  <HTML>
 8:   <BODY>
 9:      Please support my advertisers.<BR>
10:      <%= objAd.GetAdvertisement("AdList.txt") %>
11:      <P>Welcome to my site.
12:      <P>More text<P>
13:      Still more text<P>
14:      Here is my bottom ad.<BR>
15:  <%
16:      Response.Write(objAd.GetAdvertisement("AdList.txt"))
17:      Set objAd = Nothing
18:  %>
19:   </BODY>
20:  </HTML>
```

ANALYSIS   In Listing 12.2, line 4 declares objAd, and line 5 uses Set to instantiate the Ad Rotator. You then get into the HTML. Line 10 inserts a banner. Notice that this assumes that the rotator schedule file AdList.txt is in the same directory as the current page. If that is not the case, the path should be provided. Lines 11 through 14 are just generic text to take up some space, and line 16 adds the bottom banner. Line 17 is important! It frees the memory associated with objAd. You can see the output of the listing in Figure 12.1.

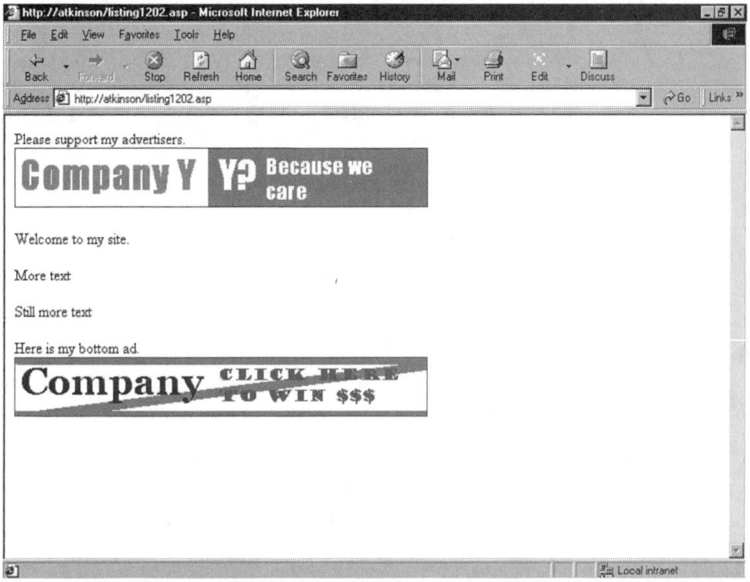

FIGURE 12.1

Page that uses Ad Rotator to display banners at the top and bottom.

If you had two separate lists of advertisers, you could display ads from both using only one instance of the Ad Rotator. Just specify the file you want to select from when you call GetAdvertisement. This gives you a little more freedom because the file specifies the banner size and the redirect page. This way, you could use the same component instance to display a 440 by 60 banner at the top and 100 by 30 buttons on the side, and use a separate redirect file for each, if you wanted. Listing 12.3 does this.

LISTING 12.3 A Page That Displays Different Kinds of Ads

```
1:  <%@ Language=VBScript %>
2:  <% Option Explicit %>
3:  <%
4:      Dim objAd
5:      Set objAd = Server.CreateObject("MSWC.AdRotator")
6:  %>
7:  <HTML>
8:   <BODY>
9:    <TABLE width=100%><TR><TD>
10:     <%= objAd.GetAdvertisement("SmallAdList.txt") %><BR>
11:     <%= objAd.GetAdvertisement("SmallAdList.txt") %><BR>
12:     <%= objAd.GetAdvertisement("SmallAdList.txt") %>
13:    </TD><TD>
14:     Please support my advertisers.<BR>
15:     <%= objAd.GetAdvertisement("AdList.txt") %>
16:     <P>Welcome to my site.
```

continues

LISTING **12.3** continued

```
17:      <P>More text<P>
18:      Still more text<P>
19:      Here is my bottom ad.<BR>
20:  <%
21:      Response.Write(objAd.GetAdvertisement("AdList.txt"))
22:      Set objAd = Nothing
23:  %>
24:      </TD></TR></TABLE>
25:  </BODY>
26: </HTML>
```

ANALYSIS Listing 12.3 displays a top and bottom banner ad, plus three small button ads on the side. The banner ads are still being read from AdList.txt, and the button ads are being read from SmallAdList.txt. Lines 9, 13, and 24 create the table structure that allows you to put the buttons running down the left side of the page. The three buttons are created with lines 10 through 12. GetAdvertisement is called three times with SmallAdList.txt. The rest of the page is the same as in Listing 12.2.

Listing 12.3 uses a second schedule file called SmallAdList.txt. You can see this schedule file in Listing 12.4.

LISTING **12.4** SmallAdList.txt Is Used in Listing 12.3

```
1:  REDIRECT AdRedirect.asp
2:  WIDTH 100
3:  HEIGHT 30
4:  BORDER 0
5:  *
6:  banners/smadvertise.gif
7:  AdvertiseHere.asp
8:  Advertise with this site
9:  15
10: banners/smcompanyX.gif
11: -
12: Sponsored by CompanyX
13: 20
14: banners/widgets.gif
15: http://www.widgetmakersinc.com
16: Need widgets?
17: 20
18: banners/winmoney.gif
19: http://www.winmoneyhere.com
20: Win up to $1000
21: 20
```

ANALYSIS Listing 12.4 displays the `SmallAdList.txt` file that is used in Listing 12.3. It uses the same redirect file as `AdList.txt`, `AdRedirect.asp`, as you can see on line 1. It specifies that the width of these images is 100 (line 2), the height is 30 (line 3), and that no border should be displayed (line 4). Line 5 is the separator. These are more generic ads like before. This list includes a smaller ad encouraging companies to advertise on the site (lines 6-9), a smaller ad for Company X (lines 10-13, again with no Web page), an ad for "widgetmakersinc.com" (lines 14-17), and an ad for some sort of giveaway (lines 18-21).

With the `SmallAdList.txt` shown in Listing 12.4, we can now correctly view Listing 12.3. Figure 12.2 shows the results of this.

FIGURE 12.2

The results of Listing 12.3.

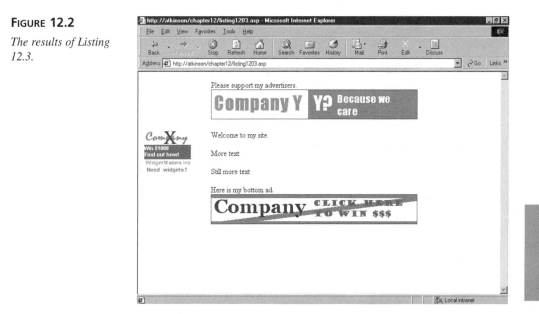

It might be nice to have a report page where advertisers could see the statistics for their ads. To do this, you would need your redirect page to record the banner that had been clicked. This allows your advertisers to determine which ads are most effective. This could be done either by writing to a text file on your server or through a database. Writing to files is discussed on Day 13, "Reading and Writing Files on the Web Server," and databases are discussed during Week 3.

Properties of the Ad Rotator

You can set a few properties of the Ad Rotator. For the most part, you should not need these. Generally, you should set the properties you need in the schedule file. But it can occasionally be handy to have a way to change them within the ASP page.

You can override the border specified in your schedule file by using the property `Border`.

`objAd.Border = 0` forcibly turns off the border around any banners that follow.

You can change whether the banner is a link by using the `Clickable` property. Setting `Clickable` to `False` guarantees that when `GetAdvertisement` is called, it does not include the `<A HREF…>`. Setting `Clickable` back to `True` will restore the settings in the file. If `Clickable` is `True` and an ad has a Web page, the link will be generated.

The third and final property of the Ad Rotator is `TargetFrame`, which is used to specify the frame that the link should be loaded into.

`objAd.TargetFrame = `*`string`* has the effect of inserting *string* into the `<A HREF=…>` tag generated by `GetAdvertisement`. It is generally used with the HTML `TARGET` property. So, for example, to load the link into a frame named `LeftFrame`, you would use the following:

`objAd.TargetFrame = "TARGET = LeftFrame"`

The name of a frame, or any of the special names such as `_self`, `_blank`, `_parent`, or `_top` may be used.

Limitations of the Ad Rotator

There is nothing to guarantee that the ads are unique. The same three buttons may be showing on the side, and the same two banners may be showing at the top and bottom. You can see this in Figure 12.3. Figure 12.3 shows the output of Listing 12.2 on an occasion when the top and bottom banners happen to be the same. If you need assurance of no duplication, do not use Ad Rotator.

NEW TERM Furthermore, it is difficult to obtain complete statistics using the Ad Rotator. It has no easy way to record the number of impressions a given banner receives. An *impression* is a single occasion of a banner being shown.

You can record each time someone clicks a banner within the redirect page. You can also approximate the number of times a given banner is displayed by putting a counter on the page and using the weight given to the ad in the schedule file. There is no easy way, though, to know for certain exactly how many times a banner is displayed. This can be important if you are promising an advertiser that you will display a banner 1,000 times. This is why many web developers go ahead and write their own banner rotation system. There are many articles on the web about how to do this, and it should not be beyond your abilities by the time you finish this book.

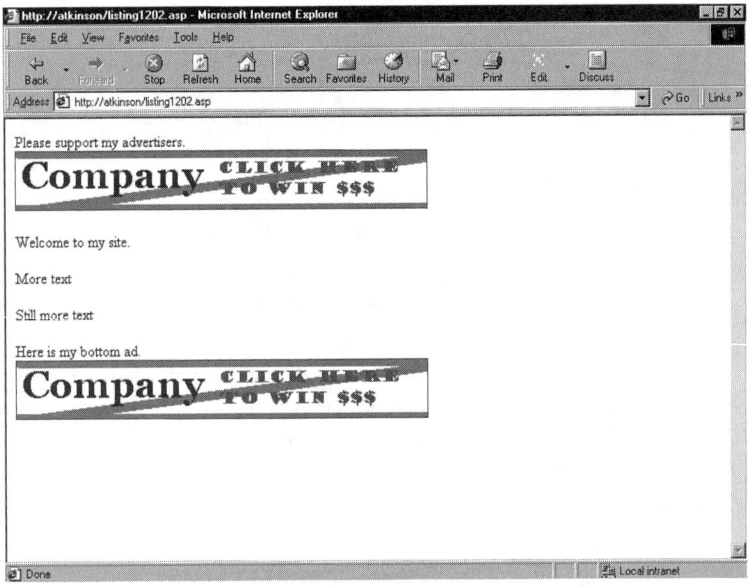

FIGURE 12.3

*There is no guarantee
that the ads will be
unique.*

Content Linker

If you have a site to which you add new content frequently, it can become a bit of a pain.
You probably have to update multiple files every time you need to add a new page.
Content Linker can make organizing a large, frequently updated site much easier. With
content linker, you update one file, and the table of contents and navigational links are
dynamically generated.

When to Use the Content Linker

The Content Linker is especially useful for Web sites that have several related pages that
can be arranged in a sequence. For example, a tutorial would work well. Visitors would
follow a sequence of pages that teach a subject. A dynamically generated link at the bottom would take them to the next chapter. The Content Linker might also be useful on a
site that sells several similar products. Visitors could cycle through the pages to see
everything the site had to offer.

The Content Linker would probably not be so useful on sites that have more of a tree
structure. For example, the typical business site with a main page, products page, locations page, and corporate philosophy page would not benefit much from applying this
component.

Figure 12.4 compares the two types of organizational structures. On the left is the tree
structure, which does not benefit much from the Content Linker. On the right is a more
horizontal structure that would benefit.

12

FIGURE 12.4

Organizational schemes like the one on the right benefit more from the Content Linker than the one on the left.

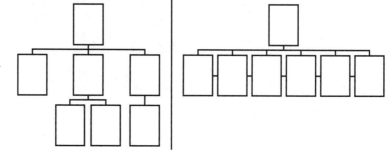

Of course many sites combine the two organizational structures. Such a site could certainly benefit by applying the Content Linker to the portion that was cyclic. Figure 12.5 demonstrates this kind of site organization.

FIGURE 12.5

Many sites combine both organizational structures.

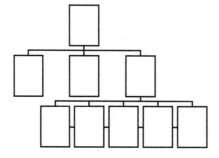

Using the Content Linker

If you want to use the Content Linker, you need a content linking list file. This file has one line per page that you want to link. Each line contains as many as three Tab-separated items:

webpage_URL   description   comment

The last two values are optional.

webpage_URL is the URL of the page you want linked. It must be a relative URL; that is, it should either be of the form *filename* or *directory\filename*. URLs that begin with http or // or \\ will not work.

> **Caution**
>
> Be careful when you create your content linking list file that you do not repeat URLs. This can cause infinite loops and other problems.

description is a text description of the page.

comment is text that describes the page. Unlike *description*, *comment* is not processed by the Content Linker. It is there only for the benefit of people trying to read the list file.

So, let's make a list file. Listing 12.5 shows one with five pages. Save it as `linklist.txt`. When you type it in, be sure that you use one tab to separate the items on each line. Do not use spaces. Do not use more than one tab. One tab exactly is used to separate the *webpage_URL* from the *description* and the *description* from the *comment*.

This example is for a Web site that sells five models of widgets. The owners want users to be able to start looking at one model of the widgets and keep cycling around until they find exactly the model that meets their needs.

LISTING 12.5   Content Linker List File

```
Standard.asp    The Standard Widget    the classic model
Deluxe.asp     The Deluxe Widget     the luxury model
Micro.asp     The MicroWidget     the miniaturized version
Lite.asp     WidgetLite     same flavor, fewer calories
Economy.asp     The EconoWidget     budget-saver model
```

Now that you have this file, what do you do with it? The Content Linker component has the following methods:

- `GetListCount(listfile)` returns the number of pages listed in *listfile*.
- `GetListIndex(listfile)` returns the index number of the current page in *listfile*.
- `GetNextURL(listfile)` returns the URL of the next page in the linker list file.
- `GetNextDescription(listfile)` returns the description of the next page listed in the linker list file.
- `GetPreviousURL(listfile)` returns the URL of the previous page listed in the linker list file.
- `GetPreviousDescription(listfile)` returns the description of the previous page listed in the linker list file.
- `GetNthURL(listfile, I)` returns the URL of the *I*th page in the linker list file.
- `GetNthDescription(listfile, I)` returns the URL of the *I*th page listed in *listfile*.

The best way to learn how to use these is to see some examples, so let's get started. Listing 12.6 shows a version of `Micro.asp`.

12

LISTING 12.6 Generic Micro.asp

```
 1:   <HTML>
 2:     <HEAD><TITLE>WidgetWorld: MicroWidget</TITLE></HEAD>
 3:       <BODY>
 4:         <CENTER>This is the MicroWidget</CENTER>
 5:         <P><HR>
 6:         <TABLE width=100%><TR><TD align=left>
 7:           <A HREF="Deluxe.asp"><<(The Deluxe Widget)</A>
 8:         </TD><TD align=right>
 9:           <A HREF="Lite.asp">(WidgetLite)>></A>
10:         </TD></TR></TABLE>
11:     </BODY>
12:   </HTML>
```

ANALYSIS Line 7 links to the previous page, and line 9 links to the next page. So what is wrong with this? Suppose that you wanted to add a new product in between the MicroWidget and WidgetLite. In addition to writing the new page, you would have to come back and change the link on line 9 of this page. You would also have to change the "previous page" link in Lite.asp. This is not too big of a problem, but imagine much longer and more complex pages. Imagine adding and removing products regularly. This is why the Content Linker can be useful. Listing 12.7 shows the same page modified to take advantage of the Content Linker.

LISTING 12.7 Micro.asp Modified to Take Advantage of the Content Linker

```
 1:   <%@ Language=VBScript %>
 2:   <%
 3:       Option Explicit
 4:       Dim objNL
 5:   %>
 6:   <HTML>
 7:     <HEAD><TITLE>
 8:       WidgetWorld: The MicroWidget
 9:     </TITLE></HEAD>
10:     <BODY>
11:       <CENTER>This is the MicroWidget</CENTER>
12:       <P><HR>
13:       <TABLE width=100%><TR><TD align=left>
14:       <A HREF="
15: <%
16:       Set objNL = Server.CreateObject("MSWC.NextLink")
17:       Response.Write(objNL.GetPreviousURL("LinkList.txt"))
18: %>
19:       "><<
20:       (<%= objNL.GetPreviousDescription("LinkList.txt") %>)
21:       </A>
22:       </TD><TD align=right>
```

```
23:     <A HREF="<%= objNL.GetNextURL("linklist.txt") %>">
24:     (<%= objNL.GetNextDescription("LinkList.txt") %>) >>
25:     </A>
26: <%  Set objNL = Nothing %>
27:       </TD></TR></TABLE>
28:   </BODY>
29: </HTML>
```

ANALYSIS Line 4 declares objNL. Lines 14 through 21 create the link to the previous page. Line 14 begins the statement. Line 16 instantiates the content linker. Line 17 writes the URL of the previous page using the GetPreviousURL method. Line 20 gets the description of the previous page using GetPreviousDescription. Lines 23 through 25 create the link to the next page. Line 23 creates the <A HREF=…> statement, getting the URL from the GetNextURL method. Line 24 writes the description of the next page using GetNextDescription. Finally, line 26 frees the memory associated with objNL. You can see the results of this listing in Figure 12.6.

FIGURE 12.6

Viewing the output of Listing 12.7 in a browser window.

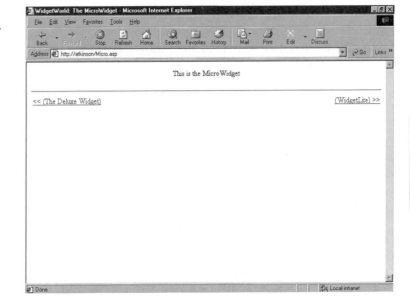

12

So now you want to create the rest of the pages. For the most part, you can copy Micro.asp. Line 7, the title, and line 10, the actual text of the page will differ from file to file.

There is one other problem with copying the code to create the other pages. Standard.asp has no "previous page"; Economy.asp has no "next page."

Notice, though, that you do not get an error. Instead, `Standard.asp` links back to `Economy.asp`, and `Economy.asp` links to `Standard.asp`. This is because an index value of zero and the real index value of the last page in the list are considered equivalent. This would allow you to have a completely cyclic site, where a user could go around in circles. Sometimes you might want that. In that case, you would not need to change anything. In this case, let's suppose that you do not want a complete circle.

You could simply take out these bits of code. This would defeat part of the purpose of using the linker, though. This linker is supposed to allow you to reorder pages, insert new ones wherever you want, and delete them, without worrying about changing the code. There is a better way. You can use the `GetListCount` and `GetListIndex` methods to write code that will be flexible. Listing 12.8 does this.

> **Note**
>
> Although an index value of zero is equivalent to the index value of the last page in the list, it does not wrap around any further. Using –1 as an index will not get you the next to last page in the list.

LISTING 12.8   `Standard.asp` Modified to Display Only Valid Links

```
 1:  <%@ Language=VBScript %>
 2:  <%
 3:      Option Explicit
 4:      Dim objNL, iIndex, iNumPages
 5:  %>
 6:  <HTML>
 7:    <HEAD><TITLE>
 8:      WidgetWorld: The Standard Widget
 9:    </TITLE></HEAD>
10:    <BODY>
11:      <CENTER>This is the Standard Widget</CENTER>
12:      <P><HR>
13:      <TABLE width=100%><TR><TD align=left>
14: <%
15:      Set objNL = Server.CreateObject("MSWC.NextLink")
16:      iIndex = objNL.GetListIndex("linklist.txt")
17:      iNumPages = objNL.GetListCount("linklist.txt")
18:      If iIndex > 1 Then
19: %>
20:      <A HREF="<%=objNL.GetPreviousURL("LinkList.txt") %>">
21:      <<(<%=objNL.GetPreviousDescription("LinkList.txt") %>)
22:    </A>
23: <%   End if %>
24:      </TD><TD align=right>
25: <%   If  iIndex < iNumPages then %>
26:      <A HREF="<%= objNL.GetNextURL("linklist.txt") %>">
```

```
27:        (<%= objNL.GetNextDescription("LinkList.txt") %>) >>
28:        </A>
29: <%    End if %>
30: <%    Set objNL = Nothing %>
31:        </TD></TR></TABLE>
32:    </BODY>
33: </HTML>
```

ANALYSIS Listing 12.8 is a good, flexible version of Standard.asp. Line 4 declares the variables. They include objNL, as before, but also iIndex and iNumpages. iIndex holds the value of the current page's index number. iNumPages holds the number of pages listed in the file. Line 15 instantiates the linker. Line 16 uses the GetListIndex method to give iIndex its correct value, and line 17 uses GetListCount to give iNumPages its value. Line 18 begins an If…Then statement. This says that if the page's index is greater than one (in other words, it is not the first page), we will display the "previous page" link. Then, lines 20 through 22 create the link the same as before. Line 23 ends the If statement. Line 25 begins a similar If statement. This one says that if the page's index is less than the total number of pages, we will display the "next page" link. Lines 26 through 28 create the link as before, and line 29 ends the If statement. Line 30 frees the memory, and the rest of the page is just HTML tags. You can see the results of this listing in Figure 12.7.

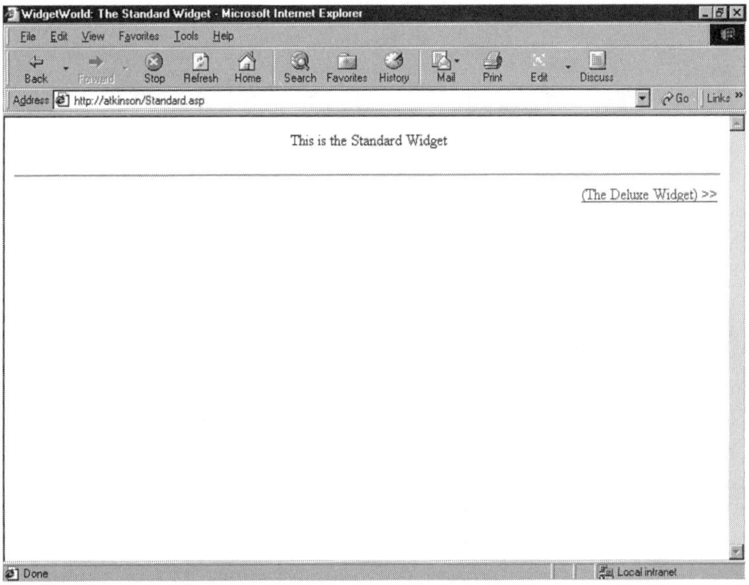

FIGURE 12.7

Viewing the output of Listing 12.8 in a browser window.

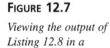

12

This code should be used for all the pages. If the order in the list file is changed, any of the pages could become the first or the last page. This allows you to change the order of the pages by only changing the linker list file.

Now the pages work pretty well. It would be nice to have a table of contents, so let's make one. Listing 12.9 does just that, so type it in and save it as Contents.asp.

LISTING 12.9 A Table of Contents Using Content Linker

```
1: <%@ Language=VBScript %>
2: <% Option Explicit %>

3:   <HTML>
4:   <HEAD><TITLE>WidgetWorld Table of Contents</TITLE></HEAD>
5:    <BODY>
6:      Table of Contents<P>
7:  <%
8:    Dim objNL, iCount, iNumPages
9:    Set objNL = Server.CreateObject("MSWC.NextLink")
10:   iNumPages = objNL.GetListCount("LinkList.txt")
11:   For iCount = 1 to iNumPages
12: %>
13: <A HREF="
14: <%= objNL.GetNthURL("LinkList.txt", iCount) %>
15: ">
16: <%= objNL.GetNthDescription("LinkList.txt", iCount) %>
17: </A><BR>
18: <%
19:   Next
20:   Set objNL = Nothing
21: %>
22:   </BODY>
23: </HTML>
```

ANALYSIS Line 8 declares objNL, which is used to instantiate the linker. It also declares iCount, which serves as a counter for a For…Next loop, and iNumPages, which represents the number of pages listed in the list file.

Line 9 uses Set to instantiate the linker. Line 10 uses the GetListCount method of the linker. Now iNumPages contains the number of pages listed in the linker file. Line 11 begins a For…Next loop. iCount will run from 1 to iNumPages.

Lines 13 through 15 create the <A HREF=…> statement. The URL for this link comes from the GetNthURL method. The corresponding description will be used for the text that is linked. This is obtained using the GetNthDescription method on line 16. Line 19 closes the loop. Line 20 is the always important memory freeing line.

Figure 12.8 shows the output of this code.

FIGURE **12.8**

Viewing the table of contents from Listing 12.9 in a browser window.

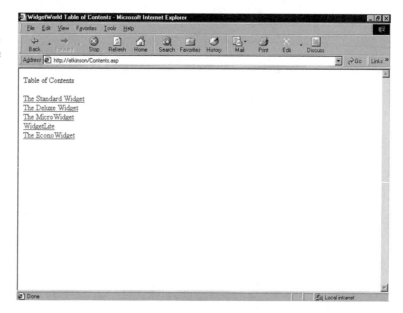

Adding a new page should be really easy now. Just copy the code from one of the other pages, change the title and the body text, and add the new page to the list. You can add it anywhere in the list you want. You can rearrange anything already in the list however you want. The links on the pages and on the table of contents will be taken care of for you.

In fact, with a little bit of fixing, you will not even need to change the title. You can generate the title dynamically from the description in the list file. All this requires is GetListIndex and GetNthDescription.

You can also add links to go directly to the first page, the last page, or the table of contents. Listing 12.10 adds these improvements to Micro.asp.

LISTING 12.10   Some Final Tweaking to Your Pages

```
 1:  <%@ Language=VBScript %>
 2:  <%
 3:      Option Explicit
 4:      Dim objNL, iIndex, iNumPages
 5:      Set objNL = Server.CreateObject("MSWC.NextLink")
 6:      iIndex = objNL.GetListIndex("linklist.txt")
 7:      iNumPages = objNL.GetListCount("linklist.txt")
 8:  %>
 9:  <HTML>
10:    <HEAD><TITLE> WidgetWorld:
11:    <%= objNL.GetNthDescription("LinkList.txt", iIndex) %>
```

continues

12

LISTING **12.10**   continued

```
12:     </TITLE></HEAD>
13:     <BODY>
14:        <CENTER>This is the MicroWidget</CENTER>
15:        <P><HR>
16:        <TABLE width=100%><TR><TD align=left>
17: <% If iIndex > 1 Then %>
18:        <A HREF="<%=objNL.GetPreviousURL("LinkList.txt") %>">
19:        <<(<%=objNL.GetPreviousDescription("LinkList.txt") %>)
20:        </A>
21: <%    End if %>
22:        </TD><TD align=right>
23: <%    If  iIndex < iNumPages then %>
24:        <A HREF="<%= objNL.GetNextURL("linklist.txt") %>">
25:        (<%= objNL.GetNextDescription("LinkList.txt") %>) >>
26:        </A>
27: <%    End if %>
28:        </TD></TR></TABLE>
29:        <P>
30:        <TABLE width=100%><TR><TD align=left>
31:         <A HREF="<%= objNL.GetNthURL("LinkList.txt", 1) %>">
32:         First page
33:         (<%=objNL.GetNthDescription("LinkList.txt", 1) %>)
34:         </A>
35:        </TD><TD align=center>
36:         <A HREF="contents.asp">Table of Contents</A>
37:        </TD><TD align=right>
38:         <A HREF="<%=objNL.GetNthURL("LinkList.txt",1 ) %>">
39:         Last page
40:        (<%=objNL.GetNthDescription("LinkList.txt", iNumPages)%>)
41: <%    Set objNL = Nothing %>
42:         </A>
43:        </TD></TR></TABLE>
44:     </BODY>
45: </HTML>
```

ANALYSIS   This listing is much like Listing 12.8. Line 11 now gets the description for the current page to use in the title. Lines 30 through 43 create the last set of links at the bottom. Lines 21 through 34 create the link to the first page. Line 36 adds a link to the table of contents page. This is a normal, static link that does not use the Content Linker. Lines 38 through 40 create the link to the last page. Otherwise, it is pretty much the same as before.

You could make further changes. You could add an If statement to keep the "go to first page" link from showing when the user is already on the first page. What you have here works pretty well, though. The only thing that needs to differ from page to page is the main body text (line 14). To create a new page, you could simply copy and paste lines 1 through 13 and 15 through 45. Try creating a new page for a product called the Super Widget. Add it to the list file. Take a look at the table of contents. Try moving the new page around in the list file.

You can see that it is easy to add a new page. If you have used server-side includes (SSI) before, you can use them to make it even easier. If you have not used SSI before, they are covered on Day 13.

Browser Capabilities Component

One issue that Web programmers must grapple with constantly is browser compatibility. Many potential visitors to your site are still using old browsers that do not support many of the more recent technologies. There are also many differences between the newest versions of the major browsers. This leaves the Web designer with a difficult decision: Is it better to write a Web site that everyone can visit or to write a powerful site that takes advantage of the latest technologies? Most designers compromise and write a site that will work for most browsers within the past year or two, but not necessarily any older ones.

Of course, ASP is a server-side technology, so it will work on any browser. Often, though, you will want to combine ASP with client-side technologies such as JavaScript and Java. In these cases, browser compatibility remains a big issue. This is why ASP comes with the Browser Capabilities component.

Basic properties you can check for using the Browser Capabilities component are as follows:

- What browser is the visitor using?
- What version number is the browser?
- Does the browser support frames?
- Does the browser support tables?
- Does the browser support background sounds?
- Does the browser support VBScript?
- Does the browser support JavaScript?

Listing 12.11 provides some examples.

LISTING 12.11 Using Basic Properties of the Browser Capabilities Component

```
1:  <%@ Language=VBScript %>
2:  <% Option Explicit %>
3:  <HTML>
4:    <BODY>
5:  <%
```

continues

12

LISTING **12.11**   continued

```
6:        Dim objBC
7:        Set objBC = Server.CreateObject("MSWC.BrowserType")
8:  %>
9:        Browser Name: <%= objBC.Browser %>
10:       <P>
11:       Browser Version: <%= objBC.Version%>
12:       <P>
13: <%  If (objBC.Frames) then %>
14:         Your browser supports frames<P>
15: <%  else %>
16:         Your browser does not support frames<P>
17: <%  end if %>
18: <%  If (objBC.Tables) then %>
19:         Your browser supports tables<P>
20: <%  else %>
21:         Your browser does not support tables<P>
22: <%  end if %>
23: <%  If (objBC.BackgroundSounds)then %>
24:         Your browser supports background sounds<P>
25: <%  else %>
26:         Your browser does not support background sounds<P>
27: <%  end if %>
28: <%  If (objBC.VBScript) then %>
29:         Your browser supports VBScript<P>
30: <%  else %>
31:         Your browser does not support VBScript<P>
32: <%  end if %>
33: <%  If (objBC.Javascript) then %>
34:         Your browser supports JavaScript<P>
35: <%  else %>
36:         Your browser does not support JavaScript<P>
37: <%
38:       End if
39:       Set objBC = nothing
40: %>
41:   </BODY>
42: </HTML>
```

Listing 12.11 uses some of the properties of the Browser Capabilities component. Line 6 declares objBC, and line 7 instantiates the component. Line 9 writes out the browser name, which it gets from the Browser property. Line 11 displays the browser version number, which it gets from the Version property.

Lines 13 through 17 test whether the browser supports frames and display an appropriate message. If objBC.Frames is True, then the browser supports frames; otherwise, it does not.

Lines 18 through 22 perform a similar test on the browser's support of tables, using `objBC.Tables`. Lines 23 through 27 use `objBC.BackgroundSounds` to test whether the browser supports the use of background sounds. Lines 28 through 38 test the browser's support of VBScript and JavaScript using `objBC.VBScript` and `objBC.JavaScript`. Finally, line 39 frees the memory associated with `objBC`.

Figure 12.9 shows the results of viewing Listing 12.11 in Internet Explorer 5.0.

FIGURE 12.9

Viewing the table of contents from Listing 12.11 in a browser window.

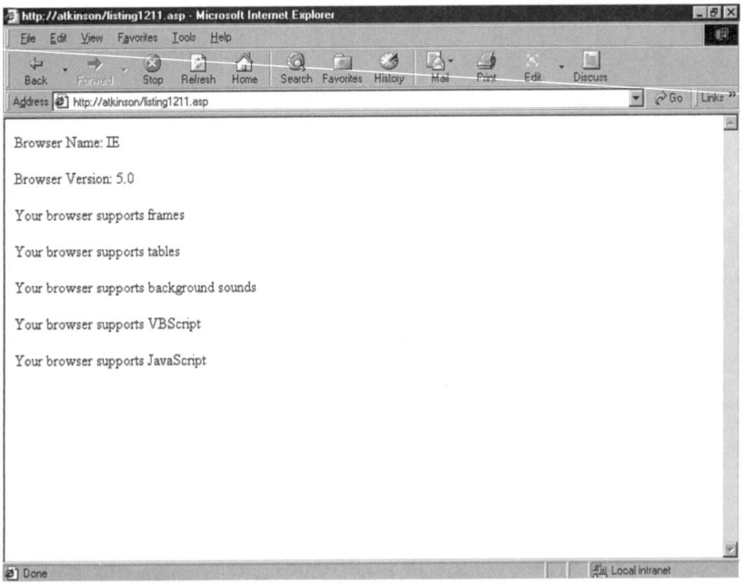

Unfortunately, it is not always as easy as this. When a new browser or a new version of a browser comes out, it will be identified as "unknown" by the Browser Capabilities component. Even minor changes will throw it off.

This is why `Browscap.ini` is used. `Browscap.ini` is a file that can be updated with new browser versions and capabilities. `Browscap.dll`, the file on the server that contains the component, compares the data in the browser's header to the data in `Browscap.ini`.

Updating your own `Browscap.ini` is a bit advanced for you at this point. However, there are several places on the Web where you can download an excellent, up-to-date `Browscap.ini`. One such place is http://www.asptracker.com. The `Browscap.ini` you can download there allows you to test for such properties as major version, minor version, cookies support, and ActiveX support.

So how could you use the Browser Capabilities component on your site? Suppose you wanted to use frames, but you know some of your users have browsers that do not support frames. Listing 12.12 shows how you could use the Browser Capabilities component to handle this.

LISTING 12.12 Using the Browser Capabilities Component to Detect Frames Support

```
1:   <%@ Language=VBScript %>
2:   <%
3:       Option Explicit
4:       Dim objBC
5:       Set objBC = Server.CreateObject("MSWC.BrowserType")
6:       If Not objBC.Frames Then
7:           Response.Redirect "nonframes.asp"
8:       End if
9:       Set objBC = Nothing
10:  %>
11:  <HTML>
12:    <BODY>
13:      Put the frames version here
14:    </BODY>
15:  </HTML>
```

ANALYSIS If the visitor's browser supports frames, Listing 12.12 displays a frames version of the site. If the browser does not support frames, the user would be redirected to a non-frames version of the page. Line 4 declares `objBC`, and line 5 instantiates the component. Lines 6 through 8 check `objBC.Frames` and, if it is false, redirect the user to the page `nonframes.asp`. Line 9 frees the memory associated with `objBC`. The rest of the page, frames and all, go where line 13 is. Only browsers that support frames will ever display this page.

Alternatively, you could put both versions of the page in the same ASP file; Listing 12.13 does this. The code for the non-frames version goes where line 10 is, and the code for the frames version goes where line 12 is.

LISTING 12.13 Another Way of Using Browser Capabilities to Handle Non-Frames Browsers

```
1:   <%@ Language=VBScript %>
2:   <% Option Explicit %>
3:   <HTML>
4:     <BODY>
5:   <%
6:       Dim objBC
7:       Set objBC = Server.CreateObject("MSWC.BrowserType")
8:       If Not objBC.Frames Then
9:   %>
10:  put the non-frames code here
11:  <% Else %>
12:  put the frames code here
13:  <%
14:       End if
```

```
15:    Set objBC = Nothing
16: %>
17:    </BODY>
18: </HTML>
```

ANALYSIS   Line 8 of Listing 12.13 checks objBC.Frames and takes the negation of it. So if objBC.Frames is false, the first block (line 10) is executed. If it is true, the second block is executed (line 12).

Which version would be preferable depends on the complexity of the pages involved. If they were complex, it would probably be better to go with the first version, to prevent the pages from becoming too large. If it is a fairly simple page, the second way might be easier.

You could just as easily determine the language you should use for your client-side scripting, as in Listing 12.14.

LISTING 12.14   Using Browser Capabilities to Check Scripting Language Support

```
 1: <%@ Language=VBScript %>
 2: <% Option Explicit %>
 3: <HTML>
 4:    <BODY>
 5: <%
 6:    Dim objBC
 7:    Set objBC = Server.CreateObject("MSWC.BrowserType")
 8:    If objBC.VBScript Then
 9: %>
10: <SCRIPT LANGUAGE=VBSCRIPT>
11:    'client-side VBScript code here
12: </SCRIPT>
13: <%
14:    Else
15:      If objBC.JavaScript Then
16: %>
17: <SCRIPT LANGUAGE=JAVASCRIPT>
18:    %client-side JavaScript code here
19: </SCRIPT>
20: <%   Else %>
21: Your browser does not support client-side scripting
22: <%
23:      End if
24:    End if
25:    Set objBC = Nothing
26: %>
27:    </BODY>
28: </HTML>
```

12

Listing 12.14 will use client-side VBScript if the browser supports it. It checks on line 8, and the VBScript code goes where line 11 is. Otherwise, it checks whether the browser supports JavaScript (lines 14 and 15). If it does, it uses JavaScript (line 18). If not, it prints a message (line 21). Do not forget to free the memory associated with the component, as in line 25.

Summary

Microsoft provides three helpful and easy-to-use components that can take a little of the work out of some common tasks.

The Ad Rotator uses a schedule file to keep track of the ads to display. Each ad can have a specified frequency to be displayed, matching text, and a specified link the user should be taken to when he clicks the ad. A special ASP file handles actually taking the user to the correct page. After these are written, the GetAdvertisement method may be used wherever an ad is to be displayed. GetAdvertisement randomly chooses an ad and generates the HTML string needed to display it.

The Content Linker is helpful when you have several pages that should be treated as a sequential list. It creates dynamically generated navigational links. This allows you to add new files to the sequence, remove files, or reorder files in the sequence without worrying about correcting the links. It can also be used to generate a dynamic and up-to-date table of contents.

The Browser Capabilities component allows your pages to determine what type of browser a user has and its capabilities. The page may then optimize itself for the browser. It reads in data about known Web browsers from a file called Browscap.ini. Because browsers and capabilities change, it is important to keep an up-to-date Browscap.ini. There are several Web sites from which one may be obtained, such as ASPTracker.com.

For these and any other components you use, be sure to correctly free the memory they use when you are finished. This is done with the following command:

```
Set instancename = Nothing
```

Failure to do this can result in problems with your server. Even if you cannot see any problems immediately, it may have cumulative effects.

Q&A

Q. Why would I want to use the Ad Rotator if I cannot keep track of impressions?

A. Some Web sites may sell ads on a per-month basis. In such cases, it would be good to know the number of impressions but not absolutely necessary. Also, you might not sell ads but rather participate in free banner exchanges. For purposes like that, the Ad Rotator should server quite nicely.

Q. **What other ways are there to find out information about a user's browser?**

A. The `User-Agent` header discussed on Day 10, "Working with the `Request` Object," is one way. Many third-party applications can also help—for example, Cyscape's BrowserHawk (`http://www.cyscape.com`).

Workshop

The Workshop provides quiz questions to help you solidify your understanding of the material covered and exercises to provide you with experience in using what you've learned. Try to understand the quiz and exercise answers before continuing to tomorrow's lesson. Quiz answers are provided in Appendix A, and exercise answers can be found at `http://www.mcp.com/info`.

Quiz

1. How is a component instantiated?

2. When should the memory associated with a component be freed?

3. What are the two major limitations of the Ad Rotator component?

4. What effect does giving one ad twice the weight of another have?

5. How do you specify in the schedule file that an ad has no associated link?

6. What method of the Content Linker is used to find out the URL of the next page in the sequence?

7. What method of the Content Linker is used to find out the index position of the current page?

8. What three things does the Content Linker list file allow you to include for each entry?

9. How is the Browser Capabilities component kept accurate and up-to-date?

Exercises

1. Assuming that the schedule file has already been written and is called `AdList.txt`, write the code to print three ads with a border thickness of 2.

2. Write the code to print out links to the previous three pages using the Content Linker. Be sure that it can handle cases where there are fewer than three previous pages.

3. Write code that will redirect Netscape users to a separate page.

12

DAY 13

Reading and Writing Files on the Web Server

Files can be used in many ways on a Web site. Some files simplify site management. Others expand the capabilities of your pages by allowing them to save and retrieve information. This is an important capability. Your sites would be limited if they could not remember data. Databases may be used for this purpose as well, as you will see in Week 3. Today, you will learn the following:

- How to use server-side includes to make your sites easier to manage
- How and when to use `Server.Execute` and `Server.Transfer`
- How to find out whether a file or folder exists on the server
- Accessing properties of files and folders on the server
- Reading from files on the server
- Writing to files on the server

Server-Side Includes

Server-side includes allow you to write some commonly used code once and have the server insert it into your pages for you. This has two major advantages:

- It makes it easier and quicker to write new pages that will use the code.
- It makes it much easier to make changes to the code. You only have to change it in one place, and all the pages that use it will reflect the change.

An include file is a file that has in it the code that you want to reuse. Any page that wants to use the code in the include file will have a special line that indicates that the code should be inserted there.

The code in a server-side include file is inserted into the pages that use it BEFORE the page's ASP code is evaluated. This means that you can put ASP code inside the include file, and it will be executed like it was part of the page that includes it. On the other hand, it means that you cannot use ASP to determine which page to include.

Using Server-Side Includes to Simplify Maintenance

Server-side includes allow you to write code once and insert it into several pages. For example, suppose that you had a set of navigational links and buttons that were to appear at the top of every page of your site. Your life would be much easier if you put the HTML code necessary to generate the navigational controls into a separate file and used include to insert it into pages where you need it. Let's look at an example like this. Save the following code as navbar.asp:

```
<A HREF="index.html">Main Page</A> ¦
<A HREF="aboutme.html">About Me</A> ¦
<A HREF="links.html">My Links</A>
```

Now, to insert this code into a page in the same directory as navbar.asp, simply use this line:

```
<!--#include file="navbar.asp"-->
```

You can also use relative URLs, such as "../navbar.asp" or "tools/navbar.shtml", depending on where navbar.asp is with respect to the page including it.

Try making up some generic index page and including the file as shown previously. It works just like you had copied and pasted the code in navbar.asp into the file where the include is. You can put the same statement in any file in the same directory.

Figure 13.1 illustrates how include has the effect of inserting another file into the current one.

FIGURE 13.1

Server-side includes let the server do your "copy-and-paste" work.

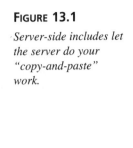
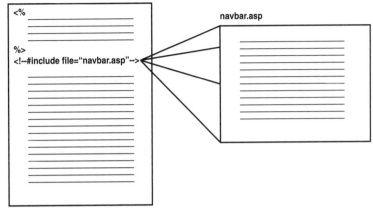

Now say that you have a fourth page you want to list at the bottom of your navigation bar. All you have to do is add it to the navbar.asp file. Compare that with the monotony of going through page after page making the same update.

You can also use include files that contain ASP code. If you have a set of functions and constants that you use throughout a site, you can put them in a file and use include in any pages where you need them. For example, save the following as functions.asp:

```
1: <%
2: Function Factorial (iNumber)
3:    Dim iCounter, iTemp
4:    iTemp = 1
5:    For iCounter = 1 to iNumber
6:        iTemp = iTemp * iCounter
7:    Next
8:    Factorial = iTemp
9: End Function
10:
11: Function RandomInt (iUpperbound)
12:    RandomInt = Cint(iUpperbound * Rnd)
13: End Function
14:
15: Function FirstDayOfWeek
16:    FirstDayOfWeek = DateAdd("d", 1 - DatePart("w", Now), Now)
17: End Function
18: %>
```

This file contains three function definitions. You should be able to tell what they do; they are not complicated. It is important that you see how you can use server-side includes to keep them separate from the rest of your code yet still use them. If an ASP page needs one of these functions, you can simply include the file at the top and use the functions whenever you need, as follows:

```
1: <!--#include file="functions.asp"-->
2: <%
```

13

```
3:  …
4:    Response.Write Factorial(8)
```

You include the file at the top of the page (line 1) and can then use the functions inside as you need (line 4). In addition to making site maintenance easier, this approach removes the clutter of having all the function definitions in the same file as the page that uses them.

If you use the word `virtual` in place of `file` in the `include` statement, you can specify absolute locations instead of relative ones. For example:

```
<!--#include virtual="/includes/navbar.asp"-->
```

This includes a file that is in a subdirectory of the root directory that is called `"includes"`. Rather than worrying about specifying a relative path, this statement works from any page on the site.

Not all files may use `include`. Certain extensions indicate that a file may contain includes. By default, those extensions are `.shtml`, `.shtm`, `.stm`, and `.asp`. This can be changed in your IIS/PWS settings. If you use includes in a file with an extension not recognized as allowing `include`, the `include` statement will not be processed. A file that is to be included in other files may have any extension, provided that it does not `include` any files itself.

> **Caution**
>
> Make sure that the file you are including is nonempty. Using an empty file causes an error.

Redirecting Users

Day 7, "Using the `Response` Object," discussed how to use `Response.Redirect` to redirect users to other Web pages. In the first section today, we discussed using server-side includes to insert code from another page into the current one. The `Server` object includes two methods that perform similar tasks to each of these: `Server.Transfer` and `Server.Execute`. Both of these are new to IIS 5.0. Under certain circumstances, these methods allow you much greater flexibility.

Executing Another ASP Page

The server-side include was used to insert code from another page into the current one. All server-side includes are carried out before any ASP code is executed. This means that if you want to use your ASP code to determine what file to include, you are in trouble. This is why you might want to use `Server.Execute`.

`Server.Execute(path)` executes the ASP script specified by `path`. If `path` is an absolute path, it should be for an ASP page within the same application space (the same folder or one of its subfolders). `path` may contain query string data.

Listings 13.1 and 13.2 demonstrate `Server.Execute`. Listing 13.1 will call a `Server.Execute` on Listing 13.2. Save Listing 13.1 as `page1.asp` and Listing 13.2 as `page2.asp`. Both listings are fairly simple.

LISTING 13.1   `page1.asp` Demonstrates How to Use `Server.Execute`

```
 1:  <%@ LANGUAGE=VBSCRIPT %>
 2:  <% Option Explicit %>
 3:  <HTML>
 4:    <BODY>
 5:    <%
 6:       Response.Write("I am in page 1 <BR>")
 7:       Server.Execute("page2.asp")
 8:       Response.Write("Back in page 1")
 9:    %>
10:    </BODY>
11: </HTML>
```

Line 6 of Listing 13.1 prints a message, then line 7 executes `page2.asp`. Once `page2.asp` is finished, line 8 will print another message.

LISTING 13.2   `page2.asp`

```
1: <HTML>
2:    <BODY>
3:    <% Response.Write("I am in page 2 <BR>") %>
4:    </BODY>
5: </HTML>
```

Line 3 of `page2.asp` simply prints a message.

Look at the output when you view `page1.asp`. The first message from Listing 13.1 is printed, then, the message from Listing 13.2 is printed. This is because of the `Server.Execute`. Finally, the second message from Listing 13.1 is printed. You can see this in the output in Figure 13.2.

Suppose for a moment that you want some information at the top and bottom of every page on your site. This might be some graphics, links, contact information, and so on. One way you could do this is to `include` some file at the top of every page and another one at the bottom. This will work, but it lacks some flexibility. You might decide that you want two different ways to view each page.

If you want to keep your options open for expansion, you might decide to use `Server.Execute`. Listing 13.3 demonstrates how you could do this.

13

FIGURE **13.2**

The output of Listing 13.1.

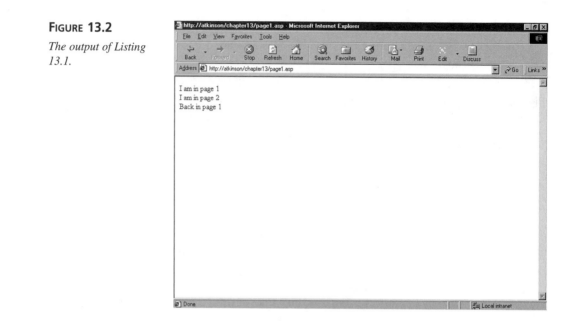

LISTING 13.3 Using `Server.Execute` Instead of Server-Side Includes

```
1:  <%@ LANGUAGE=VBSCRIPT %>
2:  <%  Option Explicit %>
3:  <HTML>
4:   <BODY bgcolor=blue text=white link=yellow vlink=yellow>
5:    <H1>Stanley's Widgets</H1><HR>
6:    <%
7:      Dim strPath
8:      strPath = Request.QueryString("URL")
9:      If Not strPath = "" Then
10:        Server.Execute(strPath)
11:      Else
12:        Response.Write "Welcome to my page"
13:      End if
14:   %>
15:    <HR>
16:    Click <A HREF=
17:      "Printpage.asp?URL=<%=Server.URLEncode(strPath) %>">
18:     here</A> to print this page.
19:    <P><CENTER>
20:    <A HREF=
21: "Showpage.asp?URL=<%=Server.URLEncode("/main.html")%>">
22:     Main Page</A> ¦
23:    <A HREF=
24: "Showpage.asp?URL=<%=Server.URLEncode("/aboutme.html")%>">
25:     About Me</A> ¦
26:    <A HREF=
27: "Showpage.asp?URL=<%=Server.URLEncode("/links.html")%>">
```

```
28:     My Links</A>
29:    </CENTER>
30:   </BODY>
31:  </HTML>
```

ANALYSIS   Save Listing 13.3 as `Showpage.asp`. Line 5 prints out a simple header at the top of the page. Line 8 retrieves the value of URL from the query string. If there is a URL, line 10 executes the page it specifies.

After you return from executing that page, you want to display some links at the bottom. Notice how the links on lines 20 through 28 are generated. You link to a new page by linking to `Showpage.asp` and passing in a new URL value.

This page has a blue background and white text, plus some extra navigational stuff that may cause it not to print clearly. So, as a favor to your users, you will provide a second version of each page that will print better. Because of how you created this site, you do not need a whole new set of pages. Instead a single page called `Printpage.asp` can be used. The link to this version is on lines 16 through 18. `Printpage.asp` displays the specified URL, much like `Showpage.asp`, only with normal colors and less extra stuff. Listing 13.4 shows `Printpage.asp`.

LISTING 13.4   Using `Server.Execute` to Offer a Printer-Friendly Version of the Page

```
1:  <%@ LANGUAGE=VBSCRIPT %>
2:  <% Option Explicit %>
3:  <HTML>
4:   <BODY bgcolor=white>
5:   <%
6:     Dim strPath
7:     strPath = Request.QueryString("URL")
8:     If Not strPath = "" Then
9:        Server.Execute(strPath)
10:    Else
11:       Response.Write "Nothing to print"
12:    End if
13:  %>
14:    Click <A HREF=
15:      "Showpage.asp?URL=<%=Server.URLEncode(strPath) %>">
16:     Here</A> to go back.
17:  </BODY>
18:  </HTML>
```

Listing 13.4 shows `Printpage.asp`. This uses `Server.Execute` pretty much the same way Listing 13.3 does. The main differences are the white background (line 4) and the lack of extra links and text at the top and bottom. Figure 13.3 shows the regular version of the page (using `Showpage.asp`). Figure 13.4 shows the printing version of the page (using `Printpage.asp`).

13

FIGURE 13.3

Using Showpage.asp *to view* main.html.

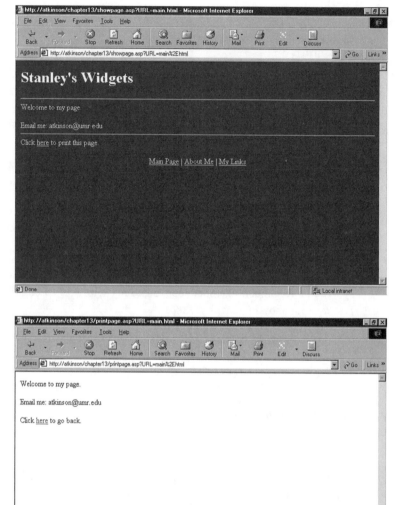

FIGURE 13.3

Using Showpage.asp *to view* main.html.

FIGURE 13.4

Using Printpage.asp *to* view main.html.

Transferring Control to Another ASP Page

Server.Transfer is used to transfer control to another ASP page. When it is called, all the data related to the calling page is transferred to the new page. This means that if variables of session or application scope have been given values, those values are kept in the new page. State information and values for the built-in objects are transferred, too. Also, the contents of the request collections are kept and are available to the new page.

You can even perform a `Server.Transfer` between two pages in separate applications (separate folders). In this case, the value of the application variables and objects will be the same as if the second page were in the same application as the first. That is, the values of application scope variables and objects are kept after the transfer.

Listing 13.5 demonstrates how `Server.Transfer` is used.

LISTING 13.5 `page1a.asp` Demonstrates How to Use `Server.Execute`

```
 1: <%@ LANGUAGE=VBSCRIPT %>
 2: <% Option Explicit %>
 3: <HTML>
 4:    <BODY>
 5:    <%
 6:       Response.Write("I am in page 1 <BR>")
 7:       Server.Transfer("page2.asp")
 8:       Response.Write("Back in page 1")
 9:    %>
10:    </BODY>
11: </HTML>
```

Save Listing 13.5 as `page1a.asp`. This page is almost identical to `page1.asp` from the previous section. The only difference is that line 7 uses a `Server.Transfer` in place of the `Server.Execute`. You can see the results of this listing in Figure 13.5. Notice that in this version, the third line is not printed. That is because you never return to the calling page when you do a `Server.Transfer`. In this regard, `Server.Transfer` may be used a bit like the `Response.Redirect`.

Recall the discussion of `Response.Redirect` on Day 7. `Response.Redirect` tells the user's browser to make a new request. This results in the creation of a new object context, which is used to contain the `Session` and `Request` objects as well as some server variables. Sometimes when you want to send the user to a different page, you will want a new object context to be created. In such cases, you should use `Response.Redirect`.

If you do not need a new object context, you are probably better off using `Server.Transfer`, which is faster because it does not involve as many communications or the creation of a new object context.

Let's look at an example to demonstrate the difference between `Server.Transfer` and `Response.Redirect`. Listing 13.6 is a simple page that prints out what it considers its URL to be.

13

FIGURE **13.5**

The output of Listing 13.5.

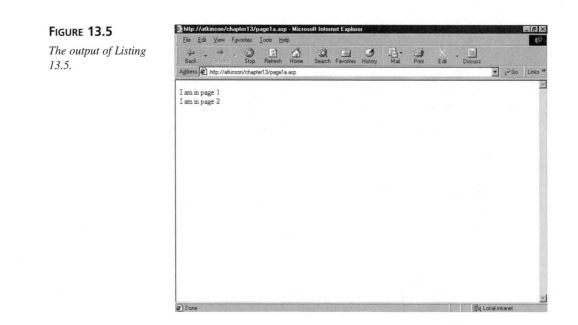

```
 1: <%@ LANGUAGE=VBSCRIPT %>
 2: <%  Option Explicit %>
 3: <HTML>
 4:    <BODY>
 5:    <%
 6:       Response.Write "My URL is "
 7:       Response.Write Request.ServerVariables("URL")
 8:    %>
 9:    </BODY>
10: </HTML>
```

Line 7 uses the `ServerVariables` collection of the `Request` object. In this case, the value you are interested in is that of "URL". Save this page as `myurl.asp`. Now create a new page and call it `UsingTransfer.asp`. It should consist of a single line:

```
<% Server.Transfer("myurl.asp") %>
```

Now create another new page and call it `UsingRedirect.asp`. It should consist of a single line:

```
<% Response.Redirect "myurl.asp" %>
```

You can see the results of viewing `UsingRedirect.asp` and `UsingTransfer.asp` in your browser in Figures 13.6 and 13.7, respectively. How are they different?

FIGURE **13.6**

Results of
UsingRedirect.asp.

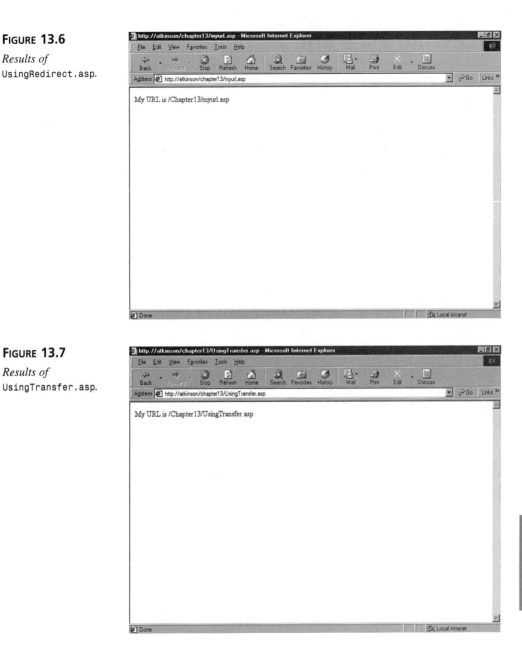

FIGURE **13.7**

Results of
UsingTransfer.asp.

13

UsingRedirect.asp actually displays the URL of myurl.asp. UsingTransfer.asp, however, displays what is really the URL of UsingTransfer.asp, even though myurl.asp does the checking. This is because when Server.Transfer is used, the object context from the first page is used in the second. So even though myurl.asp is looking up what it thinks is its URL, it is really looking up the URL in the object context, which is UsingTransfer.asp's URL.

Accessing Files and Folders

In ASP pages, you often need the capability to store and recall information. Databases, which are discussed in Week 3, are one way to do this. Another way is to use files on the server. With the file system object, ASP provides a way to access properties of files and folders, read data in from them, create new ones, write over the old ones, and more.

Determining Whether Files or Folders Exist

Before you start working with a file or a folder, you need to make sure that it exists. Trying to work with a file that does not exist causes an ugly error message. Even if you are pretty sure that the file will always exist, you need a way to make sure, so that you can protect users from having to see those ugly error messages.

The `FileSystemObject` has two methods that can be used to determine whether a file or folder exists on the server.

The `FolderExists` method takes one argument, the name of the folder with its physical path. It returns `True` if the folder is found, and `False` otherwise. To determine whether there is a folder named "`Chapter13`" within the current directory, you would do this:

```
1:  Dim objFSO
2:  Set objFSO = _
3:        Server.CreateObject("Scripting.FileSystemObject")
4:  If objFSO.FolderExists(Server.MapPath("Chapter13")) Then
5:    Response.Write "The folder exists"
6:  Else
7:    Response.Write "That folder does not exist"
8:  End if
9:  Set objFSO = Nothing
```

ANALYSIS Line 1 declares the variable that will be used to hold an instance of the `FileSystemObject`. Lines 2 and 3 instantiate the object (The line continuation character (_) is used). Line 3 uses the `FolderExists` method and `Server.MapPath` with an `If…Then` statement. `Server.MapPath` converts from a relative or virtual path to a physical one. If `FolderExists` returns `True`, a message prints saying that the folder exists (line 5). If it returns `False`, a different message prints (line 7), saying that it does not exist.

If you wanted to check for a folder in another directory, you can specify a relative path such as `"book\chapter13"` or `"..\chapter13"`, and `Server.MapPath` converts it into a physical path.

`FileExists` works pretty much the same way. As with `FolderExists`, you probably will want to use `Server.MapPath` to convert to a physical path.

Determining the Properties of Files and Folders on the Web Server

The GetFile method of the FileSystemObject can be used to create an instance of the file object. The file object has several properties and methods that allow you to work with files on the server. GetFile requires the name and path of the file as an argument. Listing 13.7 instantiates the file object and writes out one of its properties. Make sure to put a file called log.txt in the same directory.

LISTING 13.7   Using the File Object

```
 1:  <%
 2:    Dim objFSO, objFile
 3:    Set objFSO = _
 4:         Server.CreateObject("Scripting.FileSystemObject")
 5:    Set objFile = objFSO.GetFile(Server.MapPath("log.txt"))
 6:    Response.Write "log.txt was last modified "
 7:    Response.Write objFile.DateLastModified
 8:    Set objFile = Nothing
 9:    Set objFSO = Nothing
10: %>
```

ANALYSIS   Line 2 declares the two variables used for objects. Lines 3 and 4 make objFSO an instance of the file system object. Line 5 uses the GetFile method of the file system object to instantiate the file object. Notice that once again, Server.MapPath is used to convert the relative path "log.txt" to a physical path such as "C:\Inetpub\www-root\log.txt". Lines 6 and 7 write some output. Notice that line 7 uses one of the properties of the file object.

Caution   Do not confuse the file system object with the file object. They are different. The file system object represents the entire file system. The file object represents only a single file. The file system object is used in instantiating the file object.

13

The file object has the following properties:

- Attributes is used to set and return some of the special attributes of the file.
- DateCreated returns the date and time that the file was created. This property cannot be changed.
- DateLastAccessed returns the date and time that the file was last accessed. This property cannot be changed by your ASP code.

- `DateLastModified` returns the date and time that the file was last modified. This property also cannot be changed.

- `Drive` returns the letter of the drive the file is on. This property cannot be changed directly.

- `Name` is used to set or return the name of the file.

- `ParentFolder` returns an instance of the folder object corresponding to the parent folder of the file.

- `Path` returns the path for the file, including the filename.

- `ShortName` returns the version of the filename that is used by programs that do not support long filenames. This name consists of no more than eight characters, followed by a ".", followed by no more than three characters.

- `ShortPath` returns the path to the file as it is seen by programs that do not support long filenames.

- `Size` returns the size, in bytes, of the file.

- `Type` returns information that is known about the type of the file. For example, if the file is a ".txt" file, `Type` returns "Text Document".

Listing 13.8 is a simple page that demonstrates these properties. It writes out a bunch of information about `log.txt`.

LISTING 13.8   The Properties of the File Object

```
 1: <%@ LANGUAGE=VBSCRIPT %>
 2: <%  Option Explicit %>
 3: <HTML>
 4:   <BODY>
 5:   <%
 6:     Dim objFSO, objFile
 7:     Set objFSO = _
 8:         Server.CreateObject("Scripting.FileSystemObject")
 9:     Set objFile = objFSO.GetFile(Server.MapPath("log.txt"))
10:     Response.Write "log.txt was created "
11:     Response.Write objFile.DateCreated
12:     Response.Write "<BR>"
13:     Response.Write "log.txt was last accessed "
14:     Response.Write objFile.DateLastAccessed
15:     Response.Write "<BR>"
16:     Response.Write "log.txt was last modified "
17:     Response.Write objFile.DateLastModified
18:     Response.Write "<BR>"
19:     Response.Write "log.txt is on drive "
20:     Response.Write objFile.Drive
21:     Response.Write "<BR>"
22:     Response.Write "log.txt is in the folder "
23:     Response.Write objFile.ParentFolder.Name
```

```
24:    Response.Write "<BR>"
25:    Response.Write "the path to log.txt is "
26:    Response.Write objFile.Path
27:    Response.Write "<BR>"
28:    Response.Write "the short path to log.txt is "
29:    Response.Write objFile.ShortPath
30:    Response.Write "<BR>"
31:    Response.Write "the short name for log.txt is "
32:    Response.Write objFile.ShortName
33:    Response.Write "<BR>"
34:    Response.Write "log.txt is   "
35:    Response.Write objFile.Size
36:    Response.Write " bytes<BR>"
37:    Response.Write "log.txt is a "
38:    Response.Write objFile.Type
39:    Set objFile = Nothing
40:    Set objFSO = Nothing
41: %>
42: </BODY>
43: </HTML>
```

ANALYSIS Lines 6 through 9 create and instantiate the file system and file objects, just as in Listing 13.7. This code prints out the values of several properties of this instance of the file object. The properties used in this code include DateCreated (line 11), DateLastAccessed (line 14), DateLastModified (line 17), Drive (line 20), ParentFolder (line 23), Path (line 26), ShortPath (line 29), ShortName (line 32), Size (line 35), and Type (line 38). Most of these should be easy for you to understand. One that is worth taking a look at, though, is the ParentFolder property on line 23. Unlike the other properties, ParentFolder is not a string or a date. ParentFolder is an instance of the folder object. You'll learn more about folder objects in a minute. For now, just notice that you are actually using a property, called Name, of the folder object returned by ParentFolder. Figure 13.8 shows the results of Listing 13.8.

Try deleting or moving log.txt and reloading this page. You get an error message that looks like this:

13

```
Microsoft VBScript runtime error '800a0035'
File not found
/listing130b.asp, line 9
```

You do not want your users to see a message like this. Even if you are pretty sure that log.txt will always exist when they visit the page, it is good to put in some code just in case. The FileExists method from the previous section allows you to do this easily. Just add the following in between lines 8 and 9 of Listing 13.8:

```
If Not objFSO.FileExists(Server.MapPath("log.txt")) Then
   Response.Write "I'm sorry. The file could not be found."
Else
```

FIGURE **13.8**

Viewing the properties of log.txt.

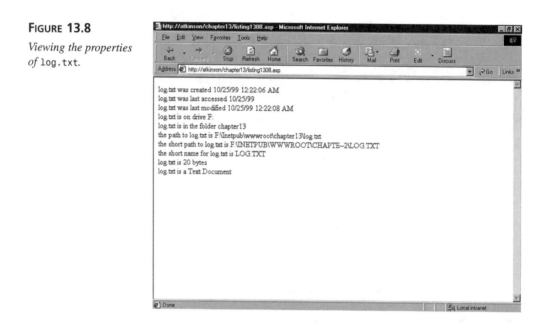

The code on lines 9 through 39 should be executed only in the case where the file exists. Since the file system object is instantiated in either case, it should be freed in either case (as on line 40). Therefore, the End if goes between lines 39 and 40.

We've mentioned the folder object a little before. Let's look at it and some of its properties:

- Attributes is used to set and return some of the special attributes of the folder.
- DateCreated returns the date and time that the folder was created. This property cannot be changed.
- DateLastAccessed returns the date and time that the folder was last accessed. This property cannot be changed by your ASP code.
- DateLastModified returns the date and time that the folder was last modified. This property also cannot be changed.
- Drive returns the letter of the drive the folder is on. This property cannot be changed directly.
- Files returns a collection consisting of all the file objects contained in the folder.
- IsRootFolder has a value of True if the folder is the root folder of the current drive.
- Name is used to set or return the name of the folder.
- ParentFolder returns an instance of the folder object corresponding to the parent folder of the specified folder.
- Path returns the path to the folder, including the name.

- ShortName returns the version of the folder name that is used by programs that do not support long filenames.

- ShortPath returns the path to the folder as it is seen by programs that do not support long filenames.

- Size returns the size, in bytes, of all the files and subfolders contained in the folder.

- Subfolders returns a collection consisting of all the folder objects contained within the folder.

- Type returns information that is known about the type of the folder. For most folders, this is simply "File Folder". Certain special folders, though, have their own type, such as "Recycle bin".

As you can see here, the folder object has many of the same properties as the file object. Three that are not in the file object are IsRootFolder, Files, and Subfolders. IsRootFolder is a simple Boolean value that indicates whether the folder is a root folder (such as "C:\"). The other two are collections. Collections were first discussed on Day 6, "Working with Objects." Files is a collection of file objects that correspond to the files found in the specified directory. Listing 13.9 demonstrates how you might write a page to display a list of files in a directory.

LISTING 13.9 The Files Collection

```
1: <%@ LANGUAGE=VBSCRIPT %>
2: <% Option Explicit %>
3: <HTML>
4:   <BODY>
5:   <%
6:     Dim objFSO, objFile, objFolder
7:     Set objFSO = _
8:         Server.CreateObject("Scripting.FileSystemObject")
9:     Set objFolder = _
10:         objFSO.GetFolder(Server.MapPath("../chapter13"))
11:    Response.Write "Directory listing for "
12:    Response.Write objFolder.Path & "<P>"
13:    For Each objFile in objFolder.Files
14:       Response.Write objFile.Name & "<BR>"
15:    Next
16:    Set objFolder = Nothing
17:    Set objFSO = Nothing
18:  %>
19:  </BODY>
20: </HTML>
```

13

ANALYSIS Lines 6, 7, and 8 declare the variables and instantiate the file system object as before. Lines 9 and 10 use the GetFolder method of the file system object to instantiate the folder object. In this case, the folder object represents a folder called "chapter13" that is contained in the current directory. A header identifying the page is printed with lines 11 and 12. Line 12 uses the Path property of the folder object, which works the same as the Path property for the file object. Line 13 uses the For Each…Next statement to iterate through all the members of the collection. Line 14 prints out the value of the Name property of the file object. The result of all this code is that a listing of all the files in the directory "chapter13" is printed out.

Notice, though, that this only prints filenames. The folders contained within "chapter13" are ignored. That is because you need the other collection included in the folder object. Listing 13.10 uses the Subfolders collection instead of the Files collection.

LISTING 13.10   The Subfolders Collection

```
1: <%@ LANGUAGE=VBSCRIPT %>
2: <% Option Explicit %>
3: <HTML>
4:   <BODY>
5:   <%
6:     Dim objFSO, objSubfolder, objFolder
7:     Set objFSO = _
8:         Server.CreateObject("Scripting.FileSystemObject")
9:     Set objFolder = _
10:           objFSO.GetFolder(Server.MapPath("../chapter13"))
11:     Response.Write "Subdirectories of "
12:     Response.Write objFolder.Path & "<P>"
13:     For Each objSubfolder in objFolder.Subfolders
14:       Response.Write objSubfolder.Name & "<BR>"
15:     Next
16:     Set objFolder = Nothing
17:     Set objFSO = Nothing
18:   %>
19:   </BODY>
20: </HTML>
```

Most of this works the same as in Listing 13.9. Now, you are looping through the subdirectories of "chapter13".

Listing 13.11 goes through the files in a specified directory and lists the ones larger than a specified size. This could be useful if you are running out of space on your site, to help find the files that are eating up the most bytes.

LISTING 13.11   Searching Through for Large Files

```
1: <%@ Language=VBScript %>
2: <% Option Explicit %>
3: <HTML>
4:   <BODY>
```

```
5:    <%
6:      Const MAX_SIZE = 1024
7:      Dim objFile, objFSO, objFolder, strFolderPath
8:      strFolderPath = "../chapter12"
9:      strFolderPath = Server.MapPath(strFolderPath)
10:     Set objFSO = _
11:         Server.CreateObject("Scripting.FileSystemObject")
12:     Set objFolder = objFSO.GetFolder(strFolderPath)
13:     For Each objFile in objFolder.Files
14:       If objFile.Size > MAX_SIZE then
15:         Response.Write "<FONT COLOR=RED>("
16:         Response.Write objFile.Size
17:         Response.Write " bytes)</FONT>"
18:         Response.Write objFile.Path & "<BR>"
19:       End If
20:     Next
21:    %>
22:    </BODY>
23: </HTML>
```

ANALYSIS Line 6 sets the maximum file size. For this example, it is 1 kilobyte. In a real-world case, you might use 50 times this number. Line 8 sets the folder that you will search. Line 9 uses `Server.MapPath` to convert this to a physical path. Lines 10 through 12 instantiate the objects you will use. Line 13 uses the `For Each…Next` statement once again to go through the files in the folder. If a file is larger than the specified `MAX_SIZE`, it will be listed along with its size. Figure 13.9 shows the results of executing this script on one system. Your results may differ, depending on the files on your system.

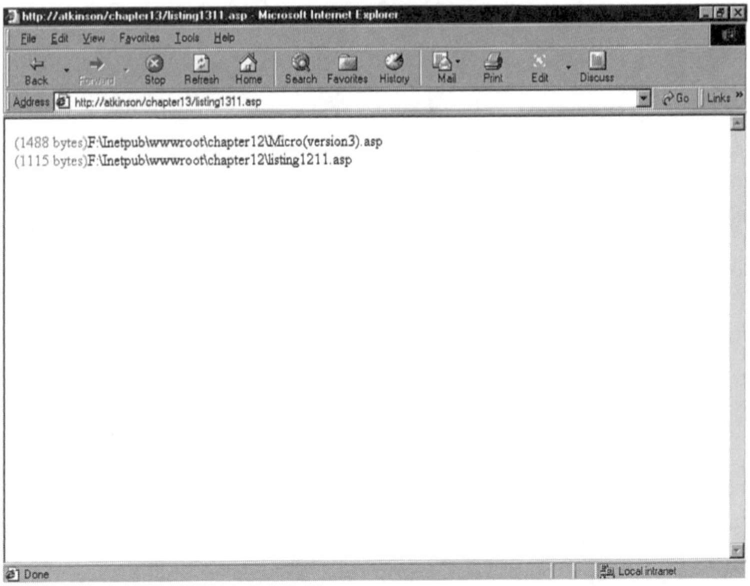

FIGURE 13.9

The results of the large file finder.

13

This script could be improved in many ways. You could change it so that you could specify a directory without changing the code. If you are familiar with recursion, you could write a recursive function to go through all the folders and subfolders on the site.

Listing 13.12 puts together some of the properties discussed in this section. This page can be used to browse the contents of your "c:\" drive.

LISTING 13.12   Properties of Files and Folders

```
 1:  <%@ LANGUAGE=VBSCRIPT %>
 2:  <% Option Explicit %>
 3:  <HTML>
 4:   <BODY>
 5:   <%
 6:      Const DEFAULT_PATH = "c:\"
 7:      Dim objFSO, objSubfolder, objFolder, objFile
 8:      Dim strCurrentPath, strPath
 9:      strCurrentPath = Request.QueryString("path")
10:      If strCurrentPath = "" Then
11:          strCurrentPath = DEFAULT_PATH
12:      End if
13:      Set objFSO = _
14:          Server.CreateObject("Scripting.FileSystemObject")
15:      Set objFolder = _
16:          objFSO.GetFolder(strCurrentPath)
17:      Response.Write "Contents of "
18:      Response.Write objFolder.Path & "<P>"
19:      If Not objFolder.IsRootFolder Then
20:          strPath = objFolder.ParentFolder.Path
21:          strPath = Server.URLEncode(strPath)
22:   %>
23:      <A HREF=
24:      "BrowseDir.asp?path=<%=strPath%>">..</A><BR>
25:   <%
26:      End if
27:      For Each objSubfolder in objFolder.Subfolders
28:          strPath = Server.URLEncode(objSubfolder.Path)
29:   %>
30:      <A HREF="BrowseDir.asp?path=<%= strPath %>">
31:        <%= objSubfolder.Name %></A><BR>
32:   <%
33:      Next
34:      Response.Write "<P>"
35:      For Each objFile in objFolder.Files
36:          Response.Write objFile.Name
37:          Response.Write "<BR>"
38:      Next
39:      Set objFolder = Nothing
40:      Set objFSO = Nothing
41:   %>
42:   </BODY>
43: </HTML>
```

ANALYSIS   Save Listing 13.12 as `BrowseDir.asp`. Line 6 sets the default path where you will start browsing as a constant. Change it if you want. Lines 7 and 8 declare the variables you will use. Line 9 retrieves the value of path from the querystring. You will use this argument, passed through the querystring, to keep track of what the current directory should be. If there is no value for `path`, the value in the `DEFAULT_PATH` constant is used (lines 10-12). Now you instantiate the file system object (lines 13-14) and the folder object (lines 15-16). Use the folder specified in the `strCurrentPath` string. Lines 17 and 18 print a header so that the user knows what he is looking at.

Now you want to print the subdirectories. If you are used to working from a command line, you probably know that at the top of a directory listing, `..` is used to indicate the parent folder. You do the same with the `BrowseDir.asp`. Lines 19 through 26 do this. If the user is already looking at the root directory, there is no parent folder to look at, and so you do not want the `..` to appear. The `If…Then` statement on line 19 takes care of this. Assuming that the user is not already at the root directory, you want to display the `..`, hyperlink to take them up a level. The link you need calls the same page, passing in a new path value. Specifically, the path value will be that of the parent folder's path. It is stored in `strPath` (line 20) and `URLEncoded` (line 21), and then used in the link (line 24). `Server.URLEncode` keeps the special characters in the path from messing up the URL (all those \'s could cause problems).

Next, for each subdirectory of the current directory, you want a link. A `For Each…Next` statement is used with the `Subfolders` collection of the folder object (line 27). `objSubfolder` takes the value of each subfolder of the current folder. Lines 28 and 30 form the link with the path to the subfolder and the name of the subfolder.

Finally, you print out a list of the files in the directory using the `Files` collection just like in Listing 13.9. As always, the script ends by setting every object instantiated with `Set` to nothing.

Figure 13.10 shows the results of executing this script and browsing to one particular folder on one system. In this case, it is being used to view the contents of a directory containing the code samples from Day 12. Your results may vary depending on the files and folders on your system.

Opening Files

Sometimes you will need to save information for future access and updating. Yesterday, Day 12, "Working with Common ASP Components," we talked about using the Ad Rotator component and mentioned that if you are going to use it, you would probably want to record some statistics. To do that, you need to be able to write to a file. Then later, in a report page, you would probably want to read in data from that file. To do either of these, you must first open the file. There are several ways to do this.

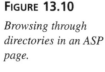

FIGURE 13.10

Browsing through directories in an ASP page.

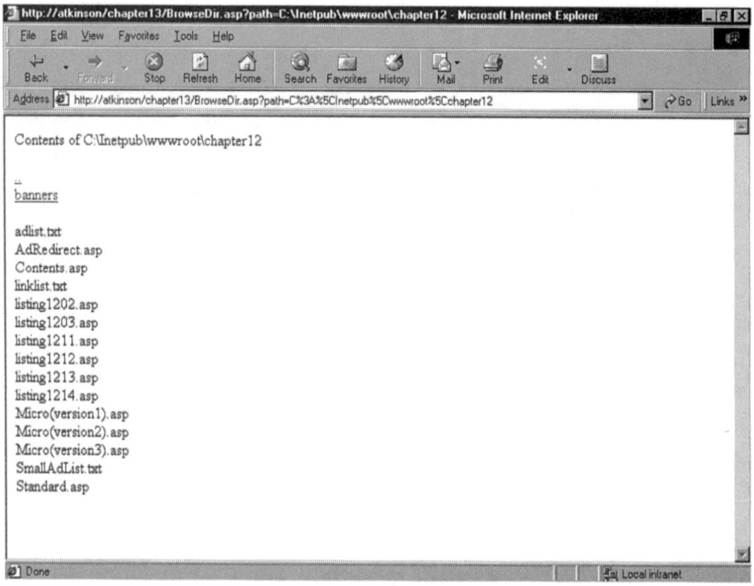

The first uses the file system object and a method called OpenTextFile. OpenTextFile has the following syntax:

```
objectname.OpenTextFile(filename, mode, create, format)
```

The last three arguments are optional. If you want to use one of them, you must use all the preceding ones, too.

filename is the name of the file to be opened. It should be a physical path, so you will probably want to use Server.MapPath with it.

mode has three possible values: ForReading (1), ForWriting (2), or ForAppending (8). These values indicate whether to open the file for reading, writing, or appending text to the end.

If the file specified by *filename* is not found, there are two options: OpenTextFile can either create a new, empty file with the name, or it can return an error message. *create* indicates which of these it should do. If *create* is True, a new file is created. If it is False, an error is displayed. The default for *create* is False.

format indicates whether to open the file as ASCII or Unicode. *format* is a Tristate value. A value of -2 specifies to use the system default. A value of 0 specifies to open the file as ASCII. A value of -1 specifies to open the file as Unicode. Unicode is a special encoding scheme. It uses more memory than ASCII to store characters, but can store a much wider variety of characters, including international characters. We will not be using this option much.

For the moment, let's just look at the first two arguments. The following code opens a file for reading:

```
1:  Dim objOpenFile, objFSO, strPath
2:  strPath = Server.MapPath("whatever.txt")
3:  Set objFSO = _
4:      Server.CreateObject("Scripting.FileSystemObject")
5:  Set objOpenFile = _
6:      objFSO.OpenTextFile(strPath, 1)
```

Line 6 uses the OpenTextFile method, passing the path and setting the mode as ForReading. OpenTextFile returns an instance of the TextStream object.

If you already have a file object that represents the file you want to open, there is another way to open it. The file object includes a method called OpenAsTextStream. OpenAsTextStream can take two arguments. The first is the mode, which works the same as with OpenTextFile. The second is the format, which also works the same as with OpenTextFile. The other two arguments are unnecessary. The file name is already known because it is part of the file object. The file must already exist because the file object instance could not have been created otherwise. Again, we are not concerned with the format at this point, so use the OpenAsTextStream method like this:

```
1:  Dim objOpenFile, objFSO, objFile
2:  Set objFSO = _
3:      Server.CreateObject("Scripting.FileSystemObject")
4:  Set objFile = _
5:      objFSO.GetFile(Server.MapPath("whatever.txt"))
6:  Set objOpenFile = objFile.OpenAsTextStream(ForReading)
```

ANALYSIS Lines 2 and 3 instantiate the file system object. Lines 4 and 5 instantiate the file object with the file whatever.txt. Line 6 uses the file object just created and the OpenAsTextStream method to instantiate the text stream object. Now you can do your reading from the whatever.txt file.

There is a third way to get an instance of the text stream object, but it is less general than the first two. There is a method of the file system object that creates a new text file and returns a matching text stream object instance.

CreateTextFile accepts up to three arguments. The first is required and is the name of the file to create. The second is optional and indicates what to do if the file already exists. If it is True, the existing file is overwritten. If it is False, and the file already exists, an error occurs. The default setting is False, but it is good to go ahead and specify a setting. The third indicates whether the file should be treated as Unicode or ASCII. Again, the default is ASCII, and that will suit our purposes.

You cannot specify ForReading or ForWriting because this method results in the creation of a new file, and there is nothing to read from it. You can use CreateTextFile like this:

13

```
1: Dim objNewFile, objFSO
2: Set objFSO = _
3:  Server.CreateObject("Scripting.FileSystemObject")
4: Set objNewFile = _
5:  objFSO.CreateTextFile(Server.MapPath("new.txt"), False)
```

This example uses the CreateTextFile method to create a new file called new.txt (line 5). Because the overwrite option is set to False, this script produces an error if new.txt already exists. To prevent users from seeing that error message, you could use the file system object's FileExists method, like this:

```
1: Dim objNewFile, objFSO
2: Set objFSO = _
3:  Server.CreateObject("Scripting.FileSystemObject")
4: If Not objFSO.FileExists(Server.MapPath("new.txt")) Then
5:   Set objNewFile = _
6:    objFSO.CreateTextFile(Server.MapPath("new.txt"), False)
7:   'insert code that uses objNewFile here
8: End if
```

This code uses the FileExists method and an If…Then statement (line 4) to make sure that the file does not exist before you try creating it.

By now you know that whenever you instantiate an object you should be sure to destroy it as soon as you are finished. Before you destroy an instance of the text stream object, you need also to close it. The Close method does this. You close an instance called objOpenFile like this:

```
objOpenFile.Close
```

Reading Files

Suppose now that there is a text file on the server and you want to print its contents within an ASP page. There are several ways for you to read in data from a file. The first step is to open the file as a text stream. No matter which way you do that, reading works the same.

There are three methods of the text stream object you can use to read in data. The first is Read(numcharacters). numcharacters is a required argument. It is an integer that specifies the number of characters to be read in. Read returns a string numcharacters in length, unless numcharacters is greater than the total number of characters remaining in the file. In that case, it returns all the remaining characters.

Let's look at an example. alpha.txt is a text file that consists of 26 characters: "abcdefghijklmnopqrstuvwxyz". The following code writes three lines of output:

```
Response.Write objOpenFile.Read(10) & "<BR>"
Response.Write objOpenFile.Read(10) & "<BR>"
Response.Write objOpenFile.Read(10)
```

The first line prints out 10 characters: `"abcdefghij"`. The second line begins reading where the first line ended and also reads in 10 characters: `"klmnopqrst"`. The third line would read in 10 characters if there were 10 characters left. There are not. So, it reads in as many characters as it can: `"uvwxyz"`.

What if there was a fourth `Read`? There would be nothing left to read in. You are already at the end of the file. An error would be generated. How can you avoid this error?

`AtEndOfStream` is a property of the text stream object. It has a value of `True` if you are at the end of the text, and `False` otherwise. `AtEndOfStream` can be useful in `If...Then` and `Do...Loop` statements to make sure that there is something to read before the `Read` is performed.

Listing 13.13 uses this property to print out characters from `alpha.txt` five at a time, and stop when it reaches the end.

LISTING 13.13 Using `Read` and `AtEndOfStream`

```
 1:  <%@ LANGUAGE=VBSCRIPT %>
 2:  <%  Option Explicit %>
 3:  <HTML>
 4:   <BODY>
 5:   <%
 6:     Dim objOpenFile, objFSO, strPath
 7:     strPath = Server.MapPath("alpha.txt")
 8:     Set objFSO = _
 9:        Server.CreateObject("Scripting.FileSystemObject")
10:     Set objOpenFile = _
11:        objFSO.OpenTextFile(strPath, 1)
12:     Do While Not objOpenFile.AtEndOfStream
13:        Response.Write objOpenFile.Read(5) & "<BR>"
14:     Loop
15:     objOpenFile.Close
16:     Set objOpenFile = Nothing
17:     Set objFSO = Nothing
18:   %>
19:   </BODY>
20: </HTML>
```

13

Lines 6 through 11 declare and instantiate everything the same as before. Line 12 begins the loop. You want to keep looping until the end of the file is reached and then stop. You can see the output from this listing in Figure 13.11. As you can see, the characters are printed five to a line until the end of the file is reached.

FIGURE **13.11**

Results of Listing 13.13.

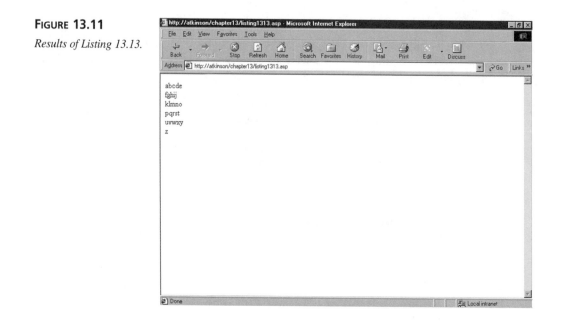

`Read` allows you to read a certain number of characters at a time. What if you wanted to read in by the line, instead? The second way of reading in from a file allows you to do just that. `ReadLine` returns a string consisting of an entire line from the file.

The third method for reading in from a file is `ReadAll`. As you may guess, `ReadAll` returns a string consisting of the entire file. Generally, it should only be used for small files. It uses quite a bit of memory to read in a whole file. It is usually better to work with the file one line at a time using `ReadLine`.

The next example is a script that prints out the source code for an ASP page. This can be especially useful if you are trying to teach visitors to a site how to use some feature of ASP. Listing 13.14 is passed a URL on the querystring and prints out the source code for the script at the URL without executing it.

LISTING **13.14**   Printing the ASP Source Code of a Script

```
1:  <%@ LANGUAGE=VBSCRIPT %>
2:  <%  Option Explicit %>
3:  <HTML>
4:   <BODY>
5:   <%
6:      Const ForReading = 1
7:      Dim objOpenFile, objFSO, strPath, strText
8:      strPath = Request.QueryString("URL")
9:      strPath = Server.MapPath(strPath)
10:     Set objFSO = _
```

```
11:          Server.CreateObject("Scripting.FileSystemObject")
12:      Set objOpenFile = _
13:          objFSO.OpenTextFile(strPath, ForReading)
14:      Response.Write "<PRE>"
15:      Do While Not objOpenFile.AtEndOfStream
16:        strText = objOpenFile.ReadLine
17:        Response.Write Server.HTMLEncode(strText)
18:        Response.Write "<BR>"
19:      Loop
20:      objOpenFile.Close
21:      Set objOpenFile = Nothing
22:      Set objFSO = Nothing
23:      Response.Write "</PRE>"
24:  %>
25:  </BODY>
26:  </HTML>
```

Save Listing 13.14 as viewsource.asp. Line 6 creates the ForReading constant. Line 7 declares the variables you will be using. Line 8 gets the URL from the querystring, and line 9 uses Server.MapPath to convert it into a physical path.

Next, the file system and text stream objects are instantiated (lines 10-13). You will be opening the page specified by the URL as a text stream. This way, you can read from the file without executing anything.

Now you need to make sure of a couple of things. First, you want the spaces within the file to display. This keeps the formatting of the file nice and readable. Second, you want to be sure that the HTML tags within the file are not interpreted. Lines 14 and 23 surround the output with <PRE> and </PRE> tags, which cause the spaces to be displayed. You will also use the Server.HTMLEncode method to ensure that the HTML tags are displayed without being interpreted by the browser.

So, although you are not yet at the end of the file, the script reads in a line (lines 15 and 16). Line 17 encodes it and sends it to the browser. Then the <BR> tag inserts a line break.

When you reach the end of the file, you exit the loop, close the file (line 20), and free the memory associated with the objects (lines 21 and 22).

13

If you had a page that you wanted users to be able to view the source code to, you would put the following link somewhere in it:

```
<A HREF=
"viewsource.asp?URL=<%=Request.ServerVariables("URL")%>">
View the source code for this page.</A>
```

This will use the querystring to pass a relative URL to the page to viewsource.asp.

Figure 13.12 uses viewsource.asp to show the source code of listing1311.asp.

FIGURE 13.12

The View ASP Source script.

Writing Files to the Server

Now you can read data in from a file, but this is only half of the coin. For your pages to record data, they need to be capable of writing to files. There are several different ways to do this. You could write data to a new file or an existing one. If it is an existing file, you could either append the new data to the end or write over data that is already there.

The `Write` method writes a string to a text file. It is used like this:

```
objTextStream.Write("your text")
```

The `WriteLine` method writes a string to a text file and then adds a carriage return. Any text added after a `WriteLine` will be on a separate line. `WriteLine` may or may not have a string argument. With no argument, it simply writes a carriage return to the file.

`WriteBlankLines(number)` writes *number* carriage returns to the file. This is not entirely the same as inserting *number* blank lines into the file.

Listing 13.15 demonstrates the use of these three methods for writing to a file.

LISTING 13.15 Ways of Writing to a File

```
1:  <%@ LANGUAGE=VBSCRIPT %>
2:  <%  Option Explicit %>
3:  <HTML>
4:   <BODY>
5:   <%
```

```
 6:        Const ForWriting = 2
 7:        Dim objOpenFile, objFSO, strPath
 8:        strPath = Server.MapPath("test.txt")
 9:        Set objFSO = _
10:            Server.CreateObject("Scripting.FileSystemObject")
11:        If objFSO.FileExists(strPath) Then
12:          Set objOpenFile = _
13:             objFSO.OpenTextFile(strPath, ForWriting)
14:          objOpenFile.Write("abcde")
15:          objOpenFile.WriteLine("fgh")
16:          objOpenFile.Write("ijklm")
17:          objOpenFile.WriteBlankLines(3)
18:          objOpenFile.Write("nopq")
19:          objOpenFile.WriteLine
20:          objOpenFile.Write("rstuv")
21:          objOpenFile.Close
22:          Set objOpenFile = Nothing
23:        End If
24:        Set objFSO = Nothing
25:    %>
26:    </BODY>
27:    </HTML>
```

ANALYSIS   Lines 6 through 12 create the constant, variables, and objects you will need. Line 14 then writes the string "abcde" to the file. Line 15 writes "fgh" to the file and then writes a carriage return. Therefore, when line 16 writes "ijklm" to the file, it will be on a separate line from the "abcdefgh". Line 17 uses the WriteBlankLines method to write three carriage returns to the file. Line 18 writes some more text to the file. Then line 19 performs a WriteLine without any text. This sends the line return to the file. Line 20 writes one last string to the file before line 21 closes it. You can see the results of this listing in Figure 13.13.

Let's go back to one of the Day 12 topics for a moment. Remember discussing the Ad Rotator and wanting to record the banners people clicked? Now you can implement that. Listing 13.16 is an improved adredirect.asp that does this.

13

LISTING 13.16   Recording Banner Click-Through Statistics

```
1:    <%@ LANGUAGE=VBSCRIPT %>
2:    <%  Option Explicit %>
3:    <%  Const ForReading = 1
4:        Dim objOpenFile, objFSO, strPath, iCount
5:        strPath = Request.QueryString("image")
6:        strPath = strPath & ".txt"
7:        strPath = Server.MapPath(strPath)
8:        Set objFSO = _
9:            Server.CreateObject("Scripting.FileSystemObject")
```

continues

LISTING **13.16** continued

```
10:     If objFSO.FileExists(strPath) Then
11:        Set objOpenFile = _
12:          objFSO.OpenTextFile(strPath, ForReading)
13:        iCount = Cint(objOpenFile.ReadLine) + 1
14:        objOpenFile.Close
15:     Else
16:        iCount = 1
17:     End if
18:     Set objOpenFile = _
19:        objFSO.CreateTextFile(strPath, True)
20:     objOpenFile.WriteLine(iCount)
21:     objOpenFile.Close
22:     Set objOpenFile = Nothing
23:     Set objFSO = Nothing
24:     Response.Redirect(Request.QueryString("url"))
25: %>
```

FIGURE **13.13**

Writing to a file.

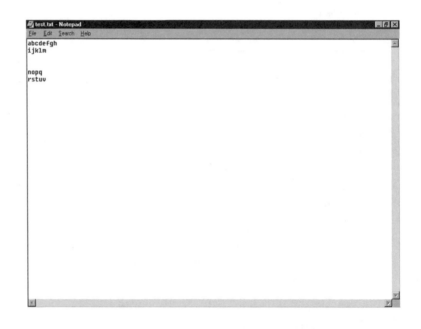

 Line 5 retrieves the image information from the querystring. Because a company might have more than one banner and you want to keep track of them separately, you identify an ad by the URL for its image. Store the click-through count for a particular image in file with the same name and path but with a ".txt" added to the end. Line 6 appends the ".txt" extension to the end of the path to the image, and then line 7 uses Server.MapPath to convert to a physical path.

Next, lines 8 and 9 instantiate the file system object, and line 10 uses its `FileExists` method to find out whether the counter file for this particular image has been created. If it has, lines 11 and 12 open the file for reading. Then line 13 reads in the number in string format (using `ReadLine`), converts it into an integer, and adds one. Line 14 then closes the file. If the file does not already exist, you can assume that this is the first time anyone has clicked-through on it and set the counter variable to one (line 16).

Now open the file for writing. Use the `CreateTextFile` method of the file system object with overwrite set to `True` (lines 18 and 19). If the file already existed, it will be overwritten and a new one created. Line 20 writes the counter value to the file, and line 21 closes the file. Lines 22 and 23 free the memory for `objOpenFile` and `objFSO`. Finally, the user is actually redirected to the page.

Appending to Files

The ways of writing to a file discussed so far all resulted in the file being overwritten. Even if you do not write anything at all to the file, as soon as you open it, specifying `ForWriting`, the old file is destroyed. Sometimes this is what you want; sometimes it is not. This is why there is a third way of opening a file: `ForAppending`.

After a file has been opened for appending, you write data to it the same as if it had been opened for writing. The only difference is that instead of replacing the text that is already there, appended text is put at the end of the file. Listing 13.17 demonstrates `ForAppending`.

LISTING 13.17   Appending to a File

```
 1:  <%@ LANGUAGE=VBSCRIPT %>
 2:  <%  Option Explicit %>
 3:  <%
 4:      Const ForAppending = 8
 5:      Dim objOpenFile, objFSO, strPath
 6:      strPath = Server.MapPath("subscribers.txt")
 7:      Set objFSO = _
 8:          Server.CreateObject("Scripting.FileSystemObject")
 9:      If objFSO.FileExists(strPath) Then
10:          Set objOpenFile = _
11:             objFSO.OpenTextFile(strPath, ForAppending)
12:      Else
13:          Set objOpenFile = _
14:              objFSO.CreateTextFile(strPath)
15:      End if
16:      objOpenFile.WriteLine Request.Form("email")
17:      objOpenFile.Close
18:      Set objOpenFile = Nothing
19:      Set objFSO = Nothing
```

13

continues

LISTING **13.17** continued

```
21: %>
22: <HTML>
23: <BODY>
24:     Thanks for subscribing!
25:   </BODY>
26: </HTML>
```

ANALYSIS Listing 13.17 uses the appending mode of the text stream object. The page assumes that the user has entered his email address into a form and adds them to a list of subscribers. Line 4 creates the ForAppending constant. Line 5 declares all the variables you will use. Line 6 converts the relative path "subscribers.txt" to a physical path, such as "c:\Inetpub\wwwroot\mailings\subscribers.txt". Remember, the file system and text stream methods require the full, physical path.

Lines 7 and 8 instantiate the file system object. Then, if the file already exists, lines 10 and 11 open it for appending. If the file does not exist, it is opened with CreateTextFile. Either way, you write to it the same, using WriteLine on line 16. Then lines 17 through 19 close the text stream and set the objects to nothing. Finally, a message displays thanking the user for signing up.

Summary

Today, we discussed how to use files on your server to store information needed by your pages as well as simplify maintenance.

Server-side includes are an easy way to simplify maintenance. They allow you to put commonly used code in a separate file. A special directive is then used to tell the server where to insert it. This is especially useful when it is code you might want to change, and the change should be reflected throughout the entire site. Instead of changing a dozen, or a hundred, or even a thousand pages, you need only change one.

Server-side includes are useful for their simplicity. If you need to include a dynamically determined file, though, they will not work. In this case, you would need Server.Execute. Server.Execute(*path*) executes the page specified by *path* as though it were part of the calling page.

Server.Transfer(*path*) is similar to Server.Execute(*path*). The difference between the two is that with Server.Transfer, control does not return to the original page after *path* is finished executing. This makes Server.Transfer a bit like the Response.Redirect. The differences between the two are that Server.Transfer does not care whether anything has been written to output, Server.Transfer is faster, and Server.Transfer does not create a new object context. This means that the session and request values are not changed.

The file system object contains several methods that you can use in accessing files on the server. FileExists and FolderExists allow you to check whether a specified file or folder exists.

GetFile returns an instance of the file object, which you can use to access a file and its properties. Some properties of the file object are DateCreated, DateLastAccessed, DateLastModified, Name, ParentFolder, Path, Size, and Type.

GetFolder returns an instance of the folder object. Properties of the folder object include all the ones associated with files, plus Files and Subfolders, which are both collections. Files contains file objects for every file in the folder. Subfolders contains a folder object for every subfolder of the folder.

OpenTextFile is a method of the file system object that is used to open a text file for reading, writing, or appending. OpenAsTextStream can be used if you already have an instance of the file object that corresponds to the file you want to open. Like OpenTextFile, it returns an instance of the text stream object. The third way to get an instance of the text stream object is with the CreateTextFile method of the file system object. It is only useful for creating a new file.

There are three different modes in which a text file may be opened: reading, writing, and appending. If the mode is ForReading, the file may be read from but not written to. If the mode is ForWriting, the file may be written to but not read from. In this case, the new data replaces what was previously in the file. The third mode is ForAppending, which allows only writing, not reading. In this case, the new data is added to the end of the file.

If you have opened your instance of the text stream object for reading, you may use the methods Read, ReadLine, and ReadAll. Read reads in a specified number of characters. ReadLine reads in a single line, and ReadAll reads in the entire file.

If the file is opened for writing or appending, use Write, WriteLine, or WriteBlankLines. Write(*string*) writes the string to the file. WriteLine(*string*) writes the string to the file, followed by a line return. WriteBlankLines(*number*) writes *number* carriage returns to the file.

13

Q&A

Q What happens if I try to open files besides my own?

A All the methods and properties of the file system, file, folder, and text stream objects apply only when you have the appropriate permissions on the server. If there are other files and folders for which you do not have the correct permissions, you will not be able to access them.

Q Why would you ever want a new object context?

A Suppose that you have an ASP page that would be passed some values on the querystring and use them to compute and pass on new values to another page. It is not possible to pass on those new values if you do not create a new object context.

Workshop

The Workshop provides quiz questions to help you solidify your understanding of the material covered and exercises to provide you with experience in using what you've learned. Try to understand the quiz and exercise answers before continuing to tomorrow's lesson. Quiz answers are provided in Appendix A, and exercise answers can be found at `http://www.mcp.com/info`.

Quiz

1. What does a server-side include do?
2. What is the difference between a server-side include and `Server.Execute`?
3. What are the differences between `Response.Redirect` and `Server.Transfer`?
4. What are the three modes in which a file may be opened?
5. What is in the `Files` collection of the folder object?
6. What is the difference between

   `objFSO.OpenTextFile("log.txt", 8, True)` and
   `objFSO.OpenTextFile("log.txt", 8, False)`?

7. How do you verify the existence of a file on the server?
8. What does `WriteBlankLines(num)` do?
9. If a file consists of the string "The quick brown fox jumped over the lazy dog," what does `Read(5)` return?
10. Why might you have trouble if you put the following statement in a file called `main.html`?

    `<!--#include file="navbar.html"-->`

Exercises

1. Write the code to convert a file called `input.txt` to all uppercase letters.
2. Write the code to print to the screen the first five lines from each of `input1.txt`, `input2.txt`, `input3.txt`, and `input4.txt`.

DAY 14

Debugging Your ASP Scripts and Handling Errors

Today we'll talk about two important aspects of application development: debugging and handling errors gracefully.

First we'll focus on debugging ASP pages. When you initially write an ASP page, chances are there are bugs within the code. A bug will come in one of two flavors: Either the bug will cause the abnormal termination of your ASP script, or it will cause the output to be different than expected. We will discuss the differences between these two types of bugs and commonly used techniques to locate and resolve them.

Then we'll turn our attention to handling errors. No matter how much debugging you do, errors will always slip by, and errors as a result of external causes are difficult to predict. Today, we'll discuss what steps you can take to gracefully handle such unexpected errors.

Today, you will learn the following:

- What types of bugs you'll commonly encounter when developing ASP applications
- The difference between a fatal and nonfatal bug
- How to debug a fatal bug
- How to debug a nonfatal bug
- How to use ASP 3.0's `ASPError` object to handle errors gracefully
- What three categories of errors can occur in an ASP page
- How to create a custom 404 error page

Debugging Your ASP Scripts

As a new hire to Acme Consulting Group, last week you were assigned to build a banner rotation system. Having studiously read Day 12, "Working with Common ASP Components," you were well versed with the Ad Rotator and decided to use that component. After completing the development of the banner rotation system, you are now prepared to display your work to your boss. However, unbeknownst to you, one of your coworkers changed the name of your Ad Rotator schedule file. When you load the first page for your boss, she is startled to see the following error:

```
MSWC.Adrotator (0x80004005)
ERROR Cannot load rotation schedule file
/adrotator.asp, line 7
```

You boss, looking over the results of your week's work, asks you why no banner is being displayed and, furthermore, wants to know what all that gobbledygook on the screen is supposed to mean!

The preceding example demonstrates that debugging and error handling are two important aspects when developing an ASP application. From an end-user standpoint, nothing is worse than receiving errors when trying to use a program. Despite the vital importance of debugging and error handling, many developers put much more time into the actual programming. Although spending time on the programming is important, it is equally important to spend as much, if not more, time on ensuring that your ASP pages are as bug-free as possible.

One of the few truisms in computer science is that no one writes flawless code. Even the most skilled programmers write code that contains bugs and software defects. Not surprisingly, the number of bugs and defects increases proportionally to the amount of code written. That means that the more code you write, the more bugs you will create, and the larger your application, the more bug-ridden it will be. Consider a large application, such as Windows or Word, which contains millions of lines of code. Although Windows and Word aren't bug-free programs, it's surprising how few bugs there are considering their vast size.

When you write an application, it is important that you take the time to reduce the number of bugs in your code. To reduce your code's bug count, you'll need to *test* your application, searching for bugs. This process of testing to locate bugs is known as *debugging*. We programmers are naturally lazy and despise any unpleasant work. Writing code is fun; finding problems in our code is not fun. Not surprisingly, debugging is often overlooked.

Imagine that you had an ASP page that printed out the current date and time. The code in Listing 14.1 would suffice.

LISTING 14.1   ASP Code that Displays the Web Server's Current Date and Time

```
1:  <%@ Language=VBSCRIPT %>
2:  <% Option Explicit %>
3:  <%
4:     Dim dtNow
5:     DtNw = Now()
6:
7:     Response.Write "The current time is " & dtNow
8:  %>
```

ANALYSIS   Look over Listing 14.1 closely. What, exactly, will its output be? It is tempting to assume that it will correctly display the Web server's current date and time. However, the script as coded in Listing 14.1 will generate an error. Look closely at line 5. The variable dtNow is misspelled there as DtNw. Because you must explicitly declare all variables (due to Option Explicit), this script will generate the following error:

```
Variable is undefined: 'DtNw'
/HiddenErrorListing1.asp, line 5
```

Although the code in Listing 14.1 is functionally correct (there is no error in the logic of the code), a typo has turned Listing 14.1 into a non-working script. No one's perfect; we all make silly typos now and then!

You need to watch out for two types of bugs when debugging your ASP application. The first type of bug is a *fatal bug*.

NEW TERM   A *fatal bug* causes the abrupt end of the execution of a program.

14

The bug in Listing 14.1 is a fatal bug. If you run the code, the ASP page stops executing at line 5 and displays an error message. These types of bugs are usually easy to locate and fix. In the next section, "Debugging Fatal Bugs," we'll discuss techniques and approaches to debugging fatal bugs.

The second type of bug is a *nonfatal bug*.

NEW TERM   A *nonfatal bug* does not halt the execution of a program; rather, it causes the program to generate the wrong output for a given input.

Nonfatal bugs can be tricky to catch. Imagine that you created an ASP page whose functionality was similar to the functionality of the Browser Capabilities component discussed on Day 12. You decide to use the User-Agent HTTP header, which was discussed on Day 10, "Working with the Request Object," to determine the client's browser type. Now, imagine that your ASP page outputs the correct browser information for all versions of Internet Explorer but does not correctly identify Netscape browsers. This is an example of a nonfatal bug because, for a given input (in this case, visiting the page with a Netscape browser), the correct output is not generated. We'll discuss some common techniques used to locate and resolve nonfatal bugs later today in the section "Debugging Nonfatal Bugs."

Debugging Fatal Bugs

Fatal bugs are defects in your code that cause the abrupt end of execution in your program. Simple testing usually exposes most fatal bugs. Fatal bugs are naturally easy to locate because when a fatal bug occurs, your ASP script will stop executing and an error message will be displayed. For this reason, anytime you can convert a nonfatal bug into a fatal bug, it is in your interest to do so.

To see a good example of converting a nonfatal bug into a fatal bug, compare Listing 14.2 to Listing 14.3.

LISTING **14.2** Nonfatal Bugs

```
1:  <%@ Language=VBSCRIPT %>
2:  <%
3:      Dim strName
4:      strNme = "Bob"
5:
6:      Response.Write "Hello, " & strName
7:  %>
```

ANALYSIS   In Listing 14.2 we commit the same type of error as in Listing 14.1, using an undeclared variable. Note that line 3 declares the only variable as strName. Then line 4 refers to a variable as strNme, a simple typo. Because we have not explicitly declared a

variable named strNme, this *should* cause a fatal bug. However, it does not because we
have not used Option Explicit. In Listing 14.2, two variables are allocated, one explicitly
(strName) and one implicitly (strNme). strNme is assigned the value Bob, whereas strName
equals the empty string. Therefore when line 6 outputs the value of strName, an empty
string will be output. The output of Listing 14.2 can be seen in Figure 14.1.

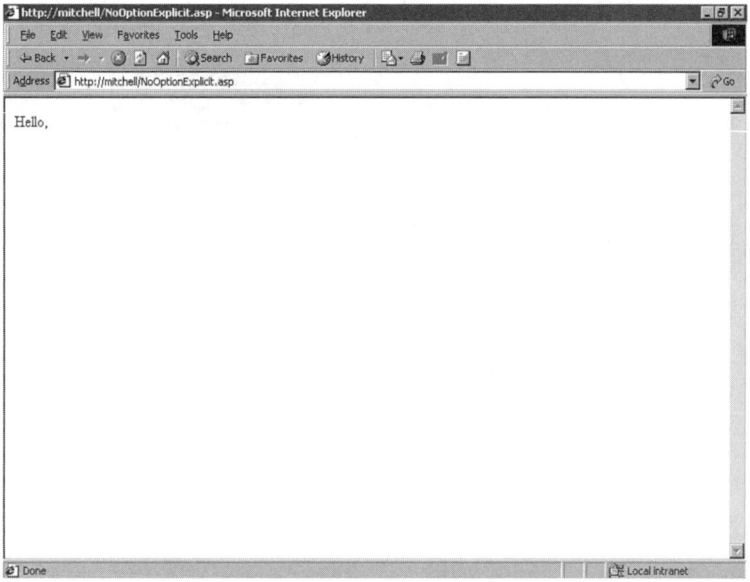

Figure 14.1

*Because strName is
never assigned a value,
a blank string is out-
putted for the value of
strName.*

Because Listing 14.2 executes completely and we did not receive the output we expected,
the bug is classified as a nonfatal bug. Although the typo on line 4 in Listing 14.2 might
be easy to catch now, it becomes much more difficult when you have such an error on an
ASP page with hundreds of lines of code. It is in your favor, then, to turn all nonfatal
bugs into fatal bugs. Listing 14.3 contains the exact same code as Listing 14.2 except for
adding Option Explicit on line 2.

LISTING 14.3   Fatal Bugs

```
1:  <%@ Language=VBSCRIPT %>
2:  <% Option Explicit %>
3:  <%
4:      Dim strName
5:      strNme = "Bob"
6:
7:      Response.Write "Hello, " & strName
8:  %>
```

14

ANALYSIS Listing 14.3 uses `Option Explicit`, thereby requiring that you explicitly declare all variables. Therefore, when line 5 is reached and an undeclared variable is referenced (`strNme`), an error is generated, and the script ceases execution. This is an example of a fatal bug because your ASP page stopped executing after it reached line 5. In Listing 14.2, we were not explicitly notified of the bug. However, with Listing 14.3, after we run the ASP script, we are immediately made aware of the bug. Figure 14.2 contains the output of Listing 14.3 when viewed through a browser.

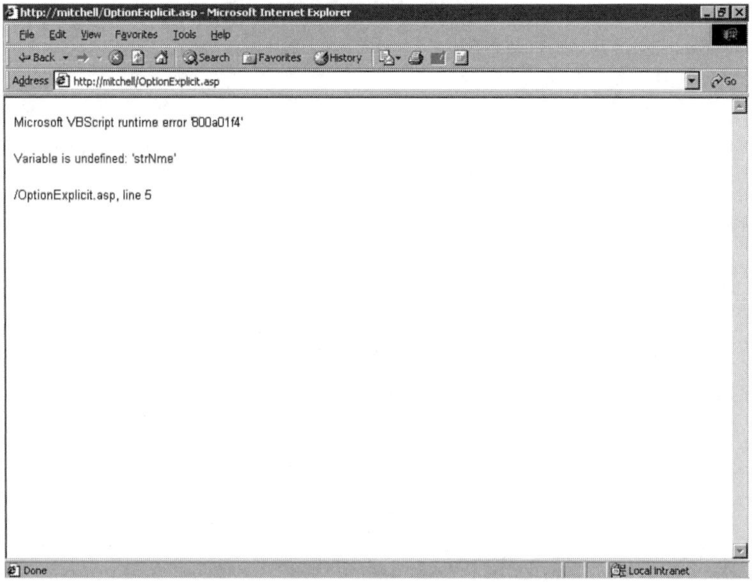

FIGURE 14.2

Because we used `Option Explicit`, *referring to a variable that hasn't been explicitly declared generates a fatal bug.*

Hopefully, the examples in Listing 14.2 and Listing 14.3 have convinced you of the importance of faithfully using `Option Explicit`. It may seem like a pain to have to add `Option Explicit` to every ASP page you create, but it is a good habit, especially as your ASP applications grow in scope and size. We cannot stress the importance of using `Option Explicit` enough. Faithful use of `Option Explicit` will save you *hours* of debugging.

Most fatal bugs in ASP pages can be found by loading the ASP page in a browser. Whenever you finish writing the code for an ASP page, take a few moments to view the ASP page in a browser, to see whether there were any fatal errors. Some common fatal errors include:

- A typo (that is, referring to a variable that has not been explicitly created).
- Trying to access an array element that does not exist. For example, the following code contains a fatal bug:

```
'The array index, 51, is out of the bounds specified
'in the array's definition
Dim aStates(50)
aStates(51) = "Guam"
```

- Referring to a nonexistent property or method of an object.

- When declaring a variable, trying to give the variable a name that is reserved. For example, if you try to create a variable named `For` (that is, `Dim For`), you will receive an error because `For` is a reserved name in the VBScript language.

Debugging Nonfatal Bugs

Nonfatal bugs are not necessarily more difficult to fix than fatal bugs but are always more difficult to locate because fatal bugs list the exact, offending line number. In fact, many nonfatal bugs find their way past even the most ardent debuggers and into the final version of the application. With nonfatal bugs, it is not a matter of catching *all* the bugs, but rather as many as you can before the product needs to ship. The only way to catch nonfatal bugs is through testing, testing, and more testing.

When debugging your ASP pages for nonfatal bugs, it helps to think in terms of input and expected output. A computer program is nothing more than an expected output for a given input. Sometimes there is no input, as in the case of the code in Listing 14.1, Listing 14.2, and Listing 14.3. In those examples, we just output some variable. If there is no input, think to yourself, "What should the output be?" Run your script and see whether you receive the output you expected.

For many ASP scripts, especially ones that collect user input through a form, there is some type of input. Identifying and documenting the input into an ASP page is the first step to reducing the nonfatal bugs in your code. After you've identified the input, determine what the acceptable input ranges are. Imagine that you created an ASP page that used a form to allow the user to enter a number, 1 through 12, into a text box. When the form was submitted, the form processing script would display the number of days in the month corresponding to the user's entry. For example, if a user entered 8 into the text box, he would see `August has 31 days` when the form was submitted. Acceptable inputs are the numeric values 1 through 12.

After you've identified the acceptable inputs, it's important that you test your ASP page using inputs that fall into each of these four categories:

- Expected input values
- Near-boundary input values
- Boundary input values
- Unexpected input values

14

Expected input values are the values that you expect users to input the majority of the time. Imagine that you had an ASP page containing a form with a text box. Into this text box the user would enter the year she was born, and the form processing script would display significant events that occurred that year. Because most people today are between the age of 9 and 99, you might define the expected inputs as the numbers between 1900 and 1990. You'd want to then test this ASP page, picking out 10 or so random values within this interval and making sure that the correct output was displayed.

If your input has specific boundaries that the input must fall within, it is important to extensively test both legal and illegal values near the boundaries. For example, if you were building a Web page on your company's intranet that would allow employees to request vacation time, you might query the user on how many days he needs off work. If the company allowed no more than 14 days of vacation for the year, 14 would be a boundary. Coincidentally, 1 would be a boundary too because why would someone ask for zero days of vacation? Tests should be run with inputs near both boundaries. For example, the following inputs should be tested: 3, 2, 0, -1, 12, 13, 15, and 16. The output for invalid inputs, such as 0, -1, 15, and 16 should generate some sort of message to the user, so that he knows the input was invalid.

Boundary input values should be tested as well. In the vacation request example, the two boundaries are 14 and 1. Both of these inputs should be tested in the system to determine whether they yield the expected output.

The last category of inputs to test is unexpected input values. If you had your users input their ages, unexpected values would include 134, -45, yellow schoolbus, and $50.00. Testing unexpected values is one of the most important categories to test when hunting for nonfatal bugs. No matter how intuitive you make your ASP application, users will enter unexpected inputs. It's important, then, to make sure that your form processing script doesn't generate an error when it is passed unexpected input.

Debugging your ASP pages thoroughly before "going live" with them is of extreme importance. Day 21, "Practicing Intelligent Application Design," discusses the software development cycle in detail. Testing, not surprisingly, is one stage of software development.

> **Note**
>
> Axiom of Programming 1: The more code you write, the more bugs you'll produce.

Handling ASP Errors Gracefully

No matter how much debugging you perform, some errors will make it into the final version of your product. Microsoft, for example, employs literally thousands of testers, and each product released has undergone hundreds of thousands of man-hours of testing. Yet Microsoft's products still contain bugs.

> **Note**
>
> Axiom of Programming 2: Bug-free programming is a myth.

Because you *know* your code will contain errors, you need to decide how to *handle* these errors. By default, when an error occurs, the ASP script stops processing and information on the error is displayed. This information contains an error number, a description of the error, the file the error occurred in, and the offending line number. For example, Listing 14.1 produced the following error message when run:

```
Variable is undefined: 'DtNw'
/HiddenErrorListing1.asp, line 5
```

Although this error message is helpful for the developer, it is an eyesore for the user. Imagine that a user has just filled out a form. After submitting the form, the user is taken to the form processing script and, due to an error, is shown an error message and nothing else. Chances are your user will be confused and annoyed and will not be happy. If you run a commercial Web site, unhappy visitors translates to unhappy customers.

Using the Err Object

With ASP 2.0, some rudimentary error handling was available with VBScript. The syntax was nearly identical to the error handling used with Visual Basic. On each page that you wanted to be able to handle an error, you had to enter the line On Error Resume Next, telling the VBScript engine that if it encountered an error, to just skip ahead to the next line. Then, usually in multiple places in your code, you would need to test to see whether an error had occurred. This was done using the Err object. Listing 14.4 contains a simple example of error handling using the Err object.

LISTING 14.4 Using the VBScript Err Object to Allow for Error Handling

```
1:  <%@ Language=VBSCRIPT %>
2:  <% Option Explicit %>
3:  <%
4:      'This tells the VBScript engine not to stop executing
5:      'when an error is encountered
6:      On Error Resume Next
7:
8:      Dim strName
9:      strNme = "Bob"
10:
```

continues

LISTING 14.4 continued

```
11:      Response.Write "Hello, " & strName
12:
13:      'Now, we need to check the Err object to see if an error occurred
14:      If Err.Number > 0 then
15:         Response.Write "<P><B>An Error Occurred!</B><BR>"
16:         Response.Write "<LI>Number: " & Err.Number
17:         Response.Write "<BR><LI>Description: " & Err.Description
18:      End If
19: %>
```

ANALYSIS Listing 14.4 uses VBScript's Err object to handle the error on line 9 gracefully. Listing 14.4, less the error handling code (line 4 and lines 14 through 18), is identical to Listing 14.3. Line 9 refers to strNme, which has not been explicitly declared. Because Option Explicit is turned on, this generates an error. Normally, the code would stop executing on line 9, and you'd see the output shown in Figure 14.2. However, because line 6 tells the VBScript engine to ignore errors using On Error Resume Next, the ASP script runs through completion. When the error on line 9 occurs, the Err object's Number property is set to 500, the error number of using an undefined variable. The Description property is set to Variable is undefined.

Line 14 checks to determine whether an error has occurred. If the Number property of the Err object is nonzero, then an error has occurred. If Err.Number is greater than 0, then lines 16 and 17 display both the Number and Description of the error. Figure 14.3 shows the output of Listing 14.4.

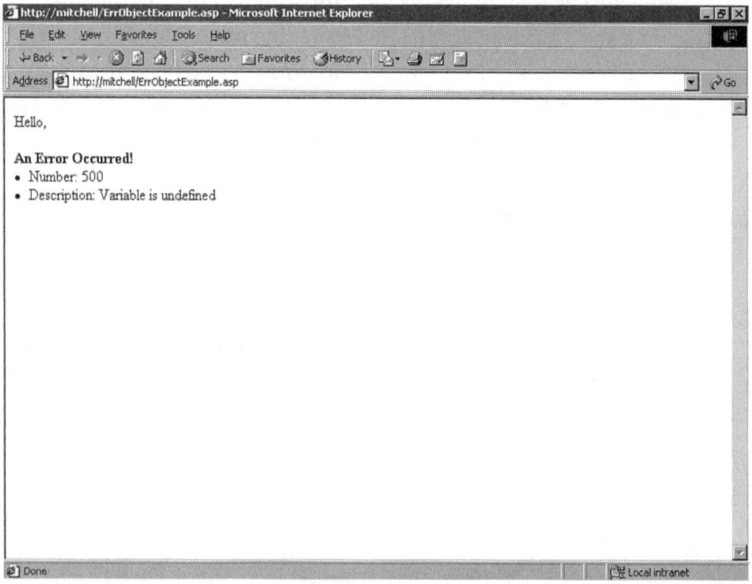

FIGURE 14.3

The Err object can be used to handle errors.

Compare the output in Listing 14.4 (refer to Figure 14.3) to that of Listing 14.3 (refer to Figure 14.2). Although Figure 14.3 might not look too different from Figure 14.2, you could alter the code in Listing 14.4 to produce a more user-friendly explanation for the error. You could let the user know that an error has occurred and provide a link to your Web site's main page and the Webmaster's email address. Using the Err object, you can handle errors gracefully, preventing abnormal terminations of your ASP pages.

Although the Err object is a nice tool for handling errors gracefully, it does have a number of drawbacks. For starters, the Err object can only be used when using VBScript as the server-side language. Also, for each page that you want to be able to handle errors gracefully, you would need to add On Error Resume Next as well as an If statement that checks Err.Number to see whether an error has occurred. With the advent of ASP 3.0, these error-handling drawbacks were addressed with the addition of a new inherent ASP object: the ASPError object.

> **Note**
>
> With version 5.0 of the JScript engine, JScript can support error handling. However, JScript uses different syntax to perform its error handling.

Using the ASPError Object

When the developers at Microsoft were working on ASP 3.0, they really did a great job with the new ASPError object. This object, the only new built-in ASP object in ASP 3.0, allows for error handling, similar to the Err object. The ASPError object, however, solves the disadvantages of the Err object.

Because the ASPError object is an intrinsic ASP object, it doesn't matter what server-side scripting language you are using. This solves the first disadvantage of the Err object, but what about the second? How can the ASPError object be used so that you don't need to include error-handling code in each ASP page? The secret lies not with the ASPError object itself, but rather with IIS 5.0. Whenever an error occurs in your ASP pages, the *HTTP error 500;100* is generated.

> **NEW TERM**   An *HTTP error* is a low-level error that occurs on the Web server in response to some unexpected or illegal behavior.

Many HTTP errors can occur. For example, a 404 error occurs when a Web server receives a request for a Web page that does not exist. All 500 HTTP errors are for internal Web server errors. 500;100 is specifically reserved for ASP errors. With IIS, you can specify one of three things to happen when an HTTP error occurs:

14

- The default error message is returned to the client.
- The contents of a file are sent to the client.
- A URL on the Web site will be visited.

If you opt to return the default error message to the client, the client's browser decides how to display the error message. If you choose to send the contents of a file, you can create a file on the Web server whose contents you want to send in the case of an error. This is usually HTML code, displaying a nicely formatted error message. Finally, you can choose to visit a URL when an error occurs. With this option, you can have an ASP page execute, from which you can access the ASPError object to perform graceful error handling.

To specify what action you want to happen for a given HTTP error, enter the Internet Information Services program in Windows 2000 (choose Start, Programs, Administrative Tools, Internet Services Manager). From there, right-click the Web site that you want to configure and select Properties. Figure 14.4 shows what you will see.

FIGURE 14.4

Open the Internet Information Services, right-click on the Web site you want to configure and select Properties.

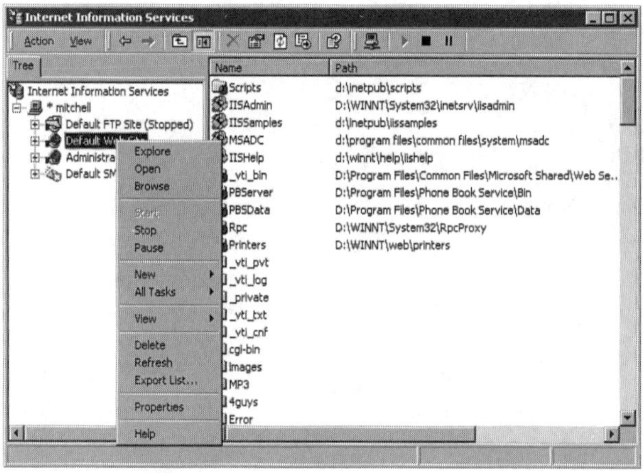

After you click Properties, a tabbed dialog box will appear. Select the Custom Errors tab. You should now see a listing of HTTP errors and the associated action with each error. Scroll down to the 500;100 HTTP error. By default, this points to a URL at /iisHelp/common/500-100.asp. Figure 14.5 shows what you should see.

To create a custom error page, assign the 500;100 HTTP error to redirect to a URL on your Web site. To do this, click the 500;100 HTTP error, and then click Edit Properties. A dialog box named Error Mapping Properties will display. The Message Type option should already be set to URL; all you need to do is change the URL option to your own custom URL. For the time being, enter /Error/ErrorHandler.asp. Figure 14.6 shows the Error Mapping Properties dialog box with the values we've entered.

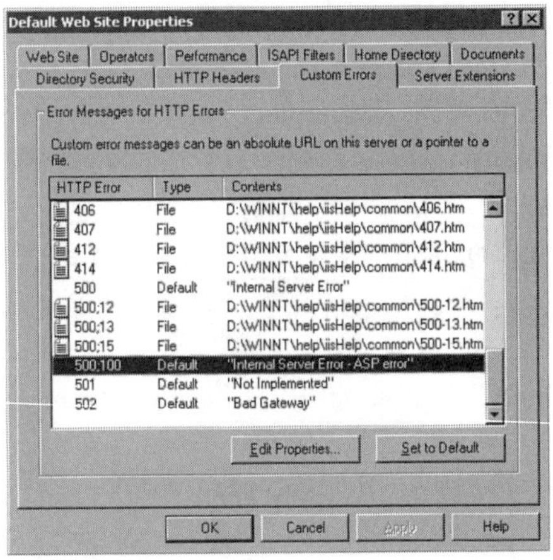

FIGURE 14.5

The Custom Errors tab allows you to determine what will happen when a specific HTTP error occurs.

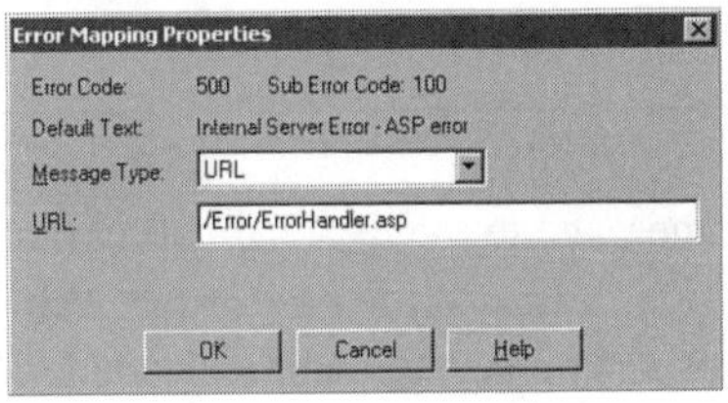

FIGURE 14.6

The Error Mapping Properties dialog box allows you to determine what action you'll take when a specific HTTP error occurs.

Now click OK on the Error Mapping Properties dialog box and the tabbed dialog box. You may be asked whether you want to apply the custom error settings to a number of virtual directory nodes on your Web site. Virtual directories serve as sub-webs on your Web site. These sub-webs may have a different physical directory from the root web's root physical directory; they also have their own Global.asa instances, and their own Session and Application object instances. If you want to have these virtual directories use the custom ASP error-handling page as well, go ahead and select the nodes and click OK.

Now whenever a 500;100 HTTP error occurs on an ASP page, /Error/ErrorHandler.asp will be called via Server.Transfer. Of course now you need to write the code for /Error/ErrorHandler.asp. If you do not create this ASP page, whenever an error occurs, the users will see the default, cryptic error message as in Figure 14.2.

Caution

Recall that ASP 3.0, by default, Buffers the output to the client until the end of a page is reached or Response.Flush or Response.End is called. If content has been written to the client when an error occurs, IIS does not load up the custom error-handling page. Rather, the default error message (refer to Figure 14.2) is displayed.

14

Let's start by creating `ErrorHandler.asp` to contain a message alerting the user that an error has occurred. You will soon employ the `ASPError` object to provide more detailed information. Listing 14.5 shows the preliminary code for `ErrorHandler.asp`. Don't forget to create the `/Error` directory and place `ErrorHandler.asp` there.

LISTING 14.5   Using `ErrorHandler.asp` to Alert the User that an Error Has Occurred

```
 1:  <%@ Language = VBSCRIPT %>
 2:  <% Option Explicit %>
 3:
 4:  <HTML>
 5:  <BODY>
 6:     <P>An Error has occurred.  We apologize for
 7:     this inconvenience.<P>
 8:     <U>Useful Links:</U><BR>
 9:     <LI><A HREF="/">Main Page</A>
10:  </BODY>
11:</HTML>
```

ANALYSIS   Listing 14.5 displays a message to the user indicating that an error has occurred (lines 6 and 7) and provides a link to the root of the Web site (line 9). Whenever an ASP page encounters an error, `ErrorHandler.asp` is loaded via a `Server.Transfer`.

Let's look at an example of executing an ASP page that contains an error. Listing 14.6 references an array element that doesn't exist—this will cause an error.

LISTING 14.6   An Index Out-of-Bounds Error

```
 1:  <%@ Language = VBSCRIPT %>
 2:  <% Option Explicit %>
 3:  <%
 4:     Response.Write "Welcome to my Array Page!<BR>"
 5:
 6:     'Create an array
 7:     Dim aStates(50)
 8:
 9:     'Reference an index out of the array bounds
10:     aStates(51) = "Guam"
11: %>
```

ANALYSIS   Listing 14.6 contains an error on line 10. Line 7 creates an array, `aStates`, whose upper bound is `50`. Line 10 attempts to assign a value to the 51st element, which is an out-of-bounds index. Trying to do so generates an index out-of-bounds error. Having altered the `500;100` HTTP error, on whatever line an error first occurs, a `Server.Transfer` occurs. So, when line 10 is reached, control is redirected to

/Error/ErrorHandler.asp. The output generated *before* the line that contains the error
is output. For example, if you were to visit an ASP page that contained the code in
Listing 14.6, you would see Welcome to my Array Page! (line 4) followed by the
output of ErrorHandler.asp. Figure 14.7 shows this output.

FIGURE 14.7

*The output preceding
the error is shown, fol-
lowed by the output of
ErrorHandler.asp.*

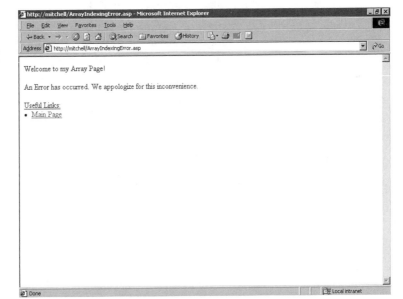

Although such an error might prove helpful for your visitors, when you are in the stages
of developing your ASP application, you will want to know the specific information about
the error. For example, it would be nice to know the line number the error occurred on and
a description of the error. You can use the ASPError object to obtain such information.

Like with any other object, to use the ASPError object you need to obtain an instance of
the object to use in your ASP page. To obtain an instance of the ASPError object that contains the error information for the latest error, use the GetLastError method of the Server
object. We will show how to use Server.GetLastError() in the ErrorHandler.asp page
shortly. First, let's examine the properties of the ASPError object.

The ASPError object contains nine read-only properties. These properties contain
detailed information about the error that occurred. Table 14.1 contains a listing of the
ASPError object's properties.

14

Table 14.1 The `ASPError` Object's Properties Containing Information Relevant to an ASP Error

Property	Description
ASPCode	Contains the error code generated by IIS when an ASP error occurs.
Number	The error number.
Source	Contains the source code of the line that caused the error.
Category	This property identifies the source of the error. There are three possible error sources: an internal ASP error, a scripting language error, or an object error.
File	Contains the filename of the ASP page that contained the error.
Line	Returns the line number on which the error occurred.
Column	Returns the column position in which the error occurred.
Description	Contains a brief description of the error.
ASPDescription	A more detailed description of the error. However, this property is only present if the error generated was an ASP-related error.

Let's add to the error handling script, `ErrorHandler.asp`, so that it uses the `ASPError` object to display detailed information about the error that just occurred. Although end users do not care about the line number an error occurs on, having such information greatly helps you and your fellow developers during the testing and debugging stages. Listing 14.7 shows the code for `ErrorHandler.asp`, updated to use the `ASPError` object.

Listing 14.7 Using the `ASPError` Object in `ErrorHandler.asp` to Present Detailed Information About the Error that Just Occurred

```
1:  <%@ Language = VBSCRIPT %>
2:  <% Option Explicit %>
3:  <HTML>
4:  <BODY>
5:    <P>
6:    An Error has occurred.  We apologize for this inconvenience.
7:    <P>
8:    <U>Useful Links:</U><BR>
9:    <LI><A HREF="/">Main Page</A>
10:
11:   <P><HR><P>
12:
13: <%
14    'Create an instance of the ASPError object
15:   Dim objASPError
16:   Set objASPError = Server.GetLastError()
```

```
17: %>
18:
19:    <CENTER>
20:    <TABLE BORDER=1 CELLSPACING=1>
21:    <TR>
22:        <TH COLSPAN=2>Detailed Error Information</TH>
23:      </TR>
24:      <TR>
25:      <TD>ASP Code</TD>
26:      <TD><%=objASPError.ASPCode%></TD>
27:      </TR>
28:      <TR>
29:      <TD>Error Number</TD>
30:      <TD><%=objASPError.Number%></TD>
31:      </TR>
32:      <TR>
33:      <TD>Source Code that caused the error</TD>
34:      <TD><%=objASPError.Source%></TD>
35:      </TR>
36:      <TR>
37:      <TD>Category</TD>
38:      <TD><%=objASPError.Category%></TD>
39:      </TR>
40:      <TR>
41:      <TD>Error Occurred in</TD>
42:      <TD><%=objASPError.File%></TD>
43:      </TR>
44:      <TR>
45:      <TD>Line Number</TD>
46:      <TD><%=objASPError.Line%></TD>
47:      </TR>
48:      <TR>
49:      <TD>Column Number</TD>
50:      <TD><%=objASPError.Column%></TD>
51:      </TR>
52:      <TR>
53:      <TD>Description</TD>
54:      <TD><%=objASPError.Description%></TD>
55:      </TR>
56:      <TR>
57:      <TD>Extended Description</TD>
58:      <TD><%=objASPError.ASPDescription%></TD>
59:      </TR>
60:    </TABLE>
61: </BODY>
62:</HTML>
```

14

ANALYSIS   Listing 14.7 is an updated version of ErrorHandler.asp, written to use the
ASPError object. Before you can use the ASPError object, you need to obtain an
instance of the object that contains the latest error information. You do this by using the

`Server.GetLastError` method. Before you can use this method, though, you need to declare a variable to hold the instance of this object. Line 15 creates such a variable, naming it `objASPError`. Then line 16 sets `objASPError` equal to the `ASPError` object instance returned by `Server.GetLastError`. Lines 20 through 60 create a table that displays each of the properties of the `ASPError` object. Figure 14.8 displays the output of `ErrorHandler.asp` when an ASP page containing a scripting error is executed.

FIGURE 14.8

`ErrorHandler.asp` *displays the nine properties of the* `ASPError` *object.*

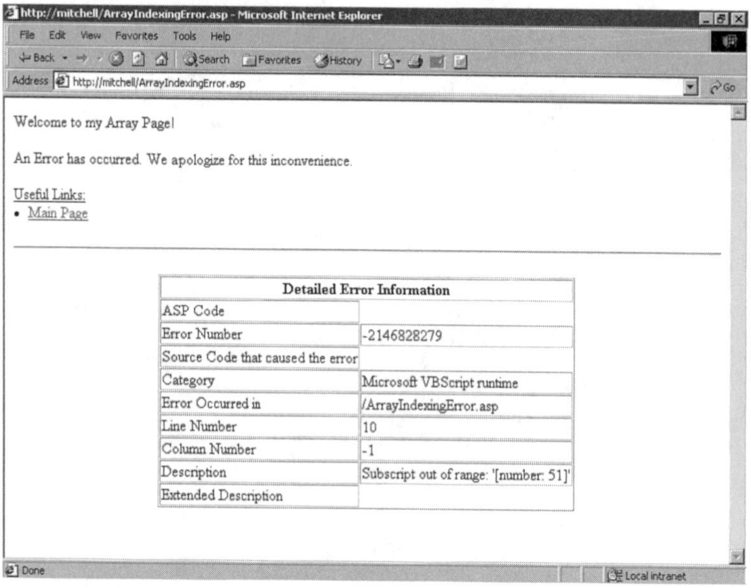

When you run an ASP page that contains an error, `ErrorHandler.asp` is called and the error information is displayed. However, what is displayed depends on what error occurs. There are three categories of errors that the `ASPError` object can detect:

- Internal ASP errors
- Scripting errors
- Errors in objects

To understand the difference between these three categories of errors, let's examine three scripts, each one causing an error in a different error category. Listing 14.8 displays the code of an ASP page, `ASPError.asp`, which contains an internal ASP error.

LISTING 14.8 The Missing Script Delimiter Generating an Internal ASP Error

```
1:  <%@ Language = VBSCRIPT %>
2:  <% Option Explicit %>
3:  <%
```

```
4:     'This will cause an ASP error:
5:
6:     'ASP requires matching script block delimiters (less than %,
7:     'greater than %). 'If we leave off the closing script block
8:     'delimiter, an ASP error will occur.
9:
10:    Response.Write("Hello, World!")
```

ANALYSIS   When creating an ASP page and using the <% and %> to denote the start and stop
of an ASP script block, it is required that for every opening script block delimiter
(<%), there needs to be a closing script block delimiter (%>). Listing 14.8 contains no
closing script block delimiter for the opening script block delimiter on line 3. For this
reason, Listing 14.8 generates an internal ASP error. Figure 14.9 shows the output for an
internal ASP error. Note that the ASPDescription property (denoted by Extended
Description in Figure 14.9) of the ASPError object contains detailed information about
the internal ASP error. This property only contains extended error information if the category of error was an internal ASP error.

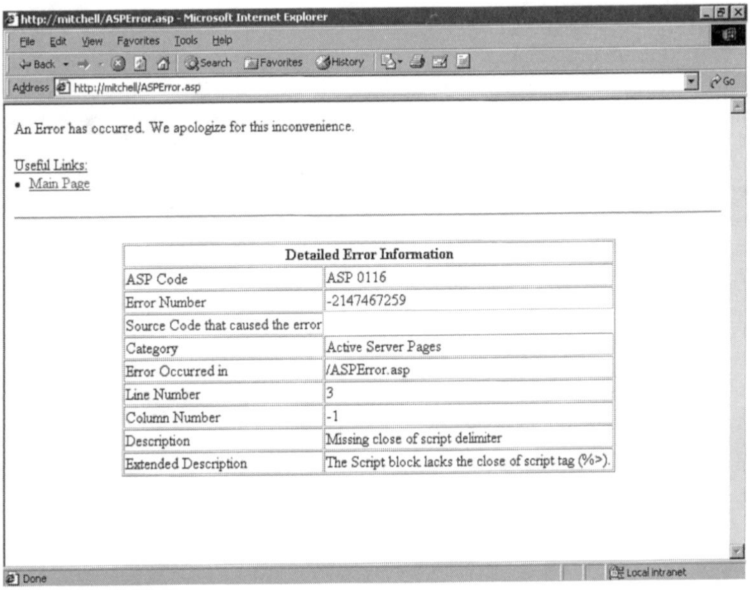

FIGURE **14.9**

*Internal ASP errors
contain an extended
description of the
error.*

If an error is not an internal ASP error, it is either a scripting language error or an object
error. A scripting language error occurs when illegal syntax is used in the server-side
scripting language you are using. For example, if you misuse a For control structure, a
scripting language error occurs. To display the results of a scripting error message, let's
create an ASP page named ScriptingError.asp, which contains the code in Listing 14.9.

14

LISTING 14.9 A Scripting Error Occurs by Passing an Incorrect Number of Parameters to the Ubound Function

```
1:  <%@ Language = VBSCRIPT %>
2:  <% Option Explicit %>
3:  <%
4:      'This will generate a scripting error:
5:
6:      'Calling a function with an incorrect number of parameters
7:      Dim iArrayUpperBound
8:      iArrayUpperBound = UBound()
9:  %>
```

ANALYSIS Calling a function with an incorrect number of parameters generates a scripting error. The UBound function, which returns the upper bound of an array, expects one parameter: the array whose upper bound you are interested in. Line 8 calls the UBound function but does not pass it an array as a parameter. This generates an error. Figure 14.10 displays the output ErrorHandler.asp generates when you attempt to run ScriptingError.asp. Note that the Category property of the ASPError object reports that a VBScript runtime error has occurred. Also, the ASPDescription property does not contain any value.

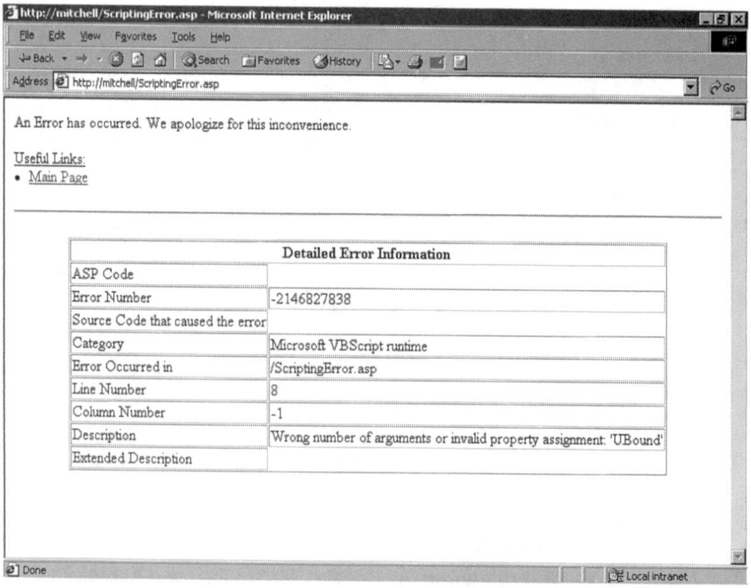

FIGURE 14.10

Scripting errors generate slightly different results than internal ASP errors.

The final type of error that can occur is an object error. On Day 12, we talked about working with several common ASP components. One component, the Ad Rotator, can be used to randomly display advertising banners. Recall that to display these banners, you need to provide an ad rotation schedule file that contains information on the URLs of the ads, how often to show each banner ad, and other pertinent information. What happens, though, if you specify an ad rotation schedule file that does not exist? This generates an error—specifically an object error because the error occurs within the compiled code of the object. Listing 14.10 displays the code of an ASP page, ObjectError.asp, which contains an object error.

LISTING 14.10 Nonexistent Ad Rotator Schedule Files Generate an Object Error

```
1:  <% @LANGUAGE=VBSCRIPT %>
2:  <% Option Explicit %>
3:  <%
4:     'This will generate an object error
5:     Dim objAdRot
6:     Set objAdRot = Server.CreateObject("MSWC.AdRotator")
7:
8:     'Since the ad rotator schedule file AdRot.txt does not exist,
9:     'an object error will be generated when the following line is
10:    'executed...
11:    Response.Write objAdRot.GetAdvertisement("AdRot.txt")
12: %>
```

ANALYSIS In Listing 14.10, an object error is generated on line 11. The object that generates the error, Ad Rotator, contains a method named GetAdvertisement. This method expects to be passed the filename of an ad rotation schedule file that contains information on what advertisement banners to display. If, however, the ad rotation schedule file does not exist on the Web server, an error is generated. When ObjectError.asp is viewed in a browser, the Ad Rotator object generates an object error on line 11 when the ad rotator file AdRot.txt cannot be found. At this point, a Server.Transfer is executed, directing execution to ErrorHandler.asp, which displays the detailed error information. Figure 14.11 shows the output of ErrorHandler.asp.

By using a custom error page, you can gracefully handle your ASP errors. There's nothing worse than showing a cryptic message to your users, so take the time to set up a custom error page. With the new ASPError object in ASP 3.0, you can access the latest error and several of its properties through the Server.GetLastError() method.

Tip

A custom ASP error page often proves useful both when developing your ASP application and after it has been released for end-user consumption.

14

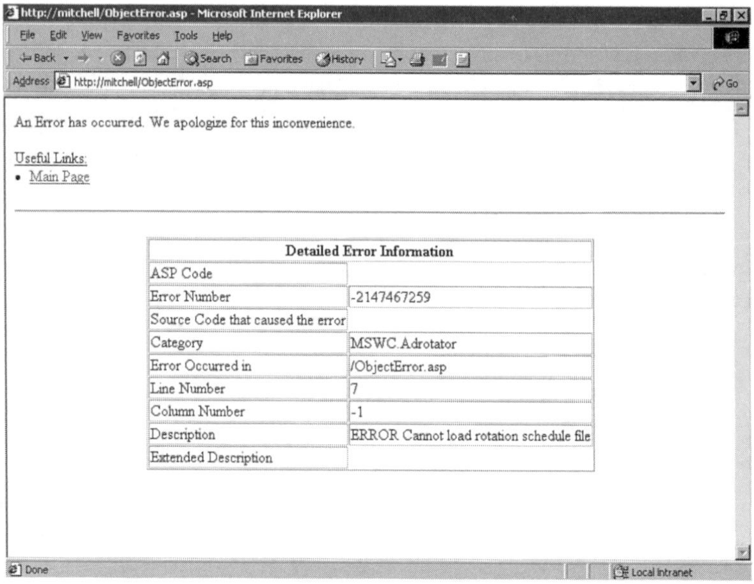

FIGURE **14.11**

When an error occurs within an object, an object error is generated by the Web server.

Handling Non-ASP Errors Gracefully

The section "Handling ASP Errors Gracefully," looked at how to react to unexpected ASP errors. By using the Custom Errors option through the Internet Information Services program, you can assign a custom file or URL for all HTTP errors, not just the one related to ASP errors (500;100).

One popular HTTP error to code for is the 404 error, which occurs when a client requests a Web page that does not exist. If a custom error page is not set for the 404 HTTP error, the user will see a pretty nondescriptive 404 error message. These 404 errors serve as a dead end for your users. Imagine that you have a broken link on one of your Web pages.

NEW TERM   A *broken link* is a link that redirects a user to a Web page that does not exist.

Let's examine the sequence of events that occur when a user clicks this link:

1. The user clicks the broken link. The user's browser makes a request to the Web server for a particular, nonexistent Web page.

2. The Web server receives the request and discovers that the Web page being requested does not exist. It sends a 404 HTTP error back to the browser.

3. The browser receives the 404 error and displays a 404 notice, alerting the user that the Web page requested could not be found.

When the user sees this message, she has reached a dead end. The user must click the Back button on the browser if she wants to return to your site. Chances are, however, that she will simply enter a different URL and be whisked away to another site, leaving yours behind. You can help prevent this dissatisfaction among your users over a 404 error by providing a custom 404 error page. A custom 404 error page alters the preceding series of steps so that the client does not receive notification of a 404 HTTP error. With a custom 404 error page, when a user clicks on a broken link, the following series of events transpire:

1. The user clicks the broken link. The user's browser makes a request to the Web server for a particular, nonexistent Web page.

2. The Web server receives the request and discovers that the Web page being requested does not exist. The browser uses `Server.Transfer` to send the output of the custom 404 URL to the client.

3. The user receives the custom 404 error page. This page can contain an explanation that the Web page requested was not found and provide a number of links to relevant pages on your site.

A custom 404 error page is preferred to sending the client the default 404 error message. Because it is relatively easy to set up through the Internet Information Services program, you have no excuse to not have a custom 404 error page. Most large Web sites these days have a custom 404 error page. To see some good example of custom 404 error pages, simply type in a URL for a large Web site that you know does not exist. For example, the following sites

```
http://www.yahoo.com/ScottMitchell.asp
http://www.excite.com/JamesAtkinson.asp
http://www.lycos.com/4GuysFromRolla
```

are all nonexistent Web pages that generate custom 404 error messages. To see some examples of Web sites that do not use custom 404 error messages, check out these:

```
http://www.amazon.com/ToddIsAGreatBowler.htm
http://www.ebay.com/ASPisFun.asp
http://www.snap.com/Custom404.asp
```

Now create your own custom 404 error Web page. Start by repeating the same steps used to create your custom `500;100` error page. Recall that to specify what action you want to happen for a given HTTP error, you need to enter the Internet Information Services program in Windows 2000 (choose Start, Programs, Administrative Tools, Internet Services Manager). From there, right-click the Web site that you want to configure and select Properties. Figure 14.4 shows what you will see.

After you click Properties, a tabbed dialog box appears. Select the Custom Errors tab. You should now see a listing of HTTP errors and the action associated with each error. Scroll down to the `400` HTTP error. By default, this points to a file in your Windows NT directory: `\WINNT\help\iisHelp\common\404b.htm`. Figure 14.12 shows what you should see.

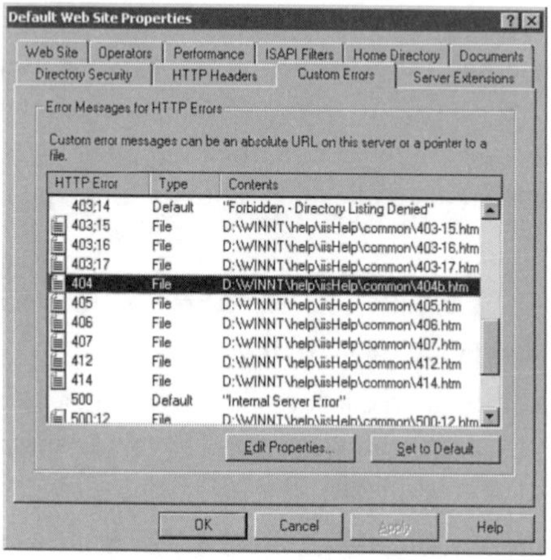

FIGURE 14.12

The custom 404 HTTP error will display a file named 404b.htm *by default.*

Now create your own 404 error page as a URL. To do this, click the 400 HTTP error and then click Edit Properties. A dialog box named Error Mapping Properties will display; change the URL option to your own custom URL. For the time being, enter /404.asp. Figure 14.13 shows the Error Mapping Properties dialog box with the values we've entered.

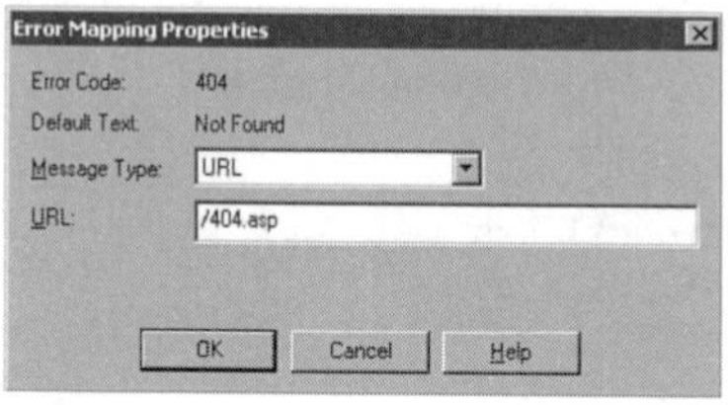

FIGURE 14.13

When a 404 HTTP error occurs, the client will be redirected to 404.asp, *which you need to place in your Web's root directory.*

Now click OK on the Error Mapping Properties dialog box and the tabbed dialog box. Again, you may be asked whether you want to apply the custom error settings to a number of virtual directory nodes on your Web site. If you want to have these virtual directories use the custom 404 error-handling page as well, go ahead and select the nodes and click OK.

Now you need to create an ASP page named 404.asp in your Web's root directory. This 404 page should first give a short explanation to the user why he is seeing this page. Let the user know that you could not locate the requested Web page. Also, the 404 page should display a list of links that the user might be interested in visiting. Create the 404.asp page and place into it the code in Listing 14.11.

LISTING 14.11 The Custom 404 Error Page Displaying Links to Popular Pages on a Web Site

```
 1:  <%@ Language = VBSCRIPT %>
 2:  <% Option Explicit %>
 3:  <HTML>
 4:  <BODY>
 5:    <FONT SIZE=+2>We cannot find the page you requested!</FONT>
 6:    <HR NOSHADE>
 7:    <LI><A HREF="<%=Request.ServerVariables("HTTP_REFERER")%>">
 8:          Return to the Page From Which you Came
 9:       </A>
10:    <P>
11:    Hot spots on our web site:<BR>
12:    <UL>
13:      <LI><A HREF="/">Start Page</A><BR>
14:      <LI><A HREF="/whatsnew">What's New?</A><BR>
15:      <LI><A HREF="/news">News Events</A><BR>
16:      <LI><A HREF="/sports">Sporting Events</A><BR>
17:    </UL>
18:  </BODY>
19:  </HTML>
```

ANALYSIS Listing 14.11 contains the contents of the custom 404 error page. An important aspect of any custom error page is letting users know why, exactly, they are seeing this page instead of the one that they expected. Line 5 informs the user the requested Web page could not be found. Then lines 7 through 9 display a hyperlink that sends them back to the referring page. This way, if a user clicks on a broken link, he will have a link on the custom 404 page that takes him back to the page that contained the broken link. Lines 13 through 16 display a series of links that the user might be interested in visiting. Figure 14.14 contains the output generated when the user attempts to visit a nonexistent Web page.

Tip

You can create custom error Web pages for all the HTTP errors. You are not restricted to custom error pages for just the 404 and 500;100 HTTP errors. To create an error for a different HTTP error, follow the same procedures outlined for creating the custom 404 and 500;100 HTTP error Web pages.

Do	Don't
DO provide a custom 404 error page. It's not difficult to implement, and your users will appreciate it if they stumble across a broken link.	

14

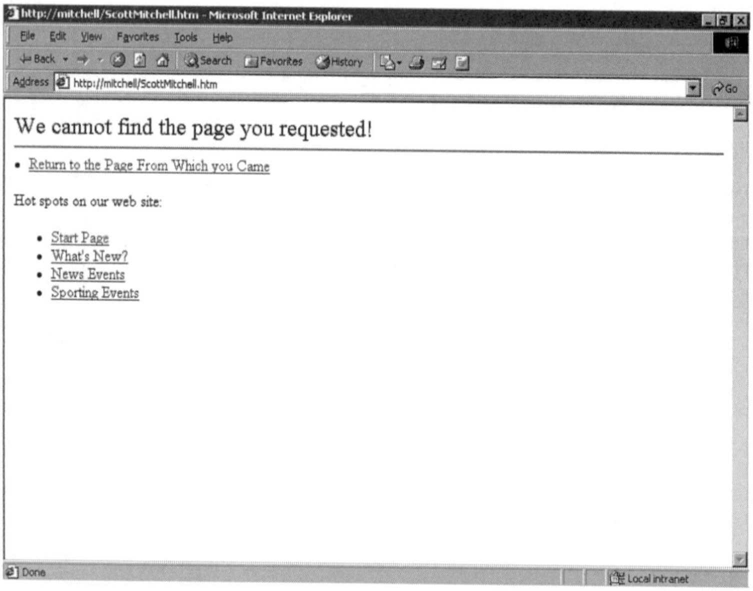

FIGURE 14.14

A custom error page proves more informative than the default `File not Found` *error message.*

Summary

Today, we discussed how to debug ASP scripts and how to handle both ASP and non-ASP errors gracefully. When developing ASP applications, an important step is testing and debugging. Through testing, you seek to reduce the number of bugs and defects present in your code. Remember, *no one* writes bug-free code, so it is important to spend the necessary time in the testing and debugging stage.

When creating ASP pages, two types of bugs can occur. The first type of bug is referred to as a fatal bug and is one that causes the abnormal termination of an ASP page. Scripting language errors, for example, are fatal bugs. If you illegally index an array, or use incorrect syntax when creating a control structure, when you view your ASP through a browser, the page will stop executing when it reaches the line with the error. Such errors are referred to as fatal bugs because they end the execution of your program.

The second type of bug that can occur is a nonfatal bug, which does not terminate the execution of your ASP page but rather generates incorrect output for a given input. Nonfatal bugs are tricky to locate because they do not cause an abnormal termination. To locate a nonfatal bug, first you need to realize that the output you are receiving is different from the output expected based on the input. After you find the nonfatal bug, knowing how to fix it is often another difficult task. Fatal bugs are preferred to nonfatal bugs during the development of an ASP application because fatal bugs can be easily traced and fixed.

When an error occurs, what should happen? With IIS, you can create a custom error page for each HTTP error. Whenever an error occurs within an ASP page, the 500;100 HTTP error is generated. If you create a custom page to handle the 500;100 HTTP error, you can display a user-friendly message alerting the user that an error has occurred. The ASPError object, new to ASP 3.0, can be used to collect detailed information about the last occurring error.

You are not limited to creating custom error pages for just the 500;100 HTTP error. Today, we looked at how you could create a custom 404 error page. A 404 error occurs when a user requests a Web page that does not exist. Without a custom 404 error page, the user is shown a cryptic message that the page was not found. With a custom 404 error page, you can explain why the user is seeing this error page in more English-like terms and provide a list of links the user might be interested in visiting.

This wraps up Week 2! Next week, you will examine how to use ASP to interact with databases. This is an exciting topic because you can accomplish profound results by being able to insert, update, delete, and read database records through ASP. Tomorrow, Day 15, "Using Databases," serves as a primer on relational databases and provides an introduction on using ASP to access such databases.

Q&A

Q Sometimes when an error occurs on my ASP page I am shown the custom error page I created. Other times, I am just shown a few lines of text containing the error description and number. Why is this?

A Remember that IIS will not transfer your user to your custom error page if you have already sent any information to the client. If the error occurs after a Response.Flush, the custom error page won't be loaded because content has already been sent to the client. Similarly, if you have Response.Buffer = False on your ASP page, buffering will be turned off, and if you have any Response.Writes or other methods that send output to the client, the custom error page won't be loaded.

Q Can I create a custom error page using Personal Web Server? What about IIS 4.0?

A You cannot create custom error pages with Personal Web Server. With IIS 4.0, you can create certain custom error pages. For example, with IIS 4.0, you can create a custom 404 error Web page; in fact, the process is identical to creating custom error pages in IIS 5.0. With IIS 4.0, though, you do not have access to the ASPError object.

14

Q **What advantages are there to creating a custom error Web page compared to creating a custom error page file?**

A Recall that when altering the mapping of a custom error, you can choose one of three options: have the default HTTP error message be sent to the client; send the contents of a file to the client; use `Server.Transfer` to return the output of a Web page to the client. When faced with the decision of whether to choose to output the contents of a file or the output of a Web page to the client, the choice you make should depend on whether you need to have the output be dynamic.

Because you can specify an ASP page as the Web page that control is transferred to when an error occurs, you can use ASPs dynamic nature. For example, in Listing 14.11, which created a custom 404 error page, the `Request.ServerVariables` collection was used to obtain the `Referer` HTTP header. This value was used to create a hyperlink back to the page the visitor came from. When an error occurs, you may want to make a note in a database, or have the Webmaster send an automatic email, indicating that an error has occurred. To have such events occur in response to an error, you need to map the HTTP error to a URL as opposed to a file. If, however, you want to output static information, a file will do just fine.

Q **I know what the `404` and `500;100` HTTP errors represent, but what errors do the HTTP errors represent?**

A There are many HTTP errors, although each shares a similar structure. Each HTTP error, by convention, is a three-digit number, with the first number representing the type of error. If the HTTP error number is between 400 and 499, it is a client error. If the HTTP error number is between 500 and 599, it is a server error. A complete list of client and server HTTP errors, respectively, can be seen at the following URLs:

```
http://www.webpartner.com/httperrors.htm#4xx
http://www.webpartner.com/httperrors.htm#5xx
```

Workshop

The Workshop provides quiz questions to help you solidify your understanding of the material covered and exercises to provide you with experience in using what you've learned. Try to understand the quiz and exercise answers before continuing to tomorrow's lesson. Quiz answers are provided in Appendix A, and exercise answers can be found at `http://www.mcp.com/info`.

Quiz

1. What two types of bugs can occur when developing an application?
2. Do programmers, on average, spend more time than needed debugging and testing

their applications, or less?

3. How can `Option Explicit` be used to convert a nonfatal bug into a fatal bug?

4. Why should you strive to turn nonfatal bugs into fatal bugs?

5. True or False: Nonfatal bugs are more difficult to locate than fatal bugs.

6. What HTTP error is generated when there is an error in an ASP page?

7. What new object to ASP 3.0 can be used to gather information about the last occurring ASP error?

8. The `ASPDescription` property of the `ASPError` object will only contain a value under what circumstances?

9. What method of the `Server` object do you need to use to obtain an instance of the `ASPError` object?

10. True or False: You should create a custom 404 error page.

Exercises

1. Locate the fatal bug in the following ASP script:

```
 1: <%@ Language = VBSCRIPT %>
 2: <% Option Explicit %>
 3: <%
 4:     Dim strNow
 5:     strNow = Now()
 6:     Response.Write "What time is it?<BR>"
 7:
 8:     Resopnse.Write "It is " & strNow & " right now.<BR>"
 9:     Response.Write "It was " & DateAdd("h",-2,strNow) & _
10:                    " two hours ago."
11: %>
```

2. Locate the nonfatal bug in the following ASP script:

```
 1: <%@ Language = VBSCRIPT %>
 2: <% Option Explicit %>
 3: <%
 4:     Dim strNow
 5:     strNow = Now()
 6:     Response.Write "What time is it?<BR>"
 7:
 8:     Resopnse.Write "It is " & strNow & " right now.<BR>"
 9:     Response.Write "It was " & DateAdd("h",-3,strNow) & _
10:                    " two hours ago."
11: %>
```

14

WEEK 2

In Review

Throughout the past 14 days, you have transformed from a beginning to an advanced ASP developer! Congratulations! You now know how to gather information from your users and process it through an ASP page. You know how to use all the built-in ASP objects. You also know how to read and write files to the Web server.

You now have a solid foundation of ASP skills. With your current skill set, you'll be able to pick up new ASP concepts. We've covered all the important ASP topics except one, database interaction, which the entire next week is dedicated to.

Bonus Project 2

Enhancing the Calendar

This week's lessons focused on how to create more user-driven ASP pages. Day 8, "Communicating with the User," looked at how to use HTML forms to collect user input. Day 9, "Collecting the Form Information," examined how to use ASP to gather and process the information entered into an HTML form. The Calendar application from Bonus Project 1 only allowed the user to view the current month. What if the user wants to see a calendar for the next month, or for six months in the future or past? One way that we are going to extend the Calendar application in today's Bonus Project is by allowing the user to selectively choose what month she wants to view.

Day 10, "Working with the Request Object," and Day 11, "Maintaining Persistent Information on the Web," discussed how to use cookies to save user-specific information over a lengthy period of time. Another extension of the Calendar application will be to use cookies to save the user's last viewed calendar month. When the user comes back to the site, rather than seeing the current month, she will be presented with the month she last viewed when visiting the site.

As with the first Bonus Project, you are invited to add enhancements. If you can think of some neat feature to add to the Calendar application that isn't covered in this Bonus Project, feel free to try adding it.

Allowing the User to Selectively View a Given Month

In the first Bonus Project, the current month was shown in a calendar view. Although this is useful, the application would be even more useful if the user could choose what month he was interested in viewing. Why restrict him to viewing only the current month?

Over the past week, we discussed a number of ways to pass information from one page to another. In today's Bonus Lesson, we are going to employ two of these approaches. First, you'll look at how to pass information through a form containing a list box. Second, you'll look at how to use the querystring to pass information.

As with Bonus Project 1, let's begin by examining what the end product should look like. Figure BP2.1 shows the enhanced Calendar application. Note the list box at the bottom of the screen, which contains the months of the year. Also note the two hyperlinks to the right and left of the month's name. Through these two mechanisms, you can allow the user to choose what month he wants to view.

You already have the bulk of the code written from Bonus Project 1. In today's Bonus Project, you don't need to worry about writing any code that will generate the HTML to construct the calendar. The first task you'll focus on is creating the list box that contains the months of the year. Note that the calendar month currently shown should be automatically selected in the list box.

Recall that in Bonus Project 1, we set dbCurrentDate to the system date. dbCurrentDate was the variable used to determine what specific month to display in the calendar. In today's Bonus Project, you are going to set dbCurrentDate to the date passed through the QueryString, if it exists. So, when the form is filled out and submitted, the current ASP page, Calendar.asp, will be reloaded and passed in the new date selected by the user. If a date is not passed through the QueryString (for example, when the user first visits the page), dbCurrentDate will be set to the current date using the Date() function.

FIGURE BP2.1

The Calendar application has been enhanced to allow the user to view months other than the current one.

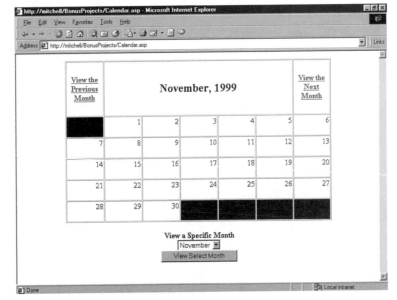

On Day 8, we discussed the list box in detail. To quickly review, a list box is comprised of two tags, a single `<SELECT>` tag and an `<OPTION>` tag for each item in the list box. To have an item in the list box selected by default, you only need to place the keyword `SELECTED` into the `<OPTION>` tag. Also, recall that each `<OPTION>` tag is uniquely identified by the `VALUE` keyword. Of course, the list box must be placed within a form. The form should specify the `METHOD` and `ACTION`. In this example, you are simply going to reload `Calendar.asp`, so the form's `ACTION` tag should be set to `Calendar.asp`. For this example, you are going to pass the form fields through the QueryString, so the `METHOD` should be set to `GET`.

Note that for each `<OPTION>` in the list box, you will need to set the `VALUE` to the correct month and year. Determining the correct month is easy enough—the month January in the list box will have a Month value of 1— but determining the correct year is not so straightforward. We will examine this later in the project. First, examine Listing BP2.1, which contains the code to create the form and list box shown at the bottom of the screen in Figure BP2.1.

LISTING BP2.1 Displaying the List Box that Contains the Months

```
1: <FORM METHOD=GET ACTION="Calendar.asp">
2:   <CENTER><B>View a Specific Month</B><BR>
3:   <SELECT SIZE=1 NAME=Date>
```

continues

LISTING BP2.1   continued

```
4:      <OPTION VALUE="<%=DateSerial(Year(dbCurrentDate), 1, 1)%>"
5:       <% If Month(dbCurrentDate) = 1 then Response.Write " SELECTED" %>>
6:         January
7:      </OPTION>
8:      <OPTION VALUE="<%=DateSerial(Year(dbCurrentDate), 2, 1)%>"
9:       <% If Month(dbCurrentDate) = 2 then Response.Write " SELECTED" %>>
10:        February
11:     </OPTION>
12:     <OPTION VALUE="<%=DateSerial(Year(dbCurrentDate), 3, 1)%>"
13:      <% If Month(dbCurrentDate) = 3 then Response.Write " SELECTED" %>>
14:        March
15:     </OPTION>
16:     <OPTION VALUE="<%=DateSerial(Year(dbCurrentDate), 4, 1)%>"
17:      <% If Month(dbCurrentDate) = 4 then Response.Write " SELECTED" %>>
18:        April
19:     </OPTION>
20:     <OPTION VALUE="<%=DateSerial(Year(dbCurrentDate), 5, 1)%>"
21:      <% If Month(dbCurrentDate) = 5 then Response.Write " SELECTED" %>>
22:        May
23:     </OPTION>
24:     <OPTION VALUE="<%=DateSerial(Year(dbCurrentDate), 6, 1)%>"
25:      <% If Month(dbCurrentDate) = 6 then Response.Write " SELECTED" %>>
26:        June
27:     </OPTION>
28:     <OPTION VALUE="<%=DateSerial(Year(dbCurrentDate), 7, 1)%>"
29:      <% If Month(dbCurrentDate) = 7 then Response.Write " SELECTED" %>>
30:        July
31:     </OPTION>
32:     <OPTION VALUE="<%=DateSerial(Year(dbCurrentDate), 8, 1)%>"
33:      <% If Month(dbCurrentDate) = 8 then Response.Write " SELECTED" %>>
34:        August
35:     </OPTION>
36:     <OPTION VALUE="<%=DateSerial(Year(dbCurrentDate), 9, 1)%>"
37:      <% If Month(dbCurrentDate) = 9 then Response.Write " SELECTED" %>>
38:        September
39:     </OPTION>
40:     <OPTION VALUE="<%=DateSerial(Year(dbCurrentDate), 10, 1)%>"
41:      <% If Month(dbCurrentDate) = 10 then Response.Write " SELECTED" %>>
42:        October
43:     </OPTION>
44:     <OPTION VALUE="<%=DateSerial(Year(dbCurrentDate), 11, 1)%>"
45:      <% If Month(dbCurrentDate) = 11 then Response.Write " SELECTED" %>>
46:        November
47:     </OPTION>
48:     <OPTION VALUE="<%=DateSerial(Year(dbCurrentDate), 12, 1)%>"
49:      <% If Month(dbCurrentDate) = 12 then Response.Write " SELECTED" %>>
50:        December
51:     </OPTION>
52:   </SELECT>
```

```
53:     <BR>
54:     <INPUT TYPE=SUBMIT VALUE="View Select Month">
55: </FORM>
```

ANALYSIS Listing BP2.1 contains the code to generate the list box that contains the 12 months. Line 1 begins by creating a form with its MEHTOD set to GET and its ACTION set to Calendar.asp. This ensures that when the form is submitted, Calendar.asp will be reloaded, containing the new date that the user wants to view in the QueryString. Next, you create the list box, which starts with the <SELECT> tag on line 3 and sets the list box's NAME property to Date . Recall from Day 8 that the NAME property is how each form field is uniquely identified.

Next, lines 4 through 51 create the 12 list box items. Each item is created using an <OPTION> tag. The <OPTION> tag VALUEs are set equal to a date created by DateSerial (line 4, for example). The date created is the 1st of the given month of the year specified by dbCurrentDate. At this point, dbCurrentDate contains the date shown in the calendar, not necessarily the current system date. So, if in the Calendar application you are examining March, 2000, the VALUE for January's <OPTION> tag will be set to 1/1/00, February to 2/1/00, March to 3/1/00, and so on.

Immediately after the VALUE tag (line 5, for example), you check to see whether the <OPTION> should be selected by default. If the current month you are viewing in the Calendar equals the ordinal month value of the given month, you need to write the keyword SELECTED before closing the <OPTION> tag. So, if you are viewing June, 2000, in the calendar, Month(dbCurrentDate) will return 6 because June is the 6th month in the year. On line 25, the following If statement

```
If Month(dbCurrentDate) = 6 then Response.Write " SELECTED"
```

will evaluate to True, and SELECTED will be outputted as part of the <OPTION> tag, which will automatically select that <OPTION> tag. If you view the HTML source code from the browser when viewing the month of November in the Calendar application, the HTML for the <OPTION> tags would look like this:

```
...
<OPTION VALUE="10/1/98"
    >
    October
</OPTION>
<OPTION VALUE="11/1/98"
    SELECTED>
    November
</OPTION>
<OPTION VALUE="12/1/98"
```

```
      >
    December
</OPTION>
```

(*Note that the* <OPTION> *tags for the months prior to October have been omitted.*) The <OPTION> tag for the month of November contains the keyword SELECTED, whereas none of the other months do. The SELECTED keyword will cause November to be selected by default from the list box.

After you've listed all the list box items, line 52 indicates that you are finished creating the list box by using the closing <SELECT> tag, </SELECT>. Next, line 54 displays the submit button. This is the button that the user will click to view the month selected from the list box.

What exactly will happen when the form is submitted? Well, because the form's ACTION tag is set to Calendar.asp, the current ASP page, Calendar.asp, will be reloaded, and the date selected in the list box will be passed through the QueryString. When first visiting Calendar.asp, you might enter the following into your browser:

```
http://localhost/Calendar.asp
```

However, after you select a month from the list box and submit the form, the URL changes to something like this:

```
http://localhost/Calendar.asp?Date=4%2F1%2F00
```

You may be wondering what those %2Fs represent. Before a form passes a variable through the QueryString, it URL Encodes it. Some browsers do not accept non-standard characters in the QueryString. For example, the forward slash constitutes as a non-standard character, and certain browsers (for example, Netscape), would not accept a URL in the following form:

```
http://localhost/Calendar.asp?Date=4/1/00
```

So, to correct for this, the form automatically URL Encodes the variables. No modification needs to be made when reading these variables from the QueryString using the Request object, though. Now that you are passing in the month and year that the user is interested in seeing a calendar for, let's examine how to set dbCurrentDate to this value. Keep in mind that when the user first visits Calendar.asp, no date information will be in the QueryString; therefore, after you set dbCurrentDate to the Date value in the QueryString, you need to determine whether dbCurrentDate contains a value. If it does not, you need to reassign dbCurrentDate to the current system date.

To clarify a little, let's look at the code. Listing BP2.2 shows what steps you'll need to take to obtain the *correct* dbCurrentDate.

LISTING BP2.2 Set dbCurrentDate to the Proper Date

```
1:  'Next, we need to obtain the date passed through the
2:  'QueryString.  To do this, we need to use the Request
3:  'object, reading in the Date variable from the QueryString
4:  Dim dbCurrentDate
5:  dbCurrentDate = Request("Date")
6:
7:  'Check to make sure that dbCurrentDate equals a value.  If Date was
8:  'not passed through the querystring or assigned a cookie value,
9:  'dbCurrentDate will be an empty string.
10: If Len(dbCurrentDate) = 0 then
11:    'Date was not passed through the QueryString
12:    'so set dbCurrentDate to the current system date
13:    dbCurrentDate = Date()
14: End If
```

ANALYSIS Listing BP2.2 assigns a date value to dbCurrentDate. If a date has been passed through the QueryString, dbCurrentDate will be assigned to this value, else dbCurrentDate will be assigned the current system date. Line 4 begins by creating dbCurrentDate. Next, dbCurrentDate is set equal to Request("Date"). Recall that when you do not specify either the QueryString or Form collection of the Request object, both collections are searched. If a form variable named Date is found in the QueryString, dbCurrentDate will be assigned its value, else dbCurrentDate will equal a blank string.

Line 7 tests whether dbCurrentDate equals a blank string. If it does, Len(dbCurrentString) will equal 0. Recall that the Len function returns the number of characters in a string variable. If dbCurrentDate equals a blank string, the code inside the If statement is executed, and dbCurrentDate is set to the result of the Date() function (line 13).

At this point, the user can select to view any month for the current year from the select box created in Listing BP2.1. After the user chooses a month to view from the list box and submits the form, Calendar.asp is recalled, with the date information passed through the QueryString in a variable named Date. Whenever Calendar.asp is loaded, dbCurrentDate is set to the Date variable passed through the QueryString, if it exists. If this variable does not exist, dbCurrentDate is set to the current system date.

Although you have added a useful feature, allowing the user to view any month in the current year, the list box implementation is a bit cumbersome. What if the user just wanted to view the next or previous month? Wouldn't it be easier to click a single hyperlink, rather than selecting a month from the list box at the bottom of the screen? Also, by being able to view the next or previous month, you can view months from other years. If you are viewing January of 2000, you could view December of 1999 by viewing the previous month. Let's look at how you can create these hyperlinks to allow the user to view the next or previous month.

Refer back to Figure BP2.1, which shows the end product. Notice the two hyperlinks to the left and right of the month name. When the user clicks the `View the Previous Month` link, the previous month should be immediately loaded into the calendar. Because you only have one ASP page, `Calendar.asp`, the hyperlink should send the user back to `Calendar.asp`, passing in the QueryString the previous month. Recall from Day 9 that the QueryString can be used to simulate form data. For example, if you want to view the calendar for August, 1978, you could explicitly enter the following URL into your browser's Address window:

```
http://localhost/Calendar.asp?Date=8%2F1%2F78
```

Remember that the `%2F`s are an encoded version of the forward slash. So, you could create a hyperlink that, when clicked, would display the calendar for August, 1978, by using the following HTML:

```
<A HREF="Calendar.asp?Date=8%2F1%2F78">View August, 1978</A>
```

If you didn't want to have to type in those strange `%2F` characters, you could use the `Server.URLEncode` method, which was discussed on Day 13, "Reading and Writing Files on the Web Server," to encode the QueryString. To use the `Server.URLEncode` function, you could use the following code:

```
<A HREF="Calendar.asp?Date=<%=Server.URLEncode("8/1/78")%>">
   View August, 1978
</A>
```

The `Server.URLEncode` function converts `8/1/78` into `8%2F1%2F78` automatically. This value will be outputted immediately after `Date=` in the HTML.

Now that you've looked at how to create a hyperlink to send a user *directly* to a specific month and year, how can you create one that will send them to either the next or previous month? Recall the `DateAdd` function from Day 5, "Using VBScript's Built-in Functions." This built-in VBScript function adds a certain number of months, days, minutes, seconds, hours, years, weeks, quarters, or just about any other interval to a given date. We'll use this function to make the `View the Previous Month` and `View the Next Month` links work.

Listing BP2.3 contains the code necessary to generate the next and previous hyperlinks.

LISTING BP2.3   Using `DateAdd` and `Server.URLEncode` to Create the Next and Previous Hyperlinks

```
1:  <%
2:    Dim strPrevMonth, strNextMonth
3:    strPrevMonth = Server.URLEncode(DateAdd("m", -1, dbCurrentDate))
```

```
4:    strNextMonth = Server.URLEncode(DateAdd("m", 1, dbCurrentDate))
5:  %>
6:
7:     <A HREF="Calendar.asp?Date=<%=strPrevMonth%>">
8:         View the Previous Month
9:     </A>
10:
11:    <A HREF="Calendar.asp?Date=<%=strNextMonth%>">
12:        View the Next Month
13:    </A>
```

ANALYSIS Listing BP2.3 creates two hyperlinks, one that reloads Calendar.asp, causing the previous month to be displayed, and one that displays the next month. To accomplish this, line 2 begins by creating two string variables, strPrevMonth and strNextMonth. These variables contain the URL Encoded text for the next and previous months. Line 3 then sets strPrevMonth to the URL Encoded version of the date one month in the past of the date dbCurrentDate. Remember, dbCurrentDate contains the date that the calendar is displaying, not necessarily the current system date. Line 4 uses DateAdd and Server.URLEncode to URL Encode the date that is one month in the future from dbCurrentDate.

What exactly is happening on lines 3 and 4? To understand, let's look at an example. Imagine that dbCurrentDate contains 12/1/00. This would cause the calendar for December, 2000, to be displayed. Performing DateAdd("m", 1, dbCurrentDate) (which we would do in line 4) would return the date that was one month in the future from dbCurrentDate, or 1/1/01. Then, applying the Server.URLEncode function to this new date, the result would end up being 1%2F1%2F01, which would be assigned to strNextMonth (line 4).

Lines 7 through 9 create the hyperlink for viewing the previous month. The Date value in the QueryString is assigned the value of strPrevMonth (line 7). This process is repeated in lines 11 through 13, except that the link is for the next month, and the Date value in the QueryString is assigned the value of strNextMonth (line 11).

At this point, the Calendar application allows the visitor to view the calendar for any month and year. The user can select a month to view, in the year being currently viewed, by selecting the month from the list box at the bottom of the screen. The user can also visit the next and previous months by clicking on the next and previous month hyperlinks. Before you complete today's Bonus Project, let's add one more function to the application. Wouldn't it be nice if, when a visitor viewed your Calendar application, rather than being shown the current month and year as the default, he was shown the calendar he last viewed when at your site? You can use cookies to save this information on the client's computer. Recall that we discussed using cookies to maintain state on Day 10 and Day 11.

To use cookies to save this information, you need to write a cookie to the client's computer each time he views the Calendar application. This cookie should contain the month and year that the user is viewing. To accomplish this, create a cookie named CalendarDate and set the cookie using the code in Listing BP2.4.

LISTING BP2.4 The CalendarDate Cookie

```
1:   'Now we need to write to our cookie, setting it
2:   'equal to dbCurrentDate
3:   Response.Cookies("CalendarDate") = dbCurrentDate
4:
5:   'Set the cookie to expire in 30 days
6:   Response.Cookies("CalendarDate").Expires = Now() + 30
```

ANALYSIS Listing BP2.4 creates a cookie named CalendarDate on the client's computer. This cookie is assigned the value of dbCurrentDate (line 3) and is set to expire 30 days in the future (line 6). By creating this cookie each time the user visits Calendar.asp, you are ensured that this cookie contains the last month and year viewed by this particular user in the Calendar application.

Now that you have the cookie stored on the client's computer, when the user visits Calendar.asp on his next visit, you can display the month and year he last viewed as opposed to the current month. There are only certain times, though, when you want to have the user view the month last stored in the cookie. For example, if the user is viewing a month and clicks on the next or previous month, you want to show the next or previous month, not the month stored in the cookie. So, you only want to display the month stored in the cookie when there is not a date passed through the QueryString. Keep in mind, though, that the user might not have the CalendarDate cookie on his computer if he has never visited the site before, or if he has his browser set up not to accept cookies.

So, when deciding what month to display to the user, you need to first check whether a date was specified through the QueryString. If there was, then display the calendar for that date, or else check to see whether date information is stored in the CalendarDate cookie. If there is, display the month corresponding to that date. Finally, if there was not a date passed through the QueryString and a CalendarDate cookie does not exist on the client's computer, display the calendar for the current system date.

Listing BP2.5 contains the code that determines what date the calendar needs to be generated for. dbCurrentDate is then assigned to this value.

Listing BP2.5 Determining what Date to Use to Generate the Calendar

```
 1:  'Next, we need to obtain the date passed through the
 2:  'QueryString.  To do this, we need to use the Request
 3:  'object, reading in the Date variable from the QueryString
 4:  Dim dbCurrentDate
 5:  dbCurrentDate = Request("Date")
 6:
 7:  'Create a cookie so that we can remember the last month.  If a
 8:  'date has been specified, set the cookie to the value, else read
 9:  'a cookie to determine what date the user is interested in seeing.
10:  'If no date was passed in, Len(dbCurrentDate) will equal 0, since
11:  'dbCurrentDate will be equal to a blank string.
12:  If Len(dbCurrentDate) = 0 then
13:    'Read in the value of the cookie
14:    dbCurrentDate = Request.Cookies("CalendarDate")
15:  End If
16:
17:  'Check to make sure that dbCurrentDate equals a value.  If Date
18:  'was not passed through the querystring or assigned a cookie value,
19:  'dbCurrentDate will be an empty string.
20:  If Len(dbCurrentDate) = 0 then
21:    'Date was not passed through the QueryString - set dbCurrentDate
22:    'to the current system date
23:    dbCurrentDate = Date()
24:  End If
```

ANALYSIS Listing BP2.5 determines what date to use to generate the calendar. Line 4 begins by creating the date variable, dbCurrentDate. Next, line 5 assigns this to the Date variable in the QueryString using the Request object. Next, determine whether dbCurrentDate contains a valid date. If a date was *not* passed through the QueryString, dbCurrentDate will be assigned to an empty string on line 5. Line 12 checks this using the Len function. If dbCurrentDate is, in fact, an empty string, meaning that the date was not passed through the QueryString, then line 14 assigns dbCurrentDate to the cookie CalendarDate. If this cookie does not exist, again, dbCurrentDate will be assigned to an empty string, in which case the If statement on line 20 will evaluate to True, and dbCurrentDate will be set to the current system date (line 23).

Take a moment to look back at Listing BP2.2, which is nearly identical to the code in Listing BP2.5. The only difference is that Listing BP2.5 has an If statement added to assign dbCurrentDate the value of the cookie CalendarDate, if dbCurrentDate was not passed through the querystring. This added If statement is shown on lines 7 through 15 in Listing BP2.5.

When the code in Listing BP2.5 has finished running, dbCurrentDate is set to the correct date, whether it is a date that was passed through the QueryString, a date stored in a cookie, or the current system date.

The Complete Code

Now that you've looked at the Calendar application code in pieces, let's look at the code in it entirety. Listing BP2.6 contains the full code, which, as you'll notice, is lengthy!

LISTING BP2.6   The Calendar Application Code in Full

```
 1: <%@ Language = VBSCRIPT %>
 2: <% Option Explicit %>
 3:
 4: <%
 5:   '**************************************************
 6:   'Display a calendar based upon a selected date
 7:   '**************************************************
 8:
 9:   'To accomplish this, we need to perform a number of tasks.
10:   'First, we will want to be able to determine the month name
11:   'for a given month.  So, let's create a function that
12:   'takes the numeric value of a month and displays the name of
13:   'the month (i.e., GetMonthName(8) would output August)
14:   Function GetMonthName(iMonth)
15:     Select Case iMonth
16:       Case 1:
17:         GetMonthName = "January"
18:       Case 2:
19:         GetMonthName = "February"
20:       Case 3:
21:         GetMonthName = "March"
22:       Case 4:
23:         GetMonthName = "April"
24:       Case 5:
25:         GetMonthName = "May"
26:       Case 6:
27:         GetMonthName = "June"
28:       Case 7:
29:         GetMonthName = "July"
30:       Case 8:
31:         GetMonthName = "August"
32:       Case 9:
33:         GetMonthName = "September"
34:       Case 10:
35:         GetMonthName = "October"
36:       Case 11:
37:         GetMonthName = "November"
```

```
38:          Case 12:
39:            GetMonthName = "December"
40:          Case Else:
41:            GetMonthName = "**INVALID MONTH**"
42:      End Select
43:    End Function
44:
45:    'Next, we need to obtain the date passed through the
46:    'QueryString.  To do this, we need to use the Request
47:    'object, reading in the Date variable from the QueryString
48:    Dim dbCurrentDate
49:    dbCurrentDate = Request("Date")
50:
51:    'Create a cookie so that we can remember the last month.  If
51:    'a date has been specified, set the cookie to the value, else
52:    'read a cookie to determine what date the user is interested
53:    'in seeing.  If no date was passed in, Len(dbCurrentDate) will
54:    'equal 0, since dbCurrentDate will be equal to a blank string.
55:    If Len(dbCurrentDate) = 0 then
56:      'Read in the value of the cookie
57:      dbCurrentDate = Request.Cookies("CalendarDate")
58:    End If
59:
60:    'Check to make sure that dbCurrentDate equals a value.  If
61:    'Date was not passed through the querystring or assigned a
62:    'cookie value, dbCurrentDate will be an empty string.
63:    If Len(dbCurrentDate) = 0 then
64:      'Date was not passed through the QueryString - set
65:      'dbCurrentDate to the current system date
66:      dbCurrentDate = Date()
67:    End If
68:
69:    'At this point, we are certain that dbCurrentDate equals a
70:    'valid date.  If the Date was not passed in through the
71:    'Querystring, we assigned dbCurrentDate to the cookie on the
72:    'client's computer which represents the last calendar date
73:    'viewed.  If no cookie existed, we set dbCurrentDate to
74:    'the current system date.  Now we need to write to our cookie,
75:    'setting it equal to dbCurrentDate
76:    Response.Cookies("CalendarDate") = dbCurrentDate
77:
78:    'Set the cookie to expire in 30 days
79:    Response.Cookies("CalendarDate").Expires = Now() + 30
80:
81:    'Now, we need to display a calendar.  At most, a calendar
82:    'can have six weeks.  Since a week contains seven days,
83:    'we will show, at most, 42 calendar cells.  We will use
84:    'a TABLE to generate this calendar
85:
86:    'We will create an array that will store the 42 possible
```

continues

LISTING **BP2.6**   continued

```
87:    'days of the month.
88:    Dim aCalendarDays(42)
89:
90:    'Into aCalendarDays, we will place the days of the current
91:    'month.  We will use the DatePart function to determine
92:    'when the first day of the month is
93:    Dim iFirstWeekday
94:    iFirstWeekday = DatePart("w",DateSerial(Year(dbCurrentDate), _
95:                           Month(dbCurrentDate), 1))
96:
97:    'Now, we want to loop from 1 to the number of days in the
98:    'current month, populating the array aCalendarDays
99:    Dim iDaysInMonth
100:   iDaysInMonth = DatePart("d",DateSerial(Year(dbCurrentDate), _
101:                          Month(dbCurrentDate)+1, 1-1))
102:   Dim iLoop
103:   For iLoop = 1 to iDaysInMonth
104:      aCalendarDays(iLoop + iFirstWeekday - 1) = iLoop
105:   Next
106:
107:   'Now that we have our populated array, we need to display the
108:   'array in calendar form.  We will create a table of 7 columns,
109:   'one for each day of the week.  The number of rows we will use
110:   'will be 6, the total number of possible rows, minus 42 (the upper
111:   'bound of the aCalendarDays array) minus the last array position
112:   'used (iFirstWeekday + iDaysInMonth) divided by seven, the number
113:   'of days in the week!  Simple, eh!!  :)
114:   Dim iColumns, iRows
115:   iColumns = 7
116:   iRows = 6 - Int((42 - (iFirstWeekDay + iDaysInMonth)) / 7)
117:
118:   'Store the next and previous months, Using Server.URLEncode
119:   'to make sure the values can be safely passed through the
120:   'QueryString
121:   Dim strPrevMonth, strNextMonth
122:   strPrevMonth = Server.URLEncode(DateAdd("m", -1, dbCurrentDate))
123:   strNextMonth = Server.URLEncode(DateAdd("m", 1, dbCurrentDate))
124:
125:   'Now, create the table
126: %>
127:
128: <HTML>
129: <BODY>
130:   <TABLE ALIGN=CENTER BORDER=1 CELLSPACING=1 WIDTH=75% HEIGHT=75%>
131:   <TR>
132:     <TH>
133:       <A HREF="Calendar.asp?Date=<%=strPrevMonth%>">
134:           View the Previous Month
135:       </A>
```

```
136:     </TH>
137:
138:     <TH COLSPAN=5>
139:         <FONT SIZE=+2>
140: <%
141:   'Display the month and year
142:   Response.Write GetMonthName(Month(dbCurrentDate))
143:   Response.Write ", " & Year(dbCurrentDate)
144: %>
145:         </FONT>
146:     </TH>
147:
148:     <TH>
149:         <A HREF="Calendar.asp?Date=<%=strNextMonth%>">
150:             View the Next Month
151:         </A>
152:     </TH>
153:     </TR>
154:
155: <%
156:   'Now, loop through 1 through iRows, then 1 through iColumns
157:   Dim iRowsLoop, iColumnsLoop
158:   For iRowsLoop = 1 to iRows
159:     'Create a new row
160:     Response.Write "<TR>"
161:     For iColumnsLoop = 1 to iColumns
162:       'Create a new column
163:       'If there is a day, display it, else black out the cell
164:       If aCalendarDays((iRowsLoop-1)*7 + iColumnsLoop) > 0 then
165:         'Display the date
166:         Response.Write "<TD VALIGN=TOP ALIGN=RIGHT WIDTH=""14%"">"
167:         Response.Write aCalendarDays((iRowsLoop-1)*7 + iColumnsLoop)
168:         Response.Write "</TD>"
169:       Else
170:         'Black out the cell
171:         Response.Write "<TD BGCOLOR=BLACK> </TD>"
172:       End If
173:     Next
174:
175:     'Close the row
176:     Response.Write "</TR>"
177:   Next
178: %>
180:
181:   </TABLE>
182:
183:   <P>
184:   <FORM METHOD=GET ACTION="Calendar.asp">
185:     <CENTER><B>View a Specific Month</B><BR>
186:     <SELECT SIZE=1 NAME=Date>
```

continues

LISTING BP2.6 continued

```
187:    <OPTION VALUE="<%=DateSerial(Year(dbCurrentDate), 1, 1)%>"
188:     <% If Month(dbCurrentDate) = 1 then Response.Write " SELECTED" %>>
189:        January
190:    </OPTION>
191:    <OPTION VALUE="<%=DateSerial(Year(dbCurrentDate), 2, 1)%>"
192:     <% If Month(dbCurrentDate) = 2 then Response.Write " SELECTED" %>>
193:        February
194:    </OPTION>
195:    <OPTION VALUE="<%=DateSerial(Year(dbCurrentDate), 3, 1)%>"
196:     <% If Month(dbCurrentDate) = 3 then Response.Write " SELECTED" %>>
197:        March
198:    </OPTION>
199:    <OPTION VALUE="<%=DateSerial(Year(dbCurrentDate), 4, 1)%>"
200:     <% If Month(dbCurrentDate) = 4 then Response.Write " SELECTED" %>>
201:        April
202:    </OPTION>
203:    <OPTION VALUE="<%=DateSerial(Year(dbCurrentDate), 5, 1)%>"
204:     <% If Month(dbCurrentDate) = 5 then Response.Write " SELECTED" %>>
205:        May
206:    </OPTION>
207:    <OPTION VALUE="<%=DateSerial(Year(dbCurrentDate), 6, 1)%>"
208:     <% If Month(dbCurrentDate) = 6 then Response.Write " SELECTED" %>>
209:        June
210:    </OPTION>
211:    <OPTION VALUE="<%=DateSerial(Year(dbCurrentDate), 7, 1)%>"
212:     <% If Month(dbCurrentDate) = 7 then Response.Write " SELECTED" %>>
213:        July
214:    </OPTION>
215:    <OPTION VALUE="<%=DateSerial(Year(dbCurrentDate), 8, 1)%>"
216:      <% If Month(dbCurrentDate) = 8 then Response.Write " SELECTED" %>>
217:        August
218:    </OPTION>
219:    <OPTION VALUE="<%=DateSerial(Year(dbCurrentDate), 9, 1)%>"
220:     <% If Month(dbCurrentDate) = 9 then Response.Write " SELECTED" %>>
221:        September
222:    </OPTION>
223:    <OPTION VALUE="<%=DateSerial(Year(dbCurrentDate), 10, 1)%>"
224:     <% If Month(dbCurrentDate) = 10 then Response.Write " SELECTED" %>>
225:        October
226:    </OPTION>
227:    <OPTION VALUE="<%=DateSerial(Year(dbCurrentDate), 11, 1)%>"
228:     <% If Month(dbCurrentDate) = 11 then Response.Write " SELECTED" %>>
229:        November
230:    </OPTION>
231:    <OPTION VALUE="<%=DateSerial(Year(dbCurrentDate), 12, 1)%>"
232:     <% If Month(dbCurrentDate) = 12 then Response.Write " SELECTED" %>>
233:        December
234:    </OPTION>
235:    </SELECT>
```

```
236:      <BR>
237:      <INPUT TYPE=SUBMIT VALUE="View Select Month">
238:      </FORM>
239:      </CENTER>
240: </BODY>
241: </HTML>
```

Tip

Wow, that's a lot of code! You'll notice that as your ASP pages grow more feature-rich, the amount of code starts to increase dramatically. One method of reducing the amount of code is to use include files to import commonly used functions. Include files were discussed in detail on Day 13.

Congratulations, you have completed the second Bonus Project! You have taken the initial Calendar application created in the first Bonus Project and extended it to allow a user to select a specific month to view. Also, two hyperlinks were added to allow the user to view the next or previous month. You greatly increased the usefulness of this application by allowing the user to choose what month and year he wants to view.

In the third Bonus Project, which is at the end of Week 3, you'll look at how to use a database to store important dates. You'll then access this database when creating the calendar to display important dates on the generated calendar, much like you write down important dates on a paper calendar.

As with the first Bonus Project, feel free to make changes to today's project. If you see any areas that new features could be added to, by all means, implement those new features. Also, when you start next week's lessons, feel free to come back and apply what you are learning to enhance the current Calendar application.

WEEK 3

At a Glance

Congratulations on completing your first two weeks! You are now, by all rights, an advanced ASP developer. You've mastered the necessary skills, and you should feel confident in your ASP expertise. Although we've covered the fundamentals of Active Server Pages, we've yet to investigate one of the most common uses of ASP pages—databases.

Throughout this entire week we will examine how to read and modify databases through ASP pages. Being able to interact with databases is the most useful feature of Active Server Pages. Most companies use databases to manage data ranging from customer information to employee information. Before the explosion of the Internet, you could only access these databases through a computer on the same network as the database. Now, with the use of ASP pages, you can let users search your database over the Internet.

Where You're Going

A *database* is a collection of organized data that can be queried and modified. There are all sorts of commercial database programs available from a number of companies. In fact, some companies, like Informix and Oracle, do nothing but databases. Other companies, like Microsoft, have database software in addition to their other product lines.

Most businesses today use databases to maintain all sorts of information. Using a Microsoft-written component known as ActiveX Data Objects, you can connect to a database through an ASP page, perform a particular query, and display its results. For example, imagine that your company has a database containing the products they sell. This database contains the description, price, and inventory of each item. By using an ASP page to query this database, you can allow users to search through the available products when they visit your Web site!

This week begins with an introduction to databases. From there we move directly into connecting and querying databases using ActiveX Data Objects. We will also look at how to insert, update, and delete information from a database through an ASP page. We'll also discuss some advanced database concepts, including SQL, the programming language used by databases.

We wrap up the week, and this book, with a discussion on designing ASP applications. Throughout this book we've discussed coding techniques; programming, however, is not the only part of a software program. When creating an application, using ASP or any other programming language, a considerable amount of time needs to be spent in other phases, such as the design phase and the testing phase. In fact, more time should be spent in these phases than in the programming phase. We'll discuss the importance of the design phase in Day 21, "Practicing Intelligent Application Design."

DAY **15**

Using Databases

During Week 2, you looked at a number of ways to store information through the use of a Web site, including using cookies, the `Session` object, and special text files.

Although all these methods can be used to store information, they all have drawbacks. Cookies only work with clients who have set up their browsers to accept cookies, the `Session` object is only good for maintaining state for the duration of a user's visit to your site, and using text files to save and retrieve data can become inefficient for large amounts of information.

Fortunately, a fourth method for preserving information is available that we've yet to discuss: using databases. Databases are specifically designed to store massive amounts of information efficiently. Many commercial databases are available, including Access, Microsoft SQL-Server, Oracle, and Informix, to name just a few.

It is possible to read and modify the contents of a database through an ASP page. This is an amazingly useful function of Active Server Pages. Today, we will discuss the differences between flat-file databases and relational databases and explore the advantages of using databases as opposed to the other three methods discussed on previous days. Finally, we will examine some examples of ASP pages interacting with databases.

Today, you will learn the following:

- What a database table is
- The differences between flat-file databases and relational databases
- What commercial relational databases are available, and how to create a database using Access 2000
- When you should choose to use a database as opposed to using a text file, cookies, or session or application variables
- What an ODBC-compliant database is
- What ActiveX Data Objects are
- How to retrieve and output the contents of a database table through an ASP page

What Are Relational Databases?

The most useful feature of Active Server Pages is the capability for an ASP page to easily interact with a *database*.

NEW TERM   A *database* is a collection of information that can easily be queried and modified.

When using a database, you can only do four things: retrieve data, insert data, update existing data, or delete existing data. Tomorrow, Day 16, "Reading from a Database Using ASP," we will discuss how to retrieve information from a database. On Day 17, "Inserting, Updating, and Deleting Database Records," we'll examine how to perform these other three tasks.

Many popular, commercial database programs are available, such as Microsoft's Access, which ships with Office; Microsoft SQL-Server; Oracle; Informix; FoxPro; DB2; and many others. Because ASP is a Microsoft technology, Microsoft databases are most commonly used. However, there is no reason why you cannot interact with a non-Microsoft database, such as Oracle.

The primary purpose of a database is to store information. Although each database system may have its own nuances, each database uses *tables* to store information.

NEW TERM   A *table* is a two-dimensional matrix that is used to store information in a database.

A table, which is a combination of rows and columns in the form of a matrix, should be thought of as a storage place for instances of objects. The columns of a table describe the properties of the object, whereas each row is a unique instance of the object. Rows in a database table are often referred to as *records*, and columns are often referred to as *fields*.

 A *record* is a single instance of an object and is represented in a database by a row.

 A *field* is a single property of an object, represented by a column in a database table.

> **Note** We will use the terms row and record interchangeably throughout the lessons this week. The same applies for the terms column and field.

For example, imagine that you wanted to store information about cars in your database. It helps to think of a car as an object that has certain properties. (We used a similar example on Day 6, "Working with Objects.") To be able to store information on particular car instances, you would need to create a Car table. This table would contain a column for each property defined for the car object. For example, you might decide to store the Manufacturer, Year, Miles, and Color properties for each car object. In this case, your Car database table would have four columns. For each car instance that you wanted to store in the database, you would need to add a row to the Car table. If you had six unique cars, you'd have six rows in your Car table.

Figure 15.1 shows a graphical representation of this table, containing no rows.

FIGURE 15.1

The columns represent the properties of the Car *object.*

Car Table

Manufacturer	Year	Miles	Color

The Car table, at this point, contains no records. The four columns of the Car table are: Manufacturer, Year, Miles, and Color. For each car instance we want to store in our database, a row will exist in this table.

A row represents an instance of the car object in the Car database table. Imagine that you wanted to store the following six cars in your database:

- A 1987, red Ford with 130,000 miles
- A 1989, black Toyota with 100,000 miles
- A 1998, yellow Volkswagen with 17,000 miles
- A 1997, black Porsche with 14,000 miles
- A 1985, white Ford with 194,000 miles
- A 1994, black Ford with 135,000 miles

To store these six instances of the car object, you would need to add six rows to the Car table. Figure 15.2 graphically represents the six new rows added to the Car table.

FIGURE 15.2

Each row in the table corresponds to an object instance.

Car Table

Manufacturer	Year	Miles	Color
Ford	1987	130,000	Red
Toyota	1989	100,000	Black
Volkswagen	1998	17,000	Yellow
Porsche	1997	14,000	Black
Ford	1985	194,000	White
Ford	1994	135,000	Black

Note that each car instance is represented by its own row in the Car table. Therefore, since we want to store information about six cars, there are exactly six rows in the database table.

Databases can consist of several database tables, and usually each database table represents a single object. However, what if an object contains instances of different types of objects? In the car example, we described a car by using four properties. What if you wanted to add a fifth property—Engine—which is an object itself? The Engine object might have properties such as Horsepower, Liters, and Cylinders. If an object's property is an entirely new object, how do you represent that in a database?

One approach is to create a new table, Engine, that would have a column for each property of an engine; however, let's look at an alternative approach first. Rather than creating a new table, let's just add three new columns to the Car table. These columns could be EngineHorsepower, EngineLiters, and EngineCylinders and would contain information about the engine for each car. We've now *merged* the Engine table into the Car table.

In the early days of databases, combining two tables into one was the commonly used approach. Merging two related database tables together into one table is a technique used with *flat-file database systems*.

NEW TERM   *Flat-file database systems* merge related tables together to form larger, all-encompassing tables.

Flat-file databases are rarely used anymore because data is often repeated unnecessarily. In the Engine example, imagine that half of the cars in the database table have identical engines. The identical engine information is repeated unnecessarily, as Figure 15.3 shows. To remove this repetitious information, we will use a process called *normalization*. A normalized database is streamlined to not contain any repetitive data. We'll discuss normalizing databases in Day 21, "Practicing Intelligent Application Design."

The flat-file databases of yesteryear have been replaced by *relational databases*, which are currently the de facto standard.

FIGURE 15.3

Flat-file databases are notorious for being clogged with duplicate data.

Car Table (with added Engine information)

Manufacturer	Year	Miles	Color	EngineHorsepower	EngineLiters	EngineCylinders
Ford	1987	130,000	Red	200	2.5	8
Toyota	1989	100,000	Black	150	2.2	4
Volkswagen	1998	17,000	Yellow	125	2.0	4
Porsche	1997	14,000	Black	275	2.5	4
Ford	1985	194,000	White	200	2.5	8
Ford	1994	135,000	Black	200	2.5	8

In this example, the three Ford cars have identical engines. By merging the car and engine tables together, we are unnecessarily duplicating the engine information for the three Ford vehicles.

NEW TERM A *relational database* represents each object, related or not, as its own database table.

In a relational database, the information about the Engine object would be stored in an `Engine` database table. Because the Engine object has three properties—Horsepower, Liters, and Cylinders—you might expect the `Engine` table to have exactly three columns. However, the `Engine` table would need four columns. The fourth column, which might be named `ID`, would uniquely identify each row in the `Engine` table.

> **Tip**
>
> Database systems allow you to create automatically incrementing ID fields. Because the field is auto-incremented each time a new record is inserted, it serves as a unique identifier.

A new column, `EngineID`, would also need to be added to the `Car` table. The `EngineID` column in the `Car` table would represent what type of engine a particular car instance had. The `EngineID` in the `Car` table would map to the appropriate `ID` in the `Engine` table.

All this talk of `ID`s and `EngineID`s can be confusing. Hopefully, Figure 15.4, which shows some sample data in the `Car` and `Engine` tables, will clear things up. Note that when multiple cars have the same engine, their `EngineID` columns contain the same value.

Can you see how relational databases do not present duplicated data among related tables? Figure 15.3 presented information on each car's engine, even if multiple cars had identical engines. In Figure 15.4, the number of rows in the `Engine` table equals the total number of unique engines. No identical engines are duplicated.

> **Tip**
>
> When designing database tables using relational databases, remember to represent each individual object with its own database table.

FIGURE 15.4

Data duplication between related tables is not a problem when using relational database.

Car Table (with a relationship to the Engine table)

Manufacturer	Year	Miles	Color	EngineID
Ford	1987	130,000	Red	1
Toyota	1989	100,000	Black	2
Volkswagen	1998	17,000	Yellow	3
Porsche	1997	14,000	Black	4
Ford	1985	194,000	White	1
Ford	1994	135,000	Black	1

Engine Table

ID	EngineHorsepower	EngineLiters	EngineCylinders
1	200	2.5	8
2	150	2.2	4
3	125	2.0	4
4	275	2.5	4

Note that the duplicates Engine information that was present in Figure 15.3 is not seen here. By using a relation database design, where each object is its own table, we reduce the amount of unnecessary duplication.

Designing relational databases is not a trivial task. Understanding how to relate various database tables to one another is an in-depth topic, and one that is beyond the scope of this book. For a good book on designing databases, read *Sams Teach Yourself Database Design in 24 Hours.*

Common Relational Databases

Many commercial relational database systems are available. Some of the most popular ones include Microsoft's SQL-Server, Microsoft Access, Oracle, and Informix. With ASP, though, you are not limited to using only these four database systems. Rather, you can access any *ODBC-compliant* database through ASP.

NEW TERM   An *ODBC-compliant database* adheres to the Open DataBase Connectivity standards outlined by Microsoft.

Because each database system might require different syntax to access its data, Microsoft set out to create a standard. This standard, known as the Open DataBase Connectivity (ODBC) standard, provides a common interface to a database so that the same chunk of code will work regardless of what database you are querying. Databases that support this standard are referred to as ODBC-compliant, and all major database systems today are ODBC-compliant. Several ODBC-compliant databases are listed below.

- Delimited text files
- dBASE
- Excel spreadsheets
- FoxPro
- Access

- Oracle
- Paradox
- SQL-Server

As the list shows, you can use a wide range of databases with your ASP application.

Note   Although many *can* be used with ASP, the most commonly used databases are Microsoft's SQL-Server, Access, and Oracle. The examples throughout this week will either use Access 2000 or SQL-Server 7.0.

Why Use Databases?

In past lessons, we've discussed how to persist data using text files, cookies, and the `Session` and `Application` objects. You may be wondering why we're discussing yet another way to save information. Why should you learn about databases, and when should you use them in place of these other methods of information persistence?

Databases, like text files, cookies, and the `Session` and `Application` objects, have their time and place. If you need to store a lot of information over a long period of time, databases are clearly the way to go. An entire branch of computer science is dedicated to studying database design and how to create efficient database systems. Due to this intense research into database systems, a database is the most effective and efficient method of storing information.

However, database use has drawbacks. Connecting to a database through an ASP page is expensive. Reading the contents of a text file or a cookie takes much less time than connecting to a database and retrieving information from a database table. For this reason, databases aren't always the best solution.

Note   Executing a database query is efficient. The inefficiency arises when you attempt to establish a connection to a database through an ASP page. Connecting to databases is discussed thoroughly tomorrow.

To help decide whether you should use a database or some other method for storing information, consult Table 15.2.

TABLE 15.2 Five Methods of Saving Data.

Method	When to Use
Cookies	When you have to save small bits of information on a user-by-user basis for lengthy periods of time, use cookies. Because cookies are stored on the client's machine, there is no guarantee that the user's cookies won't be deleted or altered. If it is vital that the information you save persists, cookies are not the best option.
	A search engine web site, like Yahoo!, might use cookies to save the last search performed for each user using cookies. When a user revisited the search page, the user's last search query could be automatically entered into the search text box.
Session variables	Session variables are ideal for storing information on a user-by-user basis for the duration of the user's visit to your site. Because session variables are preserved for only the duration of a user's visit, if you need to persist information for longer periods of time, session variables won't do. Also, session variables have a performance concern because a set of session variables is created for each simultaneous visitor on your site.
	A session variable could be used to track each web page a particular user had visited on your web site during their current visit. This list of pages could then be organized into a hierarchical structure, and presented as a navigation aid. There is a thorough article on 4GuysFromRolla.com explaining how to create a dynamic content tree using session variables at `http://www.4guysfromrolla.com/webtech/110498-2.shtml`.
Application variables	Application variables persist information from the time the Web site is started until it is shut down. Only one set of application variables exists for all users on your Web site. The values stored in your application variables are lost when the Web server is rebooted. Application variables are useful for storing global, static information on the Web server.
	Application variables come in handy when there is a changing variable that is global in scope. For example, on a message board web site, application variables could be used to store the message and author of the latest post. These application variables could then be displayed on any web page, showing the most recent post to the forum!
Text files	Text files are useful for storing small bits of information that need to persist for an indefinite amount of time. Text files are efficient, but storing information on a user-by-user basis using text files is difficult. Text files work best when storing long-lasting information that is not specific to each user.
	Imagine that you sold widgets on your web site, and had a list of credit card numbers that you did not want to accept. You could have a text file that contained this listing of credit card numbers. When a user enters her credit card number to order a widget, you could check to make sure that this credit number did not exist within the text file containing bad credit card numbers.

Method	When to Use
Databases	Databases provide the best performance for storing large, heterogeneous chunks of information. Databases are designed to simplify the process of storing and retrieving information. Connecting to a database, however, carries with it a high performance cost. Databases should only be used to store large amounts of information over indefinite periods of time. If you only need to store some temporary value, use cookies or session variables. If you need to store some small piece of global information, such as the Web master's email address, use include files or application variables. For example, if you needed to save information about the clients your company does business with, you'd want to use a database.

Table 15.2 discusses *when* to use databases and other information storage techniques, but *why* should you choose to use databases? For starters, databases are designed to do one thing and one thing only: store data. This makes databases extremely efficient at storing and retrieving information. Databases have the capacity to store large amounts of information. Some of the world's largest databases contain several terabytes of information (one terabyte is 1,000 gigabytes, or 1,000,000 megabytes)! Try to store a terabyte of information into a cookie or text file!

Another nice feature of using databases through an ASP page is that a vast number of existing applications already use databases to store information. Imagine that your company currently has a database that contains contact information for its clients. Chances are, this information is stored in a database. By interacting with this database through an ASP page, you can provide an Internet page so that your sales force, while hundreds of miles away from work, can access client information through the use of a Web browser and access to the Internet. By using databases through your ASP pages, you can tie into existing applications and present their data online.

Do	Don't
DO use a database when appropriate.	DON'T use a database when cookies, a text file, or session or application variables would suffice.

Working with Databases Using ASP

Now that we've discussed the basics of databases, it's time to get your hands dirty and begin working with them! In the remainder of today's lesson, you will learn how to create a database using Microsoft Access 2000 and then query this database through an ASP page. These topics will be discussed in much greater detail tomorrow.

Before you create your database, you need to decide what kind of information you want to store. Imagine that you wanted to create a Web page that would store contact information for your friends and loved ones. For this example, create a table named Friends that contains the following columns:

- Name
- StreetAddress
- City
- State
- Zip
- PhoneNumber

To create such a table using Access 2000, start by running Access. A dialog box appears, asking whether you want to Create a new database or Open an existing file. Figure 15.5 shows the dialog box you should see. Choose to create a Blank Access Database.

FIGURE 15.5

Start by creating a new Access database.

You are prompted with a dialog requesting a filename for your new database and a location to save the database file. Name the database file FriendsContactInfo.mdb and place it in the My Documents folder. At this point, you should be presented with three options: Create Table in Design View, Create Table by Using Wizard, and Create Table by Entering Data. Choose Create Table in Design View.

You should now see a matrix with three columns and several rows—similar to Figure 15.6.

Enter the columns for the Friends table into the rows of this matrix. Start by adding the Name column of the Friends table. This column name goes into the Field Name column of the matrix in Figure 15.6. To move between columns in the Design view, use the Tab key. Next, select the Data Type. Because you will store strings into the Name column, choose a Text data type. If you want to enter descriptive information about this column, feel free to do so in the Description column of the matrix. Enter five more rows into the matrix representing the other five columns in the Friends table. When you are finished, your screen should look similar to Figure 15.7.

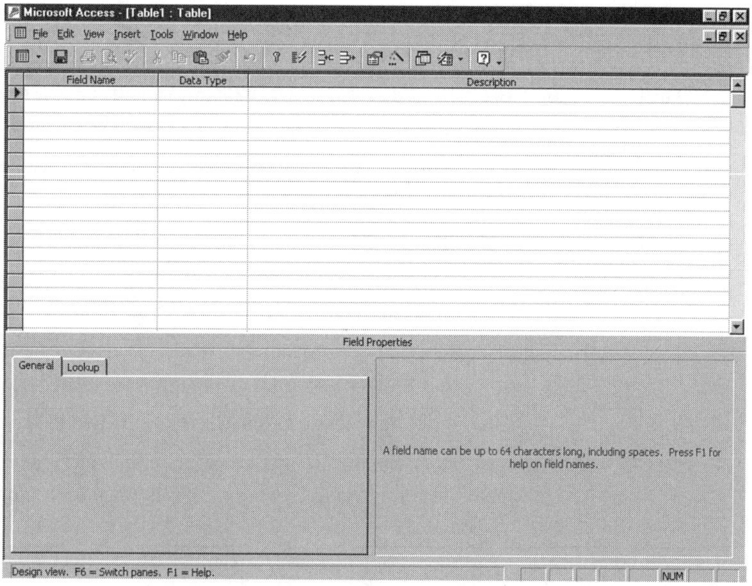

15

FIGURE 15.6

Enter the columns of your table into this matrix.

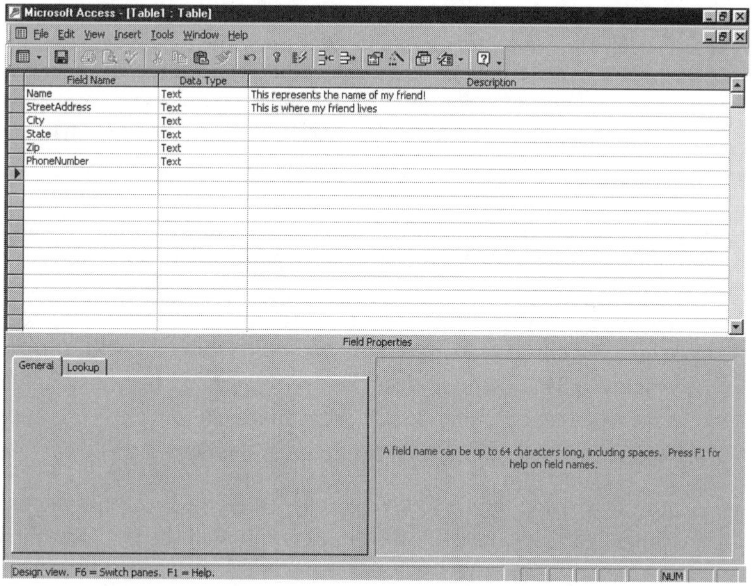

FIGURE 15.7

Each row in the matrix represents a column in the Friends table.

Note that each column in the Friends table has a Text Data Type because each column needs to store textual information. There are other Data Types you can choose. Table 15.3 lists what other Data Types you can select when creating a database through Access 2000.

TABLE 15.3 Data Types Supported by Access

Data Type	When to Use
Text	Use when you need to store 255 alphanumeric characters or less. If you need to store more than 255 alphanumeric characters, use the Memo data type.
Memo	Use when you need to store a large amount of alphanumeric characters. The Memo data type can store up to 65,535 characters.
Number	Use when you need to store numeric values.
Date/Time	Use when you need to store date and time values. A Date/Time data type in Access can store dates between the years 100 and 9999.
Currency	Use when you need to store currency values. Currency data types only support up to four digits of decimal precision.
Yes/No	Use for columns that can only have one of two values.
Autonumber	Use this automatically incrementing variable to uniquely identify each row in a table. Autonumber fields are essential when designing multiple, related tables in a relational database.

Note

Today's popular databases offer many of the same data types, although they may use different vocabulary. The data types listed in Table 15.3 are expressed in Access's vocabulary. SQL-Server, as well as other databases, use different terms for the same data types. For example, in SQL-Server, the Yes/No data type is referred to as a bit data type.

Now that you have entered all the needed information, go ahead and Save this table by choosing File, Save from the menu. You are prompted to enter a name for this table (see Figure 15.8). Type in Friends and click OK.

When you click OK to save your database table, you will be warned that no primary key is defined. This example does not need a primary key, so simply choose that you do not want to create a primary key. Congratulations! You have just created a database table. Now enter some values into your database table.

Start by closing the Design view (choose File, Close from the menu). You see the three options you were initially shown, except now there is a fourth item—the table you just created (see Figure 15.9).

FIGURE 15.8

Choose a name for your database table.

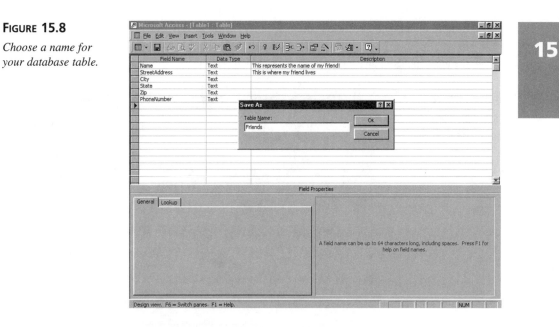

FIGURE 15.9

You are presented with a fourth option now.

Double-click this new option. Doing so opens a new window that contains a matrix representing the Friends table. Note that there are six columns, one for each column defined in the Design view (refer to Figure 15.7). Add some information for friends of yours into this table, as shown in Figure 15.10.

You now have created a database with one table using Access 2000. Now that you have a database, you can query it through an ASP page. It doesn't matter what database system you decide to use, so long as it is ODBC-compliant. Although the steps to actually create the database and a table might differ, querying the data through ASP will not be any different.

To communicate with a database through an ASP page, you need to use the ActiveX Data Objects component (ADO). This component provides a number of objects that can be used to connect to and query a database. We will discuss ADO and its associated objects in detail tomorrow. For now, just be aware that *anytime* you want to access a database through an ASP page, you *must* use ADO.

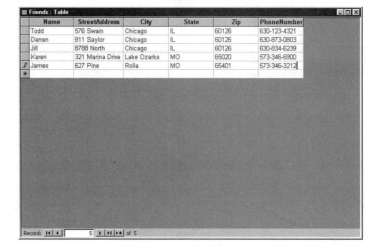

When you want to retrieve information from a database, you need to use a two-step process:

1. Establish a connection to the database.
2. Query the database, asking the database for the information you are interested in.

Imagine that you were planning to meet your friends for dinner, but you did not know what time to meet them. To determine this time, you decide to call one of your friends whom you will be dining with and ask her what time to meet. To obtain this information, you must go through a two-step process, similar to the two-step process involved with accessing a database through an ASP page. First, you must pick up the telephone and correctly dial the number so that you can speak to your friend. In this phase, you are *connecting* to your friend so that you can find out what time everyone is meeting. After you've established a connection (that is, after your friend has picked up the phone), you can then ask her when everyone is meeting for dinner. She will then (hopefully) tell you the time. When the transaction of information has been completed, you both hang up.

This is how you interface with databases through an ASP page. To help you both connect and query information, ADO provides two useful objects: the Connection object and the Recordset object. These objects' properties and methods will be discussed in detail tomorrow. For now, we will look at an ASP page that will connect to the database we just created, obtain the contents of the Friends table, and display them to the user.

15

Listing 15.1 contains the code for `DisplayFriendsTable.asp`, which uses the `Connection` and `Recordset` objects to display the `Friends` table.

LISTING 15.1 Using ADO to Connect to a Database and Retrieve the Contents of a Table

```
 1: <%@ Language=VBScript %>
 2: <% Option Explicit %>
 3: <!--#include virtual="/adovbs.inc"-->
 4: <%
 5:    'Open up a connection to our Access database
 6:    'We will use a DSN-less connection.
 7:    Dim objConn
 8:    Set objConn = Server.CreateObject("ADODB.Connection")
 9:    objConn.ConnectionString="DRIVER={Microsoft Access Driver (*.mdb)};" & _
10:                             "DBQ=C:\My Documents\FriendsContactInfo.mdb"
11:    objConn.Open
12:
13:    'Create a recordset object instance and retrieve the information
14:    'from the Friends table.
15:    Dim objRS
16:    Set objRS = Server.CreateObject("ADODB.Recordset")
17:    objRS.Open "Friends", objConn, , , adCmdTable
18:
19:    'Display the contents of the Friends table
20:    Do While Not objRS.EOF
21:        Response.Write "<B>" & objRS("Name") & "</B><BR>"
22:        Response.Write objRS("StreetAddress") & "<BR>"
23:        Response.Write objRS("City") & ", " & objRS("State")
24:        Response.Write "<BR>" & objRS("Zip") & "<BR>"
25:        Response.Write objRS("PhoneNumber") & "<P><HR><P>"
26:
27:        'Move to the next row in the Friends table
28:        objRS.MoveNext
29:    Loop
30:
31:    'Clean up our ADO objects
32:    objRS.Close
33:    Set objRS = Nothing
34:
35:    objConn.Close
36:    Set objConn = Nothing
37: %>
```

 ANALYSIS Whenever you want to access a database through an ASP page, you must use ADO. Listing 15.1 uses two ADO objects: `Connection` and `Recordset`. Recall that when you need to obtain information from a database, the following two steps must occur:

1. Establish a *connection* to the database. Use the `Connection` object to perform this task.

2. Let the database know what information you are interested in obtaining and provide a mechanism for receiving that information. The Recordset object is used to facilitate this step.

Listing 15.1 accomplishes step 1 in lines 7 through 11. Because you need to work with the Connection object, you must first declare a variable that holds an instance of this object. Line 7 creates such a variable, objConn. Next, line 8 uses Server.CreateObject to create an instance of the Connection object. Line 9 sets the ConnectionString property of the Connection object. The ConnectionString is information needed by the Connection object to establish a proper connection to the correct database. In the earlier analogy, the ConnectionString would be synonymous to the phone number of the friend you were calling. We will discuss the intricacies of the ConnectionString property in greater detail tomorrow. Finally, after you have created a Connection object instance and set its ConnectionString property correctly, you are ready to Open your connection to the database. This is done by executing the Open method of the Connection object (line 11).

On to step 2! After you've Opened a connection to your database using the Connection object, you need to let the database know what information you are interested in. You accomplish this by using the Recordset object. Line 15 begins by declaring a variable, objRS, to hold the instance of the Recordset object you are going to create. Next, line 16 uses Server.CreateObject to create an instance of the Recordset object. The Open method of the Recordset object is then used to do two things: inform the database of what information you are interested in and provide a receptacle for the information returned by the database. The Open method (line 17), takes a number of parameters. The first parameter is the name of the database table whose results you want to obtain. The second parameter is the Connection object instance that contains the physical connection to the database. The next two parameters are optional, so leave those out for now; we'll touch on these parameters later this week. Finally, the last parameter, adCmdTable, informs the database that the first parameter represents a database table name. Since we are using one of the ADO constants (adCmdTable), we've included adovbs.inc in line 3. For this script to work properly, you will need to make sure adovbs.inc is in your web application's root web directory. We will discuss adovbs.inc and what, exactly, the ADO constants are in tomorrow's lesson.

The Recordset object performs two tasks: it instructs the database as to what information you're interested in; it also stores the requested information returned by the database. Therefore, to output the information returned by the database, use the Recordset object. In Listing 15.1, the Recordset object takes a snapshot of the Friends table. After line 17 is executed, the Recordset object instance objRS contains all the data in the Friends table.

15

When working with the `Recordset` object, you can access the data on a row-by-row basis. Lines 20 through 29 iterate through each row in the `Recordset` object, displaying each of the columns. Note that you access the value of a particular column in the current row by using the following syntax:

```
objRS(columnName)
```

Line 28 moves to the next row in the `Recordset` object by using the `MoveNext` method. When we've passed the final row in the `Recordset` object, the `EOF` property, which stands for End Of File, is set to `True`, and the `Do While Not objRS.EOF...Loop`, started on line 20, ends. These topics are discussed in detail tomorrow.

After you've displayed all the contents of the `Recordset` object, `Close` the objects and explicitly free the memory associated with them (lines 32 through 36). The `Close` method of the `Recordset` and `Connection` objects disconnects the ASP page from the database. In the previous analogy, after you've obtained the information from your friend, you end the informational transaction by hanging up. Closing your `Recordset` and `Connection` objects has the same effect. After you have obtained the needed information from the database and processed it, you should "hang up." Also, as discussed on Day 6, you should *always* explicitly free your objects when you are finished using them.

Figure 15.11 shows the output of Listing 15.1, when viewed through a browser.

FIGURE 15.11

The contents of the Friends *table are displayed.*

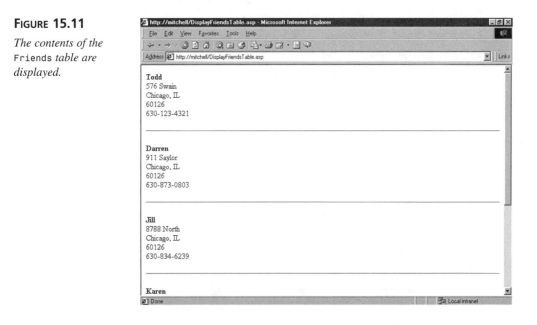

> **Caution**
>
> Listing 15.1 only works for databases created using Access. If you use another database, an error will be generated. This is due to the `DRIVER` reference in the `ConnectionString` property (line 9). We will discuss how to set up `ConnectionStrings` to use different databases tomorrow.

When closing and freeing your `Recordset` and `Connection` objects (lines 32 through 36 in Listing 15.1), be sure to close and free your `Recordset` object *before* freeing and closing your `Connection` object. Because the `Recordset` object is dependent on the `Connection` object, when you explicitly `Close` the `Connection` object, the `Recordset` object is implicitly `Closed`. If you try to explicitly `Close` the `Recordset` object *after* it's been implicitly closed, you will receive an error because you can't close something that's already closed. For example, the following syntax generates an error:

```
1:  'Close and explicitly free the Connection object
2:  objConn.Close
3:  Set objConn = Nothing
4:
5:  'Close and explicitly free the Recordset object
6:  objRS.Close
7:  Set objRS = Nothing
```

When the `Connection` object is explicitly `Closed` on line 2, the `Recordset` object will be implicitly `Closed` as well. On line 6, though, you are trying to explicitly `Close` the `Recordset` object. This generates the following error:

```
ADODB.Recordset error '800a0e78'
The operation requested by the application is
not allowed if the object is closed.
```

You cannot `Close` a `Recordset` object that is already `Closed`, so make sure that you always explicitly `Close` and free your `Recordset` object *first*, and your `Connection` object *second*.

Summary

In the past few years, ASP has really taken off to become a widely used tool for creating dynamic Web pages. One of the main reasons for this explosive growth is the fact that ASP can use ADO to connect to many databases. Being able to easily interface a Web page with any ODBC-compliant database makes ASP an invaluable tool.

Today, we discussed what databases are and what advantages they possess. We discussed the differences between the flat-file databases of yesteryear and the more commonly used relational database. We examined when to use databases as opposed to other methods of information storage. Using Access 2000, we created a sample database, and, using the

`Connection` and `Recordset` ADO objects, we connected to this database and displayed the contents of a table on an ASP page.

When you determine that your Web site needs to store information, you have a number of choices, databases only being one of the many. For example, you could use text files on the Web server, or cookies on the client's machine, to persist information. If, however, you need to maintain a large amount of information over an indefinite period of time, databases are the best option.

Next, we looked at how to create a database using Access 2000. Recall that a database is made up of tables. In the example database, we created a `Friends` table that contained six fields, identifying names, addresses, and phone numbers. We then created an ASP page that connected to this database, retrieved the results of the `Friends` table, and displayed them to the user.

When interacting with a database, a two-step process must occur. First, a connection to the database needs to be established. This connection provides a communication link between your ASP page and the database itself. Second, the ASP page should tell the database what information it's interested in and should provide a mechanism for retrieving that information. To accomplish these two tasks, ADO provides two objects: `Connection` and `Recordset`. We will discuss the use of these two objects in greater detail throughout the week.

Tomorrow, we will discuss reading the contents of a database table in much greater detail. We will discuss the role of the ActiveX Data Objects, as well as dedicate a lengthy conversation to both the `Connection` and `Recordset` objects. This week is an exciting one! Although today's lesson may have served as your introduction to databases, by the end of the week you will be working with databases through ASP pages like a database pro.

Q&A

Q When creating databases, should a relational database design be used or a flat-file database design?

A Because today's popular database systems are relational database systems, it is important to use a relational database design. Using a relational database design, though, opens up an entirely new can of worms. Correctly creating ID fields to map rows in one table to another is a skill that needs to be learned. Retrieving data from multiple, related tables is a non-trivial task.

Throughout the remainder of this book, we will only look at examples that use one database table. We decided not to include using multiple, related tables because an entire book could be written on the subject of relational database design and usage.

In fact, several have! To learn more about relational database design, be sure to read *Sams Teach Yourself Database Design in 24 Hours*.

Q **Are there other ADO objects besides the `Connection` and `Recordset` objects?**

A Yes, there are other ADO objects. However, we are going to concentrate on the `Connection` and `Recordset` objects throughout this week. On Day 20, "Using Advanced Database Techniques," we will discuss the `Command` object, which is another ADO object. Other than the `Command` object, though, we will not discuss any more ADO objects.

Q **What advantages would using a text file to save information have over using a database?**

A When needing to persist information, as a developer, you have a number of choices. One of these choices, obviously, is to use a database. Another, as discussed on Day 13, "Reading and Writing Files on the Web Server," is to create text files on the Web server.

What approach to take depends on what you need to accomplish. If you need to store vast amounts of information, a database is definitely the best solution. If, however, you only need to store small amounts of information, a text file will usually do the trick. A text file possesses one key advantage over databases: performance. Database systems are efficient at retrieving data; however, connecting to a database can be expensive and much more inefficient than opening a text file.

The approach you choose should depend on how much data needs to be stored and how important performance is. If you run a relatively small Web site, or an intranet, go ahead and use a database regardless; performance won't be an issue here. If, however, you run a large site with many simultaneous users, you'll come to appreciate the performance boost in a text file. One caveat, though: if you expect the amount of information that needs to be stored to increase, go ahead and use a database. Also, databases provide much easier mechanisms to sort and locate information than do text files.

For an example of a good use of text files in place of a database, check out `http://www.4guysfromrolla.com/webtech/070799-2.shtml`. At that URL, you will find an article that outlines an online help system that uses text files to store the help text, as opposed to databases.

Workshop

The Workshop provides quiz questions to help you solidify your understanding of the material covered and exercises to provide you with experience in using what you've learned. Try to understand the quiz and exercise answers before continuing to tomorrow's lesson. Quiz answers are provided in Appendix A, and exercise answers can be found at `http://www.mcp.com/info`.

Quiz

1. True or False: A database is comprised of one to many database tables.

2. How do flat-file database systems differ from relational database systems?

3. True or False: You can access any ODBC-compliant database through an ASP page using ADO.

4. What does the acronym ODBC stand for?

5. What does the acronym ADO stand for?

6. When should you choose to use a database to persist information?

7. What are some commonly used, commercial databases?

8. True or False: Using ADO, an ASP page can access an Oracle database.

9. To retrieve information from a database, two steps must occur. What are these two steps, and what ADO objects facilitate each of these steps?

Exercise

1. Imagine that you were asked to create a database that would store employee information. What columns would you envision needing in your Employee database table? What data types would these columns need to be?

DAY 16

Reading from a Database Using ASP

On Day 15, "Using Databases," you saw why databases are useful, and you got a quick look at how to use them. Today, we will elaborate on that and discuss how to read in tables from a database. Today, you will learn the following:

- How to connect to a database using the `Connection` object
- How to create and use System DSNs versus DSN-less connections
- What the properties of the connection are
- How to use the `Recordset` object
- How to read in and display the contents of a table

Databases and ASP

At one time, connecting to a database was difficult. Databases came in a variety of formats, and you had to know a low-level API (application programming interface) for every database you wanted to use. There was a push for a universal API that would work for a wide variety of data stores. ODBC, or Open

DataBase Connectivity, was developed as an attempt to create this universal API. Many databases conformed to the standard and became known as ODBC-compliant databases, such as Access, MS-SQL Server, Oracle, Informix, and so on.

ODBC had some faults. It still contained many low-level calls and was difficult to develop with. Developers still had to focus on low-level communications with the database. People wanted a way just to get the data they needed and use it how they saw fit. Microsoft's solution was DAO, or Data Access Objects.

DAO was followed by RDO (Remote Data Objects, targeted for distributed database architecture), and then ADO (ActiveX Data Objects). All these have shortcomings, however. According to Microsoft, "ODBC provides native access to SQL data" and "DAO provides high-level objects to data." Even DAO and RDO require the data in a data store to be in SQL (Structured Query Language) format. In response to these shortcomings, Microsoft introduced OLEDB, a COM-based data access object that provides access to all types of data and even provides access to disconnected data stores (for example, if you're on your laptop, you can easily view a snapshot of the database from the last time you synched up).

OLEDB sort of replaces ODBC. It includes an ODBC driver so that it is compatible with all the ODBC data sources. You can see how OLEDB works with your data sources in Figure 16.1.

FIGURE 16.1

The hierarchy of data access.

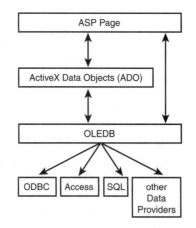

Communicating with a Database Using ActiveX Data Objects (ADO)

ActiveX Data Objects (ADO) comes with ASP and allows your pages to easily connect to databases. ADO works with any OLEDB source, which includes ODBC-compliant sources. So it will work with most databases currently being used.

The ADO model contains six objects. Of them, only the Connection object and the Recordset object will be used today.

The Connection object connects you to the data source. Obtaining a connection is the first step to working with databases.

The Recordset object allows you to work with the data in a table. The Recordset object contains a set of rows from a table. It can be used to read through the rows of a table, modify the rows of a table, or collect new data to be added to the table. Today we will just be reading through the rows. Changing and adding data to a database is covered on Day 17, "Inserting, Updating, and Deleting Database Records."

The Error object represents an error generated by the data source. The Errors collection is used when a single failed method call is allowed to generate multiple errors.

The Field object represents a single column in the table. It is discussed further on Day 18, "Examining the Recordset Object."

The Command object provides another way to create a Recordset object. It combines the Recordset object and the Connection object. It is discussed further on Day 20, "Using Advanced Database Techniques."

The Parameters collection contains any parameters needed by the command. The parameters are stored in a parameter object.

You can see a diagram of how these objects relate to each other in Figure 16.2.

FIGURE 16.2

The ADO objects and their relations.

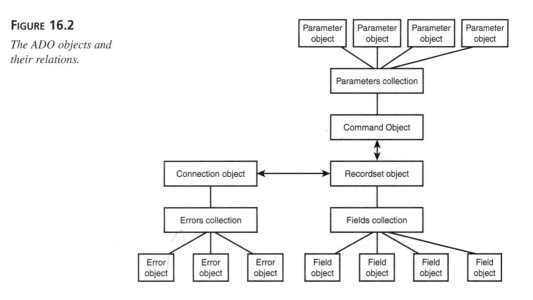

Today, you will create a new database. This one should be for the fictitious company Widget World, so use Access to create the database and call it WidgetWorld.mdb. At first, it will contain one table called tblExpenses, which will contain the employee expense reports. Table 16.1 lists the fields needed for this table.

TABLE 16.1   Fields of the Expense Report Table

Field Name	Data Type
EmployeeName	Text
EmployeeNumber	Number
ExpenseAmount	Currency
ExpenseReason	Text

This table will not need a primary key. Look at Day 15 if you need to review how to create Access databases. Be sure to remember the folder you put the .mdb file in. You will need it later.

Connecting to a Database

Before you can do anything with the database, you need to connect to it. Think of it like calling someone on the telephone. You cannot simply pick up the phone and start talking. You need to dial the number. Then the phone company computers make all the correct connections to route your call to the appropriate place. Finally, your friend hears his/her phone ringing and picks it up. Now you can have your conversation. It is similar when working with databases in ASP. Before you can talk to the database, you need to get a connection to it.

The Connection Object

The Connection object is used to hold information about the data store you want to access. It is created the same way your other components have been, using Server.CreateObject:

```
Dim objConn
Set objConn = Server.CreateObject("ADODB.Connection")
```

There may be times when you want connections to several data stores open at once. You might be using multiple Access databases, or mixing Access, Oracle, SQL, or whatever. In such cases, you would use multiple instances of the Connection object. Using multiple data sources gets a bit complicated because different sources have different capabilities. Fortunately, the need for multiple data sources in a single ASP page does not come up all that often.

Using a System DSN

A System DSN is a file that contains information about the database such as where it is and what kind of database it is. DSN stands for Data Source Name. Creating a System DSN is easy:

1. Close Access.

2. In Windows 2000, click Start; go to Settings, Control Panel, Administrative Tools, Data Sources (ODBC). Or, go to Start, Administrative Tools, Data Sources.

3. Go to the System DSN tab. You should see something like Figure 16.3. There is a listing of the system data sources currently configured. Along the right are three buttons that allow you to add a new System DSN, remove the selected one, or change the settings of the currently selected one.

FIGURE 16.3

Viewing the Data Source Administrator System DSN tab.

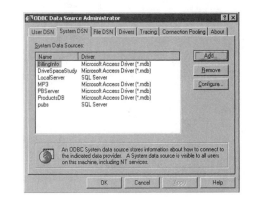

4. You want to create a new DSN, so click Add.

5. You will see a list of drivers, like in Figure 16.4. Choose Microsoft Access Driver (*.mdb) and click Finish.

FIGURE 16.4

Creating a new System DSN for the Widget World database.

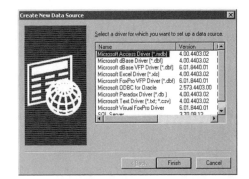

6. Now the setup box pops up. Enter **WidgetWorld.dsn** for the Data Source Name. This is the name you will use to reference the DSN in your ASP pages. You may enter a description as well. It should be something to remind you what this database and DSN are for.

7. Click Select. Now choose the `.mdb` file for the database. We named it `WidgetWorld.mdb`.

8. Click OK to select the database. Your screen should look similar to Figure 16.5. Click OK again to finish creating the DSN. You should see the DSN you just created listed under System Data Sources.

9. Click OK to exit.

FIGURE 16.5

Finishing the System DSN for the Widget World database.

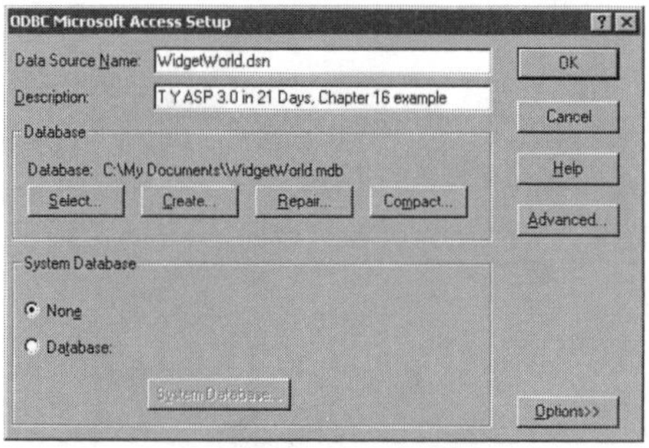

If you are using an earlier version of Windows, you can get to ODBC Data Sources like this: Click Start, then Settings, and then the Control Panel. Open up ODBC Data Sources.

Now you have a System DSN. You can tell the `Connection` object about it like this:

```
objConn.ConnectionString = "DSN=WidgetWorld.dsn"
```

Using a DSN-less Connection

There is an alternative to using a System DSN. Instead of putting the connection information into the DSN, you can put it into the connection string. You saw an example of this kind of connection yesterday. Here is the connection string we used:

```
objConn.ConnectionString="DRIVER={Microsoft Access Driver (*.mdb)};" & _
                "DBQ=C:\My Documents\WidgetWorld.mdb"
```

The `DRIVER=` line tells the `Connection` object what kind of database it is connecting to.

The `DBQ=` line indicates where on the server the database resides. This must be a complete physical path. If you do not know the complete physical path, use `Server.MapPath`.

You can specify other values in the connection string. If you are connecting to a SQL database, you may need a username and password to access it. You can specify them with UID and PWD. You would also need to specify DATABASE, DRIVER, and SERVER information.

> **Note**
>
> The connections we will discuss in this book use OLEDB's ODBC driver. This is a holdover from when it was the only OLEDB driver, but it is still used a lot. If you want to use a direct OLEDB connection to connect to an Access database, set the connection string like this:
>
> "Provider=Microsoft.Jet.OLEDB.3.51; Data Source=path_to_my_database"

16

There are drawbacks to using DSN-less connections. First of all, it requires you to figure out all the information you need. Also, if you use a DSN-less connection, the connection information must be revalidated every time. With a System DSN, this must only be done once, when creating the System DSN.

> **Note**
>
> There is a solution to the first problem, at least. It involves creating a new Microsoft Data Link. You can read about it on the Web.
>
> http://www.4guysfromrolla.com/webtech/070699-1.shtml

Opening the Connection

So far, all you have done is create the Connection object and tell it about your database. You have yet to actually open the connection. To do this, use the Open method of the Connection object:

objConn.Open

This is the same whether or not you use a System DSN.

So let's put it all together now:

```
<%
    Dim objConn
    Set objConn = Server.CreateObject("ADODB.Connection")
    objConn.ConnectionString = "DSN=WidgetWorld.dsn"
    objConn.Open
%>
```

This creates the Connection object, sets the connection string, and opens the connection. This assumes that a System DSN was used. If you prefer, you may change the connection string for a DSN-less connection.

On Web sites where several pages will access the same database, it is common to put this code in an include file (refer to Day 13, "Reading and Writing Files on the Web Server"). It saves having to remember and retype the code, and if a change needs to be made, it can be made more easily. So save this as a file called `DatabaseConnect.asp`.

> **Note**
>
> Instead of using the `ConnectionString` property, you can pass the string with the connection information to the `Open` method, like this:
>
> `objConn.Open strConnectionInfo`
>
> You can also specify a username and password with the `Open` method, if your host requires it:
>
> `objConn.Open strConnectionInfo, strUsername, strPassword`

Closing the Connection

As with any object, you need to free the memory associated with it when you are finished. However, before you do that, you need to close the connection. Freeing a `Connection` object without closing it would be a bit like walking away from the phone without hanging up. You close a connection and then free the object like this:

```
objConn.Close
Set objConn = Nothing
```

Always close and free recordsets associated with a connection before closing and freeing the connection.

If you are finished with one connection but want to open up another, you can reuse the `Connection` object you just finished with. Simply close it, set the connection information appropriately, and reopen it.

Properties of the Connection

There is a collection in the `Connection` object called the `Properties` collection. This collection contains an instance of the `Property` object for every property supported by the connection. Listing 16.1 demonstrates the use of this collection.

LISTING 16.1   Listing the Properties of a Connection

```
1: <%@ Language=VBScript %>
2: <% Option Explicit %>
3: <HTML>
4:   <BODY>
5: <!--#include file="DatabaseConnect.asp"-->
6: <!--#include virtual="/adovbs.inc"-->
7: <%
```

```
 8:      Dim objProp
 9:      For Each objProp in objConn.Properties
10:        Response.Write objProp.Name & ": " & objProp.Value & "<BR>"
11:      Next
12:      objConn.Close
13:      Set objConn = Nothing
14: %>
15:    </BODY>
16: </HTML>
```

16

ANALYSIS This simply iterates through the Properties collection, using For Each...Next (line 9). For each property, line 10 prints out its name and value. Notice that we are careful to close and free the Connection object. It can be easy to forget to do because you did not create the Connection object in this file but rather in the include file DatabaseConnect.asp.

FIGURE **16.6**

Viewing the connection properties.

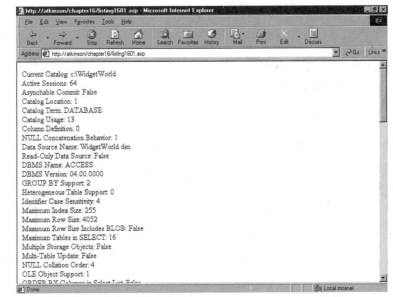

You can see in Figure 16.6 that there are many properties you can deal with. Odds are that you will never use more than a couple of these. Still, taking a look at this collection can give you an idea of what is back there, comprising this Connection object.

Reading Data from a Database

So now you know how to connect to a database. Aside from looking at all the properties, there is not much you can do with just the Connection object. To work with the data in the database, you will need another object. The Recordset object is another of ADO's objects.

The `Recordset` Object

Recall from earlier discussions that individual entries in a table are referred to as records. A recordset is, then, simply a set of records. The `Recordset` object may be used to contain a subset of the records in a table, or even all the records in the table. Often, you will use the `Recordset` object to hold a specially chosen set of records. For example, in a table containing information about users of your product, you might want to retrieve all the records pertaining to users in the Chicago area.

Today we will be retrieving the entire table. Day 18 talks about using `Filter` to filter out records you are not interested in. Day 19, "Using SQL Statements to Query Data," will also describe some ways of doing this.

First, you need to instantiate the `Recordset` object. Here is how you do it:

```
Dim objRS
Set objRS = Server.CreateObject ("ADODB.Recordset")
```

This should look familiar. Simply declare the variable that will hold the object and then use `Server.CreateObject`. The `Recordset` object is part of the ADODB package.

Creating the object instance does not fill it with any data. To do that, you need `Open`.

The `Open` Method

The `Recordset` object is filled with records by using the `Open` method. The `Open` method can accept many different sets of arguments and can be used in many different ways. Its general form is like this:

```
recordset.Open source, connection, cursortype, locktype, commandtype
```

source is either a `Command` object (discussed more on Day 20) or a string containing a recognized command.

connection is either a `Connection` object or a string containing the connection information. If the string is used, it must contain all the information that would go in the `ConnectionString` property of the `Connection` object.

cursortype indicates the way you want to move through the recordset. Its default value is the ADO constant `adOpenForwardOnly`, which is the most commonly used cursor type. This is what we will use today. `adOpenForwardOnly` indicates that you can only move forward through the recordset. The cursor type also controls how changes other users make to the table affect what you see. The cursor type is discussed in greater detail on Day 18.

locktype affects whether you can write to the table, and if so, how. Because several clients may be accessing the table at once, you need to be careful how you make changes to it. The default value of *locktype* is the ADO constant `adLockReadOnly`, which is what we will use today. This means that you can only read from the table, not write to it. Day 17 deals with writing and updating records, so when we get there we will need a new *locktype* that will allow writing to the table.

commandtype indicates how the *source* parameter should be evaluated. For the time being, we will use the ADO constant adCmdTable. This specifies that *source* should be evaluated as a table name.

For now we will omit the *cursortype* and *locktype* because the defaults suit our needs. In the days to come, though, these two options will become important.

Here is an example of a common use of the Open method:

```
objRS.Open "mytable", objConn, , , adCmdTable
```

Can you tell what this does? Notice first that the command type is specified as adCmdTable. This means that the source string should be evaluated as a table name. So if there is a table named "mytable" within the database indicated by the Connection object objConn, that table will be copied into the Recordset object objRS. The arguments for the cursor type and lock type are not specified. This means that you will only be able to move forward through objRS and that you can only read from the table.

Implicit Connections Using the Recordset Object

As you have probably noticed by now, ADO offers many ways to do the same thing. This gives you flexibility to write your code the way you want. On the other hand, you may have to read someone else's code sometimes and find it difficult to follow because it looks different.

One example of this is in the idea of implicit connections. It is not always necessary to explicitly create a Connection object to connect to a database. With the Recordset object and its Open method, you can obtain a connection to the database without creating a variable to hold a Connection object.

Here is how you do it:

```
Dim objRS
Set objRS = Server.CreateObject("ADODB.Recordset")
objRS.Open "mytable", strConnect, , , adCmdTable
```

This is all it takes. strConnect on the third line is a string containing the information that would go in the Connection object's ConnectionString. This way, you do not need objConn, or any variable to hold a Connection object. A connection to the database is still created; you just do not have any name to call it by. This is a bit of a shortcut some programmers take. In this book, we will explicitly create connections because we think it is easier to read and understand. If you are working on someone else's code, though, you might see implicit connections like this. For this reason, it is good to be aware of implicit connections.

Using `adovbs.inc`

We have been using several constants in our discussion of the `Recordset` object. These constants are not built in to ASP. You can either define them yourself whenever you need them, or you can include the `adovbs.inc` file, which contains definitions for all the ADO constants. It comes with IIS and PWS and is installed in `c:\Program Files\Common Files\System\ado\` by default. Copy it into your Web root directory and include it in any pages where you use the constants like this:

```
<!--#include virtual="/adovbs.inc"-->
```

Review Day 13's discussion of server-side includes if you need to.

If you cannot find your `adovbs.inc`, here are the definitions for the constants we will be using:

```
Const adOpenForwardOnly = 0
Const adLockOptimistic = 3
Const adLockPessimistic = 2
Const adLockReadOnly = 1
Const adCmdTable = 2
```

You could simply substitute these numbers where you need them and forget about using the constants altogether. This would not really be a good idea, though. For one thing, it decreases readability. Which of the following lines of code would be easier to figure out?

```
objRS.Open "tblUsers", objConn, 0, 1, 2
```

or

```
objRS.Open "tblUsers", objConn, adOpenForwardOnly, adLockReadOnly, adCmdTable
```

They may both be strange to you at this point, but you can probably see why the latter would be considered better. What's more, if you ever have to work with code written by someone else, they probably used the ADO constants. It is better to just go ahead and use them and become familiar with them.

METADATA as an Alternative to `adovbs.inc`

The METADATA tag may be used to import type-library constants into your pages. So as an alternative to including `adovbs.inc`, you could put the following at the top of your pages:

```
<!--METADATA TYPE="TypeLib"
FILE="C:\Program Files\Common Files\System\ado\msado15.dll" -->
```

`msado15.dll` is the ADO library file. It is put in the directory `C:\Program Files\Common Files\System\ado\` by default. Depending on what version of ADO you are using, the number may be different. Just do a Find on `msado*.dll`.

Using the METADATA tag like this in one of your pages will cause it to inherit the constants defined in the library file. You can also put this statement into your global.asa file, and the constants will be accessible in all your pages.

In this book, we will go ahead and include the adovbs.inc file. That is the most commonly used solution and is easy to do. If you decide to use the METADATA tag in your global.asa file, you will need to delete the <!--#include virtual="/adovbs.inc"--> line from any code examples in this book.

Reading and Displaying the Contents of a Database Table

Now you know how to open a recordset. The next topic is how to move through it and retrieve values from it. To do this, you will need a few more methods and properties of the Recordset object.

The Recordset object may contain several records, but you can only access one at a time. The Recordset object maintains a pointer to the current record, and you can move that pointer forward. If you have not set the recordset to forward-only movement, you can also move the pointer backward.

MoveNext advances to the next record in the recordset.

MovePrevious goes back to the previous record in the recordset. This is not valid if the recordset is set to forward-only movement.

MoveFirst is a method that moves to the first record in the recordset. MoveFirst may be used even if movement is set to forward-only movement, but it may result in re-executing the original Open method.

MoveLast goes directly to the last record in the recordset.

Move *number* goes to *number* records from the current one.

In today's examples, you will just be using MoveNext. You can see the rest of these used on Day 20.

Because trying to move to either after the last record or before the first one causes errors, you need some way of finding out whether you are at the beginning or end of the recordset. A pair of properties tells you this.

BOF is a Boolean value that is True while you are still at the beginning of the recordset.

EOF is a Boolean value that is set to True when you reach the end of the recordset.

Figure 16.7 illustrates the Recordset object. You can see in this picture a representation of the current record pointer and the BOF and EOF values.

FIGURE 16.7

A look at the Recordset *object and its properties.*

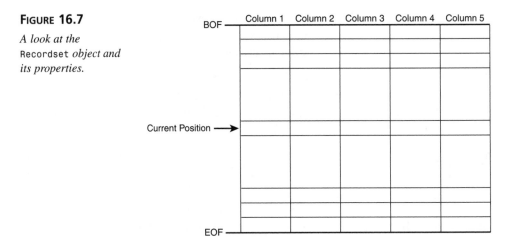

You access data from the current record like this:

RecordsetObjectName("*FieldName*")

This returns the value of the field specified by FieldName in the current row of the recordset. For example, suppose that you put the data listed in Table 16.2 into the expense report table and then retrieved the table into a recordset called objRS. Do not actually add this data to your table yet.

TABLE 16.2   Data for the Expense Report Table

EmployeeName	EmployeeNumber	ExpenseAmount	ExpenseReason
James Wright	115	$200	plane tickets
Cathy March	1192	$1200	new copier
Jane Rand	209	$50	new binders
James Wright	115	$40	motel room
Bob Roberts	598	$10	paper clips

So objRS("EmployeeNumber") will return 115, and objRS("ExpenseReason") will return "plane tickets".

If you call the MoveNext method, the current record becomes the second one. objRS("EmployeeNumber") will then return 1192.

If you call MoveNext twice more, the current record will be the fourth one, and objRS("EmployeeNumber") will return 115.

MoveNext one more time, and objRS("EmployeeNumber") will return 598. Now you are on the last record of the recordset. One more MoveNext will set EOF to True. After that, trying to continue to move forward will result in an error.

Now let's look at some complete code. Listing 16.2 prints out the records in the Widget World employee expenses table.

LISTING **16.2**   Printing the Contents of a Table

16

```
 1: <%@ Language=VBScript %>
 2: <% Option Explicit %>
 3: <!--#include file="DatabaseConnect.asp"-->
 4: <!--#include virtual="/adovbs.inc"-->
 5: <HTML>
 6:    <BODY>
 7: <%
 8:    Dim objRS
 9:    Set objRS = Server.CreateObject ("ADODB.Recordset")
10:    objRS.Open "tblExpenses", objConn, , , adCmdTable
11:    Do While Not objRS.EOF
12:       Response.Write "Name: " & objRS("EmployeeName")
13:       Response.Write " (" & objRS("EmployeeNumber") & ")<BR>"
14:       Response.Write "Amount requested: " & objRS("ExpenseAmount") & "<BR>"
15:       Response.Write "Reason for expense: " & objRS("ExpenseReason")
16:       Response.Write "<P><HR><P>"
17:       objRS.MoveNext
18:    Loop
19:    objRS.Close
20:    Set objRS = Nothing
21:    objConn.Close
22:    Set objConn = Nothing
23: %>
24:    </BODY>
25: </HTML>
```

ANALYSIS   Line 3 includes the file that establishes the connection to the database. Line 4 includes the file with the definitions of the ADO constants. Lines 8 and 9 create the Recordset object. Then you open it and fill it with the table tblExpenses. Because you omit any specified lock type or cursor type, the recordset will be opened read-only, with only forward movement allowed.

Line 11 enters a loop, which ends when you reach the end of the recordset. Lines 12 through 16 write out the data in the current record. Line 17 then moves forward to the next record in the set. If no more records are in the set, EOF will be set to True, and when line 18 takes you back up to line 11, the condition will fail, and the loop will terminate. If there are more records left, the loop will repeat and print out the next one. When finished, close the `Recordset` (line 19), set it to `Nothing` (line 20), close the connection (line 21), and set it to `Nothing` (line 22). Always do it in that order. Close before setting to `Nothing`, and take care of recordsets before the connection they are associated with.

So what do you see when you view the output of this page? Nothing? That is because the table is empty! At least you did not get an error message. Always be careful when writing your pages that an empty table does not cause your users to see an ugly error message, even if the table should never be empty. In other words, make sure that your scripts check whether there is something in the table before they try to access it. An `If...then...else` statement might be handy. Most often, a `Do...Loop` will be the best way to do things. Putting all the code that tries to access data in the table inside the loop, as we did in Listing 16.2, protects the user from these errors. If there is no data in the table, `EOF` will be True from the start and none of the code inside the loop is executed. This is the same way we dealt with the similar problem of empty text files in Day 13.

So let's put some data into the table. You will do this with Access today. On Day 17, you will learn how to write ASP pages that can add data to a table. Go ahead and enter the data from Table 16.2 now, and then try reloading the page. Your output should now look like Figure 16.8. Take a look at it and make sure that you understand what Listing 16.2 does.

FIGURE 16.8

Viewing the employee expenses table in an ASP page.

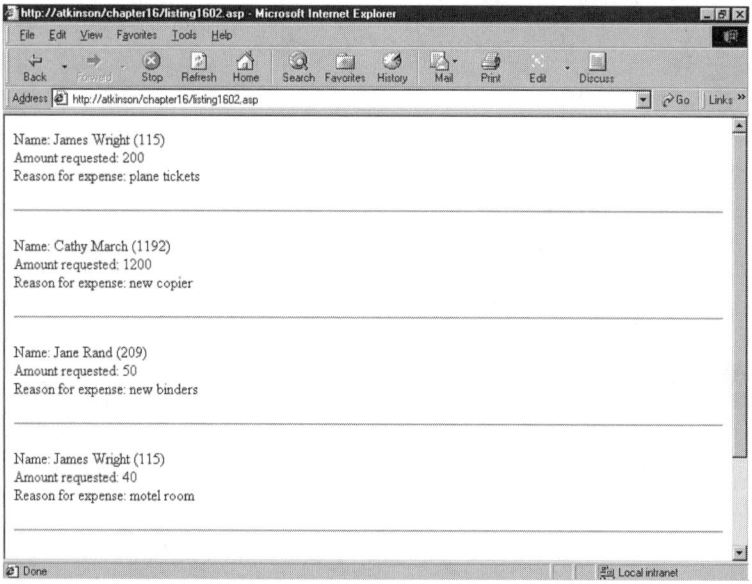

Now because these building blocks of databases are called tables, you might want to use the HTML table tags to display them. This is easily done. Listing 16.3 demonstrates how you might do it.

LISTING 16.3 Printing the Contents of a Table in an HTML Table

```
1:  <%@ Language=VBScript %>
2:  <% Option Explicit %>
3:  <!--#include file="DatabaseConnect.asp"-->
4:  <!--#include virtual="/adovbs.inc"-->
5:  <HTML>
6:    <BODY>
7:  <%
8:    Dim objRS
9:    Set objRS = Server.CreateObject ("ADODB.Recordset")
10:   objRS.Open "tblExpenses", objConn, , , adCmdTable
11: %>
12:   <TABLE border=1>
13:     <TR>
14:       <TD><B>Name</B></TD>
15:       <TD><B>Employee #</B></TD>
16:       <TD><B>Amount</B></TD>
17:       <TD><B>Reason</B></TD>
18:     </TR>
19: <%
20:   Do While Not objRS.EOF
21:     Response.Write "<TR><TD>" & objRS("EmployeeName") & "</TD>"
22:     Response.Write "<TD>" & objRS("EmployeeNumber") & "</TD>"
23:     Response.Write "<TD>" & objRS("ExpenseAmount") & "</TD>"
24:     Response.Write "<TD>" & objRS("ExpenseReason") & "</TD></TR>"
25:     objRS.MoveNext
26:   Loop
27:   objRS.Close
28:   Set objRS = Nothing
29:   objConn.Close
30:   Set objConn = Nothing
31: %>
32:   </TABLE>
33:   </BODY>
34: </HTML>
```

ANALYSIS Lines 3 and 4 include the files you need again. Lines 8 through 10 create the Recordset object and open it, the same as before. Lines 12 through 18 create the table and its top row. Then you put all the HTML tags needed for each subsequent row in the loop, with the values you want to output. If the table is empty, objRS.EOF will be True from the start, and the HTML table you create will consist of one row, listing the headings. Lines 27 through 30 handle all the clean-up, in the correct order.

Figure 16.9 shows the output of Listing 16.3. You can see from this how natural it is to use HTML tables to display database tables.

16

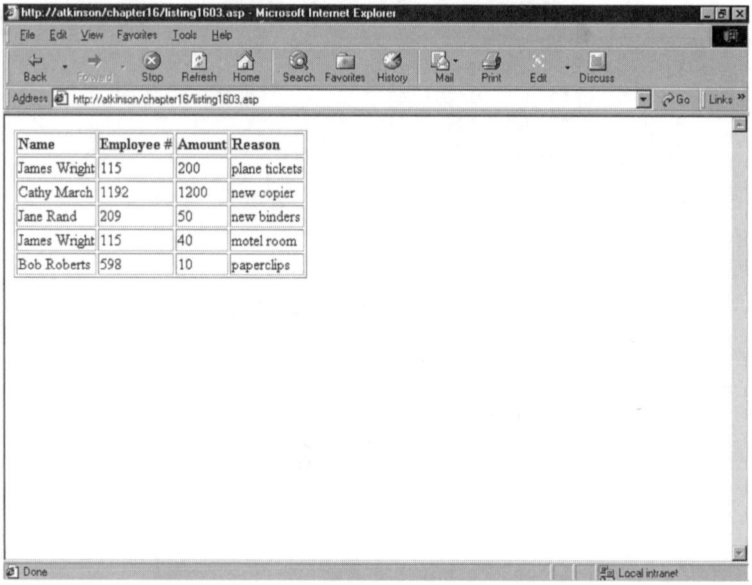

FIGURE 16.9

Viewing the employee expenses table in an ASP page, using HTML tables.

Let's look at one last example. Suppose that you want to offer your users some choices in a drop-down box. Each choice would have a text value that the user sees, plus a code used behind the scenes. In the past, you have probably written the choices into the HTML page. This works, but it is restricting. For one thing, if you use the choices in several pages, you have to keep remembering what choice each code referred to. Also, if you change a code or add a new one, you have to change several pages. If you use a database table to list the choices, though, you will gain a lot of flexibility.

For this example, you will create a drop-down box of shipping options. First, you need the database table you are going to use. Create a new table called tblShipping and make it part of the same Widget World database. It should have two fields. The first is an integer called ShippingCode and the second is a text field called Description.

Now go ahead and fill in the data shown in Table 16.3.

TABLE **16.3** Fields of the Shipping Table

ShippingCode	Description
1	US Postal
2	FedEx 2-Day
3	FedEx 1-Day
4	UPS

Listing 16.4 shows the code that will read in this table and put the options into a list box.

LISTING 16.4   Using a Table to Store Options for a List Box

```
 1: <%@ Language=VBScript %>
 2: <%  Option Explicit %>
 3: <!--#include file="DatabaseConnect.asp"-->
 4: <!--#include virtual="/adovbs.inc"-->
 5: <HTML>
 6:     <BODY>
 7:     <FORM ACTION="ProcessOrder.asp" METHOD=POST>
 8:         <SELECT NAME="ShippingChoice">
 9: <%
10:     Dim objRS
11:     Set objRS = Server.CreateObject ("ADODB.Recordset")
12:     objRS.Open "tblShipping", objConn, , , adCmdTable
13:     Do While Not objRS.EOF
14:        Response.Write "<OPTION VALUE='" & objRS("ShippingCode") &"'>"
15:        Response.Write objRS("Description")
16:        objRS.MoveNext
17:     Loop
18:     objRS.Close
19:     Set objRS = Nothing
20:     objConn.Close
21:     Set objConn = Nothing
22: %>
23:         </SELECT>
24:         <INPUT TYPE=SUBMIT VALUE="Submit">
25:     </FORM>
26:     </BODY>
27: </HTML>
```

16

ANALYSIS   Review Day 8, "Communicating with the User," if you do not remember how to create forms. Line 8 opens the select box. Lines 10 through 12 create and open the recordset. Line 13 iterates through the records in the recordset, creating a new <OPTION> tag for each. Lines 14 and 15 get the value from the record's shipping code and the text seen by the user from the record's description. Line 16 advances to the next record in the recordset. Lines 18 through 21 take care of closing and freeing memory. The list box, as the user will see it is shown in Figure 16.10.

We will not create the ProcessOrder.asp page specified on line 7. It requires topics that we have not yet covered. The important thing is that you can now pass just the integer code for the shipping choice wherever you need it. With the choices listed in Table 16.3, you do not have to worry about remembering from page to page what option 3 is.

When you want to associate values (such as integers with descriptions), it's good to use a database table. On really simple projects, it may not be worth the cost and trouble, but on something complex it is.

Figure 16.10

Using a database table to store list box values.

Testing for Empty Recordsets

In today's examples, we have been careful to protect users from ever encountering a database error message. This is important. The error messages that ASP and ADO generate are ugly. They are for programmers who are trying to debug. End-users should never see them.

One frequent cause of such error messages is trying to advance through an empty recordset. Doing so produces an error message like the one seen in Figure 16.11.

Even if the table in question should always contain at least one record, your pages should be written to make doubly sure that the user never sees a screen like this.

The examples so far today have resulted in blank screens and the like in cases of empty tables. This is better than error messages but still not good enough. The user should see a helpful, friendly message so that he knows what to do. This is not a difficult change to make.

```
1:  If objRS.EOF Then
2:      Response.Write "Sorry. No data found. If you believe this is in error, "
3:      Response.Write "please email the maintainer of this site "
4:      Response.Write "(youremail@whatever.com)"
5:  Else
6:       'put database operations here
7:  End If
```

FIGURE **16.11**

Error message from
trying to advance
through an empty
recordset.

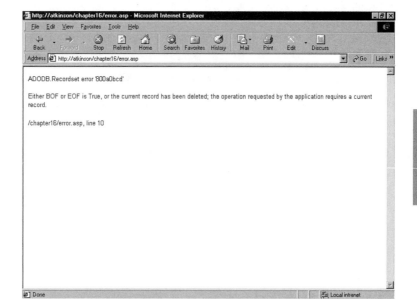

16

The best way to test whether a recordset is empty is to test the value of EOF immediately.
If you are already at the end of the recordset before you have even started going through
it, you know that it must be empty. If this is the case, an appropriate message is printed.
Otherwise, you are free to perform database operations, provided that you remain careful
to check EOF again after each MoveNext.

So let's implement this. Modify Listing 16.4 to display a nice, helpful message if the
table turns out to be empty. Listing 16.5 shows the modified version.

LISTING 16.5   Using EOF to Test for Empty Recordsets

```
1:    <%@ Language=VBScript %>
2:    <%  Option Explicit %>
3:    <!--#include file="DatabaseConnect.asp"-->
4:    <!--#include virtual="/adovbs.inc"-->
5:    <HTML>
6:        <BODY>
7:    <%
8:        Dim objRS
9:        Set objRS = Server.CreateObject ("ADODB.Recordset")
10:       objRS.Open "tblShipping", objConn, , , adCmdTable
11:       'if the record set is empty, display helpful message
12:       If objRS.EOF Then
13:    %>
14:       Sorry. No shipping options found. We will try to correct this
15:       error as soon as possible. Thanks for your patience.
```

continues

LISTING 16.5 continued

```
16:
17:  <%
18:      Else
19:      'if it is not empty, create our form and select box
20:  %>
21:      <FORM ACTION="ProcessOrder.asp" METHOD=POST>
22:        <SELECT NAME="ShippingChoice">
23:  <%
24:      Do While Not objRS.EOF
25:         Response.Write "<OPTION VALUE='" & objRS("ShippingCode") &"'>"
26:         Response.Write objRS("Description")
27:         objRS.MoveNext
28:      Loop
29:  %>
30:        </SELECT>
31:        <INPUT TYPE=SUBMIT VALUE="Submit">
32:      </FORM>
33:  <%
34:      End If
35:      objRS.Close
36:      Set objRS = Nothing
37:      objConn.Close
38:      Set objConn = Nothing
39:  %>
40:    </BODY>
41: </HTML>
```

ANALYSIS   Lines 3 and 4 continue to include the file with the database connectivity code, as we have throughout today's examples, as well as adovbs.inc. Lines 8 and 9 create the Recordset object as always, and line 10 opens it to contain the records in tblShipping. Line 12 tests to determine whether the recordset is empty. Because you have not yet done any MoveNexts, you should still be at the beginning of the recordset. If you are also at the end of it, it must be empty, and the message can be printed. If, on the other hand, you are not at the end of the recordset, it is not empty and you may proceed.

Some of the form and list box tags had to be moved so that they are all inside the Else case. Otherwise, though, the select box is created pretty much as before (lines 21 through 32). It is still important that you test EOF every time you advance the record. You know in this case that the recordset is not empty, but you could still try to go past the end of it if you are not careful.

Summary

Your pages have to go through several layers to access a data source such as a database. They use ActiveX Data Objects, which use OLEDB (which may be using the ODBC driver)—all this before you get to the actual database. Fortunately, you do not need to know too much about these middle layers.

The two ADO objects dealt with today were the Connection object and the Recordset object. The Connection object represents the connection to the database. You open it by setting the ConnectionString property and then using the Open method.

We discussed two ways to set the ConnectionString. The first is to create a System DSN. The connection information is nicely packaged on the server so that all you need to put in the connection string is "DSN=systemDSNname".

16

The alternative to the System DSN is the DSN-less connection. When you use a DSN-less connection, all the connection information has to be put in the connection string. For our purposes today, all we needed to specify was DRIVER and DBQ, which we do like this:

```
objConn.ConnectionString="DRIVER={Microsoft Access Driver (*.mdb)};" & _
                          "DBQ=C:\My Documents\myDatabase.mdb"
```

Whichever way you set the ConnectionString, to open the connection requires simply this:

```
objConn.Open
```

When you are finished with the connection, close it using the Close method and then use Set and Nothing to free its memory. Always be sure to do both, and in the correct order.

The connection would be useless without some way to get records from the database. Use the Recordset object for this. The recordset is created like this:

```
Dim objRS
Set objRS = Server.CreateObject ("ADODB.Recordset")
```

It may then be opened like this:

```
objRS.Open "mytable", objConn, , , adCmdTable
```

This puts the contents of the table mytable into the recordset objRS. Default values for the cursor type and lock type are used, which means that the recordset is read-only, and only forward movement is allowed.

There are several ways to move through a recordset, but for now we have concerned ourselves with only one: MoveNext, which simply advances to the next record.

Trying to move past the end of the recordset results in an error. To avoid this, use EOF. objectname.EOF is set to True when you run out of records. You can check EOF in Do While loops and If...Then statements to avoid going past the end of the recordset. If EOF is True at the beginning of a page, before you have performed any MoveNexts, you know that the recordset is empty.

When you are finished with a `Recordset` object, be sure to `Close` it and `Set` it to `Nothing`. Make sure that you do this before you `Close` the connection.

Q&A

Q Which is faster: System DSN or DSN-less connections?

A It is tough to say for sure which way is faster. Microsoft's performance tips page says using a System DSN is faster. Other sources disagree. Recent testing seems to indicate, though, that DSN-less connections are actually slightly better.

Q How can I improve performance when connecting to an Access database?

A The connections in this Day go through the OLEDB ODBC driver. If you are using a recent enough version of ADO, you can use a direct OLEDB connection instead. We mentioned this earlier in the Day, but if you want more information, it is available on the Web.

```
http://www.4guysfromrolla.com/webtech/063099-1.shtml
```

Direct OLEDB connections like this are more efficient for pages that will be making heavy accesses to a database.

Workshop

The Workshop provides quiz questions to help you solidify your understanding of the material covered and exercises to provide you with experience in using what you've learned. Try to understand the quiz and exercise answers before continuing to tomorrow's lesson. Quiz answers are provided in Appendix A, and exercise answers can be found at `http://www.mcp.com/info`.

Quiz

1. What does the `Connection` object do?
2. What does the `ConnectionString` property do?
3. What is a System DSN?
4. How are DSN-less connections tricky?
5. What does the `Recordset` object do?
6. What does including `adovbs.inc` do?
7. What is the alternative to including `adovbs.inc`?
8. How can you keep from moving beyond the end of a recordset?
9. How do you access a field value in the current record?

Exercises

1. Suppose that the Recordset object objRS has the following data in it:

ProductName	ModelNumber	Price
Standard Widget	A-195	$14.99
Widget Plus	T-1105	$21.95
Micro Widget	A-102	$9.99
Widget Deluxe	A-119C	$29.95

What will be the output of the following code?

```
objRS.MoveNext
Response.Write objRS("ModelNumber")
Response.Write "<BR>"
Response.Write objRS("Price")
Response.Write "<BR>"
objRS.MoveNext
Response.Write objRS.EOF
Response.Write "<BR>"
Response.Write objRS("ProductName")
Response.Write "<BR>"
objRS.MoveNext
objRS.MoveNext
Response.Write objRS.EOF
```

2. Create a new access database called JoesWidgets.mdb. Create a file called JoeConnect.asp that will open a connection to the new database. You may use a System DSN connection or a DSN-less connection, whichever you prefer.

3. Add a new table to the database called tblEmployees. It should have the following fields:

Field Name	Data Type
Name	Text
IDNumber	Number
Salary	Currency
BeganWorking	Date/Time

Write an ASP page to open the table and display at most five records. You should include the file you created in Exercise 2. Test it first with the table empty and then add at least six entries and test it again.

DAY 17

Inserting, Updating, and Deleting Database Records

Merely reading from a database is limiting. The real power of data-driven Web sites comes from the capability to add and change data in your pages. This might include allowing users to register on the site, make purchases, fill out surveys, and submit feedback. You can also use this capability to make administrative pages so that you can add or change content over the Web. Today, you will learn the following:

- How to insert new records into a database
- How to modify existing records
- How to delete existing records
- How to cancel changes made to records

While discussing these topics, we will create a system to allow users to register on a site, log on, and change options. For this, we will need a new table, called `tblUsers`. This table should have the following fields: `FirstName`, `LastName`, `Email`, `Username`, and `Password`. All of these should be text fields. It is up to you whether you want to create a new database with this table in it, or put it in your Widget World database from yesterday. If you create a new database, you will need to change your `DatabaseConnect.asp` file to open the appropriate connection.

Inserting Records

Being able to add data to the database is crucial in most data-driven sites. Registering new users, recording purchases, adding content and more hinges on this capability.

Lock Types

We talked briefly about the different types of locking yesterday. We did not talk about why locking is necessary, though. When you make a database accessible over the Web, you may have hundreds or thousands of people accessing it at once. This is fine as long as they are just reading. What do you think would happen, though, if two people tried to change the same record at the same time? This could cause all kinds of problems. To prevent this, the first person who tries to change the record puts a "lock" on it. While the lock is on, nobody else can change the record. As soon as the user is finished, the lock is removed.

Yesterday, you were simply reading from the database. Because you did not need to make any changes, you opened the recordset read-only. There is no point in putting locks on any records if you are not going to make any changes. Today, though, you need writing access. This means that the lock type used yesterday, `adLockReadOnly`, will not suffice. There are a few different types of locking that you can use. The difference between them has to do with when the lock is put on. The constant you will use for now is `adLockOptimistic`, which has a value of 3.

> **Note**　Optimistic locking means that records are locked by the provider when `Update` is called (see the next section, "`AddNew` and `Update`"). There will be further discussion of locking types on Day 20, "Using Advanced Database Techniques."

AddNew and Update

There are two methods of the `Recordset` object that you will need to make changes to the database: `AddNew` and `Update`. `AddNew` creates a new record in the recordset. The new record is not added to the database until the `Update` method is called. After `AddNew` is called, the new record becomes the current record, and it remains the current record even after `Update` is called.

Here is how you might use AddNew and Update. Assume that the recordset objRS has been correctly opened:

```
objRS.AddNew
objRS("Name") = "Bill"
objRS("Email") = "whois@nothing.net"
objRS.Update
```

AddNew creates the new, empty record and sets it as the current record. You can then assign values to the fields easily. When you are finished setting the values, add the record to the database table using Update.

If you call AddNew while you are in the middle of editing a record, Update will be called automatically. So the following has the effect of creating one new record, adding it to the table, creating a second new record, and adding it to the table:

```
objRS.AddNew
objRS("Name") = "Bill"
objRS("Email") = "whois@nothing.net"
objRS.AddNew
objRS("Name") = "Jim"
objRS("Email") = "jl@nothing.net"
objRS.Update
```

This hurts the readability of the code a little, so it is not recommended.

As an alternative to using the assignment operator to set field values, you can initialize the values of the fields using AddNew. The syntax is as follows:

```
objRS.AddNew fields, values
```

fields and *values* are either single values or arrays with the same number of elements.

So for example, calling objRS.AddNew "Name", "John" creates a new record with a value of "John" in the "Name" field. Or, you could call AddNew like this:

```
objRS.AddNew Array("Name", "Email"), Array("Joe", "jm@whatever.com")
```

In today's code examples, we will set the values of fields using the assignment operator, rather than within the call to AddNew. It's a little easier to read this way.

Listing 17.1 demonstrates the use of AddNew and Update. It adds a new record to the table and then prints out the contents of the table. This allows you to verify that the record was successfully added.

LISTING 17.1   Adding a Record Using AddNew and Update

```
1:   <%@ Language=VBScript %>
2:   <% Option Explicit %>
```

continues

LISTING 17.1 continued

```
3:   <!--#include virtual="/adovbs.inc"-->
4:   <!--#include file="DatabaseConnect.asp"-->
5:   <HTML>
6:     <BODY>
7:   <%
8:     Dim objRS
9:     Set objRS = Server.CreateObject("ADODB.Recordset")
10:    objRS.Open "tblUsers", objConn, , adLockOptimistic, adCmdTable
11:    objRS.AddNew
12:    objRS("FirstName") = "Gene"
13:    objRS("LastName") = "Williams"
14:    objRS("Email") = "blank@blah.net"
15:    objRS("Username") = "ww123"
16:    objRS("Password") = "pass"
17:    objRS.Update
18:    objRS.MoveFirst
19:  %>
20:    <B>Entries in table</B>
21:    <P>
22:    <TABLE>
23:    <TR>
24:        <TD>Name</TD>
25:        <TD>Email</TD>
26:        <TD>Username</TD>
27:    </TR>
28:  <% Do While Not objRS.EOF %>
29:      <TR>
30:        <TD><%=objRS("LastName") %>, <%=objRS("FirstName") %></TD>
31:        <TD><%=objRS("Email") %></TD>
32:        <TD><%=objRS("Username") %></TD>
33:      </TR>
34:  <%
35:      objRS.MoveNext
36:    Loop
37:    objRS.Close
38:    Set objRS = Nothing
39:    objConn.Close
40:    Set objConn = Nothing
41:  %>
42:    </TABLE>
43:    </BODY>
44:  </HTML>
```

ANALYSIS Line 3 includes the ADOVBS.inc file that contains the constants you need. Line 4 includes the file you created earlier that connects to the database. Lines 8 through 10 create and open the Recordset object you will use. Notice that lock type is specified. As discussed earlier, if you will be making changes to the recordset, you cannot use the default lock type. Line 10 specifies optimistic locking.

Now you can begin adding the new record. Line 11 invokes `AddNew`, which creates a new, empty record. Lines 12 through 16 set all the field values. Finally, line 17 saves the new record to the table using `Update`.

Now you want to verify that the record was successfully added, so have the page print out the contents of the table. Line 18 resets the cursor to the beginning of the recordset using `MoveFirst`. Then you begin moving through the recordset and displaying its contents the same way you did yesterday.

The results of viewing Listing 17.1 can be seen in Figure 17.1. You can see the record that was just added listed.

FIGURE 17.1

The results of Listing 17.1.

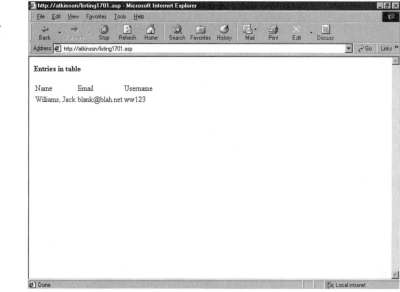

This is, of course, not a terribly useful page. The information you add to the table is coded into the ASP. More often, you would want to be able to read in data from a form and add it to the database. This is what the next example does.

You want to create a page for your users to register. This is a two-page process. The first page has the form that the user enters his information into. The form then passes that information onto the second page, which enters the information into the database.

The first page is just an HTML page with a form, as shown in Listing 17.2. Save this as `register.html`.

LISTING 17.2   Form to Collect Data for the Table

```
1:    <HTML>
2:      <HEAD><TITLE>Register</TITLE></HEAD>
3:      <BODY>
4:        <FORM METHOD=POST ACTION="RegisterUser.asp">
5:          <TABLE>
6:            <TR>
7:              <TD align=right>First name:</TD>
8:              <TD align=left><INPUT TYPE=TEXT NAME="firstname"></TD>
9:            </TR>
10:           <TR>
11:             <TD align=right>Last name:</TD>
12:             <TD align=left><INPUT TYPE=TEXT NAME="lastname"></TD>
13:           </TR>
14:           <TR>
15:             <TD align=right>Email:</TD>
16:             <TD align=left><INPUT TYPE=TEXT NAME="email"></TD>
17:           </TR>
18:           <TR>
19:             <TD align=right>Username:</TD>
20:             <TD align=left><INPUT TYPE=TEXT NAME="username"></TD>
21:           </TR>
22:           <TR>
23:             <TD align=right>Password:</TD>
24:             <TD align=left><INPUT TYPE=PASSWORD NAME="password"></TD>
25:           </TR>
26:         </TABLE>
27:         <INPUT TYPE=RESET> <INPUT TYPE=SUBMIT>
28:       </FORM>
29:     </BODY>
30:   </HTML>
```

ANALYSIS   This creates a form with five input fields—all text boxes. When the user clicks the submit button, the data will be sent to the page `RegisterUser.asp` (see line 4). The form, with some sample input, is shown in Figure 17.2.

Listing 17.3 is the page that actually adds the user to the database. Save it as `RegisterUser.asp`.

LISTING 17.3   Adding the User to the Table

```
1:   <%@ Language=VBScript %>
2:   <%  Option Explicit %>
3:   <!--#include virtual="/adovbs.inc"-->
4:   <!--#include file="DatabaseConnect.asp"-->
5:   <%
6:     Dim objRS
7:     Set objRS = Server.CreateObject("ADODB.Recordset")
8:     objRS.Open "tblUsers", objConn, , adLockOptimistic, adCmdTable
```

```
 9:    objRS.AddNew
10:    objRS("FirstName") = Request.Form("firstname")
11:    objRS("LastName") = Request.Form("lastname")
12:    objRS("Email") = Request.Form("email")
13:    objRS("Username") = Request.Form("username")
14:    objRS("Password") = Request.Form("password")
15:    objRS.Update
16:    objRS.Close
17:    Set objRS = Nothing
18:    objConn.Close
19:    Set objConn = Nothing
20: %>
21: <HTML>
22:    <BODY>
23:    Thank you for registering.
24:    </BODY>
25: </HTML>
```

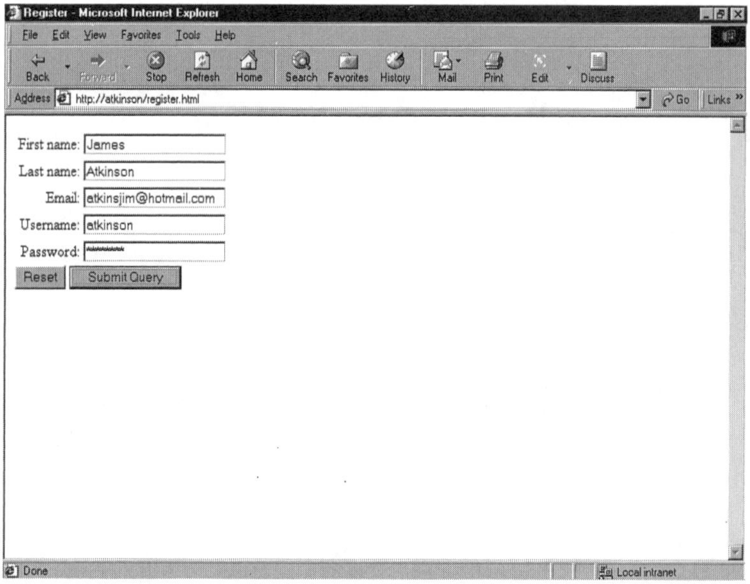

17

FIGURE 17.2

*Viewing the registra-
tion form.*

ANALYSIS Line 3 includes the file DatabaseConnect.asp. This opens a connection to the
database. Lines 5 and 6 create a Recordset object. Line 7 then opens it. Notice the
lock type and cursor type arguments that are specified. Line 9 creates a new, empty
record in the recordset. It is filled with data collected from the form in lines 10 through
14 and line 15 saves the new record to the database table. Now that you are finished with
the database work for this page, close (line 16) and set to nothing (line 17) the
Recordset object and then the connection (lines 18 and 19). Finish with a message
telling the user that he has been registered (line 23).

You can do much to improve these pages. Adding JavaScript to the first page to check
some of the form data before it is submitted would be a good idea. Client-side form validation is briefly discussed on Day 8, "Communicating with the User." If you want to
learn more about it, many Web sites discuss it and provide code examples. You might
also look for the book *Sams Teach Yourself JavaScript 1.3 in 24 Hours.*

You can make improvements using ASP. Right now, if someone tried calling the page
directly without going through the first page, she would create blank rows in your table.
Also, there is nothing to prevent several users from using the same username or one user
from accidentally registering multiple times. Listing 17.4 fixes these problems.

LISTING 17.4   Improving `RegisterUser.asp`

```
1:    <%@ Language=VBScript %>
2:    <%  Option Explicit %>
3:    <!--#include virtual="/adovbs.inc"-->
4:    <!--#include file="DatabaseConnect.asp"-->
5:    <HTML>
6:      <BODY>
7:    <%
8:      Dim objRS, bolAlreadyExists
9:      If ((Request.Form("username") = "") OR (Request.Form("password") = "") _
10:       OR (Request.Form("email") = "") OR (Request.Form("firstname") = "") _
11:       OR (Request.Form("lastname") = "")) Then
12:       Response.Write "<A HREF='register.html'>"
13:       Response.Write "You must enter values for all the fields."
14:       Response.Write "</A>"
15:      Else
16:       bolAlreadyExists = False
17:       Set objRS = Server.CreateObject("ADODB.Recordset")
18:       objRS.Open "tblUsers", objConn, , adLockOptimistic, adCmdTable
19:       Do While Not (objRS.EOF OR bolAlreadyExists)
20:        If (StrComp(objRS("Username"), Request.Form("username"), _
21:             vbTextCompare) = 0) Then
22:         Response.Write "<A HREF='register.html'>"
23:         Response.Write "Username already exists."
24:         Response.Write "</A>"
25:         bolAlreadyExists = True
26:        End If
27:        If (StrComp(objRS("Email"), Request.Form("email"), _
28:             vbTextCompare) = 0) Then
29:         Response.Write "<A HREF='register.html'>"
30:         Response.Write "Email address already found in table."
31:         Response.Write "</A>"
32:         bolAlreadyExists = True
33:        End If
34:        objRS.MoveNext
35:       Loop
36:       If Not bolAlreadyExists Then
```

```
37:            objRS.AddNew
38:            objRS("FirstName") = Request.Form("firstname")
39:            objRS("LastName") = Request.Form("lastname")
40:            objRS("Email") = Request.Form("email")
41:            objRS("Username") = Request.Form("username")
42:            objRS("Password") = Request.Form("password")
43:            objRS.Update
44:            Response.Write "Thank you for registering."
45:        End If
46:        objRS.Close
47:        Set objRS = Nothing
48:    End If
49:    objConn.Close
50:    Set objConn = Nothing
51: %>
52:    </BODY>
53: </HTML>
```

17

ANALYSIS   Lines 9 through 11 check to make sure that all the fields have specified values. If not, a message describing the problem is printed and a link back to the form is provided (lines 12 through 14). This prevents incomplete rows from being added to the table. If all the values are there, you may proceed.

Lines 17 and 18 open the recordset. Lines 19 through 35 then iterate through the recordset. Lines 20 and 21 check to see whether the current record's username is the same as the username entered in the form. If they are the same, a message is printed along with a link back to the registration page (lines 22 through 24).

Lines 27 and 28 check to see whether the current record's email address is the same as the one entered into the form. If so, a message and link to the registration pages are again printed (lines 29 through 31). This means that there may only be one registration per email address.

If either the username or the email address is found in the table, the Boolean variable bolAlreadyExists is set to True (lines 25 and 32). When either this happens or the end of the recordset is reached, the loop terminates. Then, if bolAlreadyExists is False (that is, the username and email address were not found in the recordset), AddNew is called, the field values are set, and Update is called (lines 37 through 43).

Notice that you only close the Recordset object if the request fields are all nonempty. This is because you only opened it in that case (see lines 17 and 18). The Connection object needs to be closed in any case because it was opened in the include file.

This modified version of the page will make sure that values for all the fields have been specified. This means that if someone accesses the second page directly, rather than going through register.html, no empty rows are created. Further, the record is not added to the table unless every field is specified. Even then, it is not added unless both the username and the email address are unique. It is important to take care of every circumstance when you are writing to databases. Even something that does not happen often can, over time, lead to serious clutter.

There are some easier and better ways to solve the problems we have been discussing. Day 19, "Using SQL Statements to Query Data," talks about SQL, which can simplify checking for a particular field value in a table. Again, it is worthwhile for you to learn about client-side form validation if you plan to use many forms. This allows you to perform a more rigorous check of the data entered into a form without putting added strain on your system. Also, in Access, you can set field values as required. This provides a "last line of defense" against users trying to add blank data to the table.

Canceling Changes

If you make changes to a record that you do not want saved to the database, you may call the CancelUpdate method. This only works if Update has not yet been called.

```
objRS.AddNew
objRS("username") = "Fred"
objRS.CancelUpdate
```

CancelUpdate here has the effect of undoing the preceding two lines.

```
objRS.AddNew
objRS("username") = "Fred"
objRS.Update
objRS.CancelUpdate
```

Here, however, CancelUpdate has no effect because the changes have already been saved to the database table.

Updating Records

You may also use the Update method to make changes to existing records. Instead of calling AddNew, move to the record you want to change. Set the field values with the assignment operator as in the previous section. When you are finished, call the Update method:

```
objRS("username") = "Fred"
objRS("email") = "fr2@whatever.net"
objRS.Update
```

The first two lines change the values of the username and email fields of the current record. Then, calling Update saves those changes to the database.

CancelUpdate works on changes made to existing records, too:

```
objRS("username") = "Fred"
objRS("email") = "fr2@whatever.net"
objRS.CancelUpdate
```

CancelUpdate here undoes the preceding two lines. Normally, you would not use CancelUpdate like this. What you might do, though, would be to use CancelUpdate along with an If...Then statement to handle some special circumstances, like this:

```
objRS("password") = Request("Pass")
objRS("email") = Request("Email")
If objRS("password") = "" then
   objRS.CancelUpdate
Else
   objRS.Update
End if
```

This will cancel the changes made to the record if the password is an empty string. Otherwise, the changes are saved using Update.

Let's get to an example of modifying existing records. Listing 17.5 prints the contents of the table, changes the first record, and prints the new contents of the table.

17

LISTING 17.5 Modifying Existing Records

```
1:  <%@ Language=VBScript %>
2:  <%  Option Explicit %>
3:  <!--#include virtual="/adovbs.inc"-->
4:  <!--#include file="DatabaseConnect.asp"-->
5:  <HTML>
6:    <BODY>
7:  <%
8:    Dim objRS
9:    Set objRS = Server.CreateObject("ADODB.Recordset")
10:   objRS.Open "tblUsers", objConn, , adLockOptimistic, adCmdTable
11: %>
12:   <B>Entries in table</B>
13:   <P>
14:   <TABLE>
15:   <TR>
16:       <TD>Name</TD>
17:       <TD>Email</TD>
18:       <TD>Username</TD>
19:   </TR>
20: <% Do While Not objRS.EOF %>
21:       <TR>
22:        <TD><%=objRS("LastName") %>, <%=objRS("FirstName") %></TD>
23:        <TD><%=objRS("Email") %></TD>
24:        <TD><%=objRS("Username") %></TD>
25:       </TR>
26: <%
27:       objRS.MoveNext
28:   Loop
29:   objRS.MoveFirst
30:   objRS("FirstName") = "Jack"
```

continues

LISTING 17.5 continued

```
31:    objRS("LastName") = "Miller"
32:    objRS("Email") = "blank@nobody.net"
33:    objRS("Username") = "jm33"
34:    objRS("Password") = "aaa"
35:    objRS.Update
36:    objRS.MoveFirst
37: %>
38:    </TABLE>
39:    <P>
40:    <TABLE>
41: <% Do While Not objRS.EOF %>
42:      <TR>
43:        <TD><%=objRS("LastName") %>, <%=objRS("FirstName") %></TD>
44:        <TD><%=objRS("Email") %></TD>
45:        <TD><%=objRS("Username") %></TD>
46:      </TR>
47: <%
48:      objRS.MoveNext
49:    Loop
50:    objRS.Close
51:    Set objRS = Nothing
52:    objConn.Close
53:    Set objConn = Nothing
54: %>
55:    </TABLE>
56:    </BODY>
57: </HTML>
```

ANALYSIS   Lines 12 through 28 display the entries of the recordset in an HTML table. This is done the same way as in Listing 17.1. Line 29 resets the cursor to the first record. Then lines 30 through 34 set new values for the record's fields. Calling Update on line 35 saves the changes to the database. The cursor is reset to the beginning once more on line 36. Lines 38 through 40 close the first HTML table and begin a second, which displays the new values in the recordset. The second table is created the same as the first, with a loop through the recordset.

Take a look at figure 17.3. This shows the results of viewing this page, assuming that the data in figure 17.2 has been added. You can see that the first record, with Jack Williams, has been changed to Jack Miller. The second record has not been changed.

Of course, this is not too realistic. In addition to the fact that the new values are coded into the page, this script will always modify the first record. In real situations, you will want to modify a specific record, and you must find it first.

Let's return to the user registration system. Suppose that now you want to allow the user to change the values set when she registered. This will be a three-page system. The first page is a simple HTML form where the user enters her username and password. The next page brings up the user's record and allows the user to change any of the values except the username. The username must remain constant so that you can identify the user. Finally, the third page saves the changes to the database. The first page is shown in Listing 17.6. Save it as `login.html`.

FIGURE 17.3

Viewing the results of Listing 17.5.

LISTING 17.6 User Login Page

```
1:  <HTML>
2:   <HEAD><TITLE>Log in</TITLE></HEAD>
3:   <BODY>
4:    <FORM METHOD=POST ACTION="EditUser.asp">
5:     Username: <INPUT TYPE=TEXT NAME="username">
6:     <P>
7:     Password: <INPUT TYPE=PASSWORD NAME="password">
8:     <P>
9:     <INPUT TYPE=RESET> <INPUT TYPE=SUBMIT>
10:   </FORM>
11:  </BODY>
12: </HTML>
```

ANALYSIS This is an HTML page with a simple form. It has only two input fields, one for the user's name and one for their password. When submit is clicked, the page `EditUser.asp` is loaded.

EditUser.asp is shown in listing 17.7. This page populates a form with the user's current data. They can now change any values they want, and leave the rest alone.

LISTING 17.7   Change User Settings Page

```
 1:  <%@ Language=VBScript %>
 2:  <% Option Explicit %>
 3:  <HTML>
 4:    <BODY>
 5:  <!--#include virtual="/adovbs.inc"-->
 6:  <!--#include file="DatabaseConnect.asp"-->
 7:  <%
 8:  Dim objRS, bolFound, strUsername
 9:    strUsername = Request.Form("username")
10:
11:    'make sure username was entered
12:    If strUsername = "" Then
13:       objConn.Close
14:       Set objConn = Nothing
15:       Response.Write "<A HREF='login.html'>"
16:       Response.Write "You must enter a username"
17:       Response.Write "</A>"
18:       Response.End
19:    End If
20:
21:    Set objRS = Server.CreateObject("ADODB.Recordset")
22:    objRS.Open "tblUsers", objConn, , , adCmdTable
23:    bolFound = False
24:
25:    'look for username in table
26:    Do While Not (objRS.EOF OR bolFound)
27:       If (StrComp(objRS("Username"), strUsername, vbTextCompare) = 0) Then
28:          BolFound = True
29:       Else
30:          objRS.MoveNext
31:       End If
32:    Loop
33:
34:    'if username is not found, display message
35:    If Not bolFound Then
36:       objRS.Close
37:       Set objRS = Nothing
38:       objConn.Close
39:       Set objConn = Nothing
40:       Response.Write "<A HREF='login.html'>"
41:       Response.Write "Invalid Username.<P>"
42:       Response.Write "</A>"
43:       Response.End
44:    End If
45:
46:    'if passwords do not match, display message
47:    If Not (StrComp(objRS("Password"), Request.Form("password"), _
```

```
48:                        vbBinaryCompare) = 0) Then
49:          objRS.Close
50:          Set objRS = Nothing
51:          objConn.Close
52:          Set objConn = Nothing
53:          Response.Write "<A HREF='login.html'>"
54:          Response.Write "Invalid password.<P>"
55:          Response.Write "</A>"
56:          Response.End
57:       End If
58: %>
59:    <!-- create form, fill with values from table -->
60:    <FORM METHOD=POST ACTION="ModifyUser.asp">
61:       First name: <INPUT TYPE=TEXT NAME="firstname"
62:                   VALUE="<%=objRS("FirstName") %>">
63:       <P>
64:       Last name: <INPUT TYPE=TEXT NAME="lastname"
65:                   VALUE="<%=objRS("LastName") %>">
66:       <P>
67:       Email: <INPUT TYPE=TEXT NAME="email" VALUE="<%=objRS("Email") %>">
68:       <P>
69:       Username: <%=objRS("Username") %>
70:       <INPUT TYPE=HIDDEN NAME="username" VALUE="<%= objRS("Username") %>">
71:       <P>
72:       Password: <INPUT TYPE=PASSWORD NAME="password"
73:                   VALUE="<%= objRS("Password") %>">
74:       <P>
75:       <INPUT TYPE=RESET> <INPUT TYPE=SUBMIT>
76:    </FORM>
77:    </BODY>
78: </HTML>
79: <%
80:    objRS.Close
81:    Set objRS = Nothing
82:    objConn.Close
83:    Set objConn = Nothing
84: %>
```

ANALYSIS   After the usual headers and include files, line 9 retrieves the username from the form. If it is empty, as might happen if this page were called directly, you do not go any further. The connection is closed, and a message of explanation is displayed with a link back to the login page (lines 12 through 17). Response.End is then called to make sure that the rest of the page does not execute.

If a username was entered, line 22 opens the recordset. Notice that this time the default lock type will suffice. The only thing you will be doing with the recordset is reading from it. Retrieve the password to make sure that it matches the one the user entered. If so, the form is filled with the user's data. The third page is the only one that actually needs to write to the database.

A Boolean variable is used to determine when, and if, you have found the username in the recordset. Line 23 initializes it to False. Then lines 26 through 32 iterate through the recordset, comparing each username with the one in strUsername until you find a match or reach the end of the recordset.

If, after the loop is over bolFound is still False, you never found the username in the recordset. In this case, lines 36 through 43 close the Recordset and Connection objects, display an appropriate message, and stop executing the page.

If the username is found, lines 47 and 48 compare the password entered by the user with the one found in the database. If they do not match, lines 49 through 56 close the objects, display an appropriate message, and stop executing the page .

The remainder of the page is only executed if the username is found in the database and the passwords match. That is, it is only executed if we were able to correctly log in the user. A form is created with text box inputs for the first name, last name, email address, and password. Each of these is filled-in with the values already in the database. This way, the user can see the settings and only have to type in the ones to change.

Lines 69 and 70 display the username but do not allow it to be changed. Instead of putting it into a text box, you pass it on to the next page using a hidden form input that the user cannot change.

The third page of the record updating system is in Listing 17.8. Save it as ModifyUser.asp.

LISTING 17.8   Actually Making the Changes to the Database

```
1:    <%@ Language=VBScript %>
2:    <% Option Explicit %>
3:    <HTML>
4:       <BODY>
5:    <!--#include virtual="/adovbs.inc"-->
6:    <!--#include file="DatabaseConnect.asp"-->
7:    <%
8:       Dim objRS, bolFound, strUsername
9:       strUsername = Request.Form("username")
10:
11:      'make sure all the data was entered
12:      If ((Request.Form("username") = "") OR (Request.Form("password") = "") _
13:         OR (Request.Form("email") = "") OR (Request.Form("firstname") = "") _
14:         OR (Request.Form("lastname") = "")) Then
15:         objConn.Close
16:         Set objConn = Nothing
17:   %>
18:         You must enter values for all the fields. Either hit the "back"
19:         button or click <A HREF="login.html">here to log in</A>
20:   <%
```

```
21:    Else
22:        Set objRS = Server.CreateObject("ADODB.Recordset")
23:        objRS.Open "tblUsers", objConn, , adLockOptimistic, adCmdTable
24:        bolFound = False
25:
26:        'try to find user's entry in table
27:        Do Until objRS.EOF OR bolFound
28:            If (StrComp(objRS("Username"), strUsername, _
29:                                    vbTextCompare) = 0) Then
30:                'found it
31:                BolFound = True
32:            Else
33:                objRS.MoveNext
34:            End If
35:        Loop
36:
37:        'if username not found, display message
38:        If Not bolFound Then
39:            objRS.Close
40:            Set objRS = Nothing
41:            objConn.Close
42:            Set objConn = Nothing
43:            Response.Write "<A HREF='login.html'>"
44:            Response.Write "Invalid Username.<P>"
45:            Response.Write "</A>"
46:            Response.End
47:        End If
48:
49:        objRS("FirstName") = Request.Form("firstname")
50:        objRS("LastName") = Request.Form("lastname")
51:        objRS("Email") = Request.Form("email")
52:        objRS("Password") = Request.Form("password")
53:        objRS.Update
54:        objRS.Close
55:        Set objRS = Nothing
56:    End If
57:    objConn.Close
58:    Set objConn = Nothing
59:    %>
60:    Changes made successfully.
61:    </BODY>
62:    </HTML>
```

ANALYSIS This page contains some of the same things as the other examples from earlier today. Lines 12 through 14 check to make sure that values for all the fields were specified. If not, the message on lines 18 and 19 is displayed, and the Connection object is closed (lines 15 and 16).

If all the fields have values, you may proceed. Line 23 opens the recordset, this time for writing with optimistic locking. Lines 27 through 35 then look for the record with the matching username, just as in Listing 17.7.

Lines 38 through 47 handle the case where the username is not found in the table. This would happen only in rare circumstances (such as another user is modifying the same record at the same time). Nevertheless, it is a case that must be dealt with. This is done the same as in Listing 17.7.

The rest of the page only executes if the username is found in the table correctly. The current record is the one that matches the username. The other fields are set in lines 49 through 52. Some of these may still be the same values as they originally had. It makes no difference. The call to Update on line 53 saves the changes to the database.

Deleting Records

The Delete method of the Recordset object allows for easy deletion of records. Delete deletes the current record and is called like this:

```
objRS.Delete
```

Listing 17.9 demonstrates how to use Delete. This page displays the table, deletes the first record, and displays the new table.

LISTING 17.9   Deleting Records

```
 1:  <%@ Language=VBScript %>
 2:  <% Option Explicit %>
 3:  <!--#include virtual="/adovbs.inc"-->
 4:  <!--#include file="DatabaseConnect.asp"-->
 5:  <HTML>
 6:    <BODY>
 7:  <%
 8:    Dim objRS
 9:    Set objRS = Server.CreateObject("ADODB.Recordset")
10:    objRS.Open "tblUsers", objConn, , adLockOptimistic, adCmdTable
11:  %>
12:    <B>Entries in table</B>
13:    <P>
14:    <TABLE>
15:    <TR>
16:       <TD>Name</TD>
17:       <TD>Email</TD>
18:       <TD>Username</TD>
19:    </TR>
20:  <% Do While Not objRS.EOF %>
21:       <TR>
22:          <TD><%=objRS("LastName") %>, <%=objRS("FirstName") %></TD>
23:          <TD><%=objRS("Email") %></TD>
24:          <TD><%=objRS("Username") %></TD>
25:       </TR>
26:  <%
```

```
27:        objRS.MoveNext
28:     Loop
29:     objRS.MoveFirst
30:     objRS.Delete
31:     objRS.MoveFirst
32:  %>
33:     </TABLE>
34:     <P>
35:     <TABLE>
36:  <% Do While Not objRS.EOF %>
37:        <TR>
38:          <TD><%=objRS("LastName") %>, <%=objRS("FirstName") %></TD>
39:          <TD><%=objRS("Email") %></TD>
40:          <TD><%=objRS("Username") %></TD>
41:        </TR>
42:  <%
43:        objRS.MoveNext
44:     Loop
45:     objRS.Close
46:     Set objRS = Nothing
47:     objConn.Close
48:     Set objConn = Nothing
49:  %>
50:     </TABLE>
51:     </BODY>
52:  </HTML>
```

17

ANALYSIS   This works a bit like Listing 17.5. Lines 12 through 28 first print out the table as it is initially. It then goes to the first record (line 29), deletes it (line 30), and prints out the new version of the table (lines 35 through 44).

The output of this listing can be seen in Figure 17.4. You can see in the second list of records that the Jack Miller record is now missing.

You can now add a Cancel Membership option for the users of the registration system you have been creating today. There are several ways to implement this. One simple way involves a two-page process. The first page has the user log in again for verification purposes. The second does the actual deleting. Listing 17.10 shows the delete verification page. Save it as cancel.html.

LISTING 17.10   Delete Verification Page

```
1:  <HTML>
2:     <HEAD><TITLE>User Verification</TITLE></HEAD>
3:     <BODY>
4:        <FORM METHOD=POST ACTION="DeleteUser.asp">
5:          <FONT COLOR=RED>You must log in again for verification purposes
```

continues

LISTING 17.10   continued

```
 6:          before your membership can be terminated.</FONT>
 7:          <P>
 8:          Username: <INPUT TYPE=TEXT NAME="username">
 9:          <P>
10:          Password: <INPUT TYPE=PASSWORD NAME="password">
11:          <P>
12:          <FONT COLOR=RED>Are you sure you want to proceed?
13:          This action cannot be undone. </FONT>
14:          <P>
15:          <INPUT TYPE=RESET> <INPUT TYPE=SUBMIT VALUE="Cancel Membership">
16:       </FORM>
17:    </BODY>
18: </HTML>
```

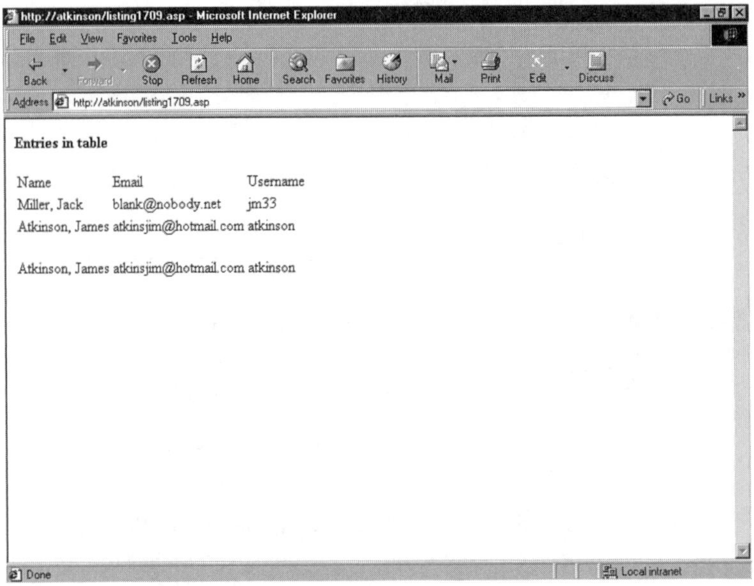

FIGURE 17.4

Viewing the results of Listing 17.9.

ANALYSIS   This is an HTML page with a simple form. It is much like the one in Listing 17.6. The main addition is warning text, reminding users what they are about to do. When submit is clicked, the page `DeleteUser.asp` is loaded.

Listing 17.11 shows the second page, which does the actual deleting.

LISTING 17.11   Actually Deleting the Record

```
1:    <%@ Language=VBScript %>
2:    <%  Option Explicit %>
3:    <HTML>
```

```
4:      <BODY>
5:   <!--#include virtual="/adovbs.inc"-->
6:   <!--#include file="DatabaseConnect.asp"-->
7:   <%
8:      Dim objRS, bolFound, strUsername
9:      strUsername = Request.Form("username")
10:
11:     'make sure username was entered
12:     If strUsername = "" Then
13:        objConn.Close
14:        Set objConn = Nothing
15:        Response.Write "<A HREF='cancel.html'>"
16:        Response.Write "You must enter a username"
17:        Response.Write "</A>"
18:        Response.End
19:     End If
20:
21:     Set objRS = Server.CreateObject("ADODB.Recordset")
22:     objRS.Open "tblUsers", objConn, , adLockOptimistic, adCmdTable
23:     bolFound = False
24:
25:     'look for username in table
26:     Do While Not (objRS.EOF OR bolFound)
27:        If (StrComp(objRS("Username"), strUsername, vbTextCompare) = 0) Then
28:           BolFound = True
29:        Else
30:           objRS.MoveNext
31:        End If
32:     Loop
33:
34:     'if username is not found, display message
35:     If Not bolFound Then
36:        objRS.Close
37:        Set objRS = Nothing
38:        objConn.Close
39:        Set objConn = Nothing
40:        Response.Write "<A HREF='cancel.html'>"
41:        Response.Write "Invalid Username.<P>"
42:        Response.Write "</A>"
43:        Response.End
44:     End If
45:
46:     'if passwords do not match, display message
47:     If Not (StrComp(objRS("Password"), Request.Form("password"), _
48:                 vbBinaryCompare) = 0) Then
49:        objRS.Close
50:        Set objRS = Nothing
51:        objConn.Close
52:        Set objConn = Nothing
53:        Response.Write "<A HREF='cancel.html'>"
54:        Response.Write "Invalid password.<P>"
```

continues

17

LISTING **17.11**   continued

```
55:        Response.Write "</A>"
56:        Response.End
57:    End If
58:
59:    objRS.Delete
60:
61:    objRS.Close
62:    Set objRS = Nothing
63:    objConn.Close
64:    Set objConn = Nothing
65: %>
66        Your membership in this site has been canceled.
67:    </BODY>
68: </HTML>
```

ANALYSIS   This is a lot like Listing 17.7. It verifies that a username was entered (lines 11 through 19). It locates the username in the table (lines 25 through 32). Notice that the table was opened using optimistic locking in this case because you may be deleting a record (line 22). If it cannot find the username, it prints a message (lines 34 through 44). It compares the password in the table to the one entered by the user, and if they do not match, an appropriate message is displayed (lines 46 through 57). Assuming that everything has worked so far, the record is actually deleted (line 59).

Note that you may not actually want to delete records. Some companies prefer to keep old records, even if they will not be used anymore. In such cases, you would probably add an extra field to the table to indicate whether the record is currently active. This would probably be an integer field that you would set to 1 initially, and set to 0 instead of deleting the record. This protects against permanent data loss in case of accidents. Should a record be "deleted" by mistake, simply setting the field value back to 1 restores it. Whether you want to use this approach depends on the importance of the data, the number of records the table might have, and how often records will be deleted.

Summary

Today, we have looked at the ways you can make changes to data in your database through ASP. This includes adding new records to a table, changing data in an existing record, and deleting records from a table.

If you will be making any changes to the recordset, the default locking type is not sufficient. Optimistic locking was used today, which means that the lock is put on when Update is called.

If the correct locking type is used, you can make changes to a field of the current record using the assignment operator. It looks like this:

```
objRS("fieldname") = new_value
```

Changes made to a record in the `Recordset` object are not immediately made to the record in the database table. Calling `Update` saves the changes made to the current record.

If you want to create a new record, call the `AddNew` method of the `Recordset` object. `AddNew` creates a new, empty record and sets it as the current one.

If you make changes to a record and decide you do not want the changes made permanently, call the `CancelUpdate` method instead of calling `Update`.

Records are deleted with, as you might guess, the `Delete` method of the `Recordset` object. `Delete` requires no arguments. It is called like this:

```
objRS.Delete
```

Calling `Delete` deletes the current record.

Be careful whenever you write ASP pages that will write to a database. Make sure that your pages will gracefully handle being used in unintended ways. It puts a real strain on performance if you accidentally add many blank lines to a table, or if you leave any connections unclosed.

17

Q&A

Q If there is an optimistic locking type, is there a pessimistic locking type?

A Yes! It is fairly commonly used, too. The difference is basically that optimistic locking puts the lock on the record when `Update` is called, whereas pessimistic locking puts the lock on when the record is first edited. We will discuss it more on Day 20.

Q What happens if I make changes to a record and never call `Update`?

A It depends on what you do after you make the changes. Calls to `Recordset` methods such as `MoveFirst` tend to have the effect of calling `Update` for you. If you simply end execution of the script, though, it may not be called, and your changes would not be saved. The upshot is that although what you intend might happen, it might not. In any case, it makes your code difficult to read and follow, so it is best to go ahead and explicitly call `Update` or `CancelUpdate`.

Workshop

The Workshop provides quiz questions to help you solidify your understanding of the material covered and exercises to provide you with experience in using what you've learned. Try to understand the quiz and exercise answers before continuing to tomorrow's lesson. Quiz answers are provided in Appendix A, and exercise answers can be found at http://www.mcp.com/info.

Quiz

1. Describe the actions performed by the AddNew method of the Recordset object.
2. What arguments can AddNew accept?
3. Why couldn't you use the default locking type in this chapter?
4. What does CancelUpdate do?
5. How do you delete a record?

Exercises

1. Create a table in your database called tblLinks. It should have the following fields: LinkID, URL, Title, Description. All are text fields except LinkID, which is an AutoNumber. Write an HTML form that a user can use to enter information about a new link. Then write the ASP page that actually adds it to the table. HINT: Because LinkID is of type AutoNumber, you do not need to set it yourself.

2. Write a page that takes the titles of the links in the table and lists them in a drop-down box. The user may then click one of the titles and then a submit button, and be taken to a page where he may edit the title, URL, or description of the specified record. Create a third page to actually save the changes to the database. HINT: Pass the LinkID between the pages to identify the correct record to edit.

3. Write a page that takes the titles of the links in the table and lists them in a drop-down box. The user may then click one of the titles and then a Delete Link button. Clicking the button opens a page that makes the change to the database and then reloads the previous page.

DAY 18

Examining the Recordset Object

This week, so far, has focused on working with a database through ASP pages. To communicate with a database through an ASP page, you need to use Microsoft's ActiveX Data Objects (ADO). ADO contains several objects to assist you with database access and information retrieval and modification.

One such ADO object is the Recordset object. Whether reading information from a database, or inserting, updating, or deleting information, you use the Recordset object. Day 16, "Reading from a Database Using ASP," looked at how to read information from a database table using the Recordset object. You also used the Recordset object on Day 17, "Inserting, Updating, and Deleting Database Records." Both lessons, though, only touched on the basics of the Recordset object.

As we discussed on Day 16, when reading information from a database table, it helps to think of a Recordset object as a matrix and each database table as the list of properties for a particular object. Each column in a database table, or in a Recordset object, represents a property of the object. Each row in a database table, or in a Recordset object, represents an *instance* of the object.

The `Recordset` object contains many methods and properties to assist with reading and interpreting data from a table. We will examine many of these methods and properties in detail. Today, you will learn the following:

- How each row in a `Recordset` object is represented by a `Fields` collection
- What the `Field` object is and what properties it contains
- What a database cursor is
- How to use the `CursorType` property to explicitly set the type of database cursor a `Recordset` object will use
- The differences between client-side cursors and server-side cursors
- How to use the `CursorLocation` property to determine whether a `Recordset` object uses a client-side or server-side cursor
- How to sort the results of a `Recordset` using the `Sort` property
- How to filter the results of a `Recordset` object using the `Filter` property
- How to enable your visitors to display rows from a database table that match a user-entered criteria

Enhancing Information Retrieval

On Day 16, we discussed the steps needed to obtain information from a database using Active Server Pages. Microsoft provides a component, ActiveX Data Objects (ADO), that you can use to communicate with any ODBC or OLE-DB compliant database. Such databases include Microsoft Access, Microsoft SQL Server, Informix, and Oracle.

Recall that a database serves as a centralized location for efficiently storing, modifying, and retrieving data. ADO contains many objects that aid you in storing, modifying, and retrieving this data. One particular object, the `Recordset` object, can be used to accomplish all three functions of a database. On Day 16, we examined how to retrieve data using the `Recordset` object, and on Day 17, we discussed how to store new data and modify and delete existing data.

When we used the `Recordset` object to retrieve data from a database, we did so by obtaining the entire contents of a particular table. It helps to think of a database consisting of a number of types of objects. For example, if you had a database that needed to only store customer billing information, you could use only one table, `CustomerBillingInformation`. Recall that a database table represents an *object class*, with each column in the table representing a property inherent in the object. Each row in a table represents an actual instance of the object.

The example `CustomerBillingInformation` table, would need properties such as `CustomerName`, `StreetAddress`, `City`, `State`, `Country`, `ZipCode`, and others. For each unique customer, you would add one row to this table. So, if your company had only three customers, you'd have only three rows in this table.

When you want to obtain the entire contents of this table through an ASP page, use the `Recordset` object. Think of the `Recordset` object as a two-dimensional matrix. When you want to obtain the contents of a particular table, use the `Recordset` object's `Open` method. When you `Open` a `Recordset` object, you create a matrix in the `Recordset` object that contains as many rows and columns as the database table contains.

When you create this matrix, you are initially positioned at the first row. To move to the next row, use the `Recordset` object's `MoveNext` method. Figure 18.1 contains a representation of the `Recordset` object in the form of a two-dimensional matrix.

FIGURE 18.1

You can think of the `Recordset` *object as a two-dimensional matrix.*

A Recordset can be thought of as a two-dimensional matrix. Each row in the table is represented by a row in the matrix. Each column in the table is represented by a column in the matrix.

Each cell in the matrix represents a specific column, row pair in the database table.

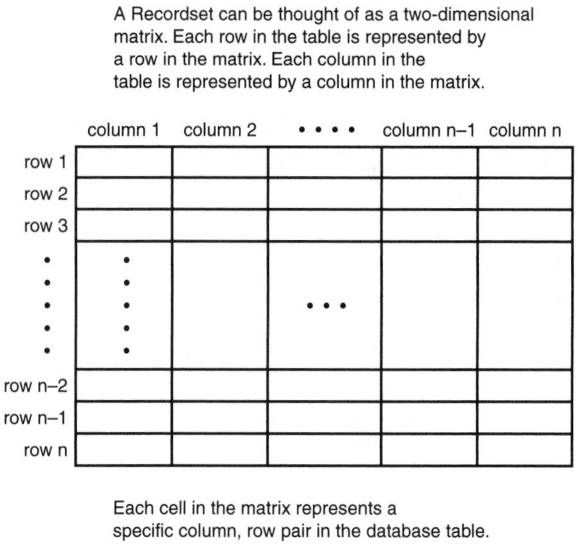

Note that if you position yourself *before* the first record in the matrix, the `Recordset` object is considered to be at the Beginning Of File. When this state occurs, the `BOF` property of the `Recordset` object will be set to `True`.

Note

You may be wondering how you can ever reach the position *before* the first record. Until now, we've only discussed how to move to the *next* row in the Recordset. However, you can move to the *previous* row. We'll discuss this briefly today, and in much greater detail on Day 20, "Using Advanced Database Techniques."

Note that if you position yourself *after* the last record in the `Recordset` matrix, you have reached the End Of File. When this position is reached the `EOF` property of the `Recordset` object is set to `True`. You examined this property on Day 16 when iterating through the contents of the `Recordset` object. To display each row of a `Recordset`, you performed a `Do While Not objRS.EOF...Loop`. Inside of the loop, you displayed the `Recordset` columns you were interested in, and then moved to the next row in the `Recordset` using the `MoveNext` method. After you processed the *last* row in the `Recordset` and issued the `MoveNext`, `objRS.EOF` returned `True`, and the `Do...Loop` aborted.

Recall that you can access each column in the current row by using the following syntax:

`objRecordsetObjectInstance(columnName)`

Imagine that in your database you had a table named `CustomerBillingInformation` that contained the following columns:

- `FirstName`—The customer's first name
- `LastName`—The customer's last name
- `StreetAddress`—The customer's street address
- `City`—The city that the customer lives in
- `State`—The state that the customer lives in
- `ZipCode`—The customer's zip code

If you wanted to display the contents of the table through an ASP page, you would need to use a `Recordset` object to `Open` a database table. Then, you would need to use a `Do ... Loop` to iterate through each row in the `Recordset` until `EOF` evaluated to `True`. Listing 18.1 contains code that displays the entire contents of the `CustomerBillingInformation` table.

LISTING 18.1   A Listing of the CustomerBillingInformation Table

```
1:  <%@ Language=VBScript %>
2:  <% Option Explicit %>
3:  <!--#include virtual="/adovbs.inc"-->
4:  <%
5:      'Open up a connection to our Access database
6:      'that stores the customer information.  We will
7:      'use a System DSN connection here.
8:      Dim objConn
9:      Set objConn = Server.CreateObject("ADODB.Connection")
10:     objConn.ConnectionString = "DSN=BillingInfo"
11:     objConn.Open
12:
13:     'Create a recordset object instance, and gather
14:     'the contents of the table CustomerBillingInformation
15:     Dim objRS
16:     Set objRS = Server.CreateObject("ADODB.Recordset")
```

```
17:    objRS.Open "CustomerBillingInformation", objConn, , , adCmdTable
18:
19:    'We are displaying our CustomerBillingInformation table
20:    Response.Write "<B>A Listing of Customers:</B><BR>"
21:    Do While Not objRS.EOF
22:       Response.Write objRS("LastName") & ", " & objRS("FirstName")
23:       Response.Write "<BR>" & objRS("StreetAddress") & "<BR>"
24:       Response.Write objRS("City") & ", " & objRS("State") & "<BR>"
25:       Response.Write objRS("ZipCode") & "<P>"
26:
27:       'Move on to the next customer
28:       objRS.MoveNext
29:    Loop
30:
31:    'Clean up our ADO objects
32:    objRS.Close
33:    Set objRS = Nothing
34:
35:    objConn.Close
36:    Set objConn = Nothing
37: %>
```

ANALYSIS Listing 18.1 displays the contents of the CustomerBillingInformation table. To list the contents of a table you need to perform a couple of steps. First, make sure that you have access to the ADO constants for the VBScript language. Line 3 includes the adovbs.inc file, which contains all the constants you'll need. Next, line 9 creates an instance of the Connection object, and line 10 sets its ConnectionString property to a DSN named BillingInfo, which points to the correct database. Finally, line 11 executes the Connection object's Open method , establishing the connection to the database.

Next, line 16 creates an instance of the Recordset object named objRS. objRS will contain the information from the CustomerBillingInformation table. To load in the contents of this table, use the Open method (line 17). Remember, when reading in the contents of a table, three parameters are required: the table name, the name of the Connection object instance to use, and the adCmdTable ADO constant, which tells ADO that you are interested in retrieving the contents of the table name specified as the first parameter.

After you have Opened the Recordset object instance, you are ready to loop through all the rows in the Recordset object. Lines 21 through 29 accomplish this with a Do While Not objRS.EOF ... Loop. Inside this loop, you need to display the Recordset information for the current row (lines 22 through 25) and then move to the next row using the MoveNext method (line 28). Finish the script by closing and explicitly freeing both the Recordset and Connection objects.

Figure 18.2 shows the output of Listing 18.1. A few records have been entered in this table to demonstrate the output. Note that *every row* in the CustomerBillingInformation is shown. When you use ADO to obtain the contents of a table, *all* the rows are returned.

A complete list of the contents of a table can be daunting for users when hundreds or thousands of records are in the database table. Later today, we'll discuss methods for limiting the records shown. Also, tomorrow, Day 19, "Using SQL Statements to Query Data," covers this topic in much greater detail.

Using the `Fields` Collection

Figure 18.1 described the Recordset object as a two-dimensional matrix that contains a mirror image of a particular database table. Although it helps to think of the Recordset object as a simple matrix, it is important to understand how the Recordset object stores this information. Each row in the Recordset object is represented by a collection that contains as many elements as there are columns in the matrix. This collection is referred to as the Fields collection. Each row in the Recordset object has its own Fields collection. Each element in the Fields collection contains specific information about a particular column.

So, Listing 18.1 displayed the contents of the CustomerBillingInformation table. This table contained six columns and four rows. The six columns were: FirstName, LastName, StreetAddress, City, State, and ZipCode. Each row represents information about a particular customer. The table contains the following four customers: Scott Mitchell, Todd Callister, Justin Miller, and Darren Maher. Figure 18.2 shows the output of Listing 18.1, which shows the six column values output for four customers.

In this example, the Recordset object in Listing 18.1, objRS, would contain four Fields collections since there are four rows. Each Fields collection would contain six items because there are six rows. Figure 18.3 illustrates what the `Fields` collection for the `Recordset` object in Listing 18.1 would look like.

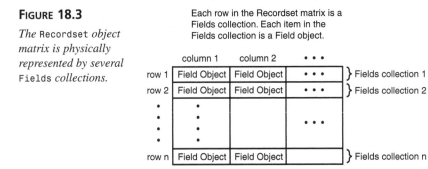

FIGURE 18.3

The Recordset *object matrix is physically represented by several* Fields *collections.*

Each row in the Recordset matrix is a Fields collection. Each item in the Fields collection is a Field object.

Understanding the internal structure of the `Recordset` object may seem daunting. However, a clear understanding is important to using the `Fields` object correctly. Recall that an item in a collection is referenced by the item's *name*. In the case of the `Fields` collection's items, the names are the column names.

The `Fields` collection is the default property of the `Recordset` object, so when we've used `objRS(columnName)` in the examples, we have been implicitly referencing the `Fields` collection. Recall from Day 6, "Working with Objects," that the default property of an object can be referenced implicitly. The following two lines of code are synonymous:

```
1:  objRecordsetInstance(columnName)
2:  objRecordsetInstance.Fields(columnName)
```

Line 1 implicitly references the `Fields` collection, whereas line 2 accesses the `Fields` collection explicitly. Both lines of code reference the item in the `Fields` collection with the name *columnName*.

The `Fields` collection contains several items, each item containing a number of properties about a particular cell in the `Recordset` object matrix. Each item in the `Fields` collection is referred to as a `Field` object. One property of the `Field` object is the `Value` property, which happens to be the default property of the `Field` object. The `Value` property for a particular cell in the `Recordset` object contains the actual data from the corresponding column, row pair in the database table. For example, Listing 18.1 presented the entire contents of the `CustomerBillingInformation` table. The `Value` of the `FirstName` column for the first customer was `Scott`. Because the `Value` property is the default property of the `Fields` collection, the following two lines of code produce the same output:

```
1:  objRecordsetInstance.Fields(columnName)
2:  objRecordsetInstance.Fields(columnName).Value
```

Line 1 implicitly accesses the `Value` property, whereas line 2 explicitly accesses it. Recall that the `Fields` collection is the default property of the `Recordset` object. Therefore, the following four lines all generate the same results:

```
1:   objRecordsetInstance(columnName)
2:   objRecordsetInstance(columnName).Value
3:   objRecordsetInstance.Fields(columnName)
4:   objRecordsetInstance.Fields(columnName).Value
```

Line 1 implicitly references both the `Fields` collection and the `Fields` collection's `Value` property. Although line 2 explicitly references the `Value` property of the `Fields` collection, it implicitly references the `Fields` collection. Line 3, on the other hand, explicitly refers to the `Fields` collection while implicitly accessing the `Value` property. Finally, line 4 references both the `Fields` collection and its `Value` property explicitly.

You may be wondering why anyone would explicitly reference either the `Fields` collection or the `Value` property. By explicitly referencing the `Fields` collection and `Value` property, your ASP code becomes easier to read. Microsoft has received a lot of flack for allowing objects to have default properties because using default properties can make your code ambiguous and difficult to read. Despite your feelings about implicitly or explicitly declaring the `Fields` collection and `Value` property, the fact remains that the vast majority of ASP developers prefer the `objRS(columnName)` syntax over `objRS.Fields(columnName).Value`. For this reason, for the majority of our scripts that access the `Value` of a particular cell, we will use the shorthand notation, `objRS(columnName)`.

If you want to access any of the other properties of the `Field` object, you *should* explicitly reference the `Fields` collection. For example, the `Field` object contains a `Name` property. This property contains the name of the column a particular cell exists in. You can access the `Name` property through the following syntax:

```
1:   objRecordsetInstance(columnName).Name
2:   objRecordsetInstance.Fields(columnName).Name
```

Line 1 implicitly references the `Fields` collection and accesses the `Name` property, whereas line 2 explicitly references the `Fields` collection. Line 2 is *much* easier to read. For this reason, in any example that uses a `Field` object property other than `Value`, the `Fields` collection will be explicitly referenced. We suggest you follow the same guidelines for your ASP pages as well.

Now that we've looked at the syntax to use when working with the `Fields` collection, let's examine what useful properties the `Field` object provides. Table 18.1 contains some of the most useful properties.

TABLE 18.1 Field Object Properties

Property	Description
Value	Contains the actual data from the database table for the particular column, row pair.
Name	Contains the name of the column that the cell exists in.
Type	Contains the type of data that exists in the cell; for example, if the cell contains a character string, a numeric value, a date value, and so on.
Precision	Represents the maximum number of digits that can be used for numeric values.
NumericScale	Represents the number of decimal places for numeric values.
DefinedSize	Contains the maximum size, in bytes, of the data the cell can contain.
ActualSize	Contains the actual size, in bytes, of the data existing in the cell.

Now that we have outlined the several properties contained by each item in the Fields collection, we can revise the graphical representation of the Recordset object once again. Figure 18.4 contains a representation of the Recordset object, now including the properties of each item of the Fields collection.

FIGURE 18.4

Each Field *object contains several properties.*

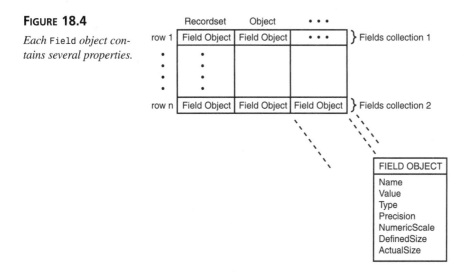

The most commonly used property of the Field object is the Value property. When you want to display the contents of a table, use the Value property. The other properties of the Field object contain information about the contents of a particular column, row pair in the table. For example, the Type property reveals what type of data is stored in the particular cell.

Because the Fields collection is a collection, it contains a Count property that returns the number of elements in the collection. The value of the Count property is the same as the number of columns in the table because a Field object exists in the Fields collection for each column in the database table.

Recall that the items in a collection can be accessed via a numeric index as well as by the name associated with each item. The `Fields` collections start indexing at `0`. You can iterate through all the items in the `Fields` collection, then, using the following code:

```
1:  Dim iLoop
2:  For iLoop = 0 to objRecordsetInstance.Fields.Count - 1
3:      'Reference the current Field object using:
4:      'objRecordsetInstance.Fields(iLoop)
5:  Next
```

Because the `Fields` collection starts its index at `0`, you need to loop from `0` through one less than the result returned by the `Count` property (line 2). Inside the loop, you can reference each `Field` object using `objRSRecordsetInstance.Fields(iLoop)`. You can use such a loop to display all the properties of each `Field` object.

> **Caution**
>
> Because the `Fields` collection starts its index with `0`, if you loop from `1` to `objRecordsetInstance.Fields.Count`, you will receive an error on the last iteration of the loop. There are exactly `objRecordsetInstance.Fields.Count` items in the `Fields` collection, but they are indexed from `0` to `objRecordsetInstance.Fields.Count - 1`.

Recall that you can also step through a collection using a `For Each ... Next` control structure. The following code steps through each `Field` object in the `Fields` collection:

```
1:  Dim strName
2:  For Each strName in objRecordsetInstance.Fields
3:      'Reference the current Field object using:
4:      'objRecordsetInstance.Fields(iLoop.Name)
5:  Next
```

Imagine that you have a table, `ProductInfo`, that contains some information on products that you sell. Specifically, `ProductInfo` contains three columns: `ProductID`, a unique identifier; `Name`; and `Weight`. Listing 18.2 contains ASP code that lists the properties of the `Field` object for each of these columns using the `For...Next` loop notation just discussed.

LISTING 18.2   The `Field` Object Properties for the `ProductInfo` Table

```
1:  <%@ Language=VBScript %>
2:  <% Option Explicit %>
3:  <!--#include virtual="/adovbs.inc"-->
4:  <%
5:      'Open up a connection to our Access database
6:      'that stores the product information.
7:      Dim objConn
8:      Set objConn = Server.CreateObject("ADODB.Connection")
```

```
 9:     objConn.ConnectionString = "DSN=ProductsDB"
10:     objConn.Open
11:
12:     'Create a recordset object instance
13:     Dim objRS
14:     Set objRS = Server.CreateObject("ADODB.Recordset")
15:     objRS.Open "ProductInfo", objConn, , , adCmdTable
16:
17:     Dim iLoop
18:     For iLoop = 0 to objRS.Fields.Count - 1
19:       Response.Write "Name - " & _
20:                       objRS.Fields(iLoop).Name & "<BR>"
21:       Response.Write "Value - " & _
22:                       objRS.Fields(iLoop).Value & "<BR>"
23:       Response.Write "Type - " & _
24:                       objRS.Fields(iLoop).Type & "<BR>"
25:       Response.Write "Precision - " & _
26:                       objRS.Fields(iLoop).Precision & "<BR>"
27:       Response.Write "NumericScale - " & _
28:                       objRS.Fields(iLoop).NumericScale & "<BR>"
29:       Response.Write "DefinedSize - " & _
30:                       objRS.Fields(iLoop).DefinedSize & "<BR>"
31:       Response.Write "ActualSize - " & _
32:                       objRS.Fields(iLoop).ActualSize & "<P>"
33:     Next
34:
35:     'Clean up our ADO objects
36:     objRS.Close
37:     Set objRS = Nothing
38:
39:     objConn.Close
40:     Set objConn = Nothing
41: %>
```

18

ANALYSIS Listing 18.2 displays the properties of each of the Field objects in the Fields collection. As with all data-driven ASP script, start by creating an instance of the Connection object (line 8), set its ConnectionString property (line 9), and Open the connection to the database (line 10). Line 14 then creates a Recordset object instance, objRS, and executes its Open method, retrieving the contents of the ProductInfo table.

Next, line 18 performs the For...Next loop, iterating from 0 to one less than the Fields collection Count property. This ensures that we'll visit every item in the Fields collection. Then, lines 19 through 32 display the seven properties of the Field object (see Table 18.1 for a listing of those properties). Finally, lines 36 through 40 close and explicitly free the ADO objects. Figure 18.5 contains the output of Listing 18.2.

FIGURE 18.5

The Field object contains several properties.

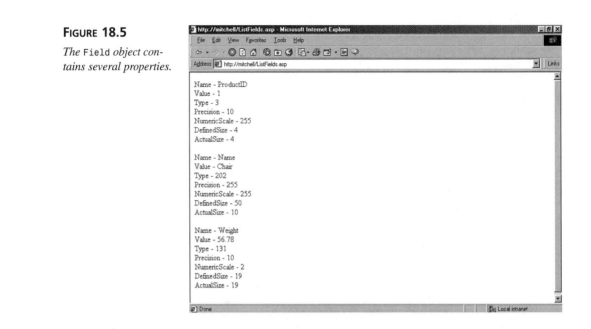

Examine Figure 18.5. The `Field` object reveals what type of data a particular cell stores. The `ProductInfo` table, which exists in an Access database, contains three columns that each can accept the following data types:

- `ProductID`—Long Integer
- `Name`—Up to 100 alphanumeric characters
- `Weight`—A numeric value with 10 digits of precision and 2 decimal digits

The output of Listing 18.2 corresponds to the data definitions listed previously. Let's examine each column specifically. The first column, `ProductID`, is defined as a long integer. Its precision is 10, and it, like all long integers, consists of four bytes. `ProductID` does not support any decimals because it is an integer. When this is the case, the `DefinedSize` property is set to `255`.

The second column in the `ProductInfo` table is the `Name`, which is defined as a `Text` field with a maximum length of 50. Note that this is the exact value of the `DefinedSize` property for the `Name` column. The `ActualSize` property represents the number of bytes currently used to store the data in the cell. Because Access 2000's `Text` fields use Unicode to represent each character, each character consists of 2 bytes. Note that the `Value` of the cell is `Chair`, so `10` bytes are required to store that `Value`. This, not coincidentally, is the value of `ActualSize`.

The third and final column, `Weight`, is defined as a `Decimal` data type, with a precision of 10 and with 2 decimal places. These values are represented by the `Precision` and `NumericScale` properties, respectively. Note that 19 bytes are required to store this value.

The one `Field` object property that we did not just analyze is the `Type` property, which determines what type of data the cell can hold. Note that the `Type` returns a numeric code. In `adovbs.inc`, several constants can be used to determine what type of data a particular cell contains. Table 18.2 contains a listing of these constants.

TABLE 18.2 Type Property Constants Found in `adovbs.inc`

Constant	Value
adEmpty	0
adTinyInt	16
adSmallInt	2
adInteger	3
adBigInt	20
adUnsignedTinyInt	17
adUnsignedSmallInt	18
adUnsignedInt	19
adUnsignedBigInt	21
adSingle	4
adDouble	5
adCurrency	6
adDecimal	14
adNumeric	131
adBoolean	11
adError	10
adUserDefined	132
adIDispatch	9
adIUnknown	13
adGUID	72
adDate	7
adDBDate	133
adDBTime	134
adDBTimeStamp	135
adBSTR	8
adChar	129
adVarChar	200
adLongVarChar	201

18

continues

TABLE 18.2 continued

Constant	Value
adWChar	130
adVarWChar	202
adLongVarWChar	203
adBinary	128
adVarBinary	204
adLongVarBinary	205
adChapter	136
adFileTime	64
adDBFileTime	137
adPropVariant	138
adVarNumeric	139

Glance back at Figure 18.5. Note how each particular column in ProductInfo has a value for the Type property that maps to a particular data type in the constants list in Table 18.2.

On detailed inspection, it may appear as though a discrepancy exists between the claimed data types for each of the three columns and the data type reported by the Type property. For example, the ProductID column is defined in Access as a long integer, yet the Type property returns a value of 3, which represents an integer. Furthermore, the Weight column is defined as a decimal in Access, whereas the Type property contains the value 131, which maps to the Numeric data type. What's going on here?

Access, unfortunately, uses a different lingo than Microsoft SQL Server to describe the data types. Therefore, there is no guarantee that the data type names chosen in Access will map to same exact name in the data type constants. This shouldn't cause much of a problem, though, because it's just a difference in the naming convention.

If you create the ProductInfo table in Microsoft SQL Server and rerun Listing 18.2, the output will differ slightly on the Name column because SQL doesn't use the Unicode character set by default. Figure 18.6 shows the output of Listing 18.2 when ProductInfo is created in a SQL Server database as opposed to an Access database. Note that the ActualSize property of the Name column is only 5, not 10, because each of the five characters in its Value, chair, takes up only 1 byte.

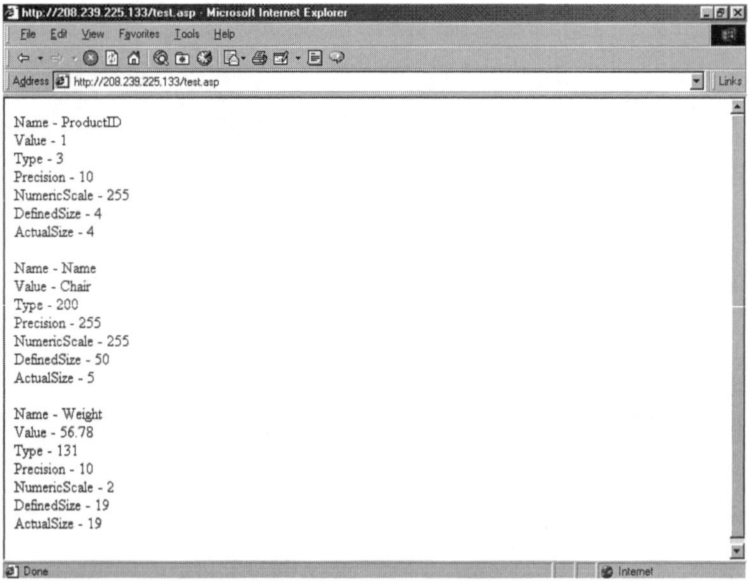

FIGURE **18.6**

There are some subtle differences between Access and Microsoft SQL Server.

Understanding the `CursorType` and `CursorLocation` Properties

When using the `Recordset` object's `Open` method, many parameters can be used. Recall from Day 16 that the `Open` method has the following syntax:

```
objRecordsetInstance.Open Source, ActiveConnection, CursorType,
                          LockType, Options
```

When using the `Open` method to read data from a database table in today's examples, we've set the `Source` to the name of the table that we're interested in, the `ActiveConnection` to the `Connection` object, and the `Options` parameter to `adCmdTable`. When reading data, we've never specified the `CursorType` or the `LockType`. However, when we've inserted and updated records, as on Day 17, we did set the `LockType`.

The `CursorType` and `LockType` play an important role in data access. The `CursorType` determines what type of *database cursor* the database uses to retrieve the information from the database table.

NEW TERM · Relational databases return *sets* of information. To step through a set of information one record at a time, a *database cursor* must be used.

When you request the contents of a table, you are actually being returned a two-dimensional matrix. Because developers usually want to deal with single records within the matrix, you need to use a cursor. Think of a cursor as a helpful person who keeps track of what record you are currently processing in a `Recordset`. Figure 18.7 shows a graphical depiction of a database cursor.

FIGURE 18.7

A database cursor "remembers" what record you are processing in a `Recordset` *object.*

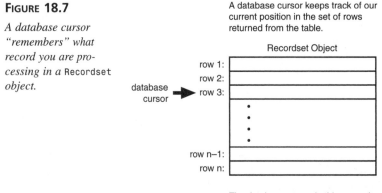

A database cursor keeps track of our current position in the set of rows returned from the table.

Recordset Object

database cursor → row 1:
row 2:
row 3:

row n–1:
row n:

The database cursor in this example points to row 3.

There are several types of database cursors, and each has advantages and disadvantages. If you don't explicitly specify a *CursorType* for a `Recordset` object, the `adOpenForwardOnly` database cursor is used. This cursor, although efficient, lacks much functionality. A forward-only cursor allows you to move the current position in the `Recordset` ahead one record at a time. This is the type of cursor used in all the examples so far. That's why we've continually used the `MoveNext` method of the `Recordset` object because the cursor we've been using only supports moving ahead one record at a time. Although the forward-only cursor limits your traversal through the `Recordset` object, it is the most efficient cursor.

> **Note**
>
> The forward-only database cursor is also referred to as a *fire hose* cursor because you can only move one direction through the `Recordset`, much like the water in a fire hose moves only one way.

Three other cursors are available, all of which are *scrollable database cursors*.

NEW TERM A *scrollable database cursor* can move both forward and backward through the `Recordset`.

These three cursors are referred to as Static, Keyset, and Dynamic. The respective ADO constants to use in the `Open` method of the `Recordset` object are `adOpenStatic`, `adOpenKeyset`, and `adOpenDynamic`. Each of these scrollable database cursors will be discussed in detail on Day 20. For the time being, we will use the `adOpenKeyset` cursor.

All three of these scrollable database cursors are less efficient than a forward-only cursor. However, many methods and properties of the Recordset object cannot be used when the Recordset is opened with a forward-only cursor. For example, the MovePrev method, which retrieves the previous row in a Recordset, can only be used with a scrollable database cursor. We will examine some properties that can be used with scrollable database cursors later today in "Sorting Recordsets."

Not only can you specify *what* database cursor to use, but you also can specify *where* the cursor should be used. Because the Internet follows a client/server model, the cursor must exist in one of two places: the client or the server. If you want to create a client-side cursor, set the CursorLocation property to adUseClient; to use a server-side cursor, either set CursorLocation to adUseServer, or don't set it to anything—a server-side cursor is created by default.

When using a client-side cursor, all the rows in the Recordset object are copied to the client's machine. If the Recordset contains a large number of records, using a client-side cursor can create considerable network overhead because the entire contents of the Recordset object must be copied over to the client's machine. However, certain Recordset object properties can only be used with the CursorLocation set to adUseClient. The only type of cursor that can be used on the client's machine is a Static cursor.

> **Tip**
>
> For performance reasons, do not use a client-side cursor unless you need the added functionality that the client-side cursor provides.

18

Sorting Recordsets

Each time we've retrieved the contents of a table, we've received the results in the order in which they were entered into the table. What if you want to sort the contents of the table, though? Imagine that you have a table called Portfolio, which has information about your personal stock portfolio. This table contains columns such as Price, Shares, and Symbol. Wouldn't it be neat if you could list the contents of this table but have it sorted by Price or Shares?

Imagine that your Portfolio table contains the following columns:

- StockID—A unique, numeric key
- Symbol—The stock ticker symbol
- Price—The price the stock was purchased at
- Shares—The total number of shares purchased
- Date—The date the transaction occurred

If your portfolio consisted of 10 stocks, there would be 10 rows in the `Portfolio` table. Table 18.3 shows the 10 rows in the table (the `StockID` is omitted because this would just contain the values 1 through 10).

TABLE 18.3 The `Portfolio` Table

Symbol	Price	Shares	Date
MSFT	79.50	100	6/1/99
YHOO	138.13	150	6/19/99
AMZN	54.00	75	9/9/99
IBM	90.50	150	9/9/99
EBAY	115.50	100	9/9/99
ZNET	16.50	100	10/16/99
DELL	44.50	100	10/16/99
SEEK	45.25	200	10/29/99
LCOS	23.00	100	11/1/99
AOL	90.75	75	11/2/99

If you were to use code similar to that in Listing 18.1 to display the contents of the `Portfolio` table, the order you would output the data would be the order in which you entered the rows into the table.

You can sort the `Recordset`; however, you have to use a scrollable database cursor on the client's machine. This is not the most efficient technique, especially if you are dealing with a large portfolio. Tomorrow, we'll look at a way to sort results from a `Recordset` using forward-only cursors on the server, a method that proves much more efficient.

To sort a `Recordset` you need to set the `Sort` property to the name of the column that you want to sort by after `Open`ing the `Recordset` object. For example, if you wanted to sort by the `Price` column, you would issue the command

```
objRecordsetInstance.Sort = "Price"
```

after executing the `Open` method. When using the `Sort` property, you need also to set the `CursorLocation` property to `adUseClient`. When using client-side cursors, you need to use the `adOpenStatic` cursor, so be sure to reference that in the `Recordset` object's `Open` method.

The `Sort` method sorts the results by a particular column in ascending order by default. To specify that you want to sort a column in descending order, append the keyword `DESC` to the column you are sorting. For example, if you wanted to sort by the `Shares` column in descending order, you would need to set the `Sort` property as follows:

```
objRecordsetInstance.Sort = "Price DESC"
```

If there is a tie between two values in the column you are sorting on, you can specify a secondary column to use to resolve the tie. To specify a secondary column to sort by, use the following syntax:

```
objRecordsetInstance.Sort = "PrimarySortColumn, SecondarySortColumn"
```

Listing 18.3 displays the contents of the Portfolio table. The Sort property is used to sort the results based on two columns: First, the number of shares is sorted in descending order; if there is a tie in that column among a set of records, those records are sorted based on their price in ascending order.

LISTING 18.3   The Field Object Properties for the Portfolio Table

```
1:  <%@ Language = VBSCRIPT %>
2:  <% Option Explicit %>
3:  <!--#include virtual="/adovbs.inc"-->
4:  <%
5:     'Create a connection to our database that contains the
6:     'Portfolio table.  Use a DSN connection
7:     Dim objConn
8:     Set objConn = Server.CreateObject("ADODB.Connection")
9:     objConn.ConnectionString = "DSN=Portfolio"
10:    objConn.Open
11:
12:    'Create a recordset object instance, objRS
13:    Dim objRS
14:    Set objRS = Server.CreateObject("ADODB.Recordset")
15:
16:    'The cursor location must be set to adUseClient for the
17:    'Sort property to work
18:    objRS.CursorLocation = adUseClient
19:
20:    'Open the recordset using the adOpenStatic cursor
21:    objRS.Open "Portfolio", objConn, adOpenStatic, , adCmdTable
22:
23:    'Sort by the Shares in descending order first, and then the
24:    'price in ascending order, if needed
25:    objRS.Sort = "Shares DESC, Price"
26:
27:    'Display the recordset in sorted order
28:    Do While Not objRS.EOF
29:      Response.Write "<B>" & objRS("Symbol") & "</B><BR>"
30:      Response.Write "Price: " & FormatCurrency(objRS("Price"))
31:      Response.Write "<BR>Shares: " & _
32:                     FormatNumber(objRS("Shares"),0)
33:      Response.Write "<BR>Date: " & FormatDateTime(objRS("Date"))
34:      Response.Write "<P><HR><P>"
```

18

continues

LISTING 18.3 continued

```
35:
36:      'Move to the next record in the recordset
37:      objRS.MoveNext
38:    Loop
40:
41:    'Clean up!!
42:    objRS.Close
43:    Set objRS = Nothing
44:
45:    objConn.Close
46:    Set objConn = Nothing
47: %>
```

ANALYSIS Until now, you've had no control over how the contents of a database table were loaded into a Recordset object. Using the Sort property, however, you can dynamically sort the records of a Recordset object. Unfortunately, to do so you must use a client-side cursor, which carries with it performance concerns. Listing 18.3 uses the Sort property to sort the output of the Portfolio table.

Line 3 starts by including adovbs.inc, because you will need to use a number of the ADO constants. Line 8 then creates an instance of the Connection object, and line 10 performs the Open method, establishing a connection to the database.

Next, line 14 creates an instance of the Recordset object, objRS. Before you Open the Recordset object, line 18 sets the CursorLocation to adUseClient. If you try to use the Sort property without having set the CursorLocation property to adUseClient, you will receive an error. After you set the CursorLocation property, you can open the Recordset object instance (line 21). Note that an adOpenStatic cursor is used. This is the type of cursor that needs to be used when using a client-side cursor. If you do not set the cursor to adOpenStatic correctly, ADO automatically changes it for you.

After you Open the Recordset, you can set the Sort property (line 25). Because, for this example, you wanted to sort on the number of shares in descending order, resolving ties by the price, in ascending order, the Sort string is Shares DESC, Price. After the Sort property is set, the Fields collections that represent each row are reordered so that they match the order specified by the Sort property.

Because the Fields collections have been reordered, you can just step through the Recordset from the beginning to the end, one record at a time, as in all the previous examples. The Do While Not objRS.EOF ... Loop starts on line 28. On lines 29 through 34, the portfolio information is displayed. Note the use of FormatCurrency, FormatNumber, and FormatDateTime. Using these functions ensures that your results are displayed in a pleasant and easy-to-read format. Line 37 uses the MoveNext method to move to the next record in the Recordset.

Finally, lines 42 through 46 close and explicitly free the ADO objects. Figure 18.8 shows the output of Listing 18.3. Only part of the results is shown, but note how these results are ordered first by descending order of the value in the Share column. If there is a tie among two or more records, the tie is resolved by sorting the Price in ascending order. Note that IBM and YHOO both contain the same number of shares, so they are sorted in ascending order by the Price.

FIGURE 18.8

The contents of the Portfolio table have been sorted!

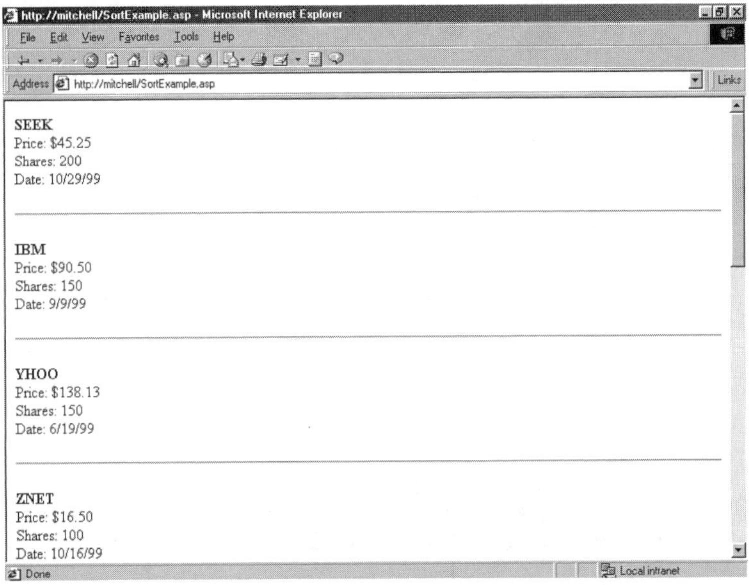

Do	Don't
DO use a client-side cursor if you need to sort the contents of a recordset.	**DON'T** use a client-side recordset if you do not care what order the contents of a table are listed in.

Filtering Recordsets

When you obtain the contents of a database table using the Recordset's Open method, you are retrieving the *entire* contents of the table. Each row from the database table makes it into the Recordset object in our ASP page. When displaying a Recordset, we've always displayed *all* the records. What if you only want to display a subset of the rows in the database table?

In "Sorting Recordsets," you learned how to order the records from the Portfolio table so that those stocks that you owned the most shares of would be displayed first. Although this is useful, imagine that you had hundreds of rows in this table. Displaying all the records would be a bit of an information overload. Wouldn't it be nice if you could filter the Recordset, so that just those stocks that you owned more than 100 shares of would be displayed?

This is possible through two means. The simplest way to do this would be to use an If statement in the Do While Not objRS.EOF ... Loop that would test to see whether the current record in the Recordset contained more than 100 shares. If it did, you would want to display the stock information, or else you would just want to skip to the next record. Listing 18.4 shows how to use such a conditional statement to limit the rows in the Portfolio table to those whose Shares value is greater than 100.

LISTING **18.4**   Using an If Statement to Show Stocks of Which You Own More than 100 Shares

```
 1:  <%@ Language = VBSCRIPT %>
 2:  <% Option Explicit %>
 3:  <!--#include virtual="/adovbs.inc"-->
 4:  <%
 5:     'Create a connection to our database that contains the
 6:     'Portfolio table.  Use a DSN connection
 7:     Dim objConn
 8:     Set objConn = Server.CreateObject("ADODB.Connection")
 9:     objConn.ConnectionString = "DSN=Portfolio"
10:     objConn.Open
11:
12:     'Create a recordset object instance, objRS
13:     Dim objRS
14:     Set objRS = Server.CreateObject("ADODB.Recordset")
15:
16:     'Open the recordset using the Forward only cursor
17:     objRS.Open "Portfolio", objConn, adOpenForwardOnly, , adCmdTable
18:
19:     'Display the recordset
20:     Do While Not objRS.EOF
21:       'Only show those records that have more than 100 shares
22:       If objRS("Shares") > 100 then
23:         Response.Write "<B>" & objRS("Symbol") & "</B><BR>"
24:         Response.Write "Price: " & FormatCurrency(objRS("Price"))
25:         Response.Write "<BR>Shares: " & _
26:                         FormatNumber(objRS("Shares"),0)
27:         Response.Write "<BR>Date: " & FormatDateTime(objRS("Date"))
28:         Response.Write "<P><HR><P>"
29:       End If
30:
31:       'Move to the next record in the recordset
32:       objRS.MoveNext
33:     Loop
34:
35:     'Clean up!!
36:     objRS.Close
```

```
37:    Set objRS = Nothing
38:
39:    objConn.Close
40:    Set objConn = Nothing
41: %>
```

ANALYSIS Listing 18.4 displays the records in the `Portfolio` table whose `Shares` column contains a value greater than `100`. One method to filter what records are displayed is to use an `If` statement to test whether the current record meets the criteria for being displayed (line 22). If it does, lines 23 through 28 display the record information; if the current record contains 100 shares or less, though, the record is not displayed, and line 29 moves on to the next record.

Because you are moving through the `Recordset` in a forward manner, one record at a time, you can use a forward-only cursor. Line 17 `Opens` the `Recordset` explicitly using the `adOpenForwardOnly` database cursor. You could leave this out because if no cursor is supplied, a forward-only cursor is used.

Other than using a forward-only cursor and an `If` statement, the code in Listing 18.4 is identical to Listing 18.3. However, due to the `If` statement on line 22, only a subset of the database table records are displayed. Figure 18.9 shows the output of Listing 18.4 when viewed through a browser.

18

FIGURE 18.9

A subset of rows from the `Portfolio` *table is shown.*

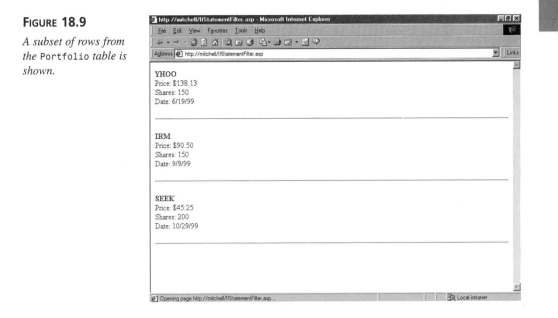

You are not restricted, however, to using an `If` statement to return only a subset of rows from a database table. The `Recordset` object provides a `Filter` property that can be used to alter the structure of a `Recordset` so that it appears to contain only the rows that meet the condition you want to `Filter` on. For example, if you wanted to use the `Filter` property to display only those stocks of which you owned more than 100 shares, you would perform the following steps:

1. Create a `Recordset` object instance and retrieve the contents of a table using the `Open` method.

2. Set the `Filter` property so that only those rows whose `Shares` column contained a value greater than `100` would be accessible.

3. Step through the `Recordset` object using a `Do While Not objRS.EOF ... Loop` control structure.

When you apply the `Filter` property to a `Recordset`, you are essentially *hiding* those rows that don't meet the condition specified by the `Filter` property. The entire contents of the database table still exist in the `Recordset` object; however, you can only visit those that meet the condition specified by the `Filter` property. When you issue the `MoveNext` command on a `Recordset` that has its `Filter` property set, you might move ahead several records, depending on where the next valid record is in relation to the current record. Figure 18.10 contains a graphical depiction of how invalid rows are hidden using the `Filter` property.

FIGURE 18.10

Those records that do not meet the condition specified by the `Filter` *property are hidden from view.*

A Filter hides rows that do not meet the specified criteria.
If we used a Filter, Price >100, our Recordset object might look like:

StockID	Symbol	Price	• • • •
1	MSFT	50.00	
2	SEEK	29.50	
row 1 → 3	YHOO	105.75	
row 2 → 4	IBM	101.50	
5	DELL	42.00	
row 3 → 6	AOL	173.25	
7	LCOS	98.75	
row 4 → 8	AMZN	119.00	

While 8 rows are loaded into the Recordset object, only 4 are visible since only 4 rows contain a Price value greater than $100.00.

When using a Do While Not objRS.EOF... Loop, we'd iterate through only the four labeled rows.

Now that you've examined the `Filter` property, Listing 18.5 shows how you could use it to display only those stocks of which you own more than 100 shares.

LISTING 18.5   Using the `Filter` Property to Show Stocks of Which You Own More than 100 Shares

```
 1:  <%@ Language = VBSCRIPT %>
 2:  <% Option Explicit %>
 3:  <!--#include virtual="/adovbs.inc"-->
 4:  <%
 5:    'Create a connection to our database that contains the
 6:    'Portfolio table.  Use a DSN connection
 7:    Dim objConn
 8:    Set objConn = Server.CreateObject("ADODB.Connection")
 9:    objConn.ConnectionString = "DSN=Portfolio"
10:    objConn.Open
11:
12:    'Create a recordset object instance, objRS
13:    Dim objRS
14:    Set objRS = Server.CreateObject("ADODB.Recordset")
15:
16:    'Open the recordset using the adOpenForwardOnly cursor
17:    objRS.Open "Portfolio", objConn, adOpenForwardOnly, , adCmdTable
18:
19:    'Return only those stocks we bought more than 100 shares of
20:    objRS.Filter = "Shares > 100"
21:
22:    'Display the recordset
23:    Do While Not objRS.EOF
24:      Response.Write "<B>" & objRS("Symbol") & "</B><BR>"
25:      Response.Write "Price: " & FormatCurrency(objRS("Price"))
26:      Response.Write "<BR>Shares: " & _
27:                     FormatNumber(objRS("Shares"),0)
28:      Response.Write "<BR>Date: " & FormatDateTime(objRS("Date"))
29:      Response.Write "<P><HR><P>"
30:
31:      'Move to the next record in the recordset
32:      objRS.MoveNext
33:    Loop
34:
35:    'Clean up!!
36:    objRS.Close
37:    Set objRS = Nothing
38:
39:    objConn.Close
40:    Set objConn = Nothing
41: %>
```

18

ANALYSIS   Listing 18.5 displays only those records whose `Shares` column contains a value greater than `100`. Listing 18.4 used an `If` statement within the `Do While Not` `objRS.EOF` ... `Loop` to display only those records that met your condition. Listing 18.5, however, uses the `Filter` property of the `Recordset` object (line 20).

Only those rows that meet the condition in the `Filter` property are viewable. Because the `MoveNext` method automatically moves to the next viewable record, you can use the same `Do While Not objRS.EOF ... Loop` that was used in Listing 18.3. You do not need a conditional statement to determine whether you need to display a row. All the rows you'll visit during the `Do While Not objRS.EOF ... Loop` will be those that meet the condition specified by the `Filter` property because all other rows will be hidden.

Figure 18.11 contains the output of Listing 18.5.

FIGURE 18.11

The `Filter` property can be used to show a subset of rows from a database table.

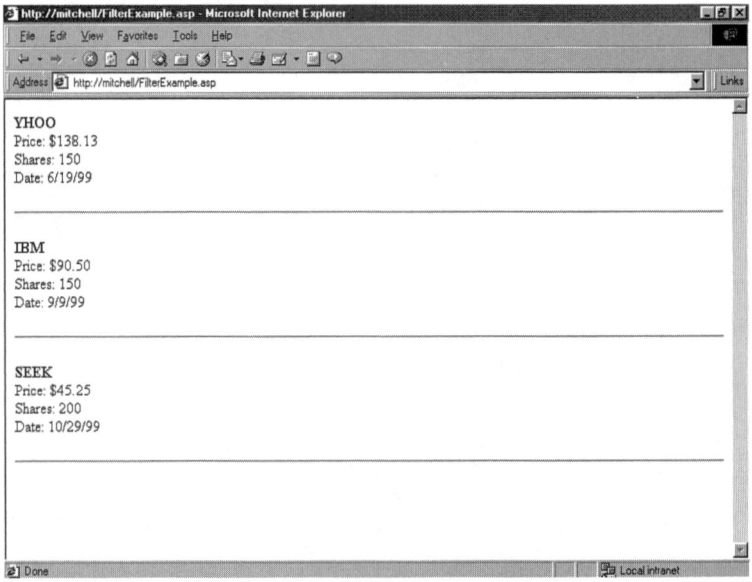

The `Filter` property may be set to any *logical statement*.

NEW TERM A *logical statement* consists of one or more statements that evaluate to true or false.

In constructing a logical statement, you can use any comparison operator to compare the value of a specific column. Each comparison can be followed by a logical operator (`AND`, `OR`, or `NOT`) to build a complete logical statement. Table 18.4 lists the comparison operators supported by the `Find` property.

TABLE 18.4 Legal Comparison Operators

Operator	Comparison Made
=	Equivalence
<	Less than
<=	Less than or equal
>	Greater than
>=	Greater than or equal
!=	Not equal
<>	Not equal

The simplest type of `Filter` consists of a single comparison. For example, Listing 18.5 uses one comparison: `Shares > 100`. However, the `Filter` property may contain numerous comparisons. When using multiple comparisons, a logical operator must exist between each comparison. Table 18.5 contains a list of the three logical comparison operators that you can use with the `Filter` property.

TABLE 18.5 Legal Logical Operators

Operator	Logical Operation Made
AND	True, only if both comparisons are true
NOT	Reverses the value of the comparison
OR	True if either comparison is true

18

Imagine that you want to refine the `Filter` statement from Listing 18.5 (line 20) to display only those stocks of which you owned more than 100 shares and cost $50.00 or more per share. To apply such a filter, you would need two comparisons:

```
Shares > 100
```

and

```
Price >= 50
```

You then would need to join these two comparisons with the `AND` logical operator because you want to show only those records for which both of these comparisons are true. To apply this filter, you would need to alter line 20 in Listing 18.5 to:

```
objRS.Filter = "Shares > 100 AND Price <= 50"
```

Regardless of what filter you use, you still iterate through the `Recordset` object using `Do While Not objRS.EOF ... Loop`. If no records meet the criteria specified by the `Filter` property, the `Recordset` object's `EOF` property will be `True` by default, and the body of the `Do While Not objRS.EOF ... Loop` will never execute.

When comparing string or date columns in the `Filter` property, you must surround the variable you are comparing the column to with single quotes. For example, if you want to return all the rows from the `Portfolio` table that have the `Symbol` `MSFT`, you would use the following conditional statement for the `Filter` property:

```
objRS.Filter = "Symbol = 'MSFT'"
```

Note the single quotes around `MSFT`. If you leave off the single quotes around the value in the `Filter` property, you will receive an error. The only time you will receive an error is if you fail to place single quotes around the value you are comparing in a column that contains string or date information. In all the examples comparing the `Shares` and `Price`, you did not surround the value with single quotes because these two columns do not contain string or date data. However, because the `Symbol` column contains string data, when using a comparison operator with this column, you need to surround the value with single quotes.

Tomorrow's lesson describes how to use SQL statements to both filter and sort `Recordsets`. The two methods described today for filtering `Recordsets` are not extremely efficient because regardless of how many filtered records are shown, the *entire* contents of the table are loaded into the `Recordset` object. Imagine that the `Portfolio` table contained 1,000 records, 10 of which had more than 100 shares. If you wanted to show just those stocks of which you own more than 100 shares, you would still have to load 1,000 records in the `Recordset` object, even though you only plan to show 10!

Also, tomorrow we'll discuss a more efficient way of sorting the records in a `Recordset`. Today, we discussed how to use the `Sort` property. However, to use this property, you need to use a scrollable, client-side cursor. This isn't as efficient as a forward-only, server-side cursor. Using SQL, which we'll discuss in detail tomorrow, you can have sorted records using a forward-only, server-side cursor.

Filtering `Recordsets` Based on User Input

Because the `Filter` property can be used to dynamically alter a `Recordset` so that only records that meet a certain set of conditions are viewable, you can allow the user to enter what conditions will apply to the `Filter` property. For example, you could provide a form where the user could enter a certain price. You could then list all the rows in the `Portfolio` table whose `Price` column matches the value entered by the user. By providing the user with a means to limit the displayed results of a `Recordset`, you allow the user to narrow the list to only the subset of records they are most interested in.

Imagine that you want to allow the user to enter the minimum number of shares he is interested in seeing stock information for. After the user enters this number and submits the form, the form processing script is loaded, and the `Filter` property is dynamically set based on the value entered by the user. The `Filter` property is set so that all records that contain a value greater than or equal to the number entered by the user is displayed.

For example, if the user enters 50, the `Filter` property needs to be set to the following:

```
objRS.Filter = "Shares >= 50"
```

To implement such a system, you need two ASP pages: the form creation Web page and the form processing script. The form creation Web page, `SelectShares.asp`, needs to contain a form with a sole text box, into which the user can enter the minimum number of shares he is interested in seeing stock information for. The form processing script, `ListShares.asp`, needs to dynamically set the `Filter` property of the `Recordset` object so that the user's input is taken into effect. Listing 18.6 contains the code for `SelectShares.asp`, the form creation Web page.

LISTING 18.6 Selecting the Minimum Number of Shares

```
1:  <%@ Language = VBSCRIPT %>
2:  <% Option Explicit %>
3:
4:  <HTML>
5:  <BODY>
6:    <FORM METHOD=POST ACTION="ListShares.asp">
7:      <B>My portfolio contains information about all of my stock
8:      purchases.  You can choose to list stocks that contain at
9:      least a certain number of shares.</B><BR>
10:
11:     Minimum Number of Shares:
12:     <INPUT TYPE=TEXT NAME=MinimumShares VALUE="50">
13:     <P>
14:
15:     <INPUT TYPE=SUBMIT VALUE="List Stock Information">
16:   </FORM>
17: </BODY>
18: </HTML>
```

ANALYSIS Listing 18.6 contains the code necessary to create the form into which the user can enter the minimum number of shares. A sole text box, created on line 12, is sufficient. This text box has a default value of 50 entered into it (line 12), to give the user an idea of what an acceptable input might be. For example, if the user entered 1,000,000 into the text box, he would *never* see any stock information, at least not with my dwarfed portfolio! Line 15 creates a submit button. When this button is clicked, the form will be submitted, and the form processing script, `ListShares.asp`, will be loaded and passed the value in the text box `MinimumShares` via a POST METHOD (line 6). Figure 18.12 shows the output of Listing 18.6, when viewed through a browser.

18

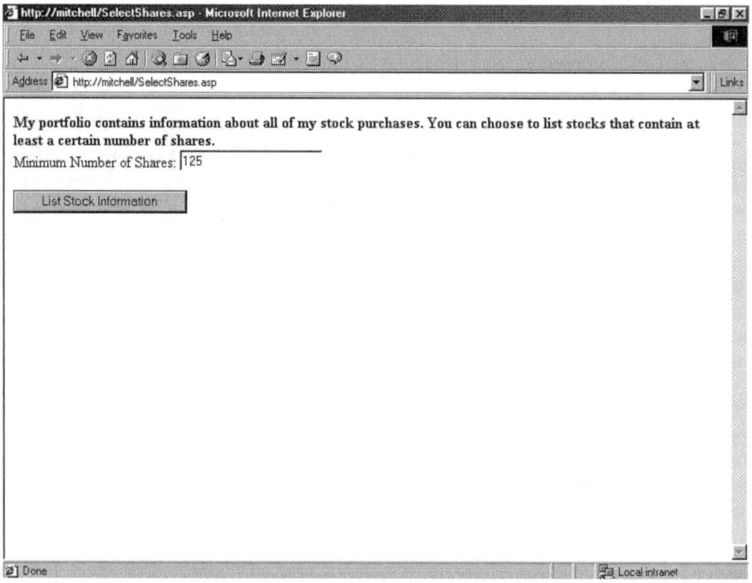

FIGURE **18.12**

The user can enter the minimum number of shares he is interested in seeing stock information for.

Now that you've completed the form creation Web page, let's turn our attention to the form processing script, `ListShares.asp`. `ListShares.asp` will be almost identical to the code in Listing 18.5; the only difference is that the `Filter` property will be set based on the user's input. Listing 18.7 contains the code for the form processing script, which displays only those records in the `Portfolio` table whose value in the `Shares` column is greater than or equal to the user's input.

LISTING 18.7   Output Based on the Users Input in `SelectShares.asp`

```
 1:  <%@ Language = VBSCRIPT %>
 2:  <% Option Explicit %>
 3:  <!--#include virtual="/adovbs.inc"-->
 4:  <%
 5:    'Create a connection to our database that contains the
 6:    'Portfolio table.  Use a DSN connection
 7:    Dim objConn
 8:    Set objConn = Server.CreateObject("ADODB.Connection")
 9:    objConn.ConnectionString = "DSN=Portfolio"
10:    objConn.Open
11:
12:    'Read in the user's input
13:    Dim iMinimumShares
14:    iMinimumShares = Request("MinimumShares")
15:
16:    'Make sure the user entered a valid value for the MinimumShares
17:    If Len(iMinimumShares)=0 or Not isNumeric(iMinimumShares) then
18:      iMinimumShares = 50
```

```
19:    End If
20:
21:    'Create a recordset object instance, objRS
22:    Dim objRS
23:    Set objRS = Server.CreateObject("ADODB.Recordset")
24:
25:    'Open the recordset using the adOpenForwardOnly cursor
26:    objRS.Open "Portfolio", objConn, adOpenForwardOnly, , adCmdTable
27:
28:    'Return only those stocks bounded by the user's requirements
29:    objRS.Filter = "Shares >= " & iMinimumShares
30:
31:    'Display the recordset
32:    Do While Not objRS.EOF
33:      Response.Write "<B>" & objRS("Symbol") & "</B><BR>"
34:      Response.Write "Price: " & FormatCurrency(objRS("Price"))
35:      Response.Write "<BR>Shares: " & _
36:                     FormatNumber(objRS("Shares"),0)
37:      Response.Write "<BR>Date: " & FormatDateTime(objRS("Date"))
38:      Response.Write "<P><HR><P>"
39:
40:      'Move to the next record in the recordset
41:      objRS.MoveNext
42:    Loop
43:
44:    'Clean up!!
45:    objRS.Close
46:    Set objRS = Nothing
47:
48:    objConn.Close
49:    Set objConn = Nothing
50: %>
```

ANALYSIS Listing 18.7 displays only those records from the Portfolio table whose Shares column contains a value greater than or equal to the value entered by the user in SelectShares.asp. The user's input is stored into a variable named iMinimumShares on line 14. Line 29 uses this variable to dynamically construct the Filter property.

However, first you must make sure that the user entered a valid, numeric value into the text box in the form creation Web page. Line 17 tests two conditions: The first condition, Len(iMinimumShares) = 0, will be True only if the user did not enter any value into the text box; the second condition, Not isNumeric(iMinimumShares) will only be True if the user entered some non-numeric value into the text box, such as Scott Mitchell. If either of these conditions is True, then you have an invalid entry for iMinimumShares. To resolve this, explicitly set iMinimumShares to 50 in line 18. If you did not check for an invalid entry, a database error will be generated. For example, trying to apply the following Filter is nonsensical and will therefore generate an error:

```
objRS.Filter = "Shares >= Scott Mitchell"
```

18

This is the `Filter` that will be applied if you allow `iMinimumShares` to contain the value `Scott Mitchell`. An error occurs if the value that `Shares` is being compared to is not numerically valid. To prevent this error, line 17 makes sure that `iMinimumShares` is valid, and, if it is not, line 18 explicitly sets it to a valid, numeric value.

Line 29 dynamically sets the `Filter`. Because you want to say:

```
objRS.Filter = "Shares >= ValueEnteredByTheUser"
```

and `iMinimumShares` contains the value entered by the user, the following line of code sets the `Filter` property to return only those records that have at least as many shares as the user entered:

```
objRS.Filter = "Shares >= " & iMaxShares
```

After you set the `Filter` property, you can loop through the `Recordset` using the `Do While Not objRS.EOF ... Loop`, displaying one record at a time, moving to the next record with the `MoveNext` method. Figure 18.13 shows the output of Listing 18.7 when the user enters `125` into the text box in `SelectShares.asp`.

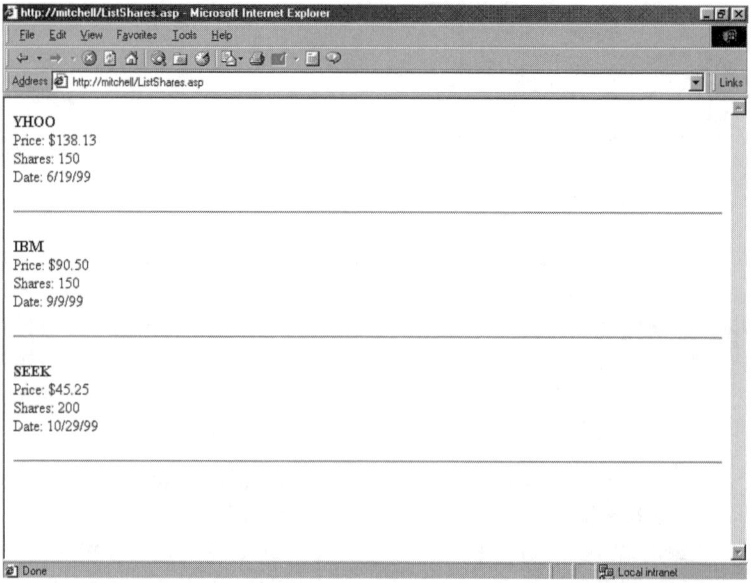

FIGURE 18.13

Only those shares that meet the user's criteria are shown.

Allowing the user to determine what subset of records he or she will see from a database table is a powerful feature of ASP. However, the method discussed today is not as efficient as the method we will discuss tomorrow. The disadvantage to using the `Filter` property, is that the entire table's contents are returned, regardless of whether the `Filter` property only makes available a small number of rows from the entire `Recordset`.

Tip

> By allowing your users to choose what information to have listed, your Web site will become more useful to the end user. Rather than having to pick through the entire Portfolio table listing, if a user can selectively choose a parameter on what results to display, she will be able to find the information much easier.

Summary

Today, we examined some advanced properties of the Recordset object. We began today's lesson by discussing how the Recordset object internally stores the information from a database table. For each record in a Recordset, a Fields collection exists, which contains as many Field objects as there are columns in the database table. The Field object has many useful properties that include information about each column in the current record. Table 18.1 contains a list of these properties, along with a description.

Next, we discussed the CursorType and CursorLocation properties of the Recordset object. When retrieving information from a relational database, you receive an entire set of information. Usually, you want to be able to step through this set of information one element at a time. To do so, you need to use a database cursor, which keeps track of what current record you're processing and provides the capability to move from one record to the next. With scrollable cursors, you can move both forward and backward through a Recordset and move more than one record forward and backward at a time. Day 20 describes database cursors in more detail.

The CursorLocation property determines where the cursor exists. Recall that the Internet is based on a client-server model. Therefore, it is not surprising that the cursor can only exist in one of two places: on the server or on the client. By default, the cursor is located on the server, which provides better performance. When a client-side cursor is used, the entire contents of the Recordset object needs to be copied over to the client. For large Recordsets this can cause an increase in network traffic and, therefore, a decrease in overall performance.

When listing the contents of a database table, there is no guarantee on the order with which the records will be displayed. This depends on the indexes used on the particular table. To force a certain type of ordering, you can use the Recordset object's Sort property. Unfortunately, to sort Recordsets, you need to use a client-side cursor. This can lead to performance degradation if your Recordset object contains many records.

Next, we discussed how to filter the contents of a Recordset using the Filter property. The Filter property expects one or more conditional statements that evaluate to either True or False. There are a number of conditional operators for comparing specific columns with either static or dynamic values. Also, three logical operators can be used to join multiple conditional statements. When using the Filter property, the rows in the Recordset object

18

that do not conform to the criteria specified are simply hidden away. This way, you can use a `Do While Not objRS.EOF ... Loop` and the `MoveNext` method to loop through all the records to display only those that meet the criteria outlined in the `Filter` property.

We also examined how to use a form to allow user input to dynamically affect the `Filter` property. When you permit the user to narrow the listing of a table, you must make sure that the user enters valid data. Listing 18.7 checks to make sure the user's input is numerically valid (line 17). If the user has input an invalid value, you need to take steps to ensure that a valid value is used instead (line 18). If you are planning to have an ASP page that will list filtered contents of a table, it is strongly recommended that you add a form creation Web page to allow users to enter their own filtering parameters.

So far, we've used objects inherent in Microsoft's ActiveX Data Objects to encapsulate data access. Tomorrow, you will learn how to use SQL, or Structured Query Language, which is a standard syntax that relational databases support to allow for data access. Using SQL, we'll examine how to sort and filter `Recordsets` more efficiently. Rather than retrieving *all* the rows from a table and then filtering or sorting the records, we'll ask the database to perform the sorting and filtering, returning a sorted and filtered `Recordset`. That way, if a table contains 1,000 records, but filtering only yields 10 records, the actual `Recordset` object will contain only 10 records, not 1,000. This proves to be a much more efficient approach than the methods discussed today.

Q&A

Q **Under what circumstances should I use the non-default cursor (recall that the forward-only cursor is the default cursor)?**

A Because the forward-only cursor only allows for movement from one record to the next, immediate record if you need to be able to move either forward or backward through the `Recordset`, or need to be able to jump forward more than one record at a time, then you will need to use a scrollable cursor. Also, if you need to use a client-side cursor (to use the `Sort` property, for example), then you cannot use the default cursor.

The default database cursor provides the best performance of all the cursors. For this reason, do not use a scrollable cursor when a forward-only cursor will do just fine. There are only a few instances when a scrollable cursor is actually needed. If, for some reason, you need to be able to move both forward and backward through your `Recordset`, use a scrollable cursor. However, you can usually remove this requirement by properly sorting your `Recordset`. Tomorrow, we'll look at how to sort a `Recordset` without using client-side cursors. With the approach we'll examine tomorrow, you can sort `Recordsets` using a forward-only cursor.

Q Is it possible to both sort and filter a `Recordset`?

A Yes, you can use both the `Filter` and `Sort` properties on a `Recordset` object. To use both properties, however, you do need to use a client-side cursor because the `Sort` property requires the use of a client-side cursor. Tomorrow, we'll examine how to sort and filter a `Recordset` using a forward-only cursor.

Workshop

The Workshop provides quiz questions to help you solidify your understanding of the material covered and exercises to provide you with experience in using what you've learned. Try to understand the quiz and exercise answers before continuing to tomorrow's lesson. Quiz answers are provided in Appendix A, and exercise answers can be found at `http://www.mcp.com/info`.

Quiz

1. What is the default property of the `Field` object?

2. How many `Field` objects exist in the `Fields` collection?

3. What does the `Name` property of the `Field` object return?

4. What is the difference between a forward-only cursor and a scrollable cursor?

5. True or False: A Static cursor is a scrollable cursor.

6. When retrieving the contents from large database tables, what will prove more efficient: a server-side cursor or a client-side cursor?

7. What property of the `Recordset` object can be used to set the cursor's location?

8. When using the `Sort` property, where does the cursor have to be located? Also, what type of cursor is required?

9. When comparing a column to a value in the `Filter` statement, under what circumstances do you need to surround the value with single quotes?

10. True or False: The `Filter` property requires the use of a scrollable cursor.

Exercises

1. The script presented in Listing 18.3 sorts the output of the `Portfolio` table using the `Sort` property of the `Recordset` object. Modify the output so that at the top of the page there are three hyperlinks. The first hyperlink should say, "Sort by Symbol," the second, "Sort by Shares," and the third, "Sort by Price." When the user clicks a hyperlink, the page is reloaded, except that the new sorting is applied.

   Hint: You will need to use the querystring to determine what column you want to sort by.

2. Create two ASP pages, a form creation Web page (`SelectPrice.asp`) and a form processing script (`ListStocksByPrice.asp`). In `SelectPrice.asp`, the user should be shown a form into which she can enter a desired maximum price. When the form is submitted, `ListStocksByPrice.asp` will list all the stocks in the `Portfolio` table that cost strictly less than the price entered by the user.

DAY 19

Using SQL Statements to Query Data

On Day 16, "Reading from a Database Using ASP," we examined how to use the Recordset object to read the contents of a database table. Reading the contents of an entire table is usually overkill. More often, you are interested in only part of the information in the table. For example, if you had a table that contained information on all the products your company carried, you might be interested in displaying only those items that cost less than $50.00.

With the methods you've learned so far, you're limited to retrieving only the entire table's contents. Although you can use programmatic logic in your ASP pages to display only certain parts of the table's contents, there is a significant performance price to pay when retrieving many records.

To selectively choose only a certain subset of a table, as opposed to the entire table, you need to let the database know what information you need exactly. You communicate with the database through a structured language known as SQL. Today's lesson focuses on the syntax of SQL and how to execute SQL statements from within ASP pages. By using SQL, you can restrict the data returned by the database to only the information you are interested in.

Today, you will learn the following:

- How to communicate to a relational database using SQL
- How to query data using SQL's SELECT statement
- The various clauses of a SELECT statement
- How to restrict data using the WHERE clause of a SELECT statement
- How to order the data returned from a database, using the ORDER BY clause of a SELECT statement
- How to execute a SQL statement in an ASP page
- How to iterate through a Recordset object that was populated with a SQL statement
- How to allow users' inputs to determine what data is displayed from a database

What Is SQL?

Recall from Day 15, "Using Databases," that relational databases store their information in structures called tables. A table can be thought of as a two-dimensional matrix that is used to store common information on an object. Each column in a table represents a property of the object being stored, whereas each row is an actual instance of the object.

On Day 16, we discussed how to read the entire contents of a table using the Recordset object. The following lines of code:

```
Dim objRS
Set objRS = Server.CreateObject("ADODB.Recordset")
objRS.Open TableName, ActiveConnection, CursorType, LockType, adCmdTable
```

return all the columns and rows for the table *TableName*. The adCmdTable at the end of the Recordset object's Open method informs the Recordset object that you want to retrieve the entire contents of the table specified by *TableName*.

No matter what information you need from a database, it can be obtained by reading the entire contents of a table. Imagine that you have a table that contains information on all your customers. One column in the table might be the customer's zip code. If you want to list *just* the customers who have a zip code of 65401, you could obtain all the customer information, and then, when looping through the Recordset object, only display those customers whose zip code is 65401. If the customer-information table were named Customer and contained the customer's first and last name and zip code, Listing 19.1 would list just those customers whose zip code is 65401.

LISTING 19.1   Customers Who Have a Zip Code of 65401

```
 1: <%@ Language=VBScript %>
 2: <% Option Explicit %>
 3: <!--#include virtual="/adovbs.inc"-->
 4: <%
 5:   'Open up a connection to our Access database that stores the customer
 6:   'information.  We will use a DSN-less connection here.
 7:   Dim objConn
 8:   Set objConn = Server.CreateObject("ADODB.Connection")
 9:   objConn.ConnectionString= "DRIVER={Microsoft Access Driver (*.mdb)};" & _
10:                             "DBQ=" & Server.MapPath("Customer.mdb")
11:    objConn.Open
12:
13:   'Create a recordset object instance, and retrieve all of the columns
14:   'and rows from the Customer table.
15:   Dim objRS
16:   Set objRS = Server.CreateObject("ADODB.Recordset")
17:   objRS.Open "Customer", objConn, , , adCmdTable
18:
19:   'We are displaying those customers whose zip code is 65401
20:   Response.Write "<B>Customers who have a Zip Code of 65401:</B><BR>"
21:   Do While Not objRS.EOF
22:       'Test to see if the current customer's zipcode is 65401
23:       If objRS("ZipCode") = "65401" then
24:         'A zip code of 65401 was found, so display this customer
25:         Response.Write objRS("LastName") & ", " & objRS("FirstName")
26:         Response.Write "<BR>"
27:       End If
28:
29:       'Move on to the next customer
30:       objRS.MoveNext
31:   Loop
32:
33:   'Clean up our ADO objects
34:   objRS.Close
35:   Set objRS = Nothing
36:
37:   objConn.Close
38:   Set objConn = Nothing
39: %>
```

ANALYSIS   In Listing 19.1, line 3 starts by including adovbs.inc. This allows you to use the ADO constants throughout this script. Next, line 8 creates an instance of the Connection object, assigning it to objConn. A DSN-less connection is used to establish the connection to the Access database that stores the Customer table. Line 16 creates an instance of the Recordset object, and line 17 retrieves all the columns and rows of the Customer table via the Open method. Line 20 displays that you are going to list all the customers whose zip code is 65401. Line 21 then begins to loop through the Recordset object instance, objRS. Line 23 tests whether the zip code is 65401. If it is, line 25 displays the customer's last and first name; if the customer's zip code is not 65401, nothing is displayed. Line 30 moves to the next customer in the Recordset. Finally, lines 34 through 38 close and explicitly destroy the Recordset and Connection objects.

Table 19.1 shows the sample data used when creating this example. Note that only half the customers have 65401 as their zip code. Figure 19.1 presents the output of Listing 19.1 with the sample data shown in Table 19.1.

TABLE 19.1   The Data Present in the Customer Table

FirstName	LastName	ZipCode
John	Doe	65401
Jane	Doe	65401
Frank	Smith	65020
Ed	Johnson	65305
Jane	Johnson	65305
Scott	Mitchell	65401
James	Atkinson	65401
Will	Johnson	65303

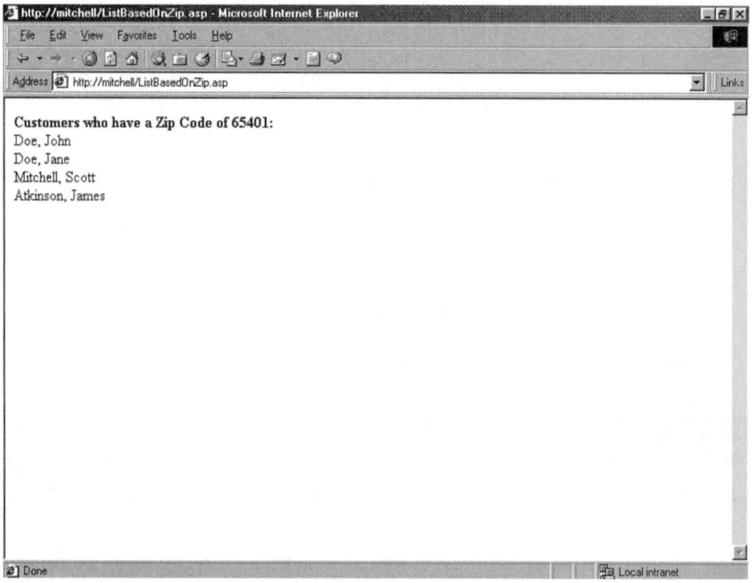

FIGURE 19.1

Only the customers whose zip code is 65401 are listed.

Although Listing 19.1 displays only the customers whose zip code is 65401, it is inefficient. Imagine that you have 1,000 customers and only one of them has the zip code 65401. You would have to obtain 1,000 records from the relational database (an expensive process) and loop through all 1,000 customers, only to display one.

You need a way to obtain only a certain number of rows or columns from a table. To accomplish this, you need to be able to ask the relational database for specific information. When asking a relational database for information, you must do so in a language that the database understands. Relational databases, from Access to Oracle to Microsoft SQL-Server, communicate via a standard language known as Structured Query Language, or SQL (pronounced *see-quill*).

> **Note**
>
> SQL can be used to retrieve specific information, delete records, update records, and insert records. We will only focus on using SQL to query data because, as discussed on Day 17, inserting, updating, and deleting records can be handled easily through ADO.

Later today, in "The SELECT SQL Statement," we will discuss the specifics of the SQL syntax needed to query data from a database. Before we do so, though, let's briefly examine how you can use ASP and ADO to execute SQL statements.

Executing SQL Statements Using ASP and ADO

Whenever you need to do *anything* concerning a database through ASP, you must use ADO (ActiveX Data Objects), which was discussed in detail on Day 16. When executing SQL statements, it comes as no surprise that you need to use ADO as well. To execute a SQL statement, follow these steps:

1. Create and open a connection to the database. To do this, use the Connection object.
2. Create a string variable to hold your SQL statement.
3. Assign your SQL statement to this variable.
4. Create an instance of the Recordset object.
5. Execute the Open method of the Recordset object.

Listing 19.2 shows these five steps in action. The entire contents of the Customer table are listed, the output shown in Figure 19.2.

19

LISTING 19.2 The Customer Table Listing via a SQL Statement

```
 1: <%@ Language=VBScript %>
 2: <% Option Explicit %>
 3: <!--#include virtual="/adovbs.inc"-->
 4: <%
 5:   'Open up a connection to our Access database that stores the customer
 6:   'information.  We will use a DSN-less connection here.
 7:   Dim objConn
 8:   Set objConn = Server.CreateObject("ADODB.Connection")
 9:   objConn.ConnectionString= "DRIVER={Microsoft Access Driver (*.mdb)};" & _
10:                             "DBQ=" & Server.MapPath("Customer.mdb")
11:   objConn.Open
12:
13:   'Create our SQL statement variable
14:   Dim strSQL
15:   strSQL = "SELECT * FROM Customer"
16:
17:   'Create a recordset object instance, and execute the SQL statement
18:   Dim objRS
19:   Set objRS = Server.CreateObject("ADODB.Recordset")
20:   objRS.Open strSQL, objConn
21:
22:   'We are displaying those customers whose zip code is 65401
23:   Response.Write "<B>A Listing of Customers:</B><BR>"
24:   Do While Not objRS.EOF
25:     Response.Write objRS("LastName") & ", " & objRS("FirstName") & _
26:                    " (" & objRS("ZipCode") & ")<BR>"
27:
28:     'Move on to the next customer
29:     objRS.MoveNext
30:   Loop
31:
32:   'Clean up our ADO objects
33:   objRS.Close
34:   Set objRS = Nothing
35:
36:   objConn.Close
37:   Set objConn = Nothing
38: %>
```

[handwritten annotation near line 15: "where usrID = " & request.queryshrpt"]

ANALYSIS Listing 19.2 demonstrates how to execute a SQL statement using ADO. Remember that you need to perform five tasks to execute a SQL statement. Step 1, creating and opening a connection to the database, is accomplished in lines 8 through 11. Note that these lines of code are identical to lines 8 through 11 in Listing 19.1. Step 2, creating a string variable to hold the SQL statement, is accomplished on line 14. The SQL statement string variable is named strSQL. Line 15 performs step 3, assigning a SQL statement to the variable. SELECT * FROM Customer retrieves every row and column from the table Customer. We will examine the intricacies of the SELECT statement later today, in "The SELECT SQL Statement."

Creating an instance of the `Recordset` object, step 4, is accomplished on line 19. Finally, the `Open` method of the `Recordset` object is executed on line 20 (step 5). Note that the first parameter is the SQL statement, `strSQL`, and the second parameter is the `Connection` object instance. It is important to realize that using a SQL statement does not change the functionality of the `Recordset` object. Rather, it simply informs the relational database what information, exactly, to place inside the `Recordset` object. A `Recordset` object is used the same if you use the `Open` method to retrieve a table, or if you use the `Open` method to execute a SQL statement. Figure 19.2 displays the output of Listing 19.2. Note that this information is identical to the information in Table 19.1.

FIGURE 19.2

A SQL statement was used to obtain all of the customers.

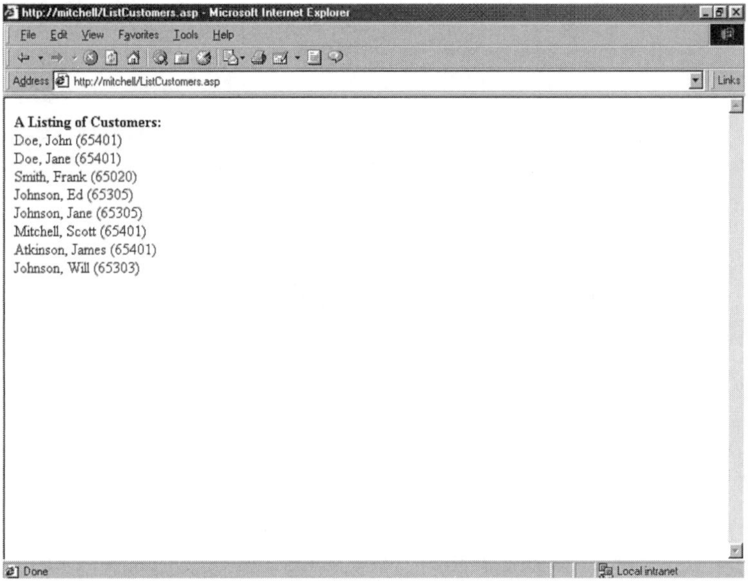

Executing a SQL statement is similar to retrieving a complete table. When retrieving a table using the `Open` method, the following syntax is used:

```
objRS.Open TableName, ActiveConnection, CursorType, LockType, adCmdTable
```

When executing a SQL statement, the syntax for the `Open` method does not change much:

```
objRS.Open SQLStatement, ActiveConnection, CursorType, LockType
```

To execute a SQL statement, you only need to remove the last parameter, adCmdTable, and change the first parameter from the table's name to the SQL statement. When executing a SQL statement, the *CursorType* and *LockType* are optional, just as when opening a table. The same considerations occur, though, when using the *CursorType* and *LockType* with a SQL statement as they do with retrieving an entire table's contents. These considerations were discussed in detail on Day 16.

Now that we've discussed the benefits of using SQL statements over retrieving entire tables, we will examine the intricacies of the SELECT statement in the following section, "The SELECT SQL Statement." We will also discuss, in greater detail, how to use SQL statements in your ASP pages. We'll look at some interesting, interactive examples showing how user input can affect the SQL statements executed. By allowing users to determine the SQL statement that is executed, users can selectively query information from your database. This is discussed in detail in "Allowing Users to Query Data."

The SELECT SQL Statement

SQL statements can be used to update, insert, delete, and query data. Entire books have been authored on how to use SQL to accomplish these functions. We will narrow our focus to querying data, and not drill down to the acute specifics.

Whenever you want to obtain data from a table in your database, you need to use a SELECT statement, which has the following form:

```
SELECT selectList
FROM TableName
[WHERE searchClause]
[ORDER BY orderExpression [ASC ¦ DESC]]
```

Although there are optional clauses of the SELECT statement, a SELECT statement must consist of at least SELECT selectList FROM TableName. Each capitalized keyword in a SELECT statement is referred to as a *clause*. A SELECT statement must contain a SELECT and FROM clause, whereas the WHERE and ORDER BY clauses are optional.

The selectList contains a comma-delimited list of the columns that you want to return, whereas the TableName is the name of the table from which you want to retrieve data. For our discussion of the SELECT statement, we will use a table named Products, which contains the data shown in Table 19.2.

TABLE 19.2 The Data Present in the Products Table

ProductID	Name	Price	Inventory
1	Monitor	195.95	100
2	Mouse	9.95	250
3	Keyboard	24.95	55
4	Scanner	149.50	15
5	CD-ROM	79.95	75
6	Printer	155.50	19
7	Sound Card	29.45	34

ProductID	Name	Price	Inventory
8	Game Pad	29.50	190
9	Zip Drive	129.95	7
10	Modem	89.90	190

If you wanted to create a SQL statement that would retrieve every column from the Products table, the *selectList* would need to contain each column of the table, each separated by a comma. The following example returns all the rows and columns in the Products table:

```
SELECT ProductID, Name, Price, Inventory
FROM Products
```

Caution

A SELECT statement that does not contain a WHERE clause returns *all* the rows in the table specified in the FROM clause. The WHERE clause is discussed in detail later today in "Using the WHERE Clause."

If you want to obtain *all* the columns, you can use the asterisk (*) in the *selectList* to denote that you want to include all the columns. The following two SQL statements are functionally equivalent:

```
1:  SELECT ProductID, Name, Price, Inventory FROM Products
2:  SELECT * FROM Products
```

Note that line 2 uses an asterisk in place of all the column names. Both SQL statements return all the columns and rows of the Products table.

If you wanted to retrieve just the Name of all products, you could modify the SQL statement's *selectList* to contain just the Name column:

```
SELECT Name FROM Products
```

If you wanted to obtain just the Name and Price of all products, you could add the Price column to the *selectList*:

```
SELECT Name, Price FROM Products
```

Using the WHERE Clause

Although the minimal SELECT statement is interesting, it really is no better than retrieving the entire table's contents. Without using the WHERE clause, a SELECT statement returns the entire contents of a table. A WHERE clause, though, specifies a single, logical

19

statement, which is used to filter the rows returned. Imagine that you wanted to display the products that cost strictly less than $50.00. The following SQL statement returns such rows:

```
SELECT * FROM Products WHERE Price < 50
```

A WHERE clause may contain any logical statement. A logical statement consists of one or more statements that evaluate to True or False. In constructing a logical statement, you can use any comparison operator to compare the value of a specific column. Each comparison can be followed by a logical operator (AND, OR, or NOT) to build a complete logical statement. Table 19.3 lists the comparison operators supported by SQL server.

TABLE 19.3   SQL's Comparison Operators

Operator	Comparison Made
=	Equivalence
<	Less than
<=	Less than or equal
>	Greater than
>=	Greater than or equal
!=	Not equal
<>	Not equal

A WHERE clause may contain numerous comparisons, but a logical operator must exist between each comparison. A logical operator performs a comparison and returns true or false based on that comparison. Table 19.4 lists the logical operators supported by SQL.

TABLE 19.4   SQL's Logical Operators

Operator	Logical Operation Made
AND	True, only if both comparisons are true
NOT	Reverses the value of the comparison
OR	True if either comparison is true

If you wanted to return rows from the Products table that cost more than $100 and had 100 items or more in inventory, you would need to use the AND logical operator between two comparisons. The SQL statement would look like this:

```
SELECT * FROM Products WHERE Price > 100 AND Inventory >= 100
```

The preceding SQL statement would return only one row, the row containing the information about the Monitor because the Monitor is the only product that has both a cost greater than $100 and an inventory greater than or equal to 100. Of course, all the columns would be returned with the preceding SQL statement because the `selectList` contains the asterisk.

If you wanted to retrieve all the rows from the Products table that do not have exactly 190 items in inventory, you could use one of the following three SQL statements:

```
1:  SELECT * FROM Products WHERE Inventory <> 190
2:  SELECT * FROM Products WHERE Inventory != 190
3:  SELECT * FROM Products WHERE NOT Inventory = 190
```

SQL supports two comparison operators for determining whether a column is not equal to a value. These comparison operators, <> and !=, differ only in syntax and are used on lines 1 and 2, respectively. Line 3 shows how to use the NOT logical operator to achieve the same results. Line 3 says, "Give me all the columns in the Products table where the statement 'The inventory is 190' is false." The intent of line 3 is not as clear as lines 1 or 2.

With multiple logical operators, which operator has precedence? For example, if you were to construct a SQL statement in the following manner:

```
SELECT * FROM Products
WHERE Price < 50 AND Inventory > 50 OR Inventory < 75
```

What, exactly, are you asking for? Do you want to retrieve the rows that have a Price less than $50 and an Inventory greater than 50, or those with an Inventory less than 75? Or do you want to retrieve those rows that have a Price less than $50, and an Inventory between 50 and 75? When using different, multiple logical operators, it is important to use parentheses to signify the operator precedence. Without using parentheses, the NOT operator has the highest precedence, followed by the AND operator, and then the OR operator.

19

If you wanted to retrieve the rows that have a Price less than $50 and have an Inventory between 50 and 75, you would use the following SQL statement:

```
SELECT * FROM Products
WHERE Price < 50 AND (Inventory > 50 OR Inventory < 75)
```

If you wanted to retrieve the products that are priced less than $50 and have an inventory greater than 50, or those products that have an inventory greater than 75, you would use the following SQL statement:

```
SELECT * FROM Products
WHERE (Price < 50 AND Inventory > 50) OR Inventory < 75
```

The preceding SQL statement is also functionally equivalent to the following:

```
SELECT * FROM Products
WHERE Price < 50 AND Inventory > 50 OR Inventory < 75
```

Because the AND operator has a higher precedence than the OR operator, the parentheses, in this example, are not needed. However, when using multiple, different logical operators, *always* use parentheses to explicitly indicate the precedence of your logical operators.

When comparing string or date columns in a WHERE clause, you will need to surround the variable you are comparing the column to in single quotes. For example, if you wanted to return all the rows from the Products table that had the Name Monitor, you would use the following SQL statement:

```
SELECT * FROM Products WHERE Name = 'Monitor'
```

If, when constructing your SQL statement in your ASP pages, you leave off the single quotes around the value in the WHERE clause, you will receive an error. The only time you need to place single quotes around the value you are comparing a column to is when the column contains string or date information. Note that in all the examples comparing the Price and Inventory, you did not surround the value with single quotes. This is because these two columns do not contain string or date data. The Name column of the Products table, however, contains string data; therefore, when using a comparison operator with this column, you need to surround the value with single quotes.

SQL offers an operator to perform pattern matching. The LIKE operator can be used in the WHERE clause to search for patterns in strings. The LIKE operator understands three simple pattern wildcards, summarized in Table 19.5.

TABLE 19.5 Wildcards the LIKE Operator Accepts

Wildcard	Description
%	Translates to any string of zero or more characters
_ (underscore)	Translates to exactly one character
[] (brackets)	Translates to any specific character within a certain range

For example, if you wanted to return all products whose Name begins with the character "M", you could use the following SQL statement:

```
SELECT * FROM Products
WHERE Name LIKE 'M%'
```

Note that the value after the LIKE operator is in quotes because you are working with the Name column, which contains string data. The preceding SQL statement asks for rows where the value in the Name column has an "M" for the first character, followed by zero or many characters. The preceding query returns all the columns for three rows: the Monitor, the Mouse, and the Modem.

> **Note**
>
> By default, SQL is not case sensitive. If a product were named microphone, it would still be returned with a WHERE clause of WHERE Name LIKE 'M%'. Some relational databases allow you to have comparisons that are case sensitive.

If you wanted to return all products that start with any character but have "ouse" as the next four characters, you could use the following SQL statement:

```
SELECT * FROM Products
WHERE Name LIKE '_ouse'
```

The underscore translates to exactly one character. With the data outlined in Table 19.1, only the Mouse row would be returned. However, if you had a product named Louse, it would be returned with the preceding SQL statement as well. If you wanted to be more specific and only return products that contain "A" through "F" as their first character and "ouse" as their next four, the following two SQL statements would do the trick:

```
SELECT * FROM Products
WHERE Name LIKE '[a-f]ouse'
```

```
SELECT * FROM Products
WHERE Name LIKE '[abcdef]ouse'
```

Braces ([ ]) can be used to specify a range of characters that are allowable. The first of the preceding SQL statements, uses the dash (-) to specify the character range from "a" through "f." The second SQL statement simply lists each of the allowable characters.

If the WHERE clause is not used in a SQL statement, *all* the rows from the table being queried will be returned. Conditional and logical operators can be used to construct a statement that evaluates to either True or False. The logical operators AND, OR, and NOT can be used to create WHERE clauses based on multiple criteria.

Working with the ORDER BY Clause

When performing a SQL statement, such as SELECT * FROM Products, there is no guarantee on what order the rows of the Products table will be returned. To return the rows in an order based on the values in a particular column, you can use the ORDER BY clause of the SELECT statement. For example, if you wanted to return all the columns from the Products table but have the products listed alphabetically by the value in their Name column, you could use the following SQL statement:

```
SELECT * FROM Products
ORDER BY Name
```

The default type of ordering is ascending ordering. Due to the *ASCII values* of the alphabet, "A" has a lesser value than "Z."

19

NEW TERM *ASCII*, or the American Standard Code for Information Interchange, is a mapping from the numbers 0 through 255 to alphanumeric characters. Each unique character in the alphabet has an ASCII value.

When performing an ORDER BY on a column containing string data, the characters are converted into their ASCII values and ordered based on that. If you wanted to list the products in reverse alphabetical order, you would need to order the Name column in descending order. To do this, use the keyword DESC after the column name in the ORDER BY clause. For example, the following SQL statement would retrieve just the Name and Price columns from the Products table and return the rows based on reverse alphabetical order of the Name column:

```
SELECT Name, Price FROM Products
ORDER BY Name DESC
```

If you wanted to order the products based on their inventory, you could use the following SQL statement, which would list the products based on the descending order of the value in their Inventory column:

```
SELECT * FROM Products
ORDER BY Inventory DESC
```

Refer back to Table 19.2, which contains the data in the Products table. Note that both the Game Pad and the Modem have the same value in their Inventory column. What one will be listed first? It depends on external variables. If multiple rows share the same value in a column being sorted, you can specify a second column to resolve the sorting on the first. Perhaps, if there is a tie in the Inventory column, you would want to have the tie resolved by ordering the Price column.

The default ordering performed by the ORDER BY clause is ascending order. For example, if you wanted to sort the rows of the Products table in alphabetical order (ascending order of the ASCII character set), either of these two SQL statements would suffice:

```
SELECT Name, Price FROM Products
ORDER BY Name
```

```
SELECT Name, Price FROM Products
ORDER BY Name ASC
```

Note that you can either explicitly state to have the results sorted in ascending order using the ASC keyword, or you can leave it off; and, by default, the results will be sorted in ascending order. Table 19.6 lists the two keywords that can be used with the ORDER BY clause.

TABLE 19.6   The ORDER BY Keywords

Keyword	Description
ASC	The default sorting order. Indicates that the column should be sorted in ascending order (from the lowest value to the highest value).
DESC	Indicates that the column should be sorted in descending order (from the highest value to the lowest value).

The ORDER BY clause expects a comma-delimited list of columns to order. The first column in the list is the primary column that the ordering is performed on. If there are ties in the primary column, the secondary column is used to resolve the tie. The secondary column comes second in the comma-delimited list. If there is a tie in the secondary column, the tertiary column is used, and so forth. If you wanted to revise the previous SQL statement so that ties in the Inventory column would be sorted based on a descending order of the value in the Price column, you could use the following:

```
SELECT * FROM Products
ORDER BY Inventory DESC, Price DESC
```

When using both the WHERE clause and the ORDER BY clause in a SELECT statement, the WHERE clause needs to precede the ORDER BY clause. For example, if you wanted to retrieve only the rows in the Products table that cost $100 or more and have those rows in order based on their price, from least expensive to most expensive, the following SQL statement would suffice:

```
SELECT * FROM Products
WHERE Price >= 100
ORDER BY Price
```

However, if the ORDER BY clause were placed *before* the WHERE clause, an error would be generated.

The SELECT statement is incredibly powerful. Today's lesson only touches on the basics of the SELECT statement. An entire book could be written exclusively on using the SELECT statement to query tables. To learn the intricacies of SQL, there are many helpful books, such as *Sams Teach Yourself SQL in 21 Days*. We have discussed some of the most common uses of the SELECT statements, the clauses that are used 95% of the time. A more thorough discussion is beyond the scope of this book.

Now that you've looked at how to use the SELECT statement, it is important that you examine how to iterate through recordsets created by SQL statements in ASP pages. This is the topic of the next section, "Iterating Through Recordsets Generated by SQL Statements." Later today, in "Allowing Users to Query Data," we will look at some real-world examples of using SQL statements to retrieve information based on user input.

19

Iterating Through Recordsets Generated by SQL Statements

We've shown how to create SQL statements that will retrieve particular subsets of tables, as opposed to the entire table. When using SQL statements in ASP pages, it is important to follow these five simple steps, which were discussed earlier today in "Executing SQL Statements Using ASP and ADO":

1. Create and open a connection to the database. To do this, use the `Connection` object.
2. Create a string variable to hold your SQL statement.
3. Assign your SQL statement to this variable.
4. Create an instance of the `Recordset` object.
5. Execute the `Open` method of the `Recordset` object.

Recall from Day 16 that the `Recordset` object should be thought of as a two-dimensional matrix. When you populate the `Recordset` object with the `Open` method, you begin by being able to read the first row of the matrix. To access any column in the current row, use the following syntax:

```
objRecordsetObjectInstance(columnName)
```

To move on to the next row in the matrix, use the `MoveNext` method of the `Recordset` object. When using a SQL statement to populate the recordset, the *selectList* in the `SELECT` statement contains each available column that you can access through the `Recordset` object instance. You iterate through a `Recordset` object the same way (via a `Do While Not objRS.EOF ... Loop`), whether the `Recordset` was generated using a SQL statement or not.

Let's look at an example of iterating through a `Recordset` object generated by a SQL statement. Listing 19.3 shows an ASP page that lists the items in the `Products` table in descending order by price.

LISTING 19.3 A Listing of the `Products` Table, Ordered by the `Price`

```
1:  <%@ Language=VBScript %>
2:  <% Option Explicit %>
3:  <!--#include virtual="/adovbs.inc"-->
4:  <%
5:      'Open up a connection to our Access database that stores the
6:      'customer information.  We will use a DSN-less connection here.
7:      Dim objConn
8:      Set objConn = Server.CreateObject("ADODB.Connection")
9:      objConn.ConnectionString = "DSN=ProductsDB"
10:     objConn.Open
11:
```

```
12:     'Create our SQL statement variable
13:     Dim strSQL
14:     strSQL = "SELECT Name, Price FROM Products ORDER BY Price DESC"
15:
16:     'Create a recordset object instance, and execute the SQL statement
17:     Dim objRS
18:     Set objRS = Server.CreateObject("ADODB.Recordset")
19:     objRS.Open strSQL, objConn
20:
21:     'We are displaying the products ordered by price
22:     Response.Write "<B>A Listing of Products:</B><BR>"
23:     Do While Not objRS.EOF
24:        Response.Write objRS("Name") & " - " & _
25:                        FormatCurrency(objRS("Price")) & "<BR>"
26:
27:        'Move on to the next customer
28:        objRS.MoveNext
29:     Loop
30:
31:     'Clean up our ADO objects
32:     objRS.Close
33:     Set objRS = Nothing
34:
35:     objConn.Close
36:     Set objConn = Nothing
37: %>
```

ANALYSIS   Listing 19.3 displays all the records in the Products table, ordered by the Price column in descending order. Note that when you use a SQL statement to populate a Recordset object, you perform the five steps outlined previously. Step 1, creating a connection to the database, is accomplished in lines 8 through 10. Next, for step 2, line 13 creates a string variable to hold the SQL statement. Line 14 performs step 3, assigning the actual SQL statement to the SQL statement variable, strSQL. Step 4, creating an instance of the Recordset object, is accomplished on line 18. The Recordset object instance is named objRS. Line 19 completes step 5, by executing the Open method of the Recordset object, populating objRS with the results of the SQL statement.

The remainder of the script iterates through objRS, displaying the Name and Price columns of each row. Remember that you only have those two columns to work with because the SQL statement on line 14 includes the Name and Price columns in the *selectList*. Lines 23 through 29 use a Do While ... Loop to iterate through the Recordset object, displaying the Name and Price on lines 24 and 25. When completed, lines 32 through 36 close and explicitly free both of ADO objects. Figure 19.3 shows the output of Listing 19.3.

19

FIGURE **19.3**

The most expensive products are listed first.

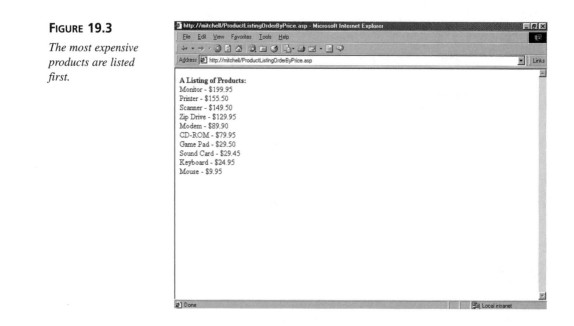

Listing 19.3 shows an example of ordering a query using the ORDER BY clause of a SQL statement. Let's now look at an example that uses the WHERE clause to limit the number of records returned. Listing 19.4 lists only the products whose Name begins with the letter "M."

LISTING 19.4   A Listing of the Products that Begin with the Letter "M"

```
1:  <%@ Language=VBScript %>
2:  <% Option Explicit %>
3:  <!--#include virtual="/adovbs.inc"-->
4:  <%
5:      'Open up a connection to our Access database that stores the customer
6:      'information.  We will use a DSN-less connection here.
7:      Dim objConn
8:      Set objConn = Server.CreateObject("ADODB.Connection")
9:      objConn.ConnectionString = "DSN=ProductsDB"
10:     objConn.Open
11:
12:     'Create our SQL statement variable
13:     Dim strSQL
14:     strSQL = "SELECT Name, Inventory FROM Products WHERE Name LIKE 'M%'"
15:
16:     'Create a recordset object instance, and execute the SQL statement
17:     Dim objRS
18:     Set objRS = Server.CreateObject("ADODB.Recordset")
19:     objRS.Open strSQL, objConn
20:
21:     'We are displaying products beginning with "M"
22:     Response.Write "<B>A Listing of Products:</B><BR>"
```

```
23:    Do While Not objRS.EOF
24:       Response.Write objRS("Name") & " - " & _
25:                      FormatNumber(objRS("Inventory"), 0) & "<BR>"
26:
27:        'Move on to the next customer
28:        objRS.MoveNext
29:    Loop
30:
31:    'Clean up our ADO objects
32:    objRS.Close
33:    Set objRS = Nothing
34:
35:    objConn.Close
36:    Set objConn = Nothing
37: %>
```

ANALYSIS Regardless of whether the SQL statement contains a WHERE clause or an ORDER BY clause, the same five steps should be followed. The code in Listing 19.4 is nearly identical to that in Listing 19.3. The only differences are the following:

- Line 14—The SQL statement has been modified to return only the products that begin with the letter "M." Also, the only two columns being returned are the Name and the Inventory.

- Lines 24 and 25—Instead of displaying the Price using FormatCurrency, the Inventory is displayed using FormatNumber.

Figure 19.4 contains the output of Listing 19.4.

FIGURE 19.4

Only the products whose names begin with "M" are shown.

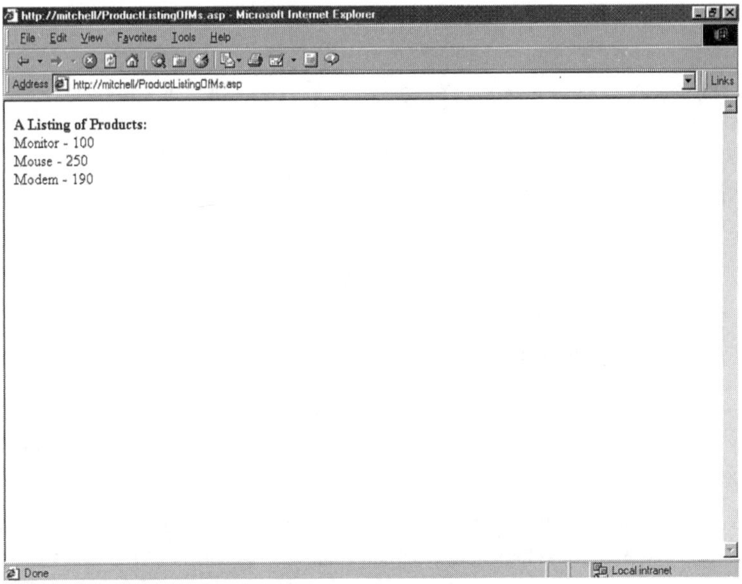

19

Note that in the WHERE clause in the SQL statement, the M% is surrounded with single quotes. Because you are performing a comparison on a column that contains string data, you need to surround the value you are comparing with single quotes. This is important! Failure to surround the value with quotes will lead to an error when you view your ASP page through a browser. Figure 19.5 contains the error message you will receive if you don't surround the values with single quotes. Remember, you only want to use single quotes around the values being compared to table columns that contain string or date data.

FIGURE 19.5

An error will occur if you leave the single quotes off the M% on line 14 in Listing 19.3.

Allowing Users to Query Data

Today, we've examined how to use SQL statements to selectively populate Recordset objects. The true power of using SQL statements is when you allow users to fill in a form to determine the data they see. Early examples today used a Products table. Wouldn't it be neat if you could allow your users to selectively list certain products? Providing such a listing mechanism is not that vital when you only have 10 products in your table, but imagine that you had 1,000. If many records are in a table, providing the user a means to refine the listing is necessary.

Do	Don't
DO provide a means of selectively listing the contents of a table if there are many rows in the table.	**DON'T** list the entire contents of a table that contains hundreds or thousands of rows.

Perhaps you want to allow users to list only the products that cost less than a certain amount. Listing 19.5 shows the form creation page, SelectMaxPrice.asp, that allows the user to select a maximum price.

LISTING 19.5 Selecting a Maximum Price for the Listed Products

```
1:  <HTML>
2:  <BODY>
3:   <FORM METHOD=POST ACTION="ListProducts.asp">
4:    <B>What is the most money you will pay
5:       for a computer item?</B><BR>
6:    Price: $<INPUT TYPE=TEXT NAME=Price VALUE="100.00" SIZE=8>
7:    <P>
8:    <INPUT TYPE=SUBMIT VALUE="List Products">
9:   </FORM>
10: </BODY>
11: </HTML>
```

ANALYSIS The code in Listing 19.5 creates a form that has one form field, a text box (line 6). Into this form field, the user enters the maximum price he is willing to pay. When the form ListProducts.asp is submitted, the form processing script is called, and a SQL statement is created with the WHERE dynamically generated based on the user's input. Figure 19.6 shows the output of SelectMaxPrice.asp when viewed through a browser.

FIGURE 19.6

The user can choose the maximum price of the products to list.

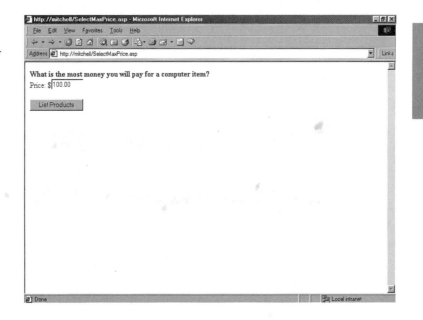

19

When the form in `SelectMaxPrice.asp` is submitted, the form processing script, `ListProducts.asp`, is called and passed the form field value the user entered. What steps does `ListProducts.asp` need to accomplish to list all the products less than the price entered by the user? All you need to do is generate a SQL statement so that you take into effect the value entered by the user in the form creation Web page. You can use the same code from Listing 19.3 to iterate through the recordset and display its contents. Listing 19.6 shows the code for `ListProducts.asp`.

LISTING 19.6 The Products Less Than the Price the User Entered

```
 1:  <%@ Language=VBScript %>
 2:  <% Option Explicit %>
 3:  <!--#include virtual="/adovbs.inc"-->
 4:  <%
 5:    'Open up a connection to our Access database
 6:    'that stores the customer
 7:    'information.  We will use a DSN-less connection here.
 8:    Dim objConn
 9:    Set objConn = Server.CreateObject("ADODB.Connection")
10:    objConn.ConnectionString = "DSN=ProductsDB"
11:    objConn.Open
12:
13:    'Read in the value max price value entered by the user
14:    Dim iMaxPrice
15:    iMaxPrice = Request("Price")
16:
17:    'Make sure that iMaxPrice is a numeric value.  If it is not, set
18:    'iMaxPrice to 100
19:    If Len(iMaxPrice) = 0 or Not IsNumeric(iMaxPrice) then
20:      iMaxPrice = 100
21:    End If
22:
23:    'Create our SQL statement variable
24:    Dim strSQL
25:    strSQL = "SELECT Name, Price FROM Products WHERE Price <= " & _
26:            iMaxPrice & " ORDER BY Price DESC"
27:
28:    'Create a recordset object instance, and execute the SQL statement
29:    Dim objRS
30:    Set objRS = Server.CreateObject("ADODB.Recordset")
31:    objRS.Open strSQL, objConn
32:
33:    'We are displaying products whose price is less than iMaxPrice
34:    Response.Write "<B>A Listing of Products less than " & _
35:                FormatCurrency(iMaxPrice) & ":</B><BR>"
36:    Do While Not objRS.EOF
37:      Response.Write objRS("Name") & " - " & _
38:                FormatCurrency(objRS("Price")) & "<BR>"
```

```
39:
40:    'Move on to the next customer
41:    objRS.MoveNext
42:  Loop
43:
44:    'Clean up our ADO objects
45:    objRS.Close
46:    Set objRS = Nothing
47:
48:    objConn.Close
49:    Set objConn = Nothing
50: %>
```

ANALYSIS   The code in Listing 19.6 is strikingly similar to that in Listing 19.3. You follow the same five steps of using SQL statements within ASP pages whether or not the SQL statements are being dynamically generated. Lines 9 through 11 start by creating and opening the connection to the database, thereby completing step 1. Before moving on to steps 2 and 3, you need to obtain the value that the user entered in SelectMaxPrice.asp. You do this by first creating a variable named iMaxPrice to hold this information (line 14). Next, line 15 retrieves the value the user entered into the form field in SelectMaxPrice.asp. Next, line 19 checks to make sure that the user entered a value into the form's text box and that this value is numerically valid. If the user has not entered a value, or has entered a non-numeric value, such as abc, line 20 sets iMaxPrice equal to 100.

After you have the user's maximum price, you can proceed to steps 2 and 3. Line 24 creates the variable to hold the SQL statement, and then line 25 dynamically creates the SQL statement. The SQL statement uses a WHERE clause to obtain all the rows whose Price is less than or equal to iMaxPrice. The SQL statement also incorporates an ORDER BY statement so that the products returned will be listed in descending order by their price.

Lines 30 and 31 complete steps 4 and 5, creating the Recordset object instance and populating it with the Open method. The remainder of Listing 19.6 iterates through the recordset and displays the Name and Price of the products returned by the SQL statement. The rest of the code in Listing 19.6 is nearly identical to the code from line 21 on in Listing 19.3.

The output of Listing 19.6, of course, depends on the input entered by the user. If the user entered in 100 as the maximum price in SelectMaxPrice.asp, the output of Listing 19.6, when viewed through a browser, would be the same as shown in Figure 19.7.

19

FIGURE 19.7

*Only those items less
than $100 are listed.*

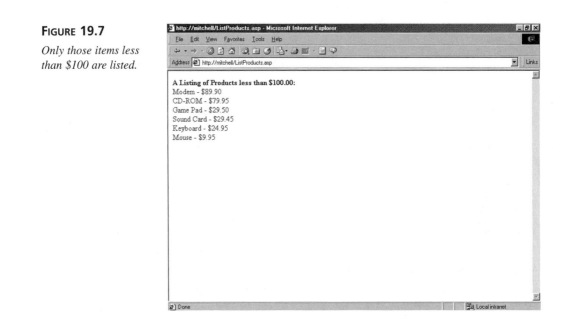

What happens if the user wants to see all products that cost less than a dollar? Because
the cheapest product in the Products table costs $9.95, this is the SQL statement that
will be executed:

```
SELECT Name, Price
FROM Products
WHERE Price <= 1
ORDER BY Price DESC
```

This will return zero rows because a row in the Products table does not exist whose
Price column has a value of 1 or less. The Recordset object objRS, then, will contain
zero records. The Do While Not objRS.EOF ... Loop on line 36 in Listing 19.6 will
not run because objRS.EOF will evaluate to True immediately. Therefore, the output
would be A Listing of Products less than $1.00:. No products will be shown
because there are no products less than a dollar.

If there are no products less than the price entered by the user, and the user sees nothing
but A Listing of Products less than $1.00: (line 34 and 35, Listing 19.6), she is
bound to think one of two things: no products are listed, therefore there are no products
costing less than a dollar; or, no products are listed, the thing must be broken! Although
nothing is technically wrong with the code in Listing 19.6 (after all, it does show all the
products less than the price the user entered!), you don't want to confuse users. If no
records are available, it is standard convention to display a message that indicates this to
the user.

To determine whether there are records in the Recordset object, you can use an If statement that checks the objRS.EOF. Recall from Day 16 that EOF returns True if you have moved through all the rows in the Recordset object matrix. If EOF evaluates to True, you want to display a message to the user. If EOF is not True, you want to perform the Do While ... Loop that will display all the records in the Recordset object. Listing 19.8 shows a code example of this.

Listing 19.6 lets the user list products based on a maximum price. What if you wanted to allow the user to list the products that start with a certain letter, or combination of letters? The user could enter mo into a text box and would be shown the Monitor, Mouse, and Modem products, along with their prices. For this, you need two pages: a form creation Web page and a form processing script. Listing 19.7 shows the form creation Web page.

LISTING 19.7   Listing Products by Their Name

```
 1:  <HTML>
 2:  <BODY>
 3:    <FORM METHOD=POST ACTION="ListProductsByName.asp">
 4:      <B>Enter the first few characters of the
 5:          product you are searching for:</B><BR>
 6:      <INPUT TYPE=TEXT NAME=ProductName SIZE=10>
 7:      <P>
 8:      <INPUT TYPE=SUBMIT VALUE="List Products">
 9:    </FORM>
10: </BODY>
11: </HTML>
```

ANALYSIS   Listing 19.7 creates a form that contains a single text box, into which the user can enter one to many letters by which to narrow the listing of products (line 6). The form, when submitted, calls ListProductsByName.asp, the form processing script (line 3). Figure 19.8 shows the output of Listing 19.7 when viewed through a browser.

When the form in SelectProductByName.asp is submitted, the form processing script, ListProductsByName.asp, is called and passed the value the user entered into the text box. The code for ListProductsByName.asp is similar to the code in Listing 19.6. To display the products that begin with a certain string of characters, you need to generate a SQL statement that returns the products whose Name column begins with the characters entered by the user. Then Open the Recordset object with the SQL statement and determine whether the Recordset object contains any records. If the Recordset object contains no records, you want to display a message to the user or else list the records. Listing 19.8 contains the code for ListProductsByName.asp:

19

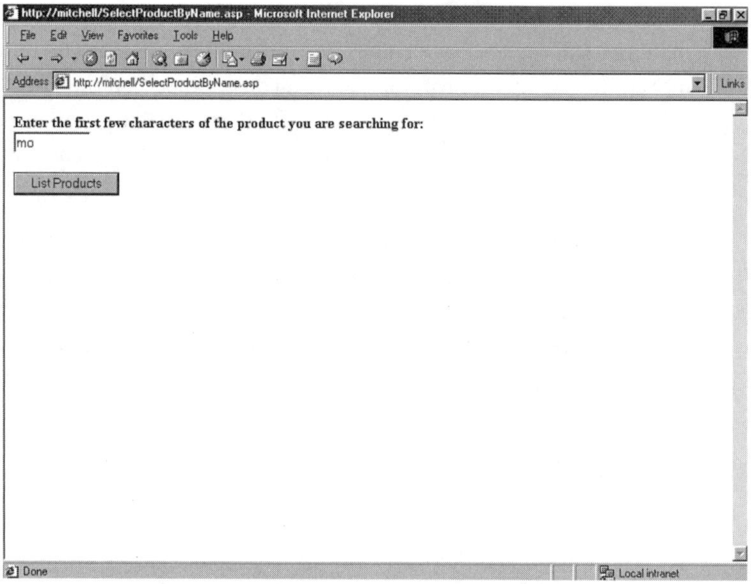

FIGURE **19.8**

The user can narrow the listing of products by entering the first few characters of the products she wants to see.

LISTING **19.8** Listing Only the Products that Start with Certain Characters

```
1:  <%@ Language=VBScript %>
2:  <% Option Explicit %>
3:  <!--#include virtual="/adovbs.inc"-->
4:  <%
5:      'Open up a connection to our Access database
6:      'that stores the customer
7:      'information.  We will use a DSN-less connection here.
8:      Dim objConn
9:      Set objConn = Server.CreateObject("ADODB.Connection")
10:     objConn.ConnectionString = "DSN=ProductsDB"
11:     objConn.Open
12:
13:     'Read in the characters the user entered
14:     Dim strProductName
15:     strProductName = Trim(Request("ProductName"))
16:
17:     'Create our SQL statement variable
18:     Dim strSQL
19:     strSQL = "SELECT Name, Price FROM Products WHERE Name LIKE '" & _
20:              strProductName & "%' ORDER BY Name"
21:
22:     'Create a recordset object instance, and execute the SQL statement
23:     Dim objRS
24:     Set objRS = Server.CreateObject("ADODB.Recordset")
25:     objRS.Open strSQL, objConn
26:
27:     'Determine whether or not there are any records in objRS
```

```
28:    If objRS.EOF then
29:      'No records were returned for the characters entered by the user
30:       Response.Write "There are no products that begin with " & _
31:                      UCase(strProductName)
32:    Else
33:      'There are one or more products that meet the condition entered
34:      'by the user.  Display these products...
35:       Response.Write "<B>A Listing of Products beginning with " & _
36:                      UCase(strProductName) & ":</B><BR>"
37:  ←  Do While Not objRS.EOF
38:        Response.Write objRS("Name") & " - " & _
39:                      FormatCurrency(objRS("Price")) & "<BR>"
40:
41:          'Move on to the next customer
42:          objRS.MoveNext
43:      Loop
44:    End If
45:
46:    'Clean up our ADO objects
47:    objRS.Close
48:    Set objRS = Nothing
49:
50:    objConn.Close
51:    Set objConn = Nothing
52: %>
```

ANALYSIS   Listing 19.8 displays only those products that begin with the characters entered by the user in SelectProductByName.asp. Listing 19.8 follows the same five steps when using SQL statements in ASP pages. The first step, creating and opening a connection to the database, is accomplished on lines 9 through 11. Before you can create the SQL statement, you need to retrieve the input entered by the user in the form in SelectProductByName.asp. Line 14 creates a variable named strProductName, and line 15 sets it equal to the form field ProductName. Note that line 15 uses the Trim function on the form field value before assigning it to strProductName. Recall that Trim strips the leading and trailing spaces from a string. You do this so that if a person enters "m" or " m", she will be shown the same product listing.

Next, line 18 creates the SQL string, strSQL (step 2). Lines 19 and 20 then assign the SQL statement to this string. The SQL statement retrieves two columns, Name and Price, from the Products table and only returns those rows whose Name column starts with the characters in strProductName. Note that the LIKE operator is used. Because you are performing a comparison on the Name column, which contains string data, you *must* place single quotes around the value you are comparing the Name column to. That is why lines 19 and 20 have WHERE Name '" & strProductName & "%'. Those single quotes before the value of strProductName and after the wildcard character %, are needed because Name contains string data. The lack of single quotes will generate an error.

19

Because you want to return all products that begin with the characters specified by strProductName, you need to use the wildcard character % following the value of strProductName. Earlier today, in "Using the WHERE Clause," we discussed the wildcard characters that can be used with the LIKE operator. The percent sign (%) is a wildcard character that translates into zero to many characters. Table 19.5 contains a list of the wildcards that can be used with the LIKE operator. So, any product that begins with the characters in strProductName and is followed by zero or more characters will be retrieved.

If the user has entered a series of characters that will return more than one product, you want to have those products ordered alphabetically. To accomplish this, the ORDER BY Name is tacked to the SQL statement after the WHERE clause (line 20). This will order the rows returned alphabetically.

Now that you've completed steps 2 and 3 (creating a variable to hold the SQL statement and assigning the SQL statement to this variable, respectively), you need to complete step 4, creating an instance of the Recordset object. This is accomplished on line 24, creating an instance of the Recordset object named objRS. Line 25 executes the Open method of the Recordset object, populating the results from the SQL query into objRS.

At this point, you need to determine whether objRS contains any records. If objRS contains no records, objRS.EOF will evaluate to True. Line 28 uses an If statement to determine whether objRS contains any records. If objRS does *not* contain any records, the code on lines 29 through 31 will be executed, displaying a message to the user. If, on the other hand, objRS does contain records, the block of code between the Else (line 32) and the End If (line 44) will be executed. This code uses a Do While ... Loop to display the records in the Recordset object objRS.

The code in Listing 19.8 ends with the all-important closing and explicit freeing of the ADO objects (lines 47 through 51). Figure 19.9 shows the output of Listing 19.8 when the user has entered mo in the form in SelectProductByName.asp. Figure 19.10 shows the output of Listing 19.8 when there are no products for the characters entered by the user.

If the user enters a few characters that do not correspond to any product in the Products table, the user is presented the output in Figure 19.10. Such a message provides much more information to the user than not listing any products whatsoever. Always add such functionality to any ASP page that lists rows from a database table. Nothing is more confusing to a user than seeing a blank Web page.

In this section, you've looked at how to allow the user to selectively list the contents of a table. If you need to display the information inside a table to your users, one option is to simply display the entire contents of the table. This quickly becomes unfeasible as the amount of data in the table grows. To provide easier-to-read information, you can collect the user's input on the subset of rows from the table he is interested in seeing.

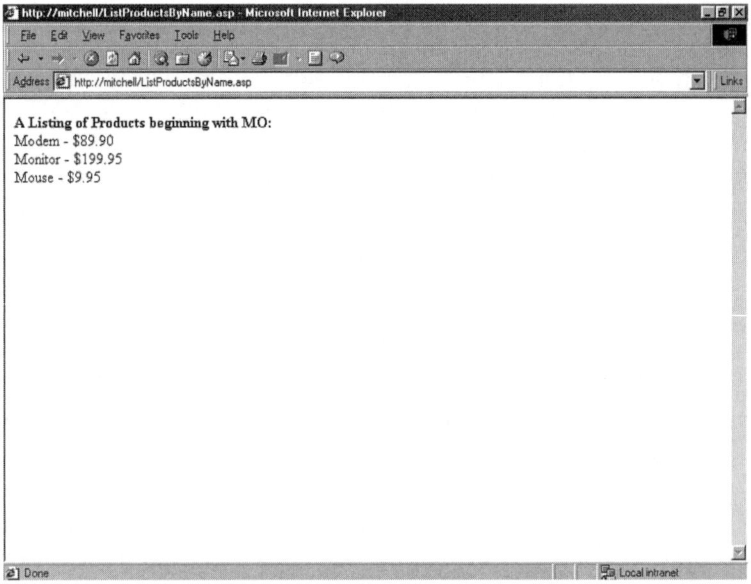

FIGURE **19.9**

Only a selective list of products are shown.

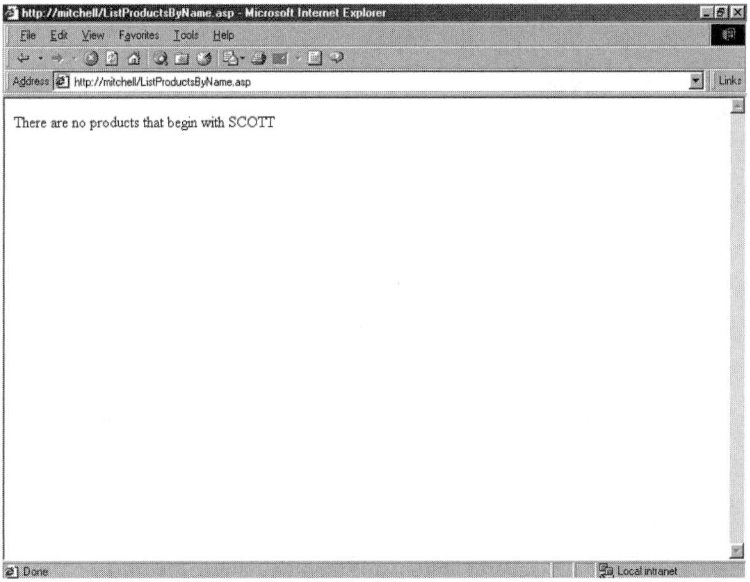

A Listing of Products beginning with MO:
Modem - $89.90
Monitor - $199.95
Mouse - $9.95

FIGURE **19.10**

When there are no products, a message is displayed.

There are no products that begin with SCOTT

19

Tip

Provide your users with multiple ways of listing items in a database table. If users are allowed to list products either by name or maximum price, it will be easier for them to find the products they are interested in.

Summary

Today, you learned how to retrieve only certain columns and rows from tables in a database. Previous to today's lesson, you were only able to retrieve the entire contents of a table. Retrieving all the rows and columns of a table is often overkill because you are usually only interested in a certain subset of information in a table. Also, if a table contains thousands of rows, retrieving all those rows takes a considerable amount of time.

To obtain a specific set of columns and rows from a table in a relational database, you need to communicate with the database in a language known as SQL, which stands for Structured Query Language. SQL is a standard language, common to all relational databases, from Access to Microsoft's SQL Server to Oracle and Informix.

SQL can be used to update, insert, delete, and retrieve records from a table. Today we focused on using SQL to retrieve records. To retrieve a set of rows from a table using SQL, the SELECT statement is used. The SELECT statement is composed of many *clauses*. These clauses determine what columns and rows are retrieved from what table. The SELECT clause determines what columns are returned. The FROM clause determines from what table the columns and rows are returned. The WHERE clause is used to limit the rows returned from a table, whereas the ORDER BY clause is used to order the rows based on the values in a particular column in the table.

A SQL statement can be used to populate a Recordset object through the use of the Recordset object's Open method. After a Recordset object instance has been populated with the results from a SQL statement, you can iterate through the Recordset object instance just as you have before, using objRS(*columnName*) to obtain a particular column in the current row and the MoveNext method to advance to the next row in the Recordset object's matrix. When using SQL statements in an ASP page, you should follow five simple steps. Following these five steps, outlined today in "Executing SQL Statements Using ASP and ADO," will make using SQL statements in your ASP pages simple.

Finally, you learned how a user's input can affect the generation of a SQL statement. By allowing your users' inputs to dynamically create SQL statements, each user can view a specific, custom set of information from a given table. Such a custom view of data in a table is a useful feature in almost any database application. Being able to create such a custom view using ASP is one reason why ASP is so powerful and useful.

Tomorrow, Day 20, "Using Advanced Database Techniques," we will discuss some of the more advanced features involved with ADO. The Recordset object has many advanced properties and methods that we have not yet discussed, which will be examined in detail tomorrow. We will also discuss the use of stored procedures, which are efficient, precompiled queries.

Q&A

Q **Where can I find more information about the SQL syntax?**

A This chapter introduced you to the SQL SELECT statement. However, only a few of the clauses of the SELECT statement were discussed in today's lesson. To learn more about the SELECT statement, or SQL's other statements, such as the UPDATE, DELETE, and INSERT statements, many Web sites have pertinent information. Some of the most information-laden Web sites are listed in Appendix D, "Helpful ASP Information on the Net." Many great books also have been written about the SQL language, such as *Sams Teach Yourself SQL in 21 Days*.

Q **When I run an ASP page that dynamically generates a SQL statement based on a user's input, I get a database error. What is the best way to debug such an error?**

A When allowing the user to enter input that will dynamically generate a SQL state-ment, an error might occur depending on the information entered by the user. For example, Listing 19.6 showed the products that are less than a certain price entered by the user. If the user enters a price of abc, the SQL statement generated will be as follows:

```
SELECT Name, Price
FROM Products
WHERE Price <= abc
ORDER BY Price DESC
```

This will cause an error because the database doesn't know how to compare abc to the Price column, which contains currency values. To prevent this error, Listing 19.6 uses an If statement on line 18 to determine whether the value entered by the user is a valid numeric value.

The best way to debug such a possible error is to place the following line

```
Response.Write "SQL String = " & strSQL
```

immediately before you execute the Open method of the Recordset object. This will display the exact value of the SQL statement that the database is receiving. You can view this SQL statement and determine what problems exist with the SQL statement.

Q **Can I use a SELECT statement to retrieve data from more than one table?**

A Yes, you can. The SELECT statement is incredibly versatile and amazingly powerful. The SELECT statement can retrieve data from multiple tables and even be used to bring back nicely formatted information on multiple, related tables. However, the syntax for retrieving data from multiple tables is not trivial and is beyond the scope of this book. Many great books on the SQL language have chapters dedicated to this topic.

19

Workshop

The Workshop provides quiz questions to help you solidify your understanding of the material covered and exercises to provide you with experience in using what you've learned. Try to understand the quiz and exercise answers before continuing to tomorrow's lesson. Quiz answers are provided in Appendix A, and exercise answers can be found at `http://www.mcp.com/info`.

Quiz

1. What does the acronym SQL stand for?
2. True or False: The only required clause of the SELECT statement is the SELECT clause.
3. What comparison operators can you use in the WHERE clause of a SELECT statement?
4. What logical operators can you use in the WHERE clause of a SELECT statement?
5. What is the order of precedence for the logical operators?
6. What does the wildcard character % do when used with the LIKE operator?
7. True or False: The ORDER BY clause can only accept a single column name to order the results by.
8. True or False: The SELECT statement consists of only four clauses—the SELECT clause, the FROM clause, the WHERE clause, and the ORDER BY clause.
9. When comparing a column to a value in the WHERE clause, under what circumstances do you need to surround the value with single quotes?
10. What five steps should you follow when using SQL statements in ASP pages?

Exercises

1. Imagine that you have a table for employee information. This table, EmployeeInfo, consists of five columns: FirstName, LastName, SSN, Age, and Salary. Write a SELECT statement that will retrieve the FirstName, LastName, and Salary columns from the EmployeeInfo table where the employee is more than 50 years old, or the employee's Salary is less than or equal to $25,000. Order the results by the Salary, in ascending order.

2. Create an ASP page that will display the results of the SQL statement from Exercise 1. Assume that a DSN named Employee exists, which you can use to connect to the Employee database, which contains the table EmployeeInfo. Be sure to use FormatCurrency when displaying the employee's salary.

3. Create two ASP pages, a form creation Web page (SelectEmployeeByAge.asp) and a form processing script (ListEmployeeByAge.asp). In SelectEmployeeByAge.asp, the user should be shown a form into which she can enter a desired age. When the form is submitted, ListEmployeeByAge.asp lists all the employees whose Age is identical to the value entered by the user. Just the employee's name and age should be shown.

WEEK 3

DAY 20

Using Advanced Database Techniques

On Day 18, "Examining the Recordset Object," and on Day 19, "Using SQL Statements to Query Data," we explored some of the more advanced database techniques. We looked at how to sort and filter results using both the Sort and Filter properties of the Recordset object, and the WHERE and ORDER BY clauses of the SELECT statement. Today, we are going to continue our foray into advanced database topics.

We will start today's lesson by discussing the advanced properties of the Recordset object in fine detail. In previous lessons, we've mentioned the CursorType, CursorLocation, and LockType properties. However, today we will examine these properties in detail. We will also discuss an alternative way to populate a Recordset object *without* using the Open method.

Until now, all of our SQL SELECT queries have been *runtime SQL statements*. That is, the database had no idea what we were going to ask it to do until we needed the information. You can make the process of querying data more efficient by using stored procedures, which precompiled SQL queries. The database *knows* more about these stored procedure queries because they have already been run at least once before. With this knowledge, the database can increase its efficiency when performing a stored procedure SQL query.

Finally, we'll discuss yet another ADO object, the Command object, which can be thought of as a combination of the Connection and Recordset objects. ADO provides many ways to accomplish the same task, and the Command object is similar in nature. There is no task that can *only* be accomplished through the use of the Command object. Regardless, it is important to examine this object and study how it can be used to query and modify information in a database.

Today, you will learn the following:

- The differences between the four types of database cursors
- How to count the number of records in a Recordset
- The differences between the four types of locks
- How to implicitly create Recordsets using the Execute method of the Connection object
- What stored procedures are
- The benefits of using stored procedures
- How to create stored procedures in Microsoft SQL Server 7.0 and Access 2000
- How to execute a stored procedure from an ASP page
- How to implicitly create Recordsets using the Execute method of the Command object

Advanced Features of the Recordset Object

Recall that the Recordset object's primary purpose is to gather the data from a database table or from a SQL SELECT statement. If there is a table in your database that you want to display through a Web page, the Recordset object should be used to gather the contents of the table. Then, through a Do ... Loop, the contents of the Recordset object could be outputted to the client.

On Day 16, "Reading from a Database Using ASP," we discussed how to read the contents of a table using the Recordset object. On Day 18, we discussed how to use the Sort and Filter properties to enhance the output of a table so that the results would be easier for a human to peruse.

The Recordset object, however, is not limited to simply reading data from a database. On Day 17, we discussed how to update, insert, and delete database records using the Recordset object. The Recordset object is fairly versatile and contains many properties—some that we've yet to discuss, such as MovePrevious, and some that we've only touched on, such as CursorType and LockType.

Throughout the next few sections, we will discuss these properties in detail. Because the `Recordset` object is used both to query and modify data from a database, having a thorough understanding of the `Recordset` object is important.

Choosing the Right Cursor

When a database is queried for information, a set of records is returned. Imagine that a database table has 20 rows. When you use the `Open` method of the `Recordset` object to retrieve the contents of that table, all 20 rows are returned in one large object. It's difficult to work with this set of information as a whole because you usually are interested in each discrete record in the set of records. A database cursor, graphically represented in Figure 20.1, indicates the individual record you're currently examining and its position relative to the other records in the set of records.

FIGURE 20.1

A database cursor indicates what record is currently being processed.

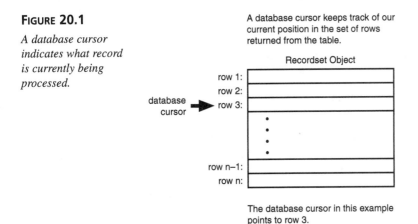

A database cursor keeps track of our current position in the set of rows returned from the table.

The database cursor in this example points to row 3.

The default database cursor used, when `Opening` a `Recordset`, is the forward-only cursor, sometimes referred to as a fire hose cursor. The forward-only cursor is the most efficient cursor but has limited movement. When using a forward-only cursor, you can only move from one record to the next. You cannot move to a previous record, or jump forward or backward several records.

The other three available cursors are referred to as *scrollable cursors* because these cursors allow both forward and backward movement. Table 20.1 lists these three cursors' functionalities.

20

TABLE 20.1 Characteristics of Scrollable Cursors

Cursor	Constant	Properties
Static	adOpenStatic	The results of the query are stored in a temporary database. The rows in this temporary database are not updated while the cursor is opened.
Keyset	adOpenKeyset	A Keyset cursor saves the keys associated with each row returned by the query in a temporary database. By just saving the keys, any changes to the data in these rows will be seen while the cursor is open.
Dynamic	adOpenDynamic	The dynamic cursor reapplies the query each time a new row is requested from the set of rows opened by the cursor. This means not only that updates are seen, but also that if new rows are added or deleted, they can affect the structure of the Recordset.

Keep in mind that multiple people can modify a database simultaneously. Imagine the following situation:

1. You use the Open method of the Recordset object to obtain the contents of a database table.

2. As you are stepping through this table, outputting the results, another user visits an ASP page that alters the value of one of the rows that has not yet been displayed by the Recordset object created in Step 1.

3. Finally, the user in Step 1 reaches this "altered" row, and outputs its value.

Should the new, updated value be displayed, or should the value of the row at the time the Open method was executed be displayed? It is up to you to decide what *should* happen. The type of cursor you use determines what *will* happen. The only cursors that will display the updated row are the Keyset and Dynamic cursors. The Static and forward-only cursors will show the value of the row when the Recordset's Open statement was executed.

Things get a bit more complicated when entirely new rows are added to a table whose contents you are viewing. Imagine the following situation:

1. You use the Open method of the Recordset object to obtain the contents of a database table.

2. As you are stepping through this table, outputting the results, another user adds a new row to the table.

3. When does your Recordset reach EOF? Is this new row displayed or not?

Only the Dynamic cursor will show this new row. With all the other cursor types, after the Recordset executes a SQL statement or obtains the contents of a table, no new rows will be added to the current set of records being referenced by the Recordset object.

> **Note** Microsoft Access does not support the Dynamic cursor. If you try to create a Recordset with a Dynamic cursor that queries an Access database, the CursorType will automatically be set to a Keyset cursor.

Each of the four cursors has its own capabilities. Which one is the best choice for an ASP application depends largely on the situation. Remember that the forward-only cursor is, by far, the most efficient type of database cursor, so, if at all possible, use a forward-only cursor. However, there may be times when you need to iterate in both a forward and backward direction.

Note that the database cursor that you tell your Recordset object to use is not always the database cursor that ends up being used. If you enter an "incorrect" value, the Recordset object automatically changes the value for you, to a "correct" value. For example, Access does not support Dynamic cursors. To see this in action, examine the code in Listing 20.1, which creates a database Connection to an Access database and attempts to Open a Recordset object using a Dynamic cursor.

LISTING 20.1   The Recordset Object Inherently "Fixes" Invalid Cursors

```
1:  <%@ Language = VBSCRIPT %>
2:  <% Option Explicit %>
3:  <!--#include virtual="/adovbs.inc"-->
4:  <%
5:     'Create a connection to an Access database
6:     Dim objConn
7:     Set objConn = Server.CreateObject("ADODB.Connection")
8:     objConn.ConnectionString = "DSN=AccessDB"
9:     objConn.Open
10:
11:    'Create a recordset object instance, objRS
12:    Dim objRS
13:    Set objRS = Server.CreateObject("ADODB.Recordset")
14:
15:    'Open the Recordset with a Dymamic cursor
16:    objRS.Open "SomeTable", objConn, adOpenDynamic, , adCmdTable
17:
18:    Response.Write "A Dynamic Cursor has the value " & _
19:                   adOpenDynamic
20:    Response.Write "<BR>The current cursor for " & _
```

20

continues

LISTING 20.1   continued

```
21:                     "<CODE>objRS</CODE> is "
22:     Response.Write objRS.CursorType & "<P>"
23:     Response.Write "<I>Note that this is a Keyset cursor being"
24:     Response.Write " used</I>."
25:
26:     'Clean up!
27:     objRS.Close
28:     Set objRS = Nothing
29:
30:     objConn.Close
31:     Set objConn = Nothing
32: %>
```

ANALYSIS   Listing 20.1 starts by creating a Connection to an Access database (lines 7 through 9). Next, a Recordset object instance is created (line 13), and the contents of SomeTable are read using the Open method (line 16). The Open method on line 16 uses a Dynamic cursor. However, Dynamic cursors are not allowed in Access. This does not cause an error, however.

Line 18 displays a message indicating that a Dynamic cursor is used. Also, the numeric value for the ADO constant adOpenDynamic is shown. Lines 20 through 22 then display the numeric value for objRS's database cursor, by outputting objRS.CursorType. If a Dynamic cursor was used to Open the Recordset, the value of objRS.CursorType and the value of adOpenDynamic should be equal. However, they are not. In fact, the value of objRS.CursorType equals 1, which is the same as adOpenKeyset. When trying to Open a Recordset with a Dynamic cursor using an Access database, a Keyset cursor is used instead.

Figure 20.2 shows the output of Listing 20.1.

Moving Through Scrollable Cursors

Scrollable cursors, unlike the forward-only cursor, can move both forward and backward. Because we've only discussed the forward-only cursor in detail, we've used just one method for Recordset navigation, namely MoveNext. Many other functions are available for iterating through a Recordset that can be used when the Recordset is Opened with a scrollable cursor. Table 20.2 outlines these functions.

TABLE 20.2   Recordset Iteration Functions Used with Scrollable Cursors

Method	Description
MoveFirst	Moves the cursor to the first record in the Recordset.
MoveLast	Moves the cursor to the last record in the Recordset.

Method	Description
MoveNext	Moves the cursor to the next record in the Recordset. That is, the cursor is moved one record forward.
MovePrevious	Moves the cursor to the previous record in the Recordset. That is, the cursor is moved one record backward.
Move	Moves the cursor forward or backward a specified number of records.

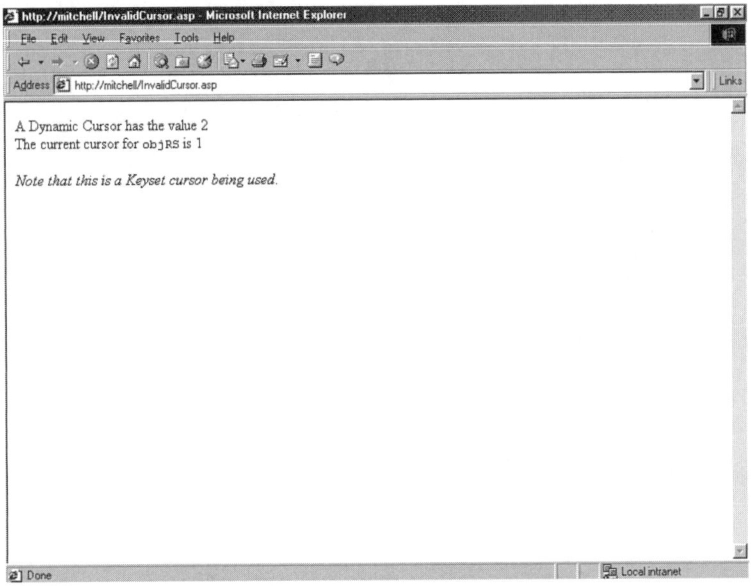

FIGURE 20.2

Access cannot use a Dynamic cursor, so a Keyset cursor is automatically selected.

Note that of these five methods, the *only* one that will work with a forward-only cursor is the MoveNext method. If you attempt to use another method with a forward-only cursor, you will receive an error. For example, if you were to replace MoveNext (line 32) with MovePrevious, the following error message would be generated when viewing the ASP page through a browser:

```
ADODB.Recordset error '800a0c93'
The operation requested by the application is not allowed in this context.
/FilterExample.asp, line 31
```

The Move method expects the following syntax:

```
objRecordsetInstance.Move NumberOfRecords
```

The Move method can be used to move both forward and backward an arbitrary number of records. To move forward, specify a positive *NumberOfRecords*; to move backward, specify a negative *NumberOfRecords*. Take the following two lines of code:

```
1:   objRecordsetInstance.Move 7
2:   objRecordsetInstance.Move -3
```

20

Line 1 moves the cursor seven records forward, whereas line 2 moves the cursor three records backward. If the cursor is moved beyond the last record, the cursor is positioned immediately after the last record, setting the EOF property to True. If the cursor is moved before the first record, the cursor is positioned immediately before the first record, setting the BOF property to True.

If you attempt to move the cursor backward, either by the Move or MovePrevious methods, when BOF is True, an error will be generated. Similarly, if the EOF property is True, and you attempt to move the cursor forward, an error will occur. For this reason, if you are using Move, MoveNext, or MovePrevious, you should test to make sure that you will not try to read beyond EOF or before BOF. In all examples using MoveNext, we loop while the EOF property is False. As soon as EOF is True, we exit the loop, so that MoveNext is not called again.

Now that we've discussed the methods that can be used to iterate through scrollable cursors, let's examine an example where we use these new methods. Listing 20.2 uses the MoveFirst and MoveLast methods to print out the first and last records in a Recordset.

LISTING 20.2   Using a Scrollable Cursor to Use the MoveLast and MoveFirst Methods

```
 1:  <%@ Language = VBSCRIPT %>
 2:  <% Option Explicit %>
 3:  <!--#include virtual="/adovbs.inc"-->
 4:  <%
 5:     'Create a connection to the Products Database
 6:     Dim objConn
 7:     Set objConn = Server.CreateObject("ADODB.Connection")
 8:     objConn.ConnectionString = "DSN=ProductsDB"
 9:     objConn.Open
10:
11:     'Create a recordset object instance, objRS
12:     Dim objRS
13:     Set objRS = Server.CreateObject("ADODB.Recordset")
14:
15:     'Open the Recordset with a Keyset cursor
16:     objRS.Open "Products", objConn, adOpenKeyset, , adCmdTable
17:
18:     'Print out the last record
19:     objRS.MoveLast
20:     Response.Write "<BR>" & objRS("Name") & " - " & _
21:                 FormatCurrency(objRS("Price"))
22:
23:     'Now print out the first record
24:     objRS.MoveFirst
25:     Response.Write "<BR>" & objRS("Name") & " - " & _
26:                 FormatCurrency(objRS("Price"))
27:
28:     'Clean up!!
```

```
29:    objRS.Close
30:    Set objRS = Nothing
31:
32:    objConn.Close
33:    Set objConn = Nothing
34: %>
```

ANALYSIS Listing 20.2 opens a connection to the same products database used on Day 19. The contents of the Products table, in fact, can be seen in Table 20.3. Imagine that you wanted to print out the last record of the Products table followed by the first record of the Products table. This would be a difficult task to accomplish with a forward-only cursor but is much simpler when using a scrollable cursor.

Start off by creating a Connection object (line 7), and Open a connection to the product database (lines 8 and 9). Next, a Recordset object instance is created (line 13), and the contents of the Products table are retrieved using a Keyset cursor (line 16). To display the last record in the Recordset, line 19 issues the MoveLast method to position the cursor on the last record. Once here, lines 20 and 21 output the Name and Price of the particular product. Then, to display the first record, line 24 uses the MoveFirst method to position the cursor on the first record in the Recordset, and lines 25 and 26 display the Name and Price.

Finally, lines 29 through 33 Close and explicitly free the ADO object. Figure 20.3 shows the output of Listing 20.2.

FIGURE 20.3

The last record is displayed and then the first.

20

Displaying only the last and first records of a Recordset is possible using a forward-only cursor. To accomplish this, the following tasks would suffice:

1. Create two variables, one to hold the Name of the first product, and the other to hold the Price of the first product. Call these variables strName and curPrice, respectively.

2. Open your Recordset object instance (objRS) using a forward-only cursor.

3. When the Recordset is initially Opened, you are positioned on the first record. Read the values of the Name and Price for the first record into strName and curPrice.

4. Create two new variables, strLastName and curLastPrice.

5. Use the following snippet of code to exhaustively move through the Recordset object:

```
Do While Not objRS.EOF
    strLastName = objRS("Name")
    curLastPrice = objRS("Price")

    objRS.MoveNext
Loop
```

This will loop through every record in your Recordset, saving the Name and Price value of the last accessed record in strLastName and curLastPrice, respectively. Therefore, after the loop has finished, strLastName and curLastPrice will contain the Name and Price of the last record in the Recordset.

6. Finally, display strLastName and curLastPrice, which contain the last record's Name and Price. Then, display strName and curPrice, which contain the first record's Name and Price.

So there you have it, a method to display information about the last and first records in a Recordset using a forward-only cursor! Although you *can* do it with a forward-only cursor, it is much easier to code and to understand what's happening when using a scrollable cursor. We find the MoveLast and MoveFirst methods easier to use and understand than having an exhaustive loop through the entire Recordset object just to reach the value of the last record.

Do	Don't
DO use the forward-only cursor when applicable. It provides better performance than a scrollable cursor.	DON'T use a forward-only cursor when a scrollable cursor would make the job easier. Code that is a little slower but much easier to understand is preferred over code that is a trifle faster but impossible to comprehend.

Counting the Records in a `Recordset`

When retrieving and displaying many records from a database table or SQL query, it would be nice to tell the end user how many records were being displayed. For example, the `Products` table from Day 19 contains columns that list the `Price` and `Inventory` of each particular object. If you had an ASP page that displayed all the products that cost under $100, it might be helpful to also show the exact number of products under $100— for example, a message that reads something like, "There were 6 products that cost less than $100."

With a forward-only cursor, the only way you can determine the number of records in a `Recordset` is by creating a counting variable and looping through the entire `Recordset`, adding one to the counting variable for each record processed. For example, Listing 20.3 displays all the records from the `Products` table and, at the bottom, the total number of records displayed.

LISTING 20.3   Count the Number of Records

```
1:  <%@ Language=VBScript %>
2:  <% Option Explicit %>
3:  <!--#include virtual="/adovbs.inc"-->
4:  <%
5:      'Open up a connection to our Access database that stores
6:      'the product information.
7:      Dim objConn
8:      Set objConn = Server.CreateObject("ADODB.Connection")
9:      objConn.ConnectionString = "DSN=ProductsDB"
10:     objConn.Open
11:
12:     'Create our SQL statement variable
13:     Dim strSQL
14:     strSQL = "SELECT * FROM Products WHERE Price <= 100" & _
15:              " ORDER BY Price DESC"
16:
17:     'Create a recordset object instance,
18:     'and execute the SQL statement
19:     Dim objRS
20:     Set objRS = Server.CreateObject("ADODB.Recordset")
21:     objRS.Open strSQL, objConn
22:
23:     'We need to create a counting variable to keep track of
24:     'the total number of records we've processed
25:     Dim iRecordCount
26:     iRecordCount = 0
27:
28:     'We are displaying products whose price is less than $100
29:     Response.Write "<B>"
```

20

LISTING 20.3 continued

```
30:    Response.Write "A Listing of Products less than $100.00:"
31:    Response.Write "</B>"
32:    Do While Not objRS.EOF
33:        Response.Write "<BR>" & objRS("Name") & " - " & _
34:                        FormatCurrency(objRS("Price"))
35:
36:        'Increment the number of records processed by 1
37:        iRecordCount = iRecordCount + 1
38:
39:        'Move on to the next customer
40:        objRS.MoveNext
41:    Loop
42:
43:    'Display how many products cost less than $100
44:    Response.Write "<P>"
45:    Response.Write "There were " & FormatNumber(iRecordCount,0)
46:    Response.Write " records under $100."
47:
48:    'Clean up our ADO objects
49:    objRS.Close
50:    Set objRS = Nothing
51:
52:    objConn.Close
53:    Set objConn = Nothing
54: %>
```

ANALYSIS Listing 20.3 begins by creating a connection to the products database (lines 8 through 10). Because you are going to use a SQL statement to query those products listed under $100, line 13 creates the SQL statement variable, and lines 14 and 15 assign the desired SQL statement to it. Next, line 20 creates a Recordset object instance, and line 21 Opens the Recordset, executing the SQL statement in strSQL. Note that you do not explicitly specify a cursor—therefore, a forward-only cursor is used.

Next, lines 25 and 26 create a counting variable, iRecordCount, and initialize it to 0. Lines 32 through 41 then perform the Do While Not objRS.EOF ... Loop, displaying each record in the Recordset. Note that for each iteration through the loop, line 37 adds one to the counting variable, iRecordCount.

After all the records in the Recordset have been displayed, lines 45 and 46 notify the user how many records were displayed. Note that iRecordCount contains the exact number of records that were displayed. The script ends by closing and explicitly freeing the ADO objects. Figure 20.4 shows the output of Listing 20.3.

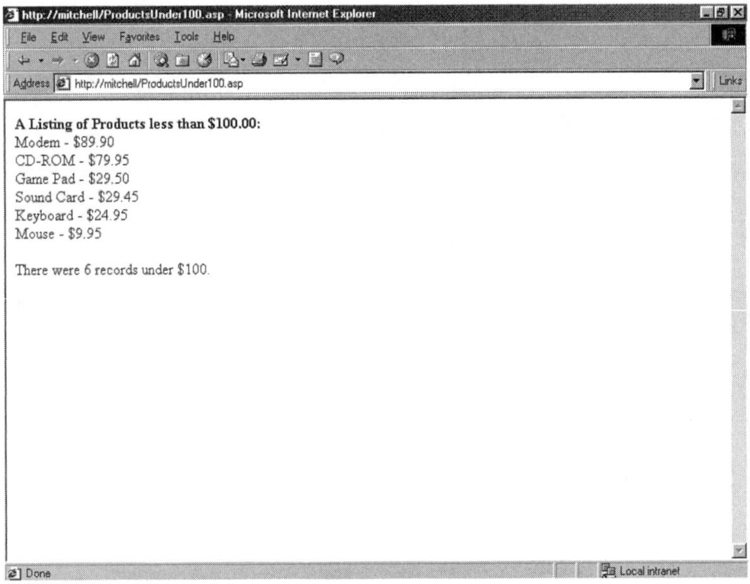

FIGURE 20.4

The number of records is displayed after the Recordset *is outputted.*

Although Listing 20.3 successfully obtains the number of records in the Recordset, you do not know how many records are in the Recordset until you've already processed all the records. This means that you could not easily display the number of records *before* listing the records in the Recordset. Also, if you just wanted to display the number of records in the Recordset without displaying the records, you would still have to loop through each record using a Do While Not objRS.EOF ... Loop and using a counting variable.

When using a scrollable cursor, however, you are not limited to this handicap imposed by the forward-only cursor. The Recordset object provides a RecordCount method that returns the number of records in the Recordset. For the RecordCount to return accurate values, a scrollable cursor *must* be used. The RecordCount property returns a value of -1 when used with a forward-only cursor.

Now that you know of the RecordCount property, let's rewrite the code in Listing 20.3 to take advantage of this property. Note that you will have to use a scrollable cursor for the Recordset. Other than that, though, very little changes. Listing 20.4 contains code that uses the RecordCount property to display the number of products less than $100.

LISTING 20.4 Using a scrollable cursor to Determine the Number of Records in the Recordset

```
1:  <%@ Language = VBSCRIPT %>
2:  <% Option Explicit %>
3:  <!--#include virtual="/adovbs.inc"-->
```

continues

LISTING 20.4   continued

```
 4:   <%
 5:       'Create a connection to an Access database
 6:       Dim objConn
 7:       Set objConn = Server.CreateObject("ADODB.Connection")
 8:       objConn.ConnectionString = "DSN=ProductsDB"
 9:       objConn.Open
10:
11:       'Create our SQL statement variable
12:       Dim strSQL
13:       strSQL = "SELECT * FROM Products WHERE Price <= 100" & _
14:                 " ORDER BY Price DESC"
15:
16:       'Create a recordset object instance, objRS
17:       Dim objRS
18:       Set objRS = Server.CreateObject("ADODB.Recordset")
19:
20:       'Open the Recordset with a Keyset cursor
21:       objRS.Open strSQL, objConn, adOpenKeySet
22:
23:       Response.Write "There were " & objRS.RecordCount & " records"
24:       Response.Write "<P>"
25:       'We are displaying products whose price is less than $100
26:       Response.Write "<B>"
27:       Response.Write "A Listing of Products less than $100.00:"
28:       Response.Write "</B>"
29:       Do While Not objRS.EOF
30:          Response.Write "<BR>" & objRS("Name") & " - " & _
31:                          FormatCurrency(objRS("Price"))
32:
33:          'Move on to the next customer
34:          objRS.MoveNext
35:       Loop
36:
37:       Response.Write "<P>There were " & objRS.RecordCount & " records"
38:
39:       'Clean up!!
40:       objRS.Close
41:       Set objRS = Nothing
42:
43:       objConn.Close
44:       Set objConn = Nothing
45:   %>
```

ANALYSIS   Listing 20.4 is similar to Listing 20.3, except that Listing 20.4 uses the
RecordCount property to display the number of records in a Recordset. Lines 1
through 20 are identical in both Listing 20.3 and Listing 20.4. On line 21, however, the
two differ. Listing 20.4 Opens the Recordset object instance using a Keyset cursor,
which is a scrollable cursor. Because the Recordset is opened with a scrollable cursor,
the RecordCount property returns the correct number of records in the Recordset.

On line 23, the number of records is displayed for the user. Lines 29 through 35 then loop through the `Recordset` using the standard `Do While Not objRS.EOF ... Loop`. You do not need to use a counting variable here because `RecordCount` provides an accurate count. Note that line 34 uses the `RecordCount` property a second time, displaying the number of records again. Finally, you `Close` and explicitly free the ADO objects.

Figure 20.5 shows the output of Listing 20.4.

For reference, the complete listing of the `Products` table is available in Table 20.3. You can compare the products listed in Figures 20.4 and 20.5 to the products whose `Price` is less than $100 in Table 20.3. You may be wondering why displaying the number of records returned in a `Recordset` is important. After all, only six products were returned, and anyone who was that interested could simply count them up.

Imagine, however, that the `Products` table contained hundreds of rows, and hundreds of rows might be displayed to the user. It would be nice, as a quick reference, to display the total number of products listed. A similar technique is used on most search engines. For example, a search on Excite.com for "ASP" yielded 53,971 matches. I know that this is the number of total matches, not because I counted every match, that would be ridiculous. Rather, Excite.com displays the total number of records on each page of results. Such a reference is handy, interesting, and useful.

20

Caution

Remember that the RecordCount property will return -1 if you use a forward-only cursor. It is easy to forget to use a scrollable cursor when using the RecordCount property. If you are using the RecordCount property and receive a value of -1, chances are you are using a forward-only cursor.

TABLE 20.3 The Data in the Products Table

ProductID	Name	Price	Inventory
1	Monitor	195.95	100
2	Mouse	9.95	250
3	Keyboard	24.95	55
4	Scanner	149.50	15
5	CD-ROM	79.95	75
6	Printer	155.50	19
7	Sound Card	29.45	34
8	Game Pad	29.50	190
9	Zip Drive	129.95	7
10	Modem	89.90	190

Understanding LockType

On Day 17, "Inserting, Updating, and Deleting Database Records," we examined how to use the Update and AddNew methods of the Recordset object to update existing records and add new records. When you want to update records or add new records, you need to specify a LockType for the Recordset object.

You need to specify a LockType because of the multi-user nature of database systems and the Internet. Imagine that you have multiple people visiting your Web site simultaneously. What happens if two users attempt to update the same record at the same time?

When a user issues a command to update a record, the database program *locks* the row that is being updated.

NEW TERM When a user *locks* a row, no other user can modify the contents of that row until the user who locked it *unlocks* it.

For example, imagine that User A and User B both want to update the Products table. Specifically, User A wants to up the Price of the Monitor to $224.99,whereas User B wants to up the Inventory to 150. When User A issues the update command, the row of the Products table being updated is locked. User B cannot update the Inventory until

User A unlocks the row. After User A finishes updating the `Price`, the row is unlocked. User B then locks the same row, updates the `Inventory`, and then unlocks the row. This process can be seen in Figure 20.6.

FIGURE 20.6

Locking protects the consistency of a database.

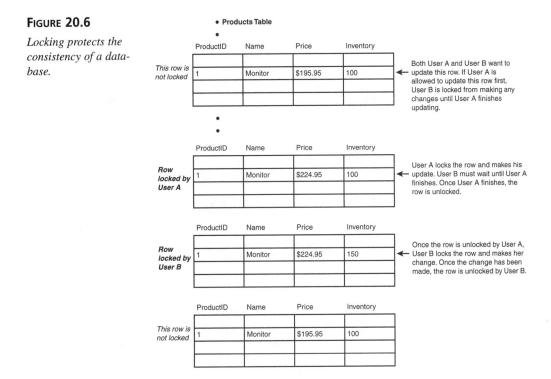

Fortunately, the database program handles locking issues. As a developer, you only need to tell the database *how* you want it to lock records. Several locking options can be specified by the `LockType` property of the `Recordset` object. You can also explicitly set the `LockType` in the `Open` method of the `Recordset` object. Recall that the syntax of the `Recordset` object's `Open` method is as follows:

```
objRecordsetInstance.Open Source, ActiveConnection, CursorType, _
                     LockType, Options
```

The default `LockType` is a read-only lock, which prevents updates altogether. You have implicitly used this `LockType` in all examples where you simply listed the contents of a `Recordset` object. In all the listings so far today, you've not explicitly specified the `LockType` property; this has the same effect as explicitly using the read-only `LockType`. If you don't plan on updating or adding any new records to the `Recordset`, there is no need for anything but the read-only `LockType`.

20

Table 20.4 shows the four LockTypes you can use. Note that, like the CursorType, each LockType is specified by an ADO constant.

TABLE 20.4   The Four Types of LockTypes

Cursor	Constant	Properties
Read-only	adLockReadOnly	The records are read-only, and cannot be modified. Also, new records cannot be added. This is the default LockType.
Pessimistic	adLockPessimistic	Records are locked immediately on editing to ensure that there are no discrepancies between when the new values were entered and when the Update command occurs.
Optimistic	adLockOptimistic	Records are only locked when the Update method is called.
Batch Optimistic	adLockBatchOptimistic	The records are not locked until a batch update occurs. This option should be used with client-side cursors and disconnected Recordsets.

Each LockType has its time and place. If you do not plan on updating or adding records, use the Read-only lock. If you are using a server-side cursor (the default) and plan on updating or adding new records, you can choose between the Pessimistic and Optimistic locks. Pessimistic locks maintain a lock from the start of editing until the record is Updated. Optimistic locks, on the other hand, don't lock the row until the Update method is executed. Examine the following code:

```
1:  'We have already opened a Recordset object instance named objRS
2:  objRS("Name") = "Scott"
3:  objRS("Age") = 21
4:  objRS("Weight") = 160
5:  objRS.Update
```

The preceding code will update the Name, Age, and Weight columns of the current record in the Recordset object instance objRS. These changes are updated in the database when the Update method is executed (line 5). When will this row be locked, though? This depends on the LockType. A Pessimistic lock locks the row as soon as editing occurs (line 2). An Optimistic lock, however, waits until the Update method is executed before attempting to lock the row (line 5).

The Pessimistic lock is not as efficient as the Optimistic lock because the row locking must occur for a longer duration. Optimistic locks, however, do not ensure data integrity. Take the following sequence of events:

1. Two users, User A and User B, each Open a Recordset object that grabs the contents from the Products table.

2. User A wants to edit the Mouse product, decreasing the Inventory column to 200. User A makes this change and executes the Update statement, storing the results in the database.

3. User B wants to increase the price of the Mouse to $13.50. This column is altered, and the Update statement is executed. Because User B performed the Update statement *after* User A had already updated the database, the Inventory value that User B assumed existed was changed by User A. When updating the database, what version of the data is correct?

Figure 20.7 shows this phenomenon graphically.

FIGURE 20.7

Optimistic locking can lead to data integrity errors in multi-user situations.

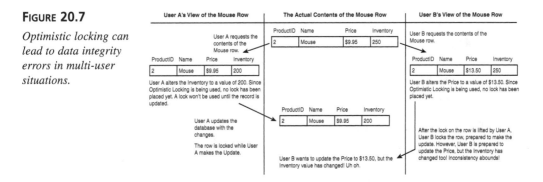

So, what LockType should you choose? If you expect many updates to occur simultaneously, it is best to use a Pessimistic lock, to ensure that no data integrity conflicts arise. If you do not expect many simultaneous updates (perhaps you only allow someone like a system administrator to perform updates to the data), then an Optimistic lock will do just fine. If you are uncertain, use a Pessimistic lock.

The last type of lock is the Batch Optimistic lock. This lock, when used with a client-side cursor, allows changes to multiple rows of data *before* the database is updated. With batch updating, many changes are made on the client-side, which are then sent in a batch to the server to be committed to the database. Batch updating, however, is beyond the scope of this book. Just keep in mind that if you decide to allow updates while using client-side cursors, you should use a Batch Optimistic lock.

20

Note

Pessimistic locking is not allowed with client-side cursors. If you choose an invalid LockType, ADO automatically alters the LockType property so that it contains a legal value.

> **Note**
> Examples of using the `LockType` property to allow for updates and additions of new records can be found in Day 17's lesson.

Creating Recordsets with `Connection.Execute`

Over the past week we've looked at several examples of retrieving and displaying database information. In all these examples, we've always performed the following steps:

1. Create a `Connection` object using

   ```
   Set objConn = Server.CreateObject("ADODB.Connection")
   ```

2. Set the `ConnectionString` property and execute the `Open` method.

3. Create a `Recordset` object using

   ```
   Set objRS = Server.CreateObject("ADODB.Recordset")
   ```

4. Populate the `Recordset` object instance with a database table or a SQL query, using the `Open` method with the following syntax:

   ```
   objRS.Open Source, objConn, CursorType, LockType, Options
   ```

   Where `Source` is the table name or SQL query.

Following these four steps is highly recommended because each ADO object is created explicitly. You can, however, create a `Recordset` object *implicitly* using the `Execute` method of the `Connection` object. We do not suggest that you create your `Recordsets` this way. Creating your `Recordsets` explicitly, in our opinion, makes the code easier to read. Also, you cannot specify the `CursorType` and `LockType` of the `Recordset` if you create it implicitly. Regardless, a great deal of ASP code uses the `Execute` method to create `Recordsets` implicitly; for this reason, you should be familiar with using the `Execute` method to create a `Recordset` implicitly.

The `Connection` object's `Execute` method can take up to three parameters, although the last two are optional. A `Recordset` object is returned. The syntax of the `Execute` method is as follows:

```
Set objRecordsetInstance = objConnectionInstance.Execute(CommandText, _
                                          RecordsAffected, Options)
```

The `CommandText` parameter can be a SQL query or a database table name. If it is a table name, the `Options` parameter needs to be set to `adCmdTable`, just like when you used the `Open` method of the `Recordset` object.

Note that you must use the `Set` keyword when assigning the results of the `Execute` method to a `Recordset` object. This is because an object instance is returned from the `Execute` method, and, as was discussed on Day 6, "Working with Objects," when assigning a variable to an object instance, you must use the `Set` keyword. Also, note the use of parentheses surrounding the parameters. You must have these parentheses there when `Setting` a variable to the `Recordset` object instance returned by the `Execute` method.

When a `Recordset` is created implicitly through the `Execute` method, the following things occur behind the scenes:

1. A `Recordset` object is created.
2. The `Recordset` object's `Open` method is executed, populating the `Recordset` with the database table or SQL query you specified as the *CommandText* in the `Execute` method.
3. This `Recordset` object is returned by the `Execute` method. At this point, it is assigned to the variable you specify with the following:

   ```
   Set variableName = objConn.Execute(...)
   ```

When creating a `Recordset` implicitly, the `Recordset` is created with the default `CursorType` and `LockType` properties. This means that the `Recordset` created by the `Execute` method will have a forward-only cursor and a Read-only lock. If you need to specify a different cursor or lock, create the `Recordset` explicitly, as we have done before, and specify the `CursorType` and `LockType` in the `Open` method of the `Recordset` object.

Because `Recordsets` created implicitly are forward-only and Read-only, you cannot use the `Update` or `AddNew` methods to alter existing records or add new ones. For this reason, when creating `Recordsets` with the `Execute` method, you can only iterate through the `Recordset` with `MoveNext`. Listing 20.3 used a forward-only, Read-only `Recordset` to list those items in the `Products` database that cost $100 or less. Listing 20.5 contains a modified version of this code, with the `Recordset` object created implicitly as opposed to explicitly.

LISTING 20.5 Implicitly created `Recordsets` have the Default Cursor and Lock Types

```
 1:  <%@ Language=VBScript %>
 2:  <% Option Explicit %>
 3:  <!--#include virtual="/adovbs.inc"-->
 4:  <%
 5:      'Open up a connection to our Access database that stores
 6:      'the product information.
 7:      Dim objConn
 8:      Set objConn = Server.CreateObject("ADODB.Connection")
 9:      objConn.ConnectionString = "DSN=ProductsDB"
10:      objConn.Open
11:
12:      'Create our SQL statement variable
13:      Dim strSQL
14:      strSQL = "SELECT * FROM Products WHERE Price <= 100" & _
```

20

continues

LISTING 20.5 continued

```
15:               " ORDER BY Price DESC"
16:
17:        'Create a recordset object instance implicitly using
18:        'the Execute method
19:        Dim objRS
20:        Set objRS = objConn.Execute(strSQL)
21:
22:        'We are displaying products whose price is less than $100
23:        Response.Write "<B>"
24:        Response.Write "A Listing of Products less than $100.00:"
25:        Response.Write "</B>"
26:        Do While Not objRS.EOF
27:           Response.Write "<BR>" & objRS("Name") & " - " & _
28:                          FormatCurrency(objRS("Price"))
29:
30:           'Move on to the next customer
31:           objRS.MoveNext
32:        Loop
33:
34:        'Clean up our ADO objects
35:        objRS.Close
36:        Set objRS = Nothing
37:
38:        objConn.Close
39:        Set objConn = Nothing
40: %>
```

ANALYSIS Listing 20.5 outputs those items in the Products database that cost $100 or less. (A listing of all the items in the Products database can be seen in Table 20.3.) Line 8 starts by creating a Connection object. Line 9 sets its ConnectionString property, and then line 10 Opens the connection to the database. Next, line 13 creates a string variable to hold the SQL SELECT statement. You then assign this variable a SELECT statement that returns all the rows in the Products table whose Price is $100 or less. These results are ordered based on the Price, in descending order.

At this point, Listing 20.3 explicitly created a Recordset object using Server.CreateObject("ADODB.Recordset"). Listing 20.5, however, uses the Execute method to *implicitly* create a Recordset object instance (line 20). Notice that all you do to obtain the Recordset object instance is create a variable (line 19) and then assign this variable to the Recordset object instance being returned by the Execute method (line 20). After you have completed this, objRS is identical to an explicitly created Recordset object that had its CursorType property set to adOpenForwardOnly and its LockType property set to adLockReadOnly.

The remainder of Listing 20.5 displays those records that meet the "$100 or less" criteria. Lines 26 to 32 perform the Do While Not objRS.EOF ... Loop, displaying each record and then using MoveNext to jump to the next record. Finally, lines 35 through 39 Close and explicitly free the ADO objects.

Figure 20.8 shows the output of Listing 20.5.

FIGURE 20.8

Those products costing $100 or less are listed.

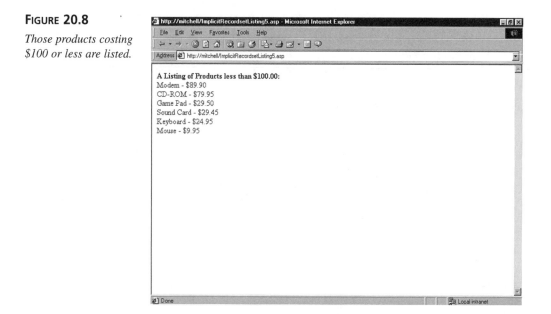

You can also use the Execute method to return the entire contents of a specific database table. If you wanted to return all the rows and columns of the Products in Listing 20.5, you could have changed line 20 from

```
Set objRS = objConn.Execute(strSQL)
```

to

```
Set objRS = objConn.Execute("Products", , adCmdTable)
```

20

> **Tip**
>
> When querying a database, strive to create your Recordsets explicitly. Creating your Recordsets explicitly makes your code easier to read and understand.

Using Stored Procedures

Throughout this week, we've examined how to use ADO and ASP to communicate with a database. We've examined how to query data, using both a database table name and a SQL statement. We've also discussed how to update records in a `Recordset` and how to add new records.

Imagine, for a moment, that you are a database. Your job in life is to sit there and wait for someone to come and ask you for some information. When they ask you for information, you scurry off, retrieve the information, and present it to them. After you hand off the information, you go back to waiting for the next request. Often you'll find that similar information is requested. For example, suppose that you have an ASP page that performs some SQL query, if 50 people visit that page in a day, the database will receive 50 identical requests throughout the duration of the day.

Wouldn't it be nice to have a plan on how to retrieve commonly requested information? Imagine a database as a gigantic warehouse crammed full of information. If a map existed that showed directions to commonly requested information, the speed with which that information was obtained would increase. You can create such a map for your database by using stored procedures.

A stored procedure is a SQL query stored by the database program. When this stored procedure is executed the first time, the database saves an *execution plan* for this query.

NEW TERM   An *execution plan* is created after the first run of a stored procedure. This execution plan serves as a guide for efficiently running the query in the future.

If you wanted to list all the rows and columns from the `Products` table, you could use the following code:

```
objRS.Open "SELECT * FROM Products", objConn
```

Or you could create a stored procedure named `ListProducts`, which would contain the SQL query `SELECT * FROM Products`. Then, to populate your `Recordset` with the results from `ListProducts`, you could use the following:

```
objRS.Open "ListProducts", objConn
```

We'll discuss how to retrieve the results from stored procedures in more detail later today in the section, "Calling Stored Procedures from ASP."

Benefits of Using Stored Procedures

Stored procedures definitely have advantages. There are many reasons why you should strive to use stored procedures religiously. One benefit of using stored procedures is that they can make your code easier to read. Imagine that you have a *very* long SELECT statement. Rather than having to assign it to a string variable in each ASP page that you want to run the query, you can simply create a stored procedure that executes the lengthy SQL query. This will make your ASP pages easier to read.

Another benefit of using stored procedures is that they provide a level of abstraction between your ASP page and the data in your database. Imagine that you've just finished creating 50 ASP pages that query data from a database without using stored procedures. Now, imagine that your boss has just informed you that the database structure is going to change slightly. You will have to go through every one of your ASP pages and edit the queries so that they do not reference database tables that no longer exist. Also, if these queries reference columns that have been removed or have had their names changed, you will need to make changes as well. When using stored procedures, however, you can protect yourself from needing to edit a number of ASP pages. This topic is discussed in detail tomorrow, Day 21, "Practicing Intelligent Application Design."

Although both of the previous benefits are compelling, the main benefit of using stored procedures is the performance increase. When a database receives a request in the form of a SQL statement or database table name, it has to parse the request and retrieve the information. When the execution of a stored procedure is requested, though, the database already has the query parsed and a plan for executing the stored procedure. This leads to an increase in performance.

Of course, the question is, "How great is the performance gain from stored procedures?" According to a case study, by using stored procedures you can boost the page requests per second rate by nearly 25 percent (http://www.asptoday.com/articles/19990601.htm).

Creating Stored Procedures in Microsoft SQL Server

Now that we've discussed what stored procedures are and why you should use them, we need to examine how to create stored procedures. In this section, we'll examine how to create stored procedures using Microsoft SQL Server 7.0. In the next section, "Creating Stored Procedures in Access," we'll examine how to create stored procedures using Access 2000. Finally, we'll examine how to call these stored procedures from an ASP page.

To create a stored procedure in Microsoft SQL Server 7.0, expand the Databases tab. You should see a listing of all the databases on the server. Expand the database to which you want to add a stored procedure. One of the nodes of the expanded database will be titled Stored Procedures; click this node. In the right pane, all the existing stored procedures will be listed. To edit an existing stored procedure, double-click the stored procedure that you want to edit. To create a new stored procedure, right-click in the right pane and select New Stored Procedure. Figure 20.9 shows the Northwinds database stored procedure listing.

20

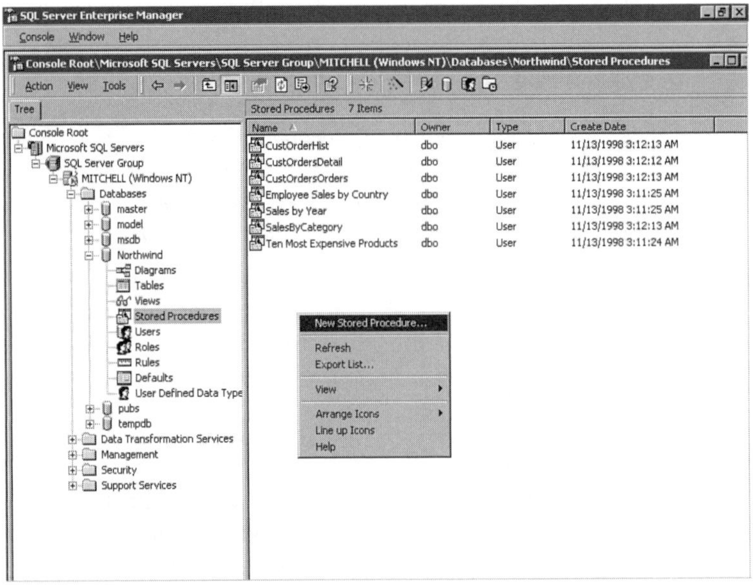

FIGURE 20.9

To create a new stored procedure click New Stored Procedure.

After you click the New Stored Procedure option, a dialog appears into which you can enter the SQL query for your stored procedure. Figure 20.10 shows the dialog that you should see.

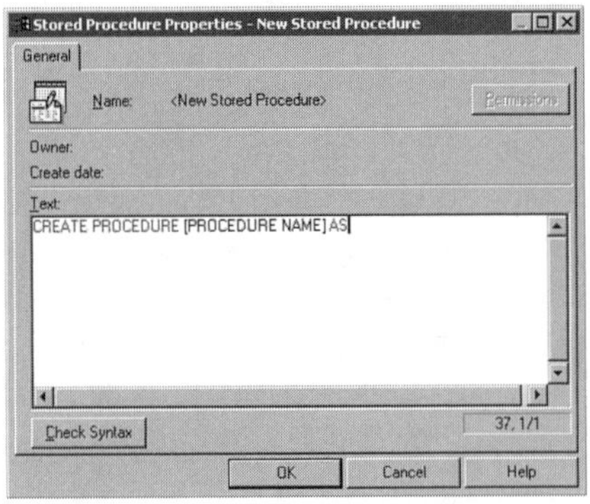

FIGURE 20.10

Enter the SQL query into the New Stored Procedure dialog.

Note that the dialog is created with some text already entered. This text reads as follows:

```
CREATE PROCEDURE [PROCEDURE NAME] AS
```

The first thing you need to do is remove the [PROCEDURE NAME] and replace it with the name of the procedure you want to create. After you've done this, place the cursor after the AS and type in the SQL query you want to execute. When you have completed typing in the SQL query, click OK. If you wanted to create a stored procedure that would list the `Name` and `Price` columns of the `Products` table, ordered by the descending value of the `Price` column, before you click OK, the New Stored Procedure dialog should contain the following text:

```
CREATE PROCEDURE ListProducts AS
SELECT Name, Price FROM Products
ORDER BY Price DESC
```

Whitespace doesn't matter when writing a SQL query in the New Stored Procedure dialog. Also, the comments can be denoted by two dashes, or can be placed between a `/*` and `*/`. For example, the following two SQL statements are synonymous:

```
SELECT Name, Price FROM Products
ORDER BY Price DESC
```

and

```
/* Select the Name and Price columns */
-- The results will be ordered by the Price in descending order
SELECT Name, Price FROM Products
ORDER BY Price DESC
```

That's all there is to it! After you've created a stored procedure, it appears in the Stored Procedures list. We'll show how to call a stored procedure from an ASP page in the section "Calling Stored Procedures from ASP."

Creating Stored Procedures in Access

You can also create stored procedures in Microsoft Access. In Access, however, the terminology is a bit different than in SQL Server. Access refers to stored procedures as Queries. To build a Query, click the Query tab in the Objects toolbar. You should see a list of all existing Queries, as well as two options: Create a Query in Design View, and Create a Query by Using Wizard. Figure 20.11 shows what you should see.

FIGURE 20.11

In Access, stored procedures are referred to as Queries.

Double-clicking the Create a Query in Design View pops up a dialog that prompts you to select which tables you want to use in your Query. Select the table or tables that you are interested in generating a Query for. This example will return a list of the items in the Products table, so we chose to add just the Products table. After you choose your table(s) and click Close, the Query Design view will be shown. Figure 20.12 contains shows the Query Design view with the added Products table.

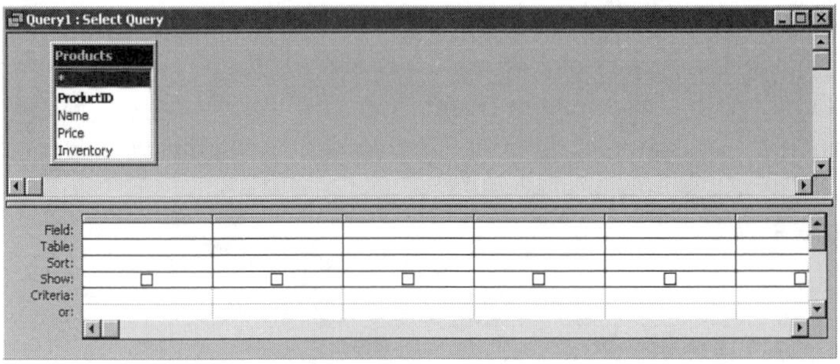

FIGURE 20.12

*You can create a
Query in Access from
the Query Design view.*

You can now choose what fields you want the Query return. A field in Access terminology is the same thing as a column in SQL terminology. So, because you want the Query to return the Name and Price columns, choose to have both these fields returned. You can also choose how you want to have the fields sorted. Because you want to order the results on the value of the Price field in descending order, choose to Sort the Price field as Descending. Figure 20.13 shows what the Query Design view should look like with the appropriate fields filled in.

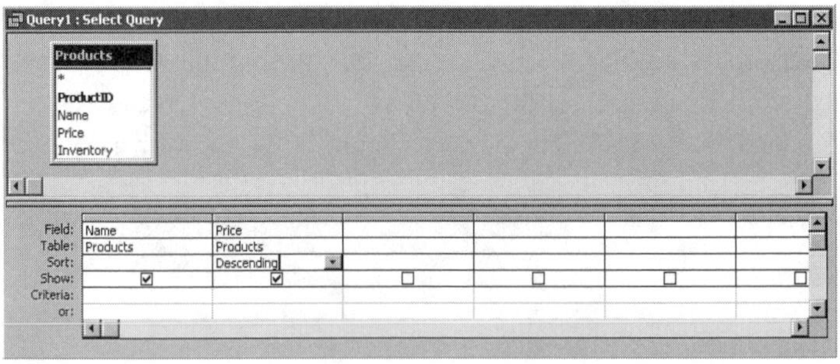

FIGURE 20.13

*Select the fields that
you want the Query to
return.*

When you've entered the information you're interested in, close the Query Design view. You are asked whether you want to save the Query. Choose Yes. You then are prompted to enter a name for the Query. For the query shown in Figure 20.13, we chose to name it ListProducts.

Calling Stored Procedures from ASP

Because a stored procedure runs a SQL query, information from the database is returned. This information is then packaged into a Recordset object by ADO. Therefore, after you execute a stored procedure and retrieve its results in the form of a `Recordset`, you can use that `Recordset` just like you've used a `Recordset` in any of the other examples.

To execute the SQL statement, you need to send the name of the stored procedure to your database just like you send a SQL query. In "Creating Stored Procedures in Access," we created a stored procedure named `ListProducts` that returned the `Name` and `Price` column of all the rows in the `Products` table. To run the stored procedure, use the following syntax:

```
1:  'Create a SQL string
2:  Dim strSQL
3:  strSQL = "ListProducts"
4:
5:  'Create a Recordset object
6:  Dim objRS
7:  Set objRS = Server.CreateObject("ADODB.Recordset")
8:  ObjRS.Open strSQL, objConn
```

The SQL string is assigned the name of the stored procedure. That's all there is to it! The results of the stored procedure are populated in the `Recordset` object instance `objRS`. Listing 20.6 shows the complete source code for executing the `ListProducts` stored procedure and displaying the results.

LISTING 20.6   Stored Procedure Results Take the Form of a `Recordset` Object

```
1:   <%@ Language=VBScript %>
2:   <% Option Explicit %>
3:   <!--#include virtual="/adovbs.inc"-->
4:   <%
5:      'Open up a connection to our Access database that stores
6:      'the product information.
7:      Dim objConn
8:      objConn = Server.CreateObject("ADODB.Connection")
9:      objConn.ConnectionString = "DSN=ProductsDB"
10:     objConn.Open
11:
12:     'Create our SQL string
13:     Dim strSQL
14:     strSQL = "ListProducts"
15:
16:     'Create a recordset object instance explicitly
17:     'The default CursorType and LockType are used
18:     Dim objRS
19:     Set objRS = Server.CreateObject("ADODB.Recordset")
20:     objRS.Open strSQL, objConn
21:
22:     'We are displaying the results of the ListProducts Query
23:     Response.Write "<B>A Listing of Products:</B>"
```

20

continues

LISTING **20.6** continued

```
24:    Response.Write "</B>"
25:    Do While Not objRS.EOF
26:       Response.Write "<BR>" & objRS("Name") & " - " & _
27:                       FormatCurrency(objRS("Price"))
28:
29:       'Move on to the next customer
30:       objRS.MoveNext
31:    Loop
32:
33:    'Clean up our ADO objects
34:    objRS.Close
35:    Set objRS = Nothing
36:
37:    objConn.Close
38:    Set objConn = Nothing
39: %>
```

ANALYSIS Listing 20.6 executes the ListProducts stored procedure and outputs the results. Line 8 begins by creating a Connection object instance, and lines 9 and 10 Open a connection to the database. Next, line 13 creates a string variable to hold the SQL statement. This string variable is assigned the name of the stored procedure, "ListProducts" (line 14). To execute a stored procedure, you need to provide only the name of the stored procedure.

To retrieve the results of the stored procedure, you need a Recordset object, which is created on line 19. Line 20 executes the Recordset object's Open method, passing in the name of the stored procedure through strSQL. This populates the Recordset with the results of the stored procedure. Note that you do not specify the CursorType or LockType in the Open statement. This has the effect of using a forward-only cursor and Read-only lock. If you needed a scrollable cursor, you could have explicitly used a different cursor type. Also, if you wanted to be able to update the results of the stored procedure, you could specify a LockType other than the Read-only lock.

After you've populated our Recordset with the results of the stored procedure (line 20), you can display the results of the stored procedure using a Do While Not objRS.EOF ... Loop (lines 25 through 31). In this loop, lines 26 and 27 output the Name and the Price , and then line 30 uses MoveNext to iterate to the next record in the Recordset. After all the records in the Recordset are displayed, lines 34 through 38 Close the ADO objects and explicitly free them.

Figure 20.14 shows the output of Listing 20.6 when viewed through a browser.

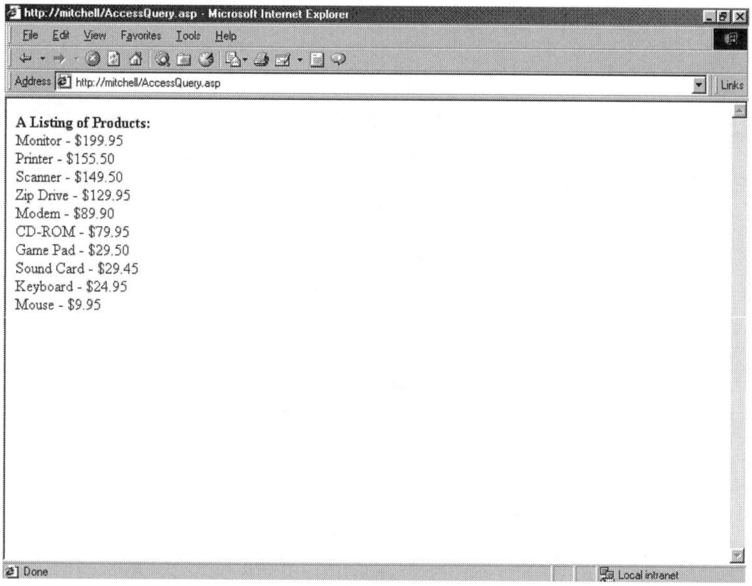

FIGURE 20.14

A stored procedure is a more efficient SQL query.

You can also use the `Execute` method of the `Connection` object to implicitly create a `Recordset` that contains the output of a stored procedure. For example, in Listing 20.6, you could have replaced lines 19 and 20 with the following:

```
Set objRS = objConn.Execute(strSQL)
```

Such a change would not affect the functionality of Listing 20.6. However, in our opinion, if you explicitly create `Recordset`s, your code will be easier to read and understand. Also, when using an implicitly created `Recordset`, you can only use the forward-only cursor and Read-only lock.

The Command Object

One interesting feature of ADO is that it provides several different ways to accomplish the exact same thing. This is a bit of a double-edged sword. On one hand, having many ways to perform a given task is a blessing: if one technique seems confusing or difficult to understand, perhaps a different technique is clearer. On the other hand, though, providing multiple ways to accomplish the same task leads to different developers writing different code. This can be a headache if you have to update a project written using techniques you are unfamiliar with.

Until now, we've looked at two ways to generate `Recordset`s. The first way was to explicitly create a `Recordset` object using the following:

20

```
Dim objRS
Set objRS = Server.CreateObject("ADODB.Recordset")
ObjRS.Open strSQL, objConn
```

The second way is to have a `Recordset` object created implicitly by the `Execute` method of the `Connection` object. After this `Recordset` object instance is created, you could assign it to a variable using the following syntax:

```
Dim objRS
Set objRS = objConn.Execute(strSQL)
```

Believe it or not, but there is *another* way to create `Recordsets`! This way is implicit as well and uses the `Command` object. As mentioned, doing the same thing different ways has disadvantages. We recommend that you choose one way to perform your data access and *stick with that method*! Personally, we prefer explicitly creating `Recordset` objects—we find that the easiest to read. It is important, however, to introduce the different ways you may see `Recordsets` being created, just in case you need to work on existing code that uses one of these alternative methods.

The `Command` object can be used to implicitly create `Recordsets`. Table 20.5 shows those properties essential to creating and populating a `Recordset`.

TABLE 20.5 Important Properties of the Command Object

Property	Description
ActiveConnection	The variable name of the database connection you want to retrieve information from.
CommandText	The table name or SQL query you want to perform to populate the implicitly created Recordset.
CommandType	This needs to be set to adCmdTable if you want to retrieve the contents of a database table.

When all these properties have been correctly set, you can issue the `Execute` method of the `Command` object, which is strikingly similar to the `Execute` method of the `Connection` object. Both implicitly create a `Recordset` and populate it with the provided SQL query.

To use the `Command` object in an ASP page, the `Command` object must be explicitly created using the following syntax:

```
Dim objCommand
Set objCommand = Server.CreateObject("ADODB.Command")
```

After you've created a `Command` object instance, you can set the properties and perform the `Execute` method to return a `Recordset` object instance.

Listing 20.5 used the `Execute` method of the `Connection` object to implicitly create a `Recordset` object. We then iterated through this `Recordset` and displayed the results. Listing 20.7 contains a modified version of Listing 20.5. The output is the same, but the `Recordset` object is created implicitly using the `Execute` method of the `Command` object.

LISTING 20.7   Creating a `Recordset` Implicitly by Using the `Command` Object

```
1:  <%@ Language=VBScript %>
2:  <% Option Explicit %>
3:  <!--#include virtual="/adovbs.inc"-->
4:  <%
5:      'Open up a connection to our Access database that stores
6:      'the product information.
7:      Dim objConn
8:      Set objConn = Server.CreateObject("ADODB.Connection")
9:      objConn.ConnectionString = "DSN=ProductsDB"
10:     objConn.Open
11:
12:     'Create our SQL statement variable
13:     Dim strSQL
14:     strSQL = "SELECT * FROM Products WHERE Price <= 100" & _
15:              " ORDER BY Price DESC"
16:
17:     'Create an instance of the Command object
18:     Dim objCommand
19:     Set objCommand = Server.CreateObject("ADODB.Command")
20:
21:     'Set the ActiveConnection and CommandText properties
22:     objCommand.ActiveConnection = objConn
23:     objCommand.CommandText = strSQL
24:
25:     'Create a recordset object instance implicitly using
26:     'the Execute method of the Command object
27:     Dim objRS
28:     Set objRS = objCommand.Execute
29:
30:     'We are displaying products whose price is less than $100
31:     Response.Write "<B>"
32:     Response.Write "A Listing of Products less than $100.00:"
33:     Response.Write "</B>"
34:     Do While Not objRS.EOF
35:         Response.Write "<BR>" & objRS("Name") & " - " & _
36:                        FormatCurrency(objRS("Price"))
37:
38:         'Move on to the next customer
39:         objRS.MoveNext
40:     Loop
41:
42:     'Clean up our ADO objects
```

20

continues

LISTING 20.7 continued

```
43:    objRS.Close
44:    Set objRS = Nothing
45:
46:    objConn.Close
47:    Set objConn = Nothing
48: %>
```

ANALYSIS Listing 20.7 displays those items in the Products database that cost $100 or less. In Listing 20.7, however, the Command object is used to implicitly create a Recordset. Line 8 begins by creating a Connection object, and lines 9 and 10 establish a connection to the database. Next, line 13 creates the string variable to hold the SQL statement. Lines 14 and 15 assign a SELECT statement to the string variable strSQL. When executed, this SELECT statement returns only those items from the Products table that have a value of 100 or less in their Price column. Also, the results will be ordered by the value of the Price column in descending order.

Next, line 19 explicitly creates a Command object instance. Line 22 then sets the ActiveConnection property to the name of the Connection object variable, objConn. Set the CommandText property to the SQL statement that you want to execute. If you wanted to retrieve the contents of a database table, you would set the CommandText to the name of the database table and the CommandType property to adCmdTable.

After you have set the Command object properties, you are ready to perform the Execute method. Line 27 creates a variable that will hold the Recordset object instance, and then line 28 assigns this variable to the Recordset object instance returned by objCommand.Execute. Recall that you must use the Set keyword because you are assigning objRS to an object.

After the Command object's Execute method has created and returned a Recordset object, you can display the results just as in past examples. Lines 34 through 40 perform the standard Do While Not objRS.EOF ... Loop, displaying the Name and Price of each product in the Recordset. Lines 43 through 47 finish the script by closing and explicitly freeing the ADO objects.

The output of Listing 20.7 is identical to that of Listing 20.5(refer to Figure 20.8).

When creating Recordsets implicitly using the Command object, the same caveats apply as when creating them implicitly with the Connection object. Explicitly created Recordsets make for straightforward, easy-to-read code. As we'll discuss in tomorrow's lesson, programs have a longer life span than expected. Chances are, someone else will be making changes to your code in the future. If you use a smattering of approaches in creating Recordsets, only those who have a solid understanding of the approaches you used can work on your programs.

Summary

Today, we talked about many advanced database topics. We started out by focusing on advanced techniques of the Recordset object, beginning with a detailed discussion of database cursors. There are four types of cursors: forward-only, which is the default cursor; Static; Keyset; and Dynamic. The last three cursors are referred to as scrollable cursors because, when they are used, movement through the Recordset is unrestricted.

There are certain uses for each cursor. The forward-only cursor boasts the best performance but allows for only forward movement through the Recordset, and only one record at a time. The other cursors differ in how they reflect changes made to the database by other users. Also, scrollable cursors allow for extra Recordset object methods and properties. For example, by using a scrollable cursor, you can obtain the number of records in the Recordset by using the RecordCount property. With scrollable cursors, you can also use the MovePrevious, MoveFirst, and MoveLast methods, which are unavailable when using the forward-only cursor.

Next, we discussed the LockType property of the Recordset object. The LockType determines how data integrity is ensured in a multi-user database system. The default LockType is a Read-only lock, which does not allow for updates. The other three types of locks are: Optimistic, Pessimistic, and Batch Optimistic. The differences between these LockTypes were discussed in Table 20.4.

We concluded the advanced Recordset techniques with a discussion on how to create Recordset objects implicitly using the Execute method of the Connection object. The Execute method provides for a shorthand way of creating a Recordset object instance with the default cursor and LockType.

Next, we turned our attention to stored procedures, which are precompiled SQL queries stored on the database. When a stored procedure is executed for the first time, the database stores an execution plan to increase the efficiency with which the query will be performed next time. For this reason, stored procedures can lead to a performance increase. Case studies have shown an increase of up to 25 percent!

20

We concluded today's lesson with a discussion of the Command object, which contains an Execute method like the Connection object. Not surprisingly, this method of the Command object can also be used to implicitly create Recordsets. It is recommended, however, that you create your Recordset objects explicitly.

Throughout the past week, you've learned several essential database skills. These skills are prerequisites to creating a robust, data-driven ASP application. Although we've discussed techniques and syntax, we've neglected to discuss what goes into a program *before* coding beings. Tomorrow, we'll discuss the most important aspect of creating applications—creating a solid design.

Q&A

Q Because forward-only cursors are more efficient than scrollable cursors, why not count the records in a `Recordset` using a counting variable and a `Do While Not objRS.EOF ... Loop`?

A If you wanted to obtain the number of records in a `Recordset`, one approach is to use a forward-only cursor and perform the following loop:

```
'Count the number of records in the Recordset
Dim iCount
iCount = 0
Do While Not objRS.EOF
   iCount = iCount + 1
   objRS.MoveNext
Loop
```

Although this approach may seem harmless, it has drawbacks. Imagine that your `Recordset` contains 100 records. To find this out, you must move through each record, one at a time. With the multi-user nature of the Internet, many people could be having this loop performed simultaneously. Such a loop can place tremendous performance degradation on your database.

Although the scrollable cursors may not be as efficient as a forward-only cursor, they can determine the number of records in a `Recordset` with much more efficiency than a forward-only cursor. For this reason, if you want to obtain the number of records in a `Recordset`, and nothing more, you should definitely use a scrollable cursor.

Listing 20.3 used a forward-only cursor to display the results of a `Recordset` *and* count the number of records. This is fine because if you're going to output all the records in the `Recordset`, it doesn't hurt to also count the records at the same time. What leads to an unacceptable performance degradation is when you loop through an entire `Recordset` *just* to obtain the number of records in the `Recordset`. If this is all you're after, use a scrollable cursor and the `RecordCount` property.

Q Should I create stored procedures for all my SQL queries, or just those used most frequently?

A We recommend that you create stored procedures for *all* your SQL queries. If you find yourself requesting the results of a SQL query or the contents of a database table, make sure that these are implemented as stored procedures before your application goes live.

Although the performance boost may not be noticeable when using stored procedures for less frequently used queries, remember that another advantage of using stored procedures is that they provide a level of abstraction between your ASP pages and the database. When database changes occur, as they almost always do, a rigid use of stored procedures will pay off. This topic is discussed in detail tomorrow.

Q What types of queries can the `Command` object be used for?

A Any type of query you can perform using an explicitly created `Recordset`, you can perform using the `Command` object. Listing 20.7 looked at performing a SQL query using the `Command` object. The code in Listing 20.7 could be altered slightly to execute a stored procedure. Replacing lines 14 and 15 with

`strSQL = storedProcedureName`

would have the implicitly created `Recordset` object instance populated with the results of stored procedure *storedProcedureName*. You can also populate the implicitly created `Recordset` object with the contents of a database table. To do this, set the `CommandText` property to the name of the database table and the `CommandType` property to `adCmdTable`.

Workshop

The Workshop provides quiz questions to help you solidify your understanding of the material covered and exercises to provide you with experience in using what you've learned. Try to understand the quiz and exercise answers before continuing to tomorrow's lesson. Quiz answers are provided in Appendix A, and exercise answers can be found at `http://www.mcp.com/info`.

Quiz

1. What are the four types of database cursors, and what is the default cursor?
2. What cursors support the `RecordCount` property?
3. What four `LockTypes` are available, and what is the default `LockType`?
4. True or False: A Pessimistic lock can be used on a client-side cursor.
5. When using the `Execute` method of the `Connection` object, what cursor and `LockType` are assigned to the `Recordset` object created?
6. True or False: The use of stored procedures can lead to improved performance.
7. What three advantages do stored procedures offer?
8. If you had explicitly created a `Recordset` object named `objRS` and had a `Connection` object named `objConn`, how would you populate your `Recordset` with the results of a stored procedure named `CustomerInformation`?
9. If you want to use the `Command` object to implicitly create a `Recordset` object instance that is populated with the results of a database table, what three `Command` object properties do you need to set before performing the `Execute` method?
10. True or False: You should strive to create all your `Recordset` objects explicitly.

20

Exercises

1. Create a Recordset with a scrollable cursor of your choice. The Recordset should then move to the *last* record and continue to move to the previous record until the Recordset object's BOF property is True. In this example, rather than moving from the start of the Recordset to the end of the Recordset, one record at a time, you are moving from the end to the beginning one record at a time.

2. Create a Recordset object implicitly using the Execute method of the Connection object. The Execute method should be used to perform a SQL query.

3. Create a Recordset object implicitly using the Execute method of the Command object. The Execute method should be used to retrieve the contents of a database table.

DAY **21**

Practicing Intelligent Application Design

Throughout the past week's lessons, you've examined how to use ASP to query, update, insert, and delete records from databases. Although knowing how to retrieve and modify information in a database through ASP is important, knowing how to design your databases is equally important.

A common misconception by developers is that their programs won't be used for any significant length of time. When designing an application, it can be tempting to think in the short term. Because programs have a lifetime much longer than initially expected, such short-term thinking can lead to disastrous problems. You need look no further than the Y2K issue to see a major problem that arose due to programmers' short-term thinking.

The viability of a database application depends largely on its initial design. If care is not taken when designing a database, it may be difficult to add new functionality to the database application. When creating applications, strive to write your code so that it can be easily understood and modified by other developers. Building a usable database application requires both a solid ASP design and database design. Today's lesson focuses on both of these issues.

Today, you will learn the following:

- Why the design of an application is more important than the code itself
- What stages are involved in the software design cycle
- What techniques to use to create maintainable and readable ASP pages
- What techniques to use to create maintainable and readable databases
- Why naming conventions should be used when creating your tables
- How stored procedures can be used as a layer of abstraction between your ASP pages and the database
- How to create modularized ASP programs

Why Design Matters

Imagine that you just started working for a consulting company as the chief intranet developer. The company wants to perform payroll over the intranet and asks you to write a database application that will collect and save employees' billing hours. The company wants to know how many hours each consultant is billed, at what rate, and to what client.

Being a skilled ASP developer who has just finished reading *Sams Teach Yourself ASP 3.0 in 21 Days*, you quickly set out on the project and have the completed payroll system online within a year. Your boss is delighted by your performance, and the entire company switches over to the intranet-based payroll system you created. The year spent developing the large payroll application was well worth your annual salary—the company expects to save one man-hour each week for each employee because of your new system!

After a couple of months, your boss comes back to you with a list of enhancements he wants see made to the payroll system. Looking over the list, you realize some of these changes will require a lot of work: some new ASP pages and a couple of new tables in your database. Being the model employee that you are, though, you take this list of enhancements and incorporate them into the payroll system in the course of a month.

Over the next two years, changes continue to be requested. With each new revision of the payroll system, the code and database structure becomes more difficult to understand, more difficult to program. However, you know your own code fairly well and can, if given enough time, poke through the source code and make the needed changes.

After several years with the consulting company, you decide that it's time to move on to a new company. Shortly after you leave, a new set of enhancements for the intranet payroll system is drafted and handed to the new hire who filled your spot. The new hire begins looking at your code, trying to understand what tables in your database store what. Your ASP pages are confusing for him, too. In the end, the new developer decides that it will be easier to rewrite the entire system than try to update your code. This new developer approaches his boss and asks to rewrite the system. The boss, flabbergasted, explains that more than a year of programming went into the current system. In the end, the payroll system is recoded.

Too often, when developing applications, programmers fail to look at the long term. With advances in hardware and software occurring frequently, it is difficult to believe that a program you write might actually be used for several years. A golden rule in computer programming is that a program's *life expectancy* will almost always be longer than expected.

NEW TERM The *life* of a program is the number of years it is used. The *life expectancy*, then, is the expected life of a program.

If, when handed a programming assignment, you are told that the program will be used for three years, you can safely bet that it will be used for at least six. Because the life expectancy of programs is usually underestimated, it is vital that when developing an application, you take steps necessary to ensure that the program will be maintainable and usable in the future.

Software development can be broken down into four general phases: design, programming, testing, and deployment. Whenever creating an application, these four steps naturally occur, although there may be some overlap. The steps involved in each of these phases are as follows:

- Design—First, make sure that you have a solid understanding of the functional requirements. What information will the application need to store? What type of ASP pages will be needed? Next, obtain the technical requirements for the project. You need to decide what Relational Database Management System (RDBMS) to use and the database structure for your application. The database design cannot be completed until you fully understand the functional requirements. You can't build your database tables if you don't know what information you need to save in your database!

- Programming—This is when you write the actual ASP pages. Before a single line of code is written, you should have listed all the ASP pages that need to be created and what functionality each page needs to serve.

- Testing—This is an important stage and can overlap with the Programming stage. This phase consists of testing your ASP pages to make sure that the expected output is generated by a given input. It is important to test all kinds of input, not just valid input. Imagine that you have an ASP page that creates a form that asks users to enter the number of hours they worked for the current week. Although you obviously want to test values such as 40, you should also try inputs like 400 and hello.

21

- Deployment—In this final phase, the application is released for public consumption. Deployment may be as simple as moving the ASP pages to a live Web server, or it may be much more complicated. Deployment should not occur until the Testing phase has been completed.

After these four steps have been completed, your job as a developer is not complete. With great certainty, you can expect to be asked to make changes. When changes need to be made, the entire four-step process begins again. For this reason, the preceding four steps are often referred to as the *software development cycle* because they repeat each time a change is needed.

> **Note**
>
> There is an entire branch of computer science that studies the development of software. The study of software engineering has yielded many different approaches to software development. The method just discussed is referred to as the *four-stage waterfall paradigm*.

Of these four steps in software development, the most important by far, and the step that you should spend the greatest amount of time on, is the first step—Design. If you rush through a particular phase, the number of software defects and bugs caused in that phase will increase. As you progress from one stage to the next, the amount of time needed to fix a given bug or software defect created in the past stage will be magnified in the new stage. Software defects created in the first stage will take much longer to fix in later stages. Figure 21.1 shows a diagram of the four stages and the time required to fix the defects and bugs created in various stages.

Note the increasing amount of time it would take to fix five bugs or defects created in the Design phase. Figure 21.1 shows the importance of fixing defects as early as possible. You will benefit greatly from being patient when designing the application. Any extra time you spend in the design phase is time well spent because it will likely save you many hours of fixing bugs in later stages.

> **Note**
>
> The Year 2000 (Y2K) problem arose due to an underestimated program life expectancy. Developers in the 1960s, '70s, and even '80s, represented dates with only two digits for the year. It was obvious back then that this would cause problems when the century ended, but who expects a program to be used for upwards of 40 years?
>
> Such a lack of foresight can cause major problems and great sums of money to fix. If you ever find yourself skimping on the Design phase of your application, simply remind yourself of the Y2K fiasco!

FIGURE 21.1

It's best to fix bugs and defects in early stages!

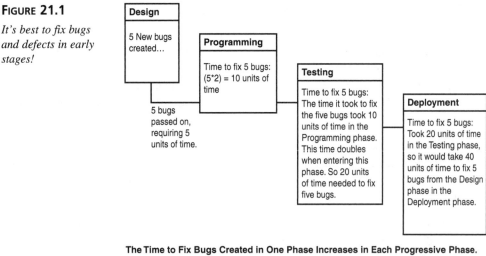

The Time to Fix Bugs Created in One Phase Increases in Each Progressive Phase.
Imagine that each bug takes one time unit to fix and that between each stage, the time needed to fix bugs from the previous stage doubles. You can see how the time needed to fix just a few bugs created in the Design stage increases dramatically!

When working in the Design phase, one of the most important things to do is document, especially if you're working on a project with multiple developers. In the Design phase, you should answer the following questions:

- What ASP pages will be needed?
- What database tables and columns will need to be created?
- What information will the ASP pages need from the database?

When you make a decision on one of these questions, it is important to document your decision. If you decide that the current project needs to have three ASP pages, one that lists all the information in each of the three database tables, how can you expect another developer to know this if you don't document it? Even if you are working alone on a project, chances are someone else will need to make changes to your project at a later date. These changes are easier to make if there is adequate documentation, explaining what ASP pages have been created and why, what database tables and columns have been created and why, and what information the ASP pages need from the database and why.

Note

Documentation should occur in all phases of the software development cycle. The two phases where documentation is the most important, though, are the Design and Programming phases. The Programming phase is briefly discussed later today in the section "Practiced ASP Programming Techniques."

21

Making Changes to Your Database

When you create an application, you can be sure of one thing: As soon as you finish your project, you will be asked to add new functionality. It would be nice if program requirements were set in stone, but it simply doesn't work this way. For this reason, it is important to build your ASP database applications to accommodate future changes. If your programming is so rigid that a change requires the complete system to be reprogrammed, chances are you spent too little time in the Design phase.

With ASP database applications, two types of changes generally will be requested. The first type of change has to do with the information stored by the database. Usually, you will be asked to grow your system so that it can include more information. Such an increase usually requires additions to the database.

Depending on how you designed your database structure, adding new tables, or adding new columns to existing tables, can either be simple, or an excruciating chore. A good database design also is easy for others to understand. If others cannot comprehend your database design unless they receive a lengthy explanation from you, what will happen after you leave the company and the project still needs to be maintained? We will discuss the techniques needed to create a solid database design later today in the section "Good Database Design Techniques."

Making Changes to Your ASP Pages

You also may be requested to change your ASP pages. Perhaps no new information needs to be saved, but a different report needs to be generated. Such a change should only require a minor change to one of your ASP pages. Of course, the severity of the change needed depends on the design of your ASP pages.

When designing ASP pages, your efforts should be largely directed toward making the ASP pages maintainable. As many developers know, nothing is more difficult than picking through another's source code trying to grasp what the code is supposed to accomplish. More often than not, due to poor design, it is quicker and easier to recode another's ASP page than to take the time to understand the code and make the needed changes. Recoding, of course, is wasted time, because it repeats the work that someone has already done. To prevent your ASP pages from be rewritten by the next developer, it is important to have a solid design before programming your ASP pages.

Today's lesson, if you hadn't guessed, focuses on this Design phase. We've already spent 20 days discussing the Programming phase, and Day 14, "Debugging Your ASP Scripts and Handling Errors," discussed the Testing phase. Because many developers find programming more interesting and more fun than software design, there is a temptation to jump right into the coding when handed a project. It is vital that adequate time be spent on the design, though, before a single line of code is written.

Because ASP is used primarily to develop distributed database applications, we will focus on design techniques for databases and ASP pages. Creating a robust database design is as important to the maintainability of your program as creating robust ASP pages. In the remainder of today's lesson, we will discuss these two topics.

Good Database Design Techniques

Now that you now *why* it is important to invest the time to create a solid database design, we need to discuss *how* to create such a design. Many techniques are available for creating a useful database design. Remember that your goal is to create a database design that can be easily maintained and updated by *other* developers. A solid database design allows other developers to easily accomplish the following tasks:

- Add new columns to existing tables
- Create new tables
- Obtain an understanding of what purpose each table and each column serves
- Make changes to the database without requiring a vast number changes to the ASP pages

To ensure a high-quality database design, there are a number of commonly practiced techniques used by database developers. The first, and most important, technique is *normalization* of your database. This technique is discussed in the section "Normalizing Your Database" later today. Normalizing your database allows you and others to add new columns and create new tables with greater ease. Also, when viewing someone else's database, having it normalized makes it easier to interpret and understand.

A technique similar to normalization is the use of *lookup tables*. Imagine that you have a table with a column that can only be equal to a predetermined set of values. For example, you might have users fill out a form on your Web site. You would then want to store this information in this database table. If, on the form, you asked users how they had heard about your Web site, you would want to present them with a list of options from which to select. Such options might include, `From a Search Engine`, or `From a friend`. In any case, the options they may choose from are restricted; often, these types of questions are asked using a list box.

Because you are storing the users' responses into a table, one of the table columns needs to store the value indicating how users heard about the Web site. Think for a moment, what will you store in this column? One option is to store the option they selected as a string. So, if a user had heard of your site through a search engine, the string `From a Search Engine` would appear in the column. This approach is restrictive, though, for what

21

happens if you want to reword the options, add new options, or remove existing options? A more robust approach is to use lookup tables. A thorough discussion of lookup tables and how they can be used occurs later today in the section "Using Lookup Tables."

Another common technique that makes it easier for others to understand your database is the use of naming conventions. A database that consists of logically named columns and tables is easier to read than one that contains nonsensical names. Imagine that you needed to create a table to contain a list of customers. It would make sense to name the table tblCustomers and to have column names such as FirstName, LastName, Age, and other such information. With such table names and column names, it is easy to understand what information the table holds and what information is in each column. How easy to understand would it be if you named the table T1, and the columns C1, C2, through CN? Anyone but you, the creator of this table, would be utterly confused when looking at this table definition. Advice on proper naming conventions is discussed later today in "Naming Conventions."

A common problem when designing ASP database applications is that when the database design changes, many changes are required in the ASP pages that are responsible for displaying, updating, inserting, and deleting database information. Although it is nearly impossible to have to make no changes to your ASP pages when your database design changes, there are steps you can take to minimize the number of changes that need to be made. By using stored procedures, discussed yesterday, Day 20, "Using Advanced Database Techniques," you can place a level of abstraction between the database queries and the ASP pages that process information from those queries. We will discuss this topic in more detail later today in "Using Stored Procedures."

Normalizing Your Databases

When creating relational databases, a common error is to have unneeded data. For example, a table may contain two columns: one might be a particular person's birth date, and another her age. This information on the person's age is redundant because you can easily compute someone's age if you know her birth date. To weed out redundant information, a technique known as *normalization* is used.

There are different degrees of normalization. The higher the degree of normalization, the less redundant data your database will contain. However, each successive degree of normalization is exceedingly difficult and complex to perform. Table 21.1 contains an explanation of the first three degrees of normalization.

TABLE 21.1 The First Three Degrees of Normalization

Normalization	Description
First Normal Form	To achieve first normal form, each field in a table must convey unique information. If you had a table that stored customer information and contained two identical columns for the customer's name, the database would not be in first normal form. By simply removing one of the duplicate columns, however, the database could be classified as first normal form.
Second Normal Form	No fields in a table can be derived from another field in that table. Returning to the birth date and age example earlier in this section, if one column contains information that can be derived from another column in the table, then the database is not in second normal form.
Third Normal Form	No duplicate information is permitted throughout the entire database. Imagine that you wanted to create a database that would track customers and their purchases. First, you created a table named `Customer` that contained the customer's name, billing, and shipping information. Next, you created a table named `Purchases` that contained the name of an item for sale, the customer's name, the customer's billing address, and the customer's shipping address. Note that the customer name, billing, and shipping address in the `Purchases` table are redundant if a relationship is set up between the `Customer` and `Purchases` tables. If a database contains such duplicate information across tables, it is not in third normal form.

Always normalize your database design. It is recommended that you normalize your database to third normal form, but you need to at least normalize it to second normal form. There are normal forms beyond third normal form; however, databases are not often normalized beyond third normal form.

When using an RDBMS such as Microsoft SQL Server, Microsoft Access, Oracle, or Informix, take advantage of the relational nature of the database. In fact, to carry your database design to third normal form, a solid understanding of relational databases is needed. Such a discussion on relational databases is beyond the scope of this book. The details of relational databases and of SQL, the language of relational databases, are discussed in detail in *Sams Teach Yourself SQL in 21 Days*.

Using Lookup Tables

When working on your database design, remind yourself of your objective: to build a database that is easy to maintain and update. To be easy to maintain, a database needs to be easy to understand by outside developers. If the names of your columns or tables or the

21

data in your columns or tables are ambiguous, your database will not be easy to maintain. If adding new data, altering existing data, or removing old data is difficult to do, your database is not easy to update. A poor database design can lead to such problems.

Imagine that you need to create a table, tblUserInformation, that will hold information about your visitors, including their education level. On a form, you ask the users what level of education they possess: Some high school, Completed high school, Some College, or Completed College. Think, for a moment, how you would store their responses in tblUserInformation. You'd need to create a column to store the education information, which we'll call EducationInformation, but what data, exactly, would EducationInformation need to hold?

One option would be to store a single character. If the person had Some high school, store an S; those who Completed high school would have a C stored in the education column; those who had Some College would get a B; finally, those who had Completed College would have a D stored. If you took this approach, would a different developer be able to ascertain what each character stood for? Would you remember what each character stood for after not working on the project for several months?

A better approach might be to store the entire string. Those who chose Completed College on the form, would have Completed College stored in the database. Although this is obviously easier to read than the character code, it is still difficult to update. Imagine that you wanted to add another option, Completed Masters Degree. You wouldn't have to change your database design, but you would have to edit the ASP page that has the form listing the education levels. Other changes, such as changing the title of an education level, or removing an education level option, require at least a change in the ASP page that displays the form. Also, some of these approaches would require a change to the data in the table.

The *best* solution is to use a lookup table. A lookup table is a table that contains the allowable options. In the education example, you would want to create a lookup table named tblEducationLevel that contains two columns: a unique ID named EducationLevelID (an IDENTITY field), and a string containing the education level choice, Description. Figure 21.2 shows the table definition of tblEducationLevel and the data it contains.

Now that you have a lookup table, how do you reflect what education level a user has in tblUserInformation, the table containing the visitors' information? Because you have a unique identifier for each row in tblEducationLevel, why not simply store that ID in EducationInformation? In fact, you'd want to make a relationship between these two tables, relating the EducationInformation column in tblUserInformation to the EducationLevelID column in tblEducationLevel.

FIGURE 21.2

The definition of
Education Level
and its data.

tblEducationLevel
EducationLevelID int IDENTITY
Description   varchar(100)

EducationLevelID	Description
1	Some high school
2	Completed high school
3	Some College
4	Completed College

You could now use the `tblEducationLevel` table to populate the list box in your form.
The code in Listing 21.1 would dynamically populate the list box.

LISTING 21.1 The List Box Containing the Values of `tblEducationLevel`

```
1:  <%@ Language=VBScript %>
2:  <% Option Explicit %>
3:  <!--#include file="adovbs.inc"-->
4:  <%
5:      'Open a connection to the database
6:      Dim objConn
7:      Set objConn = Server.CreateObject("ADODB.Connection")
8:      objConn.ConnectionString = "DSN=UserInformation"
9:      objConn.Open
10:
11:     'Create a recordset, retrieve the tblEducationLevel table
12:     Dim objRS
13:     Set objRS = Server.CreateObject("ADODB.Recordset")
14:
15:     objRS.Open "tblEducationLevel", objConn, , , adCmdTable
16: %>
17:
18: <HTML>
19: <BODY>
20:   <FORM METHOD=POST ACTION="SaveUserInformation.asp">
21:     ...
22:
23:     <SELECT NAME=EducationLevel>
24: <%
25:     Do While Not objRS.EOF
26:         Response.Write "<OPTION VALUE=" & objRS("EducationLevelID")
27:         Response.Write ">" & objRS("Description")
28:
29:         objRS.MoveNext
30:     Loop
31:
32:     'Clean up
33:     objRS.Close
34:     Set objRS = Nothing
```

continues

21

LISTING 21.1   continued

```
35:
36:        objConn.Close
37:        Set objConn = Nothing
38: %>
39:        </SELECT>
40:
41:        ...
42:    </FORM>
43: </BODY>
44: </HTML>
```

ANALYSIS   As with all the ASP scripts we've written that use ADO to access the database, start off by including ADOVBS.INC (line 3). Line 7 creates an instance of the ADODB.Connection object, and line 8 sets its connection string equal to a DSN created for this example). Line 9 Opens the connection to the database. Next, you need to create a Recordset object that obtains the values in the tblEducationLevel table. The Recordset object is instantiated in line 13, and the table data is obtained on line 15.

The form for requesting the user's information begins on line 20. The other form fields are cut out because you are just interested in populating the education level list box (line 23). Line 25 begins a Do While ... Loop to iterate through all the records in the recordset objRS. Lines 26 and 27 print out the <OPTION> tag, setting its VALUE to the current row's EducationLevelID value, and having the Description value displayed in the list box. Line 29 moves to the next row in the recordset using the MoveNext method. Lines 33 through 37 close and explicitly destroy the ADO objects.

Because the EducationInformation column in tblUserInformation is a foreign key to tblEducationLevel's column EducationLevelID, the value returned by Request("EducationLevel") in the form processing script is the value that we will set EducationInformation to. Figure 21.3 shows the output of Listing 21.1.

If you want to add a new education level option—Completed Masters Degree—to the form, what steps will you need to take? Because the values in the form list box are obtained via a database query, you would only need to add a single row to tblEducationLevel. Specifically, that row would contain Completed Masters Degree in the Description column of tblEducationLevel (the EducationLevelID column would be automatically entered because it is defined as an IDENTITY field). The ASP page doesn't need to be modified to accommodate any changes in the education level options.

Another benefit of using lookup tables is the increased readability of the database tables. If you had used character codes to denote the various education levels, a developer new to the database would have a difficult time discerning what characters stood for what education options. With a lookup table, though, you can quickly see what values in the `EducationInformation` column correspond to what `Descriptions` in `tblEducationLevel`.

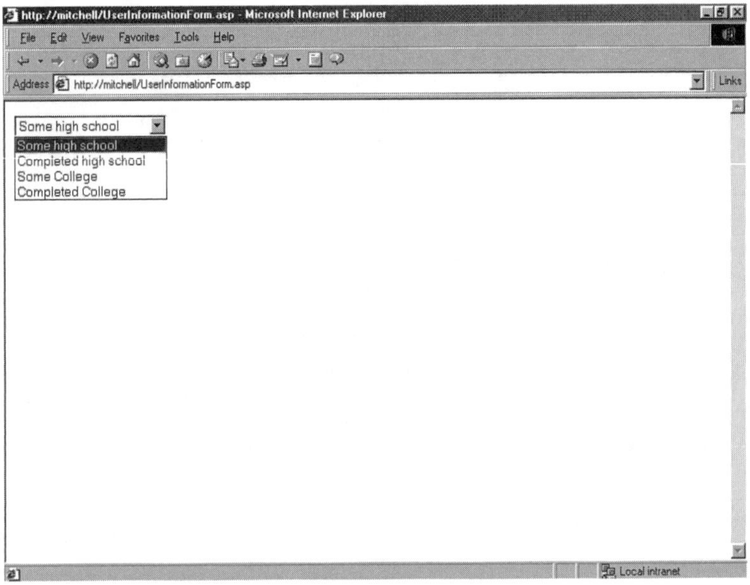

FIGURE 21.3

The list box contains the contents of `tblEducationLevel`.

When developing a database table with a column that can only contain one value out of a set of predefined values, a good database design will use a lookup table. A lookup table should contain a unique identifier in addition to the list of acceptable values. Using the lookup table approach will make your database easier to understand. Also, adding, editing, or removing education level options do not require any ASP page updates.

Naming Conventions

When designing your database, it is important to create logically named tables and columns. Because your database should be easy to read and understand, even for someone who has not worked on your database before, using a standard set of naming conventions will help greatly. To increase the readability of your database, be sure to use a consistent set of naming conventions and choose logical names for all your database objects.

Deciding what naming convention to use is not nearly as important as using the convention faithfully. Table 21.2 contains a list of recommended naming conventions for all the database objects. Do not feel compelled to use the conventions listed in Table 21.2. If there is a set of conventions that you find easier to use, by all means, use those. Just be

21

consistent. If you choose to use a `tbl` prefix for your table names, be sure to give all table names the `tbl` prefix. Nothing is more confusing than viewing a database design that does not adhere to a single naming convention.

TABLE 21.2 Suggested Naming Conventions for Database Objects

Prefix	Database Object
tbl	Table
sp	Stored procedure
vw	View

Table 21.2 lists the naming conventions used for database design throughout this book. Adhering to this naming convention, tables are named `tblTableName`, stored procedures are named `spStoredProcedureName`, and views are named `vwViewName`. Throughout this book, we have not ascribed a naming convention to columns in tables, although some developers use a modified form of *Hungarian notation* when naming columns.

NEW TERM *Hungarian notation* uses a specified prefix to illustrate the type of data the column stores.

Table 21.3 contains a list of commonly used prefixes for column names.

TABLE 21.3 Suggested Naming Conventions for Column Datatypes

Prefix	Data Type
b	bit
s	varchar
c	char
t	text
i	integer
f	numeric
dt	date/time

Using Hungarian notation on column names, developers can determine what *type* of information belongs in those columns.

Note Charles Simonyi, a Hungarian programmer at Microsoft, created Hungarian notation. His style of prefixing variables to represent their type is commonly used in C and C++ programming.

Finally, no matter what naming convention you choose, make sure that you give logical names to your columns and database objects. If a table contains a listing of the products your company sells, name the table tblProducts, not something ambiguous, like ProdListFY00. By following a naming convention, an outside developer should be able to know what purpose a particular column or table serves. For this reason, naming conventions are an important part of a good database design.

Do	Don't
DO use a naming convention when naming your database objects.	DON'T waiver from the naming convention you choose. Pick a naming convention and stick with it.

Using Stored Procedures

Yesterday, we discussed what stored procedures are and how to create them using Microsoft SQL Server 7.0. In the discussion, we focused primarily on the performance benefits of using stored procedures rather than queries.

Although improved performance is reason enough to use stored procedures, there is also another convincing reason. Stored procedures serve as a layer of abstraction between a database query and the returned results. When you write a SQL query directly in an ASP page, you have to know the names of the columns and tables that you want to retrieve data from. What happens if the table name changes, or if an existing column is removed? You would have to rewrite your ASP pages to conform to the new database design. If you use stored procedures, however, there is a good chance that you would only have to modify the stored procedure itself.

Earlier today, in "Why Design Matters," we used the example of building an online payroll system. Imagine that this system contains an ASP page that displays all employees and their employee numbers, which are used by the accounting department to uniquely identify each employee. Listing 21.2 shows some code that might be used to list the employee's name and number.

LISTING 21.2 A Query to List the Employee's Name and Number

```
1: <%@ Language=VBScript %>
2: <% Option Explicit %>
3: <%
4:      'Open a connection to the database
5:      Dim objConn
```

21

continues

LISTING 21.2 continued

```
6:          Set objConn = Server.CreateObject("ADODB.Connection")
7:          objConn.ConnectionString = "DSN=EmployeeInformation"
8:          objConn.Open
9:
10:         'Create a SQL string that will get the employee's
11:         'name and number
12:         Dim strSQL
13:         strSQL = "SELECT Name, EmployeeNumber " & _
14:                  "FROM tblEmployeeData ORDER BY Name"
15:
16:         'Create a recordset, retrieve the tblEducationLevel table
17:         Dim objRS
18:         Set objRS = Server.CreateObject("ADODB.Recordset")
19:         objRS.Open strSQL, objConn
20: %>
21:
22: <HTML>
23: <BODY>
24: <%
25:     Do While Not objRS.EOF
26:         Response.Write objRS("Name") & " - " & _
27:                        objRS("EmployeeNumber") & "<BR>"
28:
29:         objRS.MoveNext
30:     Loop
31:
32:     'Clean up...
33:     objRS.Close
34:     Set objRS = Nothing
35:
36:     objConn.Close
37:     Set objConn = Nothing
38: %>
39: </BODY>
40: </HTML>
```

ANALYSIS Listing 21.2 is written to display each employee's name and number. This information is stored in the `tblEmployeeData` table. To accomplish the full listing of employees, line 6 starts by creating an instance of the `ADODB.Connection` object. Line 7 sets its connection string to a DSN, and line 8 opens the connection to the database. Next, line 13, creates the SQL string to retrieve the employee names and numbers. Line 18 then instantiates a `Recordset` object, and line 19 retrieves the results of the SQL statement using the `Open` method of the `Recordset` object.

Line 25 starts a `Do While ... Loop` to iterate through the recordset values. Lines 26 and 27 display the `Name` and `EmployeeNumber` columns, whereas line 29 retrieves the next record in the recordset. Finally, lines 33 through 37 clean up the ADO objects by closing them and explicitly freeing the memory associated with them.

Although Listing 21.2 does a fine job of listing all employees' names and numbers, what would happen if the accounting department switches to using social security numbers for identification? They might want a report that lists each employee and his social security number. This would require you to do three things:

1. Create a new column named SSN in the EmployeeData table.
2. Enter the employees' social security numbers into the SSN column.
3. Modify the query in the ASP page that generates the report.

Although this might not seem too bad, what if you have a dozen ASP pages that display the employees' numbers and need to be changed to display the social security numbers?

Imagine if a stored procedure were used instead of a direct query in the ASP pages that needed the employees' names and employee numbers. The syntax in the ASP pages wouldn't change much. In fact, you could write a stored procedure to return two columns, Name and EmployeeNumber. If you created such a stored procedure and named it spGetEmployeeNamesAndNumbers, you would only need to change the SQL statement on lines 13 and 14 in Listing 21.2. If you changed the SQL statement to the following:

```
spGetEmployeeNamesAndNumbers
```

and created spGetEmployeeNamesAndNumbers with the query:

```
SELECT Name, EmployeeNumber
FROM EmployeeData ORDER BY Name
```

the output of Listing 21.2 would not change. Now if the accounting department asks you to use employee social security numbers, you need only do the following steps:

1. Create a new column named SSN in the EmployeeData table.
2. Enter the employees' social security numbers into the SSN column.
3. Modify the stored procedure spGetEmployeeNamesAndNumbers to return SSN rather than EmployeeNumber.

Because the ASP page is expecting a column named EmployeeNumber, in the stored procedure the query must rename the SSN column EmployeeNumber. The modified query for spGetEmployeeNamesAndNumbers is as follows:

```
SELECT Name, SSN AS EmployeeNumber
FROM EmployeeData ORDER BY Name
```

That one simple change to spGetEmployeeNamesAndNumbers saves you from having to go through all your ASP pages, find where you referred to EmployeeNumber, and change that to SSN. Using a stored procedure adds a level of abstraction between the database and the

21

ASP page. When writing a database application with ASP, ASP should be responsible only for properly displaying the data. The database itself should be used to store the data. A middle layer should be used to collect the data and present it to ASP in a defined format. Stored procedures can be used as this middle layer. Figure 21.4 displays how stored procedures can be used as a layer of abstraction between a database and an ASP page.

FIGURE 21.4

Stored procedures serve as a layer of abstraction.

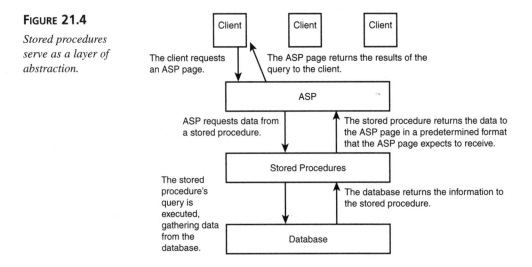

Using stored procedures within your ASP application has two benefits:

- As discussed yesterday, database queries run faster when using a stored procedure.
- Stored procedures provide a means of abstraction between the raw data in the database and the ASP pages. For this reason, a good database design should include a number of stored procedures.

Good ASP Design Techniques

As your program ages and changes are requested, those changes can usually be placed into one of two categories. Either a change to the database structure is needed, or a change to the presentation of the database information is requested. Sometimes, however, such a requested change requires that both the database and ASP pages be modified. When changes to the database are needed, a solid database design makes those changes easier. When a change is requested for the presentation of database information, a change to one or more ASP pages is needed, and a good ASP design simplifies the process. A well-thought-out ASP design will reap the same benefits as a good database design.

Recall from "Why Design Matters" earlier today that the Design phase is the most important part of the software design cycle. The Design phase occurs before any actual programming is done. It is important to dedicate sufficient time to this phase before you begin to program your various ASP pages.

The first step in ASP design is to decide what ASP pages you will need for your project. Imagine that you received the following email from your boss:

"Our sales reps in the field have asked for an Internet site that would allow them to query our Products database. We don't want any changes to be made to the Products database. What we need is a listing of all our products, with a way for our reps to obtain more information on each individual product."

After you have a description of the requirements, spend some time thinking about how many ASP pages you will need. What will each page need to display? Write down your thoughts on paper so that when you arrive at the Programming phase, you will know what pages, exactly, you'll need to write. For the preceding example, you will need two ASP pages: one that lists all the company's products, and one that lists detailed information about a particular product. Figure 21.5 shows the two ASP pages and how they relate to one another.

FIGURE 21.5

For this example project, you need two ASP pages.

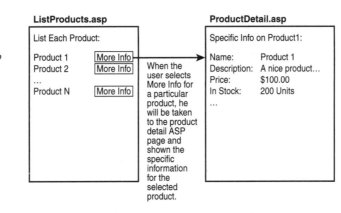

The first ASP page will be used to display each product in the Products database. Each product will have a More Info hyperlink next to it. When clicked, the second ASP page will be displayed, showing the detailed information on the particular product. Although you may think that such an early analysis isn't needed, imagine what would happen if you started programming immediately and, after writing a couple of ASP pages, realized that you needed some new ones, or you didn't need some of the ones you already wrote. The time that you wasted with extraneous ASP pages could have been better spent in the Design phase. This is especially the case as your ASP projects become larger.

21

Practiced ASP Programming Techniques

The Design phase consists of planning for your future ASP pages and constructing a database design. With ASP pages and databases, creating a solid design before moving on to the Programming phase ensures maintainability and readability. When you do reach the Programming phase for your ASP pages, though, you still need to practice techniques that will augment the readability of your ASP pages.

Documentation, an important aspect of the Design phase, is equally important in the Programming phase. With the Design phase, documentation is in the form of function and technical specification documents; in the Programming phase, documentation exists within the code. To document the source code of your ASP pages, use *comments*.

Comments, signified by the apostrophe (') in VBScript, should be used often. Whenever you can logically group together a few lines of code, you should place a comment at the beginning of that block of code, explaining what, exactly, the code does. For example, if you created an ASP page that read all the values from a particular table in a database, your source code might look like the code in Listing 21.3.

LISTING 21.3   Code Listing a Table in a Database

```
 1:  <%@ Language=VBScript %>
 2:  <% Option Explicit %>
 3:  <!--#include file="adovbs.inc"-->
 4:  <%
 5:      Dim objConn
 6:      Set objConn = Server.CreateObject("ADODB.Connection")
 7:      objConn.ConnectionString = "DSN=UserInformation"
 8:      objConn.Open
 9:
10:      Dim objRS
11:      Set objRS = Server.CreateObject("ADODB.Recordset")
12:      objRS.Open "tblEducationLevel", objConn, , , adCmdTable
13:
14:      Dim iLoop
15:      Do While Not objRS.EOF
16:          For iLoop = 0 to objRS.Fields.Count - 1
17:              Response.Write objRS.Fields(iLoop).Name & " - "
18:              Response.Write objRS.Fields(iLoop).Value & "<BR>"
19:          Next
20:
21:          Response.Write "<P><HR><P>"
22:          objRS.MoveNext
23:      Loop
24:
25:      'Clean up
26:      objRS.Close
```

```
27:     Set objRS = Nothing
28:
29:     objConn.Close
30:     Set objConn = Nothing
31: %>
```

ANALYSIS   Listing 21.3 lists all the columns in all the rows of the tblEducationLevel table. We looked at a similar script earlier in Listing 21.1; however, the code in Listing 21.3 is not commented at all. Glancing through the code, it might seem easy to ascertain what is happening without comments. With a short ASP script, commenting may seem like wasted time. Don't fall into this trap. If you do not comment short scripts, you will soon find yourself not commenting longer ones. *Always* comment *every* ASP script, even if it is only a few lines long.

Commenting is especially essential with lengthy ASP scripts. When designing complicated ASP pages, it is not unlikely for there to be hundreds of lines of code. Commenting does help the readability of ASP pages, even if they are under 100 lines of code, as is Listing 21.3. Compare Listing 21.3 to Listing 21.4. Listing 21.4 contains the same functional code as Listing 21.3 but includes commenting.

LISTING 21.4   Using Comments to Make Listing 21.3 Easier to Read

```
1: <%@ Language=VBScript %>
2: <% Option Explicit %>
3: <!--#include file="adovbs.inc"-->
4: <%
5:     'Open a connection to the database
6:     Dim objConn
7:     Set objConn = Server.CreateObject("ADODB.Connection")
8:     objConn.ConnectionString = "DSN=UserInformation"
9:     objConn.Open
10:
11:     'Create a recordset, retrieve the tblEducationLevel table
12:     Dim objRS
13:     Set objRS = Server.CreateObject("ADODB.Recordset")
14:     objRS.Open "tblEducationLevel", objConn, , , adCmdTable
15:
16:     'Loop through the recordset
17:     Dim iLoop
18:     Do While Not objRS.EOF
19:         'Loop through each field in the recordset object
20:         For iLoop = 0 to objRS.Fields.Count - 1
21:           'Display the name and value of the field
22:           Response.Write objRS.Fields(iLoop).Name & " - "
23:           Response.Write objRS.Fields(iLoop).Value & "<BR>"
24:         Next
```

21

continues

LISTING 21.4 continued

```
25:
26:            'Print a dividing line and move to the next record
27:            Response.Write "<P><HR><P>"
28:            objRS.MoveNext
29:        Loop
30:
31:        'Clean up
32:        objRS.Close
33:        Set objRS = Nothing
34:
35:        objConn.Close
36:        Set objConn = Nothing
37: %>
```

ANALYSIS The functionality of Listing 21.4 is identical to that of Listing 21.3 because only comments were added. These comments have been placed immediately above logically related blocks of code. The first comment, which appears on line 5, describes what the next four lines of code are going to do. The comment on line 11 explains what lines 12 through 14 are doing. With comments present, a new developer can quickly skim through the source code, reading just the comments, and obtain an understanding of the code. Reading an English explanation of the source code is much easier than trying to determine the purpose of the source code by reading through ASP syntax.

The use of good comments leads to explicitly documented code. You should also aim at writing *self-documenting code*.

NEW TERM *Self-documenting* code is well formatted and consists of logically named variables with proper notation.

In all the code examples throughout this book, we've striven to use self-documenting code. Note how we indent each loop, function, and If statement and how we place a blank line after groups of commonly related code. Code that uses white space to enhance its readability is said to be well-formatted code. We also give variables logical names. If a variable serves as a counter in a loop, we choose a name like iLoop or iCounter. Choosing such a name makes it easier to understand the purpose of the variable.

Also choose a naming convention for your variables. Throughout the book, we've used a modified Hungarian notation, prefixing each variable to represent the type of information the variable will hold. Using such a notation is useful in VBScript, where all variables are of type Variant. By having a prefix, developers can quickly determine what type of information you are storing in the variable. Table 21.4 lists the naming convention used throughout this book.

TABLE 21.4   Type Prefixes for Variable Names

Variable Type	Prefix
Integer	i
Single	sng
Double	dbl
String	str
Date	dt
Boolean	bol
Currency	cur
Object	obj

Note

Do not feel compelled to use our variable naming convention if you'd rather use a different one. The important thing is not what naming convention you choose to use, but rather that you do choose a naming convention and faithfully use it throughout all your ASP pages.

Another good technique to practice when programming your ASP pages is *modularization*.

 A *modularized* program is one that is broken down into discrete modules. Each individual module serves a sole, unique purpose.

Having your program comprised of several modules is good for development for several reasons. First, it allows for code reuse. Imagine that if a currency value were less than zero you'd want it to be displayed in red as opposed to black. You could write the following function:

```
Function CurrencyDisplay(cCurrencyValue, iNumDigitsAfterDecimal)
   If cCurrencyValue < 0 then
     Response.Write "<FONT COLOR=RED>" & _
       FormatCurrency(cCurrencyValue, iNumDigitsAfterDecimal) & _
       "</FONT>"
   Else
     Response.Write "<FONT COLOR=BLACK>" & _
       FormatCurrency(cCurrencyValue, iNumDigitsAfterDecimal) & _
       "</FONT>"
   End If
End Function
```

which will display a currency using `FormatCurrency`. Negative currencies will be displayed in red, whereas nonnegative currencies will be displayed in black. This function can be placed in a module and reused. Code reuse provides two major benefits: first, it

21

saves time because you don't have to rewrite code; second, it's less error-prone. The more code you write, the greater the chance that code will contain a bug or defect. If you reuse code, the bugs are worked out, and, before too long, your reusable code is bug free.

You are probably wondering what, exactly, modules are in ASP and how you can use them. ASP does not have true modules, as Visual Basic does, but you can create module-like behavior using a server-side include to import a common function or common set of functions into your ASP pages. Recall from Day 13, "Reading and Writing Files on the Web Server," that server-side includes import existing ASP pages into the currently executing ASP page.

To use module-like programming practices with ASP, simply create an ASP page for each module you need. Then, to use that module in a given ASP page, include the module that is needed. For example, if you had a number of currency-formatting functions, similar to the CurrencyDisplay function mentioned previously, you could place all these functions in a file named CurrencyFunction.asp within a directory named /include. Then, if you needed to use one or many of these currency-formatting functions in an ASP page, you would only need to add the following line of code:

```
<!--#include virtual="/include/CurrencyFunction.asp"-->
```

After this line of code was added in an ASP page, the currency-formatting functions could be used as if they had been declared in the ASP page itself.

> **Tip**
>
> It is recommended that you create a directory named /include and place all your module files there. This makes it easy to include the module and clearly illustrates to other developers that commonly used functions can be found in the /include directory.

By using such modularization techniques, you will not only save time through code reuse but also have fewer bugs in your code. By faithfully commenting your code, it will be easier to read and understand, thereby simplifying changes and updates to the code. These two techniques are both highly recommended during the Programming phase of the software development cycle.

Summary

Today, we examined why the design of your ASP database application is vital. The applications you build today will be around for years, if not decades. Also, rarely will a project only be seen by one pair of eyes. For this reason, it is important to design maintainable and readable applications.

When designing an ASP database application, there are two parts of the Design phase: the database design, and the design of the ASP pages. When designing a database, maintainability and readability are the two goals to be striven for. To make a database as maintainable as possible, it is important to normalize the database. It is recommended that your database be put in third normal form. Also, the use of lookup tables can help make a database both easier to read and easier to update. Finally, to help with the readability of your database, be sure to follow a set of naming conventions.

The other part of the ASP database application Design phase is the design of the actual ASP pages that will present the database's data. Before you write a single line of code in an ASP page, be sure to have documented all the ASP pages that you will need for your project. Having a listing of each ASP page needed and what each ASP page will accomplish will save you a great deal of time during the Programming phase.

When you do begin programming your ASP pages, it is important to document your source code with the use of comments. Comments should precede every logically related group of code. When trying to determine the purpose and functionality of an ASP page, it is much easier to read English comments instead of picking through VBScript syntax. Also when developing your ASP pages, be sure to take advantage of code reuse. Place commonly used functions and subroutines in different files, or modules. Then, whenever you need to use one of those common functions in an ASP page, you can use a server-side include to import the contents of the file that contains the needed function.

When you set out to create an ASP database application, keep in mind that the most important part of the entire project is not the coding, but the design. A well-thought out design will give the application a lengthier life span because the application will be easier to maintain. For every minute spent in the Design phase, you'll save 10 minutes in later updates of the application! For this reason, make sure that more than enough time is spent designing the application.

Q&A

Q What other software development methodologies are there besides the four-stage waterfall paradigm discussed in today's lesson?

A There are many other commonly used software development methodologies. In fact, an entire branch of computer science is dedicated to the study of software engineering. One of the most popular software development methodologies is a five-stage waterfall paradigm. The five-stage waterfall paradigm is identical to the four-stage waterfall paradigm discussed today, except that it adds a Systems Analysis phase prior to the Design phase. Another popular methodology is the

21

four-stage spiral methodology. This methodology contains the same four stages as the four-stage waterfall paradigm, but each phase is repeated several times during the creation of the application.

Just like naming conventions, the software development methodology you choose to use is not of great consequence. What is drastically more important is that you adhere to the methodology you choose.

Q What kind of documentation should be generated in the Design phase?

A Documentation is a vital part of the design phase, especially when multiple developers are on a project. When updating another developer's application, without sufficient documentation, the only way to determine how the database is designed, or how the ASP pages work, is to meticulously study each database table and every ASP page. With proper documentation, however, a quick assessment of the application can be made.

When designing your application, two types of documents are usually generated: a functional specification and a technical specification. The functional specification usually contains a high-level view of the purpose of the application. It should also delve into each ASP page, discussing what tasks the page needs to perform. The technical documentation should contain specifics of the database, including the database table structure. With these two documents, future developers will find your application much easier to maintain.

Q Is there any performance concern to using server-side includes to import several modules?

A Each time a page that contains a server-side include is requested, the Web server needs to grab a file off of the disk and insert its contents into the ASP page before the ASP engine can process the requested ASP page. Using modules is slightly less efficient than having the actual function declarations contained in the ASP page. However, the performance loss is not great enough to offset the benefit gained from modularizing your ASP scripts.

Remember that a Web server is designed to read files from the hard drive and send them to the client that requested it. Therefore, you could expect that when a file needs to be imported into an ASP page, the Web server could efficiently retrieve the file off the hard drive and include its contents. I have developed ASP applications that have used upwards of five server-side includes on each ASP page. I have talked to developers who have created applications with 10 to 20 server-side includes and still did not see any noticeable performance degradation.

Workshop

The Workshop provides quiz questions to help you solidify your understanding of the material covered and exercises to provide you with experience in using what you've learned. Try to understand the quiz and exercise answers before continuing to tomorrow's lesson chapter. Quiz answers are provided in Appendix A, and exercise answers can be found at `http://www.mcp.com/info`.

Quiz

1. What is the most important phase of the software development cycle?

2. True or False: The actual life expectancy of your program is often less than the estimated life expectancy.

3. Why is it important to fix bugs and software defects as soon as possible?

4. What criteria does your database need to meet to be considered in second normal form?

5. True or False: The highest normal form your database can be in is third normal form.

6. How do stored procedures provide a level of abstraction between the database and ASP pages?

7. In the Design phase, half of your efforts should be directed toward database design. Where should the other half of your efforts be directed?

8. Why is it important to comment your ASP pages?

9. What advantages are achieved through code reuse?

10. True or False: Server-side includes can be used to allow for modular ASP scripts.

Exercise

1. Using the programming techniques discussed in the section "Practiced ASP Programming Techniques," rewrite the following code:

```
1:  <%@ Language=VBScript %>
2:  <% Option Explicit %>
3:  <%
4:      Dim a, b
5:      b = 1
6:      For a = 1 to 10
7:          Response.Write b & " squared equals " & b * b & "<BR>"
8:          b = b + 1
9:      Next
10: %>
```

21

WEEK 3

In Review

Congratulations on completing your first 21 ASP lessons! Over the past three weeks, you have acquired the skills to create professional ASP pages that can accomplish a wide range of functions. With the skills you have learned, you can create just about any ASP page you'll ever need to code.

Where do you go now, though? We covered those ASP topics most often used throughout the past three weeks; however, several topics still remain that deserve inspection. With your acquired ASP skills, you can quickly pick up these new topics. To learn new topics, we recommend starting on the Net and checking out the Web sites listed in Appendix D, "Helpful ASP Information on the Net."

Bonus Project 3

Adding Events to the Calendar

This last Bonus Project ties together all the skills you've learned over the past three weeks. Today's Bonus Project will enhance the Calendar application by using a database to store date-specific events. In `Calendar.asp`, these date-specific events will be shown in the appropriate `TABLE` cell, as if someone had written down an important event on a paper calendar.

When beginning a project, recall from Day 21, "Practicing Intelligent Application Design," that the *most* important phase is the Design phase, where you decide what code you will need to write and what database tables you'll need to create. The upcoming section, "Designing the Event Database," in today's Bonus Project focuses on the database design and the actual creation of the database. The section "Displaying the Events" deals with code design and implementation.

15

16

17

18

19

20

21

As with the first two Bonus Project, you are encouraged to add enhancements to the presented designed. In fact, a couple of possible improvements are listed in the final section of today's Bonus Project, "The Calendar Application: Where to Go Next."

Designing the Event Database

In the first Bonus Project, the current month was shown in a calendar view. With the second Bonus Project, you added functionality to allow the user to switch what month she was currently viewing. You also used cookies to "remember" what month the user last viewed. In today's Bonus Project, you are going to greatly extend the usefulness of the Calendar application by allowing the calendar to display date-specific events.

I am a very busy man, and people sometimes have a hard time getting in touch with me. I want to provide some way for my associates to know my future schedule without them having to query me directly. One solution is to simply post my itinerary to a personal Web site. This itinerary might list what activities I have planned in the present and near future. For example, when visiting my page on March 5, the visitor might see an output similar to Figure BP3.1.

FIGURE BP3.1

Interested in my future plans? Check my Web page!

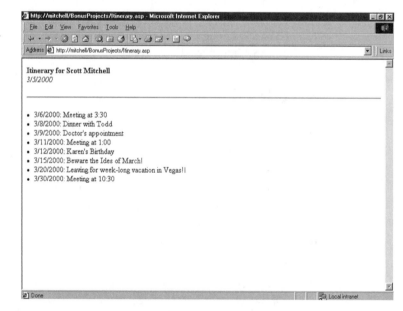

Although Figure BP3.1 does display, in detail, my future plans, it is not extremely easy to read. If someone is wondering what my time looks like on 3/9, he has to pick through the output, looking for a specific reference to 3/9. Or, if someone is interested in seeing what days are free between 3/11 through 3/15, it would not be an overly simple task.

I could simplify these requests, though, by putting my itinerary in calendar form. That way, a visitor can quickly look at a specific date and determine what my schedule for that day looks like. Because we already have a Calendar application from the first two Bonus Projects, we will build on our previous work, adding functionality to list what events I have planned.

To do this, we will use a database. In this case, it makes sense to use a database because we can expect a large amount of information needing to be stored indefinitely. Also, I will be making frequent changes and additions to my schedule, so it is important that the event information be easily updateable. Using a database is wise in this scenario.

What will the database need to consist of? Before you can answer that question, you need to understand what will be happening in the ASP page, `Calendar.asp`. When the user visits `Calendar.asp`, whether for the first time, or after choosing to view a different month through the list box or hyperlinks in the Calendar application, the variable `dbCurrentDate` contains the month and year of the calendar the user is viewing. To display the calendar, you use an HTML `TABLE`, looping through an array, `aCalendarDays`.

To be able to display date-specific events, you need to first be able to get the appropriate events from the database when `Calendar.asp` is loaded. For example, if the user is viewing the calendar for April, 2000, you want to query the database, retrieving all events that occur in April, 2000. Then, as you loop through `aCalendarDays`, if the day being outputted matches the day that an event occurs, you want to display that event's title.

To accomplish this, you need just one table, which we'll call `Event`. This table will need to contain information on the month, day, and year that a particular event occurs, and a title for that event. Therefore, the `Event` table will have four columns: `Month`, `Day`, `Year`, and `EventTitle`. Figure BP3.2 shows the columns I created for the `Event` table in the Access 2000 Design view.

You could use just two columns in the `Event` table, `EventDate` and `EventTitle`, where `EventDate` was a Date/Time field. However, the SQL needed to obtain just those records that have a certain month and year is a bit more complex when using an actual Date/Time than when using three fields, one for the year, month, and day.

For this Bonus Project, populate the `Event` table with the information shown in Table BP3.1.

TABLE BP3.1 The Data Present in the `Event` Table

Month	Day	Year	EventTitle
11	19	1999	Beer Night
11	20	1999	Justin visiting for the weekend

continues

TABLE BP3.1 continued

11	22	1999	Pick up Lolita from the airport
11	23	1999	Head home for Thanksgiving
11	30	1999	Give the Web site presentation at 3:30
12	1	1999	Meeting at 2:45
12	4	1999	Pearl Harbor Party!!

FIGURE BP3.2

The Event table needs only four columns.

As you can see, the Event database contains records detailing my scheduled events.

Caution

The Calendar application is designed to handle only one scheduled event per day. Creating multiple events that occur on the same day causes events after that day not to be shown. We will discuss how to enhance the application to handle multiple dates in the final section, "The Calendar Application: Where to Go Next."

Displaying the Events

To display the events, you first need to obtain the set of events that coincide with the month and year being viewed. Recall that dbCurrentDate contains a date within the month and year of the calendar being viewed. So, you can obtain all the events for the month and year being viewed by using the following SQL statement:

```
SELECT *
FROM Event
WHERE Month = MonthBeingViewed
  AND
Year = YearBeingViewed
```

Refining this SQL statement, note that the month being viewed is Month(dbCurrentDate), and the year being viewed is Year(dbCurrentDate). Also, you really don't need to retrieve *all* the columns from the Event table, rather just the Day and EventTitle. Finally, you need the events returned to be ordered by the day they occur on, in ascending order. Because our loop to display the calendar displays the first day of the month, then the second, and so on, you want the Recordset containing the events to be ordered so that the events that occur earlier in the month appear before those that occur later. To accommodate this, add an ORDER BY clause to the SELECT statement; specifically, ORDER BY Day ASC.

Listing BP3.1 contains the code that will obtain all the events for the month and year being currently viewed, ordered by the day that they occur.

LISTING BP3.1 A SQL Statement Used to Obtain Those Events That Occurred

```
1:  'Now that we have the Date we're interested in viewing, we need
2:  'to grab the events from the database that correspond to the
3:  'month and year of dbCurrentDate.  We'll begin by creating our
4:  'Connection object
5:  Dim objConn
6:  Set objConn = Server.CreateObject("ADODB.Connection")
7:  objConn.ConnectionString = "DSN=CalendarEvents"
8:  objConn.Open
9:
10: 'Now, we need to create our recordset object, grabbing all of the
11: 'events whose Month column equals Month(dbCurrentDate) and whose
12: 'Year column equals Year(dbCurrentDate).  We'll use a SQL statement
13: 'to accomplish this, since there may be many records in the Event
14: 'table
15: Dim strSQL
16: strSQL = "SELECT Day, EventTitle FROM Event WHERE Month = " & _
17:   Month(dbCurrentDate) & " AND Year = " & Year(dbCurrentDate) & _
18:   " ORDER BY Day ASC"
19:
20: 'Now, we need to create and open our recordset object.  We can use
21: 'a forward-only cursor and read only lock, so we'll simply not
22: 'specify them, since they are the default
23: Dim objRS
24: Set objRS = Server.CreateObject("ADODB.Recordset")
25: objRS.Open strSQL, objConn
```

ANALYSIS Listing BP3.1 retrieves those records from the `Event` table that fall within the month and year being viewed; these results are ordered by the day they occurred on in ascending order. As with the SQL examples on Day 19, "Using SQL Statements to Query Data," to retrieve database information, a `Connection` and `Recordset` object are often used. Line 6 in Listing BP3.1 creates the `Connection` object, and line 7 sets its `ConnectionString` property to a System DSN. For more information on creating System DSNs, revisit Day 16's lesson, "Reading from a Database Using ASP."

Next, you create the SQL string that will be used to populate the `Recordset` object. Line 15 starts by declaring the string variable, `strSQL`. Next, line 16 sets `strSQL` equal to the finalized SQL string. This SQL string retrieves all the events that occurred in the month and year of `dbCurrentDate` and will order those results by the day they occurred in ascending order.

After you have the SQL statement, you're ready to create the `Recordset` object and `Open` it. Line 24 creates the `Recordset` object instance, `objRS`. Line 25 executes the `Recordset` object's `Open` method, populating the `Recordset` with the results from the SQL query.

To better understand what data the `Recordset` object will retrieve from the database, let's look at a specific example. Imagine that the user is viewing the calendar for November, 1999. From the `Event` table, whose contents are shown in Table BP3.1, the `Recordset` object will contain the data shown in Table BP3.2.

TABLE BP3.2 The Contents of the `Recordset` Object When the User Views the Calendar for November, 1999

Day	EventTitle
19	Beer Night
20	Justin visiting for the weekend
22	Pick up Lolita from the airport
23	Head home for Thanksgiving
30	Give the Web site presentation at 3:30

Now that you have this information, you can display it as you work through the two nested loops responsible for displaying the calendar. When you iterate through each day, you can check to see whether the `Day` field in the current record in the `Recordset` is equal to the day that you are currently displaying in the calendar. If it is, you want to display the `EventTitle` and move to the next record in the `Recordset`.

Let's look at the two loops that display the calendar and the added code to display the database events. Listing BP3.2 contains this code, and Figure BP3.3 shows the Calendar application in action.

LISTING BP3.2   Check if an Event for the Current Day Exists

```
1:    'Keep track of how many events we display
2:    Dim iEventCount
3:    iEventCount = 0
4:
5:    'Now, loop through 1 through iRows, then 1 through iColumns
6:    Dim iRowsLoop, iColumnsLoop
7:    For iRowsLoop = 1 to iRows
8:       'Create a new row
9:       Response.Write "<TR>"
10:      For iColumnsLoop = 1 to iColumns
11:         'Create a new column
12:         'If there is a day there, display it, else black out the cell
13:         If aCalendarDays((iRowsLoop-1)*7 + iColumnsLoop) > 0 then
14:            'Display the date, and determine whether or not there is
15:            'an event in the database for this date
16:            Response.Write "<TD VALIGN=TOP ALIGN=RIGHT WIDTH=14% " & _
17:                           "HEIGHT=" & FormatPercent(1/iRows,0) & ">"
18:            Response.Write "<TABLE CELLSPACING=0 CELLPADDING=0 BORDER=0 " & _
19:                           "WIDTH=""100%"">"
20:
21:            'Write the day in the upper-right hand corner
22:            Response.Write "<TR><TD ALIGN=RIGHT><B>"
23:            Response.Write aCalendarDays((iRowsLoop-1)*7 + iColumnsLoop)
24:            Response.Write "</B></TD></TR>"
25:
26:            'Write the calendar event for that day, if it exists
27:            'First check to make sure objRS is not at the end of file
28:            If Not objRS.EOF then
29:               'Now, check to see if the current record contains the
30:               'current date for its day column
31:               If objRS("Day") = _
32:                aCalendarDays((iRowsLoop-1)*7 + iColumnsLoop) then
33:                  Response.Write "<TR><TD VALIGN=TOP ALIGN=LEFT>"
34:                  Response.Write "<FONT SIZE=2>"
35:
36:                  Response.Write objRS("EventTitle")
37:                  objRS.MoveNext
38:
39:                  'Increment how many Events we're showing
40:                  iEventCount = iEventCount + 1
41:
42:                  Response.Write "</FONT>"
43:                  Response.Write "</TD></TR>"
44:               End If
45:            End If
46:
47:            Response.Write "</TABLE>"
48:            Response.Write "</TD>"
```

continues

LISTING BP3.2   continued

```
49:        Else
50:           'Black out the cell
51:           Response.Write "<TD BGCOLOR=BLACK> </TD>"
52:        End If
53:     Next
54:
55:     'Close the row
56:     Response.Write "</TR>"
57:   Next
58:
59:   'We can close and explicitly free our recordset and connection
60:   'objects now!
61:   objRS.Close
62:   Set objRS = Nothing
63:
64:   objConn.Close
65:   Set objConn = Nothing
66: %>
67:
68:   </TABLE>
69:
70:   <CENTER>
71:   <FONT SIZE=2>
72:      <%=FormatNumber(iEventCount,0)%> Events in
73:      <%=GetMonthName(Month(dbCurrentDate))%>, <%=Year(dbCurrentDate)%>
74:   </FONT>
75:   </CENTER>
```

ANALYSIS Listing BP3.2 displays the code that inserts the event titles into the correct days on the calendar. Take a moment to examine Figure BP3.3 to see what events will be listed. Note the text at the bottom of the calendar: 5 Events in November, 1999. To ascertain the total number of events that were processed, you *could* have opened the Recordset with a scrollable cursor, which would have allowed you to use the .RecordCount property. However, because you are not going to display this value until you completely loop through the Recordset, you can use the forward-only cursor and just increase the counting variable each time you process a record from the Recordset. The code starts by creating (line 2) and initializing (line 3) this counting variable, iEventCount.

Next, the two nested loops begin, looping from 1 to the number of rows in the calendar, and then looping from 1 to the number of columns in the calendar. We looked at this loop in great detail in Bonus Project 1 and will not delve into it here. I do, however, want to draw your attention to line 18, which creates an HTML TABLE *inside* the calendar cell. So, for each date on the calendar, a TABLE will exist inside it. This inner table will contain two rows. The first will be right justified and display the date in the upper right-hand corner.

The second row, if it is needed, will be left justified and will be used to display the event title for that day.

Line 23 displays the date for a given calendar cell, using the same method as in the previous two Bonus Projects. You then need to determine whether an event exists for this date. Start by checking to see whether any records are left for processing in the Recordset. Check this by testing whether objRS.EOF is True or False. You know that there are no more events to process if objRS.EOF returns True, so line 28 has an If statement to make sure objRS.EOF is *not* True.

If you still have records to process, check the current record's Date field, seeing whether it is equal to the date just processed (lines 31 and 32). If it is, then you need to display the EventTitle, and the code from line 33 to line 43 will be executed. This code displays the event's title (line 36), moves to the next record in the Recordset (line 37), and increments iEventCount (line 40).

When the loops have finished, you have finished using the Recordset object, so Close and explicitly free the Recordset and Connection objects (lines 61 through 65). Finally, you are ready to display the total number of events listed for the month. After you close the TABLE (line 68), you're ready to display the message. Line 72 outputs the value of iEventCount, using the FormatNumber function to format the value.

Figure BP3.3 shows the calendar from November, 1999. Note that only those events in the Event database that are scheduled for November, 1999 are listed. This is because the Recordset object was populated with only those records from the Event table that occurred in the month we were viewing (refer to Listing BP3.1).

The Calendar Application: Where to Go Next

One major strength of Active Server Pages is the ease with which you can use a database. Only a few changes were needed to integrate a database-driven event display for the calendar. With these small changes, you have an easy to use, powerful application!

The Calendar application has its limitations, however. Most notable is the inability to display multiple events on one day. With some slight modifications of the code shown in Listing BP3.2, you can have the application handle multiple dates per day. I leave this as an exercise to the reader. However, let me give you a couple of hints on how to solve this problem. Starting on line 28 in Listing BP3.2, you check to see whether objRS.EOF is False. If it is, then you check to see whether the current record's Day field matches the current day. Rather than just checking once, you may need to check multiple times, if there are multiple events for the current day. Rather than using an If statement on line 31, you will need to use some kind of loop.

FIGURE BP3.3

Looks like a busy month!

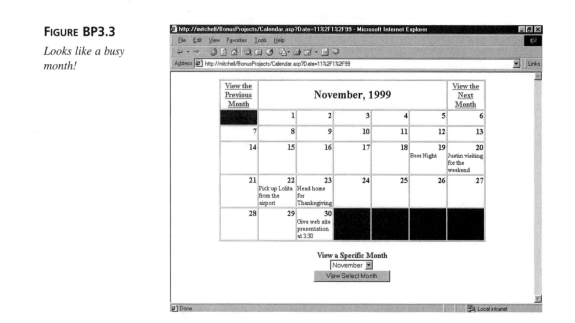

Also, the application isn't as efficient as it could be. Every time you perform an iteration in the loop, you perform at least one access to the `Recordset` object, even if the month contains no events. You could increase the efficiency of this by using the following steps:

1. Read in the first record's `Day` and `EventTitle` columns before you reach the loop, storing them into variables `iDay` and `strTitle`.

2. When in the loop, check to see whether the current day equals `iDay`. If it does, output `strTitle`, move to the next record, and store the next record's `Day` and `EventTitle` fields into `iDay` and `strTitle`, respectively.

Again, I will leave this as an exercise to the reader. If you can think of any other enhancements you'd like to see added to the Calendar application, feel free to tweak the code.

This concludes the Calendar application. This application, which was built piece-by-piece, starting from Bonus Project 1, illustrates many of the lessons covered throughout this book. This project is a good representation of a real-life application you might be asked to program one day. The project used cookies to maintain state information, used an HTML form, passed information through the QueryString, and read information from a database. In closing, be sure to challenge yourself by adding new functionalities to the Calendar application. Happy programming!

APPENDIX A

Answers to the Quiz Questions

This appendix provides answers to the quiz and exercise sections at the end of each chapter

Day 1

Quiz

1. True or False: The Internet is based on the client-server model.

   True.

2. How does a Web server handle ASP page requests differently than static HTML page requests?

   When a static HTML page is requested, the Web server simply sends the exact contents of the page requested to the client (refer to Figure 1.1). When an ASP page is requested, however, the Web server processes the programmatic code first and *then* sends the resulting HTML output to the client (refer to Figure 1.2).

3. What Microsoft Web server is needed to run ASP pages on Windows 95, Windows 98, or Windows NT Workstation?

   Personal Web Server (PWS).

4. What version of Internet Information Server do you need to be running to use ASP 3.0?

   To use version 3.0 of ASP, you need to be running Internet Information Server (IIS) 5.0.

5. True or False: ASP pages can only be run on Microsoft Web servers.

   False. Using third-party products from Halcyon Software or Chili!Soft, you can run ASP pages on non-Microsoft Web servers and non-PC platforms.

6. What is the default root physical directory when installing both Personal Web Server and Internet Information Server?

   `\InetPub\wwwroot`

7. If you created an ASP file in `C:\InetPub\wwwroot\scripts\hello.asp`, where `C:\InetPub\wwwroot` was your Web's root physical directory, what URL could you use to access `hello.asp` from your machine?

   `http://localhost/scripts/hello.asp`

8. True or False: Notepad can be used to create and edit ASP pages?

   True. Any text editor can be used because ASP pages are nothing more than text files.

Day 2

Quiz

1. What is wrong with this code:
   ```
   <% Response.Write "Hello, World"
      %>
   %>
   ```

   The extra `%>` will cause an error.

2. What kind of scripting is the `<SCRIPT>` tag used for?

   Both. It is client-side by default, but if you add `RUNAT=SERVER`, it can be used for server-side scripting.

3. How are comments written in VBScript?

   They are preceded by the single quote (').

4. What does the underscore character mean?

   It means that the statement is continued on the next line.

5. What does `Response.Write` do?

   It writes output from the ASP block to the HTML.

A

6. What is the shortcut alternative to `Response.Write`?

    It is `<%= whatever %>`

    It can only be used outside an ASP block.

7. Is it possible to write a page that displays the current time using ASP?

    Yes.

8. Is it possible to write a ticking clock using ASP?

    No. ASP is a server-side technology. This means that ASP cannot do any more after the page reaches the user.

Day 3

Quiz

1. What effect does putting `<% Option Explicit %>` at the top of your page have?

    It causes VBScript to require you to declare all your variables explicitly. It is used to make debugging easier.

2. What does 5 `Mod` 2 evaluate to? 7 `Mod` 9?

    1 and 7

3. What does 3 * 5 + 2 ^ 2 – 6 evaluate to, according to the rules of precedence?

    13

4. How would you parenthesize 3 * 5 + 2 ^ 2 – 6 to make its meaning clearer?

    One good answer is (3 * 5) + (2 ^ 2) - 6

5. What does ("Banana" < "banana") AND (4 < 4) evaluate to?

    False (4 < 4 is false, and both must be true for the statement to be true in an AND statement.)

6. What does ("Banana" < "banana") OR (4 < 4) evaluate to?

    True (Only one needs to be true in an OR statement.)

7. What data type do the comparison and logical operators evaluate to?

    Boolean (True or False)

8. What is 5 / 2? 5 \ 2?

    2.5 and 2

Day 4

Quiz

1. Under what circumstances is it better to use a `For...Next` than a `Do While...Loop`?

   `For...Next` is better when the number of times the loop must execute can be determined before it executes.

2. What is wrong with this code?
```
If (sngArea > 5)
   Response.Write("Big")
Else
   Response.Write("Small")
End if
```

   `If` requires a `Then`.

3. What does it mean for a variable to be global?

   It means that any code on the page can access that variable.

Day 5

Quiz

1. What function would you use to find out how many weeks there were between September 19, 1999, and April 15, 2000?

   `DateDiff`

2. What function would you use if you had an array of names and you wanted to find all the Johnsons?

   `Filter`

3. What function would you use if you wanted to change every mention of Frank Johnson to Frank Smith in a particular string?

   `Replace`

4. What function would you use to find out what day of the week your birthday will fall on in the year 2020?

   `Weekday`

5. What are the differences between `InStr` and `InStrRev`?

   `InStr` starts looking for the sub-string from the beginning of the string. `InStrRev` starts from the end. They also accept their arguments in different orders.

6. What function would you use to perform comparisons between two strings without distinguishing between upper- and lowercase letters?

   `StrComp`

A

7. Describe what the `Split` function does.

   `Split(string, delimiter, count, comparetype)` breaks up *string* into an array of strings. It breaks it up using *delimiter* to determine where one string ends and another begins. If *count* is specified, it is broken up into no more than *count* strings. If *count* is -1 or not specified, it is broken up completely. *comparetype* indicates whether to consider uppercase letters and lowercase letters the same.

8. What is the term for converting one data type to another?

   Typecasting.

Day 6

Quiz

1. What is a collection?

   A collection is a set of name/value pairs.

2. What three things make up an object?

   Properties, methods, and events

3. What does `Set objectVariable = Nothing` do?

   It frees the memory used by *objectVariable*. It should be used as soon as *objectVariable* is no longer needed.

4. What built-in object would you use to read a client's cookies?

   `Request`

5. What built-in object is used to share data among clients?

   `Application`

6. What method of `Server` converts virtual paths to physical paths?

   Server.MapPath(*VirtualPath*)

Day 7

Quiz

1. If you have a long block of HTML code and you need to retrieve a single ASP value, which should you use: `Response.Write` or `<%=...`?

   You should use the shortcut `<%=...`.

2. What is the difference between `Response.Flush` and `Response.Clear`?

   `Response.Flush` sends the contents of the buffer to the client before it empties it. `Response.Clear` just empties the buffer, destroying the contents.

3. What is the difference between `Response.Expires` and `Response.ExpiresAbsolutely`?

   `Response.Expires` specifies a number of minutes from now that the cached page should expire. `Response.ExpiresAbsolutely` specifies a date and time.

4. Why should a negative value for `Response.Expires` be used to force the page to expire immediately?

   A negative value should be used in case the client's clock is a little behind that of the server. Using zero in this case would cause the page to be cached for a couple of minutes. To be really safe, -1500 should be used.

5. True or False: Using `Response.Flush` without buffering turned on will produce an error.

   True. If there is no buffer, there is nothing to flush.

6. True or False: Using `Response.End` without buffering turned on will produce an error.

   False. `Response.End` can still stop execution without anything in the buffer.

7. True or False: Using `Response.Clear` without buffering turned on will produce an error.

   True. If there is no buffer, there is nothing to clear.

Day 8

Quiz

1. What are the two properties for the `<FORM>` tag?

   `METHOD` and `ACTION`.

2. What are the roles of the form creation web page and the form processing script?

   The form creation web page is responsible for the HTML that when viewed in a browser will display the various form fields. The form creation web page can be an HTML page or an ASP page. The form processing script is an ASP page that collects the information from the form creation page and makes programmatic decisions based upon the data received.

3. How can you create a text box that is 50 characters wide?

   `<INPUT TYPE=TEXT NAME=TextBoxName SIZE=50>`

4. Can you have the form processing script exist in a different directory than the form creation web page?

   Specify the directory and filename of the form processing script in the form's `ACTION` property. For example, you could set the form processing script to an ASP page named `FormProcessingScript.asp` in the `/scripts` directory by using the following `<FORM>` tag:

   `<FORM METHOD=POST ACTION="/scripts/FormProcessingScript.asp">`

A

5. What property of the `<INPUT>` and `<SELECT>` tag uniquely identifies each form field, or each group of related form fields?

   The `NAME` property.

6. Given a group of related radio buttons, how can you ensure that a user will select one of these radio buttons?

   Put the `CHECKED` keyword in one of the radio buttons. This will select that radio button by default. Since a user cannot *unselect* a radio button once it has been selected, the user will be forced to have one of the related radio buttons selected.

7. How do you create a submit button in a form?
   ```
   <INPUT TYPE=SUBMIT VALUE="Title On Submit Button">
   ```

8. How do you create a checkbox that is checked by default?

   Add the `CHECKED` keyword in the `<INPUT>` tag. For example:
   ```
   <INPUT TYPE=CHECKBOX NAME=CheckboxName VALUE=SomeValue CHECKED>
   ```

9. What property of the `<OPTION>` tag is used to uniquely identify what list box option was selected by the user?

   The `VALUE` property uniquely identifies each list box option.

10. How do you create a text box that has a value entered by default?

    You specify the default value in the `<INPUT>` tag's `VALUE` property. For example:
    ```
    <INPUT TYPE=TEXT NAME=TextBoxName VALUE="Default Value Here!">
    ```

Day 9

Quiz

1. What is the difference between the `Request.QueryString` collection and the `Request.Form` collection?

   The `Request.QueryString` collection reads form values from forms that have their `METHOD` property set to `GET`. For forms that have `METHOD=POST`, the `Request.Form` collection should be used.

2. How can you read the entire querystring into a single variable?
   ```
   <%
     Dim strQueryString
     strQueryString = Request.QueryString
   %>
   ```

3. The querystring is made up of name/value pairs. What character separates one name/value pair from another in the querystring?

   The ampersand (&).

4. If you created a form with a text box whose NAME property was set to TextBox, how would you read the contents of the text box into a variable named strTextBox?

```
<%
  Dim strTextBox
  strTextBox = Request("TextBox")
%>
```

5. Why do you need to use the split function when you create multiple form fields with the identical NAME properties?

When multiple form fields have the same NAME property, the Request object reads the fields as comma-delimited list. The split function converts a delimited string into an array. You use the split function to convert the comma-delimited list into an array, so that you can easily iterate through the values.

6. What are related radio buttons?

Related radio buttons are a set of radio buttons from which only one radio button can be selected.

7. How do you create a group of related radio buttons?

You give related radio buttons the same NAME. The following code creates three related radio buttons:

```
I own my own business<BR>
<INPUT TYPE=RADIO NAME=BusinessOwner VALUE=Yes>Yes<BR>
<INPUT TYPE=RADIO NAME=BusinessOwner VALUE=No>No<BR>
<INPUT TYPE=RADIO NAME=BusinessOwner VALUE=Maybe>Maybe?
```

8. What is the syntax needed to loop through all the form field values from a form that had its METHOD property set to POST?

A For Each ... Next loop is needed.

```
Dim strName
For Each strName in Request.Form
   ...
Next
```

9. If you fail to explicitly specify the VALUE property in a check box, what is it implicitly set to?

If you fail to explicitly specify the VALUE of a check box, it is implicitly set to on.

10. If you had the following code:

```
What is your gender?<BR>
<INPUT TYPE=RADIO NAME=Gender VALUE=Male>Male<BR>
<INPUT TYPE=RADIO NAME=Gender VALUE=Female>Female
```

could the form send the following querystring to the form processing script?

```
Gender=Male&Gender=Female
```

No, this could not happen. Because you've created two related radio buttons, only one option could be selected at most. Therefore, the querystring could only be one of three values:

```
Gender=Male
Gender=Female
```

Or a blank string.

Day 10

Quiz

1. What is the name of the response header that sends detailed information about the browser and operating system being used by the client?

   The response header is named User-Agent. It contains information on the client's browser and operating system. Its value can be read using:

   ```
   Response.ServerVariables("HTTP_USER_AGENT")
   ```

2. What HTTP header can you check to determine whether your visitor reached your page through a hyperlink on a different Web page?

   If a Web page was reached through a hyperlink on another page, the Referer header returns the full URL of the page with the hyperlink. You can access the value of the Referer variable with the following code:

   ```
   Response.ServerVariables("HTTP_REFERER")
   ```

3. What environment variable returns the physical address of your Web's root directory?

   The APPL_PHYSICAL_PATH environment variable returns the full physical address of the Web's root directory. The environment variable is read using the following code:

   ```
   Response.ServerVariables("APPL_PHYSICAL_PATH")
   ```

4. When using the ServerVariables collection to obtain an HTTP header, what five characters must prefix the name of the HTTP header?

   When reading an HTTP header using Request.ServerVariables, you must prefix the header name with HTTP_. For example, the Referer header is obtained with Request.ServerVariables("HTTP_REFERER")

5. What does the URL environment variable contain?

   The URL environment variable contains the part of the full URL of the executing ASP page. The part of the URL is from the hostname up until the querystring. For example, if you created an ASP page in the /scripts directory named MyASPPage.asp, with the following code:

   ```
   <%= Response.ServerVariables("URL")%>
   ```

and then visited the following URL:
`http://www.myserver.com/scripts/MyASPPage.asp?Age=21`, the output would be
`/scripts/MyASPPage.asp`.

6. What kinds of data types can a cookie not store?

   A cookie cannot store array or object variables.

7. When writing a cookie to a client's computer, what properties can you set?

   You can set four properties when writing a cookie to a client's computer. These
   properties are `Expires`, `Domain`, `Path`, and `Secure`. The majority of the time, you
   will only need to set the `Expires` property because the defaults for the other three
   properties are probably already set correctly.

8. If a cookie is created with its `Expires` property set to some date in the past, when
   will the cookie expire?

   If a cookie's `Expires` property is set to a date in the past, or if the `Expires` property is not set at all, the cookie will expire when the user closes her browser.

9. What happens to a cookie when it expires?

   When a cookie expires, it automatically deletes itself from the client's computer.

10. What functionality does the `HasKeys` property serve?

    The `HasKeys` property determines whether a cookie has keys. If a cookie has keys,
    the `HasKey` property for that cookie returns `True`. If the cookie does not have keys,
    the `HasKeys` property returns `False`. The following code determines whether a
    cookie named `MyCookie` has any keys:

```
If Request.Cookies("MyCookie").HasKeys then
    Response.Write "Egad!  I have keys!"
Else
    Response.Write "No keys for me..."
End If
```

Day 11

Quiz

1. Will the querystring method of maintaining state work if the user has configured
   her browser not to accept cookies?

   Yes. Because the querystring method passes the persistent information through the
   querystring, it doesn't matter whether the user supports cookies.

2. If you need to maintain user-specific state for weeks at a time, should you use the
   querystring method, the cookies method, or the `Session` object?

A

To maintain a user's state for any duration lengthier than a visit to your site, you need to use cookies. Therefore, if you need to persist user-specific information for weeks at a time, cookies need to be used.

3. What does the `Timeout` property of the `Session` object do?

The `Timeout` property determines the length of time that must pass between a user's last request and when that user's `Session` is freed from the Web server's memory.

4. True or False: Objects should be put into the user's `Session`.

False. Try to keep objects out of the user's `Session`, due to performance concerns.

5. Why is it important to `Lock` and `UnLock` the `Application` object before altering the values of application variables?

Because only one instance of the `Application` object exists for the entire Web site, each user, when altering any given application variable, is altering the same variable. Therefore, to prevent corruption of the variable when two users attempt to update the application variable at the same time, it is important to first `Lock` the `Application` object before updating an application variable. After the variable is updated, you should `UnLock` the `Application` object. The following code is an example of updating an application variable:

```
Application.Lock
Application(SomeVariable) = 5
Application.UnLock
```

In line 1, the `Application` object is `Locked`. In line 2, the application variable `SomeVariable` is updated, and in line 3, the `Application` object is `UnLocked`.

6. In what file should you place the code for the `OnStart` and `OnEnd` events of the `Application` and `Session` objects?

The two events handlers for the `Application` and `Session` objects need to be placed in a file named `Global.asa`, which needs to belong in your Web's root directory.

7. What is Cookie Munger used for?

Cookie Munger is an ISAPI filter, written by Microsoft, to provide `Session` support for users who don't accept cookies.

8. What collection, present in both the `Session` and `Application` objects, contains all the non-object variables?

The `Contents` collection contains all the non-object variables. Specifically, `Session.Contents` contains all the non-object session variables, whereas `Application.Contents` contains all the application variables.

9. What property of the `Session` object uniquely identifies each `Session` instance?

Each `Session` object instance is uniquely identified by the `SessionID` property. This ID is also written to the client's computer in the form of a cookie, so that a particular user can be mapped to a particular `Session`.

10. When does the `Application` object's `OnEnd` event fire?

    The `Application` object's `OnEnd` event is fired once when the Web server is being restarted. It fires after the last user's `Session_OnEnd` event fires.

Day 12

Quiz

1. How is a component instantiated?

   First the variable should be declared and then the `Set` statement is used like this:
   ```
   Set variablename = Server.CreateObject(classname.componentname)
   ```

2. When should the memory associated with a component be freed?

   As soon as you are finished using it!

3. What are the two major limitations of the Ad Rotator component?

   It does not guarantee that an ad will not appear twice on the same page, and it does not easily allow you to keep track of impressions.

4. What effect does giving one ad twice the weight of another have?

   The ad with the double weight will appear twice as often as the other.

5. How do you specify in the schedule file that an ad has no associated link?

   Use a hyphen (-). `GetAdvertisement` will then know not to create the link.

6. What method of the Content Linker is used to find out the URL of the next page in the sequence?
   ```
   GetNextURL(listfile)
   ```

7. What method of the Content Linker is used to find out the index position of the current page?
   ```
   GetListIndex(listfile)
   ```

8. What three things does the Content Linker list file allow you to include for each entry?

   Relative URL, Description (optional), and a comment (optional)

9. How is the Browser Capabilities component kept accurate and up-to-date?

   With the `Browscap.ini` file

Day 13

Quiz

1. What does a server-side include do?

   It inserts the code inside the specified file into the current page.

2. What is the difference between a server-side include and `Server.Execute`?

   `Server.Execute` can use dynamically generated filenames. Server-side includes cannot.

3. What are the differences between `Response.Redirect` and `Server.Transfer`?

   `Response.Redirect` creates a new object context for the new page. `Server.Transfer` reuses the old one. Also, you may only use `Response.Redirect` before any output has been sent to the client.

4. What are the three modes in which a file may be opened?

   It may be opened for reading, writing, or appending.

5. What is in the `Files` collection of the folder object?

   It contains file object instances that correspond to every file in the folder.

6. What is the difference between

   `objFSO.OpenTextFile("log.txt", 8, True)` and
   `objFSO.OpenTextFile("log.txt", 8, False)`?

   If `log.txt` does not exist, the first statement will create it, but the second will not.

7. How do you verify the existence of a file on the server?

   Use the file system object's `FileExists` method.

8. What does `WriteBlankLines(num)` do?

   It writes *num* carriage returns to the file.

9. If a file consists of the string "The quick brown fox jumped over the lazy dog," what does `Read(5)` return?

   It will return the string `"The q"`.

10. Why might you have trouble if you put the following statement in a file called `main.html`?

    `<!--#include file="navbar.html"-->`

    Only files with certain extensions may use server-side includes. Unless your settings have been changed from the default, files that end in `.html` cannot use them.

A

Day 14

Quiz

1. What two types of bugs can occur when developing an application?

   The two types of errors that can arise when developing an application are fatal bugs and nonfatal bugs. Fatal bugs cause an abrupt termination in program execution, whereas nonfatal bugs result in incorrect output for the given input.

2. Do programmers, on average, spend more time than needed debugging and testing their applications, or less?

   Programmers, on average, spend *far less* time than needed on debugging and testing.

3. How can `Option Explicit` be used to convert a nonfatal bug into a fatal bug?

   When `Option Explicit` is used, mistyping a variable name results in a fatal bug. Without using `Option Explicit`, such a mistake results in a nonfatal bug.

4. Why should you strive to turn nonfatal bugs into fatal bugs?

   Fatal bugs are much easier to locate and fix than nonfatal bugs because when a fatal bug occurs, you are immediately notified of the offending error and the line on which the error occurred.

5. True or False: Nonfatal bugs are more difficult to locate than fatal bugs.

   True. Nonfatal bugs are *much* more difficult to locate than fatal bugs.

6. What HTTP error is generated when there is an error in an ASP page?

   `500;100`

7. What new object to ASP 3.0 can be used to gather information about the last occurring ASP error?

   The `ASPError` object.

8. The `ASPDescription` property of the `ASPError` object will only contain a value under what circumstances?

   The `ASPDescription` property of the `ASPError` object will contain a value when the error that occurred belongs in the category of internal ASP errors. See Listing 14.8 and Figure 14.9 for an example of an internal ASP error and the output of the `ASPDescription` property.

9. What method of the `Server` object do you need to use to obtain an instance of the `ASPError` object?

   The `GetLastError` method of the `Server` object is used to obtain an instance of the `ASPError` object that contains information about the latest error.

10. True or False: You should create a custom 404 error page.

    True. Your users will greatly appreciate a custom 404 error page.

Day 15

Quiz

1. True or False: A database is comprised of one to many database tables.

   True.

2. How do flat-file database systems differ from relational database systems?

   When two or more objects share relationships among each other, two approaches can be taken: the related objects can be merged into one large table, or each object can be represented in its own table. A flat-file database system would merge the tables, whereas a relational database system would create a table for each unique object.

3. True or False: You can access any ODBC-compliant database through an ASP page using ADO.

   True.

4. What does the acronym ODBC stand for?

   Open DataBase Connectivity.

5. What does the acronym ADO stand for?

   ActiveX Data Objects.

6. When should you choose to use a database to persist information?

   If you need to store a large amount information over an indefinite period of time, databases are the way to go.

7. What are some commonly used, commercial databases?

   The most commonly used commercial databases for ASP pages are Microsoft's SQL-Server and Microsoft Access. Oracle databases are also used, though, and many other databases can be used. In fact, *any* ODBC-compliant database will do.

8. True or False: Using ADO, an ASP page can access an Oracle database.

   True.

9. To retrieve information from a database, two steps must occur. What are these two steps, and what ADO objects facilitate each of these steps?

   Step 1: A connection must be made to the database.

   Step 2: A request to the database for particular information should be made, and a mechanism for storing the information retrieved should be available.

   These two steps are completed with the help of two ADO objects. The `Connection` object establishes the connection to the database, whereas the `Recordset` object sends the information request to the database and, secondarily, holds the results returned by the database.

Day 16

Quiz

1. What does the `Connection` object do?

   The `Connection` object stores information about a connection to a data source.

2. What does the `ConnectionString` property do?

   The information the `Connection` object needs to make the connection is put in `ConnectionString`.

3. What is a System DSN?

   It is a file on your system that packages the necessary connection information together.

4. How are DSN-less connections tricky?

   They require you to handle putting in the needed information yourself. There is a greater risk of human error when using DSN-less connections.

5. What does the `Recordset` object do?

   It is used to hold a set of records from a data source. The records may be read or changed, or new ones added.

6. What does including `adovbs.inc` do?

   Several constants are needed that are not part of ASP or VBScript. `adovbs.inc` contains the definitions for the constants, so including it allows you to use them in your pages.

7. What is the alternative to including `adovbs.inc`?

   `METADATA`, along with the ADO `.dll` file, can be used in every page as an alternative to including `adovbs.inc`. Better yet, you can put `METADATA` in your `global.asa` file, and all your pages will have the appropriate constants defined automatically.

8. How can you keep from moving beyond the end of a recordset?

   Use the `EOF` property. Check it before making any moves or trying to read any fields. `If…Then` statements and `Do While…Loop` are often helpful.

9. How do you access a field value in the current record?

   Like this: recordsetName("FieldName")

Day 17

Quiz

1. Describe the actions performed by the `AddNew` method of the `Recordset` object.

   It creates a new, empty record in the recordset and sets it as the current record.

A

2. What arguments can AddNew accept?

   It can accept either a single field name and a single value, or an array of field names and an array of values. The fields of the new record are then initialized using the matching value. The same number of fields and values must be specified.

3. Why couldn't you use the default locking type in this chapter?

   The default locking type is read-only. This works fine if all you are doing is displaying the data. If you want to change any of the data in the table, it is insufficient.

4. What does CancelUpdate do?

   It cancels any unsaved changes to the current record.

5. How do you delete a record?

   Move to the record you want to delete and call Delete.

Day 18

Quiz

1. What is the default property of the Field object?

   The Value property is the default property of the Field object.

2. How many Field objects exist in the Fields collection?

   There are exactly as many Field objects in the Fields collection as there are columns in the database table being queried.

3. What does the Name property of the Field object return?

   The Name property of the Field object returns the name of the database table column.

4. What is the difference between a forward-only cursor and a scrollable cursor?

   A forward-only cursor can only move from one record to the next in a Recordset. A scrollable cursor has no restrictions to its movement: you can move forward or backward, and you can jump forward or backward several records at a time.

5. True or False: A Static cursor is a scrollable cursor.

   True. The Keyset and Dynamic cursors are the other two scrollable cursors.

6. When retrieving the contents from large database tables, what will prove more efficient: a server-side cursor or a client-side cursor?

   Server-side cursors are more efficient than client-side cursors because with client-side cursors, the contents of the Recordset object must be copied to the client.

7. What property of the Recordset object can be used to set the cursor's location?

   The CursorLocation property of the Recordset object can be used to set the cursor's location.

8. When using the Sort property, where does the cursor have to be located? Also, what type of cursor is required?

   When using the Sort property, you must use a client-side cursor. When using a client-side cursor, a Static cursor must be used. It doesn't matter whether you specify to use a Static cursor when Opening the Recordset. When you use a client-side cursor, a Static cursor is automatically selected.

9. When comparing a column to a value in the Filter statement, under what circumstances do you need to surround the value with single quotes?

   When comparing a column to a value in the Filter statement, you *must* surround the value with single quotes if the column contains string or date data. Failure to do so will result in an error.

10. True or False: The Filter property requires the use of a scrollable cursor.

    False.

Day 19

Quiz

1. What does the acronym SQL stand for?

   Structured Query Language

2. True or False: The only required clause of the SELECT statement is the SELECT clause.

   False. The SELECT statement requires at minimum two clauses: the SELECT clause and the FROM clause.

3. What comparison operators can you use in the WHERE clause of a SELECT statement?

   SQL allows for a number of comparison operators in the WHERE clause. They are: <, <=, >, >=, =, <>, and =. They are listed in Table 19.3.

4. What logical operators can you use in the WHERE clause of a SELECT statement?

   The logical operators allowed by SQL that we discussed include: NOT, AND, and OR. These operators are listed in Table 19.4.

5. What is the order of precedence for the logical operators?

   NOT; AND; OR.

6. What does the wildcard character % do when used with the LIKE operator?

   The wildcard character % translates into zero to many characters. So, if you had a WHERE clause like this:

   ```
   WHERE ColumnName LIKE 'Duck%'
   ```

rows such as `Duck`, `Ducked`, `Ducks`, and `Duckdljsafdlkfjadfl` would be returned. As long as the row's first four characters in the `ColumnName` column were `Duck`, the `WHERE` clause would include the row.

7. True or False: The `ORDER BY` clause can only accept a single column name to order the results by.

   False. The `ORDER BY` clause can accept several columns, in the form of a comma-delimited list.

8. True or False: The `SELECT` statement consists of only four clauses—the `SELECT` clause, the `FROM` clause, the `WHERE` clause, and the `ORDER BY` clause.

   False. In Day 19, we discussed only four clauses of the `SELECT` statement, but actually, the `SELECT` statement can accept many more clauses.

9. When comparing a column to a value in the `WHERE` clause, under what circumstances do you need to surround the value with single quotes?

   When comparing a column to a value in the `WHERE` clause, single quotes *must* be used if the column being compared stored either string or date data. Failure to surround a value with single quotes when comparing it to such a column will result in an error.

10. What five steps should you follow when using SQL statements in ASP pages?

    Create and open a connection to the database. To do this, use the `Connection` object. Create a string variable to hold your SQL statement. Assign your SQL statement to this variable. Create an instance of the `Recordset` object. Execute the `Open` method of the `Recordset` object.

Day 20

Quiz

1. What are the four types of database cursors, and what is the default cursor?

   The four database cursors are forward-only, Static, Keyset, and Dynamic. The forward-only cursor is the default database cursor.

2. What cursors support the `RecordCount` property?

   Only scrollable cursors support the `RecordCount` property. Recall that the scrollable cursors are the Static, Keyset, and Dynamic cursors.

3. What four `LockTypes` are available, and what is the default `LockType`?

   The four types of available `LockTypes` are Read-only, Optimistic, Pessimistic, and Batch Optimistic. The Read-only lock is the default `LockType`.

4. True or False: A Pessimistic lock can be used on a client-side cursor.

   False.

5. When using the `Execute` method of the `Connection` object, what cursor and `LockType` are assigned to the `Recordset` object created?

   The default `LockType` and cursor are used when implicitly creating a `Recordset` object using the `Connection` object's `Execute` method. Therefore, this implicitly created `Recordset` object has a forward-only cursor and a Read-only lock.

6. True or False: The use of stored procedures can lead to improved performance.

   True. In fact, case studies have shown an improvement of up to 25%.

7. What three advantages do stored procedures offer?

   Stored procedures allow for easier-to-read code, provide a layer of abstraction between an ASP page and the database, and offer increased data access performance.

8. If you had explicitly created a `Recordset` object named `objRS` and had a `Connection` object named `objConn`, how would you populate your `Recordset` with the results of a stored procedure named `CustomerInformation`?

   ```
   objRS.Open "CustomerInformation", objConn
   ```

9. If you want to use the `Command` object to implicitly create a `Recordset` object instance that is populated with the results of a database table, what three `Command` object properties do you need to set before performing the `Execute` method?

   The three `Command` properties that must be set before using the `Execute` method are `CommandText`, `ActiveConnection`, and `CommandType`. The `CommandText` is the table name or SQL query to be executed; the `ActiveConnection` is the variable name of the `Connection` object; and the `CommandType` represents the type of query to be done. If you plan to read the contents of a database table, `CommandType` needs to be set to `adCmdTable`. For example, the following lines of code would implicitly create a `Recordset` object, assigning it to the variable `objRS`:

   ```
   'Explicitly create our Command object
   Dim objCommand
   Set objCommand = Server.CreateObject("ADODB.Command")

   'Set the three properties
   objCommand.ActiveConnection = objConn
   objCommand.CommandText = TableName
   objCommand.CommandType = adCmdTable

   'Assign the implicitly created Recordset object to objRS
   Dim objRS
   Set objRS = objCommand.Execute
   ```

10. True or False: You should strive to create all your `Recordset` objects explicitly.

    True.

Day 21

Quiz

1. What is the most important phase of the software development cycle?

   The Design phase.

2. True or False: The actual life expectancy of your program is often less than the estimated life expectancy.

   False. The life actual expectancy of your program is usually *much* longer than the estimate life expectancy!

3. Why is it important to fix bugs and software defects as soon as possible?

   The time it takes to fix bugs and software defects created in one phase of the software development cycle increases between stages. If it would take 15 minutes to fix a bug that was created in the Design phase, it might take an hour to fix the same bug if it was not detected until the Programming phase.

4. What criteria does your database need to meet to be considered in second normal form?

   For a database to be in second normal form, for a given table in the database, no fields can be derived from another field in that table.

5. True or False: The highest normal form your database can be in is third normal form.

   False. There are many higher forms of normalization, dealing with advanced topics of topology.

6. How do stored procedures provide a level of abstraction between the database and ASP pages?

   A stored procedure can be created to return a defined set of information. If the database experiences minor changes in its structure, the stored procedure can be altered slightly to still return the same set of information, even though the underlying structure has been altered. Such a minor change in the database structure would not require a change in the ASP pages that reference the stored procedures.

7. In the Design phase, half of your efforts should be directed toward database design. Where should the other half of your efforts be directed?

   To the design of your ASP pages.

8. Why is it important to comment your ASP pages?

   If you don't comment your source code, how are other developers supposed to know the purpose of the code? With comments, the purpose of the code is outlined in simple English.

9. What advantages are achieved through code reuse?

   Code reuse offers two advantages. First, code reuse saves time because every line of code reused is a line of code that doesn't need to be typed. Second, code reuse leads to fewer bugs. The more code you write, the more bugs you will create. If you write less code by reusing more, the number of bugs will decrease.

10. True or False: Server-side includes can be used to allow for modular ASP scripts.

    True.

APPENDIX B

VBScript Reference

This appendix covers the VBScript keywords, operators, functions, and control structures as well as the file system object and related file scripting objects.

Statements and Keywords

Dim is used to declare variables. VBScript variables are variants, which means that they do not have to have a fixed data type.

Const is used to declare constants, which are like variables except that they cannot be changed in the script.

Option Explicit is put at the top of a page to force explicit declaration of all variables.

Operators

Table B.1 lists the VBScript operators in order of precedence.

TABLE B.1 Operator Precedence

Precedence	Operators
Highest (done first)	Anything in parentheses
	Exponentiation (^)
	Negation (-)
	Multiplication, Division (*, /)
	Integer Division (\)
	Modulus (Mod)
	Addition, Subtraction (+,-)
	String Concatenation (&)
	Comparison Operators(=, <>, <, >, <=, >=)
	Not
	And
	Or
	Xor
	Eqv
Lowest (done last)	Imp

VBScript Functions

This will provide you with a quick look at the more important VBScript functions. They include functions for type checking, typecasting, formatting, math, date manipulation, string manipulation, and more. If you need more explanation, many of these are discussed in Day 5.

Type Checking Functions

These functions allow you to determine the data subtype of a variable or expression.

VarType(*expression*) returns an integer code that corresponds to the data type. Table B.2 lists these integer codes.

TABLE B.2 VarType Codes for Data Types

Value	Constant	Data Type
0	vbEmpty	Empty (This is the type for a variable that has not been used yet. In other words, Empty is the default data type.)
1	vbNull	Null (No valid data)

Value	Constant	Data Type
2	vbInteger	Integer
3	vbLong	Long
4	vbSingle	Single
5	vbDouble	Double
6	vbCurrency	Currency
7	vbDate	Date
8	vbString	String
9	vbObject	Object
10	vbError	Error
11	vbBoolean	Boolean
12	vbVariant	Variant (used with vbArray)
13	vbDataObject	Data Access Object
14	vbDecimal	Decimal
17	vbByte	Byte
8192	vbArray	Array (VBScript uses 8192 as a base for arrays and adds the code for the data type to indicate an array. 8204 indicates a variant array, the only real kind of array in VBScript.)

TypeName(*expression*) returns a string with the name of the data type rather than a code.

IsNumeric(*expression*) returns a Boolean value of True if the *expression* is numeric data, and False otherwise.

IsArray(*expression*) returns a Boolean value of True if the *expression* is an array, and False otherwise.

IsDate(*expression*) returns a Boolean value of True if the *expression* is date/time data, and False otherwise.

IsEmpty(*expression*) returns a Boolean value of True if the *expression* is an empty value (un-initialized variable), and False otherwise.

IsNull(*expression*) returns a Boolean value of True if the *expression* contains no valid data, and False otherwise.

IsObject(*expression*) returns a Boolean value of True if the *expression* is an object, and False otherwise.

B

Typecasting Functions

Typecasting allows you to convert between data subtypes.

Cint(*expression*) casts *expression* to an integer. If *expression* is a floating-point value or a currency value, it is rounded. If it is a string that looks like a number, it is turned into that number and then rounded if necessary. If it is a Boolean value of True, it becomes -1. False becomes 0. It also must be within the range that an integer can store.

Cbyte(*expression*) casts *expression* to a byte value provided that *expression* falls between 0 and 255. *expression* should be numeric or something that can be cast to a number.

Cdbl(*expression*) casts *expression* to a double. *expression* should be numeric or something that can be cast to a number.

Csng(*expression*) casts *expression* to a single. It works like Cdbl(), but must fall within the range represented by a single.

Cbool(*expression*) casts *expression* to a Boolean value. If *expression* is zero, the result is False. Otherwise, the result is True. *expression* should be numeric or something that can be cast to a number.

Ccur(*expression*) casts *expression* to a currency value. *expression* should be numeric or something that can be cast to a number.

Cdate(*expression*) casts *expression* to a date value. *expression* should be numeric or something that can be cast to a number, or a string of a commonly used date format. DateValue(*expression*) or TimeValue(*expression*) can also be used for this.

Cstr(*expression*) casts *expression* to a string. *expression* can be any kind of data.

Formatting Functions

FormatDateTime(*expression*, *format*) is used to format the date/time data in *expression*. *format* is an optional argument that should be one of the following:

- vbGeneralDate—Display date, if present, as short date. Display time, if present, as long time. Value is 0. This is the default setting if no format is specified.
- vbLongDate—Display date using the server's long date format. Value is 1.
- vbShortDate—Display date using the server's short date format. Value is 2.
- vbLongTime—Display time using the server's long time format. Value is 3.
- vbShortTime—Display time using the server's short time format. Value is 4.

FormatCurrency(*value*, *numdigits*, *leadingzero*, *negparen*, *delimeter*) is used to format the monetary value specified by *value*.

numdigits specifies the number of digits after the decimal place to display. -1 indicates to use the system default.

Tristate options have three possible values. If the value is -2, it means use the system default. If it is -1, it means turn on the option. If it is 0, turn off the option.

leadingzero is a Tristate option indicating whether to include leading zeroes on values less than 1.

negparen is a Tristate option indicating whether to enclose negative values in parentheses.

delimeter is a Tristate option indicating whether to use the delimiter specified in the computer's settings to group digits.

FormatNumber is used to format numerical values. It is almost exactly like FormatCurrency, only it does not display a dollar sign.

FormatPercent works like the previous two. The options are the same, but it turns the value it is given into a percentage.

Math Functions

Abs(*number*) returns the absolute value of *number*.

Atn(*number*) returns the arctangent, in radians, of *number*.

Cos(*number*) returns the cosine of *number*. *number* should be in radians.

Exp(*number*) returns e (approx. 2.71828) raised to the power *number*.

Fix(*number*) returns the integer portion of *number*. If *number* is negative, Fix returns the first integer greater than or equal to *number*.

Hex(*number*) converts *number* from base 10 to a hexadecimal string.

Int(*number*) returns the integer portion of *number*. If *number* is negative, Int returns the first integer less than or equal to *number*.

Log(*number*) returns the natural logarithm of *number*.

Oct(*number*) converts *number* from base 10 to an octal string.

Rnd *number* returns a random number less than one and greater than or equal to zero.

If the argument *number* is less than 0, the same random number is always returned, using *number* as a seed.

If *number* is greater than zero, or not provided, Rnd generates the next random number in the sequence.

If *number* is 0, Rnd returns the most recently generated number.

Randomize initializes the random number generator.

Round(*number*) returns *number* rounded to an integer.

Round(*number, dec*) returns *number* rounded to *dec* decimal places.

Sgn(*number*) returns 1 if *number* is greater than zero, 0 if *number* equals zero, and –1 if *number* is less than zero.

Sin(*number*) returns the sine of *number. number* should be in radians.

Sqr(*number*) returns the square root of *number. number* must be positive.

Tan(*number*) returns the tangent of *number. number* should be in radians.

Date Functions

Date returns the current date on the server.

Time returns the current time on the server.

Now returns the current date and time on the server.

DateAdd(*interval, number, date*) is used to add to the date specified by *date. interval* is a string that represents whether you want to add days, months, years, and so on. *number* indicates the number of *interval*s you want to add; that is, the number of days, months, years, and so on.

DateDiff(*interval, date1, date2, firstDOW, firstWOY*) is used to find the time between two dates. *interval* is one of the interval values from Table B.3. DateDiff returns the number of *interval*s elapsed between *date1* and *date2*. The optional integer *firstDOW* specifies what day of the week to treat as the first. Values for this may be found in Table B.4. The optional *firstWOY* specifies which week of the year to treat as the first. Values for this may be found in Table B.5.

DateSerial(*year, month, day*) takes the integers *year*, *month*, and *day* and puts them together into a date value. They may be negative.

TimeSerial(*hour, minute, second*) is similar to DateSerial.

Timer returns the number of seconds elapsed since midnight.

DatePart(*interval, datetime, firstDOW, firstWOY*) allows you to retrieve the part of *datetime* specified by *interval*. The valid values for *interval* are listed in Table B.3. The optional integer *firstDOW* specifies what day of the week to treat as the first. The optional *firstWOY* specifies which week of the year to treat as the first. Again, these values are listed in Tables B.4 and B.5.

TABLE B.3 Interval Codes for the Date Functions

Value	Meaning
"yyyy"	Year
"q"	Quarter
"m"	Month
"y"	Day of year
"d"	Day
"w"	Weekday
"ww"	Week of year
"h"	Hour
"n"	Minute
"s"	Second

TABLE B.4 Day of the Week Constants

Value	Name	Meaning
0	vbUseSystem	National Language Support API Setting
1	vbSunday	Sunday (default)
2	vbMonday	Monday
3	vbTuesday	Tuesday
4	vbWednesday	Wednesday
5	vbThursday	Thursday
6	vbFriday	Friday
7	vbSaturday	Saturday

TABLE B.5 First Week of the Year Constants

Value	Name	Meaning
0	vbUseSystem	National Language Support API Setting
1	vbFirstJan1	Week of January 1
2	vbFirstFourDays	First week with four days of new year
3	vbFirstFullWeek	First full week

Year(*date*) returns the year portion from *date* as a number.

Month(*date*) returns the month portion from *date* as a number.

`MonthName(date)` returns the month portion from *date* as a name.

`Day(date)` returns the day portion from *date* as a number.

`Weekday(date)` returns the day of the week of *date* as a number.

`Hour(time)` returns the hour portion from *time*.

`Minute(time)` returns the minute portion from *time*.

`Second(time)` returns the second portion from *time*.

String Functions

`UCase(string)` returns *string* with all its lowercase letters converted to uppercase letters.

`LCase(string)` returns *string* with all its uppercase letters converted to lowercase letters.

`LTrim(string)` removes all the spaces from the left side of *string*.

`RTrim(string)` removes all the spaces from the right side of *string*.

`Trim(string)` removes spaces from both the left and the right sides.

`Space(number)` returns a string consisting of *number* spaces.

`String(number, character)` returns a string consisting of *character* repeated *number* times.

`Len(string)` returns the number of characters in *string*.

`Len(variable)` returns the number of bytes required by *variable*.

`LenB(string)` returns the number of bytes required to store *string*.

`StrReverse(string)` returns *string* with the characters in reverse order.

`StrComp(string1, string2, comparetype)` is used to perform string comparisons. If *comparetype* is zero or omitted, the two strings are compared as if uppercase letters come before lowercase letters. If *comparetype* is one, the two strings are compared as if upper- and lowercase letters are the same. `StrComp` returns –1 if *string1* is less than *string2*. It returns 0 if they are the same, and 1 if *string1* is greater than *string2*.

`Right(string, number)` returns the *number* rightmost characters of *string*.

`RightB(string, number)` works like `Right`, but *number* is taken to be a number of bytes rather than characters.

`Left(string, number)`, as you may guess, returns the *number* leftmost characters of *string*.

`LeftB(string, number)` works like `Left`, but *number* is taken to be a number of bytes rather than characters.

Mid(*string*, *start*, *length*) returns *length* characters from *string*, starting at position *start*. When *length* is greater than the number of characters left in the string, the rest of the string is returned. If *length* is not specified, the rest of the string starting at the specified starting position is returned.

MidB(*string*, *start*, *length*) works like Mid, but *start* and *length* are both taken to be byte numbers rather than character numbers.

InStr(*start*, *string1*, *string2*, *comparetype*) is used to check if and where *string2* occurs within *string1*. *start* is an optional argument that specifies where in *string1* to start looking for *string2*. *comparetype* is an optional argument that specifies which type of comparison to perform. If *comparetype* is 0, a binary comparison is performed, and uppercase letters are distinct from lowercase letters. If *comparetype* is 1, a textual comparison is performed, and uppercase and lowercase letters are the same. InStr returns zero if *string1* is empty (""), if *string2* is not found in *string1*, or if *start* is greater than the length of *string2*. It returns Null if either string is Null. It returns *start* if *string2* is empty. If *string2* is successfully found in *string1*, it returns the starting position where it is first found.

InStrB works like InStr except that the start position and return value are byte positions, not character positions.

InStrRev(*string1*, *string2*, *start*, *comparetype*) starts looking for a match at the right side of the string rather than the left side. *start* is by default –1, which means to start at the end of the string.

Replace(*string*, *find*, *replace*, *start*, *count*, *comparetype*) is used to replace occurrences of *find* with *replace* in *string*. *start*, *count*, and *comparetype* are optional, but if you want to use one, you must use the ones that come before it. *start* indicates where the resulting string will start and where to start searching for *find*. It defaults to 1. *count* indicates how many times to perform the replacement. By default, *count* is –1, which means to replace every occurrence. If *comparetype* is 0, a binary comparison is performed, and uppercase letters are distinct from lowercase letters. If *comparetype* is 1, a textual comparison is performed, and uppercase and lowercase letters are the same.

Filter(*arrStrings*, *SearchFor*, *include*, *comparetype*) searches an array of strings, *arrStrings*, and returns a subset of the array. *include* is a Boolean value. If *include* is True, Filter searches through all the strings in *arrStrings* and returns an array containing the strings that contain *SearchFor*. If *include* is False, Filter returns an array of the strings that do not contain *SearchFor*. *include* is optional and defaults to True. *comparetype* works the same as in the other string functions we have discussed. If you want to use *comparetype*, you must use *include*.

Split(*expression*, *delimiter*, *count*, *comparetype*) takes a string and splits it into an array of strings. *expression* is the string to be split up. If *expression* is zero length, Split returns an array of no elements. *delimiter* is a string that indicates what is used to separate the sub-strings in *expression*. This is optional; by default the delimiter is the space. If *delimiter* is zero length (""), an array of one element consisting of the whole string is returned. *count* is used to specify a maximum number of sub-strings to be created. The default for *count* is –1, which means no limit. If *comparetype* is 0, a binary comparison is performed, and uppercase letters are distinct from lowercase letters. If *comparetype* is 1, a textual comparison is performed, and uppercase and lowercase letters are the same. *comparetype* is only useful when the delimiter you have chosen is a letter.

Join(*stringarray*, *delimiter*) does just the opposite of Split. It takes an array of strings and joins them into one string, using *delimiter* to separate them. *delimiter* is optional; the space is the default.

Other functions

LBound(*array*) returns the smallest valid index for *array*.

UBound(*array*) returns the largest valid index for *array*.

Asc(*string*) returns the ANSI character code for the first character of *string*.

Chr(*integer*) returns a string consisting of the character that matches the ANSI character code specified by *integer*.

Array(*value1*, *value2*, ..., *valueN*) returns an array containing the specified values. This is an alternative to assigning the values to array elements one at a time.

Control Structures

Control structures allow you to control the flow of execution of your scripts. You can specify that some code should be executed only under certain circumstances, using conditional structures. You can specify that some code should be executed repeatedly, using looping structures. Lastly, you can specify that code from somewhere else in the script should be executed using branching controls.

Conditional Structures

The If…Then…Else construct allows you to choose which block of code to execute based on a condition or series of conditions.

```
If condition1 Then
  code block 1
ElseIf condition2 Then
  code block 2
```

```
Else
   code block 3
End If
```

If *condition1* is true, *code block 1* is executed. If it is false, and *condition2* is true, *code block 2* is executed. If *condition1* and *condition2* are false, *code block 3* executes. An If…Then construct may have zero or more ElseIf statements, and zero or one Else statements.

In place of some really complex If…Then constructs, you can use a Select Case statement. It takes the following form:

```
Case Select variable
Case choice1
   code block 1
Case choice2
   code block 2
...
Case choicen
   code block n
Case default
   default code block
End Select
```

This compares the value of *variable* with *choice1*, *choice2*, and so on. If it finds a match, it executes the code associated with that choice. If it does not, it executes the default code.

Looping Structures

Looping structures allow you to execute the same block of code repeatedly. The number of times it executes may be fixed or may be based on one or more conditions.

The For…Next looping structure takes the following form:

```
For counter = start to stop
   code block
Next
```

code block is executed with *counter* having the value *start*, then with *counter* having the value *start*+1, then *start*+2, and so forth through the value *stop*.

Optionally, you may specify a different value to increment *counter* by. In this case the form looks like this:

```
For counter = start to stop Step stepvalue
   code block
Next
```

Now *counter* will take the values *start+stepvalue*, *start+stepvalue+stepvalue*, and so forth. Notice that if *stepvalue* is negative, *stop* should be less than *start*.

The For Each…Next looping structure takes the following form:

```
For Each item In set
   code block
Next
```

code block is executed with *item* taking the value of each member of *set*. *set* should be an array or a collection.

The Do While…Loop looping structure has the following form:

```
Do While booleanValue
  code block
Loop
```

code block is executed as long as *booleanValue* is True. If it is False to begin with, the loop is not executed at all.

The While…Wend looping structure has the following form:

```
While booleanValue
  code block
Wend
```

code block is executed as long as *booleanValue* is True. If it is False to begin with, the loop is not executed at all.

The Do…Loop While looping structure has the following form:

```
Do
  code block
Loop While booleanValue
```

code block is executed as long as *booleanValue* is True. The loop is executed at least once no matter what.

The Do Until…Loop looping structure has the following form:

```
Do Until booleanValue
  code block
Loop
```

code block is executed as long as *booleanValue* is false. If it is true to begin with, the loop is not executed at all.

The Do…Loop Until looping structure has the following form:

```
Do
  code block
Loop Until booleanValue
```

code block is executed as long as *booleanValue* is false. The loop is executed at least once no matter what.

Branching Structures

Branching structures allow you to jump from one position in the code to another.

A subroutine does not return a value. It simply executes. Subroutines look like this:

```
Sub name (argumentlist)
   code block
End Sub
```

Functions do return values and have the following form:

```
Function name (argumentlist)
   code block
   name = expression
End Function
```

File System Object

The file system object is used to access the files and folders of the server.

Methods

BuildPath(*path*, *name*) appends name onto path, fixing the path separator if necessary.

CopyFile *source*, *destination*, *overwrite* copies the file specified by *source* to *destination*. If there is already a file by the same name in the destination, and overwrite is True, the file is overwritten. If it is False, the file will not be overwritten.

CopyFolder *source*, *destination*, *overwrite* copies the folder specified by *source* to *destination*. If there is already a folder by the same name in the destination, and over-write is True, the files in it are overwritten. If it is False, they will not be overwritten.

CreateFolder(*foldername*) creates a folder.

CreateTextFile(*filename*, *overwrite*, *unicode*) creates a text file and returns the TextStream object for it. *overwrite* is an optional Boolean value that indicates if the file should be overwritten, if it already exists. True indicates the file should be overwritten, False indicates it should not be. The default value is False. *unicode* is an optional Boolean value that indicates whether the file is created as Unicode or ASCII. True indicates Unicode, False indicates ASCII. The default is False.

DeleteFile(*path*, *force*) deletes the file(s) specified by *path*. *path* may contain a wildcard character at the end. *force* is an optional parameter that is set to True to force read-only files to be deleted.

DeleteFolder(`path, force`) deletes the folder(s) specified by `path` and their contents. `path` may contain a wildcard character at the end. `force` is an optional parameter that is set to `True` to force read-only folders to be deleted.

DriveExists(`path`) returns a Boolean value indicating whether the drive specified by `path` exists.

FileExists(`path`) returns a Boolean value indicating whether the file specified by `path` exists.

FolderExists(`path`) returns a Boolean value indicating whether the folder specified by `path` exists.

GetAbsolutePathName(`pathspec`) returns a complete path given a specification. For example, if `pathspec` is "c:", it returns the full path to the current directory on the c drive. If it is "c:..", it would return the parent of the current folder.

GetBaseName(`path`) returns the base (no extension) of the filename pointed to by `path`.

GetDrive(`path`) returns the Drive object for the drive containing `path`.

GetDriveName(`path`) returns a string containing the name of the drive for `path`.

GetExtensionName(`path`) returns the extension of the file specified by `path`.

GetFile(`path`) returns the File object corresponding to the file specified by `path`.

GetFileName(`path`) returns the last filename or folder of `path`. So, for example, GetFileName(`"c:\Inetpub\wwwroot\default.asp"`) would return `"default.asp"`.

GetFolder(`path`) returns the Folder object corresponding to the folder specified by `path`.

GetParentFolderName(`path`) returns a string containing the parent folder of the file or folder specified by `path`.

GetSpecialFolder(`spec`) returns the path to the specified special folder. `spec` can have one of three values: `WindowsFolder`, `SystemFolder`, `TemporaryFolder`. These constants have the values 0, 1, and 2, respectively. With these, you can get the path to the server's Windows directory, system directory, or temporary directory.

MoveFile `source, destination` moves the file specified by `source` to `destination`.

MoveFolder `source, destination` moves the folder specified by `source` to `destination`.

OpenTextFile(`filename, iomode, create, format`) returns an instance of the TextStream object corresponding to `filename`. `iomode` specifies whether the file should be opened for reading (1), for writing (2), or for appending (8). `create` indicates whether to create the file if it does not already exist. If `format` is –1, it opens the file as Unicode. If it is 0, it opens it as ASCII. If `format` is –2, the file is opened according to the system default.

Collections

`Drives` contains all the drive objects available on the machine.

File Object

The file object is used to represent a single file (usually a text file) on the server.

Properties

`Attributes` is used to set and return some of the special attributes of the file.

`DateCreated` returns the date and time that the file was created. This is a read-only property.

`DateLastAccessed` returns the date and time that the file was last accessed. This is a read-only property.

`DateLastModified` returns the date and time that the file was last modified. This is a read-only property.

`Drive` returns the letter of the drive the file is on. This is a read-only property.

`Name` is used to set or return the name of the file.

`ParentFolder` returns an instance of the folder object corresponding to the parent folder of the file.

`Path` returns the path for the file, including the filename.

`ShortName` returns the version of the filename used by programs that do not support long filenames. This name consists of no more than eight characters, followed by a ".", followed by no more than three characters.

`ShortPath` returns the path to the file as it is seen by programs that do not support long filenames.

`Size` returns the size, in bytes, of the file.

`Type` returns information that is known about the type of the file. For example, if the file is a ".txt" file, `Type` returns "Text Document".

Methods

`Copy(destination, overwrite)` copies the file to the specified destination, overwriting any existing file by the name if overwrite is set to `True`.

`Delete(force)` deletes the file. If *force* is True, the file is deleted even if set to read-only.

`Move(destination)` moves the file to *destination*.

OpenAsTextStream(*iomode, format*) returns a text stream object for the file. *iomode* indicates whether the file should be opened for reading (1), for writing (2), or for appending (8). If *format* is –1, it opens the file as Unicode. If it is 0, it opens it as ASCII. If *format* is –2, the file is opened according to the system default.

Folder Object

The folder object represents a single folder on the server.

Properties

Attributes is used to set and return some of the special attributes of the folder.

DateCreated returns the date and time that the folder was created. This is a read-only property.

DateLastAccessed returns the date and time that the folder was last accessed. This is a read-only property.

DateLastModified returns the date and time that the folder was last modified. This is a read-only property.

Drive returns the letter of the drive the folder is on. This is a read-only property.

Files returns a files collection consisting of all the file objects contained in the folder.

IsRootFolder has a value of True if the folder is the root folder of the current drive.

Name is used to set or return the name of the folder.

ParentFolder returns an instance of the folder object corresponding to the parent folder of the specified folder.

Path returns the path to the folder, including the name.

ShortName returns the version of the folder name that is used by programs that do not support long filenames.

ShortPath returns the path to the folder as it is seen by programs that do not support long filenames.

Size returns the size, in bytes, of all the files and subfolders contained in the folder.

Subfolders returns a folders collection consisting of all the folder objects contained within the folder.

Type returns information that is known about the type of the folder. For most folders, this is simply "File Folder." Certain special folders, though, have their own type, such as "Recycle bin."

Methods

Copy(*destination*, *overwrite*) copies the folder to the specified destination, overwriting any existing folder by the same name if overwrite is set to True.

CreateTextFile(*filename*, *overwrite*, *unicode*) creates a text file and returns the text stream object for it. If the file already exists, the Boolean value *overwrite* determines whether the file is overwritten. *unicode* is a Boolean value that, if true, causes the file to be created as Unicode, and if false, causes it to be created as ASCII. The default is ASCII.

Delete(*force*) deletes the folder. If *force* is True, the folder is deleted even if set to read-only.

Move(*destination*) moves the folder to *destination*.

Drive Object

The drive object may represent either an actual drive or a network share.

Properties

AvailableSpace returns the amount of space available to the user on the drive or network share.

DriveLetter returns a string containing the drive letter. If the object is not associated with a drive letter, the result is a zero-length string ("").

DriveType returns a string indicating the type of the drive ("Removable" or "CD-ROM," for example).

FileSystem returns the type of file system in use on the drive.

FreeSpace returns the amount of free space on the drive or network share.

IsReady is True if the specified drive is ready. This is useful in dealing with removable drives and CD-ROM drives.

Path is a string containing the drive's path.

RootFolder returns a folder object containing the root folder.

SerialNumber contains the serial number used to identify the drive.

ShareName returns a string containing the share name of the object. If the object is not a network drive, the result is a zero-length string ("").

TotalSize returns the total size of the drive or network share in bytes.

VolumeName returns the volume name of the drive.

TextStream Object

The TextStream object is used for reading data in from a file and writing data out to a file.

Properties

AtEndOfLine is True if the pointer is at the end of a line in the file.

AtEndOfStream is True if the pointer is at the end of the file.

Column contains the column number of the current position in the file.

Line contains the line number of the current position in the file.

Methods

Close closes the file.

Read(*num*) reads in the next *num* characters from the file into a string.

ReadAll reads the entire file into a string.

ReadLine reads in a single line of text into a string.

Skip(*num*) skips *num* characters when reading the file.

SkipLine skips a single line of text.

Write(*string*) writes *string* to the file.

WriteLine(*string*) writes *string* followed by a carriage return to the file. *string* is optional.

WriteBlankLines(*num*) writes *num* carriage returns to the file.

APPENDIX C

Built-in ASP Objects

This appendix will provide you with quick, at-a-glance information about the seven objects built into ASP. These objects are the `Application` object, the `ASPError` object, the `ObjectContext` object, the `Request` object, the `Response` object, the `Server` object, and the `Session` object. For each object, the properties, methods, collections, and events are discussed.

Remember, you access members of an object like this: *objectname.member*

Application Object

The `Application` object is used to share data among several users visiting the same group of pages. Only one instance of the `Application` object is created per application, and it is shared among all the clients accessing that application.

Collections

`Contents` contains all the non-object application's variables.

`StaticObjects` contains all the application's objects.

Methods

Contents.Remove(*item*) removes the item from the Contents collection. *item* is either a string or an integer representing an index number.

Contents.RemoveAll removes all items from the Contents collection.

Lock prevents all other clients from modifying values in the Application object.

Unlock releases the lock and allows other clients to modify values in the Application object.

Events

Application_OnStart occurs when an application is started before the session starts.

Application_OnEnd occurs when the application quits, after all the sessions have ended.

ASPError Object

The ASPError object is new in IIS 5.0. It allows you to obtain information about errors that have occurred in the script.

Properties

ASPCode returns a string with the error code.

ASPDescription is a long string that describes the error that occurred.

Category returns a string indicating whether the error is from the scripting language, ASP, or an object.

Column returns the column number responsible for the error.

Description is a short string that describes the error that occurred.

File returns a string indicating the name of the file responsible for the error.

Line returns the line number responsible for the error.

Number returns the error number returned by a COM component.

Source returns the code responsible for the error.

ObjectContext Object

The ObjectContext object is used to link ASP and the Microsoft Transaction Server.

Methods

SetAbort aborts the transaction.

SetComplete declares that the transaction should complete, overriding any prior use of SetAbort.

Events

OnTransactionAbort occurs if the transaction is aborted.

OnTransactionCommit occurs after the transaction commits.

Request Object

The Request object is used to access data the client sent when it requested the current page.

Collections

ClientCertificate contains certification values sent by the client.

Cookies is used to read in the values of cookies that were sent with the request.

Cookies(*name*).HasKeys allows you to find out whether the specified cookie has keys.

Form contains the values entered into a form that uses the POST method.

QueryString contains the values passed to the page on the query string.

ServerVariables contains the values of the environment variables.

Properties

TotalBytes specifies the number of bytes sent in the client's request.

Methods

BinaryRead retrieves the data sent by the client in a POST request and stores it into a special kind of array called a SafeArray.

Response Object

The Response object is used to send output to the client. It also allows you to control how and when the output is sent.

Collections

`Cookies` is used to set cookie values.

`Cookies(name).Domain` allows you to specify that only a particular domain can access the cookie.

`Cookies(name).Expires` allows you to set the date that the cookie expires. If it is not set, the cookie will expire when the session ends.

`Cookies(name).HasKeys` allows you to find out whether the specified cookie has keys.

`Cookies(name).Path` allows you to specify that only a particular path can access the cookie. The default of this is the application path.

`Cookies(name).Secure` allows you to specify whether extra precautions are taken to ensure the security of the cookie.

Properties

`Buffer` specifies whether buffering is turned on.

`CacheControl` specifies whether proxy servers are able to cache the page.

`Charset(name)` appends the name of the character set (specified by *name*) to the content-type header.

`ContentType` is used to specify the HTTP content type for the output. Default is text/HTML.

`Expires` specifies the length of time, in minutes, before the cached version of the page expires.

`ExpiresAbsolute` specifies the date and time when the cached version of the page expires.

`IsClientConnected` is a Boolean value that indicates whether the client is still connected to the server.

`Pics(label)` will add *label* to the PICS-label response header.

`Status` is the value of the server's status line.

Methods

`AddHeader name, value` adds an HTML header with the specified name and value.

`AppendToLog string` adds *string* to the end of the server log entry.

`BinaryWrite data` writes *data* to the HTTP output without performing any character conversion.

`Clear` deletes all the buffered output that has not been sent.

End halts execution of the script and sends all buffered output.

Flush sends all the buffered output and clears the buffer.

Redirect *path* tells the client to make a request for the page specified by *path*.

Write *string* writes *string* to the HTTP output.

Session Object

The Session object carries values needed by a single client over the entire session, which may be several pages.

Collections

Contents contains all the non-object session variables.

StaticObjects contains all the session objects.

Properties

CodePage is used to specify the page that defines the character set.

LCID specifies the location identifier to be used.

SessionID returns a numerical session identifier.

Timeout specifies the time, in minutes, until the session timeout.

Methods

Abandon causes the session object to be destroyed on completion of the current page.

Contents.Remove(*item*) removes the *item* from the Contents collection. *item* is either a string or an integer representing an index number.

Contents.RemoveAll removes all items from the Contents collection.

Events

Session_OnEnd occurs when a session ends, either by Abandon or a timeout.

Session_OnStart occurs when a new session is created.

Server Object

The Server object provides access to some basic tools on the server.

Properties

ScriptTimeout specifies the amount of time, in seconds, a script will be allowed to run before timing out.

Methods

CreateObject(*componentname*) is used to instantiate a server component.

Execute(*path*) executes an ASP page as though it were part of the calling page. This is more flexible than server-side includes because the filename can be dynamically generated.

GetLastError() returns an instance of the ASPError object that describes the last error to occur.

HTMLEncode(*string*) encodes *string* so that the browser will not interpret it as HTML.

MapPath(*path*) maps the specified virtual path, either a relative one or an absolute one, into a physical path.

Transfer(*path*) transfers control to another ASP page without creating a separate object context.

URLEncode(*string*) applies encoding rules so that the string may be put safely into the query string.

APPENDIX D

Helpful ASP Information on the Net

Because Active Server Pages are used to build dynamic Web sites, it is fitting that there is a vast amount of ASP information on the Internet. Many small Active Server Pages information sites have sprung up, providing a plethora of useful information. Over the years, some of these small, homegrown sites have matured into extensive information resources.

It's amazing how much Active Server Pages information is available on the Internet. At least a dozen Web sites add new ASP articles on nearly a daily basis. Going to any popular search engine and entering "ASP" as the search term yields an incredible listing of sites and articles.

When installing IIS or PWS, you can choose to have the ASP documentation installed as well. This documentation contains an online technical reference for the built-in ASP objects. Also included are technical references for the VBScript and Jscript languages.

Here, now, is a list of some of the best ASP resources on the Internet:

- `4GuysFromRolla.com`—This site is our own. We, Scott Mitchell and James Atkinson, run `4GuysFromRolla.com`. In September 1998, we started 4Guys as a hobby site. Since then, it has grown into one of the most popular ASP resources. On 4Guys, we concentrate on writing articles that cover all skill levels. When you think ASP, think `4GuysFromRolla.com`!

- `ASPMessageBoard.com`—Got a question on Active Server Pages? Chances are, there's an answer on `ASPMessageBoard.com`. This is the Internet's busiest message board site dedicated to Active Server Pages. Hundreds of questions are asked and answered each day.

- `LearnASP.com`—This site is run by Charles Carroll and is *the* place to go if you are learning ASP. Also, if you have a question on syntax or semantics, chances are you will find your answer on `LearnASP.com`.

- `ASP101.com`—`ASP101.com` is another site focused on teaching ASP to the beginner. At `ASP101.com`, focus is placed on explaining each article and providing both the code and a working example of the lesson learned.

- `15Seconds.com`—`15Seconds.com` contains advanced articles on many ASP topics that aren't covered on other ASP Web sites. If you have a question on any advanced ASP topic, such as ADSI or LDAP, `15Seconds.com` is the place to find the answer.

- `ASPIn.com`—`ASPIn.com` is a comprehensive index of ASP information on the Internet. `ASPIn.com` organizes its information in a table of contents fashion, similar to Yahoo! If you need to find more information on a particular topic, `ASPIn.com` is a good place to start.

- `ASPFree.com`—Steve Schofield, an IT expert hailing from Detroit, runs `ASPFree.com`. `ASPFree.com` contains a plethora of great articles, providing excellent explanation and examples for each subject discussed. New articles are added to `ASPFree.com` on nearly a daily basis.

- `ASPTracker.com`—This site is known for having up-to-date BrowseCap.ini files. This site was mentioned in Day 12's lesson when discussing the Browser Capabilities component.

Unfortunately, Microsoft doesn't provide a centralized collection of Active Server Pages articles and tutorials. Throughout Microsoft's Web site you will find some Web development articles that deal with ASP, but, unfortunately, an ASP Start Page does not exist. A good place to start looking for ASP-related articles on Microsoft's site is the Microsoft Developer Network (MSDN) at http://msdn.microsoft.com.

INDEX

Symbols

4GuysFromRolla.com, 13
<%= shortcut, 42-43
**<%=expression %,
180-181**
**@LANGUAGE directive,
10, 43-45**

A

<u>Abandon</u> **method
(Session object),
347-348, 745**
**Abs() function, 130-131,
727**
Accept header, 302
**Accept Language header,
302**
Access, 651-652

accessing
databases, 497-502
environment variables,
309-310
object members, 741
**ACTION property
(<FORM> tag),
224-225, 235-237**
**action statements, 91,
102, 109-110**
argument passing,
114-120
Do, Loop statements,
102-105
ElseIf statements, 97-99
For Each, Next state-
ments, 107
For, Next statements,
106-107
functions, 120-122
If, Then statements,
92-94

If, Then, Else state-
ments, 94-97
infinite loops, 107-108
nesting loops, 108-110
Select Case statements,
98-102
subroutines, 110-113
While, Wend state-
ments, 105-106
**Active Server Pages
(ASP)**
.ASP extension, 7, 14
caching, 193-195
creating
requirements, 29-31
with FrontPage, 28
with Notepad, 24-26
with Visual InterDev,
26-28
and databases, 507-508

Other Related Titles

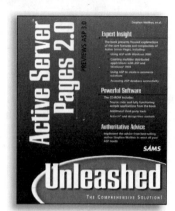

Active Server Pages 2.0 Unleashed
Steve Walther
ISBN: 0-672-31613-7
$49.99 US/$71.95 CAN

Sams Teach Yourself SQL Server 7.0 in 21 Days
Rick Sawtell and Richard Waymire
0-672-31290-5
$39.99 USA/$57.95 CAN

Java Security Handbook
Jamie Jaworski
0-672-31602-1
$39.99 USA/$52.95 CAN

Building Enterprise Solutions with Visual Studio 6
G.A.Sullivan
0-672-31489-4
$49.99 US/$71.95 CAN

Sams Teach Yourself CGI in 24 Hours
Rafe Colburn
0-672-31880-6
$24.99 USA/$37.95 CAN

Microsoft Windows 2000 Troubleshooting and Configuration
Robert Reinstein
0-672-31878-4
$49.99 USA/$74.95 CAN

Visual InterDev 6 Unleashed
Paul Thurrott, et al.
0-672-31262-x
$49.99 USA/$74.95 CAN

Sams Teach Yourself E-Commerce Programming with ASP in 21 Days
Eric Richardson and Stephen Walther
ISBN: 0-672-31898-9
$39.99 US/$57.95 CAN

Sams Teach Yourself ADO 2.5 in 21 Days
Christoph Wille and Christian Koller
ISBN: 0-672-31873-3
$39.99 US/$57.95 CAN

SAMS

www.samspublishing.com

All prices are subject to change.